MASTERPLOTS II

SHORT STORY
SERIES

MASTERPLOTS II

SHORT STORY SERIES

1

A-Cri

Edited by

FRANK N. MAGILL

SALEM PRESS

Pasadena, California   Englewood Cliffs, New Jersey

Library of Congress Cataloging-in-Publication Data
Masterplots II: Short story series.
  Bibliography: p.
  Includes index.
  Summary: Examines the theme, characters,
plot, style and technique of more than 700 nine-
teenth- and twentieth-century works by prominent
authors from around the world.
  1. Fiction—19th century—Stories, plots, etc. 2.
Fiction—19th century—History and criticism. 3.
Fiction—20th century—Stories, plots, etc. 4. Fic-
tion—20th century—History and criticism. 5.
Short story. [1. Short stories—Stories, plots, etc. 2.
Short story] I. Magill, Frank Northen, 1907-   .
II. Title: Masterplots 2. III. Title: Masterplots two.
PN3326.M27 1986   809.3   86-22025
ISBN 0-89356-461-3 (set)
ISBN 0-89356-462-1 (volume 1)

PREFACE

This six-volume set is the second entry in the new Masterplots II Series, and it comprises critical evaluations of 732 outstanding short stories from world literature. The format is uniform, with a heading that consists of the author's professional name and his date or dates, the type and time of plot, the locale of the action, the date of first publication, and a list with identifications of the principal characters involved in the story.

Articles vary in length but are usually within the limits of fifteen hundred to two thousand words, totaling well over a million words for the set. Following the top matter, articles are divided by sections: (1) *The Story*, (2) *Themes and Meanings*, and (3) *Style and Technique*, a format useful for review of particular aspects of the piece. At the end of the set appears a carefully selected bibliography, whose focus is on recent scholarship.

Selections of the lists of authors and titles to be dealt with in this work required substantial research and extended consultations in order to arrive at a representative collection suitable for academic reference as well as general inquiry. The vast amount of material to be researched was narrowed considerably through the use of guidelines that defined the special scope sought: the short story as a distinct literary genre that originated in the nineteenth century.

The short-story form has great appeal for many novelists because of the freedom it offers their imagination and the opportunity it provides for depicting succinctly the essence of reality: The narrator and the protagonist can engage each other in an atmosphere devoid of "rules of the genre" often required in the novel. Indeed, Edith Wharton has been quoted as claming that, unlike the novel, in the short story situation is more important than character development.

This is not to imply that the short story is a creative work of simplified dimensions. On the contrary, the successful short-story writer must manipulate the reader's point of view, and it is also the author's job to create, and maintain, the *tone* of the story. The use of metaphor is often extremely effective here; also, the author's special vision must sometimes be transferred to the narrator and the protagonist in order to reduce the demands on the reader.

Among major critics, some claim that the short story and the novel are really based on the same characteristics of fictional development and that neither is necessarily unique in style. This is a debatable, if interesting, concept which many writers proficient in both genres might question sharply. While it is true that many great novelists are also great short-story writers, success in one form does not necessarily assure success in the other. Nor does failure in one negate chances of success in the other.

In the work at hand, of the 275 authors represented, ninety-six had three or more of their short stories chosen for inclusion here—in fact, Ernest Hemingway had twelve chosen, Henry James eleven, and John Cheever, Nathaniel Hawthorne, James Joyce, and Franz Kafka ten each. Forty-four of the ninety-six authors referred to above are very successful novelists, a high percentage of crossovers in genres.

Historically, the short story has always had peaks and valleys in the measure of its popular interest, but after the mid-century loss of favor—perhaps caused in part by the novelty of the new television fad—the 1980's have provided a sharply revived interest in the short story as preferred entertainment. Because the genre makes possible such a flexible style of literary expression, the best way to deal with it is to examine individual short pieces and explore the reactions such study inspires. Herewith are some examples.

Greenleaf. Flannery O'Connor. One of the great short stories of mid-twentieth century American literature, this work embodies the combination of violence, humor, and realism that makes much of O'Connor's work distinctive.

The Lady or the Tiger? Frank R. Stockton. The classic tour de force of fairy tales—seemingly simple yet maddeningly provocative.

Lamb to the Slaughter. Roald Dahl. At last, a "perfect crime" story that seems infallible; yet, the guilty conscience sometimes does play tricks.

Rip Van Winkle and *The Legend of Sleepy Hollow.* Washington Irving. The former is considered the first successful American short story, by the "Father of American Literature"; Irving's report of Ichabod Crane's midnight encounter with the headless horseman was equally popular with readers in 1819.

The Murders in the Rue Morgue. Edgar Allan Poe. Considered to be the first American detective story, "the standard for its type."

Night-Sea Journey. John Barth. A highly imaginative interior monologue of a spermatozoan swimming toward an ovum, told with great discernment and discrimination.

An Occurrence at Owl Creek Bridge. Ambrose Bierce. The ultimate in surprise-ending short stories. The author is in such firm control that the reader never suspects the outcome until the last sentence is reached.

The Other Two. Edith Wharton. One of this finished novelist's most charming short stories, for those who fancy the turn-of-the-century New York social scene.

The Outcasts of Poker Flat. Bret Harte. This dark story depicts the early California vigilante mind at work in its most vicious pattern. Influential in shaping the image of the "wild West" for Easterners.

Patriotism. Yukio Mishima. A fictional depiction of a ritual suicide of husband and wife as an act of loyalty to the Emperor. An incredible deed to most Western audiences.

The Queen of Spades. Alexander Pushkin. One of the first great short stories in Russian literature—a true masterpiece and a bellwether of the coming fruitful tradition of Russian short fiction.

Rain. W. Somerset Maugham. Certainly one of Maugham's most famous literary works. A classic display of "evil" over "good," a bleak reminder of the weakness of the flesh.

The Short Happy Life of Francis Macomber. Ernest Hemingway. This is "typical Hemingway," an ideal example of how the author wanted to be viewed by his reading audience.

The Tell-Tale Heart. Edgar Allan Poe. Another of Poe's classics of morbidity, this one centering on a deranged mind that is helpless before its compulsion to murder.

Typhoon. Joseph Conrad. One of Conrad's finest short stories, this dramatic portrayal of a vicious storm in the China Seas stresses the competence of the stolid captain, MacWhirr, whose qualities of leadership had been questioned by his brash young first mate. An admirable example by a master of the short story.

Where Are You Going, Where Have You Been? Joyce Carol Oates. A bitter report on the rancid element that preys on a teenage society bent on recreating the pop-culture illusion of glamour.

Young Goodman Brown. Nathaniel Hawthorne. In this dramatic example, a progenitor of the American short story brings to the reader his theory that man is naturally depraved, that "Evil is the nature of mankind."

Yermolai and the Miller's Wife. Ivan Turgenev. The sad story of the serf Arina, later the miller's unhappy wife, who when young was unable to marry her young lover of ten years because her master objected. The story later appeared in Turgenev's highly regarded *A Sportsman's Sketches*, a popular work said to have been influential in the decision of young Alexander II to abolish serfdom in Russia in 1861.

We are indebted to the many contributing reviewers whose expertise forms a vital element of this work. Also deserving our sincere appreciation are the many staff members who have helped bring this set to completion.

Frank N. Magill

CONTRIBUTING REVIEWERS

Brenda B. Adams

Michael Adams

Kerry Ahearn

P. Angelo

Stanley Archer

Edwin T. Arnold

Dorothy B. Aspinwall

Bryan Aubrey

S. Badrich

Joachim T. Baer

Louise S. Bailey

James Baird

Dean Baldwin

Thomas Banks

Dan Barnett

Harold Barratt

Jane M. Barstow

Miriam Bat-Ami

E. Beatrice Batson

Thomas Becknell

Joseph Benevento

Robert Bensen

Mary G. Berg

Anthony J. Bernardo, Jr.

Robert L. Berner

Jerry M. Bernhard

Dale B. Billingsley

Rochelle Bogartz

Robert L. Bowie

Marion Boyle

Harold Branam

Gerhard Brand

Jeanie R. Brink

J. R. Broadus

Lawrence Broer

Keith H. Brower

Rosemary M. Canfield-Reisman

Krista Ratkowski Carmona

David A. Carpenter

John R. Carpenter

Jerome Cartwright

Jocelyn Creigh Cass

Dennis C. Chowenhill

John R. Clark

Bruce Clarke

Julian W. Connolly

Elizabeth Cook-Lynn

Janice B. Cope

F. A. Couch, Jr.

Catherine Cox

Don Richard Cox

Virginia Crane

Lee B. Croft

Donald A. Daiker

J. D. Daubs

Paul B. Davis

Susan Davis

Frank Day

A. Bruce Dean

A. A. DeVitis

Sally V. Doud

Leon V. Driskell

Charles Duncan

Gweneth A. Dunleavy

Ann Edward

Bruce L. Edwards, Jr.

Robert P. Ellis

Thomas L. Erskine

Donald M. Fiene

Patricia A. Finch

Beverly A. Findley

Edward Fiorelli

Robert J. Forman

Leslie D. Foster

Edgar Frost

Frank Gado

Greg T. Garrett

Helen S. Garson

Charles J. Gaspar

Betty G. Gawthrop

Roger Geimer

Jill B. Gidmark

Jonathan A. Glenn

Joseph Gold

Sidney Gottlieb

William E. Grant

Gerald R. Griffin

Drewey Wayne Gunn

Charles Hackenberry

Donna B. Haisty

Cathryn Hankla

Natalie Harper

Sandra Hanby Harris

Terry Heller

Walter Herrscher

Erwin Hester

Nina Hibbin

Hal Holladay

Ronald W. Howard

Linda Humphrey

Helen Jaskoski

D. Barton Johnson

Ronald L. Johnson

Sheila Golburgh Johnson

Albert E. Kalson

Sita Kapadia

Carola M. Kaplan

Cynthia Lee Katona

Stephen Katz

William P. Keen

Steven G. Kellman

Richard Kelly

Paul Kindlon

Cassie Kircher

Wm. Laird Kleine-Ahlbrandt

Edgar C. Knowlton, Jr.

Stephen W. Kohl

James B. Lane

Michael J. Larsen

Donald F. Larsson

CONTRIBUTING REVIEWERS

Anne Thompson Lee

Leon Lewis

Merrill Lewis

James L. Livingston

Eileen Lothamer

Michael Loudon

Barbara A. McCaskill

Mark McCloskey

Mary Davidson McConahay

Dennis McCormick

William J. McDonald

John L. McLean

A. L. McLeod

David Madden

Paul D. Mageli

Philip Maloney

Martha Manheim

S. Elaine Marshall

Anne Laura Mattrella

Charles E. May

Laurence W. Mazzeno

Jeffrey Meyers

Walter E. Meyers

Jane Ann Miller

Leslie B. Mittleman

Peter Monaghan

William E. Morris

Robert E. Morsberger

Edwin Moses

James V. Muhleman

Eunice Myers

D. G. Nakeeb

Peter West Nutting

George O'Brien

J. D. O'Hara

I. T. Olken

William O'Rourke

Sylvia G. O'Sullivan

Cóilín Owens

David B. Parsell

David Peck

Robert C. Petersen

Leonard Polakiewicz

Patricia A. Posluszny

David Powell

Norman Prinsky

Charles H. Pullen

Rosamond Putzel

David J. Quinn

Sanford Radner

Victor J. Ramraj

K. S. Narayana Rao

John D. Raymer

Bette Adams Reagan

Michael D. Reed

Ann E. Reynolds

Richard Rice

Betty Richardson

R. E. Richardson

Jerome J. Rinkus

Michael Ritterson

Joan A. Robertson

David E. Robinson

St. John Robinson

Charlene Roesner

Mary Rohrberger

Carl E. Rollyson, Jr.

Joseph Rosenblum

Sandra Rosengrant

Dale H. Ross

Diane M. Ross

Arthur M. Saltzman

Denis Sampson

E. San Juan, Jr.

Mark Sandona

James C. Schaap

Joachim J. Scholz

Noel Schraufnagel

Thelma J. Shinn

T. A. Shippey

R. Baird Shuman

Anne W. Sienkewicz

Charles L. P. Silet

Marjorie Smelstor

Elton E. Smith

Gilbert Smith

Ira Smolensky

James Smythe

Katherine Snipes

Nancy Sorkin

Michael Sprinker

Larry L. Stewart

Gerald H. Strauss

Mary J. Sturm

James Sullivan

David Sundstrand

Sheila Ortiz Taylor

Zacharias P. Thundy

Jonathan Tittler

Lewis W. Tusken

Shelly Usen

George W. Van Devender

Dennis Vannatta

A. M. Vázquez-Bigi

Michael Verdon

Jon S. Vincent

J. M. Walker

Jane B. Weedman

Manfred Weidhorn

James M. Welsh

Terry White

Bruce Wiebe

Barbara Wiedemann

Ora Williams

Resa Willis

Jerry W. Wilson

John Wilson

Philip Woodard

Rhona E. Zaid

LIST OF TITLES IN VOLUME 1

LIST OF TITLES IN VOLUME 1

MASTERPLOTS II

MASTERPLOTS II

SHORT STORY
SERIES

A & P

Author: John Updike (1932-   )
Type of plot: Initiation story
Time of plot: The 1950's
Locale: A small coastal town near Boston
First published: 1961

> *Principal characters:*
> SAMMY, a nineteen-year-old checker at the A & P
> LENGEL, the middle-aged manager of the supermarket
> THREE GIRLS, unnamed teenagers from the nearby summer
> beach colony

The Story

"A & P" is a short initiation story in which the young protagonist, in a gesture of empty heroism, quits his job at the supermarket because the manager has embarrassed three girls—and learns just "how hard the world was going to be to him hereafter."

Most of the action in the story takes place in the short time Sammy stands at his cash register on a summer afternoon watching three girls from the nearby beach colony, dressed in "nothing but bathing suits," wander the store in search of a jar of "Fancy Herring Snacks in Pure Sour Cream." By the time the three reach his checkout stand, Sammy is halfway in love with their leader, a girl he nicknames "Queenie," who has "nothing between the top of the suit and the top of her head except just *her*." Sammy is attracted to the girl not only by her physical beauty but also by her regal bearing and by her clear disdain for small-town mores. Sammy is highly sensitive to the class differences between "the Point," where the three are apparently vacationing ("a place from which the crowd that runs the A & P must look pretty crummy"), and the supermarket where he works (where "houseslaves in pin curlers" push shopping carts up and down the aisles, followed by squalling children).

Sammy's fantasies are rudely interrupted when Lengel, the officious supermarket manager (and Sunday school teacher), notices and reprimands the girls for their dress: "We want you decently dressed when you come in here." Queenie blushes, and Sammy jumps to their defense in the only way he can: "I say 'I quit' to Lengel quick enough for them to hear, hoping they'll stop and watch me, their unsuspected hero." They do not, and Sammy is left to confront Lengel. "You didn't have to embarrass them," he says. Lengel explains, in defense of the town's provincial mores, "It was they who were embarrassing us." Lengel reminds Sammy that his impulsive action will hurt his parents and that he will "feel this" for the rest of his life, but Sammy is trapped by his own chivalric gesture, and by the romantic code of which it is a part and by which he swears: "It seems to me that once you begin a gesture it's fatal not to go through with it." Remembering how Lengel "made that pretty girl blush," Sammy punches "the No Sale tab" on his register and walks out into the hot and empty parking lot.

Themes and Meanings

On its simplest level, "A & P" is a humorous adventure story, in which a young protagonist acts in the name of romantic love—and pays the price. The optimistic reader may feel that a sensitive hero has been freed from a dead-end job and a restrictive moral code, but a more realistic response will also recognize that Sammy's act has left him in a kind of limbo: He now belongs neither to the world of Lengel and his parents (because he has quit the job they hoped he would keep) nor to the world the girls represent and to which, through his romantic gesture, he aspires. Like Sarty in William Faulkner's "Barn Burning" (another story about a young boy acting against his parents), Sammy's act takes him, not from one world to another, but to a place in between—and nowhere.

Like so many short stories, both European and American, "A & P" is primarily a story of initiation, as a young boy moves from innocence (and ignorance) to experience (and knowledge). Like the young boy in James Joyce's "Araby," perhaps the quintessential initiation story, Sammy has gained some knowledge (through what Joyce called an "epiphany" or revelation) both of himself and of adulthood, but he has also discovered "how hard the world was going to be" to those who cling to their romantic notions about life. Lacking as yet the maturity to accept compromise or to live with the world's injustices, this noble and still uncorrupted youth has acted rashly and lost everything, except perhaps himself. The reader implicitly feels that Sammy's initiation into the adult world will continue long after this short story is over.

Short as it is, the story has a number of classical overtones. Like the hero in an Arthurian legend, Sammy is on a romantic quest: In the name of chivalry, he acts to save the "queen" (and her two consorts) from the ogre Lengel. At the same time, Sammy is tempted by the three Sirens from "the Point," and rejects his mentor (or older guide), Lengel, to follow them; from this perspective, Sammy's initiation comes when he recognizes the futility of this quest and returns to Lengel, who presents him with the truth. Such mythical possibilities point up the richness of Updike's prose.

There are also sociopsychological implications in this initiation story. Although Sammy defends the three girls against the provincial morality of Lengel and the town ("Poor kids, I began to feel sorry for them, they couldn't help it"), it is only Sammy who holds to the outmoded romantic code; the three girls ignore him. Sammy, in other words, is a working-class "hero" defending a privileged upper class that does not even acknowledge his existence. In the medieval romance, *all* the characters were aristocratic. Here Sammy loses his job because of romantic notions to which only working-class characters, apparently, still subscribe.

Style and Technique

Style *is* meaning in "A & P." The story opens abruptly—"In walks these three girls"—and maintains that vernacular, conversational, ungrammatical voice throughout its 250 lines. The point of view is strictly Sammy's and, while tense shifts occasionally from past to historical present (as it would in such a retelling), Sammy's voice has an authenticity and immediacy that is matched in very few twentieth century stories. That voice can be both pedestrian ("I thought that was so cute") and poetic (as when Sammy describes Queenie's bare upper chest as "a dented sheet of metal tilted in the light").

Sammy's voice is also explicitly humorous. When he first sees the girls, he cannot remember whether he has rung up the box of HiHo crackers under his hand.

> I ring it up again and the customer starts giving me hell. She's one of these cash-register watchers, a witch about fifty with rouge on her cheekbones and no eyebrows, and I know it made her day to trip me up. She's been watching cash registers for fifty years and probably never seen a mistake before.

When Lengel tells the girls, "this isn't the beach," it strikes Sammy as humorous, as if the thought had just occurred to Lengel, "and he had been thinking all these years the A & P was a great big dune and he was the head lifeguard."

All the characters, in Sammy's language, become animals: Lengel is about to "scuttle" crablike into his office when he first sees the girls; the other customers group like "sheep" and "pigs in a chute" when they see the trouble at the front register; the three girls "buzz" to one another, like a queen bee and her two drones. Sammy's voice, his humor, and his detailed descriptions of the supermarket setting undercut the implicitly romantic and sentimental situation of the story.

What Updike has achieved in "A & P" is a story of richness and ambiguity. The girls and Lengel argue the meaning of "decent," for example, and the word reverberates with socioeconomic import; Sammy jumps to the defense of the girls, but he has earlier shown that his attitude toward the dress code is similar to Lengel's ("You know, it's one thing to have a girl in a bathing suit down on the beach").

"A & P" works well as a story because the tone, the language, and the point of view are so appropriate to and consistent with the subject. Updike, in writing a seriocomic story on the common theme of initiation, has achieved a small masterpiece through a rich, supple prose that conveys the story's comic tragedy through its very language and imagery.

David Peck

ABSOLUTION

Author: F. Scott Fitzgerald (1896-1940)
Type of plot: Romantic realism
Time of plot: The early twentieth century
Locale: A small town in the Dakotas
First published: 1926

Principal characters:
RUDOLPH MILLER, the protagonist, a boy of eleven
FATHER ADOLPHUS SCHWARTZ, a priest of Rudolph's parish
CARL MILLER, Rudolph's father, a freight-agent

The Story
"Absolution" begins with Rudolph Miller's visit to Father Schwartz's room to reveal to the priest a terrible sin which Rudolph has committed and which is retold along with the events following it in a flashback. One Saturday afternoon Rudolph's father, a devout Catholic, orders him to go to confession. In the confessional, Rudolph recites to Father Schwartz a list of minor sins, reflecting his romantic, imaginative nature as when he says that he believed he was too good to be the real son of his parents. He also tells the priest that he never lies, which is itself a lie. Rudolph does not realize this until his confession is nearly over and he is unable to confess this sin before the priest closes the confessional slat. Rather than feeling guilty, Ralph takes refuge, as at other times, in daydreams in which he is the debonair Blatchford Sarnemington.

With such a sin on his conscience, Rudolph must avoid going to communion the next day, so he resolves to drink a glass of water "accidentally" before going to church, since, under the Catholic law of the time, this prevents him from going to communion. Thus, early Sunday morning he sneaks into his kitchen to drink a glass of water and lend his story verisimilitude, when he is surprised by his father, Carl, just before he can put the glass to his lips. Seeing Rudolph about to disregard a religious injunction for no apparent reason, Carl verbally abuses his son and then beats him as punishment for defiantly throwing the glass into the sink. This is not an uncommon occurrence between the frustrated Carl and his willful son.

As they enter the church, Carl forces Rudolph to go to confession for his offense that morning, thus providing Rudolph with the opportunity to confess to lying so that he can go to communion with an easy conscience. Instead, Rudolph enters the confessional and lies a second time. This deliberate violation of religious practice marks a turning point in Rudolph's life: "The pressure of his environment had driven him into the lonely secret road of adolesence." A greater self-confidence enters him and he begins to recognize his own daydreams and ambitions. Ironically, Carl, seeing his son come back from confession, begins to regret his anger toward the boy. Rudolph receives communion with great trepidation and afterward believes that he is damned. Whereas the rest of the communicants are alone with God, Rudolph is alone with himself. He resolves to confess his sins to Father Schwartz the next day.

This brings the story back to its beginning: The reader now knows the events that Rudolph has been telling the priest. Father Schwartz, instead of giving conventional comfort or admonishing the boy, begins to speak in a strange fashion about parties and amusement parks and how "when a whole lot of people get together in the best places things go glimmering all the time." At first the priest's chaotic mumblings frighten Rudolph, but then he realizes that Father Schwartz is simply expressing his own romantic, imaginative longings. Yet Father Schwartz also warns Rudolph not to become too closely involved with these beautiful things, "because if you do you'll only feel the heat and the sweat and the life." Father Schwartz collapses under the strain of releasing his own feelings to the boy. Rudolph, terrified, runs out of the rectory with his sins absolved in a strange fashion.

Themes and Meanings

The principal theme of "Absolution" is the conflict between the conventional world and the romantic imagination, a conflict that runs throughout Fitzgerald's fiction. Indeed, this story was originally written as the prologue to *The Great Gatsby* (1925), with the young Gatsby as the central character; this plan was discarded, and the story was altered and published separately. Thus, the novel informs the story, adding an extra dimension to this tale of a young boy's coming to terms with his fantasies.

Rudolph Miller is a romantic dreamer of the type often found in Fitzgerald's fiction. He creates for himself a daydream existence in which he is Blatchford Sarnemington and not the son of a frustrated, ineffectual railroad clerk, living in a small Midwestern town. This is a form of escape, of avoiding responsibility, or so Rudolph originally believes, for his religious tradition and his father have told him that these fictions are lies. Yet the events of the story lead him to a kind of "absolution" for his sins.

Lying plays an integral part in this story. Rudolph's first sin is to lie to his confessor about never telling lies. Next he lies to his father about drinking water, and finally he lies a second time in the confessional. Lying is conventionally seen as evil, but Fitzgerald treats it paradoxically, saying that Rudolph is a habitual liar with a great respect for the truth. Fitzgerald sees lying as part of the romantic imagination, the ability to see things greater than the common and everyday. Rudolph realizes that his lies in the confessional were a way of making life seem grander. When Father Schwartz tells him about the glories of an amusement park, this affirms that there does exist a world outside Catholic theology and Midwestern small-town life. Father Schwartz himself has great longings, but they have been sublimated to his duties as a priest. Rudolph's confession, however, raises his feelings to an uncontrollable level, and he has a nervous breakdown—the fate of a romantic nature which has denied itself. Carl Miller has also suppressed his romantic dreams into an intense Catholicism, as well as hero-worship of railroad magnate James J. Hill, so that he must take out his frustrations on his son. Rudolph comes to believe that his "unrealistic" ideals are not unattainable or evil and that they may eventually be realized.

Fitzgerald, however, does not suggest that the conflict between imagination and reality can be resolved simply by the former's unwillingness to conform to the latter. If Rudolph's romanticism is not foolishness, neither is it a substitute for knowledge of the real world. Rudolph is said to have entered the state of adolescence, not adulthood, and there is no guarantee that as he gets older his confidence in his dreams will not fade away. Moreover, Father Schwartz, while telling Rudolph about the glimmering world, warns him about giving himself wholly over to it, since such a world cannot be concrete without coming to terms with "the heat and the sweat and the life." This double vision of involvement in and detachment from romantic idealism is one of the central themes of Fitzgerald's fiction.

Style and Technique

The style of "Absolution" makes great use of detailed descriptions of states of mind, since its central theme is a young boy's entrance into adolescence, a time when the imagination sometimes dominates one's perception of the real world. Rudolph's fear of having offended God for his childish offenses is described as if it were the fear of eternal damnation, for so it seems to Rudolph; similarly, when Father Schwartz's raving confirms Rudolph's faith in imaginative reality, it is presented as an entrance into a world of chivalric glory. These devices provide a sympathetic but detached view of Rudolph's consciousness. Father Schwartz's own consciousness is also dwelt upon as an example of the romantic nature that suppresses itself and is continually assaulted by the sensuous world. The story begins, "There was once a priest with cold watery eyes, who, in the still of the night, wept cold tears." The fairy-tale-like opening and lyric, evocative quality of the prose establish the pervasiveness of the romantic imagination in the world of "Absolution."

Fitzgerald also weaves elements of Catholicism throughout the story to suggest that Rudolph, in abandoning his old religion, is entering a new religion of the imagination. The story's title is the formal term for the remission of sins in the sacrament of penance, but here it refers to Rudolph's absolution for the "sin" of romantic idealism. Rudolph's statement that he never lies is seen as an affirmation of "immaculate honor." Thus, the story also suggests the power of Catholicism upon the imagination, stylistically presenting unrestrained romanticism and the discipline of organized religion as the two polarities of "Absolution."

Anthony J. Bernardo, Jr.

ACE IN THE HOLE

Author: John Updike (1932-   )
Type of plot: Psychological realism
Time of plot: The 1950's
Locale: Olinger, Pennsylvania
First published: 1955

> *Principal characters:*
> FRED "ACE" ANDERSON, a twenty-six-year-old who prefers to ·
>   relive his high school days rather than to face the present
> MOM, his mother, who defends her son against Evey
> EVEY, his wife, who is upset about Ace losing another job
> BONNIE, their baby daughter

The Story

Ace Anderson is a former star high school basketball player. As the story opens, he is driving home after being fired. Fearing the wrath of Evey, his wife, he finds some consolation in listening to "Blueberry Hill" on the car radio, while he sucks powerfully on a cigarette. Reverting to adolescence, Ace challenges the teenager in the fat car in the next lane, emerging triumphant when his opponent's vehicle stalls. He then decides to stop at his mother's house to pick up Bonnie, the baby. His mother offers him the consolation that he was probably seeking by welcoming his dismissal from a job that had no future. She also states that he and Bonnie are welcome in her house if Evey is too angry. Evey, she suggests, is a wonderful girl, but she is a Catholic and should have married one of her own kind.

When Ace declines his mother's offer, she changes the subject by informing him that his name is in the newspaper. Ace, remembering a former coach's advice about avoiding cars when you can make it on foot, sets out for home at a gallop, with Bonnie in his arms. At home, he indulges in the ritual of combing his hair in an attempt to get the look of Alan Ladd, the popular film star. Worried about Evey's impending arrival, he turns on the television, opens a beer, and finds the newspaper article, which states that a current basketball player has come within eighteen points of the county scoring record set by Olinger High's Fred Anderson in the 1949-1950 season. Ace is angered at being referred to as Fred, however, and the article only increases the tightness in his stomach, which is similar to the pregame jitters of high school days.

When Evey arrives, Ace feigns nonchalance, but she has already heard about the loss of the job from his mother. Ace sees that Evey is in a sarcastic mood ("thinking she was Lauren Bacall," he observes to himself—again, the unreal world of films, television, and popular music provides his frame of reference), and an argument is inevitable. She states that she is fed up with his stunts. She is ready to let him run right out of her life. He ought to be making his plans for the future immediately.

Ace attempts to divert Evey's anger by turning on the charm and turning up the volume of the radio, which is playing romantic music. The mood of the moment seduces Evey into her husband's arms. As they dance, Ace seems to return to greatness. He imagines his high school friends forming a circle around them; in this fantasy world, he is once more the center of attention.

Themes and Meanings

The major conflict in "Ace in the Hole" is between the juvenile mind of Ace and the business mentality of Evey. Like Updike's Flick Webb in the poem "Ex-Basketball Player" and Harry "Rabbit" Angstrom in Updike's novels *Rabbit, Run* (1960), *Rabbit Redux* (1971), and *Rabbit Is Rich* (1981), Ace suffers from the former-jock syndrome. He is unable to cope with life after his athletic career is over. The excitement of life during the high school basketball seasons makes everything else seem anticlimactic. There is nothing in the ordinary world of making a living that can compare to being a hero. All of his basketball skills, however, are irrelevant in his current situation. Thus Ace feels uncomfortable, perhaps incompetent, in the job market. In his effort to overcome his feelings of inferiority, he reverts to the past. In his dress, hair style, language, and mannerisms, Ace is still existing in the teenage environment of his days of glory. He is a victim of the emphasis that society puts on sports. Now that he is no longer a sports hero, there is no place for him. He fails to make the adjustment from the realm of a high school star to the business world. Besides Flick Webb and Rabbit Angstrom, Ace is similar, in his predicament, to Christian Darling in Irwin Shaw's short story "The Eighty-Yard Run," and to Tom Buchanan in F. Scott Fitzgerald's classic novel *The Great Gatsby* (1925).

Evey, on the other hand, is concerned with more practical matters—such as why her husband got fired and what he is going to do for employment. She proclaims that he is no longer the most important thing in her life. She has a life of her own, and, if he wants a part in it, he will have to change. There will be no Fred, Junior, in their lives, since Ace has trouble adequately supporting one child. Evey's values are centered on money and social position. Because Ace has been a failure in the business world, he is a handicap in her plans for upward mobility. While Ace lives in the past, she exists in her dreams of the future. There is no room in her world for a loser. At the end of the story, she momentarily yields to Ace's charisma, but she is too obsessed with business to linger for long.

The tension between Ace and Evey, then, is not likely to disappear. Ace's romanticism, involving a glorification of the past, is supported by his mother.

She apparently has been overprotective of Ace during his childhood, and she refuses to help make him an adult. Her attack on Evey's Catholicism and her invitation to Ace to move into her house illustrate her disruptive influence on the marriage. Evey is not the right wife for her wonderful son. It is doubtful if any woman could live up to her expectations. Ace's mother consciously puts more pressure on her son's marital situation in an effort to win him back.

The baby daughter also creates added pressure. To the obsessed Evey, she represents the further necessity of economic security. The loss of the job is made more critical by Bonnie's presence. Evey has to work to keep the family solvent, and now her husband has increased the problem. She is saddled with a spiteful mother-in-law and an incompetent husband. Evey does not want to spend her time cooking, baby-sitting, or dancing. She wants to get ahead in what she perceives as the real world.

Ace, who is indeed "in the hole," pulls out one more ace from his deck of tricks to divert Evey's wrath temporarily. Yet her version of his domestic responsibilities is still the trump card. Thus, the battle continues.

Style and Technique

Updike is particularly proficient in choosing words and gestures to emphasize the outstanding qualities of his characters. In depicting the immaturity of Ace Anderson, the author uses words that are associated with the teenage milieu of about 1950. Ace feels crowded by Evey and his mother. He feels threatened by the teenager in the next lane and calls him a miserable wop. When he tries to turn on the charm, Evey becomes "Baby." In his view, it is not his fault that he was fired. In the lingo of the jock, Ace calls attention to the terrific hands of Bonnie, claiming that she is a natural.

Ace resembles a teenager, too, in his gestures. He flicks on the radio and beats time to the popular song. He sucks on a cigarette and snaps the match out the window, scoring two points in the perennial basketball game in his mind. He runs from his mother's house to his own with Bonnie in his arms. Ace makes a ritual out of combing his hair. He whips it back and flips it out of his eyes. He seizes Evey and spins her into a dance routine in the concluding scene. He is continually in motion, as if his physical activity will conquer the strength of Evey, who prefers to see his energy channeled into the proper course of making money. Thus, the details of the story unobtrusively work together to create a coherent pattern of imagery.

Noel Schraufnagel

THE ADMIRAL AND THE NUNS

Author: Frank Tuohy (1925-   )
Type of plot: Social realism
Time of plot: 1952
Locale: Brazil
First published: 1960

> *Principal characters:*
> BARBARA WOROSZYLSKI, an English-born housewife living in
>   Brazil
> STEFAN WOROSZYLSKI, her Polish husband
> FERNANDO FERREIRA, their neighbor
> DORALICE FERREIRA, his wife
> THE NARRATOR, an English visitor to Brazil

The Story

An unnamed English visitor to a South American country which seems to be Brazil unintentionally becomes involved in the lives of Stefan Woroszylski, a Polish laboratory assistant at a remote industrial development project, and Barbara, his English wife. Barbara insists upon inflicting on her fellow Englishman the "emotional confusion" built up over two years in a strange country. In contrast, Stefan is relatively comfortable in Brazil, since several Poles are there.

The daughter of an admiral, educated in a convent, Barbara desperately misses the active social life associated with her upper-middle-class background. Even with a husband, three children, and a fourth on the way, she is lonely in a place so different from that to which she has been accustomed, not only in Kensington but also in such places as Malta, Gibraltar, and Alexandria. "Perhaps I'm just not the pioneering type," she explains to the narrator. Barbara does all she can to inform the narrator of her former status so that he will "perhaps, later, commiserate with her for her present circumstances."

The narrator can sympathize with Barbara up to a point, especially when he accompanies Stefan on a hunt for wild dogs: "You can judge your distance from civilization by the state of the dogs: Tonight we were very far away." This distance becomes even clearer when Stefan declines to finish off a dog he has wounded because of the expense of the extra bullet, explaining that the dog's "friends will kill him for us." The distance increases when Stefan interrupts a dinner conversation between Barbara and the narrator to tell his guest about the quality of the local prostitutes.

The Woroszylskis live only one hundred yards from Fernando and Doralice Ferreira, but Barbara is almost entirely isolated from them and everyone else in the settlement. The wives consider Barbara an incompetent housekeeper and mother and feel only contempt for her. Barbara looks forward to a ball at the local British Club in celebration of the coronation of Queen Elizabeth II. She imagines that she will find there those who will "accept her in the way she wanted to be accepted as a person."

Stefan takes the narrator on a tour of his world: a meal of cabbage and sausages, heavy drinking, and the Polish prostitutes at the Bar Metro. The narrator narrowly escapes spending the night with one of the whores. Barbara later thanks the narrator for looking after her husband: "You boys seem to have had a whale of a time together."

The Woroszylskis have difficulty getting into the ball since Stefan, in his shabby brown suit, is not dressed properly. Inside, because Stefan flirts with a seventeen-year-old blonde, Barbara tries to make him jealous by dancing closely with the narrator, but they are forced to leave shortly when the girl becomes upset by Stefan's advances.

The narrator suspects that Barbara's patience with her philandering husband has finally come to an end. When Fernando brings her to him looking forlorn, the narrator expects her to say that she is leaving Stefan. Instead, she reveals that her husband has decided to return to Poland. Stefan's exile will then have ended; Barbara's will continue, probably for the rest of her life.

Themes and Meanings

Because Frank Tuohy has taught in Finland, Poland, Brazil, Japan, and the United States, his stories and novels frequently contrast cultures and examine how social, sexual, and cultural distinctions alienate people from one another. Tuohy's characters who attempt to embody two cultures at once are seen as absurd for doing so. Fernando Ferreira is "the traveling salesman of a progressive North-Americanized civilization" yet is "full of Latin prejudices, without having any idea they made nonsense of his smart Americanism." The humorless, unimaginative Fernando judges the Europeans he encounters as types rather than individuals: "He accepted every remark one made as a representative national judgment." Seeing himself as a sophisticated man in a primitive land, Fernando devotes himself to "preserving the formalities" of civilization but is bewildered by the Woroszylskis since they, as Europeans, should be at least as civilized as he but seem much less so. Barbara, as usual, is oblivious to the possibility of any superiority on the part of the Ferreiras and acts like one who considers "it her right to intrude into the houses of her inferiors," thereby lowering their opinion of her even further.

Stefan is perhaps more at home in South America than Fernando because he refuses to acknowledge the distinctions observed by his wife, the Ferreiras, and even the Bar Metro prostitutes. He is "perpetually the peasant arriving in the great cities of the world and staring uninvolved at the palaces or skyscrapers." He cannot understand the people at the British Club, since getting drunk and chasing women is the most natural behavior for him regardless of his surroundings. The narrator admires Stefan for being himself, for being immune to alienation, and sees him, ironically, as having "more standards" than those who expel him from the British Club.

Barbara's standards, on the other hand, intensify her isolation. It is clear from the beginning of "The Admiral and the Nuns" that her background has left her unprepared for life in Brazil and perhaps for marriage as well. Yet Barbara has more complexity, if not depth, than the other characters. She seems stupid to the narrator but has a strength the others lack. She has committed herself to a marriage with a man completely unlike herself and will try to make the best of it not only because her Catholicism will not allow her to consider divorce but also because of her personal code of behavior. This code makes her outraged when other Englishmen dare to slight her husband in her presence, and she stands up for him even when he embarrasses her at the coronation ball.

Barbara lacks self-knowledge, persisting in considering herself the best possible thing that could ever have happened to Stefan, yet she refuses to ask for help from her family or friends because she would be letting them down: "I feel kind of responsible to them all. I'm sure they've all been praying for me such a lot." Her marriage makes her an exile whether she is in Brazil or Poland. Yet she becomes almost admirable to the narrator for her willingness to endure everything that life throws at her. Her philosophy that "everything'll turn out right in the end" is too shallow to help her do much more than survive, but Tuohy knows, even if his narrator does not, that such self-deception is an inescapable part of life, a necessary weapon against the sterility and isolation of the human condition.

Style and Technique

"The Admiral and the Nuns" begins with Barbara's pearl necklace breaking for the second time since the narrator has known her. The pearls are the main symbol in the story, signifying Barbara's superficial, pretentious values. "They're artificial," she explains to the narrator. "But good artificial, if you see what I mean." They also suggest that Barbara's life is more than only her ill-suited relationship with Stefan and her endless talking about the convent nuns; she tells the narrator that the pearls have a sentimental value, and he guesses this sentiment is not connected to her husband. The story ends with this same second breaking of the pearls, ironically providing it with a structure missing from Barbara's life. The pearls underscore her inability to use her background to impose any order on her life.

Tuohy's other major stylistic device is the use of his sympathetic yet impatient, judgmental narrator. This character cannot decide what to make of

Barbara. One minute he despises her arrogance; the next he feels sorry for the predicament into which she has gotten herself. As he is kept off balance by her, so is the reader. When she says she must keep Stefan from sin, the narrator wonders if she truly believes this or has "returned to her usual game of lying to herself." The narrator wants a simple explanation for everything, but his intelligence makes him realize the foolishness of this need.

Michael Adams

THE ADMIRER

Author: Isaac Bashevis Singer (1904-   )
Type of plot: Domestic realism
Time of plot: 1975
Locale: New York City
First published: 1975

> *Principal characters:*
> "I," the narrator, a writer
> ELIZABETH ABIGAIL DE SOLLAR, a thirty-three-year-old
>   woman who admires the narrator's work
> OLIVER LESLIE DE SOLLAR, her husband
> MRS. HARVEY LEMKIN, her mother
> HOWARD WILLIAM MOONLIGHT, Mrs. Lemkin's lawyer
> DR. JEFFREY LIFSHITZ, an assistant professor of literature at
>   the University of California and an admirer of the narrator

The Story

Elizabeth Abigail de Sollar writes to the narrator to express her admiration for his books. Then she calls to arrange a meeting. In the course of the conversation, he mentions his fondness for Thomas Hardy; she soon sends him a beautifully bound set of Hardy's works. Finally, after a number of delays, she arrives at the narrator's West Side Manhattan apartment.

As she had in her letter, Elizabeth tells the narrator how much she likes his writing. She also gives him another present, a Ouija board, because he seems interested in the occult.

He asks about her life, and she willingly replies. She is the granddaughter of a Polish rabbi but has married a Christian. Her husband taught philosophy but has quit his professorship to write about astrology and numerology. Soon she is revealing more intimate details, including the information that she is a virgin, that she has never slept with her husband, and that she daydreams about "passionate affairs" with the narrator. She adds, however, that she has not come to seduce him.

The visit is repeatedly interrupted by telephone calls. Even before Elizabeth arrives at the narrator's apartment, her husband, Oliver Leslie de Sollar, calls, saying that their daughter (his child from a previous marriage, Elizabeth claims), is suffering an asthma attack and that Elizabeth must come home with the medicine which she carries in her purse. Later, Mr. de Sollar calls again to warn the narrator to beware of Elizabeth: "She lives in a world of illusions. . . . If . . . you became involved with her, your talent would be the first casualty." He denies that he is writing about astrology; he claims that his book concerns Isaac Newton's religious views.

The narrator hangs up and goes looking for Elizabeth, whom he finds in his bedroom. She has overheard her husband's statements and vows never to return to him. She and the narrator begin to act out her passionate daydreams when the phone rings yet again. This time her mother has called to repeat Mr. de Sollar's warning. Elizabeth grabs the phone, shouts insults at her mother, and then crashes to the floor in an epileptic fit.

The narrator desperately seeks help. In a nightmarish sequence of events, his phone goes dead. He then knocks at a neighbor's door, but no one answers. Turning to go back to his apartment, he notices that the door is closed, locking him out. The elevator will not come, so he runs down eleven flights of stairs to the superintendent's office, but when he reaches the lobby his path is blocked by furniture. He races back to the sixth floor to ask a friend to call the superintendent, but further complications ensue. The narrator finally returns to the lobby, secures a duplicate key, and gets into his apartment, where he finds Elizabeth lying on his couch. She looks at him "with the silent reproof of a wife whose husband has left her sick and alone and gone off somewhere for his own pleasure." She tells him that she wants to stay with the narrator and offers to type, clean, and cook for him.

Before he can reply, someone knocks at the door and again the phone rings. The call is from the lawyer of Elizabeth's mother; the narrator mistakes the visitor at the door for Elizabeth's husband and begs him to take her home. In fact, the man proves to be Dr. Jeffrey Lifshitz, a professor of literature and another admirer of the narrator's work. Elizabeth, realizing from what the narrator has told Lifshitz that she is not wanted, leaves, promising to call if she does not go mad. The narrator never hears from her again.

Themes and Meanings

On one level, the story is a comic portrayal of the harried life of a popular writer. The constant ringing of the phone, the appearance of one admirer at the beginning of the story and a second at the end, the narrator's frantic efforts to secure help for Elizabeth, who recovers without assistance and seems to reproach him for going off on a lark, all these incidents are the stuff of farce.

Yet the story has its menacing aspect. Elizabeth may be viewed as the stereotypical crazed admirer and the narrator the conventional beleaguered writer who wants to be polite—and left alone. On a deeper level, though, Elizabeth suggests the Lilith of Jewish legend. In the Cabala, Lilith was the first wife of Adam and the arch-seductress. She has also been identified with the Queen of Sheba, who, like Elizabeth, journeyed to see a man she admired and put questions to him. Like the Queen of Sheba and Lilith, Elizabeth tests the narrator's knowledge. She asks him to explain the theological tract that her grandfather wrote, and, more subtly, she challenges him to decipher her true character. Is she telling the truth about herself and her husband? Is her husband's version the correct one? What about her mother's account?

Singer's use of the Lilith legend stresses a recurring idea in his fiction: Man is never free from the struggle between the divine and the demonic, not even in a West Side Manhattan apartment. Elizabeth represents temptation, particularly of the flesh but not limited to that. She has apparently cost her husband his teaching job and has caused her mother to leave New York for Arizona. Combatting her are other forces, apparently providential. Elizabeth's mother calls just as the narrator is about to go to bed with his visitor; the second admirer comes as Elizabeth is trying to persuade the narrator to let her stay with him. His apartment thus becomes a battleground between the forces of light and dark fighting for his very soul.

The narrator escapes. Or does he? Tomorrow he has an appointment with another admirer, whom he has mistaken for Elizabeth's husband. Lifshitz is not in fact Mr. de Sollar, but might he be Asmodeus, king of the demons and the legendary husband of Lilith?

Style and Technique

As he so often does, Singer has woven a complex message into a seemingly simple tale. "The Admirer" finally—and finely—questions the narrator's ability to judge and perceive. Perhaps Providence does intervene to save him from the destruction that befell Oliver Leslie de Sollar. Certainly, the narrator would not have been able to save himself, since he repeatedly demonstrates his lack of judgment. He mistakes Dr. Jeffrey Lifshitz for Mr. de Sollar. He misdiagnoses Elizabeth's fit. He gets no answer when he knocks on his typesetter's door because he has sought him on the wrong floor.

Yet is the narrator saved? Might he be wrong to reject Elizabeth, who offers services he needs? His apartment is a mess, and his larder is decidedly limited. Since Singer tells the story through the filter of a first-person narrator who is obviously flawed, the reader cannot be certain that sending Elizabeth away is the right decision.

Like the narrator, the reader must decide about Elizabeth. He knows no more than "I"; for the reader, as for the narrator, Elizabeth comes and then vanishes, leaving behind questions about herself. Ultimately, she also leaves doubts about the realms of appearance and reality.

Joseph Rosenblum

THE ADULTEROUS WOMAN

Author: Albert Camus (1913-1960)
Type of plot: Fable, domestic realism
Time of plot: The early 1950's
Locale: Algeria
First published: "La Femme adultère," 1957 (English translation, 1958)

> *Principal characters:*
> JANINE, the title character, a childless married woman in her
> forties
> MARCEL, her husband, a textile merchant

The Story

Taking its ironic title from the parable that is related in John 8:3-11, "The Adulterous Woman" describes a day of sensual and spiritual crisis in the life of a middle-aged, faithful wife who, until the time of the story, has had little reason or occasion to question the basic facts of her existence.

Narrated in the third person, although from the limited viewpoint of the title character, known only as Janine, the story tells of Janine's inner and outer adventures during the course of a business trip on which, however reluctantly, she has agreed to accompany Marcel, her husband of some twenty years.

Although French by origin and culture, both Janine and Marcel are *pieds-noirs* (black feet), presumably born and reared in Algeria during the period of French domination which still continues. Neither Janine nor her husband has ever managed to master the native language of Algeria's Arab majority; throughout their marriage, Janine and Marcel have lived all but confined to their apartment in one of Algeria's northern, Europeanized cities, intent upon the precarious textile trade that Marcel has inherited from his family. The trip described in the story is in fact their first venture into the Algerian interior, prompted by Marcel's long-planned determination to eliminate the "middleman" in his transactions with rural Arab merchants.

During the course of a long, difficult bus ride, Janine finds herself recalling the years of her marriage to Marcel and, for the first time, questioning her attachment to him. Marcel is shorter than she is, with irritating mannerisms; what is more, he has long since abandoned his legal studies in favor of the business in which Janine often assists him. Under the frank gaze of a jackal-faced French soldier seated across from her on the bus, Janine begins simultaneously to doubt and to reaffirm her sexual desirability: Tall and far from slender, she is, she reasons, probably still attractive in a mature, full-bodied way.

At one point, the soldier distractedly offers Janine a hard candy from a box in his pocket, proceeding thereafter to lose interest in the woman as he stares at the road before him. Janine's preoccupation with the soldier, never fully acknowledged, gives way to her visual and tactile impressions of the trip, and of their eventual stop at a somewhat drab and inhospitable hotel. Janine, feeling somewhat spurned by the soldier, becomes increasingly aware of her weight and clumsiness, her thoughts returning as before to the athletic fitness and well-being of her adolescent years, before she joined her future to that of the law student Marcel whom she may or may not have loved.

Despite the ironic "promise" of the story's title, Janine's adultery is and remains purely internal and symbolic, quite possibly informed and infused by her own recollections, however unconscious, of the biblical parable deliberately recalled in the author's choice of title. Like the biblical adulteress who is about to be stoned, Janine feels a strong sense of guilt, if only for perceiving vague intimations of a freedom of which she has never even dreamed. As her thoughts run on, for once unchecked by habit, she is increasingly aware of her femininity, incongruous in a male-dominated world. The language of the story, reflecting Janine's thoughts, grows increasingly sensual, culminating in a scene of almost ritual abandonment. Janine, having encouraged Marcel to visit with her the ramparts of a fortress recommended for its sweeping view of the desert, returns alone to the fort after Marcel has fallen asleep in their hotel room. Surprisingly light of step, running faster than she would ever have dreamed possible, Janine seeks desperately to reexperience the sense of release, of freedom, that had briefly overtaken her there hours earlier, at the side of her reluctant, uncomprehending husband.

Returned to the fort, Janine experiences an even greater sense of freedom than before, a simultaneous revelation of fitness and release: "After so many years of mad, aimless fleeing from fear, she had come to a stop at last. At the same time, she seemed to recover her roots and the sap rose again in her body, which had ceased trembling." Increasingly filled with "the water of night," Janine begins to moan in ecstasy. "The next moment, the whole sky stretched over her, fallen on her back on the cold earth."

Back in the hotel room with her sleeping husband, Janine watches as Marcel rises from the bed in a nearly somnambulistic state. By the time he returns, having slaked his thirst from a bottle of mineral water, Janine is weeping uncontrollably. "It's nothing, dear," she attempts to reassure him, "It's nothing." The story thus ends on an intentionally ambiguous note, raising more questions than it answers. Will Janine return to her "normal" state, assailed by guilt, or profit from her newly discovered freedom? The story's resolution, it seems, is left to the reader to decide.

Themes and Meanings

First in the series of thematically linked short stories gathered in *L'Exil et le royaume* (1957; *Exile and the Kingdom*, 1958), "The Adulterous Woman" adumbrates and announces the prevailing themes of the collection. Janine, "exiled'" like Marcel among the ethnic French born and reared in Algeria, perceives on both of her visits to the fort a greater "kingdom" of nature and humanity than she has hitherto even suspected. The innumerable Arabs, predominantly male, and the rockbound, evidently hostile land that they inhabit provoke in the sheltered Janine a sudden awareness of human possibility, of unnoticed opportunity, occasioning a "moment of truth" that is quite unforeseen.

Despite his repeated rejections of the "existentialist" label, followed by repudiations on the part of the existentialists themselves, Camus' mature work developed from, and significantly contributed to, the postwar intellectual climate most commonly associated with Jean-Paul Sartre and his followers. Faithful in spirit to Camus' own early essay *Le Mythe de Sisyphe* (1942; *The Myth of Sisyphus and Other Essays*, 1955), "The Adulterous Woman," like most of the tales in *Exile and the Kingdom*, delineates the contrast between freedom and habit, between "authentic" response and "conditioned" human behavior. Janine's "moment of truth," however unique and memorable, demonstrates both the "authenticity" and the unpredictability of human behavior "in situation," a theme frequently encountered in the works of both Camus and Sartre. Presumably, Janine's incipient discovery of her "authentic" self will uproot her from the "inauthenticity" formed by years of habit; the author, however, is careful to leave the situation open. It is up to both character and reader to ponder what will happen next.

Like Camus' novel *La Chute* (1956; *The Fall*, 1957), originally planned as a short story to be included in *Exile and the Kingdom*, "The Adulterous Woman" derives no small part of its impact and resonance from the author's skillful infusion of biblical themes and references. Although a professed unbeliever, Camus often tended to reinterpret his observations in terms and structures drawn from Scripture; in the present story, the parable related in John's Gospel is inscribed within the narrative or, more specifically, within Janine's recorded observations: In symbolic replication of the scriptural stoning, the bus on which Janine and Marcel are riding is frequently pelted by wind-driven sand; upon reaching the heart of the desert, Janine is surprised to find that it is composed largely of rock. The predominance of male characters, mostly faceless, who fail to notice Janine's imposing female presence recalls the tribunal of men who would stone the biblical adulteress. An even deeper inscription of the parable occurs when Janine perceives undecipherable writing in the sand, recalling Jesus' "earthly" rewriting of the Law as described in the Gospel verses. Should Janine be "condemned" like her biblical predecessor, Camus strongly suggests, the condemnation would be of her own doing, a voluntary if unconscious choice to resume the patterns of behavior that have promised her security, however false that security may be. At the end, having glimpsed the "kingdom," Janine is, ironically, still "free" to prolong her lifelong "exile" by forgetting what she has seen and felt.

Style and Technique

An acknowledged master of many styles and voices, Camus in "The Adulterous Woman" chose to use the neutral, "affectless" third person. Although limited to Janine's "uninformed," instinctive, often uncomprehending viewpoint, the narrative hints often at the presence of an omniscient, objective, yet generally sympathetic observer and recorder. The style is generally terse, matter-of-fact, yet as Janine travels deeper into the desert and farther from home, her thoughts are set down in increasingly sensual, even erotic language, culminating in the frank and lyrical description of her symbolic seduction when she returns to the fort. By implication, the subject of language itself also figures prominently in the story's development: Janine and Marcel are "exiled" from the Arab majority by their dependence upon French, yet at the end of the story they experience an even wider "communication gap" within their common language, a gap widened still further by their perfunctory lovemaking preceding Janine's return visit to the fort.

David B. Parsell

THE ADVENTURE OF THE DANCING MEN

Author: Arthur Conan Doyle (1859-1930)
Type of plot: Mystery
Time of plot: The late 1890's
Locale: London and Riding Thorpe Manor, Norfolk
First published: 1903

> *Principal characters:*
> SHERLOCK HOLMES, a private detective
> DR. JOHN H. WATSON, Holmes's roommate and trusted friend
> HILTON CUBITT, a wealthy landowner
> ELSIE CUBITT, his wife
> ABE SLANEY, a Chicago gangster
> INSPECTOR MARTIN, a Norfolk constable

The Story

Like almost all the Sherlock Holmes stories authored by Arthur Conan Doyle, this one is presented as a memoir written by Watson, the first-person narrator. The story begins in Holmes and Watson's Baker Street apartment in London. Holmes, who appears to be deeply engrossed in his chemicals and test-tubes, surprises Watson by apparently reading his mind: "So, Watson . . . you do not propose to invest in South African securities?" Watson, astonished by Holmes's remark, demands an explanation, and Holmes complies, relating an intricate chain of reasoning that begins with the presence of chalk on Watson's left hand the previous night and concludes with his investment decision.

Holmes then hands Watson a sheet of paper bearing some stick figures and asks him what he makes of it. Watson believes it to be a child's drawing, but Holmes tells him that a client, Mr. Hilton Cubitt, is calling on them soon to seek an explanation of the stick figures drawn on the paper, figures that seem to resemble dancing men. When Cubitt arrives, he explains that he has been married for about a year to a young American woman. He knew little about his wife, Elsie, when they met, and she requested that he not ask her about her past, a past she says she would like to forget. He has honored her request, but recently she seemed quite shaken after receiving a letter from the United States. Shortly after she read and burned that letter, the dancing men hieroglyphics were found written in chalk on the window sill. Cubitt washed them off but noticed his wife's dismay when he told her about them. Then the paper that Holmes had shown Watson was found on the sundial in the garden. When Cubitt found it and showed it to Elsie, she promptly fainted. He does not wish to violate his promise to his wife and ask whether these dancing men are related to her unknown past, so he has come to

Holmes for help in understanding this apparent mystery involving the woman he loves so dearly.

Holmes asks Cubitt some questions about the neighborhood and sends him home, asking him to watch for more dancing men drawings and urging Cubitt to copy down faithfully any that he finds. Holmes studies the drawing silently and makes no remarks about the case to Watson. About two weeks later, Cubitt returns with more hieroglyphics; some have been written in chalk on a door, others have been scrawled on a paper left on the sundial. One night, Cubitt reports, he saw a figure moving through the darkness in the yard; he took his pistol and, despite his wife's protests, went after the man. He did not find anyone, but the next morning more dancing men, apparently drawn by this mysterious visitor, were found chalked on the door. Cubitt believes that his wife possibly knows who this man is; he remains true to his promise, however, and refuses to interrogate her about the matter.

Cubitt returns to his home—Riding Thorpe Manor—on the train, and Holmes puzzles over the drawings some more. When Cubitt mails him another set of drawings found on the sundial, Holmes examines them and decides that he has the key to the mystery and needs to visit Norfolk immediately. When he and Watson arrive at Riding Thorpe Manor, they find Inspector Martin of the local police. Martin reports that Cubitt has been shot dead; Mrs. Cubitt has also been shot but remains alive in critical condition. It is assumed that Mrs. Cubitt murdered her husband and then attempted to take her own life. Holmes is stunned by this news and immediately examines the scene of the crime and questions the staff about the shooting. After close scrutiny of the room where the murder took place, Holmes discovers that three shots were fired, rather than only two as the police assume. Because only two bullets were fired from the revolver found with the bodies, Holmes concludes that another person with a gun was present at the time of the murder. The third person perhaps fired into the house through an open window, he reasons, a thesis confirmed by a spent cartridge found in the garden. Testimony from the staff that they heard a loud explosion, followed by a second explosion not nearly so loud, establishes that there were two shots fired almost simultaneously, followed shortly by a single third shot.

Holmes questions the stable boy about the inns and farms in the area and then sits down and writes a brief note, which he sends off to a nearby farm, addressed to a Mr. Abe Slaney. Holmes remarks that they will have about an hour before anything happens; he uses the time to explain the secret of the dancing men. The individual dancing figures are symbols substituted for letters of the alphabet. Because the most frequently used letter in the English alphabet is "E," Holmes assumed that the dancing man hieroglyph that appeared most often stood for the letter "E." By substituting other letters for symbols, using the frequency with which these letters normally appear in the language as a guideline, Holmes was able to break the code and decipher the messages. Finding the name Abe Slaney in one of the messages, and, knowing that the original letter that had disturbed Mrs. Cubitt had come from the United States, Holmes then cabled New York to ask a police friend there whether Abe Slaney was known to him. When the response indicating that Slaney was "the most dangerous crook in Chicago" came on the same night that Holmes received the last dancing man message from Cubitt, a message saying "Elsie prepare to meet thy God," Holmes realized that there was no time left to waste. Unfortunately, he explains, he and Watson arrived too late to prevent a murder.

Holmes's explanation is interrupted by the appearance of Slaney, who is immediately apprehended. He was summoned to the house by Holmes's message, written in dancing man hieroglyphics; Slaney had assumed that Elsie Cubitt had sent the message. The dancing man code was developed in Chicago by Elsie's father, the leader of the criminal gang to which Slaney belonged. Elsie was at one time engaged to marry Slaney but decided that she wanted no part of his criminal life, so she fled the country and attempted to start over in England, marrying Cubitt, who agreed to raise no questions about her past. When Slaney finally tracked her down and began to leave her messages in the code she had learned as a child, she panicked. She wrote him and asked him to leave, then asked him to meet her so she could attempt to bribe him into disappearing.

It was during this late-night meeting that Hilton Cubitt surprised his wife and Slaney arguing. Slaney and Cubitt exchanged shots, but Slaney ran without knowing whether Cubitt had been seriously wounded. Elsie Cubitt, unknown to Slaney, shot herself with her husband's revolver when she saw that her secret past had indirectly brought the life of her trusting husband to an end.

After explaining how the pieces of the puzzle fit together, Holmes hurries Watson off for the train back to London. Slaney is given a life sentence, and Mrs. Cubitt survives her self-inflicted wound to live out her life as a despondent widow.

Themes and Meanings

This story resembles many other stories in the Holmes series in that it revolves around a secret past, an apparently forgotten indiscretion. Time and again Holmes is called upon to piece together a series of seemingly unconnected clues. The key to these puzzles is frequently, as it is here, a past action—a love affair, a theft, a personal injury—that one of the participants hopes will remain undiscovered. Past secrets always have a way of coming back to haunt people, Doyle believed. In this story, for example, Mrs. Cubitt will not be able to escape her past, no matter how badly she wishes to do so. If she had told Cubitt about her involvement with Slaney in Chicago, her husband would probably have loved her just the same. Because she attempts instead to keep the past concealed, she loses her husband and is condemned to live out the rest of her life without the one man who loved her so dearly that he would never break the promise he had made.

Style and Technique

It is generally agreed that one of the most important factors in the success of Doyle's Sherlock Holmes stories is the use of Watson as narrator. Doyle wrote a few stories with Holmes himself narrating, but they are not successful. Watson is a pleasant sort, but he is not terribly perceptive when it comes to understanding the puzzles he is called upon to investigate. His guesses about the significance of clues are frequently wrong, as they are in this story when he first assumes the dancing men are a child's drawing. Watson's stolid and somewhat plodding personality provides a reassuring contrast to the brilliance of Holmes. Readers can identify with Watson's misperceptions because they themselves cannot follow Holmes's lightning-quick deductions. Watson's literal-mindedness provides an anchor that both secures Holmes to the world of plausibility and accentuates the marvelous powers of the famous detective's mind.

Watson's narration also maintains the suspense of the mystery that is unfolding. In this story, for example, Holmes works out the secret of the code, but the answers are kept from Watson (and the reader). The ominous message contained in the last set of hieroglyphics and the fact that Holmes has been in touch with New York and knows of a gangster named Slaney are not revealed until Doyle allows Holmes to explain the case to Watson. The structure that Doyle developed for the Holmes stories—an opening in Baker Street, the appearance of a client with a mysterious problem, a visit to the scene of the crime, misperceptions of the clues by Watson, the sudden revelation of the mystery followed by a detailed explanation by Holmes—was a formula that was repeated fairly consistently throughout the sixty adventures that make up the Holmes and Watson series. Using an omniscient narrator (who would have to tell the reader all the facts) or using Holmes as narrator (and thereby revealing how the detective is working his way through the puzzle) would not keep the reader guessing the way that Watson's narration does. If people read mysteries so that they can attempt to solve the puzzles before the characters in the stories do, then Doyle discovered the nearly perfect technique for prolonging the suspense and mystery by using Watson as first-person narrator; the proof is that the Holmes stories are the most famous, and most widely read, detective stories in the world.

Don Richard Cox

ADVENTURE OF THE GERMAN STUDENT

Author: Washington Irving (1783-1859)
Type of plot: Gothic horror
Time of plot: The late eighteenth century, during the French Revolution
Locale: Paris, France
First published: 1824

> *Principal characters:*
> GOTTFRIED WOLFGANG, the German student studying in Paris
> THE MYSTERIOUS WOMAN, found seated on the steps of the
> guillotine
> THE NARRATOR, the "old gentleman with the haunted head"

The Story

This story, one of a number of tales and sketches collected in *Tales of a Traveller* (1824), is narrated by an old man to a group of listeners. The story concerns a young student from the German university town of Göttingen. The student, Gottfried Wolfgang, is described as a man of good family, but also as one given to intense speculation on the dark, mystical side of existence. Indeed, he is shown to have dedicated himself in these studies to such an extent that both his physical health and his imagination have become "diseased." As the narrator tells his audience, "He took up a notion, I do not know from what cause, that there was an evil influence hanging over him; an evil genius or spirit seeking to ensnare him and ensure his perdition."

In order to combat Wolfgang's melancholy and morbid obsessions, his friends and family send him off to France to continue his studies at the Sorbonne. They hope that, removed from the gloomy German environment, he will be more happily influenced by the new surroundings of the school and by the "splendors and gayeties of Paris." Unfortunately, Wolfgang arrives in Paris at the beginning of the Reign of Terror, and the scenes of butchery and cruelty which follow cause him to withdraw even more into his own private, dark world of the imagination. Again, in the words of the narrator, "Sometimes he spent hours together in the great libraries of Paris, those catacombs of departed authors, rummaging among their hoards of dusty and obsolete works in quest of food for his unhealthy appetite. He was, in a manner, a literary ghoul, feeding in the charnel-house of decayed literature."

In addition to his constant musings on the metaphysical and demonic, the student is also sexually obsessed. Although he is too shy actually to approach a woman, he gives himself over to romantic and erotic dreams when safely ensconced in his room. One female face in particular becomes the focus of his desires; he dreams about her night after night until he nears the point of madness.

Finally it happens that on one stormy night Wolfgang, making his way from the library to his room, finds himself at the Place de Grève, the site of the daily executions performed on the guillotine. As he reluctantly crosses the square, he sees a dark figure collapsed on the steps leading up to the horrible instrument of death. Motivated by an uncommon feeling of sympathy, he approaches the figure to offer help or condolence, but when he speaks he sees, to his amazement, that the person is the haunting and enticing young woman whose face has filled his dreams. He asks her if she has a home, a place to stay on such a stormy night. "Yes—in the grave!" she answers, and Wolfgang, touched by her despair, impulsively offers his own room as temporary shelter. The beautiful woman accepts.

Once Wolfgang and his guest reach his boardinghouse, he is better able to appraise her appearance, which is both alluring and disturbing. She has long, raven-black hair, eyes "large and brilliant," and a striking figure. Most remarkable, however, is the "broad black band . . . clasped by diamonds" which she wears around her neck. Although somewhat perplexed, Wolfgang is immediately captivated by the strange woman. As they talk, he gives over all of his doubts and fears; soon he expresses his love and passion for her, and she in return avows her desire for him. "I pledge myself to you forever," he tells her. "Forever?" she asks seriously. "Forever!" he answers, whereupon she gives herself to him as his bride for the remainder of the night.

The next morning Wolfgang goes out before his bride awakes, but when he returns he finds her sprawled across the bed, her head hanging over one side, her face "pallid and ghastly." Horrified, he calls for help and waits in shock for the authorities. When a policeman arrives, he too is stunned at what he sees, for he recognizes the corpse as that of a recent victim of the guillotine. As the policeman unclasps the black band around her neck, the strange woman's head drops onto the floor, and Wolfgang shrieks in despair, remembering his old nightmare of damnation. "He was possessed with the frightful belief that an evil spirit had reanimated the dead body to ensnare him," the narrator explains. Driven now into total madness, the student is finally placed in an asylum, where he remains until his death.

Is the story true? "I had it from the best authority," the narrator replies. "The student told it me himself. I saw him in a mad-house in Paris."

Themes and Meanings

The stories in *Tales of a Traveller* strongly reflect the influence that the European Gothic horror story, with its emphasis on psychological as well as physical terror, played on Irving. Gottfried Wolfgang is an "enthusiast," one given to extremes rather than carefully reasoned actions. He has devoted himself to unhealthy studies, and they have made him into a kind of monster—a "literary ghoul," as Irving bluntly puts it, feeding on dead and putrid thoughts just as an actual ghoul would feed on dead bodies. Thus, the student is shown from the beginning to be of unsound mind, bordering precariously on the edge of madness.

Irving also makes clear, however, the student's sexual obsession, which is equally unhealthy. His lack of restraint as he thinks about women, and especially about the one ravishing female of his dreams, shows yet again the diseased state of his imagination. Indeed, these two fascinations—mystical speculation and sexual fantasies—are linked in the student's mind: His ghoulish tendencies are easily transformed into necrophilic desires.

Finally, when Wolfgang gives himself to the mysterious woman, he does so by denying time-honored social and religious beliefs and ceremonies. "What need is there of sordid forms to bind high souls together?" he asks before consummating his marriage night with his "bride." Since the woman is likely dead, although possibly inhabited by an evil spirit, this sexual consummation is an act of incredible horror: Wolfgang becomes a necrophiliac and must pay for his rashness with his sanity.

Thus, in addition to being a thrilling horror story, "Adventure of the German Student" is a warning against enthusiasm, loss of balance, lack of reason. For Irving, who grew up in the Age of Reason, Wolfgang represents the dangers of extreme liberality, whether in philosophy, sex, or religion, just as the French Revolution illustrates the madness of a society which rejects a rational manner of government. The story shows Irving's uneasiness with many aspects of the Romantic movement, which he helped to usher in.

Style and Technique

The most striking aspect of the story is its use of narrator. The chief speaker is the "old gentleman with the haunted head," who tells the story to a group of other men. Among them is the "inquisitive gentleman" who questions the truth of the story after the narrator has finished. The narrator then replies that he heard it from the most reliable source, Wolfgang himself. Thus, Irving gives the reader several possible explanations for the events in the story and also imparts a fascinating ambiguity to the tale.

The reader may, for example, simply accept the student's story as a true example of demonic possession: The woman was indeed a reanimated corpse sent specifically to ensnare Wolfgang's soul. Given the student's already established precarious mental state, however, the reader might address even more disturbing possibilities. Was the woman ever truly alive in Wolfgang's presence? Since he has necrophilic tendencies, could he have appropriated a corpse and imagined it alive? The fact that the portress at his hotel sees Wolfgang and the woman arrive might bring this reading into question. Is it then possible that Wolfgang himself murders the woman after he brings her to his apartment? Perhaps, but the police officer identifies the woman as one executed previously on the guillotine, so once again this rational answer seems unlikely.

The reader, however, must remember that the source of all this information appears to have been Wolfgang himself, a madman incarcerated in an insane asylum. The narrator says that the student is the best authority, but how reliable can Wolfgang be? Moreover, what does the reader make of the narrator himself: the "gentleman with the haunted head"? What relationship is there between this man and Wolfgang? Why was he in the asylum in the first place? Why is he "haunted"? Should not the reader, like the "inquisitive gentleman," wonder at the events he relates?

"Adventure of the German Student," then, is a deceptively complex story, suggesting a great deal more than Irving chooses to make clear. It is the forerunner of the psychological horror story that Edgar Allan Poe would perfect in such works as "Ligeia" and "The Fall of the House of Usher," stories in which the mental state of the narrator is often as intriguing as the events he relates. Although Irving uses traditional folklore in this story, he employs it to reveal his awareness of the dark side, of the terrors that may hide inside every man.

Edwin T. Arnold

THE ADVENTURE OF THE SPECKLED BAND

Author: Arthur Conan Doyle (1859-1930)
Type of plot: Detective story
Time of plot: 1883
Locale: London and Surrey, England
First published: 1892

Principal characters:
SHERLOCK HOLMES, the world-famous English detective
DR. WATSON, Holmes's companion and confidant, the
    narrator of the story
HELEN STONER, a young English lady who fears for her life
SIR GRIMESBY ROYLOTT, Helen's stepfather and the master of
    Stoke Moran

The Story

Sherlock Holmes and Dr. Watson rise unusually early one morning to meet Helen Stoner, a young woman who fears that her life is being threatened by her stepfather, Sir Grimesby Roylott, a doctor who practiced in India and who was married to Helen's mother there. Helen's sister has died almost two years earlier, shortly before she was to be married. Helen had heard her sister's dying words, "The speckled band!" but had been unable to understand their meaning. Now Helen, too, is engaged, and she has begun to hear strange noises and to observe strange activities around Stoke Moran, the estate where she and her stepfather live.

Sir Grimesby Roylott does keep strange company at the estate. He befriends a band of Gypsies on the property and keeps as pets a cheetah and a baboon. For some time, he has been making modifications to the house: Before Helen's sister's death, he had modifications made inside the house, and now he is having the outside wall repaired, forcing Helen to move into the room where her sister died.

Holmes listens carefully to Helen's story and agrees to take the case. He plans a visit to the manor later in the day. Before he can leave, however, he is visited by Roylott, who threatens him should he interfere. Undaunted, Holmes proceeds, first to the courthouse, where he examines Helen's mother's will, and then to the countryside.

At Stoke Moran, Holmes inspects the premises carefully inside and out. Among the strange features that he discovers are a bed anchored to the floor, a bell cord that does not work, and a ventilator hole between Helen's room and that of Roylott.

Holmes and Watson arrange to spend the night in Helen's room. In darkness they wait; suddenly, a slight metallic noise and a dim light through the ventilator prompt Holmes to action. Quickly lighting a candle, he discovers on the bell cord the "speckled band"—a poisonous snake. He strikes the snake with a stick, driving it back through the ventilator; agitated, it attacks Roylott, who had been waiting for it to return after killing Helen. Holmes reveals to Watson that Roylott plotted to remove both daughters before they married because he would have lost most of the fortune he controlled when the daughters took with them the money left them by their mother.

Themes and Meanings

To understand the theme of "The Adventure of the Speckled Band" and to appreciate the levels on which the story operates, one must view it as representative of its genre, the detective story. Like all formula fiction, it is intended by its author to conform to the traditional requirements of that genre.

Formula fiction provides its readers a certain kind of satisfaction: Those familiar with the formula know what to expect, in a general sense, from any story that follows the pattern. In the case of detective fiction, readers may not know how a particular case will be resolved, but they are assured that certain common elements will be present in every such story, and that certain expectations will be raised and satisfied. Most readers seek out detective stories to satisfy their inquisitive nature: People like to have their intellectual faculties challenged. They like to attempt to solve the mystery before the hero does. This they do through careful reading and clever analysis of clues presented by the author, often through a narrator who is aware of the facts but not always able to make the proper deduction. Hence, the "meaning" of most detective stories is usually discoverable on the surface: The denouement gives the reader a sense of completeness, and rereadings simply provide better opportunities to discover carefully disguised clues that make the solution of a particular case more plausible. Readers are not usually challenged to think about larger issues, as they might be by stories dealing with more complex social or philosophical issues.

At the end of the tale, Holmes himself supplies the moral, observing that "Violence does, in truth, recoil upon the violent, and the schemer falls into the pit which he digs for another." The events of the story support this claim, as Roylott dies by the agent he had planned to use against his stepdaughter. While such an explicit conclusion might be out of place in other forms of literature, it is expected in detective fiction, especially in early examples of the genre.

This is not to say that the story itself is simplistic, or that Doyle is interested only in showing that "good will out." "The Adventure of the Speckled Band" explores a universal problem that transcends its genre: the tendency of individuals to jump to conclusions based on insufficient or misleading evidence. Even the great Sherlock Holmes is temporarily led to a wrong conclusion by evidence that suggests a solution which, in reality, is far from the truth. Not only can physical evidence be misunderstood—the sinister combination of the Gypsies, the cheetah, and the baboon in this story certainly provides a wonderful opportunity for such misguided reasoning—but also words themselves are subject to misinterpretation, with potentially deadly results. Only by examining every piece of the puzzle and carefully evaluating each item in relationship to all other clues and circumstances is Holmes able to solve the mystery and, in this case at least, save an innocent life. "The Adventure of the Speckled Band" provides its readers with a vivid lesson in the importance of sound reasoning and careful, unprejudiced observation—something that is not simply the purview of detectives.

Style and Technique

Arthur Conan Doyle's works provide a touchstone for the reader seeking a guide to the formula for good detective fiction. Many classic elements of style and technique are used with great success in the Holmes stories.

Characteristic of this story and of other Holmes adventures is the use of the first-person narrator who is not the detective. Watson, less observant than Holmes, presents the clues for the reader's benefit; part of the thrill of reading is in solving the crime, using information provided by Watson without benefit of the doctor's analysis. The first-person narrator also allows Doyle to mask information from the reader, since Watson is limited in knowing what Holmes discovers when he is away, or of knowing what Holmes is thinking.

This tale also contains another familiar device of the detective story: the presence of "red herrings," false clues drawn across the trail to distract the unwary reader from evidence that is germane to solving the crime. The baboon, cheetah, and band of Gypsies are all false clues. In this story, though, the false clues serve a dual purpose: They also throw Holmes off the trail momentarily, adding to the suspense and, ultimately, to the realism of the adventure.

Extensive dialogue is the primary method for presenting background information and for revealing the detective's method of operation, providing readers with details essential to solving the crime and explaining how evidence should be interpreted. This dialogue is balanced with extended, minute descriptions of locale and character. The thrill of reading such stories is in making proper deductions from this plethora of information—and misinformation. As in all first-rate detective stories, the evidence provided in "The Adventure of the Speckled Band" allows the careful reader to arrive at the right answer. No tricks are introduced at the end of the tale. One need only exercise one's skills in inductive reasoning to become equal in skill to the world's most successful detective.

Laurence W. Mazzeno

THE AEROPLANES AT BRESCIA

Author: Guy Davenport (1927-   )
Type of plot: Surreal historical narrative
Time of plot: 1909
Locale: Riva, Austria, and Brescia, Italy
First published: 1970

> *Principal characters:*
> FRANZ KAFKA, the protagonist, a young lawyer and aspiring
>   writer, on vacation from Prague
> MAX BROD, a friend of Kafka, also on vacation
> OTTO BROD, the younger brother of Max, also on vacation
> BLÉRIOT, a French aviator at Brescia
> G. H. CURTISS, an American aviator, the winner of the
>   Brescia airshow

The Story

Standing on a seawall in Riva, Franz Kafka, the story's protagonist, and Otto Brod, his friend, conclude their morning walk. They are on vacation from Prague and decide to finish their discussion over a beer. En route, their conversation turns from moving pictures to the modern, cubelike architecture of Riva. This style creates, in contrast to Prague's older architecture, a sense not only of freedom but also of emptiness. As the two arrive at the café, they learn from Max Brod, Otto's brother, that there will be an airshow at Brescia. The attraction of the new flying machines, and the possibility of seeing internationally recognized aviators, convinces the three vacationers to travel to Brescia.

On the first stage of their journey, the trio board an ancient steamboat which ferries them across the lake to Salò. More important, the miniature odyssey is a mental one: Kafka, recalling the previous evening's conversation about the Wright brothers, falls into a daydream that mixes people, places, times, and themes. He wonders about what Orville and Wilbur's plane looked like, imagines what they could see while flying above an American community, and thinks about their pragmatic study of previous pioneers of flight—Leonardo da Vinci, Benjamin Franklin, and Samuel Pierpont Langley. He considers also the influence of the brothers on each other, and he hints at a rivalry between the Wright brothers and another early American flyer, G. H. Curtiss.

More pessimistically, he thinks of the loneliness and monotony which could be inspired in modern classrooms. Unlike the Brods, who are "modern men" (Otto is comfortable with the "hollow thought of Ernst Mach," and Max dreams of a new Zionist state in Tel Aviv), Kafka is burdened by this modern sense of loneliness. Although he is becoming a successful lawyer, and although he can mentally create stories, he is deeply frustrated by his inability to put his ideas onto paper.

At Salò, the journey shifts from boat to train, and the three soon arrive in Brescia. There a comic interlude gently satirizes the bustle of this modern city. Newspapers are not read privately here, but are rather declaimed from the sidewalks; the militia has been called in to keep order in the restaurants; that night, several policemen frantically chase two individuals down a street outside the trio's hotel. The three travelers also experience a similar distortion of reality: Their driver takes a convoluted path to a building where the airshow's organizing committee assigns them to a dirty hotel; later, through a hole in the floor of their room, they observe a pizza being cut with such an enormous knife that it causes Otto to indulge in unexplained hysterical laughter.

Still, this surreal world has a darker side, as Kafka begins to realize. Spatially, the streets of Brescia seem to come together at one focal point. Temporally, the "Italian continuity of things" is one in which "accident and order were equally impossible." This is juxtaposed to Berlin and Vienna, where there is a facile dichotomy between the new and the old. Yet now Kafka is confused: He believes that any narrative produced in an Italian setting would be devoid of meaning—"gratuitous figures in an empty *piazze*" or "an empty room in an empty building in an empty novel." Thus, Kafka's nightmare that evening, instead of providing insight, only further confuses him. In his dream he is alone (when he had expected to be in the company of statues of poets and statesmen), and Kafka hears Johann Wolfgang von Goethe reciting a poem in a language so alien that it is incomprehensible.

In the morning, however, the humorous tone returns. Resuming their train journey to the aerodrome, the three pass a comic mélange of travelers: goggled automobile drivers desperately trying to maintain their composure in speeding cars, passengers in carriages swaying along the road, and a strange congregation of bicyclists. Others like these individuals have already created a carnival atmosphere at Brescia itself. All of Europe, apparently, has joined in the festivities. There are Gypsies and royalty, the obese Countess Carlotta Primoli Bonaparte; the musician Giacomo Puccini is there, as is the philosopher Ludwig Wittgenstein. The planes seem incongruously insignificant; the great Blériot's craft is "alarmingly small, scarcely more than a mosquito magnified to the size of a bicycle."

Counterpoised with this comic commotion is the composure of the aviators. Blériot, the Frenchman who successfully overflew the English Channel after eighty unsuccessful attempts, has an "athlete's sureness." Prior to the competition, the American Curtiss displays a "professional nonchalance" by remaining detached, with his feet propped on a gasoline tin, reading a newspaper. Even when mechanical problems frustrate Blériot, the first flier, he simply removes himself from the aircraft until the plane is ready to be flown. Curtiss, in contrast, starts his engine on the first attempt and taxis smoothly across the field, becoming airborne almost effortlessly.

Yet if Otto is entranced with the ground operations, clearly it is Kafka who learns the most from the airshow. To be sure, Curtiss performs cleanly, almost magically, and looks, as he flies overhead, "peculiarly familiar and wildly strange" simultaneously. Indeed, his five circuits in less than fifty minutes virtually assures his victory in the Grand Prix de Brescia. His performance is important, yet it is two other fliers—Blériot and another Frenchman, Rougier—who teach Kafka something more immediately relevant. In flying his ungainly machine, Blériot appears to be dividing his attention equally among three activities simultaneously; to Kafka, he seems like a scholar working heroically at his desk. Rougier, who also has difficulty controlling the many levers and gears of his flying machine, manages successfully and seems, ultimately, "like a man for whom writing with both hands at once is natural." Still, Kafka's understanding of what he has learned from these three aviators is imperfect at this stage; in the last line of the story, he tells Max that he does not know why he is quietly crying. The ending is thus problematic: It remains unclear, in this open-ended narrative structure, whether Kafka will return from the airshow, and from his vacation, with the ability to work as a writer in the modern world. If he can, then Kafka's tears become tears of joy.

Themes and Meanings

In his important essay "Ernst Machs Max Ernst," Guy Davenport points out that when he collected the stories for *Tatlin!* (1974), in which "The Aeroplanes at Brescia" appears, he consciously arranged these narratives to circumscribe the history of flight, from its early days to Commander Neil Armstrong's first step onto the moon. His purpose, he notes, is to demonstrate that the "*logos* hides in technology in our time." This view makes the airplane, the technological symbol of the twentieth century, representative of the essence of this society. It is at once both an exciting attraction and a fear-inducing new technology.

That the twentieth century's predicament is troublesome for Kafka may be seen in the dichotomy Davenport establishes between Prague and Riva. In the former, older city, there is a "glittering richness," yet one may discover only the "half-truths of the cut-glass sunlight"; in the latter, there is "truth in the light," but, as Kafka himself notices in Brescia, there is a disturbing emptiness and loneliness in this modern existence. Indeed, Kafka is the only character who shows, in his quiet tears at the story's end, any emotion. In addition, his contact with others— including his good friends, the Brods— seems curiously sterile. While many of the incidents in Brescia have a comic tone, Kafka is unable to communicate his innermost concerns—his daydreams, his nightmares, and his meditations about the aviators—to his fellow travelers.

As Davenport mentions in his essay, "The Aeroplanes at Brescia" evolved from a previous study of the writer Franz Kafka, who was, in 1909, actually suffering from a serious writer's block. Davenport thus transmutes a real historical event—Kafka's attendance at the airshow—into an imaginative re-creation of his protagonist's inspiration from the aviators. Davenport's Kafka begins to learn from those he watches: from Blériot that perseverance is needed; from Rougier that a beginning writer must concern himself with many actions simultaneously; from Curtiss that a polished writer can gracefully provide fresh insight about familiar subjects. He learns from those he sees only imaginatively as well: from the Wright brothers of the need for study and pragmatic practice; even from Leonardo da Vinci's and Icarus and Daedalus' early errors. By examining these aspects of flight, he discovers that technology, like the writer's imagination, must be actively employed if one is to survive in the modern world.

Style and Technique

As might be expected from a writer who announces that "a page could be dense in various ways," the style of "The Aeroplanes at Brescia" is one which challenges the reader. On the one hand, Davenport uses similes and metaphors often, and in this way he helps the reader visualize unfamiliar objects. Such, for example, occurs when he describes Blériot flying "around them like an enormous bee." Conversely, Davenport's numerous passing allusions to figures as diverse as the Goncourt brothers, Alfred Löwry, and the Roman poet Cinna require the reader to pause to consider their implications. It is important to note that these allusions encapsulate individuals from a wide variety of historical and cultural contexts, and thus Davenport brings many disparate epochs together. In essence, he is conflating time and space as the architecture of Brescia seems to do.

The reader, then, is invited to perform an imaginative act that links him with the writer. The surreal images of life in Brescia, combined with Kafka's dreams and thoughts, begin to make sense when the careful reader correlates these ideas and facts in new ways. The main theme—how an imaginative individual is able to survive in a culture based on technology—only gradually surfaces, from Kafka's daydreams and nightmares, as the central concern of the story. Davenport's answer is optimistic, but conditional: The legacy of the past and the technology of the present must be combined in new, imaginative ways.

Charles J. Gaspar

AFTER SATURDAY NITE COMES SUNDAY

Author: Sonia Sanchez (1934-   )
Type of plot: Social realism
Time of plot: April in the late 1960's
Locale: Indianapolis
First published: 1971

> *Principal characters:*
> SANDY, the protagonist, a single black mother with twin baby
> boys, who lives with Winston
> WINSTON, the antihero, a thirty-eight-year-old unemployed
> black, a former convict, and a heroin addict
> ANTHONY SMITH, the antagonist, a middle-aged white drug
> dealer

The Story

As the story opens, Sandy has gone indignantly to the bank to correct what she believes to be a bank error showing her checking account to be three hundred dollars overdrawn. To her humiliation, the bank officer confronts her with five checks—all bearing the signature of Winston, the man with whom she lives. She reacts to the officer's condemning stare with a stupor of silence and immobility, so that someone must be called to drive her home. Ironically, Anthony Smith, Winston's drug connection, arrives and Sandy rides silently home while contemplating the first spring with Winston, wondering "if it wud be beautiful."

Amid Sandy's own despairing confusion and Winston's crying, he confesses that *"I'm hooked again on stuff."* Having been first addicted at seventeen, he explains that he realizes that he *"shouldn't have done that"* this time: He has used heroin with his friends from prison because he felt sorry for them, because he had wanted to help them overcome their self-hatred and their addiction. He claims, however, that he has not been addicted long and that he will withdraw from the habit the next day, on Saturday. Swearing that he loves Sandy and her children, Winston begs her forgiveness and promises to stop hitting her, to get a job, and to spend more time at home.

Sandy's first response is to ask about the welfare of her children, but she stutters so badly that she must resort to writing Winston a note; learning that her babies are asleep, Sandy writes that she is tired, has a headache, and wants only to sleep. As Winston leaves to get sleeping pills for her and for himself (to use in his withdrawal the next day), Sandy drifts off to sleep. When she awakes, it is already dark and Winston has returned but, instead of sleeping pills, he has brought her a morphine tablet, and she realizes that he is high again. While Winston explains alternative ways in which Sandy can use the tablet, she sees his needles and blood-soaked cotton.

Again Sandy attempts to speak, only to suffer once more her childhood malady of extreme stuttering. She writes another note, demanding that Winston throw away the tablet and promising to help him through the withdrawal. He reads her note meekly, and she hears the toilet flush before he returns with two cold beers. Believing that Winston has resigned himself to the difficult struggle of withdrawal, Sandy hears a cry upstairs and feeds the twins their bottles.

When she finishes, Winston is in the bathroom, but he will not permit her to enter. A half hour later, he comes out, high again. Sandy, out of sorrow and desperation, tries to make love with him. Winston, however, cannot perform because of the drug's effects; Sandy feels guilty and ashamed, "as if she had made him do something wrong." Still unable to enunciate clearly, she listens as Winston tells her that she is "unlucky," having lost her husband to "*a rich/wite/woman*" and now having a "junkie" as an inept lover. Before they slip into an uneasy sleep, Winston once again proclaims his love and begs Sandy for help.

When Winston awakes the next morning, he kisses Sandy in the kitchen, where she is feeding the boys, and she watches him go outside and throw away the envelope containing his drug apparatus. In order to be with Winston throughout most of the day, Sandy has arranged for a baby-sitter, so that they can go to the country. The car will not start, however, and Winston is too weak from the initial withdrawal to push it to a service station for help in starting it. Instead, they walk to a park, where Winston's attention and their horseplay suggest to Sandy that he will finally conquer his addiction. When he grows too weak from the progressing withdrawal to continue their play, she helps him walk home.

After Sandy has cooked supper, she checks upstairs on Winston, who is now bedridden, engulfed in his "Saturday/nite/pain." Proud of his struggle, she massages him and brings sherry to ease the pain; as he thanks her, she says "*any ol time, man*" and realizes that she has not stuttered for the first time in twenty-four hours. Having fed the babies, she returns to check on Winston, whose condition has deteriorated to nausea and chills. Sandy adds an extra blanket and, taking off her clothes, tries to warm him with her body. Fearful and crying, she is unsure how to comfort Winston, so she sings to him as if he were a child. Having quieted him, Sandy succumbs to her own exhaustion, falling asleep while calling his name as he gets up to regurgitate in the bathroom.

When one of the babies wakes her, it is very early Sunday morning. While she hands the baby his bottle of milk, Sandy realizes that the house is dark and silent. Frantically, she turns on the lights to find an empty bed and, downstairs, her open purse with an empty wallet. Knowing that Winston has failed, she walks out on the porch and, despite her nakedness, stares for a moment at the empty street. Vulnerable but strengthened by the ordeal, Sandy returns to the children.

Themes and Meanings

Although Sonia Sanchez has worked in several genres, poetry is her primary craft; the story "After Saturday Nite Comes Sunday" might then best be considered an autobiographical prose poem, for her childhood years were spent in a New York tenement, where drug addiction was an everyday reality. In her essay "Ruminations/Reflections," she asserts that "the poet is a creator of social values." The story, without recourse to blunt didacticism, addresses from "a Black woman's view of the world" the struggle to avert the breakdown of the black family in the social context of white oppression.

The story's opening clarifies that context when Sandy is confronted by "that undersized/low expectation of niggahs/being able to save anything" at the bank. When she discovers that Winston is responsible for the missing money, it is not only his drug addiction which she must confront, but also the legacy of his frustrated dreams, *"like some childhood disease,"* which have culminated in heroin fantasies from an early age. Those fantasies, based on the fear of failure and a sense of hopelessness, have led to drug-related crime, conviction, and prison—metaphors for being born black, for racism, and for exclusion. Having served his sentence, Winston remains criminally irresponsible and unemployed: He has confirmed the white stereotype of prejudice, which ignores the fact that he has grown up in a society that discriminated against him both legally and socially.

Sandy's self-induced silence, her stuttering, and her dependence on the white drug dealer Smith (an Everyman figure for racists) reenact symbolically Winston's entire fragmented life in the course of two hours and, further, the two days that follow. From the humiliating stare at the bank to her vacant gaze on the empty streets of the white world that consumes her lover, the story is framed by a white society which encourages blacks to become addicts to its own values, among which is the implicit inferior social status of the black man. As Sanchez asserts in her essay: "The most fundamental truth to be told in any art form, as far as Blacks are concerned, is that America is killing us."

Sandy's solitary struggle to free Winston from his cycle of self-hatred and self-destructive drug addiction is not a struggle *against* him so much as it is a loving struggle of selflessness *for* him. Despite his lies, theft, and betrayal, she respects Winston's attempt to affirm blackness, through his empathy for his friends and for her, far more than she respects her former husband, who has left her for a rich white woman and, subsequently, feeds the addiction to white values. Sandy, however, knows that Winston may fail again, and her struggle for a loving black unity of the family centers not only on him but also on her twin boys, who will inherit Winston's legacy. When Sunday—a day of thanks and rest—comes, Sandy will have practiced the black aesthetic, which Sanchez defines in part as "a clarion call to the values of change while it also speaks to the beauty of a nonexploitative age." In the midst of the mutual despair, Sandy nurtures the destiny of the black male—and family—offering to her boys a model of care, attention, commitment, self-reliance and, most important, unwavering love.

Style and Technique

While Sanchez's third-person narrator reflects Sandy's point of view, Sanchez gives both of the central characters voices in their own right. Italicized passages permit Winston a tenuous dignity appropriate to this desire for psychological freedom and trace Sandy's conquest of her stuttering as she becomes confident in her commitment to him. These passages blend indistinguishably dialogue and interior monologue; the characters speak directly from within to each other and to the reader. Consequently, the reader knows that these characters are aware of their efforts to shape their own lives. Just as Sandy must overcome her stuttering in favor of clear self-expression to endure the emphatic images of emptiness which close the story, Sanchez must subvert standard English to find a language suitable to her characters.

Sanchez's language alternates between clashing images of a harsh reality, such as the spots of blood seeping through the envelope that contains Winston's needles, and of tender commitment, such as Sandy's naked vulnerability of selflessness while he is in the throes of withdrawal. Within this imagistic tension, Sanchez develops her images of drug addiction into a complex, dominant metaphor of nearly absolute evil: the living death of an individual or a people when they become dependent on values which they have had no role in creating. To underscore the need for self-definition in order to gain self-determination, Sanchez frequently uses unusual spellings, slang, and compressed phrasing: The spellings "wuz," "wud," "cuz," and "sed" echo not only black speech, but also her devotion to the improvised sound poem in which her cries and moans are impossible to capture on the printed page, thereby affirming the black oral tradition; her phrases such as "wite/dude" and "yo/woman" indicate not only the previous sound technique but also a semantic compression in which "wite/dude" connotes a clever, exploitative bigotry—the mask of friendship worn by Smith, at whose "crib" Winston and his friends inject heroin. This latter example of slang contributes both to the frequent intermeshing of drug users' slang and black slang for realism in the speech rhythms and to the irony which Sanchez achieves through repetition; Smith's "crib" is the living death that awaits Winston, while the boys' crib is the living beauty that Sandy is determined to create for them.

Even straightforward repetition works ironically and symbolically, for as Sandy turns on lights all over the house, only to find emptiness, she gains an inner illumination and a strength that allows her to stand naked boldly—not submissively—before the world. She returns to her boys with a greater resolve than ever to secure their future, whether or not Winston returns to continue his struggle. Like Sanchez turning her experience into a distinctive language of the black aesthetic, Sandy transforms her disappointment with Winston into an ethic for those who will follow her.

Michael Loudon

AFTER THE FAIR

Author: Dylan Thomas (1914-1953)
Type of plot: Sketch
Time of plot: 1933
Locale: Wales
First published: 1934

Principal characters:
ANNIE, the protagonist, a homeless young mother
THE FAT MAN, a circus freak who befriends her

The Story

After the crowd goes home from a local fair and the booths and rides are closed down, a young girl named Annie remains behind. Surrounded by the shapes of wooden horses and fairy boats, she begins to look for a place to sleep for the night. Peeping into tents and behind stalls shrouded in canvas, she continues searching for a suitable bed but fails to find a comfortable place. When she comes to the Astrologer's tent, she discovers a bundle of straw in the corner. When she touches the straw it begins to move. She then kneels by its side, puts out her hand, and feels a baby's hand touch her own.

Having nowhere to sleep now, she decides to walk toward the trailers where the workers from the fair make their homes. Most of the trailers are dark, so she chooses to knock at the door of one of the only two that still have their lights on. The fattest man she has ever seen in her life opens the door and invites her in. After they share some buttered toast, the large host explains to Annie that he is the Fat Man. As he puts it, "I've always been a fat man . . . and now I'm the Fat Man; there's nobody to touch me for fatness." When he asks her why she left her home in Cardiff, Annie simply replies, "Money." He, in turn, tells her about the fair, the places he has been, and the people he has met. Annie finally tells him about the baby in the Astrologer's tent. "That's the stars again," he replies. Annie merely says, "The baby'll die."

When the Fat Man suddenly leaves the trailer Annie assumes he is going after the police, and the narrator explains that she does not want to be caught by the policeman again. It is not clear why she is sought by the police, but her earlier remark that she left Cardiff because of money implies that she may have stolen some cash. One is also led to assume that she is now down on her luck, a vagrant, and that the abandoned baby is hers.

The Fat Man, however, returns to the trailer smiling and carrying the baby in his arms. "See what the stars have done," he announces. She takes the child, which has begun to cry, and holds it against her small breast. She tells the Fat Man that a policeman is after her, but when he asks her why the police want her, she does not answer but holds the child closer to her "wasted breast."

As the baby's cries grow louder, both Annie and the Fat Man become distressed. Annie decides that the only thing they can do to silence the child is to take it on the merry-go-round. The three of them move through the darkness of the deserted fair toward the place where the wooden horses stand waiting. With the baby clutching her neck, Annie climbs into the saddle of one of the horses and calls out for the Fat Man to start the engine. The machinery set into motion, the Fat Man gets up by her side, pulls the main lever, and climbs into the saddle of the smallest horse of all.

As the merry-go-round picks up speed, the baby stops crying and begins to clap its hands out of sheer excitement and pleasure. The noise of the ride brings out the men from the other trailers who see this amazing spectacle: the Fat Man and a thin girl dressed in black with a baby in her arms, racing round and round on the wooden horses to the blaring music of the organ.

Themes and Meanings

In both his poetry and his fiction, Dylan Thomas celebrated the animal joy and vitality that human beings embody when they are in harmony with the cosmic cycle of life and death. As a young boy, Thomas took great joy in going to the local fairs. The spectacle of the crowds, lights, music, and exotic people (such as the Fat Woman) presented life in a rich, compressed form that dazzled the boy from Swansea. In his essay "Holiday Memory" (1946), he recorded the excitement that he and his friends had shared during a visit to the fair on a bank holiday.

In "After the Fair," Thomas focuses on the intense loneliness experienced by a young woman when the bright wonders of the fair are closed down. Annie's life is one of fear and alienation from the community. Hungry and homeless, she leaves her baby in the Astrologer's tent, presumably hoping that someone will find it and be able to care for it. Thomas, who later emphasized the symbolic importance of the constellations in his poem "Altarwise by Owl-Light" (1936), suggests the providential nature of the stars in this story. When the Fat Man fetches the baby and announces, "See what the stars have done," he is simply being considerate of Annie's feelings by jokingly attributing the baby to the stars rather than to its actual mother. Thomas, however, implies that the stars do, indeed, help to shape the destiny of this lonely woman and her abandoned child.

Annie, her baby, and the Fat Man bring the sleeping fair to life when they start up and ride the merry-go-round. The wooden horses come alive as they are ridden by this bizarre "family." The story ends with the celebration of life as the baby claps its hands and Annie and the Fat Man become one through the ever-increasing music, speed, and exhilaration of the ride. The circular motion of the merry-go-round suggests the great cycle of life itself. The ecstasy of Annie, the child, and the Fat Man reflects the pulsing energy of the primitive life force that drives all creatures under the stars.

Style and Technique

"After the Fair" was the first short story that Thomas published. Presented from the third-person, omniscient point of view, the narrative is seemingly straightforward. There is, however, an interesting ambiguity in the story. The narrator never states outright that it is Annie's baby lying in the straw in the Astrologer's tent, and never explains why Annie is being sought by the police. The reader can, therefore, interpret the Fat Man's remark, "See what the stars have done," as having symbolic significance. As a "star child," the baby brings Annie and the Fat Man together in a symbolic union of life-giving energy.

The story has the form of a sketch, a small slice of life. The reader is never informed of Annie's background and only a few details are given about the Fat Man's past. The focus is upon the present, and in concluding the story with the night ride of the merry-go-round still in progress, Thomas suggests the endless nature of this exhilarating moment. Thomas, displaying a Romantic sensibility (with his interest in children, freaks, common people, and the mutability of life), freezes in a timeless action a circus fat man and a lonely girl clutching her baby. In so doing, he moves from his straightforward prose style to a lyrical, celebratory, poetic style rich in metaphors and rhythmic cadences.

Richard Kelly

AFTER THE STORM

Author: Ernest Hemingway (1899-1961)
Type of plot: Realism
Time of plot: The late 1920's or early 1930's
Locale: The Florida Keys
First published: 1932

> *Principal character:*
> THE NARRATOR, an unnamed sponger

The Story

The story opens with two men fighting over very little, something that has to do with making punch. One man is getting the better of the other by choking him. This man, however, manages to get his knife out, and he slashes the arm muscles of his attacker, after which he leaves the bar where the fight has taken place. He gets into his skiff, which is full of water from a recent storm, bails it out, and sails toward the open sea.

First he sees a three-masted ship that has sunk during the storm. He can see the stumps of the ship's spars sticking out of the water, but the vessel itself rests in water too deep for him to have any hope of reaching it and claiming the salvage. Then he notices a huge congregation of birds in the distance. He sails toward them and eventually comes upon the wreckage of the largest steamer he has ever seen. The ship is lying on its side in sand, some of it close enough to the surface of the water that he can stand on it and be only chin-deep in water. He can see rows of sealed portholes as he looks at the side of the ship down through the clear water.

He speculates on what riches the ship might have been carrying. After he tries unsuccessfully to break one of the porthole windows with a wrench tied to a pole, he strips and dives into the water carrying the wrench with him. He gets a grip on the edge of one of the portholes and tries to break the glass, but it will not yield. He can see through the window. On the other side is a dead woman, her hair floating languidly in the water.

He makes several dives to the porthole and succeeds only in cracking it. He cannot break it. His nose is bleeding badly from staying under the water so long and from diving so deep. He cuts the grapple from his anchor to use as a tool and goes back under with it, but he cannot hold on to the grapple. Next he lashes his wrench to the grains pole and tries to use it to get into the porthole, but the wrench slips from the lashing and sinks to the bottom. He is forced to abandon for the time his attempts to penetrate the ship. He speculates that the liner must have had five million dollars' worth of loot on her. He wonders why there are no sharks in the vicinity.

When he gets back to port, he learns that the fellow he cut with his knife is all right except for his wounded arm. The narrator is placed under a five-hundred-dollar bond for his part in the fight, but some of his friends perjure themselves and testify that the wounded man had come after him with an ax and that he had acted in self-defense, so he is not held culpable. The weather is foul for all the next week, and by the time he is able to return to the site of the wreck, "the Greeks had blown her open and cleaned her out. They got the safe out with dynamite. . . . She carried gold and they got it all. They stripped her clean."

The narrator speculates on what must have happened on the night of the storm. The night was too wild for anyone to be out on deck. The ship, out of Havana, could not make port. The captain was trying to get through a channel and missed it by only a hundred yards, but what the ship hit was quicksand. Probably the captain ordered the ballast tanks opened, and when that happened, the ship went down. The boilers then likely exploded, killing many of the 450 passengers on board as well as all the crew. Those who did not die in the explosion soon drowned.

The reader is told that the hull, which is still there, is now inhabited by huge jewfish, some weighing three to four hundred pounds. The narrator complains that he was first at the wreck after the birds, but that the Greeks got all the booty. He reflects, "even the birds got more out of her than I did."

Themes and Meanings

"After the Storm" tells about a catastrophic event, the sinking of a large ocean liner during a storm. The loss of life is in excess of 450 passengers as well as the entire crew. Readers are dependent, however, on the narrator to tell them about the catastrophe, and he views his loss of the booty as more catastrophic than the loss of life incurred in the sinking.

The narrator is a sponger, and the double meaning of the word is quite intentional. He makes a living harvesting sponges, but he also is not above living off carrion, just as do the birds that first attract him to the wreck. This man is willing to engage in a potentially fatal fight which is, by his own admission, not about anything. If he has any emotions about the deaths of those who went down with the ship, they are not revealed in this carefully controlled and tightly written story.

The story is essentially about predators: the narrator, the birds, the jewfish, and the Greeks. The narrator is an embryonic version of Harry Morgan in Ernest Hemingway's later novel *To Have and Have Not* (1937). He is a man whose only hope of real wealth comes from the possibility of plundering something. His only obstacle to doing this in "After the Storm" is that he does not have the equipment to carry out the job, so that others beat him to the plunder. It is not unusual in the Hemingway canon to find characters whose success in an important venture is blocked by their lack of equipment or, in the case of Hemingway's writing about wars, lack of adequate weapons.

The solitary qualities of this story remind one of those found in *The Old Man and the Sea* (1952), in which Santiago hooks his dream fish but does not have the equipment to land it, so he drags it behind his ketch while it is eaten away by sharks. By the time Santiago reaches the dock, little is left of the majestic fish with which he had his greatest and most threatening combat.

In "After the Storm," the narrator is a loser, the captain of the sunken liner is a loser, and all those on board are losers. The birds win by getting the carrion that first attracts them to the wreck, the jewfish prosper afterward by living in the battered hull, and the Greeks succeed best of all, because they have the equipment necessary to salvage the treasure.

Style and Technique

Hemingway's mastery of understatement as a controlling literary device is evident throughout "After the Storm." Akin to the understatement is the strong irony within the story. Events that have cost the lives of all the people on the sunken ship are minimized by Hemingway's choice of narrator. Because the narrator's focus is self-serving, materialistic, and essentially meretricious, the information given about the shipwreck is minimal, and its scope is limited by the vision of the low-life person who tells it. The secondary action of the story, that of the actual shipwreck, is the larger, more dramatic action of the two story lines Hemingway develops here, but by downplaying it, he asserts his stylistic control.

The story's narrator is a crude, brutalized person, someone who will fight over nothing and whose moral code is as debased as his speech, which throughout the story gives subtle insights into his personality. The birds flock around the ship to eat carrion because they must live; they are morally neutral. The narrator, however, does not have their moral neutrality and is, hence, more culpable than they.

Despite the ironic contrast between the main action and the secondary action, in fact, perhaps because of it, the reader develops a growing sense of horror at what happened. This sense of horror continues to develop in one's mind long after one has read the story. The impact is remarkably long-lasting because the reader keeps supplying details from an imagination that Hemingway has piqued and set in motion.

Hemingway's language in this story, as in most of his work, is simple and direct. His sentence structure is unornamented. The ironies of the story are convoluted and intertwined with one another. Hemingway controls them with precision, as he controls the two story lines with a deftness and economy that one finds in few other authors.

R. Baird Shuman

THE ALBATROSS

Author: Susan Hill (1942-   )
Type of plot: Social realism
Time of plot: 1968
Locale: A fishing village in northeast England
First published: 1969

> *Principal characters:*
> DUNCAN PIKE, the protagonist, a simpleminded workman
> HILDA PIKE, his mother
> TED FLINT, a fisherman

The Story

Duncan Pike is an eighteen-year-old young man with limited intelligence and thus an outsider to himself and to the small fishing village in which he lives. His agonizing feeling of being an outcast is reinforced by his domineering mother, Hilda, who constantly reminds him, "We keep ourselves to ourselves in this town." His mother wants him to be alone; she clings to him for several reasons. For one, she is handicapped, like her son. Because she is confined to a wheelchair, she depends on Duncan to help her through each day. She also underestimates her son: She thinks him incapable of performing the simplest task without her instructions. This is also the attitude of the villagers toward Duncan; he can only feel further isolated because of this.

For Duncan, any contact with the villagers is extremely painful. "He dared not wonder what they really thought of him, or how they talked, as he went away. . . . He has almost come to hate himself and doubt his abilities because he has listened too long to his mother and to the other residents of the village.

An incident at the opening of the story illustrates this well. Each Wednesday, Hilda sends her son to buy fish in the market for their supper. She writes down "not cod" as "she wrote everything down for him, every message, every demand, every list." Duncan resents this treatment; no matter where he goes, he thinks, he takes his mother with him. He has given up trying to defend or explain himself to her or anyone else. The villagers speak to him clearly, loudly, and slowly, thinking that he cannot understand them if they do not. He buys cod because that is all that is being sold, not bothering to ask for anything else or to go to another fish seller. Too mentally beaten down to explain the circumstances, Duncan endures the verbal abuse of his mother when he returns home.

Understandably, at eighteen, Duncan is beginning to want some independence, to break away from his mother and the village. His desire is particularly acute because of his isolation and his feelings of inferiority. He sits in rapture when his boss speaks of the outside world, which Duncan sees as "new, miraculous." He stands and looks out at the sea, longing for a new life. Slowly, reluctantly at first, Duncan begins to see that "I could go anywhere." His mother seems to sense his desire to leave, for she repeatedly reminds him that he could not make it at sea or anywhere else. "You stay as you are," she chides him. Duncan's desire to leave his old life nevertheless remains strong. With each view of the sea he reminds himself that "he could go anywhere, by himself."

Ted Flint, a fisherman, is Duncan's idol. He has done everything and been everywhere that Duncan would like to go. Ted treats Duncan as an equal. He offers to take him out in his boat, but Hilda's relentless words, "You leave going in boats alone," stop Duncan.

He continues to be fascinated by Flint, and Flint befriends the boy because he feels sorry for him. He good-heartedly offers to buy Duncan a drink at the local pub. He does not fear Hilda Pike, but Duncan does, and so he does not accept the invitation. Still, Duncan is thrilled, for he has had the chance to go, to be with the men, to assert his independence. It reinforces his feeling that perhaps he could do something about his life.

The turning point of the story, and of Duncan's life, happens when Flint is drowned in a sea storm. The incident crystallizes in Duncan's realization that he, too, could die without ever having lived. He is so affected by Flint's death that he leaves his mother in her wheelchair alone at the funeral because she taunted him, saying that he understood nothing about death. It is Duncan's first act of defiance.

The act of ignoring his mother's abuse and leaving her helpless in church is followed by Duncan's going by himself to the pub to buy a drink. He repeatedly tells himself, as if to convince himself, that he can do what he wants. Ultimately, a sense of calm overcomes him. "He was no longer anxious, he felt a new person, strong, by himself."

"Duncan thought of nothing, felt nothing. He had decided what he should do and could not remember a reason." What Duncan decides to do is to free himself, and he does that by poisoning his mother and burning all the things in the house that he hates and that remind him of her. Ceremoniously, he removes her sewing materials, her furnishings, and burns them in the grate. Then he dresses his mother, places her in her wheelchair, and pushes her into the sea. Duncan then gets into a boat and goes to sea himself—something his mother would never allow him to do.

That Duncan is limited mentally is apparent in his solution to his problems. He can be free only by killing his mother. He makes no plans for his future beyond being at sea in a boat. He is later found huddled in a grainbarn. The reader must assume that he will be tried but found mentally incompetent.

Themes and Meanings

The title "The Albatross" immediately evokes Samuel Taylor Coleridge's poem *The Rime of the Ancient Mariner* (1798). In the poem, the mariner is cursed to wear an albatross, a seabird, around his neck because he has callously killed the bird. Only when he appreciates the beauty and power of nature and of life is the curse lifted: The albatross falls from his neck.

The two themes of burden and the power of nature are central to this short story. Hill very carefully lets the reader decide who is an albatross to whom. Hilda Pike sees her son as a burden. She is ashamed of his limited mental ability. She believes that she has sacrificed her life to give him a home because he could not possibly make it in the world on his own. Similarly, Duncan sees his mother as the albatross. Her dependence on him and her constant harping on his inabilities to survive are his curse. Finally, he believes that in order to have any freedom he must kill her. The irony here is apparent in relation to the Coleridge poem: The mariner gains freedom through an appreciation of life, while Duncan thinks that he is gaining life through death; in fact, he has merely exchanged one kind of prison for another.

Style and Technique

Hill's straightforward, easy-to-read prose has the resonance of a folk ballad. In part, this effect is achieved by her use of traditional symbolism.

The sea is the predominant symbol in the story. It represents both freedom and death. It gives life to the village, but it also takes life because of its power. Descriptions of the turmoil of the sea reflect the inner emotional turmoil of the characters involved. When Duncan sees the dead body of Ted Flint, he can only compare it to the deaths he has known, that of dead fish, "dead white cod."

Further symbolism of the sea and nature is achieved in the use of the characters' names. Hilda and Duncan Pike see each other and themselves as useless. A pike fish in England is a freshwater fish that is good for nothing, including food, and is bothersome and caught only by mistake. Ted Flint is as tough and strong as his name implies. He is the flint that starts the spark in Duncan, provoking him to want life.

The final words of the story show that life goes on just as nature endures. Hilda Pike is dead, Duncan Pike has been apprehended, but the land, the sea, the seasons, and the elements are eternal. "Later that day, the wind veered west, blowing in soft-bellied rain clouds. The thaw began."

Resa Willis

THE ALEPH

Author: Jorge Luis Borges (1899-1986)
Type of plot: Fantastic literature
Time of plot: February, 1929–March, 1943
Locale: Buenos Aires, Argentina
First published: "El Aleph," 1945 (English translation, 1962)

> *Principal characters:*
> BORGES, the narrator and protagonist, a writer
> BEATRIZ VITERBO, his beloved
> CARLOS ARGENTINO DANERI, her cousin and a writer of
>   questionable merit

The Story

"The Aleph" begins with the narrator, Borges, recalling that on the February morning of Beatriz Viterbo's death, a billboard advertisement in the Plaza Constitución was being changed. The observation prompts him to vow not to allow himself to be changed by life, and thus he intends to consecrate himself to the memory of his beloved. Every year on Beatriz' birthday (April 30), Borges returns to the house of her father and her cousin, Carlos Argentino Daneri. Whereas in the past it had been necessary to devise pretexts for his visits, the new circumstances permit him to carry on his devotion to Beatriz while seeming to perform an act of courtesy and respect. With each successive visit, he arrives later and stays longer. Gradually he gains the confidence of Carlos Argentino.

Beatriz' cousin is in effect her antithesis: Beatriz possessed an ethereal quality that almost transcended reality, while Carlos Argentino is altogether too human, as is suggested by his entirely ordinary physical presence and his pointless existence. His remarks about modern man (that it is unnecessary for him to travel since the advent of the telephone, telegraph, radio, cinema, and so forth) cause Borges to make a connection between Carlos Argentino and literature: Both are equally inept, pompous, and vast. When Borges asks why Carlos Argentino does not write down his ideas, Carlos Argentino predictably responds that he has, in a poem entitled "The Earth." As Carlos Argentino reads and comments on the verses, the consummate mediocrity of the work becomes evident. The real task involved in the poem, decides Borges, has been, not its composition, but rather the invention of reasons to explain why it is so admirable. Carlos Argentino's purpose in his encyclopedic enterprise is to versify the face of the earth, which he does in a boring, unskillful, and chaotic way.

Several Sundays after Borges hears about the poem for the first time, Carlos Argentino unexpectedly requests a meeting between the two, which is to take place in the establishment of Zunino and Zungri. After censuring critics and the practice that he refers to as "prologuemania," Carlos Argentino comes to the point of the interview: He would like Borges' assistance in securing a prologue for his poem from Alvaro Melián Lafinur, a literary figure of renown. Borges agrees to help, but without any actual intention of doing so.

The following October, the protagonist receives the second call that he has ever received from Carlos Argentino, who this time is extremely upset because Zunino and Zungri are about to demolish his house in order to expand their business. Borges thinks that he understands the cousin's consternation until Carlos Argentino explains the real cause of his distress: He cannot finish the poem without the Aleph (one of the points in space which contains all points), which is located in the basement. An accidental discovery of his childhood, it now serves as the source of material for the poem.

Borges tells Carlos Argentino that he will be over immediately, and, upon hanging up, it occurs to him that Carlos Argentino is insane, which would account for his seemingly inexplicable behavior. Once in the house, Borges engages in a conversation with a large portrait of Beatriz until he is interrupted by Carlos Argentino, who is obsessed with the idea of losing the Aleph. After a glass of wine and some instructions about how to view the phenomenon, Borges goes down to the basement and settles into the position that Carlos Argentino has designated. Just when he fears that he has been poisoned and buried by a madman, he sees the Aleph, a small, iridescent sphere of nearly intolerable brilliancy, which reveals the inconceivable universe. He gropes for some emblem or image which might enable him to communicate the experience of witnessing the ineffable, infinite, and vertiginous Aleph, but at the same time he fears contaminating his report with the falseness of literature. Also, he feels despair in the knowledge that the successive nature of language makes it an inadequate vehicle for conveying the simultaneity of spectacle that is the Aleph.

Overcome by feelings of veneration and pity, Borges is once again rudely interrupted by the voice of Carlos Argentino. At that moment, he plots his revenge: He refuses to talk about the Aleph with Carlos Argentino and recommends repose in the serenity of the country. Yet despite his pretense, Borges has indeed been transformed by the experience: All faces seem familiar and nothing surprises him; all is return. Fortunately, however, memory yields to forgetfulness after a few nights of insomnia.

A postscript from the first of March, 1943, updates the report. Carlos Argentino's poem has won the Second National Prize for Literature, something which Borges ascribes to misunderstanding and envy. Finally, he poses some questions about the Aleph: Did Carlos Argentino choose that name for the sphere, or did he see it used elsewhere applied to the same sort of phenomenon? If, as Borges suspects, the latter is the case, does a genuine Aleph exist, and did he see it and forget it?

Themes and Meanings

"The Aleph" is a fictional rendering of a universal metaphor as outlined by Borges in an essay published in 1952 entitled "La esphera de Pascal" ("Pascal's Sphere"). The essay traces the development of the image of God as an endless sphere from six centuries before the Christian era to Blaise Pascal. Borges first cites Xenophanes of Colophon, who proposed to the Greeks the concept of one God who might subsume all the gods of their mythology, a single, perfect divinity in the form of a sphere and conveying solidity. Analogous images are found in the classical verses of Parmenides of Elea, in the Egyptian *Hermetica*, in the twelfth century poem *Roman de la rose*, and in the Book of Kings. The medieval interpretation of this idea was the presence of God in all of His creatures without being limited by any one of them, a reaffirmation of Scripture. When the cosmic vision represented in *The Divine Comedy* (the earth as the immobile center of the universe around which nine concentric circles revolve) ceded to Copernican space, the initial sense of liberation eventually turned into anguish: Man felt lost in time and space, alone in a universe that resembled a labyrinth and an abyss.

As Beatrice led Dante through the spheres to a vision of God, so does Beatriz Viterbo serve as the link between the character Borges and the Aleph: Her clairvoyance helps Borges to see. Images of light, agony, ecstasy, and eternity are common both to her and to the sphere, which is also prefigured by the collage of photographs that capture Beatriz' multiple attitudes in frozen time. Her death removes her from time or its passage (which is marked through change). The large portrait which Borges addresses shows her smiling out of time rather than out of date. She stands still, so to speak, while life goes on; she has entered eternity.

If Beatriz expresses the Aleph, Carlos Argentino misunderstands it. Her notable lack of interest in books and her desire to live life contrast with his obsession with literature, which, in his case, equals an avoidance of contact with life. His conclusions about twentieth century man show an enthusiasm for substituted forms of experience and an inability to distinguish them from reality. During all the years that he has spent in the basement observing the Aleph, he has been incapable of interpreting it because his deficient intellect dwells on its millions of individual details, which he then records. His attempts to turn revelation into reason are misdirected, a distortion of the original subject. The poem presumes to be a faithful reproduction of life but merely accumulates facts at the expense of essence.

Borges' description of the Aleph is an unrhymed enumeration in which events are seemingly unordered and unrelated—in other words, meant to simulate the experience itself. He despairs of communicating what he has witnessed because he is acutely aware of the limitations of language and the falseness of literature. The religious and literary precedents which he invokes do not betray the verbal ostentation of Carlos Argentino but rather are intended to refer to a shared past. At the same time that he relies on that past, however, he also recognizes the importance of forgetting: As the twilight blurs distinctions in the photographs and the colors of the portrait fade, so does time corrupt his memory of the Aleph—a release for which Borges is grateful. To him, this godlike knowledge is an intolerable burden to be forgotten.

Style and Technique

One of the most striking aspects of "The Aleph" is the quantity of allusions made to the world outside the text, be they literary, historical, religious, philosophical, or geographic. Most are explicit, such as the epigraphs which preface the story or the numerous proper names mentioned, but implicit reference is also made, for example, to *The Divine Comedy* by the presence of certain structural and thematic elements (Beatriz, the sphere, the descent, and the name Daneri). Literary precedents are summoned by Carlos Argentino as well as by Borges, although their respective reasons for doing so differ substantially: ostentation versus the quest for answers. In addition to texts, place-names appear with some regularity, contributing to the would-be veracity of Borges' report (a veracity which is completely at odds with the report's fantastic central episode).

The range and quantity of factual information are complementary to the story's elaborate temporal framework, both being dimensions which would normally help to orient the reader with respect to the events recounted. Throughout, the narrator remains highly conscious of years, months, days, hours, minutes, times of day, and segments of time, thereby enhancing the illusion of accuracy. There is also a thematic function involved: The contrast between time and eternity, like that between geographic locations and infinity, manifests the arbitrariness and artificiality of those human inventions.

Carlos Argentino is the symbol of such absurd endeavors, the epitome of misguided activity, and through him the futility of man's efforts becomes amusing. Meaninglessness, insignificance, affectation, obsession, mediocrity, and complacent stupidity are identified as humankind's characteristic traits and as a way of coping with existence: Man focuses on small, immediate concerns because the larger questions cannot be answered. The somber, melancholy tone set by the agony and death of Beatriz is pervasive and bespeaks other losses (of innocence and faith, for example). In juxtaposing two elements as incongruous as profound sadness and absurdity (a technique that recurs throughout the story), the author illuminates otherwise undiscernible qualities and relationships in an ironically humorous way.

Krista Ratkowski Carmona

THE ALIEN CORN

Author: W. Somerset Maugham (1874-1965)
Type of plot: Realism
Time of plot: The early 1920's
Locale: London and Sussex, England, and Munich, Germany
First published: 1931

> *Principal characters:*
> FERDY RABENSTEIN, a worldly and affluent London Jew
> GEORGE BLAND, his great-nephew
> SIR ADOLPHUS (FREDDY) BLAND, a country squire of Sussex
> and George's father
> MURIEL (MIRIAM) BLAND, Sir Adolphus' wife
> LADY HANNAH BLAND, the mother of Sir Adolphus and the
> sister of Ferdy Rabenstein
> LEA MAKART, a concert pianist and a friend of Ferdy
> Rabenstein

The Story

The narrator, a successful middle-aged novelist, tells the story from his point of view in episodes that span about three years. He reminisces about his long-standing acquaintance with Ferdy Rabenstein, a cultured and affluent Jewish bachelor of London who moves in the best social circles. From Ferdy, the narrator learns that the Blands, who have invited him to Tilby, their estate in Sussex, are Ferdy's relatives, Sir Adolphus Bland being his nephew. Unlike Ferdy, they have concealed their Jewish identity and have led the lives of English country gentry.

Eminently successful, Sir Adolphus, a conservative member of Parliament, served as minister of munitions during World War I. Muriel, his wife, has converted to Catholicism. Their two sons, who bear the quintessentially English names George and Henry, are enrolled in elite educational institutions. Henry attends Eton, and George, the elder son, has just been sent down from Oxford, where he wasted his time and his father's money. Family ties with Ferdy have been broken, in part because he would not change his name during World War I, but also because the Blands want no association with unassimilated Jews.

Since George will inherit the estate, his father wants him to follow a suitable profession, such as the diplomatic service. George has other ideas. He asks permission to go to Munich to study languages and prepare for an Oxford examination, a request his family reluctantly grants.

A few days after his return from the Blands', the narrator sees Ferdy in London and is invited to dinner. At the dinner he finds George present, a surprising turn because George's parents have rejected Ferdy's invitation, sent through the narrator himself. Ferdy has interceded with his sister, Lady Hannah Bland, George's grandmother, who arranged the meeting. Yet the dinner is not a success because Ferdy embarrasses George, whom he has just met for the first time, by telling humorous Jewish stories.

When the narrator next sees Muriel, he learns that George has spent his time in Germany studying music in the hope of becoming a concert pianist. The parents turn their energies to discouraging him from a course that they regard as unsuitable and demeaning. When George returns to Tilby for his twenty-first birthday celebration, however, he is heaped with gifts. On this occasion he causes consternation when he informs his family that he intends to return to Munich, saying that he knows he has genius. Even Ferdy, who is now on speaking terms with Sir Adolphus, sides with the family against George's ambition. After George remains unmoved by pleas and threats, his grandmother, Lady Bland, suggests a compromise. He will be allowed two years' study in Munich and will return home at the end. If it is not apparent by then that he has genuine talent, he will give up music and assume the duties of an elder son on a landed estate.

Later, the narrator visits George in Munich at the request of his mother, since the agreement with George stipulated that members of the immediate family would not visit him. He finds George living a bohemian life-style but conscientiously applying himself to his piano. He also learns that, unlike his parents, George is concerned with his Jewish identity and heritage and takes pride in his friendship with Jewish students, artists, and intellectuals. He no longer thinks of himself as English. The narrator hears George play the piano, and, although he is no critic of music, concludes that George's hands are not well coordinated. When he returns to England, he tells the family only that George is well.

At the end of two years George returns to Tilby, and the family gathers to judge his talent. With his concurrence, they have invited the concert pianist Lea Makart to hear him play and to make the judgment about his career. The narrator notices the same lack of coordination that he had noticed before. When George finishes playing, Lea Makart inquires, "What is it you want me to tell you?" He replies that he wants to know whether he can become a first-rate concert pianist. Her devastating response is, "Not in a thousand years." George accepts this profoundly disappointing news in good form. When she suggests that he ask for another opinion, he admits that her assessment agrees with that of his teacher in Munich. She points out to him that he does not have a pianist's hands and, before leaving for her scheduled concert, plays for the assembled family. In her performance, the narrator clearly discerns the difference between the professional artist and the amateur.

Sensing his son's deep pain and disappointment, Sir Adolphus offers to give him another year in Munich or to send him around the world with a friend from Oxford. Deeply moved, George embraces his father and says he will take a walk; instead, he goes to the gun room. Afterward, hearing a report, servants go to the room and find George shot through the heart.

Themes and Meanings

Maugham's title is taken from John Keats's "Ode to a Nightingale," which contains a poignant reference to the biblical character Ruth, who stood with heavy heart in Judah amid the alien corn. Although Maugham finds his chief talent in telling a story in a memorable way, he considers characters that are alienated from society the most interesting. In other narratives he writes of unassimilated but changed Englishmen in the colonies, particularly in Asia and the South Pacific. He likes to depict characters who are in a sense outsiders, who have a kink or unusual streak in their personalities. In this story, the narrator identifies with the Blands, calling himself an alien because of his aesthetic detachment, yet he shows the reader, by probing beneath the surface of the characters, by catching them off guard, that they are not as assimilated as they think. As self-conscious outsiders, the Blands (the name they have chosen seems symbolic) are unusual because they strive so hard for assimilation. Their very striving to shut themselves off from their past creates tensions within the family involving three generations and leading to their son's tragic death.

More than alienation, however, the quest for an ideal contributes to the tragedy. Another common and significant theme in Maugham is art, especially its power to attract absolute commitment. While the Blands think the performing arts too trivial for their son, Lea Makart, the gifted pianist, expresses the view embraced by George. Artistic genius is all that matters. Other people are only the artist's raw material in the creation of beauty. If one has genius, all sacrifices to further it pale into insignificance. Like other characters in Maugham's works, George is willing to pin all of his hope on artistic success. A character such as Charles Strickland in *The Moon and Sixpence* (1919) takes a desperate gamble and succeeds, establishing himself as a renowned painter. In *Of Human Bondage* (1915), however, Fanny Price, seeking to become a painter despite her lack of talent, experiences a fate similar to George's. When he discovers that he cannot attain his only ambition, George concludes that life is not worthwhile, despite the wealth, status, and security assured him by his doting family.

Style and Technique

The story is narrated in the lucid, fluent, and idiomatic English that one usually finds in Maugham, who is not known for figurative language or for poetic passages. Yet one passage from the story, that describing the narrator's response to the playing of Lea Makart, has been noted as one of

Maugham's most artful. It is filled with images, associations called up by the music, and flights of imagination, leading up to generalized impressions. Its rhythm is artfully complex. The plot reveals extensive use of foreshadowing and irony.

Yet Maugham's narrative art is perhaps most evident in the narrator, a type often designated a Maugham persona because he bears a striking resemblance to the author. He is an established and successful author who moves with ease in upper-class society. He is tolerant, urbane, skeptical, and somewhat detached. The narrator interacts with the characters, advising them, even disagreeing with them, but never becoming insistent or intense. Some of his comments are only for the reader, differing from those he addresses to the characters. He sizes up situations and characters in frank and critical revelations to the reader.

The narrator tells the story in episodes, beginning with a leisurely account of his acquaintance with Ferdy Rabenstein. A series of episodes exploiting dramatic conflicts then follows, with effective and sparkling dialogue. It is typical of Maugham that much of this dialogue occurs during dinners with Ferdy, with the Blands, and with George. Maugham's early success as a dramatist appears to have exerted a strong influence on his later fiction.

Stanley Archer

ALL THE YEARS OF HER LIFE

Author: Morley Callaghan (1903-   )
Type of plot: Domestic realism
Time of plot: 1935
Locale: Unspecified; probably New York City
First published: 1935

> *Principal characters:*
> ALFRED HIGGINS, the protagonist, a young man apparently
>   destined for serious trouble
> MRS. HIGGINS, his mother
> MR. SAM CARR, his employer

The Story

Late in the evening, a drugstore owner and his assistant are closing up for the day. Sam Carr, the small, gray-haired proprietor, stops Alfred Higgins, his adolescent helper, just as the young man is leaving for home. Alfred has worked there for six months, and this is the first time Mr. Carr has ever varied the evening routine of bidding his employee "good night" without even looking at him. Alfred is unnerved by his boss's softly menacing manner as he blocks his exit.

Mr. Carr asks Alfred to empty his pockets before he leaves. When Alfred feigns surprise and then indignation, Mr. Carr reveals that he knows the exact items that Alfred has stolen that evening: a compact, lipstick, and toothpaste. Moreover, he tells Alfred that he has suspected him of petty thievery for some time but wanted to be proved wrong because he liked him. Now, he believes, he has no alternative but to call in the police.

Mr. Carr pauses to let Alfred absorb the full impact of his sense of betrayal and disappointment. Alfred admits to himself that repeatedly he has been in serious trouble since leaving school and has been unable to hold on to a job. He feels afraid and ashamed. Mr. Carr seems to sense Alfred's emotional pain and decides to call Alfred's mother before summoning the authorities. Clearly, Alfred is at a decisive point in his life.

Anxious to appear indifferent and self-reliant, Alfred is nevertheless hoping desperately to be rescued from police and courts by his mother. He expects her to rush in, hysterical and pleading; while he hopes she will save him from the law, he anticipates his embarrassment at her abject behavior to Mr. Carr and her contempt for him. She soon arrives; although it is obvious that she has hurriedly dressed, her poise and calm dignity are a surprise to them both.

She confronts her son, who does not deny his guilt or attempt to mitigate it. She then speaks to Mr. Carr with such unaffected humility and understanding that he is somewhat awed by her. She asks for compassion, which she receives for her son. Mr. Carr dismisses Alfred from his job but lets him go home. On their way home, Alfred's relief verges on hilarity, but he is restrained by his mother's obvious pain and anger. Her silence abashes him.

At home, Mrs. Higgins calls Alfred "a bad lot" and sends him to bed while she goes to the kitchen to make some tea. In his room, the fear and shame Alfred felt earlier in the evening begin to dissipate, and he longs to tell his mother how he admired her smooth handling of the situation. He quietly goes to the kitchen, and there, undetected, he observes his mother's face, the face behind the mask she had worn earlier in the evening. It is "a frightened, broken face utterly unlike the face of the woman who had been so assured a little while ago in the drugstore." Her hands tremble as she pours tea and draws the cup unsteadily toward her lips. At that moment, Alfred has a sudden, crucial insight. He comprehends the hard reality of his mother's life as well as the effect of his actions on her. He knows, too, that in an important sense his own youth is over. An evening that began with a shabby crime culminates in a moment of sympathetic identification that marks Alfred's passage to manhood and maturity.

Themes and Meanings

In this story, Morley Callaghan focuses on a rather commonplace and distressing experience during which a young man's character begins to take a definite moral form. The boy's petty thievery, false bravado, and emotional dependency are highlighted early in the story. There is little to suggest the possibility of genuine moral growth except for the boy's capacity for honest self-evaluation when he is first confronted by his employer, and his ready admission of guilt to his mother.

Alfred does mature, however, and it is important to recognize that his moral development owes very little to the fear and shame that suffuse him upon being caught and imagining his punishment or his mother's contempt for him. Fear and shame prompt him at first to indulge in some defensive role-playing, and these emotions quickly dissipate once the immediate threat of arrest is removed. In this interlude of relaxation from tension, however, Alfred is surprised by an insight that transforms him.

When he discovers his mother, alone and vulnerable, he sees for the first time the hard path she has walked "all of the years of her life." This capacity for responding deeply and fully to the imagined life of another is, Callaghan implies, the beginning of maturity. Thus, for Callaghan, maturity depends essentially on a sense of solidarity with others as opposed to a feeling of anarchic individualism, which sees others as simply obstructions or conveniences. All of Alfred's anger, shame, despair, and elation earlier in the evening subside eventually, allowing his innate capacity for sympathetic identification with another to reach expression. This capacity may seem as commonplace as the crime that Alfred commits, but Callaghan convincingly suggests that it is at the root of the moral imagination.

Style and Technique

As in most of his stories, Callaghan's style here is objective, concise, and unadorned. He strives to present the essential, illuminating experience directly to his reader. Much depends on the reader's sensitivity to implications and undercurrents, which is entirely consonant with a story about a young man's discovery of the poignant reality underlying his mother's apparently routine existence.

The story is written in the third person, with Alfred as the central consciousness, as befits a story about his moral growth. The clipped dialogue, unmetaphorical prose, and paucity of specific details regarding time, place, characters, atmosphere, and so on allow Callaghan to highlight those moments when the central character's consciousness expands under the impact of experience.

Structurally, "All the Years of Her Life" develops through a series of surprises moving toward a crucial revelation. Alfred is surprised by his employer, surprised by Mr. Carr's inexplicable reluctance to prosecute, surprised by his mother's deft handling of the situation, and, finally, surprised by his discovery of the pain and suffering his mother endures. Though compact and spare, the story convincingly suggests the potential in humanity for significant moral development.

Michael J. Larsen

"ALL YOU ZOMBIES—"

Author: Robert A. Heinlein (1907-   )
Type of plot: Science fiction
Time of plot: 1945-1993
Locale: Cleveland, Ohio; New York City; somewhere under the Rocky
    Mountains
First published: 1959

Principal character:
THE NARRATOR, an agent of the Temporal Bureau

The Story

"'All You Zombies—'" takes full advantage of the cause-and-effect paradox inherent in the concept of time travel. The tale assumes not only the
existence of time travel but also its necessity. In order to forestall the atomic
destruction of the earth, for example, agents of the Temporal Bureau must
selectively manipulate what becomes the past, taking care not to leave too
many anachronisms. Temporal agents do not change the past, for that is
impossible; rather, it is their hidden presence in past events that ensures that
history turns out as it really does. For example, the intervention of a temporal agent turned what could have been the nuclear disintegration of New
York into what became known as the Fizzle War of 1963. The Mistake of
1972 (which apparently led to forced labor and a shortage of food in 1974),
however, did take place. It is history, and no temporal agent can undo it.

More temporal agents are needed to prevent another Mistake. Thus, the
narrator is sent from 1993 back to 1970 to recruit a likely candidate: himself.
Central to the fun of the story is the revelation of how significant a part the
agent played in the very existence of the raw recruit. The recruit actually
comes into the world as a baby girl, Jane. She is stolen from the hospital in
1945 by a mysterious man, the temporal agent, who places her as a foundling
on the steps of an orphanage in Cleveland. Though she is determined to keep
her virginity until she is married, Jane realizes after lonely years in the
orphanage that her rather severe, mannish appearance will do little to attract
a potential husband. The alternative is to enlist in W.E.N.C.H.E.S., the
Women's Emergency National Corps, Hospitality & Entertainment Section,
to provide on-board relief of sexual tensions for pilots who must spend years
in space. The Corps takes good care of its own, and many end up getting
married to pilots.

Jane's dream, though, is shattered in 1963. She is seduced by a mysterious
man and becomes pregnant. Her baby girl is delivered by cesarean section,
and the surgeon points out to Jane that she has apparently grown up with
both male and female organs. In fact, though Jane did become pregnant,

"she" is really a man. Worse, a month later Jane's daughter is stolen from the hospital nursery. Jane is determined to find the man who seduced her and brought ruin to her life. Now maturing as a male, Jane changes his name and moves to New York and, unable to secure a decent job, becomes a confession writer. Now, in 1970, at twenty-five, he spills out his life story to the barkeeper at "Pop's Place" in New York. The man behind the counter, the temporal agent, offers this potential recruit a chance to come face-to-face with the seducer.

That requires a time jump for both of them back to 1963. Sent out by the agent, the potential recruit finds not a mysterious man, but Jane. She is irresistible. As the agent later reflects: "It's a shock to have it proved to you that you can't resist seducing yourself." After such a realization, the young man is ready to be recruited into the Temporal Bureau. The agent returns to 1993 with his recruit, who is sent off for processing.

The agent returns to his own quarters, determined to give up recruitment for some other work at the Bureau. Thirty years of recruiting have soured him on the job. Besides, once one has recruited oneself, completing the circle, what is there left to accomplish? The young man will make a good agent, of course; he already knew that.

Self-doubt and loneliness wash over the agent. He glances down at his belly, finding the scar from the cesarean section, and something in him aches for Jane. Those around the agent, and presumably the readers of the story as well, are to him little more than zombies, animated corpses, less than human, with their origins unknown. Now, in the darkness, the agent has a frightening thought, and he addresses the reader: "*You* aren't really there at all. There isn't anybody but me—Jane—here alone in the dark. I miss you dreadfully!"

All the main characters in the story—the agent, the recruit, the baby girl, the woman, the seducer—are the same person. A few other supporting characters are briefly mentioned in the story, such as the doctor at the hospital and an officer at the Temporal Bureau, but the question of their identity is left open. The events in the story form a closed loop, and it is in that loop that the agent is caught. Everyone else is excluded from that loop; the very existence of others, from the agent's perspective, is questionable indeed.

Themes and Meanings

Robert A. Heinlein has dealt with the convolutions of time travel before, most notably in the novel *The Door into Summer* (1957) and in "By His Bootstraps," a story published in 1941. "'All You Zombies—'" takes full advantage of those convolutions but is much more than the work of a gifted writer who has taken on an imaginative challenge. At the beginning of the story, the temporal agent refers to the odd ring he is wearing. A gift from another operative, it pictures the World Snake consuming its own tail, symbolizing the time-travel paradox. It is in a sense also symbolic of a favorite kind of Heinlein character, the self-made individual, one who by force of intellect and will is able to create his own environment. In *Starship Troopers* (1959), for example, published the same year as "'All You Zombies—',", Heinlein glorifies the individual combatant in his fight against the Bugs. The world of the starship trooper is all that matters.

It is to the author's credit that he realizes the darker side of the self-made individual. In the end, such a person is condemned to a solipsistic universe. A culture which exalts individualism, self-achievement, and even eccentricity, also produces alienation, disenchantment, and loneliness. The ultimate end of the work ethic, the pressure for individual accomplishment, is the salvation of the world, over and over and over again, by the temporal agent. It is at once the highest calling and yet the most meaningless of tasks, for if all but the agent are mere zombies, for whom is the world to be saved? Fittingly, the word "zombie" refers not only to talking corpses, the soulless ones, but also to a snake, the python god of West African origin.

Style and Technique

The story is told in a brusque, no-nonsense manner, with each of its seven divisions headed by time and location. There is playfulness in Heinlein's depiction of the young recruit, who as a confession writer has taken to calling himself the "Unmarried Mother," reminiscent perhaps of the author's own early days as a pulp writer at four cents a word. "Unmarried Mother" refers not only to the point of view taken in the young man's published stories but also to his experience as Jane, pregnant (it turns out) with himself. Here the writer is truly the creator.

Heinlein peppers his story with intriguing glimpses of a future society. In his version of 1970 (the story was published eleven years earlier), space travel is routine, with the need for female companionship spawning such organizations as W.E.N.C.H.E.S. and, in 1993, the elite Women's Hospitality Order Refortifying & Encouraging Spacemen. At Pop's Place in 1970, a song entitled "I'm My Own Grandpaw!" keeps blaring from the jukebox. The mysterious Temporal Bureau headquarters under the Rocky Mountains hints of increasingly complex loops. Are operatives from the farther future at work in 1993 to ensure the workings of temporal agents in 1970?

Against this background, the events leading to the Unmarried Mother's self-creation are played out. The agent recounts his activities with a serious, though wry, tone. His emotions at the end of the story suggest a lonely, world-weary cry, yet even here the cry is for the self, for Jane. "'All You Zombies—'" is a cautionary tale as well as one of the finest time-travel yarns in science fiction.

Dan Barnett

AN ALPINE IDYLL

Author: Ernest Hemingway (1899-1961)
Type of plot: Realism
Time of plot: The early 1920's
Locale: The Austrian Tyrol
First published: 1927

> *Principal characters:*
> NICK and
> JOHN, young American men
> AUSTRIAN INNKEEPER
> SEXTON
> OLZ, an Austrian peasant

The Story

"An Alpine Idyll" belongs at the end of the Nick Adams cycle of stories. A now mature Nick has come down from a month's skiing in the mountains with a friend, John. They witness a peasant burying his wife and the reader experiences an epiphanic moment of recognition shared with Nick, though not with his friend.

The story opens in the early morning with two young men carrying their skis as they are climbing down from the mountains into the valley. They pass a churchyard just as a burial is ending. The narrator, who remains unnamed throughout the story but who is clearly Nick Adams, greets the priest but does not receive a greeting in return. The young men stop to watch the sexton shoveling earth into the new grave. When the sexton rests, a peasant standing at the grave takes over, spreading the soil as evenly as he would manure in a garden.

The grave filling looks unreal to the young men, and they cannot imagine being dead on such a beautiful May morning. They walk up the road to the town of Galtur; the narrator explains that they were skiing in Silvretta for a month, but that with the coming of the warmer weather the skiing was spoiled. It was too late in the spring to be up in the Silvretta; they stayed too long, and the May morning in the valley seemed more natural than the spring in the high mountains.

They arrive at an inn, and, after greeting the owner, who gives them their mail, they go inside to drink beer while they read the accumulated post. During an exchange of conversation, John notes that it is no good doing a thing too long, such as skiing in the mountains in the spring. The open window draws Nick's attention to the white road and dusty trees and the green field and stream beyond. Inside, the sunlight filters through the empty glasses. John is asleep with his head on the table. Two men come into the inn: the sexton and the bearded peasant from the burial. Both order drinks, for which, after a brief argument, the peasant insists on paying, and he abruptly leaves to drink at a gasthaus up the road. The innkeeper, after a brief exchange in a local dialect with the sexton, asks when the young men want to eat. John is still asleep on the table, but he awakens when the menu is brought by the waitress. Nick asks the innkeeper to join them for a drink.

As the innkeeper is taking a seat, he calls peasants beasts. Nick confesses that he and John saw the funeral as they were coming into town; he is informed that it was for the peasant's wife. Again, the innkeeper calls the peasant a beast. "How do you mean?" asks Nick. The innkeeper calls over the sexton to meet Nick and John, and the sexton accepts a drink and agrees to tell the two gentlemen about the peasant; he must do so, however, in a dialect unintelligible to John. The peasant, the innkeeper begins, brought his wife in for burial that day. She died the previous November. No, it was in December, the sexton corrects him, but the peasant was not able to bring her to be buried until the snow was gone from the pass over the Paznaun, for although the peasant lives over the mountain, he belongs to their parish. The sexton explains that some difficulty arose when the priest saw the condition of the dead woman's face. The priest asked her husband if she had suffered much (since she was known to have had a heart condition, nobody was surprised by her death); no, she had not suffered, the priest was told. Then the priest asked how her face had got into such a condition.

The peasant responded that, after his wife died and he realized that he could not move her body across the pass until spring, he placed her body in the woodshed on top of the big logs. Later that winter, when it came time to use the big logs, he stood his wife's body against the wall. Her mouth was open and, when he came in to cut wood at night, he started hanging his lantern from her frozen mouth. He did this every time he went to the woodshed to work. Upon hearing this, the priest was furious and told the man that he had done wrong. The peasant, however, claimed that he loved his wife and apparently felt little remorse.

John interrupts the story to ask when they are going to eat. Nick tells him to order and asks the innkeeper whether the story is true. Certainly, he is told; the peasants are beasts. Again, John says that they should eat, and Nick agrees.

Themes and Meanings

Although several critics have noted the importance of this grotesque Tyrolean tale, "An Alpine Idyll" contains more than the mordant humor of the folk story. The central theme, which is introduced in the opening paragraphs, is the need to return to an active life after a period of rest and pleasure. Nick and John have already stayed too long in the mountains and are regretting that they did not leave earlier: It is not good to extend pleasure beyond a certain point. This theme is reinforced by the references to descending from the mountain into the valley, where the May sunshine seems more natural. The accumulated letters which the two young men read while drinking beer also recall the outside world awaiting them. It is a world of obligations and responsibilities.

Little attempt has been made to understand the macabre story-within-the-story as in any way integrated with such larger themes. Yet there are many connections. The first and most obvious is to see the folktale also reflecting the theme of something overstayed or prolonged beyond what is natural. The peasant, like the young men, had to remain too long in the mountains with his dead wife before he could descend into the valley to discharge his duty and bury her, thereby putting a closure to her death. With the funeral completed, he is free to get on with life's obligations.

"An Alpine Idyll" was first published in book form in the collection *Men Without Women* (1927), and the peasant's story may also suggest the grotesqueness of men living without women, providing a clue to some of the unmentioned obligations to which Nick must return—namely, those of wife and family. The "unnaturalness" of the spring skiing also makes a connection here with the unnaturalness of the peasant's behavior in using his wife's dead body as a lantern stand. In both cases, the light of the past experience illuminates something strange in the mountains, a something put into perspective in the cleansing light of the valley below.

Style and Technique

It is commonplace to notice that Hemingway used nature as a reflector of his characters' moods and feelings. "An Alpine Idyll" is a story whose meaning hinges on an evocative description of a pastoral scene out a window which Nick observes while reading his mail. It is an especially telling scene, since it so expertly illustrates Hemingway's pictorial style, a style he likened to the paintings of Paul Cézanne.

This passage opens with the sun streaming through the window and through the half-full beer bottles on the table. It ends with Nick's attention drawn back inside the window to the empty beer glasses on the table and to John asleep with his head resting on his arms. What Nick sees outside the window does indeed look like a painting described plane by plane: the white road and dusty trees, the green field and stream beyond, the mill with the untended log bobbing in the water, the five crows—one separate (like Nick) looking at the others in the green fields—the porch of the inn and the men sitting on it and finally, John asleep at the table. It is as though a motion picture camera were making an excursion out into nature and back in again; Nick ties together his own life and thoughts with the Cézanne-like outdoors, and the empty/full tension of the Jan Vermeer-like still life indoors.

The log rocking in the mill water recalls the peasant's wife, frozen and unattended in the woodshed. The wetness and greenness of the fields and stream contrast with the cold sterility of the mountains which Nick has left behind. All this is made clear through Nick's painterly synoptic vision. The scene is a moment of calm recognition which is broken by the arrival of the peasant and the sexton, who will tell their strange story of death—a story which, like the gravesite scene which greets the young men just down from the mountain, provides both protagonist and reader with a grim reminder of life's final obligation.

Charles L. P. Silet

THE ALTAR OF THE DEAD

Author: Henry James (1843-1916)
Type of plot: Psychological realism
Time of plot: Late Victorian period
Locale: London
First published: 1895

> *Principal characters:*
> GEORGE STRANSOM, the protagonist, who maintains a
>   memorial altar to his dead friends
> THE YOUNG LADY, a nameless female character who becomes
>   a friend of Stransom and a fellow worshiper at the altar
> MARY ANTRIM, Stransom's deceased fiancée
> ACTON HAGUE, a former friend to Stransom and lover to the
>   nameless female character

The Story

Fifty-five-year-old George Stransom is obsessed with observing the anniversary of his fiancée Mary Antrim's death, a fact which leads him to expand his commemorative pantheon to include all the other departed friends who live on in his memory. Imbued from an early age with what he terms "the religion of the Dead," he decides to provide a material sign of his remembrance in the form of a private altar in a church, which he endows on the condition that he be allowed to stipulate the number of candles to be lit there.

Stransom, after a time of worshiping privately at his altar, notices that a lady somewhat younger than he has been as frequent a worshiper at his altar as he. One day he notices her at a concert and inquires if she recognizes him, which she does. They strike up a friendship subsequently, although Stransom, in his reserve, takes considerable time even to learn her name. She lives with an elderly aunt, who acts as an obstacle to their further intimacy until her death, after which the young lady invites Stransom to her lodgings. On this occasion, in showing Stransom her room, it is brought out that the young lady was the lover of Acton Hague, and it is to his memory that she has been devoted in her observances at Stransom's altar. More powerfully than the deceased had in life, the ghost of Acton Hague rises up between Stransom and the lady and separates them for an extended period. This gulf is fixed between them because of Stransom's hatred of Hague (who injured him in a way that is never specified) and the lady's refusal to abandon the memory of her lover.

Separated for many months, the pious couple are reunited finally when Stransom journeys to his altar to complete the array of lighted candles which lacks but one more for perfect symmetry. Drawn by some mysterious instinct, the young lady discovers Stransom at the altar, now committed to adding a final candle to the group. The young lady believes at first that the addition is to be the memorial to Acton Hague that she had demanded of him, but she discovers her error upon realizing that the final candle is to light the memory of Stransom's own death, which occurs as the story closes.

Themes and Meanings

The story is perhaps the most powerful presentation in Henry James's entire oeuvre of two of his most important themes: mourning and renunciation. Stransom's obsession with the memory of his departed friends is linked to his having abandoned any other form of living, to his characteristically Jamesian renunciation of an active life for one of contemplation and privacy. Even the bond that is forged, then broken, between Stransom and the nameless young lady depends crucially on their mutual recognition that the truly human act is the abandonment of life in favor of memorializing the dead. Her career as a writer and his vaguely specified affairs do not impinge in any significant way upon the main action, which is focused on their mutual mourning and the conflict that arises out of their inability to share a single attitude toward one of their dead.

Like many of James's shorter tales, this one, too, is concerned with the life of the artist, although here the figure of the artist is represented in the pious Stransom, whose work of art is neither novel nor painting but the very altar which he endows and in a way even creates. The clear emphasis on the importance of symmetry and harmony among the lighted candles, on the price which Stransom must pay in order to achieve this perfection (his death is necessary to complete both the altar and the tale itself)—these in other contexts are characteristic features of James's conception of the artist's life and work. For James, the artist must renounce participation in the active affairs of the world and devote himself to the solitary and generally unappreciated labor of aesthetic understanding. The nameless young lady's profession as a writer serves to counterpoint the genuine devotion to art that she and Stransom share against the false labors of commercial scribbling. As in many other contexts throughout the James canon (most graphically in the short story "The Next Time"), public fame and commercial success are at absolute loggerheads with authentically aesthetic achievement. The price of such devotion, as the fate of Stransom illustrates, is ultimately life itself. One could say that Stransom's death is merely the logical and necessary outcome of a life which has effectively renounced the living from the moment that its focus became exclusively the mourning over the memory of departed friends.

Style and Technique

James was a notable theoretician of fictional technique, particularly of so-called narrative point of view. Taking his cue from the "free indirect style" inaugurated by Gustave Flaubert, James stipulated again and again that the adoption of a limited point of view in which the narrator was privy to the innermost thoughts of a single character but more or less deprived, except from the evidence of conversation and gestures, of any information about the thoughts and feelings of other characters was the key to realistic and aesthetically powerful narrative. "The Altar of the Dead" adopts exclusively the point of view of Stransom, whose speculations, emotions, and intuitions are all made entirely lucid for the reader, at the same time that he acts as what James often called the "reflector" of the deeds and the possible thoughts of the other principal character. Her remaining unnamed throughout the story is possibly mannered, but it does reinforce the point that for the reader she is never fully embodied but remains an object of attention only insofar as she is of interest to and helps to illuminate the character of Stransom.

The adoption of limited omniscience serves other purposes in the tale as well, and James characteristically practices his craft with consummate skill. The entire narrative turns, in one sense, on the meaning of the character of Acton Hague, who is both the bond and the barrier between Stransom and the young lady. Given Stransom's long-standing grievance against Hague, and his effectively having written Hague out of existence (for Stransom himself, that is), it is perfectly plausible that the reader will never learn any more about Hague than Stransom's vague feeling of having been wronged. A different view of Hague would have been possible were the reader to have access to the nameless young lady's thoughts, but this is precisely what the narrative technique, rigorously limiting point of view, denies the reader. The mystery of Hague, which is in a way the mystery of the entire tale, is protected by the device of narrative technique.

James's major fiction (the bulk of his novels and some two dozen of the tales, including "The Altar of the Dead") is dominated by the device of the secret. Diane Arbus' famous remark about a photograph's being "a secret about a secret; the more it tells you, the less you know," applies with equal rigor to the fictional world of Henry James. In learning that Acton Hague was the lover of Stransom's younger friend, one is more, not less, in the dark about Hague than before. This is made clear in Stransom's puzzlement over what his lady friend might have loved in his enemy, as well as in Stransom's desire to know precisely the details of their relationship. All that the revelations in this story, including the final revelation of Stransom's own death as the fulfillment of the design of the altar, reveal is the extent of the reader's ignorance about the meanings of the lives of the characters. There would have been a variety of ways in which this sense of ultimate and irresolvable mystery could have been achieved, but surely the device of limited narrative point of view is one of the more effective means of maintaining the sense of ignorance and wonderment which animates James's fiction. James's stories manifestly reach a point of climax, customarily in the final paragraphs, but they signally lack any definitive factual or diegetic resolution. In this way, his narratives are less contemporary with those of Arthur Conan Doyle than with the antinovels of Alain Robbe-Grillet.

Michael Sprinker

ALYOSHA THE POT

Author: Leo Tolstoy (1828-1910)
Type of plot: Satiric fable
Time of plot: Nineteenth century
Locale: Rural Russia
First published: "Alyosha Gorshok," 1911 (English translation, 1944)

> *Principal characters:*
> ALYOSHA, the protagonist, a simple, good-hearted, and
>   uncomplaining peasant lad
> ALYOSHA'S FATHER, who is selfish and neglectful of his son
> A TOWN MERCHANT, the employer of Alyosha at age nineteen,
>   who, as well as his family, overworks the lad
> USTINYA (or USTINJA), the orphaned young cook for the
>   merchant's family, who is in love with Alyosha

The Story

In simple language, this compact narrative presents the correspondingly uncomplicated and short life of Alyosha, from his early years with his family in a village to his death at age twenty-one from an accident while working in town. The plot can be divided into three phases, in each of which the protagonist is abused in some way. The first phase shows Alyosha's life from early childhood through his eighteenth year, as the spindly lad grows up with his peasant family in a village. Despite his build, he is hardworking and is abusively overtaxed with farm chores by his mother and father, leaving him little if any time for school, which Alyosha has found difficult from the beginning. Because of his cheerfulness (derived from good-heartedness, the narrator implies), Alyosha uncomplainingly bears his labors, his parents' habitual, overly severe chastisement, and the mockery from other youths about his homeliness and clumsiness. The latter occasions his nickname, when after accidentally breaking a pot filled with milk Alyosha is not only beaten by his mother but also tauntingly dubbed "the Pot" by his peers, whose childhood cruelty complements that of the adults.

In the second phase of the plot, Alyosha is apprenticed by his father to a town merchant, replacing Alyosha's brother, who has been drafted into the army. Despite initial doubts and insults about Alyosha's physical capacity for labor, the merchant, along with the rest of the household, quickly falls into the pattern of Alyosha's parents, assigning the ever-cheerful and obedient youth an unending series of toils. Once again, Alyosha is incessantly criticized and taken for granted, never thanked, and shown kindness only by the young cook, who, though working Alyosha like the rest of the household, makes an effort to see that he is properly fed and clothed.

In the third phase of the plot, Alyosha discovers for the first time a relationship not based on family or necessity but on love. Though his clumsy marriage proposal is accepted by the cook, Ustinya, who returns his feeling, the couple is thwarted by the callous self-interest of those around them. The merchant and his wife object to the marriage, fearing a lessening of productivity in their servants. When their complaint is made to Alyosha's father, who has only been interested in collecting the entirety of his son's wages and has even reproved his son for the expense of a new pair of boots (the old ones, hand-me-downs from his brother, were literally worn out in Alyosha's ceaseless labors), the father forbids the marriage. Always obedient, Alyosha agrees, though both he and Ustinya are grieved, and for the first time in his life, Alyosha's smiling gives way to weeping when he answers affirmatively the question put to him by the merchant's wife about whether he will mind his father.

The narrative states that Alyosha's life returns to what it had been, but the reader knows that Alyosha suffers the added injury of losing his loved one in addition to his regular maltreatment by family and employers. Only a short time later, Alyosha falls from the rooftop of the merchant's store, where he has climbed to clear off snow, as ordered by the merchant's clerk. At the conclusion of the story, Alyosha's simple piety is demonstrated when on the third day of his incapacitation Alyosha thanks Ustinya for her kindness, vindicates the thwarting of their marriage (since his fatal injury would have ended it anyway), prays wordlessly with the priest who has been summoned, and then dies peacefully.

Themes and Meanings

The fundamental goodness, patience, meekness, and altruism of Alyosha highlight in satiric contrast the moral defects of the story's other characters. The impatience and ungentleness of Alyosha's mother are stressed by the opening picture of her thrashing of her son for dropping the pot, though later in the story Alyosha fleetingly recalls moments of maternal kindness or pity. Alyosha's father is depicted as self-interested and materialistic, concerned only with how much work and money he can get out of his son. Similarly, the merchant and his wife care only about how much labor they can be spared as a result of Alyosha's toils, at the least possible expense. The rest of the household, with similar lack of compassion, take advantage of Alyosha, even (in the beginning) the sympathetically portrayed Ustinya, whose acceptance of Alyosha's proposal by striking him on the back with a towel (or a ladle, depending on the particular translation of the story) seems to symbolize her partial affiliation with the world of force and self-assertiveness for which Alyosha is a foil.

Alyosha's noteworthy special definition of love as not only being affectionate or tender but also serving or looking after another emphasizes altruism.

Another inner value from the "heart" (a key word in the story) is the simple uneducated piety of the peasant class, a theme in several of Tolstoy's works. Like the three hermits (the title characters of Tolstoy's story "The Three Old Men") who show their inner holiness by running on top of the sea after an educated bishop because they have forgotten the formal prayer that he has taught them, Alyosha merely folds his hands in prayer twice a day, and finally at his death, and lets his heart speak, having long forgotten the words his mother taught him.

Alyosha's meekness, or not talking back, is repeatedly emphasized in the story. The prevention of his marriage and his sadly premature death cut Alyosha off from the pleasures of earthly life, but the story implies that Alyosha will gain entry into Heaven (which he thinks of only as "the world beyond" or "there"). All of Alyosha's attributes enable him to accept death peacefully, an encounter that preoccupies Tolstoy in many of his stories.

Style and Technique

Symbolism is pervasive in the story, including many religious allusions. References to Shrovetide and Lent put Alyosha's death at Easter time, while Alyosha's death on the third day after his fall (as well as his final request for something to drink) also suggests an analogue to the gospel story of Christ. Ironically, while Jesus arose to life, the downtrodden Alyosha falls and dies; yet if a cruel material world has been persecuting Alyosha in life, death promises escape and possibly reward, which parallels Jesus' life and message. Even a mark of Alyosha's homeliness, his large or lop ears, which evoke the ridicule of the other village children, by implication of the simile "stuck out like wings" may ironically suggest not only the manner of his death but also his angelic qualities and future.

The most far-reaching symbolism in the story is that embodied in Alyosha's nickname, "the Pot." The pot corresponds to many of Alyosha's physical features: the prominence of his nose and ears, giving his head a pot or pitcherlike appearance; a certain clumsiness, resulting in the dropped milk pot at the beginning of the story and Alyosha's own fall and breakage at the end; and a poignant reference to his physical slightness, contrasting with the fullness or heaviness of a filled pot. Furthermore, the pot symbol conveys many attributes of Alyosha's personality or spirituality. It intimates his capacity to bear, both in physical labor (Alyosha's incessant hard work) and in suffering or endurance (his toleration of all the injustices continually heaped on him). It suggests that despite his appearance of empty-headedness, Alyosha, whose mouth gapes in a perpetual grin (comparable to the open mouth of a pot or jar), has the capacity to be filled by pleasure from simple things in life or by the tranquillity from an influx of the spiritual. Finally, the pot symbol points to the cycle of emptiness and fullness in Alyosha's discovery of love, its removal, and his final transcendence to "the world beyond." Alyosha's true love is a cook, whose occupation revolves around pots; after the opening paragraph, she is the only character who explicitly mentions Alyosha's nickname, doing that, significantly, when she accepts his marriage proposal. At the end of the story, after the loss of Ustinya and any earthly pleasures, the dying Alyosha repeatedly asks for something to drink, reminiscent of Jesus' words in John 19:28-30 and suggestive of a different sort of fulfillment that is to become Alyosha's.

Contributing to the story's fablelike or fairy-tale quality are its telling in simple language and its purposeful deletion of much realistic specificity. All other characters besides Alyosha, his brother, and Ustinya are unnamed, being referred to merely as "Alyosha's father," "the merchant," "the merchant's wife," or "the clerk." Moreover, places are similarly unspecified (only "the village" or "the town"), nor are there any references that would pinpoint the time. Such devices also help to create the satiric dimension of the story, which does not have the conventionally happy ending of the prince and princess getting married and living happily ever after. Perhaps most important, this parabolic quality contributes to the universality of the story, which was a principal aim of Tolstoy's last works, including among them many children's or fairy tales, folktales, and legends.

Norman Prinsky

THE AMBITIOUS GUEST

Author: Nathaniel Hawthorne (1804-1864)
Type of plot: Domestic realism
Time of plot: The early 1800's
Locale: Notch of the White Hills, Massachusetts
First published: 1835

Principal characters:
THE AMBITIOUS GUEST, a visitor to a remote cottage inhabited
by a gregarious family
MOTHER
FATHER
ELDEST DAUGHTER
AGED GRANDMOTHER
YOUNGER CHILDREN

The Story

"The Ambitious Guest" begins in a moment of great tranquillity, with a family cozily gathered around their hearth. Father and mother, eldest daughter and aged grandmother, are briefly described as assuming the guises of persons of their ages who are filled with great contentment. Although they are entirely comfortable, mention is made of the harsh winter weather and the dangerous position of the cottage, over which towers a mountain. The noise of stones tumbling down the mountain has often startled the family at midnight.

Throughout the story, a contrast is made between the cozy harmony within and the stormy conditions of nature outside. The wind rattles their door, and they are glad of the company of a young traveler, who proceeds to make himself at home in the welcome atmosphere of the friendly family.

The Ambitious Guest is "frank-hearted" and quickly engages the family in a discussion of his plans to make a reputation for himself. He finds in them a responsive mood that encourages his conversation about how a person must make his mark on life. As they are caught up in his enthusiasm, several family members express very personal feelings about their lives. The father would like a better property and a better title (Squire)—in short, a station in life that would command the respect of his community. One of the younger children, excited by all this discussion of life's possibilities, calls out to his mother that he would like everyone, the guest included, to "go and take a drink out of the basin of the Flume!" His seemingly extravagant notion of visiting a brook that spills over into a "deep precipice" amuses the others, who cannot imagine leaving the presumed safety and comfort of the cottage.

One by one, however, the family members forsake their usual placid acceptance of things as they are and admit to various fancies, so that, as the mother says, "we're in a strange way, to-night." The guest himself is portrayed as having "a high and abstracted ambition." A solitary wanderer, his dreams of making his mark are just that—dreams, reveries removed from the concreteness of domestic life as it is evoked at the beginning of the story.

The talk turns to death, as the grandmother confesses to a strange preoccupation with a superstition of her youth, that a corpse cannot rest in the grave if it suspects that something about its appearance is awry. She asks her children to make a point of holding a looking glass over her face to get a glimpse of herself after she is laid out for the grave. "Old and young, we dream of graves and monuments," murmurs the guest, who has stimulated the whole family to think about how it wants to be remembered.

Reminders of the roaring wind and of the harsh, inhospitable elements outside finally culminate in the "awful sound" of a slide. The family rushes from the cottage seeking a safer haven but, in fact, flees "right into the pathway of destruction." The whole mountain falls upon them. In the aftermath, their cottage remains intact and the circumstances of their lives are apparent to all who observe the tokens the family has left behind. Only the identity of the guest remains in doubt, his ambition having come to nought.

Themes and Meanings

The title of the story focuses on the disturbing element: ambition. The guest's ambition is equated with his solitariness, his wandering, and his separation from the community of feeling enjoyed by the family. Ambition, in itself, is abstract. It seems to have nothing to do with the way this family lives; indeed, as the mother remarks, she feels a sense of strangeness when the family begins to talk in the guest's terms about what it wants as opposed to what it already has.

The eldest daughter is aware of the guest's disturbing ideas when she replies, "It is better to sit here by this fire . . . and be comfortable and contented, though nobody thinks about us." The guest, on the other hand, thinks of "Earthy Immortality," as the narrator puts it. The guest rejects her acceptance of the status quo in favor of a sense of destiny. He ignores, however, the signs of fate that Hawthorne infuses into the sounds of nature: "There was a wail along the road, as if a funeral were passing." What the family has forsaken, under the temporary influence of the guest, is its own attunement to the world.

By not naming his characters, Hawthorne gives his story a universal dimension. It is about the family, about ambition, and about how human beings both place themselves in and abstract themselves from the world at large. As the narrator remarks of the family in this story, "Though they dwelt in such a solitude, these people held daily converse with the world."

"The Ambitious Guest" is a fable, but it is also a folktale with its origins, the narrator implies, in fact—not in fancy or in abstractions. Of the family, for example, the narrator comments: "All had left separate tokens, by which those who had known the family were made to shed a tear for each. Who has not heard their name?" They have become the subject of poets, the narrator notes, so that their fate becomes everyone's fate, human fate—or, as the narrator puts it earlier in the story while commenting on the affinity of the family for the guest, "Is not the kindred of a common fate a closer tie than that of birth?"

Style and Technique

Hawthorne's style is ironic. The common fate he speaks of at the beginning of the story, for example, is not simply the meeting of minds between the guest and his hosts but also the death they will share, that everyone must ultimately share. Such a terse style allows the narrator to comment subtly on the characters without ever seeming intrusive or impeding the flow of the story. His technique is to understate the theme, giving over most of the narrative to description and dialogue. Nearly every paragraph is carefully balanced between the ease with which the characters behave and speak, on the one hand, and the disruptive, saddening sounds of nature that punctuate the human conviviality, on the other hand.

Always a master of sly, subtle repetition, Hawthorne is able to insert several references to discordant sound that serve as a counterpoint to the human harmony. Even that human harmony is usually shaded by qualifying phrases, such as the one that introduces the lively guest: "His face at first wore the melancholy expression, almost despondency, of one who travels a wild and bleak road, at nightfall and alone, but soon brightened up when he saw the kindly warmth of his reception." Thus, sentences as well as paragraphs are set off against one another, the first part establishing a mood that gives way to its opposite in the second part.

Hawthorne's style, in other words, aims to capture the rhythms of existence itself, rhythms which are contradictory and reversible and which elicit the intense concentration of the ironist. The implication is that all human beings are on the verge of confronting the end of their world. As the grandmother thinks of her death, the guest thinks of how "mariners feel when the ship is sinking." It is almost as if these words occasion the story's ending—so tightly has Hawthorne constructed the denouement. The house trembles and the earth shakes "as if this awful sound were the peal of the last trump." The biblical phrasing here emphasizes the parabolic nature of the author's style and themes. In his mind, the short story itself becomes the synecdoche of human fate.

Carl E. Rollyson, Jr.

AMERICA! AMERICA!

Author: Delmore Schwartz (1913-1966)
Type of plot: Reflective narrative
Time of plot: 1934
Locale: Brooklyn
First published: 1940

> *Principal characters:*
> BELMONT WEISS, a musician recently returned from Paris
> MRS. WEISS, his mother
> MR. BAUMANN, the insurance salesman
> MRS. BAUMANN, his wife
> DICK BAUMANN, the oldest son
> SIDNEY BAUMANN, the youngest child
> MARTHA BAUMANN, the daughter

The Story
    Belmont Weiss returns from Paris to a world changed by the effects of the Depression. Unable to fit into the changed situation among friends whose hopes have been "wholly modified," he takes it easy by enjoying long break-fasts, during which he listens to his mother's stories. The story of the Baumann family is told to him one morning as his mother irons.
    Mr. Baumann, a cultivated immigrant, was known for his sociability, his appearance, and his ease of living. With little effort, he sold insurance policies, consoled the grieving at funerals, and accumulated a comfortable income from the premiums. His life was leisurely. The family often took four vacations a year, often entertained, and indeed became celebrated for their Sunday evening gatherings, where immigrants shed the loneliness of people who have been cut off from the old country ways and then thrust into the "immense alienation of metropolitan life."
    As his mother irons, she tells Belmont that Mr. and Mrs. Baumann "shared so many interests that there was naturally a good deal of antagonism between them." Other people might regard her husband as a sage, but Mrs. Baumann sought out the rabbi, read Sigmund Freud and Henri Bergson, and relished all things and people Jewish. Their children, Belmont is told, reflected the attitudes of their parents. The oldest, Dick, moved from job to job but made little headway, except by marrying a successful beauty-parlor owner, Susan. When Mr. Baumann and Dick became involved in a real-estate partnership with Belmont's father, Mr. Weiss soon tired of their casual attitude toward business hours and responsibilities, terminating the partner-ship with a summary letter of dismissal. This ended the Weiss-Baumann friendship only briefly, however, because seemingly no one could stay angry

with affable Mr. Baumann.

The youngest child, Sidney, followed an even more disastrous course of action, finding some jobs unbearable because of the class of people with whom he worked, others because of the summer heat. Sent to Chicago to find his feet, he failed there and returned to a series of temporary jobs, becoming embittered by his father's "limited success." After a quarrel over the seemingly trivial—a pair of shoes—the father and son fought, and the son "unsuccessfully" attempted suicide and was sent to a mental asylum.

Only their daughter, Martha, the plain intellectual, managed her life by increasing her separation from the family and by marriage to a doctor who, despite her bitterness, enjoyed the family atmosphere at the Baumanns. Although twenty years younger, Mrs. Weiss had offered advice through the years to Mrs. Baumann and continues to share her insights with Belmont (though she would have preferred talking with her older lawyer son).

The reader learns only in passing that Belmont's father left the family in the 1920's, but as this short story draws to an end, Belmont's reflections shape the plot. Sitting in the bedroom that he is sharing for a time with his brother, he examines the conflicting emotions generated by the morning's saga of the Baumann family and the whole panorama of immigrant expectations about America. The reader hears no more about the Baumanns but turns inward to the real purport of the story—what Belmont has learned about others and about himself.

Themes and Meanings

Although Schwartz added a disclaimer that "the characters in this story are not to be identified with actual persons," and that it is "a work of fiction in the fullest sense of the word," readers will see possible parallels between the musician-listener (Belmont) and any poet-creator, especially in the concluding reflections concerning Belmont's sense of differentness, society's lack of appreciation, and its failure to acknowledge the importance of art.

Even if readers honor the disclaimer, they will still notice the juxtapositions of the personal and the social. Schwartz sets his story during the first part of the twentieth century, ending with the Depression, and fills it with details about the aspirations of a typical immigrant family. Himself a third-generation American, Belmont Weiss learns not only about the changes which affected the Baumanns but also about those which have shaped his own life. As he hears more and more about the Baumanns, he acquires a growing understanding of his own life until finally he is overcome by a "profound uneasiness" and realizes that the contempt which he had directed toward the Baumann way of life is in reality self-contempt.

Belmont finds it difficult to put himself in the place of his forebears. Gradually, however, he begins to see a pattern in the experience of the immigrants and their children—a pattern that is evident not only in the failure of the younger Baumanns but also in his own life. Mr. Baumann was satisfied with an unreflective materialism, but his children, the next generation, judged and weighed him, finding much out of balance. What once had succeeded for Mr. Baumann (hence by implication, for that generation of immigrants) no longer served. His sons' mistakes mirror the changing attitudes of society.

Thus, when Mrs. Weiss comments that "a certain refinement" could "be a severe and even a fatal handicap," the social and personal levels of meaning are joined. As Belmont's reflections on his mother's storytelling (her attitude, her "irony and cruelty") increase in length, the reader moves toward an understanding of the estrangement that Belmont had expressed at the start of the story. He now sees his own life from the same ironic perspective from which he has viewed the Baumanns and realizes that he, too, may have been ruined by his "finest qualities." No longer the passive listener to the story of others, he realizes that he is those others and that "their America would always be present in him."

Style and Technique

Schwartz establishes a framework of storyteller and listener, with the third-person point of view focused on Belmont Weiss so that the reader, too, increases his understanding of the "meanings" of what Belmont hears. As Belmont increasingly fits himself into the story which his mother tells, Schwartz can insert time clues. The reader sees the span of generations in the account of the two women, Mrs. Baumann and a fellow "shipsister," who came by boat to the United States in 1888, were separated in 1911, and reunited in 1930. These structural clues are kept within the plausible context of remembrance and event.

Because of Schwartz's repetition of the word "irony," the reader notices Belmont's interaction with his mother's narrative and her ironic perspective. His mother's aural memory captures the nuances of the speech of the earlier immigrant generation, their becoming "American," and Schwartz has Belmont note that the mother imposes "her own variety of irony upon the irony which sang in Belmont's mind at every phase of her story." Brief at first, Belmont's ruminations increase page by page until they consume the final two pages. At first uncertain "whether the cruelty of the story was in his own mind or in his mother's tongue," he is finally convinced that the irony and contempt with which he has listened to the story applies to himself and to his own awareness of self-contempt.

The telling concluding analogy has Belmont acquiring the "curious omniscience" gained by looking at an old photograph. Much as Belmont has judged the failure and waste of the Baumanns, so might the viewer of an old photograph look condescendingly on the people pictured there, finding their clothes and their very posture ridiculous—until, moving beyond this superficial vision of past time, he might recognize "that the very act of looking has . . . in its time, the same character."

The passive viewer of the photograph of past times, as Belmont has been the passive listener to tales of past times, achieves his enlightenment: "And now it seemed to him that all those lives inhabited the air he breathed and would be present wherever he was." The framework, therefore, embraces both the social and the personal, inviting all readers to reflect and to achieve awareness of the forces that have shaped them.

Eileen Lothamer

AMONG THE DANGS

Author: George P. Elliott (1918-1980)
Type of plot: Parody
Time of plot: From 1937 to after World War II
Locale: The United States and the eastern foothills of the Andes
First published: 1958

Principal characters:
THE NARRATOR, a graduate of Sansom University in search of
a vocation
DR. SORISH, the narrator's sponsor at Sansom
REDADU, the narrator's wife among the Dangs
VELMA, the narrator's North American wife

The Story

The I-narrator, the story's central character and only developed personality, is an Everyman with needs to satisfy. His quest depicts the relative capacity of two different societies to fulfill his needs and to bring him to full humanity. Upon graduation from Sansom, he requires a job and will take what he can get, no matter how unpromising it seems. When the doing brings him to a greater truth than he had aimed at and through a path of apparent improbabilities, the result is nothing short of miracle or comedy in the Dantean sense, but it is tinged finally by his reversion to the values of the lesser civilization. This story realizes the full potential of I-narration by bringing the unwitting modern through his society's delusions and his own limitations toward the will to faith. His dramatized example witnesses that, of all the stories having more than passing value, the deepest and most satisfying—toward which others lead—is the Christian mystery. His return to something less, though certainly human, is a letdown.

To run the course of his discovery, the narrator makes three trips to the primitive Dangs, about whom little is known except their appetite for prophecy and hostility toward intruders. Surprisingly, he makes three returns, though one seems unlikely, his qualifications to do anthropological research among the primitives being merely that he is a "good mimic, a long-distance-runner, and black." These seem less than sufficient, considering the problems: He has no zeal for the quest but goes because he needs money and has no other prospects; he doubts that the "brick dust" black Dangs will spot a relative in his "granite dust" black skin and ersatz primitive getup. All this points to a comedy of snafus by a reluctant volunteer.

Surprisingly, virtually everything goes his way. Entering primitiveness, he makes enough errant gestures to get a troop of searchers killed but without that conclusion. Apparently, the Dangs are broader-minded about accepting other humans than he and his educated tutors had assumed; when he unwittingly assumes the "prophetic squat" and commits additional natural gestures in which the Dangs see significance, he has assured himself of success. Throughout his first visit, comedy issues from the Dangs' seeming gullibility in accepting his ways. They even bend the rules for his satisfaction. For example, when the narrator accepts the advances of the girl Redadu and satisfies himself prodigiously, the Dangs accommodate the couple by condoning their irregular mating, going so far as to find a substitute for his "Methodist mother" to sit outside the marriage hut and listen for the "orgastic cries" of consummation. Because these primitives honor naturalness and accept others easily, the narrator does not grasp the firmness of purpose beneath their smoothing of his way to prophecy. After all, the advanced civilization which has sent him forth is not particularly compliant or flexible; it bent him from his desire to study history into a tool of social science. Finally prepared for the vatic role, he chants *St. James Infirmary*, and the Dangs accept that good story by incorporating its rhythms into their daily drumming.

One might expect the narrator's departure to end this relationship as a grade-B comedy, but he returns to the Dangs and is accepted, as are his explanations, by this people who put so high a premium on artful telling. Given these conditions, he works toward greater efforts, shifting from the blues to the Christian Passion and moving toward an understanding of what he has been doing. The wisdom and patience of the primitives has produced an artist who satisfies his audience as well as himself.

The returns to modernity, handled briefly, serve to illustrate the superficiality of values in a civilization where marriage, money, and vocational acceptance fail to stimulate the passion and satisfaction produced by the narrator's relationships among the Dangs. Consequently, it is a sad irony that hovers over the ending. Back home at Sansom, he has employed his experience to make an "honorable contribution to knowledge" and has gained a "tenure to a professorship—thereby pleasing" his "wife." There are no "orgastic cries" from the bedroom, nor do his two daughters match the aspiring-prophet son he has left among the Dangs. The narrator's defense for his final return to Sansom—his fear that he would "revert" until he became "one of them"—is a spiritual letdown. The Dangs had led him into his vocation, a process of their primitive society, not his social science, being the power which promoted the loss of self "utterly" in religious truth.

Themes and Meanings

"Among the Dangs" is an argument for the primacy of story among humanity's ways of knowing and for the primacy of the vatic teller among the world's knowers and tellers. The story suggests that the data of the modern social scientist is not wisdom, that advanced civilization does not satisfy, and that the persistent ritual of primitives who know what they want can lead man, through the habituation of doing, to spiritual understanding. The "Dangs make no separation between fact and fantasy, apparent reality and visionary reality, truth and beauty," suggesting a connection between them and a more romantic stage of civilization that modern man has fallen away from—much to the chagrin of such thinkers as Matthew Arnold, William Butler Yeats, and W. H. Auden as well as George P. Elliott. The Dangs's seemingly "mindless holding of the same position hour after hour" and the monotony of their melodies can blot out the noise, however unique, of modern delusions and can make the prophet aware, through subtle rhythms, of the mystic truth.

The Dangs, so improbably helpful to the intruder, are so cast to call attention to the limitations of advanced society's assumptions and values; their behavior also represents an educational philosophy—help the willing to find the way by patience and flexibility—from which any society could benefit. There is also in the story a chastening of blind belief in uninterrupted progress. Since the religious knowing pictured here depends upon a creative interaction between the individual and the whole society, when the individual flags in his pursuit of the truth and steps down to lesser values, the society may have to wait for another generation to produce a new performer. To be "among the Dangs" is to be within the possibility of integrity; to leave is to impede the best hope.

Style and Technique

Elliott's style, which promotes irony, satire, and other deflators of pretentiousness, thus functioning as a pathway to moral judgment, has been called "cool." Elliott himself has described his medium as "formal seeming, of a certain polish," and has explained that his didacticism depends upon "the complex relationships among storyteller, characters, and readers" and an "aesthetic distance," without which "there is not likely to be much moral clarity." In "Among the Dangs," the narrator's discoveries act as adjustments of the moral focus until aesthetic distance is achieved. Contrasts, both within the narrator and outside in his world, are essential.

The comedy of the narrator's encountering primitive humanity employs sharp contrasts between frightening expectation and actuality. Equally important for aesthetic distance are muted contrasts introduced at varying removes: Consider, for example, that a life of floating corpses and the possibility of mutilation and even sacrificial death brings the narrator only to the scratch-wounds of sexual ecstasy and a stubborn rash, whereas a return to civilization involves him in World War II, "in which" his "right hand" is "severed above the wrist," a fact he relates almost incidentally among a list of supposed accomplishments.

Moral clarity increases when, through the narrator, truth momentarily shines forth from beneath the mix of styles. Modern man in need bares his motives: "After I'd got them to throw in a fellowship of some sort for the following year I agreed. It would pay for filling the forty cavities in my brothers' and sisters' teeth." The budding anthropologist describes a primitive event: "They could not possibly just assimilate me without marking the event with an act (that is, a ceremony) signifying my entrance." Then the growing prophet discovers real values: "*If the conditions of my being elevated,* I said to myself, *are the sufferings of the people, Redadu's death, and the sacrifice of an old man, then I must make myself worthy of the great price. Worthy*—a value word, not a scientific one."

Then the moral instrument achieves its full aesthetic distance by the deflating rhythm of the ending: ". . . if I had stayed there among the Dangs much longer I would have reverted until I had become one of them, might not have minded when the time came to die under the sacrificial knife, would have taken in all ways the risk of prophecy—as my Dang son intends to do— until I had lost myself utterly."

William P. Keen

...AND THE EARTH DID NOT PART

Author: Tomás Rivera (1935-1984)
Type of plot: Fantasy and social realism
Time of plot: The 1950's
Locale: Chiefly Texas
First published: "...y no se lo tragó la tierra," 1971 (English translation, 1971)

> *Principal characters:*
> A CHICANO BOY, the protagonist
> HIS COMMUNITY, Chicano migrant workers

The Story

"...and the earth did not part" is the title story in a book of linked stories, a sequence of vignettes in which an unnamed Chicano boy confronts his memories of the past year in an attempt to define himself and to understand more fully the lot of his people. In each of these brief pieces, averaging four or five pages in length, Tomás Rivera presents one facet of the life of a community of migrant workers. The workers and their children—who are indeed workers themselves—are exploited by seemingly uncaring or blatantly callous American bosses. Brutality, however, is not limited to Anglo-Chicano relations, and the author also shows Chicanos exploiting their own people. "...and the earth did not part," which appears midway in the sequence, recounts a crucial experience in the young protagonist's life, a decisive change in his outlook.

The story begins with a directness characteristic of the volume: "The first time he felt hate and anger was when he saw his mother cry for his uncle and for his aunt." The fate of the aunt and uncle is quickly sketched: Having contracted tuberculosis, they were sent to separate sanatoriums, their children "parceled out" among various relatives; the aunt died, and the uncle, allowed to go home, was spitting blood. The boy's mother was "crying all the time," and it was then, he recalls, that he began to be angry—"angry because he could not strike back at anyone."

These emotions clearly signal the onset of critical awareness, the full development of which is traced in the course of the story. When his father is temporarily felled by sunstroke, the boy becomes angrier—even his father is not exempt from pointless suffering—and he is angrier still when both his mother and his father repeatedly call upon God, asking for His mercy. The boy confronts his mother, raging against her, against their fate, against God. Frightened by his words, she tells him that he must not blaspheme: "The ground might open up and devour you for talking like that." Her fatalistic faith, however—"Only death can bring us rest"— does not persuade him.

The climax of the story comes when the boy goes out to work in the fields with his brothers and sisters; their father is still too sick to work, and their mother must stay with him. The day is hot, and the youngest brother, nine years old, becomes sick, vomiting and then fainting. The boy must carry his sick brother home, and as he does his anger comes to a head. Finally, he finds an outlet, someone to "strike back at": He curses God. For a moment, he feels "the fear instilled in him by time and by his parents," but the earth does not open; indeed, he "felt himself walking on very solid ground; *it was harder than he had ever felt it.*" His anger rises again and, emboldened, he again curses God; far from suffering retribution, he notices that his brother appears to be better.

That night, he feels a sense of peace, and he goes to work the next morning with a man's self-confidence. The story concludes with a symbolic expression of that confidence and of his mature awareness of life and death; he kicks at the ground and taunts it: "Not yet, you can't eat me yet. Someday. But I won't know."

Themes and Meanings

Many Chicano stories and novels present an adolescent character, usually a boy, in the throes of discovering his own identity in a world which is not of his making but which he must make sense of. This adolescent moves between two worlds, that of his parents and that of his own adulthood, and in the process often confronts the relative nature of good and evil, deception and reality, morality and immorality; in short, he must rethink and reevaluate what he sees and experiences. The position of the Chicano, caught in the tension of his dual (Mexican and American) heritage, is analogous to that of the adolescent in that the Chicano must evaluate the cultural trappings passed on to him and must decide which ones to keep and which to reject as he sets about defining himself anew.

This is precisely the issue faced by the nameless Chicano character who recalls, synthesizes, and eventually evaluates the experiences of a year in his and his community's life. Paramount in the young Chicano boy's recollections is the cyclical pattern of suffering and disillusionment suffered by the boy's community. At first, he is unable to understand why he and his community suffer, but his review of the year allows him to discover that suffering is not unique to Chicanos and that brutality and exploitation know no boundaries of race, place, or time.

Indeed, these vignettes are above all directed at Chicano readers, urging them to self-awareness. The periodic ills of the Chicano community are caused by the economics of migration and peasant labor, neither of which fosters the building of strong individuals or communities and both of which prevent the acquisition of a good education. Ignorance of the lands where the migrants work and of the world beyond their community exposes them to economic exploitation, while an almost stereotypical passivity, ingrained by the free admixture of superstition and a Catholicism which leaves all events in the hands of God, prevents the members of the community from acting to change their lot. With his curses, the protagonist redefines himself as a young man capable of decisive action; it is this liberating knowledge which gives him hope both for his own future and for the future of his community.

Style and Technique

... *and the earth did not part* (1971), the volume in which this story appears, was one of several works published in the 1970's that brought to the tradition of Chicano fiction a new degree of artistic quality.

Chicano fiction, that literature by and about Americans of Mexican descent, began to make great strides in the 1960's. With the founding in 1969 of Quinto Sol, a publishing house dedicated to Mexican American, or Chicano, literature, and the subsequent institution of the Quinto Sol Prize, Chicano fiction of high artistic quality received a needed boost. ... *and the earth did not part* was one of the first works to receive this prize.

In terms of structure and narrative technique, ... *and the earth did not part* is highly unusual. As noted above, it is a cycle of linked stories: twelve vignettes, formed by a very brief opening "chapter" (about a half-page long) and a longer concluding chapter. The opening chapter presents the problem of the young boy's confusion and his need to resolve the problem through recalling the events of the past year. In the last chapter, he recapitulates the contents of the twelve vignettes and forms his conclusions. Each of the vignettes (and the concluding chapter as well) is preceded by a self-contained, brief italicized passage, only a few lines long, which plays against the piece that follows.

The author employs a wide variety of narrative techniques, among them dialogue, interior monologue, contrapuntal setting of both, and a number of third-person narrators. His combination of some of these within any one vignette or chapter allows for a variety of points of view of a particular incident; this in turn allows the incident or the character to acquire new dimensions and to free itself from the control of the author.

Multiplicity of point of view, however, introduces the possibility of ambiguity. In the opening chapter, the author consciously blurs the lines between reality and dream and reinforces this ambiguity with multiple points of view; one is never quite sure whether what is reported actually happened.

Rivera, as a true Chicano writer, shows the influences of both American and Mexican writers: of Sherwood Anderson and William Faulkner in his use of monologues and the creation of a community with mythic proportions, and of Juan Rulfo, the Mexican novelist and short-story writer, in his use of simple peasant language in dialogue combined with an overwhelming variety of narrative techniques.

St. John Robinson

ANGEL LEVINE

Author: Bernard Malamud (1914-1986)
Type of plot: Fantasy
Time of plot: Twentieth century
Locale: New York City
First published: 1955

Principal characters:
MANISCHEVITZ, a tailor
FANNY, his wife
ALEXANDER LEVINE, a black angel

The Story
Manischevitz has lost everything. His son was killed in the war, and his daughter left home. After a lifetime of work, his tailor shop burned to the ground and could not be rebuilt; his own health is so broken that he can work only a few hours a day as a clothes presser; his wife, Fanny, ruined her own health by taking in washing and sewing, so she is now confined to her bed. Always a religious man, Manischevitz cannot understand how God can have allowed such unreasonable suffering to come to him. In desperation, Manischevitz first prays for an explanation from God, but he quickly changes his prayer to a simple appeal for relief.

Later, while reading the newspaper, Manischevitz has a premonition that someone has entered the apartment. Entering the living room of his small and shabby flat, he discovers a black man sitting at the table reading a newspaper. At first Manischevitz assumes that the visitor is an investigator from the welfare department. When this proves not to be the case, the tailor again asks the man's identity. This time the man answers with his name, Alexander Levine. Manischevitz is surprised to discover that the black man is a Jew, and even more surprised when Levine tells him, "I have recently been disincarnated into an angel. As such, I offer you my humble assistance, if to offer is within my province and power—in the best sense."

Manischevitz is unwilling to accept Levine's characterization of himself, suspecting that he may be the butt of some joke or prank, so he tests him with such questions as "Where are your wings?" and "How did you get here?" Levine answers rather lamely, and even though he is able to recite correctly in Hebrew the Jewish blessing for bread, Manischevitz is unconvinced of his visitor's authenticity. As the interview reaches a conclusion, Manischevitz accuses Levine of being a fake, and the angel, disappointment registering in his eyes, announces, "If you should desire me to be of assistance to you any time in the near future... I can be found... in Harlem." He then disappears.

For a few days after Levine's visit, both Manischevitz and Fanny seem better, but their condition soon reverts to its former state. The tailor laments his fate, questioning why God should have chosen him for so much unexplained and undeserved suffering. Eventually he comes to wonder if he was mistaken in dismissing Alexander Levine, who indeed might have been sent to help him. In his desperation, he decides to go up to Harlem in search of Levine.

At first he cannot find Levine in Harlem. When he goes into the familiar setting of a tailor shop and asks for Levine by name, the tailor claims never to have heard of him. Yet, when Manischevitz says, "He is an angel, maybe," the tailor immediately remembers Levine and indicates that he can be found in a local honky-tonk. Making his way there, Manischevitz peers through the window to see Levine dancing with Bella, the owner of the bar. As they dance by the window, Levine winks at Manischevitz, and the latter leaves for home, convinced of the failure of his mission.

When Fanny is at death's door, Manischevitz goes to a synagogue to speak to God, but he feels that God has absented himself. In his despair, Manischevitz suffers a crisis of faith and rails against God, "cursing himself for having, beyond belief, believed." Later that afternoon, napping in a chair, the tailor dreams that he sees Levine "preening small decaying opalescent wings" before a mirror. Convinced that this may be a sign that Levine is an angel, he makes his way again to Harlem in search of him. This time, before arriving at Bella's honky-tonk, he enters a storefront synagogue, where four black Jews sit studying the Holy Word. Again he asks for Levine—identified by one of the congregation as "the angel"—and is told to look at Bella's down the street.

Since the previous visit, when Levine was shabbily dressed, things appear to have changed. He now is attired in fancy new clothes and is drinking whiskey with Bella, whose lover he appears to have become. As Manischevitz enters the bar, Levine confronts him, demanding that he state his business. First the tailor acknowledges that he believes Levine is Jewish, to which the black replies only by asking if he has anything else to say. When Manischevitz hesitates, Levine says, "Speak now or fo'ever hold off." After an agonizing moment of indecision, Manischevitz says, "I think you are an angel from God."

Levine changes back into his former clothes and returns to the tailor's flat with him. When Manischevitz asks him to come in, the angel assures him that everything has been take care of and tells him to enter, while he "takes off." Instead, Manischevitz follows him to the roof, only to find the door padlocked. Peeping through a broken window, the tailor believes that he can see "a dark figure borne aloft on a pair of strong black wings." A feather drifts downward, but when Manischevitz catches it, it proves to be only a snowflake.

Returning to his flat, Manischevitz finds Fanny up and about, busily cleaning. "A wonderful thing, Fanny," Manischevitz says, "Believe me, there are Jews everywhere."

Themes and Meanings

Perhaps the most ubiquitous figure in Bernard Malamud's fiction is the person, usually Jewish, who suffers, like Job in the Old Testament, without any apparent reason. Manischevitz is not a bad man; no sin accounts for his fall. As he complains, he suffers far more than would seem to be just.

The tailor's mistake is in wanting to understand why he should suffer, and in expecting there to be some cause and effect in life. Just as he will want proof that Levine is an angel, he wants some sign that God exists. When he fails to achieve either of these assurances, Manischevitz undergoes a crisis of faith when he renounces his belief in God and surrenders to despair. It is then that his dream vision of Levine preening his wings gives him new hope and sends him in search of the angel. Still, his faith must be tested, so Levine forces him to acknowledge before the assembled crowd in the honky-tonk that the black is an angel. At this point, not only is Manischevitz's problem solved, Levine casts off the clothes of a pimp and becomes the angel he is meant to be. Faith is necessary both for God and for man.

Manischevitz final realization that there are Jews everywhere reflects Malamud's theme that all men are Jews. Jews, in Malamud's fiction, are those who suffer without cause and who maintain their faith in humanity (or in God) despite the injustice of their plight. Manischevitz does not suffer because he is a Jew; he is a Jew because he suffers. He does not believe because he is a Jew; he is a Jew because he believes.

Style and Technique

Though it deals with purely imaginary events, Malamud tells his story in the straightforward manner of literary realism. The language and grammar are those appropriate to someone of Manischevitz's background, because, though the story is told in the third person, Manischevitz is clearly the center of consciousness, and the dialect in the story is his. This is an appropriate method, as it enables the reader to reach his own determination as to whether he is reading of an episode imagined by this broken old man or whether the event occurred as reported. In the final analysis, it makes little difference, as Malamud's theme does not rely for its effectiveness on the "reality" of the situation so much as on the reader's understanding of the humanizing quality of faith.

William E. Grant

THE ANGEL OF THE BRIDGE

Author: John Cheever (1912-1982)
Type of plot: Psychological realism
Time of plot: Mid- to late twentieth century
Locale: New York City
First published: 1964

Principal characters:
THE NARRATOR, a businessman and the protagonist
THE NARRATOR'S OLDER BROTHER, also a businessman
THE NARRATOR'S MOTHER
THE HITCHHIKER, a young woman and folksinger

The Story
The story begins with the narrator being embarrassed that his seventy-eight-year-old mother likes to ice-skate in Rockefeller Center in New York City. He shortly discovers, while he is waiting with her in the Newark airport to put her on a plane to visit some friends of hers in Ohio, that she is mortally afraid of flying. His next revelation is that his older brother, more successful in business than he and their mother's favorite, has recently developed an intense fear of high buildings, especially the elevators in them. While the narrator's confrontation with his mother's phobia has given him an insight into her fragility, his brother's neurosis—perhaps because the narrator feels in competition with him—strikes him as absurd.

The narrator is afraid of neither heights nor planes. His business requires that he fly frequently to the West Coast and to Europe. He romanticizes flying: He enjoys comparing the simultaneous activities in different time zones, the way the sky appears at high altitudes, and the way night moves across a landscape seen from the air. Without warning, however, on the way back with his wife and children from a visit in New Jersey, the narrator undergoes a strong emotional and physical reaction to the George Washington Bridge as he drives across it. From then on he is afraid of large bridges, especially high ones.

He informs the family doctor, who in effect informs him that he is being cowardly. When a psychiatrist suggests that the anxiety behind his fear will need long-term analysis, the narrator backs off, unwilling to spend the time and money, or to entrust his problem to psychiatric procedures.

The narrator's phobia changes his view of himself and of the world. He begins to doubt the joy that he finds in living and to see the world as emotionless and chaotic. He senses that the high point of a bridge symbolizes for him his loathing of the complexity and banality of modern civilization. He tells no one of his phobia other than the doctor and the psychiatrist, and he takes extravagant means to avoid driving on bridges; he drives twenty miles out of his way on a trip to Albany, New York, and he leaves his rented car in San Francisco to take a cab across the Oakland Bay Bridge.

The narrator's fear comes to a head on a Sunday morning when he drives his daughter back to a convent school in New Jersey. He does not remember his phobia until he is actually on the George Washington Bridge. Managing to hide the symptoms, he makes it across. He decides to return on what he thinks is the easier Tappan Zee Bridge farther north. Everything he thinks of either to avoid the bridge or to console himself fails. His wife might send someone for him, but the shame he would feel would damage his marriage. He might stop at a friend's house for a drink, but he would have to explain why he needed one so early in the day. When he stops for gas, he finds the gas station attendant too withdrawn for conversation. He might wait for the bars to open in the afternoon, but he has spent all his money on gas.

Finally, he arrives at the bridge and begins to cross. It upsets him more than he has ever been upset on a bridge since his phobia began, and he is forced to pull over. A young woman gets into his car, thinking that he has stopped to pick her up. She is a hitchhiker and a traveling folksinger who plays in coffeehouses. Besides her cheap suitcase, she carries a harp with her. She turns out to be the "Angel of the Bridge," for she sings him a folksong as he drives, and this not only calms him completely but also leads him to see order and beauty in the bridge and the river. The singer leaves at the toll station, and the narrator from then on is able to cross bridges without fear, though he still avoids the George Washington Bridge.

Themes and Meanings

One of John Cheever's favorite subjects is the middle class, and the locale of many of his stories is New York City and the suburbs north of it. His stories often focus on the eccentricities and failures of these people, and on how they endure. The major motif of "The Angel of the Bridge" is fear, and it is pictured as both an eccentricity and a failure. The story presents eccentricity as odd behavior in the early scene in which an elderly woman is committed to doing something that the young normally do: ice-skating. It is soon clear that the narrator's mother's odd behavior includes her phobic reaction to flying. The narrator and his older brother are also eccentric in their respective phobias. The fears of all three have two things in common besides their eccentricity: all three are afraid of heights and—if their disinclination to talk about their phobias is any sign—they regard their fears as personal failures.

In the narrator's case, his fear of heights not only is triggered by bridges but also signals a change in his vision of the world from a romantic to a terrifying one. Before the change, he was safe in his habits and regarded aberrant behavior as partially distasteful, partially amusing. The world was beautiful because his life was orderly, if somewhat boring. After the change, the world seems chaotic to him, a failure resting on his own failure to take in stride such implicit dangers in it as high bridges. His comfortable expectations and habits are turned upside down as he goes to extravagant lengths to avoid bridges.

It takes an example of courage in an eccentric form to reverse the fear and horror in the narrator. The appearance of the young folksinger when the narrator is finally all but paralyzed by his fear is enough to cure him. She is eccentric because she pursues an abnormal—that is, an adventurous—career. She is courageous because she does this on her own, hitchhiking from place to place, enthusiastically taking what the world has to offer rather than imposing meanness or paranoia on it. Her daring is what makes her angelic to the narrator and what saves him from his phobia, restoring him to a sense of well-being and giving him a new appreciation of daring behavior such as his mother's. He has realized, in short, that the human world is lovely precisely because of the unpredictability in it, and that the function of fear and failure is to make one see this.

Style and Technique

Paradox is the chief stylistic device that Cheever uses in this story. The characters demonstrate it to a marked degree. The narrator's mother is old yet pursues a sport that is dangerous for someone her age. Moreover, she radiates youth and a kind of sexiness by putting herself on display in a skating costume that reminds the narrator of "a hat-check girl." The paradox continues in his mother's case in that she is not afraid of the real danger of falling in the ice-skating rink but is afraid of the remote danger of falling in an airplane. The narrator's brother is also paradoxical. While he is "higher," so to speak, than the narrator in their mother's esteem, and higher than the narrator on the scale of worldly success, he is also so terrified of high buildings and of elevators falling that he interrupts his career and success by quitting his job when the firm for which he works moves to the upper level of a skyscraper.

The paradox in the narrator is twofold. His own success in life is fairly humdrum and earthbound, yet it involves much flying, which at first gives him, despite the mild discomfort he feels toward the end of flights, a sense of well-being. After his phobia develops, the second part of the paradox shows itself. Not only does the fear he shares with his mother and older brother fail to draw them all closer together, but also he is returned to his normal way of life by an abnormal event—the appearance of an "angel" (the young folksinger with her harp). She is paradoxical in the narrator's mind in that her beauty and power do not fit into his original vision of the world's order. Finally, the paradox embedded in the narrator is meant to suggest that modern civilized man himself is paradoxical, pursuing a restricted and orderly life but projecting a romantic vision on the world and, on the other hand, experiencing chaos and profound anxiety.

Mark McCloskey

APOCALYPSE AT SOLENTINAME

Author: Julio Cortázar (1914-1984)
Type of plot: Autobiographical fantasy
Time of plot: The mid-1970's
Locale: Costa Rica, Nicaragua, and Paris
First published: "Apocalipsis de Solentiname," 1977 (English translation, 1980)

> *Principal characters:*
> THE NARRATOR, an unnamed but renowned writer and the protagonist of his own narration
> CLAUDINE, his companion

The Story

The narrator, a celebrated Latin American cultural figure—he shares with Julio Cortázar the honor of having written the short story "Las babas del diablo" ("Blow-Up")—recounts a journey that he has made to Central America. Upon arriving in Costa Rica, he is met by several friends who are important members of the Sandinista movement, some of whom escort him to the island of Solentiname, off the coast of Nicaragua. During his visit, one of the purposes of which is to demonstrate solidarity with the Sandinistas in their protracted armed struggle against the Somoza dictatorship, he notices some naïve paintings done by the humble inhabitants of Solentiname. Struck by their unashamed innocence and enthusiasm, he photographs the paintings as souvenirs. After several intermediate stops, he returns to his home in Paris, where his life resumes its normally hectic rhythm. One day, when he recalls having left the roll of film to be developed, he retrieves it and settles down for a comfortable and nostalgic viewing. Approximately halfway through the roll of slides, however, just when the pleasantly ingenuous pictures should appear, the narrator is dismayed to witness projected scenes of unspeakable violence and cruelty: Soldiers murder peasant children in cold blood, cadavers are piled in tall mounds, women are tortured and raped. The arrival of his companion Claudine coincides with the end of the brutal spectacle. Too upset to speak, the narrator reloads the projector for her and retreats hastily to the bathroom, where (here his memory fails him) he may have vomited, cried, or simply sat in disbelief. After recomposing himself, he returns to Claudine's side and learns that she has seen nothing but the charming paintings that the narrator photographed when at Solentiname. Not wanting to appear foolish before Claudine (or the reader), the narrator says nothing to explain his uncanny experience. This aporetic conclusion is highly appropriate, since for those who share his revolutionary social concerns there remains nothing to say, and for those who do not, the whole matter is inexplicable and, perhaps, meaningless.

Themes and Meanings

Cortázar's writing generally sorts itself into one of two categories: the fantastic-mythical, as characterized by many of his early stories in such collections as *Final del juego* (1956; *End of the Game and Other Stories*, 1963) and *Todos los fuegos el fuego* (1966; *All Fires the Fire*, 1973), or the political-historical, best seen in his novel *Libro de Manuel* (1973; *A Manual for Manuel*, 1978). "Apocalypse at Solentiname," which first appeared in *Alguien que anda por ahí* (1977), constitutes an extraordinary synthesis of these two major tendencies within one brief tale. The ascending portion of the narrative is uniformly in the historical mode. Easily recognized and politically significant names (Sergio Ramírez, Ernesto Cardenal, and Roque Dalton) and places (San José, Solentiname, and Havana) inform the reader of the theater and the principal actors in this highly charged ideological drama. The narrator's deep affection for the Sandinista leaders and his admiration for the unpretentious artwork of the common folk of Solentiname create reader sympathy for the insurgents' cause (in 1976, when the story was composed, the Somoza regime still held absolute power in Nicaragua). Fantasy would appear to have no place in this palpable and contemporary conflict.

Only when the narrator attempts to relive his trip does an irrational element enter. No logical explanation for the intrusion of the scenes of officially sanctioned atrocities is possible, since the first half of the roll of film offers the narrator no surprises, and Claudine sees nothing unusual in her viewing of the same roll. This overlaying of the marvelous on the mundane is quite characteristic of Cortázar's fiction (he contends, in consonance with the surrealists, that a more real superreality is always there, lurking below or behind our everyday, impoverished conception of existence). Some of his most frequently anthologized stories, such as "La noche boca arriba" (The Night Face Up") and "Instrucciones para John Howell" ("Instructions for John Howell"), follow that very pattern. What is especially well achieved in "Apocalypse at Solentiname," however, is the creation of a highly tendentious, but still verisimilar, initial setting, the political impact of which is enhanced rather than undercut (or rendered irrelevant) by the climactic revelation (implicit in the term "apocalypse"). The literary mode of socialist realism is thus dealt as severe a blow by the Utopian visionary as is capitalist market theory.

The playful treatment which Cortázar affords so serious a theme as civil war finds an antecedent in his master piece *Rayuela* (1963; *Hopscotch*, 1966), in which the author uses a puerile game as a stunning metaphor for mankind's search for identity and meaning in life. A highly fragmented and polymorphous text (the reader has endless options as to the inclusion and ordering of the parts), *Hopscotch* irreverently calls into question some of the classical tradition's most cherished assumptions: what constitutes literature, the wisdom or possibility of exercising free will, the value of reason itself.

Bridging such discrete domains as theory and practice, on the one hand, and the metaphysical and the physical (erotic play is not the least of Cortázar's concerns), on the other, *Hopscotch* has come to enjoy the status of a secular Bible of the contemporary Latin American novel. It lacks, however, the explicit commitment to social justice of "Apocalypse at Solentiname," a story that captures in miniature the major issues in the author's mature, politicized worldview.

Style and Technique

Without a doubt, Cortázar has one of the most kindly authorial personas in modern literature. An analysis of that benignity, on whose convincing portrayal the story's success is greatly dependent, reveals three chief components: colloquial diction, intimacy with the reader, and self-deprecating humor. The illusion of a spoken rather than a written text is achieved by the first-person narration through the frequent use of diminutives (which are extremely common in spoken Spanish) and slang (especially with respect to nationalities: Nicas, Ticos, and Gringos for Nicaraguans, Costa Ricans, and Americans, respectively). The reader's confidence is gained principally through direct address ("You're probably saying I'm boiling over with false modesty, but let's face it, old man"), and by means of the "vos" (a very familiar form of the second-person singular pronoun that is archaic in mainstream Spanish but still current in Argentina, among other places). In addition to several humorous asides along the way and a confession of incredible naïveté where Polaroid cameras are concerned, the author makes himself the butt of his own joke at the conclusion. He confides to the reader his temptation to ask Claudine if she did not see a picture of Napoleon on horseback, in essence a confession of the absurdity of his situation vis-à-vis his companion.

A fourth ingredient in the author's winning repertoire, no less significant but certainly more diffuse, could be called deceptive simplicity. Although there are numerous instances of recognizable cultural allusions (the references to the author's story "Blow-Up," to Roque Dalton and Ernesto Cardenal, as well as to other lesser known writers, for example), Cortázar is sure to avoid appearing bookish or excessively cerebral, as might his compatriot Jorge Luis Borges, the immensely respected but much more politically conservative dean of postmodern Latin American literature. Despite the story's brevity and folksy tone, though, the simplicity is decidedly deceptive, for the layers of representation evoked in the final scene outstrip many a full-length novel. When the narrator (who is and is not Julio Cortázar: his wife at the time was named Carol) describes his hallucinatory vision, the reader receives a verbal (sequential) rendition of iconic (spatial) perceptions or conceptions. These images, in the normal course of events, should have been mere filmic reproductions of the amateur pictorial artwork produced in Solentiname, and those canvases, in turn, would be based on the imagined or lived experiences of their painters. The multiple intermediate levels of interpretation, both actual and hypothetical, between the reader and the event related in the text, disclose the true complexity of the author's thinking. A master ironist and rhetorician, Cortázar means in "Apocalypse at Solentiname" much more to the "accomplice reader" (a term he coins in *Hopscotch*) than meets the untrained or passive reader's eye.

Jonathan Tittler

THE APRIL WITCH

Author: Ray Bradbury (1920-   )
Type of plot: Fantasy
Time of plot: The 1920's or 1930's
Locale: Green Town, Illinois
First published: 1952

> Principal characters:
> CECY ELLIOTT, the protagonist, a remarkable seventeen-year-old with magical powers
> ANN LEARY, the nineteen-year-old girl whose body Cecy possesses
> TOM, a twenty-two-year-old man who is in love with Ann

The Story

In April, the spring of the year when gentle breezes blow and flowers begin to bloom, young girls everywhere dream of falling in love. Young seventeen-year-old Cecy Elliott, from whose point of view the story is told, also desperately desires to fall in love. Cecy, however, is unlike other girls. She possesses magical powers. She can travel through space and time, she can soar in doves, stop in trees, and she can become one with frogs, dogs, grass, moles, and every living thing. She sleeps by day and flies by night. She can leave her plain, bony body and spiritually possess any living thing. Yet Cecy cannot marry a mortal. As Cecy's parents warn: "We'd lose our magical powers if we did."

Despite her parents' warnings to be careful, to be patient, telepathic Cecy satisfies her longings for love in a special way. Because Cecy cannot experience love for herself, she decides to experience love through a human. She promptly dispatches her mind and quickly possesses the body of nineteen-year-old Ann Leary, a girl quite unwilling to have Cecy possess her. When Ann drinks from a well, Cecy enters her body and, through Ann, comes to cherish human love.

Cecy must work hard to experience and to maintain this love, however, and herein lies the story's intrigue. Cecy forces Ann to accept a date with an admirer, Tom, a twenty-two-year-old whom Ann has never really liked. While inhabiting Ann's body before and during the date, Cecy faces a constant struggle in trying to develop and nurture the relationship between Tom and Ann. When Ann spills water at the well, Tom wipes her shoes with a kerchief. Unappreciative of his kind gesture, Ann kicks at Tom and then thanks him only because Cecy forces her to respond.

Cecy is ecstatic when Tom asks a reluctant Ann to the dance that evening. Cecy has never worn a long gown, and she has never danced. Cecy controls

Ann's movements as Ann prepares for the dance. They heat water for a bath, iron a gown, and prepare for Tom to arrive with his horse and buggy. During the evening, Ann and Cecy dance with Tom. Both have a wonderful time even though Tom wonders about Ann's new demeanor.

As they return home from the dance, Tom confesses that he still loves Ann, despite her fickle nature and despite his fear of being hurt. Inside Ann's "roundly fleshed" body, Cecy tries to force Ann to return Tom's love. Nothing happens. Tom reveals that he plans to accept a job a hundred miles away and asks Ann whether she will miss him. Both girls reply in the affirmative. When Tom asks Ann if he may kiss her good night, Cecy answers affirmatively "before anyone else could speak."

After the kiss, Ann sits motionless, unwilling to move and unwilling to embrace Tom despite Cecy's pleading. At this point, a lonely Cecy realizes that, despite her parents' warnings, she would indeed risk everything—all of her magical powers—for love. "I'd need only to be with him. Only him. Only him," she decides.

As Tom and Ann approach her home, Ann, directed by Cecy, makes Tom promise to visit a friend of hers a few miles away in Mellin Town, Illinois. Reluctantly, Tom finally agrees. On a piece of paper, Ann scratches the name of her friend: Cecy Elliott.

When midnight approaches, a tired Cecy, like Cinderella just returned from the ball, feels her magical powers waning. Before she leaves Ann's body, though, Cecy and Ann again kiss Tom good night. During this kiss, Cecy tells an unsuspecting Tom, "This is *me* kissing you."

As Tom sleeps, he clutches the paper Ann gave to him and never stirs when a blackbird pauses wondrously at his windowpane and gazes softly at him before flying away toward the east.

Themes and Meanings

In "The April Witch," Bradbury readers will recognize familiar themes: initiation into maturity and metamorphosis. Bradbury's young people, whose emotions largely control their actions, frequently struggle for rather than against adulthood.

Nostalgic Cecy, who can metamorphose at will according to her desires and needs, has a large capacity for wonder. During her journeys through time and space, she looks at the world, wonders at the world, participates in the world, and cannot look away. She yearns desperately for her innermost desire: to be loved. This love, as she has been warned by her parents, surely will destroy her magical powers; nevertheless, as a typical teenager, she fails to heed their warnings and rushes to embrace life and experience a love she has never known. At the end of the story she wonders whether Tom will love her "with all his heart for all time" as she loves him. Symbolically, Bradbury suggests that he will. The bird that gazes softly at Tom flies toward the east, a symbol of new beginnings and of renewal.

Because of Cecy's special qualities, reality in this story is relative. To the readers, reality is determined by what Cecy needs and wants. First she flies into the air, then she lives in blossoms, perches in frogs, and lives in new April grasses. Finally, however, she embraces the reality of a teenager in love, a young lady who yearns for a special kind of love: one that will last forever.

Style and Technique

A lyrical writer, Ray Bradbury uses strong sensory images, particularly nature imagery, which he combines with rich metaphors and similes, with a poet's attention to the sound of words, with nostalgic scenes, and with frequent juxtapositions. An impressionistic writer, Bradbury builds his scenes via a deluge of images which suggest rather than directly relate.

Bradbury begins his story with nature imagery: Cecy inhabits air, valleys, stars, rivers, winds, fields, and various animals. These images convey both the advent of spring and the magical powers of Cecy; they suggest spring and, by extension, the season of love. Cecy longs to embrace both love and life despite her parents' warnings. Cecy views the world through sensory imagery: She sits in Ann's eyes, and in the eyes of insects and animals. These images also form similes. Cecy is "invisible as new spring winds," she "soars in doves as soft as white ermine," and she perches in a frog "cool as mint."

Moreover, Bradbury juxtaposes Cecy with Ann Leary, a girl who shrinks from life and love. Ann's body is "roundly fleshed," whereas Cecy's body is plain and bony. A pretty girl, Ann stands in direct contrast to the less attractive Cecy, who, like most people in springtime, wants to dance, to kiss, and to fall in love.

Bette Adams Reagan

ARABY

Author: James Joyce (1882-1941)
Type of plot: Symbolic realism
Time of plot: c. 1894
Locale: Dublin, Ireland
First published: 1914

Principal characters:
A YOUNG BOY, aged about twelve
A YOUNG GIRL, the sister of a playmate named Mangan

The Story

The little boy lives with his aunt and uncle on a dead-end street in Dublin, in a house formerly occupied by a now deceased priest. The boy is impressed and somewhat mystified by the moldy books—a historical romance, a pious tract, and a detective autobiography—and other reminders of the previous tenant.

The action of the story begins with the children's games, played in the lanes and backyards of the neighborhood during the winter twilight. These games end when the sister of one of the boys—named Mangan—calls her little brother in to his tea. The image of this girl standing in the lighted doorway so fixes itself in the boy's imagination that he begins to pursue her shyly in the street. Even in the bustle of the weekly grocery shopping, he carries with him a feeling about her which amounts to something like mystical rapture.

Then, one day, while the other little boys are playing, she asks him if he is going to a bazaar, named Araby. She is unable to go because of religious activities at her school, but he undertakes to go and bring her a gift instead. This brief conversation and the prospect of the trip to the bazaar causes the boy to lose concentration on his lessons and regard his playmates with disdain.

The Saturday of the bazaar is acutely agonizing for the boy. He has to wait all day long for his uncle to come home and give him the required pocket money. He withdraws from play and wanders through the upper empty rooms of the house, dreaming of the girl. His apprehension during supper-time is compounded by the chatter of a visiting woman. Finally, at nine o'clock, his uncle arrives home, somewhat drunk, for his dinner. He greets the boy's anxious reminder of his trip with some patronizing clichés.

When he sets out at last, the boy finds that he is alone on the special train arranged for the bazaar, and finally arrives there at 9:50 P.M. In his haste, he pays the adult fee at the turnstile, only to find that the bazaar is just about to close and the day's take is being counted. Hesitantly, he approaches one of the few stalls still open, one selling pottery. The young lady in charge of this stall pauses momentarily in her flirtatious banter with two young men to attend to the boy's diffident interest in her wares. He is so put off by all his disappointments and her tone of voice, however, that he at once decides not to buy anything. Instead, he simply stands there in the middle of the darkening bazaar, incensed at the betrayal of his hopes and the shattering of his illusions.

Themes and Meanings

This is a story of the loss of innocence and the frustration of first love. The young boy's exaggerated expectations about the emotional rewards of his devotion to the little girl are cruelly deflated. He interprets the disappointing circumstances of his journey as a sign of the hollowness of the ideals with which he undertook that quest. He thus connects the frivolous banter among the young people and his own earlier brief conversation with Mangan's sister and thinks that he has perceived the banal reality behind the romantic image. Yet his perceptions in each case are unreliable: His immaturity causes him to overreact in each direction. The story, then, shows that the temptations to both the romantic inflation and to the cynical devaluation of experience are but two sides of the same false coin.

"Araby" is the third of the fifteen stories in *Dubliners* (1914). These stories examine the hazards of the various stages in life, and "Araby" marks the end of childhood and the beginning of adolescence. This protagonist begins his story as a boy amid his peers, full of childish energy and short-lived attention. The image of Mangan's sister gradually emerges from these confused impressions, however, gathering itself into a vision of desire, both erotic and religious. The growth of these feelings soon sets the boy apart from his fellows, and becomes even more consuming at the mention of the bazaar. He now connects his attitude toward the transcendent with the popular mystique of the Orient, each with an awakening sexual longing. No sooner are these connections made, however, than they are compromised: The girl cannot be possessed (because of her "retreat"), and in the compromise—the material gift—lie the seeds of the destruction of the dream. The rest of the story dramatizes the painful deflation of that dream: the human limitations of his uncle and aunt and the natural limitations of time and space all conspire to thwart the boy's search for fulfillment. He is therefore emotionally disposed to interpret the material elements of his adventure (the adult admission fee, the falling coins, the extinguishing lights, the casual talk of fibbing) as the signs of the end of the childish idealization of human values. From such a point of view, this is a story of initiation, marking the rites of passage from the Edenic domain of home to the uncertain terrain of adult life.

Similarly, the story can be viewed as a version of the medieval romance. The hero sets forth from surroundings of blissful innocence in pursuit of a distant ideal. In his solitary adventure through dark places, his spirits are buoyed up by the vision of remote beauty with which he hopes eventually to commune. He encounters and overcomes various obstacles and adversaries on his journey, finally gaining possession of the symbol of the truth which liberates him from ignorance and unites him with the beauty he desires. This literary mode is predominantly melancholic and nostalgic, focusing on the consciousness of the narrator or hero, emphasizing the chivalric virtues, and embracing a sense of Christian mystery. In its broad terms as well as in scores of details, "Araby" may be seen as designed in accordance with this story type, though rendering it in an ironic vein. The promise of spiritual bliss is made but not delivered: The hero's aspirations are cultivated and then denied. The cacophony of the modern city clashes and breaks the harmony of the mood of nostalgia for a faith in an ideal order of nature and grace. Thus, the story conjoins the personal and archetypal stories in a beautiful blend of realistic detail, tonal control, and symbolic design.

Style and Technique

Told from the first-person point of view, the story is a convincing representation of the voice of an observant, impressionable, naïve young boy. At the same time, through the deft use of language, symbol, and allusion, a world of feeling beyond the boy's experience is conveyed to the attentive reader.

First, the story is firmly rooted in time and place: The Joyce family lived on North Richmond Street in 1894, and the young James (then twelve years old) attended the actual Araby bazaar held between May 14 and 18 of that year. All the historical, geographical, and cultural references in the story are true to life.

Second, the language is carefully designed so as to convey a complex, yet highly controlled range of meanings. Consider, for example, the use of the words "blind," and "set . . . free" in the first sentence, the various uses of "stall" in the body of the story, and "driven" and "eyes" in the last sentence. These motifs support the chivalric and religious themes in the story and subtly link them to its emotional core.

Third, the story is rich with the symbolism of romance, Roman Catholicism, and the orientalism popular at the end of the last century. The various allusions—to Sir Walter Scott, James Clarence Mangan, *The Arab's Farewell to his Steed*, the Freemasons, Mrs. Mercer—can enlarge the relevance and appeal of the boy's private adventure for the attentive reader.

Finally, the story reaches its climax with what Joyce calls an "epiphany": a term borrowed from theology and applied to a moment of unexpected revelation or psychological insight. Such moments are not conventionally dramatic, nor are they explained to the reader. Here the epiphany occurs in the boy's consciousness when he overhears the petty and incomplete conversation at the bazaar. He believes himself to have been self-deluded: He has placed too much faith in Mangan's sister and the values she represents. His early religious training and ignorance of human relations have caused him to adore a mere petticoat.

Cóilín Owens

ARK OF BONES

Author: Henry Dumas (1934-1968)
Type of plot: Experimental fable in black dialect
Time of plot: Probably the mid-twentieth century
Locale: The Rural American South, probably Arkansas
First published: 1971

Principal characters:
  FISH-HOUND, the narrator, a young black male
  HEADEYE, his friend, another young black male with the
    powers of a seer

The Story

Because the actual language of "Ark of Bones" is its primary virtue, the story is difficult to describe. It is a first-person account of Fish-hound, a young black male, who goes fishing one day and is followed by his friend Headeye, who claims to have supernatural powers because he possesses a mojo bone, a totemistic object of African superstition. The story attempts to create the rhythm and idiom of Southern black dialect and to emulate the syntax and digressions of an uneducated black youth. Although the ages of Fish-hound and Headeye are not revealed, their language and actions suggest that they are in their early teens.

The plot of the story at first seems aimless, with Fish-hound describing how Headeye follows him to the Mississippi River and how Fish-hound tries to dodge him so as not to reveal the best fishing spots. Events take a turn toward the metaphoric, however, when Headeye catches up with Fish-hound and tells him that the mojo bone is a key to the black experience, the only one in the world. Headeye recounts the story of Ezekiel in the valley of dry bones, in which it is foretold that the bones shall be bound up and shall rise again. Headeye himself prophesies that Noah's Ark will come again and seems to be watching for it to appear on the river, while Fish-hound tries to ignore him and continues fishing. The story moves into fable when Fish-hound indeed sees a gigantic boat floating on the water, moving and standing still at the same time.

Fish-hound assumes that they are both dead and that the boat is the glory boat to take them to Heaven—until he sees a rowboat drawing up to them (rowed by two black men) which takes them to the Ark. After climbing aboard on steps that seem to be numbered for various years, they meet an old, long-haired black man dressed in skins, who talks to Headeye while Fish-hound hangs back frightened. When Fish-hound and Headeye go down into the Ark, they find bones stacked to the top of the ship; crews of black men handle the bones as if they were babies, while the old man reads from a long parchment. The men on the ship speak in a foreign tongue, which sounds as if it might be an African dialect and which Fish-hound cannot understand. As Fish-hound watches the men haul bones from the river and lay them out, he recalls a sermon about Ezekiel in the valley of dry bones, a theme frequently repeated throughout the story.

The old man tells Headeye that he is in the house of generations, that every African who lives in America has a part of his soul on the Ark and that God has called Headeye to be anointed. The old man makes Headeye promise to consecrate his bones and to set his brother free. He then engages in a ritual ceremony with the mojo bone before the two leave the Ark. Several days later, Headeye comes to tell Fish-hound that he is leaving, that he will someday be back, and that Fish-hound is his witness. The story ends with people asking Fish-hound where Headeye has gone, but he answers only by telling them about Ezekiel in the valley of dry bones, which makes people think he is crazy.

Themes and Meanings

Although "Ark of Bones" is based on a common short-story convention of a central character who undergoes a mysterious and unexplained experience, and although it makes use of a fablelike form common to the short story since its beginning in biblical parables, Henry Dumas adapts these conventions to a uniquely black idiom and theme. The story depends on that unique blend of African black magic and Christian religion that creates the spiritualism that often characterizes black religion in America. The black magic of the mojo bone is connected to the idea of the dry bones in the Old Testament, and Headeye is both an Old Testament prophet and an African witch doctor. Dumas combines these two folk traditions of the supernatural to create a parable of the black experience in America. The notion of the dry bones being like little babies combines the idea of the death of the black man in white America with the promise that he will rise again and take his rightful place; thus, the bones are scrupulously cared for, as if they were incubating for a rebirth. Although the story does not make clear how Headeye is qualified to fulfill such a role, he is the chosen prophet for black resurrection, a seer who hears the moans and cries of his people and sets off in the end to fulfill his sacred promise to "set my brother free."

Fish-hound is the one who remains behind to tell the story of the sacred encounter and of Headeye's holy mission. Headeye is special because, as his name suggests, his eyes are large enough to see what no one else can or wants to see—the soul and spirit of the black man in America. The notion of the Ark still traveling the water is a metaphor for the idea of there being no place for the black man to land, no home for him until his bones can be bound up together and he can rise whole again. Fish-hound has several intimations of the meaning of Headeye's encounter and mission, but he keeps them to himself, for he is a sacred witness, the one allowed to see the encounter, although he is unable to understand or explain it fully. He never tells anyone about the Ark, only the story of Ezekiel in the valley of dry bones. Indeed, "Ark of Bones" strangely combines black versions of both the Ezekiel story and the Noah story to serve as a subtle and submerged metaphor of the black experience in America. Thus, although "Ark of Bones" is not an explicit outcry against injustices against the black man, it is a sly and sacred parable of those injustices.

Style and Technique

Style is crucial in this story. Fish-hound tells the tale in a manner and dialect that is typically black. Dumas creates the feel of oral speech, even as he gives Fish-hound's spoken tale a biblical rhythm. Thus, the story combines the oral with the written, the informal with the formal, the everyday with the ritualistic. "Ark of Bones" also blends the naturalistic with the fabulistic and the everyday with the supernatural. The linking of these two realms of the profane and the sacred is typical of short-story technique, and Dumas makes use of the combination to address the black experience.

The story is somewhat difficult to read, not because the dialect is hard to understand but because of the elliptical nature of Fish-hound's speech and the abbreviated and cryptic nature of the dialogue between Fish-hound and Headeye. It is also difficult to determine the nature of Headeye's experience because so much of the story depends on a religious view of reality in which signs are manifested in everyday life, in which ordinary objects have totemistic value, and in which Old Testament religion is taken literally and thus is very much a part of external reality.

To respond to the story appropriately, one must be willing to enter completely into the seemingly aimless, but actually quite formal and stylized, language of the young narrator. As in many similar first-person narrator stories (for example, those by Sherwood Anderson) one must accept the values of the narrator, at least temporarily, as a way into the worldview of the story. Fish-hound is a young man trying to understand, trying to make sense of his experience and to communicate that experience to others. That Headeye's confrontation with his own special destiny goes beyond commonsense understanding adds poignancy to Fish-hound's apparently stumbling and wandering story line. Consequently, more than simply a commonsense understanding is required to accept this highly stylized spiritual/social parable.

"Ark of Bones" is the title story of Henry Dumas' only short-story collection, published after his death at age thirty-four. It is typical of other stories in the collection in its focus on the oral nature of the black culture in America, particularly the Gospel tradition and the tradition of black blues. Thus, although the language of the young narrator may appear uneducated and aimless, there is a sense of ritualized music, almost a chant, in the sound of his tale. What the story ultimately attempts to do is create a sense of the very source of folktale and legend as Fish-hound watches the birth of a heroic figure for the twentieth century black, as Headeye is consecrated to go out and "set my people free."

Charles E. May

THE ART OF LIVING

Author: John Gardner (1933-1982)
Type of plot: Social realism
Time of plot: The early 1970's
Locale: Upstate New York
First published: 1981

> *Principal characters:*
> ARNOLD DELLER, the protagonist, a cook in an Italian
> restaurant
> FINNEGAN, the narrator, a member of a motorcycle gang
> ANGELINA DELLAPICALLO, a high school senior and cocktail
> waitress in the restaurant
> FRANK DELLAPICALLO, the owner of the restaurant
> JOE DELLAPICALLO, a bartender in the restaurant, Frank's son
> and Angelina's father

The Story

An Italian restaurant in a town in northern New York State has acquired a certain local fame because of its cook, Arnold Deller. A veteran of World War II, in which he was an Army cook in Europe, Deller is fascinated by the art of cooking, and though the special dishes he prepares each week for the restaurant are not elaborate, they are unusual and meticulously researched. Deller has worked in the restaurant for twenty years. He is an avid reader, something of a philosopher, and a political idealist. He has three young daughters, and his son Rinehart has been killed in the Vietnam War.

Finnegan, the narrator, belongs to a teenage motorcycle gang called the Scavengers. Beneath their braggadocio, they are a harmless bunch; their custom is to visit the Italian restaurant in the afternoon to have a beer and listen to Deller hold forth in his eccentric but literate manner while he takes a break from work.

One afternoon, he harangues the boys with his notion of "the art of living." Also present are Joe Dellapicallo, the owner's son, a bartender, and Joe's daughter Angelina, a cocktail waitress in the restaurant. While Joe seems indifferent to, and Angelina coldly irritated by, Deller's lecture, Finnegan is nonplussed by its intensity. Deller's argument is that the art of living is the ability to absorb rather than fight foreigners and foreign ways of thinking. His assumption is that man has always been both a social and a warlike creature. The need to have and protect children is at the root of this dual aspect of man's nature, according to Deller. The social contract has arrived at the point, however, where a man has to accommodate those he once regarded as his enemies if children are to be successfully nurtured in the modern world.

The emotional force behind Deller's point is the fact that his son has been killed in a war that is primarily racial, and therefore anachronistic. That is, the social instinct is now more important than the warlike instinct, for if children are to be given a chance to survive, the former must be enlarged deliberately (through "art," a willfully intentional process) and the latter must be forsworn.

That evening, Angelina approaches Finnegan in his father's garage, where he is working on his motorcycle. Finnegan has been attracted to Angelina for some time, but he has kept the attraction a secret—or so he believes. At dinner earlier, his sister Shannon teased him about it and his mother suggested that he invite Angelina to dinner. So far, Finnegan has expressed his interest only by driving his motorcycle by Angelina's house at night or near the places where she might be attending a party. He is, in his own eyes, concerned for her safety, as though he were a surrogate for her father. They have not been together—even to talk—before she arrives at the garage.

Angelina tells Finnegan about an ancient Chinese dish called "Imperial Dog." It requires a completely black dog, and she asks him to find one that night so that Deller may prepare the dish. Vaguely scandalized, but not wanting to alienate Angelina, Finnegan, along with the other Scavengers, breaks into a pet shop, steals a black dog, and brings it to the restaurant after hours. Deller is waiting for them, and as he continues his harangue from the afternoon, he butchers the dog and cooks the exotic dish. Besides the Scavengers, his audience consists of Frank Dellapicallo, his son Joe and granddaughter Angelina, Deller's three daughters, and his kitchen helper Ellis. Frank insists that, according to the long contract Deller has with him, the dish must be eaten. He himself eats nothing but spaghetti, and after he sees that everyone present except his son has sat down to eat the dish, he leaves, as does Joe himself.

The story ends with Finnegan commenting on how good the Imperial Dog tastes, and with various toasts and the approval—as Finnegan reports—of the shadows beyond the candlelight, which are the ghosts of Deller's son and of numerous Asians.

Themes and Meanings

This story's theme concerns the meaning of art: Art is essential to life itself, John Gardner believes, for it connects human beings to one another. Not only is it social in this respect, but it also requires that artists practice their art with this concern in mind, controlling their instinct to be defensive and allowing their instinct to benefit mankind to predominate. There are various kinds of art in the story that serve as examples of the "the art of living." The main one is Arnold Deller's cooking; it is meaningless unless there is someone for whom to cook. The Scavengers work, like Finnegan, to make their secondhand motorcycles function well, and they do this to cement the social bond among them: This, too, is art. Angelina is not only a work of art in that she is beautiful and attracts others to her, but also an artist insofar as she actively promotes social ideals (especially, as the reader learns, when she goes to college) and functions as mediator between clashing social units (Deller, her father, and the Scavengers).

Art is based on the love for children—that is, on concern for the future of mankind. Those who are without feeling and who mechanically accept the status quo, and those who thoughtlessly hate strangers and unfamiliar customs, are against art in its true social sense. These are the antagonists in the story, and they are represented by Joe Dellapicallo, Angelina's father. He pretends not to listen to Deller when the latter is talking about art in the bar; he seems not to care, but it soon becomes clear that he is passionately against the idea of cooking a dog, and later, when the dish is ready to eat, he refuses to take part and walks out of the restaurant. Ironically, as Finnegan notes, Joe is civilized (to the extent supporting the idea of art as the suppression of the primitive destructiveness built into the human psyche) in refusing to eat "man's best friend," but he is also the servant of unexamined assumptions, suggested by his robotlike movements as he withdraws from the banquet. His father, Frank, represents a middle position: He accepts art and its social function by allowing Deller to prepare special or unusual dishes as part of the restaurant's menu, but he refuses to eat these dishes himself. He is the kind of conservative (a condition underlined by the fact that he is old, sick, and withdrawn) who supports art but does not act on its implications—who does not, in short, partake of art.

Style and Technique

"The Art of Living" uses two aspects of plot, foreshadowing and climax, to embody its meaning. The potential merging of perspectives in the story is foreshadowed by what some of the major characters are and how they behave. Arnold Deller is a cook, which means that his art is to do something for others; he also makes his appeal to those who are much younger than he—Angelina and Finnegan. Angelina is a social idealist, which means that she is open to Deller's appeal. Though she belongs to a tightly knit Italian family, she acts on the basis of Deller's values by putting in motion the theft of the dog for his recipe. Finnegan himself is half-Irish and half-Italian, a racial mixture to begin with, and since his mind and his attraction for Angelina enlarge his perspective beyond the confines of his gang he procures the dog for Angelina and Deller.

The climax of the story is the ultimate realization of all these tentative mergings, the moment in which the barriers between the characters (with the exception of Angelina's father) break down. They all participate in the same difficult dinner: The young gang members cooperate with the older and more established Deller; Deller's daughters come out of their seclusion to be with

the others; Finnegan and Angelina cement a friendship; the shadows of the
dead merge with the high spirits of the living at the ceremonial dinner.

Mark McCloskey

THE ARTIFICIAL NIGGER

Author: Flannery O'Connor (1925-1964)
Type of plot: Psychological realism
Time of plot: Probably the 1940's or 1950's
Locale: Atlanta, Georgia
First published: 1955

Principal characters:
MR. HEAD, a sixty-year-old man living in rural Georgia
NELSON, his ten-year-old grandson

The Story

Flannery O'Connor's own favorite among her stories, "The Artificial Nigger" is really two stories in one: the saga of Nelson's initiation into the world of experience and the tale of Mr. Head's fall from righteousness to emptiness. The two journeys parallel each other, just as the railroad tracks, which play an important part in this story, parallel each other; unlike the tracks, however, which never intersect, Mr. Head's and Nelson's journeys coalesce in their shared visions of the mysterious statue which provides the title of the story.

In the opening scene, Mr. Head and Nelson, who live together in rural Georgia, are preparing for a trip to Atlanta, each motivated to make this monumental expedition for different reasons. Mr. Head, proud of his independence and omniscience (he does not even need an alarm clock to awaken him), sees the trip as a "moral mission" during which he will guide his grandson through the complexities of the city, helping him see everything so that Nelson will never again want to visit the city and will, instead, be content to live forever with his grandfather. Nelson, for his part, wants to see the city where he believes he was born; for him, the trip is a journey into his past.

Traveling to Atlanta by train, the pair experience their first shared event—an event which, ironically, separates them. Mr. Head has been warning Nelson about seeing "niggers," telling him that the city is full of these people, who were run out of the county two years before Nelson was born. Nelson, confident that he will be able to identify a black person when he sees one, observes but does not recognize the first black man he sees on the train. Mr. Head asks him, "What was that?" and Nelson responds, "A man." Pushed to be more specific, Nelson says that the man is "fat" and that he is "old," but never does he identify him as black. As Nelson tries to rationalize when told by his grandfather what he was supposed to have seen, "You never said they were tan. How do you expect me to know anything when you don't tell me right?" Mr. Head, the guide, righteously enjoys his knowledge at the expense of his grandson's ignorance.

The next episode continues to distinguish the guide from the follower. The two weigh themselves on a scale in front of a store, and though the machine is inaccurate in its numbers, Mr. Head is sure it is accurate in its words because the ticket says that he is "upright and brave" and that all of his friends admire him. Nelson's fortune, by contrast, is ominous: "You have a great destiny ahead of you but beware of dark women."

As the two pursue their journey, Nelson becomes increasingly enamored of the wonders of the city, horrifying his grandfather by his positive reaction to the place Mr. Head believes is evil. To shock his grandson, Mr. Head takes Nelson to a sewer entrance and forces him to look into the depths of the underground system. Explaining to him the terrors of that underbelly, Mr. Head unknowingly teaches Nelson that there is indeed a dark underside to the wonders of existence. The lesson, however, requires more experience before Nelson truly understands its implications.

One of these experiences occurs when Nelson and his grandfather, lost in the city, meet a black woman whose presence confuses Nelson because of her maternal yet sensuous presence. Wanting to be comforted and seduced by her, a feeling he has never had before, Nelson nearly collapses from the sensation, remembering the fortunes on the scale that told him to beware of dark women but told his grandfather that he was upright and brave. Nelson decides to trust his mentor once again.

His mentor, however, betrays that trust. In a subsequent episode, Nelson collides with a woman, knocking her down and incurring her wrath. She accuses Nelson of breaking her ankle and tells Mr. Head that he will have to pay the doctor's bill. When Mr. Head responds that Nelson is not his boy, that he "never seen him before," the biblical echoes of Peter's and Judas' betrayals resound. Nelson is devastated.

Guide and follower are now separated by a monumental chasm. The relationship between the two is literally and figuratively severed, with Mr. Head walking ahead of his grandson, the young boy trailing behind. As the two individuals proceed in this fashion, they see a statue whose image and significance provide the climax of the journey and the story. A plaster figure of a black boy about Nelson's size, the statue has "a wild look of misery," and its misery, viewed by two human beings who are themselves miserable, becomes the vehicle by which Nelson and Mr. Head transcend their particular situation. Grandfather and grandson sense that they are "faced with some great mystery, some monument to another's victory that brought them together in their common defeat. They could both feel it dissolving their difference like an action of mercy."

The two return to their life in rural Georgia, Nelson having been initiated into the world of good and evil, Mr. Head having been initiated into the world of humanity. Each recognizes his need of the other; both realize that they do not understand the mystery of a world that contains sewers and illuminating visions.

Themes and Meanings

Two worlds are juxtaposed in "The Artificial Nigger": the world of the machine, with its alleged accuracy and predictability, and the world of mystery, with its ambiguity and spontaneity. In the first world, the railroad train arrives on time and, like the best of technological inventions, transports its passengers efficiently and safely to their destinations. The scale, another mechanical device, provides weight and fortune, both for a mere penny. The train, however, delivers Mr. Head and Nelson to a place that they had not expected to visit—their inner selves—and the scale gives numbers that are not accurate and fortunes that are ambiguous.

In the other world, the world of mystery, there is no pretense of accuracy or clarity. A black man on a train is not really black; he is tan. A black woman leaning in a doorway is not simply seductress or mother; she is both. A statue, appearing miraculously on the lawn of someone's yard, is not merely terrifying or purifying; it is an ambiguous combination of both emotions.

Like William Faulkner, another Southern writer, Flannery O'Connor celebrates those qualities that distinguish human beings from machines, those qualities that are most closely connected to mystery and ambiguity. When Mr. Head and Nelson return from their trip to the city, they are interdependent because they have been touched by the mysterious, shared vision that connects them.

Style and Technique

Flannery O'Connor adapts various traditional literary devices to her story of Mr. Head and Nelson. The most obvious strategy is the idea of a journey, which provides both the structure and the content of the tale. Just as Don Quixote and Huckleberry Finn travel to make external and internal discoveries, so grandfather and grandson in "The Artificial Nigger" voyage to foreign territory and see not only new sights but also new selves.

In the classical version of the journey, a guide plays an important role in helping the traveler find his way and his goal. Ironically adapting the figure of the guide, O'Connor describes the grandfather as "Vergil summoned in the middle of the night to go to Dante, or better, Raphael, awakened by a blast of God's light to fly to the side of Tobias." Mr. Head does indeed lead Nelson, but he guides him to wonders that neither mentor nor follower anticipates.

Still another traditional image is that of moonlight, which both distorts and illuminates. At the beginning of the story, when Mr. Head awakens to discover "half of the moon five feet away in his shaving mirror," he finds in its "dignifying light" confirmation of his delusive self-image, his self-righteous notion that he is "one of the great guides of men." At the end of the story, when the travelers return from their trip, the moonlight is once again shining, but this time the light is clarifying, not misleading. Nelson and Mr. Head have returned, a reminder of T. S. Eliot's words in *Four Quartets* (1943): "Home is where one starts from/ . . . And the end of all our exploring/ Will be to arrive where we started/ And know the place for the first time." Nelson says this in his own words: "I'm glad I've went once, but I'll never go back again!"

Marjorie Smelstor

THE ARTIST OF THE BEAUTIFUL

Author: Nathaniel Hawthorne (1804-1864)
Type of plot: Allegory
Time of plot: c. 1840
Locale: New England
First published: 1844

Principal characters:
OWEN WARLAND, the protagonist, a watchmaker, dreamer,
and the artist of the beautiful
PETER HOVENDEN, Owen's former employer, now a retired
watchmaker
ANNIE HOVENDEN, Peter's daughter, whom Owen loves
ROBERT DANFORTH, a blacksmith, Owen's childhood friend
and rival for Annie's hand

The Story

Even as a child, Owen Warland enjoyed carving intricate figures of birds and flowers and showed mechanical ability. Hence, he is apprenticed to Peter Hovenden, a master watchmaker, with whom, his relatives hope, he will be able to make practical use of his delicate talents.

Peter, however, is not impressed with Owen's character. He recognizes his apprentice's considerable talents but senses that Owen does not care to apply them in a conventional way. When failing eyesight forces Peter to surrender his shop to Owen, the young man confirms his master's fears. Owen's business declines because his customers do not appreciate the way he trifles with their beloved timepieces, which he tends to embellish fancifully.

Far from regretting this lack of customers, Owen rejoices in the free time he now has to pursue his goal of creating an object so like its natural original that it will be indistinguishable from it. The first attempt fails after Robert Danforth comes to deliver a small forge ordered from the blacksmith. Danforth's brute strength so disturbs Owen that he carelessly demolishes the artifact.

For some months Owen returns to watchmaking, abandoning any artistic pretense. Slowly, however, he recovers his interest in his project and is about to begin again when Peter visits him. His former master's skepticism toward anything lacking utilitarian value so upsets Owen that he relinquishes his dream.

In the summer he once more takes up his task, but again he is frustrated, this time by Annie Hovenden, who has come to his shop to have her thimble repaired. Owen loves her and wonders whether she might be a worthy partner for him. She provides the answer by touching Owen's delicate device, thus ruining it. Enraged and disappointed, Owen sends her away and resigns himself to a winter of dissipation.

With the return of spring, Owen resumes work on the intricate device. One evening Peter comes to tell him of Annie's engagement to Robert Danforth. Though Owen does not betray his disappointment to Peter, he himself destroys the mechanism in a fit of despair. For a while he ridicules his former dream of rivaling nature, but at last he decides to produce his imitation as a wedding gift for Annie.

By the time he delivers the present, Annie and Robert already have a child. As Annie, Robert, Peter, and the child look on, Owen opens an elegantly carved ebony box; out flutters a butterfly, more beautiful than any to be found in the woods or meadows. While all admire Owen's handiwork, none recognizes its true genius. As it hovers about the room, the infant grabs it and crushes it in his fist. Owen is not troubled, though, for in creating the butterfly he had achieved his dream.

Themes and Meanings

As in many of his works, Hawthorne here explores the artist's life, which Hawthorne defines in true Romantic fashion. Owen takes nature as his model, devoting his summers to the careful observation of butterflies. His examination is not scientific; he does not dissect or analyze. Rather, he draws inspiration from the butterflies and seeks to comprehend their essential qualities.

This quest for understanding has no monetary or utilitarian value. Again showing himself a product of the Romantic era, Hawthorne stresses Owen's desire for self-satisfaction. Owen rejects the practical: He has no interest in using his talents to regulate machinery, and the sight of a steam engine, that most useful of devices, makes him physically ill. His concern is with the spirit, chiefly his own. Hence, he feels no regret when the physical manifestation of his art is destroyed; all that matters is fulfilling his dream.

Yet if Owen enjoys the success of the Romantic artist, he also suffers from the artist's failure. To become an artist of the beautiful he must sever his ties with his fellowmen. He cannot be bothered with customers, with would-be friends like Robert Danforth, even with love. He creates the artificial butterfly, but he loses Annie. Because Owen does not isolate himself for any evil purpose, Hawthorne does not condemn him as he does Ethan Brand (in the story of that title) and Chillingworth (*The Scarlet Letter*, 1850), who have also cut themselves off from humanity. Still, Owen pays a price for his victory, and Hawthorne leaves open the question of whether it is too high.

Style and Technique

To make his point about art and the artist, Hawthorne uses allegory. Each of the characters in the story represents an attitude or principle. Owen embodies the artistic quest. Robert Danforth, strong and earthy, is brute force. Peter Hovenden, who devotes his considerable skill to regulating the temporal world rather than changing it, stands for materialistic skepticism; Annie is the force of love. Each of these last three challenges and threatens Owen, and each is responsible for the destruction of the mechanism in the course of the story. Owen's self-doubt also threatens his success, as indicated by his destroying the artifact after he learns of Annie's engagement when, presumably, he questions the value of his enterprise if it costs him so dearly.

Owen's device takes the form of a butterfly emerging from a black box, an allegory of the soul escaping, transcending, the body. Owen has worked to release his spirit from its prison, and he finally succeeds. Because the butterfly is only the physical manifestation of the concept, its fate, once the dream has been made real, cannot affect Owen, who remains free—and alone.

Nature, too, assumes an allegorical aspect. In the winter, symbol of the soul's dark and unproductive period, Owen abandons his project. When spring returns, Owen's creative spirit is renewed, indicated by the reappearance of butterflies in the fields. Owen's struggles, his periods of doubt and achievement, are those of any artist who would create beauty. "The Artist of the Beautiful" demonstrates Hawthorne's faith in the artistic principle, but also his clear-sighted understanding of the struggles which the artist must endure.

Joseph Rosenblum

THE ASPERN PAPERS

Author: Henry James (1843-1916)
Type of plot: Psychological realism
Time of plot: Near the end of the nineteenth century
Locale: Venice, Italy
First published: 1888

> *Principal characters:*
> THE NARRATOR, an American editor who never reveals his
> name
> MRS. PREST, his American confidante in Venice
> JULIANA BORDEREAU, an elderly American lady, the former
> love of Jeffrey Aspern
> TITA BORDEREAU, Juliana's niece and companion in Venice

The Story

This is a tale of a man obsessed. The narrator, an American editor, is completely controlled by his desire to know all that can be known about Jeffrey Aspern, a deceased American poet. Determined to publish the definitive biography and collected work of his idol, the editor assumes a false identity in order to move into the dilapidated apartments of Juliana Bordereau, an elderly lady reputed to be Jeffrey Aspern's lover before 1825. Juliana lives in near isolation with only her niece and a maid for companions. Refusing the company of other Americans in Venice, including Mrs. Prest, the editor's confidante, Juliana is considered eccentric and stingy. Using these characteristics to his advantage, the editor offers to pay extravagant rent for her extra rooms, claiming that he is a writer who needs the inspiration of the garden attached to Juliana's property. Juliana acquiesces, much to the surprise of her niece, Miss Tita Bordereau, and the editor begins his summer-long campaign to capture any of Aspern's papers that might be in Juliana's possession.

The editor embarks on this adventure expressly to deceive. Not only does he conceal his true name and vocation, but also he decides that if nothing else succeeds, he will feign romantic interest in the niece and steal the papers if necessary. His adoration for Aspern is so intense that he despises the women who may have been involved with him as inferior creatures. Indeed, one of his reasons for seeking out Juliana is to prove that Aspern, reputed to have treated her badly, behaved like a gentleman throughout their relationship. Yet he is also fascinated with Juliana and desires to touch the hand that once touched Aspern's; through her, the editor feels closer to Aspern than he ever has before.

So obsessed with his project is he that the editor only gradually comes to realize that he is being manipulated by Juliana. She extorts increasingly large amounts of rent from him as the summer progresses, encourages him to cultivate the garden at great expense, and finally suggests that he should entertain Miss Tita. This vaguely middle-aged niece has always lived in the shadow of her critical, domineering aunt. When the editor takes her into his confidence, she considers ways to make the papers available to him, yet even when her aunt becomes ill and lies semiconscious in her bed, Tita is controlled by her. Despite the editor's wooing, Tita is hesitant to look for the papers; her timidity frustrates the editor, whose impatience impels him to act.

Angry at Juliana's manipulations and Tita's cowardice, the editor disregards their privacy and makes up his mind to steal the papers. Already a liar and a con man, he does not scruple to become a thief. Aware that his actions are morally suspect, the editor nevertheless defends himself by claiming, "I think it was the worst thing I did; yet there were extenuating circumstances." He creeps into Juliana's room and approaches the desk where he knows the papers are concealed; as he reaches out to open her desk, he hears a noise and turns to find Juliana glaring at him furiously. She condemns him as a "publishing scoundrel" and falls into a dead faint.

Appalled, the editor flees from Venice, but returns after some days when he hears that Juliana is dead. He decides to appeal once again to Tita, and is surprised to discover that she has acquired some of her aunt's subtlety. Glad to see him, Tita explains that she has saved the papers from her aunt, who tried in her last moments to burn them. Yet Tita does not feel right about simply handing over the papers to the editor. She suggests that her aunt, who tried to provide for Tita's future by collecting exorbitant rent, would understand if Tita shared the papers with a husband. Faced with the implications of his romantic charade, the editor panics, leaving Tita in confusion. At last, he seems about to recognize the extent of his obsession: "I could not, for a bundle of tattered papers, marry a ridiculous, pathetic, provincial old woman." He wishes he had never heard of the papers and thinks himself strange for caring so much about them. Freed from his only desire, he becomes suddenly aware of Venice, for the first time acknowledging the delight of his surroundings.

Yet this reprieve from his fanatical idea is only temporary. He suddenly becomes more determined than ever to obtain the papers and returns to Tita determined to do whatever is necessary to achieve his goal. In this frame of mind, he sees Tita—who receives him without reproach—as almost angelic, altered by her forgiveness into a younger, more lovely being. In short, he begins to believe he could marry her, and that Aspern, were he alive, would approve his actions. Tita, however, has finally recognized the hypocritical nature of the man. Humiliated by him, she rises above him morally at the end by destroying the weapon he has used against her—the papers. Slowly, determinedly, she has burned everything, taking a long time, she notes, because there was so much. Her revenge for being manipulated is complete, and the editor leaves Venice with nothing but bitterness and chagrin.

Themes and Meanings

The namelessness of the narrator is in direct contrast to the prominence of Jeffrey Aspern, who, though long dead, is named continually. This suggests that the narrator is a cipher, a man with little sense of himself who absorbs his identity from his idol. His work as an editor depends on Jeffrey Aspern's creativity as a poet; his work as a biographer depends on the interesting travels and romances of Aspern's life. The narrator tries to mold his own life to the shape of Aspern's and even begins to imagine Aspern condoning his behavior and urging him on. The narrator is not only obsessed with Aspern's papers; he wants to become Jeffrey Aspern.

The theme of such a gross obsession is explored through the fate of its victims, the most significant of whom is the narrator himself. The progress of his moral degradation controls the order of the story as he lies, orchestrates deception, commits bribery, and attempts thievery. Throughout the tale, he tries to justify his actions by implying that Juliana is a worse manipulator than himself, but after her death, the destructiveness of his obsession is fully revealed in his treatment of Tita.

James uses Tita to demonstrate how someone accustomed to being controlled by others can mature into a self-determined person. Tita's existence has all been dependent on her aunt's, and she leaves to Juliana plans for the future. She knows that she will inherit the editor's rent payments but warns him nevertheless of Juliana's manipulations, signaling her own dislike of such tricks. Very trusting, she accepts the editor's assurances that he understands and does not mind continuing the arrangement, and believes in the sincerity of his attempts to flatter her and show her something of Venice. Falling in love with him, Tita resorts to manipulation of her own and attempts the feeble stratagem of offering him the papers if he will marry her. This moral slip, however, is only temporary. Embarrassed and disgusted with herself, Tita develops a sense of dignity by choosing to destroy the papers when they would still bring her either great wealth or a husband. With this act, she rises above the muddied morality of her aunt and the editor and recognizes the self-worth which has been denied her for a lifetime.

Style and Technique

The reader's interest in this tale is maintained in two ways: first, through the external drama of the narrator's quest for the papers; second, through the internal drama of his moral decline. James intentionally draws out the action, building suspense by allowing the narrator a summer to win his landlady's trust and to ascertain that the papers do exist. Parallel to this quest is the slow erosion of the narrator's code of social behavior. He jokes at the beginning of the summer that he will do anything to get the papers, but clearly he does not mean it; by the end, he is willing to marry a woman he finds repulsive.

James emphasizes this change in his narrator by employing first-person narration and creating the character of the confidante, Mrs. Prest. As the narrator explains, and tries to justify, his motives to Mrs. Prest, he exposes all of his prevarication and male chauvinism. He tries to blame his actions on Mrs. Prest, saying that she is the one who suggested that he go to live with the Misses Bordereau, an idea which would not have occurred to him otherwise. Throughout the tale, he implies that women are more deceptive than men, and blames his final defeat on Juliana and Tita rather than identify his lack of honesty as the source of the problem. He is, indeed, a publishing scoundrel, but he admits only to being "not very delicate." In his voice at the end can be heard, not the wisdom of a man who has learned the dangers of manipulating others, but the bitterness of a man who will never fully understand himself.

Gweneth A. Dunleavy

AN ASTROLOGER'S DAY

Author: R. K. Narayan (1906-   )
Type of plot: Social realism
Time of plot: Probably the 1920's and 1930's
Locale: Southern India
First published: 1947

Principal characters:
THE ASTROLOGER
THE ASTROLOGER'S WIFE
GURU NAYAK, a client of the Astrologer

The Story

The story begins with a description of the place and environment in which the astrologer meets his clients and does his work. He begins his work every day at midday in a public place under a large tree that is close to a public park in his town. The place chosen for his work is generally full of people who pass by or gather there, such as customers attracted by vendors of nuts, sweetmeats, and other snacks. It is a place poorly lighted in the evening, and since the astrologer has no light of his own, he must depend on what light comes from the flickering lamps kept by neighboring vendors; a dully lighted, murky place is best for his purpose. He is not an astrologer by profession, but was led into it by circumstances which forced him to leave his village, where, if he had stayed, he would have settled down to a life of tilling the land.

He has a practical knowledge of the common problems of most people: "marriage, money, and the tangles of human ties." His sharp eyes, used to scanning for customers, make people believe he has an unusual ability to tell people's fortunes.

"An Astrologer's Day" opens as its title character arrives at his workplace, at midday, and as usual spreads his charts and other fortune-telling props before him, though no one comes seeking his aid for many hours. Later, with nightfall approaching, he begins preparing to go home when, all of a sudden, he beholds a man standing in front of him. In the exchange of talk that ensues, the astrologer carefully tries to spread the net of his craft around the client, and the client, Guru Nayak, responds with a challenge: Would the astrologer tell him whether he, Guru Nayak, will be successful in a search he is carrying out, returning double the fee he has paid if the prediction cannot be made? The astrologer alternately accepts, declines, and feigns indifference, all the more to whet Nayak's appetite and make him press his offer. The astrologer then catches a glimpse of Nayak's face (previously shrouded in darkness) in the light of the match Nayak has struck under his cheroot, and, though at first chilled by the sight, decides to play out Nayak's game: The astrologer tells him that he was once left for dead by another man, who had attacked him with a knife; Nayak, astonished, bares his chest to show the scar and wants to know if his assailant is alive. The astrologer, addressing him by name (to his further surprise), adds that his assailant is now dead and that he, Guru Nayak, should go back to his village and live out his life peacefully. To placate the still angry Nayak, who demands to know if the assailant met the kind of death he deserved, the astrologer replies that he was crushed under a lorry (truck). Nayak pays him the fee and hurriedly departs. The astrologer returns home late to his anxious wife and gives her the money he earned that day, adding that it all came from one client. The wife is happy, but notices a slightly changed expression on her husband's face; she asks him if there is something wrong. "Nothing," he says, but after dinner tells her that he is relieved that the man he killed in a drunken brawl many years earlier is, in fact, alive. He says that it is late and goes to sleep on a *pyol* (mat).

Themes and Meanings

The story turns on a most important human weakness: the desire to know the future. This weakness is greater among the sick, the suffering, and the poverty-stricken. In a poor country such as India, astrologers, palmists, and numerologists, as well as others who claim to know the future (for example, fortune-tellers assisted by birds in drawing cards), assume a great significance in society. Fortune-tellers offer hope to those leading tragic lives, giving them reason to continue their existence, and offer solace where it otherwise does not exist. They also find a means of survival in taking advantage of the misfortunes of millions, by listening to their tales of woe (particularly significant in a culture where psychiatrists are not common and would not command confidence even if they were). Astrology, in particular, has played a crucial role in the lives of many, and has long been an integral part of Indian life (so much so that, tradition has it, the horoscopes not only of Buddha—who lived five hundred years before the birth of Christ—but even of epic heroes dating back at least a thousand years before Christ have been maintained). In "An Astrologer's Day," Narayan not only touches on a tradition that has existed since antiquity, but also comments on its debased modern version. Emphasizing a social reality, Narayan exploits, with a comic eye, a common foible of Indians and writes a happy-ending story with a double twist and double surprise. The astrologer in the story is not a Brahman (a traditional astrologer), but one of the more common kind found on the roadside who has been forced to run away from an appointed role to a new destiny, and who adroitly uses the opportunity to thwart permanently a calamity that was hanging over his head. Even as others have their ups and downs, the astrologer has his ups and downs in life, and as the narrator says, "He knew no more of what was going to happen to others than he knew what was going to happen to himself next minute." In the story, significantly enough, the astrologer's would-be assailant unwittingly comes to the man whom he is seeking in revenge and misses the opportunity to kill him. Astrology deflects him from his violent purpose, giving him the illusion of tasting revenge, and also helps the astrologer to resolve an old, burning conflict; so, both are happy.

Style and Technique

"An Astrologer's Day" is the title story of a collection by Narayan published in 1947 (in Great Britain but not in the United States); it is also the first story in *Malgudi Days* (1982), a retrospective volume that includes stories from several decades. It is typical of Narayan's work not only in its themes but also in its style and structure.

The distinctive appeal of Narayan's stories derives in part from the tension between their strong emphasis on plot and their extreme brevity. "An Astrologer's Day," like most of Narayan's stories, is very short, less than five pages long. Most modern short stories of this length are sketches, tending toward the plotless; in contrast, Narayan's stories almost always have a clear dramatic action in which (in Narayan's words) "the central character faces some kind of crisis and either resolves it or lives with it."

"An Astrologer's Day" features a plot twist worthy of O. Henry, but the brevity and conciseness of the tale and its low-key ending save if from the air of contrivance to which O. Henry was prone. Also notable is the irony that can be appreciated only in rereading—particularly the exchange in which the astrologer assures Guru Nayak that his enemy met the fate he deserved.

K. S. Narayana Rao

AT THE BAY

Author: Katherine Mansfield (Kathleen Mansfield Beauchamp, 1888-1923)
Type of plot: Epiphanic
Time of plot: Early twentieth century
Locale: New Zealand
First published: 1922

> *Principal characters:*
> LINDA BURNELL, a woman who embodies a female mystique
> STANLEY BURNELL, her husband
> ISABEL, their oldest daughter
> KEZIA, the middle daughter, much like her mother in
> temperament
> LOTTIE, the youngest daughter
> MRS. FAIRCHILD, Linda's beloved mother, the stabilizing
> female force in the household
> BERYL FAIRCHILD, Linda's unmarried younger sister, a central
> figure in the story
> ALICE, the servant girl

The Story

Although written four years later, "At the Bay" was conceived as a continuation of "Prelude." Like the earlier story, "At the Bay" is organized around time in all of its various aspects, the design of the story functioning symbolically as part of the overall meaning that derives from the integration of themes. The story begins at the moment the sun rises over Crescent Bay and concludes on the evening of the same day.

The meticulous record of that day in terms of time and the household routines of the Burnell family provides a summary of the action of the story, the careful delineation of sequential time causing plot to become symbolic action. Stanley, the first to arise, goes to the beach in order to swim in the bay, but he finds his brother-in-law, Jonathan Trout, there before him. After his swim, Stanley returns to the cottage and dresses while breakfast is being prepared by Beryl and Mrs. Fairchild. Stanley allows twenty-five minutes to have breakfast with them and the children. Linda remains in bed. After much frenzied activity, Stanley leaves for work, and the children are sent out to play. The women relax with another cup of tea. At exactly eleven o'clock, they all go to the beach—except Linda, who sits in the garden while the new baby sleeps. The children play at the beach with their cousins, Rags and Pip, and Beryl, despite her mother's disapproval, leaves the family group to swim with Mrs. Harry Kember.

After lunch, Mrs. Fairchild and the children take an afternoon rest. Beryl washes her hair and then goes out to play bridge with Mrs. Kember. Alice, the servant girl, has the afternoon off and goes into town to visit with Mrs. Stubbs. After tea, the children go out to play in the garden, while Mrs. Fairchild gives the baby his bath. Linda walks in the garden until sunset, when Jonathan comes to take the boys home, and Stanley returns from the city. After dinner the day has ended for everyone except Beryl, who, late at night, after everyone is asleep, walks with Mr. Kember in the garden.

Although in both "Prelude" and "At the Bay" it is difficult to name a protagonist (all the female characters seem to merge into a collective identity, with each single character suggesting an aspect of the female psyche), if it is necessary to name a protagonist, it is arguable that in "At the Bay" Beryl emerges as the principal figure. For Beryl, the day is one of disquieting discovery and frustrated attempts to find a life and a lover of her own.

Early, at breakfast, Stanley is aware that something is wrong with Beryl. She is unmindful of him and cross with Kezia. Her mood changes when she stops the coach and has the chance to talk and laugh with one of the passengers. She is happy to have Stanley leave, to be free from his demands and authority. At the beach, Beryl disregards her mother's wishes and moves beyond the family circle to join Mrs. Harry Kember. Fascinated by what she sees as masculine qualities in Mrs. Kember, Beryl becomes shy and reckless. Defiant of the other women on the beach, she undresses boldly and goes into the water with Mrs. Kember. For Beryl, Mrs. Kember's face in her black bathing cap as it emerges from the water is an image of Satan, constantly shifting form in a manner that is for Beryl both horrible and fascinating.

Later that night in her bedroom, Beryl recalls the day and in her imagination puts Mrs. Kember's compliments on the lips of a lover. In the midst of Beryl's fantasy, a real man appears, Harry Kember. When he calls to her, Beryl goes out to him, but she is not prepared for his aggressiveness, and she runs inside. Kember is a horrible caricature of a fantasy lover; the episode seems like a dark and disturbing dream.

Themes and Meanings

From the moment "At the Bay" opens, readers are introduced to the geographical area where the story takes place and to the emotional climate which will prevail. From the merging images of earth and sea arise the major symbol of the story. Throughout the narrative, the activities of the characters will be seen against the background of the rise and fall of the tides of the ocean, and, as in "Prelude," are in time with the movement of the sun and moon through the heavens. Life moves along a path between birth and death and is no more than the rising and setting of the sun. As the images of sea and earth merge, so life and death are unified; the manifestations of sex, male and female, merge also, so that distinctions disappear.

The opening paragraph of the story, in which sea and earth are merged, is a metaphorical statement of the mutability of time and life. In the microcosm, the members of the Burnell family react to the symbolic situation and setting with varying degrees of awareness and acceptance. In "Prelude," the house and garden are surrounded by the dark bush, and the story moves back and forth between them. In "At the Bay," the action moves in and out of the house to the sea and seashore. The characters continue the same concerns, seeking answers to the same questions.

Style and Technique

One of the characteristic devices used by Mansfield in her fiction is the disruption of normal time sense. Often within a sequence of events defined in terms of clock time, Mansfield provides knowledge of another time, one not bound by ordinary rules of motion and space but rather existing apart from perception or the record of time passing. Thus, immediately at the beginning of "At the Bay," when Jonathan calls out to Stanley, the reader experiences a dislocation from normal sequential time. Jonathan's voice is totally unexpected as it booms over the water and thus destroys the normal time sequence, which has been carefully built up. Time doubles back; other doors are opened; another character has emerged and made his way to the water to join Stanley. The time in which this has happened is unexperienced by a reader, since the author has not provided necessary sense data to fill in the interval.

Another, and more striking, example of the disruption of the normal time sense, when time is stripped of its ordinal and metrical qualities, occurs in the scene with Linda in the garden under the manuka tree. In the garden there is an abrupt shift of geographical place that ignores the ordinary relationships of distance, time, and motion. Without transition in the narrative, Linda is seen as a child leaning against her father's knee. The reader's imagination accomplishes the sudden movement into past time because Linda's does, but simultaneously the reader is led to experience events that never took place, that existed only in Linda's imagination. As a result of this manipulation of time, the reader experiences a release from normal sequential time perception. The ordinal and metrical limitations are destroyed, and when they cease to exist, so do the boundaries which separate the real from the unreal and life from death.

Katherine Mansfield's role in the development of the short story was profound. Concentrating on a single moment in time, eliminating a strongly plotted action line, and using imagery and metaphor to expand the moment and give it significance beyond itself, Mansfield helped to move the short story away from the formulaic, shaping it as an art form whose aesthetic value was sufficient to place it beside the other and older literary genres.

Mary Rohrberger

AT THE BOTTOM OF THE RIVER

Author: Jamaica Kincaid (1949-   )
Type of plot: Idyllic surrealism
Time of plot: Mid-twentieth century
Locale: St. Johns, Antigua, West Indies
First published: 1982

>   *Principal characters:*
>   THE UNNAMED PROTAGONIST, at times the first-person
>   narrator, a young adult woman
>   THE UNNAMED MAN, her father at middle age, seen from a
>   child's perspective
>   THE UNNAMED WOMAN, her mother at middle age, seen from a
>   child's perspective

The Story

In the first of the six sections which constitute this story, the third-person narrator defines a "terrain" that is at once external and internal. From the mountains of its origin to the flat plain of its mouth, the river poses a philosophical riddle of its own cycle of creation and destruction, which awaits the human sensibility "that shall then give all this a meaning." The unnamed narrator then shifts abruptly to describe "a man who lives in a world bereft of its very nature." As an individual, the man is incapable of reconciling his own alienated existence with his participation in the larger cycles of natural and human history. He "cannot conceive" of a contentment that comes from "the completeness of the above and the below and his own spirit resting in between." Further, he is unaware even of his own alienation or of a contradiction within him; consequently, he "sits in nothing, in nothing, in nothing."

While the second section continues the third-person narration, the mood and tone of the narrative voice become more familiar, even autobiographical, than they were in the first section. The scene shifts to a detailed but detached domesticity: a man, his wife, and his child. As the father, a skilled carpenter and a subsistence farmer, contemplates what he has accomplished, he meditates on the joy and futility which seem to possess him: "First lifted up, then weighed down—always he is so." He delights in the beauty of ordinary events—the color of a sunset, the flight of birds, and the dance of insects—but he mourns the passing of the natural world. Despite a loving family and his domestic stability—he has built his own house, read books, planted fruit trees, educated his child, and provided food—the father seems to stand uncertainly "on the threshold" of spiritual identity, for he "imagines that in one hand he holds emptiness and yearning and in the other desire fulfilled."

Analogous to the first section, which offered a universalized figure, this section offers a particular man who succumbs to the futility of an amorphous but vast silence, to "Nothing."

As the third section begins, the tone becomes even bleaker: The narrator recites a litany on the inevitability, the ultimacy of death. The mood deepens from futility to despair as the narration changes in mid-paragraph to the first-person interior monologue of the man, who decides that "life is the intrusion," and, subsequently, so, too, is his sense of beauty and truth in his own accomplishments and in his love for his family, an intrusion into the absolute context of death. Sorrow, grief, and regret as well as joy, innocence, and knowledge are "bound to death." The speaker here, however, claims to regret, not this awareness of the pervasive presence of death, but the powerlessness of "my will, to which everything I have ever known bends." The fragility of human will and achievement constitutes despair, not the fact of death itself.

Midway through this third section, a folk parable intervenes in the manner of a riddle. An exotic caterpillar is stung by a honeybee; its pain becomes pleasure as it balances "remembering and forgetting" in its life "inside and outside" the mound in which it lives, until it vanishes, leaving only a faint glow in the darkness around it. The speaker, still in the first-person voice, says that she has "divined this" and wishes to share her knowledge with "a monument to it, something of dust"; yet this interior monologue is not that of the man, her father, but that of the daughter, who feels that she has been mocked by her father's explanation: "Death is natural." She rejects death as a natural occurrence: "Inevitable to life is death and not inevitable to death is life." In her own echoic parable, she describes—amid a tentative, majestic imagery—a worm (symbolic of death) overcome by a bird (symbolic of the soul's flight), but a boy enters the scene and shoots the bird with his bow and arrow. Bluntly, she concludes that the boy's own "ends are numberless. I glean again the death in life." For the child's sensibility of the speaker, all life yields to death, but she rejects the inevitability as a natural process.

The brief fourth section clarifies the point of view of the first-person speaker, who now reveals the reflection in process: "I see myself as I was as a child." Here, focusing on the innocence of love in the memory of her mother rather than on the alienation of her father, the recollection is one of unquestioned contentment; yet the mature narrator notes that even as she sang harmoniously with other girls at a celebration, she and the others did so with "minds blank of interpretation." They were oblivious to an image of the grave within the song. The threat of death never intruded into the childhood reveries of joyous expectation.

In the complex epiphany of the fifth section, the narrator stands on the river's bank looking below into the mouth of her own experience. At the bottom of the river, she sees a detailed vision of her childhood house, her personal memory, situated "near the lime-tree grove," her cultural memory. (Limes were a principal crop of the colonial economy.) In the motionless world that she views below, she realizes that she experiences "something new: it was the way everything lit up." This illuminated, expansive sense of the past brings her a sense of unity with her mother, the natural world, and her own destiny. As she watches the woman below looking to the horizon, she too sees what the woman sees: the simultaneous shining of the sun and the moon beneath the water. In the transparent light of the epiphany, "the sun was The Sun, a creation of Benevolence and Purpose," and "the moon, too, was The Moon, and it was the creation of Beauty and Purpose." Having symbolically reconciled her father's alienation (the sun) and her mother's innocence (the moon), her vision of harmony expands to embrace the whole of the natural world, and she is "blessed with unquestionable truth" in a "world not yet divided, not yet examined, not yet numbered, and not yet dead." Simply viewing this world, however, is not enough; she yearns to enter it in order to discover her purpose.

While still in the first person, the narrative perspective once again shifts— to a vantage point from the bottom of the river: "I stood above the land and the sea and looked back up at myself as I stood on the bank of the mouth of the river." Disassociated now from the egocentric self, the narrator sees herself merging with her cultural history and the natural world. While she burns in transforming flames, she experiences herself as an enlightened, pure will over which she has "complete dominion," and she enters the sea, merging fearlessly with it to touch "the deepest bottom." In the freedom of "a mind conscious of nothing," she embodies the paradox of the creation of being out of nothingness. She becomes an unnamed medium of light, beyond contradiction and time, much like the glow of the caterpillar in the earlier parable.

In the brief closing section, the narrator questions the new light of which she is made, a light that might lead her "to believe in a being whose impartiality I cannot now or ever fully understand and accept." From the "pit" of her paradoxically liberating repressed memories, primordial as well as personal and cultural, she steps into a room and, in the light of a lamp, sees a few simple things: books, clothes, a table and a chair, and a flute and a pen. At this moment, she knows that she is bound to the history of "all that is human endeavor" and to all that will perish without a trace. Uncertain but assured, she asserts the will to purpose which she has experienced as her spiritual identity: "I claim these things then—mine—and now feel myself grow solid and complete, my name filling up my mouth."

Themes and Meanings

What remains unanswered at the end of Jamaica Kincaid's imagistic yet abstract story is the question of the name which creates her identity anew.

When the narrator's final persona emerges from her transforming vision at the bottom of the river, she accepts her own inevitability of death in the knowledge that she can create herself beyond it: She accepts the mature artist's role of creating works in the midst of a modern world marked by alienating futility. In order to achieve the confidence of the creative will, the narrator had to endure passage through a number of identities, which led from her own childhood innocence through the pain of both her father's and her own experience of pain and death to the uncertainty with which she must live. Seized by the reluctance to acknowledge the limits of creation, to face death, the narrator must immerse herself in the unconscious psychological and spiritual turmoil that she imagines in her father and experiences within herself.

The reader is privileged, then, to witness the birth of an artist and to experience—through an empathetic identification with the narrator—the struggle of the creative will to come into being. Obliquely autobiographical, the narrator describes an island world where natural beauty threatens to overwhelm the creative energies of humanity. Constrained by an implied experience of isolating poverty, the narrator knows too well the agony of her father's alienation and the futility which has imprisoned him. Consequently, once she can move beyond the naïve rejection of death, created by the sheltering love for and from her parents, the narrator is free to enter the sea, symbolic of both the unconscious and death itself. Her epiphany is the dissolution of the ego and the death of the body, a vulnerability that, conversely, opens new possibilities of power; experiencing primordial, cultural, and personal unity, she is capable of seeing herself anew, organizing an informed innocence—through her creations—of light, the spiritual awareness of truth, which she now reflects to achieve beauty and purpose. Nothingness, however, has been prerequisite to that light; interpretation and meaning originate in darkness, consistently calling the self into question. To create being is to name it, and to name is to engage continuously in the creative will necessary to both aesthetic and spiritual being: They are one and the same. The artist overcomes death by creating even as the creations disappear into death, into nothingness. The artist achieves the will to purpose by giving up the will to immortality, thereby—paradoxically—gaining immortality for the creative process itself.

Style and Technique

Kincaid's style embodies the very process of creation that the story describes, for she re-creates elements from traditional and modern genres. On one hand, she draws upon the pastoral mode of the idyll, framing scenes of a rural, tranquil beauty which are emblematic of a simple happiness; yet, in contradiction, she further extends her pastoral images into biblical echoes of incantatory repetitions to emphasize the complexity of those magical moments of earthly content. Moreover, she evokes the historical development of the idyllic mood, perhaps reminiscent of Robert Browning's *Dramatic Idyls* (1879-1880), to juxtapose psychological crisis and the innocent rapture of the Caribbean folktale. On the other hand, the haunting images and fractured narrative voices recall the surrealism of the early twentieth century, which sought to heal, through disruption of ordinary perception, the fragmented consciousness of modernity. With narrative perspective that ranges from a detached observer through the alienated unconscious of the father to the naïve, the disembodied, and the mature selves of the narrator herself, these rapidly transforming personas demonstrate the very growth—through creation and dissolution—of the artist about which the story concerns itself.

Kincaid's creative process, then, consists of reconstructing the various elements of passing traditions and "monuments," works of art, in a "terrain" that contradicts them, within the creative will and without, on the page (the story at hand), so that what constitutes making something new is also the unmaking of it, which, in turn, is the preservation of the traces of the past. The author achieves exactly what the young girl wishes to do in remembering the caterpillar and inventing the story of the boy who kills the bird: She compounds a compressed, concise language that is at once intensely concrete and profoundly abstract into a self-definition of the artist and, in so doing, illuminates the contentment in the process of fiction itself. Yet, to underscore the death of the author, she appears as the mature artist only when the fiction is complete.

Michael Loudon

BABYLON REVISITED

Author: F. Scott Fitzgerald (1896-1940)
Type of plot: Social realism
Time of plot: 1931
Locale: Paris
First published: 1931

Principal characters:
CHARLIE WALES, a thirty-five-year-old businessman, formerly
from the United States, now from Prague, Czechoslovakia
HONORIA WALES, his nine-year-old daughter
MARION PETERS, Charlie's sister-in-law
LINCOLN PETERS, Marion's husband
DUNCAN SCHAEFFER, a friend of Charlie from his earlier days
in Paris
LORRAINE QUARRLES, also a friend of Charlie from his former
days in Paris

The Story

Charlie Wales has returned to Paris after a three-year absence in the hope of taking his nine-year-old daughter, Honoria, back to live with him in Prague. He remembers with regret that his former life in Paris was a life of dissipation and wildly extravagant spending. Paris then was awash with Americans who had achieved almost instant wealth on the stock market. The Paris to which Charlie returns, however, is a changed Paris, now almost empty of Americans, since most of those who had lived so extravagantly had lost everything in the stock market crash of 1929. Charlie himself has come back a changed man. He has replaced his wild, drunken sprees with the stable life of a successful businessman who consciously takes only a single drink each day to help keep the idea of alcohol in proportion in his mind. He hopes that the change will convince Marion Peters, his sister-in-law, to relinquish to him the legal guardianship of Honoria, which Marion assumed at the death of Charlie's wife, Helen.

Marion has persisted in unfairly holding Charlie responsible for the death of his wife. Charlie and Helen had argued while dining out one night in February, and he had gone home without her, locking the door behind him, not knowing that she would arrive there an hour later, wandering about in slippers in a sudden snowstorm and too drunk to find a taxi. As a result, Helen had barely escaped pneumonia, and Marion has never forgiven Charlie, taking the scene as typical of their turbulent life together. Charlie must now break through Marion's reservations to the maternal part of her nature, which Charlie knows must acknowledge that Honoria's proper place is with her father. Charlie fears that if he does not get his daughter soon, he will lose all of her childhood and she will learn from her aunt to hate him. He is relieved and gratified when, on an outing with him, Honoria expresses a desire to come and live with him.

Charlie knows that he can win his battle with Marion if he shows her that he is now in control of his life. She is skeptical about his even entering a bar, after his earlier extravagances, but he convinces her that his drinking is under control. During Charlie's lush years, Marion and Lincoln had ample reason to envy his wealth, but now it is clear that his is not a precarious income based on the fluctuations of the market, but the stable income of a hard-working businessman, and that he can indeed provide a good life for Honoria. Charlie makes it clear that he is in control of his emotions when he listens to Marion attack him one more time for his role in Helen's death, and he calmly responds, "Helen died of heart trouble."

Charlie has the battle won when suddenly there intrude two ghosts from his past in the form of two friends whom he cannot control. Early in his visit to Paris, Charlie leaves his address at his brother-in-law's with a bartender in case some of his former friends want to get in touch with him. Later, when he actually encounters two of these old friends, Duncan Schaeffer and Lor-raine Quarrles, he realizes how far he has progressed beyond where they still are and how uncomfortable he is in their presence. He shocks them with his sobriety and amuses them with his fatherly concern for Honoria, but they are drawn to him because he possesses a strength that they know they do not have. Charlie avoids giving them his address, but they get it from the bar-tender, and just as Charlie is making arrangements for Honoria's move to Prague, into the Peterses' home they burst as drunken reminders of Charlie's dissipated past. Charlie, as angry as his relatives about the intrusion, rushes them out, but it is too late. The damage has been done. Marion is so upset that she retires to bed, and any further arrangements have to be postponed. The next day, Lincoln informs Charlie that they must put off any decision about Honoria for six months. Charlie sits in a bar, disillusioned and alone, but still in control of himself as he says no to a second drink and tells himself that he will come back for Honoria some day, that they cannot keep her from him forever.

Themes and Meanings

In this story that recalls Fitzgerald's own alcoholic existence in Paris in the 1920's, Charlie Wales learns how truly relative wealth is. In losing, for at least a while longer, the future that he hopes to share with Honoria, he is paying for his past.

Charlie recalls his earlier dissipated life and suddenly realizes the meaning of the word "dissipation": to make nothing out of something. As Charlie sits alone in a bar at the end of the story, he seems left with nothing. He is not without wealth. He now makes through hard work as much money as he made through luck during the boom days of the stock market. The way of life that came with sudden fortune, however, destroyed his chance to enjoy things of more lasting value. He remembers the money frivolously thrown away on wild evenings of entertainment and knows that it was not given for nothing: "It had been given, even the most wildly squandered sum, as an offering to destiny that he might not remember the things most worth remembering, the things that now he would always remember—his child taken from his control, his wife escaped to a grave in Vermont." Just when he hopes to get Honoria back and establish a future with her, his past intrudes, and he is unfairly kept from doing so. The ill-timed appearance of Duncan and Lorraine convinces him of the impossibility of ever outliving his past.

Charlie is alone and frustrated at the end, but he is not defeated. He has learned to "trust in character again as the eternally valuable element," and he has faith in his own reformed character. He knows that he has much to offer Honoria: a home, love, and values. He is disillusioned, but, in his new strength, he will not slip back into the destructive habits of his past. For the time being all that he can offer Honoria are things, and he knows how little value there is in the things that money can buy.

Style and Technique

Contrast plays a major part in Fitzgerald's technique as he presents both Charlie and Paris as they were before the crash of 1929 and as they are at the time of the story. The language of the stock market adds a note of irony as Charlie applies it to the rise and fall of his fortune—both his monetary fortune and his fate in general.

On his return, the reformed Charlie sees Paris through new eyes. With the majority of the wealthy Americans gone, Paris is indeed a changed city, but even what remains unchanged looks different to Charlie when seen with the clarity of sobriety rather than through a drunken haze. He sees his former outlandish behavior from a more serious point of view and shies away from contact with his friends, who seem never to have changed. He can even see his old self as he must have appeared to the Peters, who did not share in the wealth that seemed to come to him so easily. Helen's death is presented from two different perspectives—Charlie's and Marion's. Her obvious jealousy and his remorse shift the balance in favor of support for Charlie and belief in his version of the story.

Charlie sees the error of his former ways and the ephemeral nature of his life prior to 1929. He recalls the snowstorm that almost caused Helen's death and the fantasy world that surrounded the incident: "The snow of twenty-nine wasn't real snow. It you didn't want it to be snow, you just paid some money." Money was not a problem during two dazzling, extravagant years in Paris: "He remembered thousand-franc notes given to an orchestra for playing a single number, hundred-franc notes tossed to a doorman for calling a cab." Having too much money, ironically, was the source of Charlie's greatest losses. As he sits in a bar realizing that he has once again lost Honoria, at least for a time, the bartender offers his regrets for a different loss: "I heard you lost a lot in the crash." Charlie responds, "I did," and adds, "but I lost everything I wanted in the boom."

Donna B. Haisty

BAD CHARACTERS

Author: Jean Stafford (1915-1979)
Type of plot: Psychological realism
Time of plot: Early twentieth century
Locale: Adams, Colorado
First published: 1954

>   *Principal characters:*
>   EMILY VANDERPOOL, the narrator and protagonist
>   LOTTIE JUMP, an eleven-year-old vagabond
>   JACK, Emily's brother
>   STELLA and
>   TESS, Emily's sisters
>   THE VANDERPOOLS, Emily's parents

The Story

The bad characters in this fictional autobiography are two young girls: Emily Vanderpool, the protagonist and narrator, and Lottie Jump, an eleven-year-old vagabond from the lower-class section of town. A brash, impudent, yet privileged girl, Emily has not yet learned to maintain friendships. Because she believes that she needs frequent solitude, she insults her friends until she loses their friendship. Always Emily repents of these impetuous actions, but always too late; she indeed alienates all of her friends. Even her brother and sisters are targets of Emily's vituperation.

Emily has one friend—her cat, Muff. Muff dislikes all humans except Emily, mirrors Emily's need for self-inflicted privacy, and, by extension, mirrors Emily herself. Because Muff and Emily are mirror images, Stella, her sister, frequently refers to Emily as "Kitty" whereas Jack, her brother, calls Emily "Polecat."

As the Christmas holidays approach, Emily, without a friend, sits home alone with Muff. When she investigates a sound coming from the kitchen, she quickly discovers a young girl stealing a piece of cake. Tall, sickly looking, ragged, and dirty, this girl, Lottie Jump, is the antithesis of Emily. Lottie frequently lies, steals, has ragged teeth, and comes from a lower-class family. Lottie's mother is a short-order cook in a dirty café; her father has tuberculosis; her brother has received no education. By contrast, Emily has a good home, wears nice clothes, attends a good school, attends church regularly, and has educated, healthy parents. Yet, during the course of one afternoon's conversation, the spirited Lottie, who explains that she appeared in Emily's kitchen not to steal but to visit Emily, manages to convince the vulnerable Emily to become her friend. Incredible as the story may appear, Emily acquiesces.

That afternoon, the girls search through Emily's mother's bureau drawers. Emily, however, fails to notice Lottie stealing Mrs. Vanderpool's perfume flask. Emily's many advantages make Emily feel guilty, which is why, perhaps, she succumbs so easily to Lottie's proposition. To remain friends, Lottie threatens, Emily must not only join in a shoplifting spree at the local dime store but also bring along money for the trolley fare. Reluctantly, Emily agrees to the plan.

Before she leaves the Vanderpool home, Lottie steals the cake she initially sought earlier that day. That evening, Emily allows her parents to believe that a vagrant stole the cake and, because of her guilty conscience, has a tantrum when her mother worries about the loss of the perfume flask.

In the following few days, ordinary events cause Emily to feel even more conscience-stricken with regard to her approaching day of shoplifting. Her dad's visiting friend, a respectable judge, discusses vandalism and punishment of criminals; Emily steals her Sunday-school offering to pay for both trolley fares; and on the fatal day, she begs off from baby-sitting for her younger sister. Most of all, she worries about the Sunday-school offering she has taken to pay for the trolley ride, money intended for widows. Ironically, she does not want to steal anything and certainly does not need anything. Repelled by Lottie's suggestion, she does not even wish to see Lottie again. Yet she feels mesmerized and fascinated by this clever girl's persuasive personality, by her thieving, by her unfortunate background, and by her colloquial Oklahoma dialect.

On Saturday, Emily meets Lottie and is astounded to discover Lottie wearing a huge hat. Emily does not realize that Lottie's hat is a repository for the day's stolen articles. In the trolley car, Lottie, adept at stealing, carefully explains Emily's role. In exchange for half of the stolen articles, Emily is to divert the clerk's attention while Lottie steals the articles and hides them under her huge hat.

By late afternoon, and after several articles have been successfully stolen, Emily suddenly and characteristically needs to be alone. This time, however, she insults Lottie at the same moment Lottie attempts to hide a string of pearls. Whirling around to notice the target of Emily's insults, the clerk catches Lottie in the act of stealing the pearls.

Although she has been caught stealing, Lottie cleverly pretends to be deaf and dumb and points an accusing finger at her young accomplice: Emily Vanderpool. Because the authorities believe that a more powerful and advantaged Emily has victimized an obviously handicapped Lottie, they reward Lottie with a bag of candy and send her home.

Since this is Emily's first offense, she is remanded to her father's custody. Subsequently, she faces her father's friend, Judge Bay, who lectures to her on the subject of thievery. Then she faces her wounded mother's recriminations and those of her brother and sisters.

Emily, however, has learned important lessons from this experience. She no longer thoughtlessly insults her friends when she wishes to be alone. Instead, like adults, she feigns a headache or a dentist appointment. She has also learned to maintain more than one friendship.

Meanwhile, her mirror image, Muff, has also grown up. Rather than miss Emily's infrequent companionship, Muff has been busy herself—having kittens.

Themes and Meanings

Jean Stafford depicts two young girls who are approaching puberty. One girl, who has every advantage a girl could desire, is trapped by her antithesis, a girl who has had no advantages in life. By contrasting the girls' backgrounds, values, manners of speech, and personalities, Stafford can examine Lottie's corrupt, emotionally bereft nature. When she is caught stealing, Lottie, who has initiated the dishonesty, pleads a physical handicap and allows Emily to bear the responsibility alone. Lottie has clearly taken advantage of Emily and has felt her expertise superior to that of Emily's. By revealing her obvious disadvantages and thereby appealing to Emily's propensity for guilt, Lottie, left unpunished for her crimes, does not mature or learn from the experience. For Emily, this has been an important learning experience: She faces a crisis in her young life, resolves that crisis, and, as a result, gains both experience and maturity.

Style and Technique

Stafford employs both dramatic irony and symbolism to give the story resonance. Through the device of dramatic irony, the reader learns immediately important information that Emily learns only at the end of the story. More pervasive is the use of symbolism. Muff and Emily, for example, are symbolically compared: Both are unkind to humans; Emily is referred to as Kitty and Polecat; Lottie dislikes cats. Moreover, Jack insists that Emily likes fish. As Muff matures, she becomes less dependent on Emily and, finally, has kittens. At the same time, Emily matures and spends her time maintaining friendships.

Other uses of symbolism are Lottie's stealing devil's food cake, which foreshadows her tempting Emily and further suggests Lottie's devilish nature. At Emily's house, Lottie admires herself in the mirror as if she has never really seen herself. Symbolically, she has not. The evening before the shoplifting spree, Emily does cross-stitch embroidery, a symbolic foreshadowing of the next day's deceit. Also, the story takes place during the Christmas holidays, a time for renewal. Together, these and other symbols create a pattern that reinforces the story's themes.

Bette Adams Reagan

THE BALLAD OF THE SAD CAFÉ

Author: Carson McCullers (Lula Carson Smith, 1917-1967)
Type of plot: Domestic tragedy
Time of plot: The 1930's
Locale: Central Georgia
First published: 1943

> *Principal characters:*
> MISS AMELIA EVANS, the owner of the Sad Café
> COUSIN LYMON WILLIS, the hunchbacked, beloved cousin of
> Amelia
> MARVIN MACY, Amelia's former husband

The Story

The action of the story covers the period from the time Cousin Lymon arrives in town until his departure with Marvin Macy almost seven years later. The narrative, however, includes incidents and explanations of circumstances from Amelia's early childhood until several years after Lymon and Marvin have gone. The story begins with a description of the dreary, isolated town, the hostile climate, and the central building there—a shabby, boarded-up former café. From the upstairs window the dim, grief-stricken face of Miss Amelia can occasionally be seen gazing out. The story of the café and the story of Miss Amelia are one. She was born there in the upstairs living quarters, was reared as a solitary child by her widowed father, and was heiress to both the property and the business when her father died. She is a woman of many talents: a sharp business negotiator, a renowned liquor distiller, a compassionate and knowledgeable doctor, and a strong and independent person.

Amelia's independence and solitary habits of existence are well-known, and when Lymon, the little sickly hunchback, arrives and claims to be her cousin, the townspeople are astonished and baffled that she takes him in. He quickly becomes the center of her life and encourages her to convert the store into a combination store-café, where not only the traditional supplies and moonshine are dispensed, but also meals are served and a general festive gathering of the townsfolk takes place on Saturday nights. Lymon is the center of the café activities. He enjoys the company of the townsfolk, and Amelia becomes more sociable and friendly, even to the extent of wearing dresses instead of the rough, masculine work clothes she had always worn before.

Her love for Cousin Lymon is obvious, though incredible, to the townspeople, especially as they recall her one previous experience with love, when she was courted and wed by Marvin Macy. Marvin was a wild young man who had been abandoned by his parents when he was a small child. He was handsome, reckless, and a notorious seducer of romantic, trusting young women. When Marvin Macy met Amelia, however, his life changed. He fell in love with her, reformed his character and behavior, and patiently waited two years before declaring his love and asking her to marry him. Amelia did marry him, but with the belief that the marriage was a business arrangement, and she aggressively resisted his efforts to consummate the marriage physically. In his efforts to win her over, he gave her all that he owned: his money, property, and gifts that he bought for her. After ten days of this uneasy relationship, with Marvin the lover trying earnestly to win over his beloved, she threw him out but kept all that he had given her. He left town, and rumors subsequently went around that he was in the penitentiary for robbery. Amelia's life continued as before until the arrival of Lymon.

After six years of happiness and contentment between Amelia and Lymon, during which time the café flourishes and the townsfolk enjoy the social activity each Saturday night, Marvin Macy abruptly returns. Lymon is entranced; he adores this arrogant, swaggering, handsome outlaw. Marvin, for his part, ignores and even abuses the little hunchback.

During the winter, Lymon, undaunted by Marvin's scorn, invites him to come and live in the café. Amelia makes no protest, not daring to insist that Marvin leave, for fear that Lymon might go with him. Instead, she begins to practice boxing. She is an inch taller than Marvin Macy and solidly built; the townspeople speculate that she will precipitate a fight when she feels confident that she can whip Marvin.

Finally that day arrives, and the townspeople gather to witness the fight. Amelia and Marvin exchange hundreds of blows over the course of a half hour or so; they are so nearly equally matched that no apparent advantage can be seen. Then the fighters shift to wrestling, grappling in intense effort and concentration. Finally, Amelia proves to be the stronger and pins Marvin to the floor. Just as she has her hands around his throat and is on the verge of victory, however, Lymon, who has been standing on the counter in order to see better, leaps onto Amelia's back and grabs her around the throat. This intervention turns the course of the fight, and Amelia is decisively beaten— left lying on the floor of her café. Marvin and the spectators leave, and Lymon hides underneath the back steps outdoors.

Later that same night, Marvin and Lymon return and with Amelia closeted in her small office, they ransack the café, destroying what they do not care to take. As a final expression of their hatred, they prepare Amelia's favorite dish—grits and sausage—mixed with poison.

Amelia becomes more and more isolated. She raises her prices, and people can no longer afford to eat at the café or shop at her store. She loses her interest in healing and in helping small children. For three years, she simply sits on the front steps, waiting, but Lymon never returns. Finally, she has the building boarded up, and she retreats to the upper story, whence she occasionally looks out over the town.

The town itself loses its spark of life as the life goes out of the café. It becomes a dispirited and isolated place, and the only pleasure the people find is in walking out to the highway, where a chain gang of twelve men is working at patching the road. The men in the gang begin singing, and as they sing, their song fills the listeners and the earth and sky with the music of human voices telling of the joys and sorrows of life. It is the music of men chained together.

Themes and Meanings

The love theme is unquestionably the most important of several themes interwoven in this richly symbolic story. The author not only demonstrates through her characters her distinctive view of love relationships, but also, at one point in the novel, digresses into a brief essay on the nature of love and how it affects people who love and are loved. She distinguishes the lover, who is free to love and to demonstrate this love and is thus in control of the relationship, from the beloved, who is in danger of being possessed by the lover. The lover is the happier one in the relationship always, and the beloved fears and even hates the lover.

There is no place for reciprocal relationships in this concept of love. Marvin Macy loves Amelia and she rejects him. Amelia loves Lymon and he uses and finally attacks her. Lymon loves Marvin, but Marvin despises and abuses Lymon. Love is a pleasure for the lover as long as the beloved will tolerate the lover. For the beloved, the relationship is no pleasure at all, and the only reason to tolerate it is for some perceived material gain.

A very insistent theme is that of isolation. The town is isolated, Amelia is isolated in many ways from the other people of the town, Marvin Macy was isolated in prison, the members of the chain gang are isolated from other people in society, Lymon is isolated by his handicap and ill health. All attempt to overcome the isolation by love, social intercourse with other people, and singing in harmony, as the case may be. Yet the story ends with Amelia in ever more profound isolation, with the townspeople seeking to relieve their loneliness by leaving the town to go listen to the chain gang singing. Love, the author suggests, can overcome this sense of isolation, and being together, even in a chain gang, is preferable to the intolerable loneliness of isolation. Amelia's isolation is destroying the life of the town as it has destroyed the social center of the town.

Another important theme is that of the grotesque. Each of the major characters is manifestly grotesque in certain ways. The little hunchback who is less than four feet tall is certainly grotesque. To add to his oddity, he dresses in grotesque clothing not at all appropriate to the time, place, or climate. Amelia is grotesque also. She is not built like an ordinary woman, being too tall, too strong, too brawny, and she dresses and acts like a man. Amelia's talents for commerce, healing, moonshining, fighting, and self-sufficiency all set her apart from the ordinary. Marvin Macy is also grotesque, in his outlaw behavior, his defiance of social mores, and his cruelty to people who care about him. Indeed, the town and the climate itself seem grotesque in that they depart manifestly from the usual. The author seems to suggest that isolation stems from differences and that love does provide a bond to enable people to share and be together, but as the love is not reciprocated, the chain is weak and will be broken, incurring even more profound isolation, and even more grotesque behavior.

Style and Technique

The author is acutely concerned with presenting an atmosphere within which rather bizarre characters can interact and seem plausible. She undertakes detailed descriptive passages to bring into focus the aspects of the town, the café, and the people, which enables the reader to comprehend and believe the action of the story. Although the story is told from a third-person point of view, there is not an omniscient narrator, but rather one who observes acutely and from time to time digresses to comment on the action, or even on the philosophy of the events of the story. The strength of the characterizations depends to a large extent on this skillful control of descriptive passages. The movement of the action is well paced, and the flashbacks to earlier episodes in the major characters' lives are never intrusive, but seem necessary and well integrated into the story line.

Betty G. Gawthrop

THE BAMBINO

Author: May Sinclair (1863-1946)
Type of plot: Psychological realism
Time of plot: c. 1920
Locale: London and a country house in Buckinghamshire, England
First published: 1920

Principal characters:
ROLAND SIMPSON, an artist and the narrator of the story
THE BAMBINO, a five-year-old boy, the title character
ADELA ARCHDALE, the Bambino's mother
JACK ARCHDALE, Adela's husband and the Bambino's father
FRANCES ARCHDALE, Jack's sister, an artist and the painter of
a portrait of her sister-in-law and nephew

The Story

Told in the first person by artist Roland Simpson to an unidentified listener, "The Bambino" is less a plotted story than a sketch revealing a dramatic situation and a set of characters. The anonymous listener prompts the story by asking Simpson if he painted a portrait hanging on his studio wall. Simpson replies that it is a study of Adela Archdale and her infant son painted by Frances Archdale, sister of Adela's husband and at one time Simpson's fiancée. Jack Archdale collects modern pictures, and Simpson explains to the listener the circumstances that explain why he has not purchased this one.

According to Simpson, the key to the situation can be seen in the composition of Frances' portrait of Adela and her son. The child is naked, standing between his mother's knees, but the visual focus of the picture is Adela's hands. "They're in the centre of the picture, large and white and important, as if Frances had known." For Simpson, the portrait captures the deadly combination of Adela's chief traits. The first is her beauty; he describes her as a "slender Flemish Madonna" and implies that Jack Archdale married her because she appealed to his collector's taste. The second is her clumsiness, both verbal and physical. Adela's hands are always in motion and always dropping things; she does not seem to understand the extent of the damage she does when she drops an antique Chinese bowl, left to Simpson in the will of a friend, and replaces it with a modern blue and white bowl from a department store.

The conflict Simpson observes between Jack and Adela is objectified in a dispute in London about who should hold the baby, thirteen months old at the time. Jack is angered when Adela says that the boy is "more mine than yours" and confides to Simpson that he cannot wait until the baby, whom they both call the Bambino, grows up. "I can't wait twenty years to know what he's going to do, the sort of things he'll say, what his mind'll be like." On the other hand, Jack continues, Adela would like to keep the boy a baby for the rest of his life. While this tension between Jack and Adela, on the surface, represents the rather normal friction between the mother and father of any child, Simpson sees the conversation with Jack Archdale as ironic in the light of the Bambino's fate.

Four years later, Simpson meets Jack in his sister Frances' studio and accepts an invitation to drive down to the house in Buckinghamshire that Jack had purchased as a family home. Simpson, who has been out of touch with all the Archdales, notices a great change in Jack. He is short-tempered, withdrawn, and clearly under some sort of strain. The reason becomes clear when Simpson, upon their arrival, asks to see the Bambino, who is now five years old. He was not prepared, he remarks to the listener, to see Adela return "with a baby in her arms—a baby too young to display excitement, too young to talk." It is the Bambino, however, and not a second child. Simpson perceives immediately, "She had got her way. The Bambino would be a baby all its life. Its mind had stopped dead at fifteen months." Adela, however, seems not to acknowledge this fact, attributing the child's physical and mental slowness to the size of his brain, but Jack Archdale is fully aware of the significance of his son's condition.

Frances Archdale explains to Simpson that when the Bambino was fifteen months old, Adela dropped him down a staircase. "She was coming down [the stairs] with the Bambino on one arm and the tail of her gown on the other. He caught sight of Archdale in the hall, and was struggling to get to him. . . ." Jack clings to every shred of medical evidence that suggests that the effects of that accident will not be permanent, and he struggles with his negative feelings for his wife. Simpson tells his visitor of the terror on Jack's face when, during that visit to Buckinghamshire, he saw Adela enter a room with a burning lamp in her hands. Frances explained then to Simpson that Jack lives in fear of the consequences of his wife's every action. He does not want her to have any more children, Frances added: "He simply couldn't stand seeing her hold them." Painful as the effects of the Bambino's condition are on Jack, Simpson tells his listener, he agrees with Frances that the greater potential for tragedy lies in Adela's situation. Oblivious to the consequences of her actions, as she has been throughout her life, Adela faces the most painful realization when the Bambino is too old for her to rationalize away his mental retardation. She will have to face the terror and hatred she engenders in the husband who cannot bear to look at her hands.

Themes and Meanings

In its broadest sense, the theme of "The Bambino" is the artist-observer's capacity to see the truth more clearly than do the participants in a particular situation. This generalization is supported by May Sinclair's use of Simpson as the narrator of this and a number of the other stories collected in *Tales Told by Simpson* (1930). Simpson and Frances Archdale, both of them paint-ers, arrive at the insights concerning Jack and Adela with which the story ends; indeed, the entire story hangs upon Simpson's assumption that the pose which Adela and the Bambino take in Frances' portrait provides a key to understanding the Archdales' situation.

The emphasis on the psychology of Jack Archdale is characteristic of Sinclair's novels and stories. She has a nearly scientific interest in the inter-play of biological heredity and environment in the development of human personality. This is seen in Jack Archdale, the man who married a woman who was an art object and whose son becomes in time "like a porcelain idol, doing nothing but wag his head." One of the ironies at work in "The Bam-bino" is the fact that Jack gets exactly the wife and son his aesthetic taste craves, and then learns how life-denying aestheticism is. Sinclair's treatment of psychology is less complex in "The Bambino" than in *The Three Sisters* (1914), *Mary Olivier: A Life* (1919), and *Life and Death of Hariett Frean* (1922), novels written at approximately the same time she was working on the Simpson stories. All three novels discuss the relationship of child and adult; like the protagonists of the novels, the Bambino is shaped by factors of heredity and environment beyond his control.

Style and Technique

In "The Bambino," Sinclair does not use the stream-of-consciousness nar-rative technique which she employed in novels such as *Mary Olivier: A Life.* The style of the story develops from her use of Simpson as first-person narrator and of the painting as the visual focus of Simpson's conversation with the unidentified listener. In technique, the story most resembles the dra-matic monologues of Robert Browning; Simpson, like the speaker in "My Last Duchess," uses the art object as a point of departure.

As a narrator, however, Simpson is more self-aware than the speaker in Browning's dramatic monologue. His sensitivity to the irony in the situation, and to the nuances of character found in the simplest words and actions, be-trays his affinity with the narrator of Ford Madox Ford's *The Good Soldier* (1915). Essential to each is achievement of insight into others and into self. Simpson tells the story of "The Bambino" because he is reliable and honest, and is able to show the dishonesty with which others live.

Robert C. Petersen

BARBADOS

Author: Paule Marshall (1929-   )
Type of plot: Psychological realism
Time of plot: 1958
Locale: Barbados
First published: 1961

> *Principal characters:*
> MR. WATFORD, the seventy-year-old owner of a coconut plantation
> MR. GOODMAN, a local shopkeeper
> THE GIRL, an eighteen-year-old who is sent by Goodman to keep house for Watford

The Story

The title suggests a story that treats life in the Caribbean island of Barbados, perhaps on the microcosmic scale that suits the scope of the short story. Yet the main character, Mr. Watford, deliberately lives far outside the mainstream of Barbadian society. He lives alone in an ostentatious plantation house with stone walls, large windows, and a columned portico, which is set far back from the gate that separates it from the crude wooden houses of the village. He tries to live like a white man. His house is an emblem of such a life, with size and pretense, with its furniture from Grand Rapids, Michigan, and its enormous parlor, where in the evenings he reads the newspapers from Boston. He is pleased when the boy who comes to order coconuts for Mr. Goodman shows him deferential gestures usually reserved for whites. Although he worked in a Boston hospital until he retired at sixty-five and although he has kept his American accent, furniture, and newspapers, he had been as detached from American life as he is from life in Barbados, the homeland to which he returned to buy his plantation and live five years before the story begins.

Alone, he works his five hundred trees all day, from dawn to dusk. At seventy, his vigor is fading, though he works ever harder to deny it, driving his body to perform as it did when he was much younger. His lean body is filled with tension, as if he could clench into himself all of his strength and prevent himself from breaking down in exhaustion and despair.

His solitude, his independence, his routine, and his forced energy all isolate him from the village. His disdain for his own people lies in his inability to hate the white family who forced him into servility when he worked for them as a yard boy. His hatred was redirected toward his own race, even toward his mother, who had given birth to nine stillborn children and whose only child to survive was himself. His terrible fear of death, his racial disgust, and his self-loathing drive him to work like a young man, a slave to his weakness and fear.

The antithesis to Watford is Goodman: corpulent, full of lusty vitality and magnanimity, with a rum shop and a coconut booth at the racetrack, a wife, two mistresses, and fourteen children. Goodman dispensing coconuts to the loud, sweating vulgar crowd at the track is the very image of sociability—an image that disgusts Watford. When Goodman comes to buy Watford's coconuts for resale, Watford criticizes as an idler the young man whom Goodman had sent to order the coconuts. Goodman replies that people such as Watford and himself, who have money, must provide work for those who need it. Watford balks at Goodman's assertion that they are responsible for helping others and becomes nauseous with rage when Goodman says that he will send a girl the next day for Watford to hire as a servant.

To have a servant in the house would violate the isolation that Watford has built around himself, would deny his complete self-reliance. To reveal the slightest need for the aid of another human might well lead to his confronting his true self as a mortal, black, aging man.

The servant appears the next day, a young woman barefoot in the driveway, standing as she must have stood, in the sun, from her arrival until his return at noon from the grove. Her stillness and self-possession contrast with Watford's frenetic activity. He tries to send her away, but she replies that she will be beaten if she does not work at least one day. After she fixes his lunch, he decides to send her back at the end of the day with a dollar in payment. She prepares his tea and a late supper, but when he looks for her to send her away, he finds her in an unused room under the stoop, asleep on a cot. He feels like an intruder in his own house. He decides to send her away the next morning.

When he descends at his customary 5:00 A.M., he smells breakfast and finds her sweeping the corridor. He thrusts the dollar at her and orders her out, but she tells him that it is raining. Her faint trust dies at that moment. Though she remains to cook and keep house, she becomes silent and more a part of the house than a human presence, because Watford refuses to converse with her.

He preserves his isolation even in her company, yet something about her, the tilt of her head, which reminds him of his mother, works on his affections. After many weeks of her working every day, she goes on a bus excursion on the August bank holiday. Her absence is suddenly more of a disruption than her presence ever was. He feels betrayed by her eagerness to take the day off. He dresses carefully for her return, cleans his nails, and brushes his hair. The feelings mounting in him are those that he has repressed all his life, those of both father and lover, wanting to punish and to protect her.

After watching for some time for her return, he sees her in the moonlight with the boy whom Mr. Goodman had sent, the two of them laughing and frolicking and dancing. The tension with which Watford has held himself together as he has grown old goes limp, and he is unable to speak or act. Unnerved and unmanned, Watford sinks into his bed, aroused and tormented by the thought of the two outside. Sensing them inside the house, he dashes toward her room, preparing his anger for his discovery, but she is alone instead, her clothes twisted about her, and womanly in a way he has not seen before in her. His anger fails him, and he supports himself against the wall. In his weakest moment, he recognizes that she is his last chance to live, but he cannot find the strength to win her, to approach her as a man. He must first defeat her, so he reproaches her and flings her onto the cot. That is the last exercise of his strength. She stands and slaps his hand aside, halting him with her first assertion of selfhood, calling him a "nasty, pissy old man." Her greatest condemnation of him is uttered in language that sums up his predicament exactly, the result of his own confused racial identity: "You ain't people, Mr. Watford, you ain't people."

The charge crushes him. The audacity of her rebellion strikes him hard, but even harder is the epiphany of the "waste and pretense which had spanned his years." His heart gives out, and he dies with a great moan that fills the house and yard with his anguish.

Themes and Meanings

Paule Marshall identifies two sources for the character of Watford. In her 1983 essay "From the Poets in the Kitchen," she recalls a West Indian custodian at the public library in Brooklyn who would give her orders as if he were the librarian himself. The other model, as she wrote in the preface to "Barbados," was her landlord for a year in Barbados, an old man who scarcely spoke to her and who lived in a plantation house such as a black man "playing white" would have.

These two sources suggest that Marshall is examining in her main character the weakness that underlies a particular kind of angry, arrogant, male authority. Watford is portrayed as a strong, energetic man who is accustomed to having things exactly his way. His essential isolation undermines his power, until finally the girl brushes him aside and he collapses. His hatred of his people, his mother, and even himself prevents him from participating in his community, both in the United States and in Barbados. He holds himself above everyone through his cold, facile cynicism. He will not converse with the girl or even ask her name because he cannot allow anyone living so close to him her own personhood. Significantly, her first self-assertion destroys him. The kind of black manhood that is based on racial loathing corrupts every aspect of Watford's personality. His authority is hollow, his strength a mask for weakness.

Style and Technique

Marshall embodies her theme in her characters' physical surroundings and in their physiques. Watford's estate and house are a barrier between himself and the people he despises, but even that distance is not enough. He hardens even his body against the world, but the tension with which he holds himself eventually squeezes the life out of him.

His leanness is the opposite of Goodman's expansive robustness, the physical equivalent of Goodman's outgoing nature and his embracing of the life available to him in Barbados. What Goodman has dissipated through luxurious, sensuous living, Watford has hoarded, but it has dried up in his arid spirit. The house that he has built remains unfinished, the walls unpainted, the furniture unarranged. The magnificent but excessive exterior hides his loss of purpose. He has no one for whom to finish the house. His work in the coconut grove is obsessive, joyless, and dull, his movements mechanical.

Into that life comes the young woman, and as sternly as he tries to drive her off, her humble trust, ease of being, and grace embody a self-acceptance that undermines the basis of Watford's self-contempt. She is the ultimate danger as well as his only possible salvation. Only by letting her destroy his pretenses can he hope to stop wasting his life. To the end, he cannot unclench his body or his grasp on those protections he has built around himself. His strength has been exhausted in the effort, and when at last the girl's dismissive blow flings him aside, his very heart is squeezed dry.

Robert Bensen

BARN BURNING

Author: William Faulkner (1897-1962)
Type of plot: Psychological realism
Time of plot: Post–Civil War
Locale: Mississippi
First published: 1939

> *Principal characters:*
> COLONEL SARTORIS "SARTY" SNOPES, the protagonist, a ten-year-old boy
> ABNER SNOPES, his father
> LENNIE SNOPES, his mother
> MAJOR DE SPAIN, a wealthy Southern landowner, Abner Snopes's most recent employer
> MRS. LULA DE SPAIN, Major de Spain's wife

The Story

As the story opens, ten-year-old Colonel Sartoris Snopes (he is named for Colonel John Sartoris, one of the central figures in William Faulkner's fiction) sits in a makeshift courtroom in a dry goods store and listens as his father is accused of burning a neighbor's barn. Young Sarty is called to the stand, but because the plaintiff is ultimately unwilling to force him to testify against his own father, the case is closed, and the father, Abner Snopes, is advised to leave that part of the country. As the family—Sarty, his parents, two sisters, an older brother, and an aunt—camp out that night on their way to their next home, Snopes, for whom barn burning seems to have become a habitual means of preserving his integrity in the face of men who have more power and wealth than he does, is absolutely cold and unemotional as he strikes Sarty and accuses him of having been prepared to betray his father back in the courtroom. He warns his son, "You got to learn to stick to your own blood or you ain't going to have any blood to stick to you."

Moving from one run-down tenant farmer shack to another has become a way of life for Sarty: He and his family have moved at least a dozen times within his memory. When Sarty and his father first approach the home of Major de Spain, on whose land they have most recently come to labor, Sarty finally feels that here are people to whom his father can pose no threat, that their mansion exists under a spell of peace and dignity, *"rendering even the barns and stable and cribs which belong to it impervious to the puny flames he might contrive."* Snopes, in his pride and envy, however, immediately forces a confrontation between the landed de Spain and himself, the landless tenant. As Snopes and Sarty walk up the drive, Snopes refuses to alter his stiff stride even enough to avoid some fresh horse droppings and then refuses to wipe his feet before he walks across the pale French rug that graces Mrs. de Spain's entrance hall. The shaken Mrs. de Spain asks the Snopeses to leave her house, and later in the day her husband brings the rug to their home, ordering that it be cleaned. In spite of his wife's pleas that she be allowed to clean it properly, Snopes sets his lazy and inept daughters to work cleaning the rug with harsh lye and, to be sure that it is ruined, scars it himself with a piece of stone.

Major de Spain seeks reparation for the damaged rug in the form of twenty bushels of corn from Snopes's next crop. He is amazed when Snopes, instead of accepting the fine, has him brought before a justice of the peace on the charge that the fine is too high. The justice finds against Snopes, but lowers the fine to ten bushels. Any fine at all, however, is too much of an affront to Snopes's dignity. He goes home that night and, once more against his wife's protestations, gathers the kerosene and oil that he will use in burning de Spain's barn.

Sarty is faced with a decision that will shape the rest of his life. His father already knows what the decision will be. Snopes orders his wife to hold the boy so that he cannot warn de Spain. As soon as Snopes leaves, that is exactly what Sarty does. He wrenches himself free from his mother's grasp, warning her that he will strike her if necessary to free himself, and runs to alert the Major. As Sarty runs back toward the barn, de Spain, on his horse, passes Sarty on the road. Sarty hears first one shot and then two more. When he starts to run again, this time it is away from the fire, its glare visible as he looks back over his shoulder.

At midnight, Sarty is sitting on the crest of a hill, his back toward his home of four days and his face toward the dark woods. He tries to convince himself that his father was brave, that he even served nobly in the recent war. Later he will know that his father was in the war only for the booty it had to offer. For now, though, Sarty dozes briefly and then, near dawn, as the morning birds start to call, he walks off into the woods, not looking back.

Themes and Meanings

Young Sarty Snopes describes his own inner conflict as "*the being pulled two ways like between two teams of horses.*" On one side is "the old fierce pull of blood"—family loyalty. On the other are truth and justice. The pull of family ties is strong, but Sarty is old enough to have started to realize that what his father does is wrong.

In the first courtroom scene, Sarty finds himself thinking of the plaintiff as his father's enemy and consciously has to correct himself: "*Ourn! mine and hisn both! He's my father!*" Leaving the courtroom, he attacks a boy half again his size who calls Snopes a barn burner. Throughout the story, a pattern is established. Sarty keeps trying to defend, through his speech and actions, the father to whom he knows he owes his life and his loyalty. His thoughts, however, and what Faulkner projects will be his future thoughts once he has reached manhood, reveal the ultimately stronger pull of truth and justice. When, after the first trial, his father strikes him and tries to convince him that the men who bring him to trial are only after revenge because they know that ultimately Snopes is in the right, Sarty says nothing, but Faulkner knows that twenty years later, Sarty will tell himself, "If I had said they wanted only truth, justice, he would have hit me again." The de Spain mansion immediately appears to Sarty as a symbol of hope that perhaps here is a power too great—a power with which his father cannot even hope to contend. What he cannot yet comprehend, in his childish innocence, is that the greater the wealth, the greater the gulf between the landowner and the landless Snopes, and thus the greater his father's jealous rage—a rage that Snopes keeps tightly in check until it bursts out in the flames of the fires he sets.

The battle goes on as Sarty continues outwardly to defend his father while inwardly his doubts grow stronger and stronger. When de Spain imposes the fine, Sarty protests to his father that de Spain should have told them how to clean the rug, that the fine is too high, that they will hide the corn from de Spain. When the fine is lowered, he still protests that the major will not get a single bushel. His outbursts in his father's behalf almost cause more trouble for Snopes when Sarty loudly protests, "He ain't done it! He ain't burnt. . . ." when the issue at hand this time is the damaged rug, not a burned barn.

Sarty still seems to be supporting his father when he runs to get the oil to burn de Spain's barn. During the short trip, however, he decides that he can neither simply run away nor stand by idly as his father burns the barn. He returns with the oil to defy his father openly for the first time, and he takes his stand firmly on the side of truth and justice when he runs to warn the major. By the end, he has turned his back both literally and symbolically on his home and on what remains of his family. His turning away from his family, however, is presented as a sign of hope as he walks off into the woods as dawn breaks and morning birds' calls replace those of the birds of night.

Style and Technique

The story is not narrated by the ten-year-old Sarty, but Faulkner calls attention to the boy's thoughts and thus to the inner conflict they represent by italicizing them. Subtle word choices also help trace Sarty's move toward maturity and responsibility. Hearing the shots that announce his father's death, Sarty first cries, "Pap! Pap!" but seconds later shifts to the more mature sounding "Father! Father!"

Images of cold and heat, of stiffness and metal, help characterize Abner Snopes. Snopes walks stiffly because of a wound suffered when he was caught stealing a horse during the war. Yet stiffness describes his character as well as his walk. His voice is cold, "harsh like tin and without heat like tin."

His wiry figure appears "cut ruthlessly from tin." This man who burns barns seems to save his fire for his crimes; all else he does without heat or emotion—whether it is talking, whipping a horse, or striking his son. Even the campfires he builds are niggardly. For him, fire is a means of preserving his integrity and "hence to be regarded with respect and used with discretion."

A little of Snopes's stiffness seems to have carried over to his son at the end of the story. When Sarty awakens after the night of the fire, he is described as being a little stiff. For Sarty, however, the stiffness will not last: "Walking would cure that too as it would the cold, and soon there would be the sun."

Donna B. Haisty

BARTLEBY THE SCRIVENER
A Story of Wall Street

Author: Herman Melville (1819-1891)
Type of plot: Psychological realism
Time of plot: The 1840's
Locale: New York
First published: 1853

Principal characters:
THE NARRATOR, a successful Wall Street lawyer
BARTLEBY,
TURKEY, and
NIPPERS, his scriveners
GINGER NUT, his office boy

The Story

"Bartleby the Scrivener" is narrated by a prosperous Wall Street lawyer who, in "the cool tranquillity of a snug retreat," does "a snug business among rich men's bonds, and mortgages, and title-deeds." Among his clients, the nameless narrator is proud to report, was John Jacob Astor, the richest man in America at the time of his death.

The narrator's employees, as the story begins, are Turkey and Nippers, who are scriveners, or copyists, and Ginger Nut, a young office boy. The Dickensian copyists present problems for their employer, for each displays a different personality during each half of the working day. Turkey, who is short and fat, works quickly and steadily before noon but becomes clumsy and ill-tempered after his midday meal. At the opposite extreme is the dyspeptic Nippers, nervous and irritable in the mornings but mild and productive in the afternoons. Since they are regular in their inconsistent behavior, the narrator reports that he "never had to do with their eccentricities at one time," and the work of the office proceeds, with Ginger Nut keeping the scriveners under some control by supplying them with cakes and apples.

The unusual order of the office is disrupted when the lawyer, because of extra work created by his being appointed a Master in Chancery, hires an additional copyist. At first, Bartleby works constantly, but one day he suddenly declines to compare a copied document and its original, offering no explanation, saying simply, "I would prefer not to." Gradually, he prefers not to perform any of his tasks. His employer also discovers that Bartleby has no home other than the office and is sleeping there nights and weekends, eating little more than ginger nuts (small, spicy cakes).

The lawyer pleads with Bartleby to work or leave, but the obstinate scrivener continues to pursue his preference not to do anything. Growing increasingly distraught over these circumstances, the lawyer finally moves his chambers to another building. When Bartleby is expelled from the office by the new tenant, he remains in the building. The lawyer makes final pleas, even offering to take Bartleby home with him. Still, the scrivener prefers not to make any change, and the narrator flees the city in his frustration. On his return, he learns that Bartleby has been taken to the Tombs, the forbiddingly named city prison, as a vagrant.

The lawyer bribes a Tombs employee to take care of Bartleby, but the prisoner refuses to eat, preferring to stand beside and stare at the prison wall. The narrator tries to convince him that his surroundings are not that depressing; the prisoner replies, "I know where I am." Eventually, he dies.

After Bartleby's death, the lawyer learns that he had previously been a clerk in the Dead Letter Office in Washington and thinks that such a melancholy duty explains the poor man's peculiar behavior. He ends his story by proclaiming its pathetic universality: "Ah, Bartleby! Ah, humanity!"

Themes and Meanings

The wealth of thematic possibilities in "Bartleby the Scrivener" has made it perhaps the most analyzed of all American short stories. Much of this analysis centers on the title character, who is seen as a forerunner of alienated modern man, as the victim of an indifferent society, as a nonconformist— perhaps even a heroic one—who becomes isolated simply for daring to assert his preferences. Another interpretation, built around Bartleby's role as a writer of sorts, claims that Herman Melville's story is a parable of the isolation of the artist in a materialistic society which not only is indifferent to its writers but also is bent on their destruction.

Such views, while having varying degrees of validity, ignore the fact that "Bartleby the Scrivener" is dominated by the sensibility of its narrator and his search for the truth, a search which is ironic because he is incapable of any objective understanding of Bartleby and his seemingly perverse preferences. Not Bartleby's actions or passivity but the narrator's responses to his copyist are what is important.

Early in the story, the lawyer describes himself as "an eminently *safe* man," one "who, from his youth upwards, has been filled with a profound conviction that the easiest way of life is the best." He makes allowances for Turkey and Nippers because that is the easiest way to deal with them, but he is unable to understand why he cannot similarly control Bartleby.

When his initial efforts with Bartleby fail, he attempts to turn the predicament to his advantage. The sentimental narrator tries to change the scrivener from an intractable problem to an opportunity for compassion. Yet this compassion, as is appropriate for a man of Wall Street who exults in John Jacob Astor's name, "for it hath a rounded and orbicular sound to it, and rings like unto bullion," is selfish: "Here I can cheaply purchase a delicious self-approval. To befriend Bartleby; to humor him in his strange willfulness, will cost me little or nothing, while I lay up in my soul what will eventually prove a sweet morsel for my conscience." For him, the moral and the financial seem inseparable.

When compassion proves insufficient, the narrator resorts to philosophical explanations. Reading Jonathan Edwards' *The Freedom of the Will* (1754) and Joseph Priestley's *The Doctrine of Philosophical Necessity Illustrated* (1777) convinces him that Bartleby has been "billeted upon me for some mysterious purpose of an all-wise Providence, which it was not for a mere mortal like me to fathom." This evasion of responsibility is not the answer, however, because people are talking about him; since the good opinions of others are essential to his business and his self-esteem, the lawyer is finally forced to act.

Melville is satirizing the materialistic society of his time, but in a much larger sense than merely its indifference to writers. Melville is attacking its smug morality, its pomposity, its sentimental, patronizing attitude toward its individual citizens, its simplistic view of the complex and the ambiguous, its persistent ignorance of its responsibilities. Not Bartleby but the self-deceiving narrator is the absurd, pathetic protagonist.

Style and Technique

Wall imagery dominates this "story of Wall Street." The narrator describes the location of his chambers in detail. At one end is seen the white wall of a large skylight shaft: "This view might have been considered . . . deficient in what landscape painters call 'life.'" At the other end is an ugly brick wall, blackened by age, ten feet from the window. Bartleby's desk is inside the lawyer's office, so that he can be within easy call, but is in a corner by a small window, which "commanded at present no view at all" because another wall is three feet from the panes. Bartleby stares at this wall when he prefers not to work. He is separated from his fellow copyists by a ground-glass door and is isolated from his employer, "a satisfactory arrangement," by a high, green folding screen, suggesting the lawyer's monetary obsession. Thus, there are walls within walls within walls within Wall Street.

The impossibility of the absence of walls is emphasized when Bartleby is removed to the Tombs, where he ignores the limited space in the exercise yard, choosing to stand beside the exterior wall, which both keeps him and protects him from society. He dies there curled into the fetal position (suggesting a possible tomb-womb pun), as if he could return to a state of innocence only in death.

These walls represent more than mere isolation; they are barriers to communication, to understanding, especially in a story told by a man who understands much less than he thinks he does. As in Melville's greatest achievement, *Moby Dick* (1851), the walls imply that man is incapable of true perception, that understanding the purpose of existence is impossible.

The other major stylistic device employed by Melville is his unreliable narrator, who sees only what is on the surface. It is ironic that in his quest for the easy explanation he decides that Bartleby refuses to work because something is wrong with his eyes. Melville helps establish the tradition of having a tale told by someone who is accurate about facts but who is very subjective in interpreting the motivations not only of others but also of himself. This self-justifying narrator creates the story's irony, its humor, its greatness.

Michael Adams

THE BASEMENT ROOM

Author: Graham Greene (1904-   )
Type of plot: Psychological realism
Time of plot: The 1930's
Locale: London
First published: 1935

> Principal characters:
> PHILIP LANE, seven years old, who loves Baines
> BAINES, the butler
> MRS. BAINES, the housekeeper
> EMMY, the girl Baines introduces to Philip as his niece

The Story

Left by his parents in the care of their butler and housekeeper, seven-year-old Philip Lane excitedly anticipates exploring the large Belgravia house while learning something about the adult world. Philip loves Baines, the butler, whose adventurous tales about Africa entrance him, but he dislikes and fears Mrs. Baines, whose very presence terrifies him in the same way that the demons that people his nightmares do.

Once his parents leave the house on their holiday, Philip seeks out Baines in the basement room, entered through a green baize door that separates the family rooms from the servants' quarters. In the basement room, Philip's fear and dislike of Mrs. Baines are reaffirmed as he watches Baines efface himself in her presence. Philip begins to appreciate the conflicting claims of adulthood in a world he yearns for yet fears to enter. He begins to understand fear and coercion and to intuit the meaning of evil. He suspects that undiluted joy, his feeling for Baines, can be threatened by the very presence of those such as Mrs. Baines.

Philip asks Baines to take him for a walk, but Mrs. Baines interferes. The boy escapes alone into the world beyond the Belgravia mansion rather than witness their disharmony. Too timid to venture far, he begins to retrace his steps. In a tea shop he sees Baines, not the cowering individual he recently left but a concerned and affable lover pressing jars of discarded cosmetics, rescued and then rejected by Mrs. Baines from the upstairs rooms in the process of housecleaning, on a young and unattractive girl. Philip thinks that it would be amusing to intrude on Baines and his "niece" in Mrs. Baines's voice. He invades their moment of happiness, returning them to reality with a fearful thud. Baines introduces Philip to Emmy, offers him a cake with pink icing, and asks him to keep Emmy a secret from Mrs. Baines.

Later, in the nursery, Mrs. Baines manages to trick Philip into revealing the secret he shares with Baines. She bribes him with a Meccano set. The pressures of adult responsibility invade his innocent sphere of love and trust, and he wonders about his place within the adult world. "Baines oughtn't to have trusted him; grown up people should keep their own secrets," he thinks. He betrays Baines by failing to tell him about Mrs. Baines's invasion of his dreams.

Mrs. Baines devises a simple plan to trap her husband and Emmy. She pretends to leave London to care for an ailing mother, then sends a telegram saying that she is delayed and will return the following day. Although she is gone, her presence pervades the house. Baines and Emmy and Philip spend a delightful day exploring London; that night, however, after Philip has been put to bed, Mrs. Baines comes once more into his room and confirms the reality of his nightmares. She again promises him a Meccano set if he will tell her where Baines and Emmy are. Terrified, Philip screams, then watches Baines grapple with Mrs. Baines on the landing. Philip sees her go over the banister "in a flurry of black clothes" and fall into the hall below.

Once again, Philip escapes into the world beyond the Belgravia house. He is found by the police, who learn of the "accident," reported by Baines. They return him to the house.

In attempting to shield Emmy, Baines has moved the body from the hall into the basement room. When confronted by Mrs. Baines's death, Philip refuses Baines's mute plea to keep yet another secret. He has learned that to love is to accept the burden of trust in and responsibility for another, for which life has not yet prepared him. Philip extricates himself from Baines— from love and life. He dies sixty years later, still asking about the girl, Emmy, who had unwittingly unleashed fear into his innocent world and forced him to choose a life of lonely noninvolvement.

Themes and Meanings

"The Basement Room" is the dramatization of a traumatizing event which inhibits the individual from achieving human contact in the future. The situation presented deals with the souring of innocence and the consequent fear of life which it occasions. The theme is best expressed in the narrator's statement: "Life fell on him [Philip] with savagery and you couldn't blame him if he never faced it again in sixty years." Philip Lane is portrayed as an imaginative and sensitive boy who has not yet learned to distinguish good from evil and right from wrong. The story's central meaning has to do with his sudden awareness that life is a series of compromises, and that adulthood forces one into commitments and allegiances that one does not always understand. Philip learns that good and evil are not as clear-cut as his feelings for Baines, whom he loves, and Mrs. Baines, whom he fears. When he unwittingly betrays Baines, he does not understand that choice has been thrust upon him too soon; rather than commit himself in trust and love to another human being in the future, he chooses to remain isolated from human life. The story focuses on the theme of betrayal, agonizingly complicated to the boy Philip, provocative to the reader.

Style and Technique

The action is presented by an omniscient narrator as he presents the events that inhibit the boy from fulfilling himself in the sixty years he lives following the traumatizing experience which constitutes the story's main action. The narrative shifts from an acute and psychologically perceptive account of the boy's refusal to accept Baines's appeal to keep yet another secret, to a view of the dying man who has managed, at best, a life of dilettantism. The contracting and expanding focus allows the reader to appreciate the traumatizing incident and to realize its results on the character of the man that the boy becomes.

The story can also be read as an exercise in meaningful symbolism. The house in Jungian terms can loosely be seen as the integrated personality. The green baize door through which the boy passes to the basement room serves as a Freudian device to distinguish between the conscious and the subconscious, while the sweet cake and the Meccano set with which he never plays function as comments on the nature of existence. The experience of betrayal denies Philip both the sweetness of life and the ability to create. The city beyond the house can be interpreted as the region outside the self, where good and evil exist in mutual tolerance of each other. Outside the house, Philip agrees to keep Baines's secret. Mrs. Baines, however, invades his psyche and catalyzes in the boy a fear of life. Insofar as Philip becomes Mrs. Baines's accomplice by failing to tell Baines that he has inadvertently betrayed their secret, he is in complicity with evil; later, he suffers the death of the heart when he refuses the responsibilities and consequences of an adulthood which he is unprepared to accept. Dream and nightmare, furthermore, afford a coherent imagery that emphasizes the power of evil. As such, the story serves as an epitome of favorite themes and preoccupations that characterize Greene's fictional universe.

Perhaps the story's greatest accomplishment is the immediacy with which the traumatizing episodes are presented. The reader is convinced of the tale's psychological validity as he appreciates and acknowledges the nature of a betrayal that destroys innocence and dooms the individual to a life of waste and loss.

A. A. DeVitis

THE BEAST IN THE JUNGLE

Author: Henry James (1843-1916)
Type of plot: Psychological realism
Time of plot: Late nineteenth century
Locale: England
First published: 1903

> *Principal characters:*
> JOHN MARCHER, an English gentleman of leisure
> MAY BARTRAM, his friend and confidante

The Story

At a party in one of the stately homes of England, John Marcher meets May Bartram, and they realize that they had met years before in Italy. She recalls a strange confession he made on that occasion—that he had always felt the deepest thing within him was a sense of being reserved for a unique fate, "something rare and strange, possibly prodigious and terrible," that eventually would happen to him and perhaps overwhelm him. Whatever the fate is, it is not anything he is to do or accomplish; his role is to wait, and he asks if she will wait and watch with him. Like most people in James's fiction, they do not have to work for a living; Marcher seems to be well-off, and Miss Bartram, though less well-to-do, can get by in a genteel fashion on a modest income. Whatever Marcher's fate is to be, it has not happened yet, and in response to her query, he says that it has not been to fall in love.

Thus they begin a long, intimate, but uncommitted relationship, from which she gets nothing but the dubious pleasure of his company. He can give her nothing more, since he must reserve himself wholly for the revelation of his destiny. At first, Marcher is as much hopeful as apprehensive; he believes that when it comes, his special fate will cause him to have "felt and vibrated . . . more than any one else." As the years go by and nothing happens, however, his feeling changes to dread, and he abandons the dream and waits for "the hidden beast to spring." He now sees this moment as the deadly leap of something sinister that "lay in wait for him, amid the twists and turns of the months and the years, like a crouching beast in the jungle." He does not know whether he will slay it or it will slay him; the crucial thing is the ultimate and inevitable spring. He has some qualms of conscience about having Miss Bartram accompany him on a "tiger-hunt," even if it is a psychological one, but he continues to exploit her, unable to give her anything in return because he must reserve himself for his great climactic moment.

As that moment continues to recede, they drift into the beginning of old age. (As the story opens, he is thirty-five and she is thirty.) Gradually, he becomes aware that she knows something about his fate that he does not. Her concern is to help him "to pass for a man like another," but he fails to understand her. While they continue to grope as if in a dark valley, he begins to feel that he has been cheated. Yet May assures him that his fate is indeed special, that it is on the verge of happening, and that it is the worst thing possible. Still, she cannot tell him; he must find it out for himself. He will not consciously suffer, but his destiny is more monstrous than anything they could imagine. Yet she assures him that the door is still open, that he can still escape. She is too ill to tell him how, however, and when he still fails to understand, she says that the beast has now sprung, the moment has passed. Perhaps he could have saved her, but he is too obsessed with himself to understand how, and she dies. So tenuous was their intimacy that Marcher is excluded from her funeral.

For a year, he travels around the world. On his return, he pays a visit to her tomb. At a nearby grave, he sees a man suffering from acute bereavement. From the other man's intense grief, he gets the revelation of his own fate. His life has been a void, untouched by passion; he is "*the* man, to whom nothing on earth was to have happened." Too late, he realizes that May Bartram had loved him, that his escape would have been to love her, that had he done so, he might have saved her, that the moment when he failed to understand this was the moment when the beast sprang. Suddenly overwhelmed by despair, he flings himself upon her tomb.

Themes and Meanings

James seems to have been going through an emotional crisis when he wrote "The Beast in the Jungle," for *The Ambassadors* (1903), the novel that he completed just before it and to which, in a way, the short story is a pendant, is also concerned with the waste of life. Its protagonist, Lambert Strether, has known love, but for a generation he has been a widower whose only role in life has been to edit a little magazine in a bleak New England town. When he goes to Paris at the age of fifty-five, he too has an emotional crisis that causes him to cry out, "Live all you can; it's a mistake not to. It doesn't so much matter what you do in particular, so long as you have your life. If you haven't had that what *have* you had?" Strether feels that for him, it is too late; he has, so to speak, missed the train. In fact, however, he still has a chance, whereas for Marcher, it is indeed too late. May Bartram is dead, the chance of love irrevocably beyond recall. His special fate is not to have had his life. The irony is that he has not even missed it until the final revelation. James valued his characters by their degree of awareness, and Marcher is supremely unaware until too late. His obsession with the special fate that he calls the beast in the jungle has so absorbed him that he has not realized that in waiting for it, he has lost everything else. At the end, he does not even have the beast to wait for any longer; it has already sprung, and he is left utterly bereft. A monstrous egotism has wasted not only his own life but also that of the woman who loved him and to whose love he was unable to respond. As scholar F. O. Matthiessen puts it, for James "the wasting of life is the implication of death."

Though classified as a realist, Henry James wrote a number of ghost stories, the most famous of which is *The Turn of the Screw* (1898). In these tales the realism comes from the psychological subtlety, which makes it sometimes questionable as to whether the ghosts have any external reality or are only in the mind of one or more of the characters. "The Beast in the Jungle" has no ghosts, but it is generally included among the ghostly tales. The beast is purely in John Marcher's mind; he has, so to speak, conjured it up, but it destroys him just as surely as if this were an African or Asian adventure, not a story devoid of action and set on the fringes of British society. Marcher is surely haunted by his obsession, and May Bartram is the victim he has sacrificed to it. Though James enjoyed the adventure fiction of his friends Robert Louis Stevenson and Joseph Conrad, he himself preferred narratives in which very little happens externally, writing that "a man might have . . . an amount of experience out of all proportion to his adventures." Thus "The Beast in the Jungle" and *The Ambassadors* are full of the imagery of adventure fiction, though the only adventure in the narratives is in the mind. James said of himself that he stood "on the rim of the circle" of life and that "the only form of riot or revel ever known to . . . [him was] that of the visiting mind."

Despite an active artistic and social life, James ultimately found this life of the visiting mind to be inadequate. Critics said that Henry James had the mind of an eavesdropper, and Max Beerbohm once drew a cartoon of James eavesdropping. The main deficiency in the life of the visiting mind, however, is the lack of love and of the sort of commitment to someone else that James could never give. Another novelist, Constance Fenimore Woolson (1840-1894), the grandniece of James Fenimore Cooper, was apparently in love with James, who could not wholly respond, and she committed suicide; scholar Leon Edel suggests that John Marcher's failure to perceive and respond to the love of May Bartram is in part a reflection of the relationship between James and Woolson.

Style and Technique

"The Beast in the Jungle" is a product of what critics call James's third and final phase. Some consider this his richest phase; others find it flawed by excessive narrative and indirection, implausibly mannered dialogue, a fussy and cobwebby style, and a pretentious ponderousness. James Thurber, who admired James, parodied this style and technique in "The Beast in the Dingle."

"The Beast in the Jungle" does have some shortcomings. James's late works are an acquired taste, and though the denouement and message of the story are extremely powerful, they are delayed so long and the situation leading up to them is so farfetched that a reader unaccustomed to James may be frustrated. James was unable to place it in a magazine, and it had to wait a year to be published in a collection of his stories. Despite its length, the characters are never fully developed as three-dimensional individuals. Their lives and relationship are so anemic as to seem almost disembodied. May Bartram, as she is declining and trying to make Marcher aware of her love and his danger, does become poignant, but until the end, Marcher seems almost an abstraction, more the embodiment of an idea than a flesh and blood human being. He is wintry March; Miss Bartram is May. On the other hand, the story gradually generates considerable suspense as the reader waits to discover what the beast is and when it will spring, especially when Miss Bartram becomes aware of it and tries to warn Marcher, who continues to lack all comprehension. Even the labyrinthine style and the dialogue that seems more verbalized intuition than realistic conversation gradually take hold of the reader and appropriately create a sort of twilight world. Frustrating though its slow progress is, the story finally delivers a devastating conclusion. It lingers in the mind long after stories with more lively but superficial narrative are forgotten.

Robert E. Morsberger

THE BECKONING FAIR ONE

Author: Oliver Onions (George Oliver, 1873-1961)
Type of plot: Horror
Time of plot: Early twentieth century
Locale: London
First published: 1911

Principal characters:
PAUL OLERON, a forty-four-year-old novelist
ELSIE BENGOUGH, a journalist

The Story

In "The Beckoning Fair One," Paul Oleron, a novelist who has not catered to popular taste, becomes fascinated with the spirit that he detects occupying his apartment. He believes that the beckoning fair one is the spirit of a woman, and he tries to court her; the spirit appears, instead, to take possession of him and to drain him of his energy and his will. Under the influence of that spirit, he apparently murders the woman who loves him and nearly starves himself to death.

The process of Oleron's decline begins when he is attracted to an old, decaying building as an inexpensive way to solve his problem of living and working in different places. To unite living and working, he takes a single larger apartment in the otherwise abandoned building. He makes this move when he is fifteen chapters into what he believes is his greatest novel, *Romilly*. Upon completing the move, he discovers that he is unable to continue working on that novel.

The heroine is based on his journalist friend Elsie Bengough. As he attempts to continue writing, he finds himself dissatisfied with the heroine. He wants to begin again with a new heroine quite different from Elsie. Just as Elsie fits less well into his novel and his imagination after he moves, so too does she feel unwelcome in his new dwelling. She cannot be comfortable there. During two visits, she is injured in unaccountable ways, nails appearing where he is sure he had already removed them, and a step that had seemed perfectly sound to him suddenly breaking.

Oleron's attitude toward Elsie has always been ambivalent. Though he likes Elsie, she strikes him as too worldly for his austere taste. Similarly, his attitude toward his career has grown ambivalent. He confesses to her that he has become weary of his writing. He has not achieved the comfort and success which would make the effort seem worthwhile, and the effort itself has become an intolerable burden. Writing no longer provides him enough of the glow and thrill that it offered when he was younger.

Gradually, Oleron comes to believe that the opposition between the old and the new *Romilly* arises from an opposition between Elsie and a being occupying his rooms, a being whom he calls "the beckoning fair one." Her name comes from the title of a song that he hears in the sound of water dripping from a faucet and which is identified by a neighbor when he spontaneously hums it. This opposition also exists within himself, in his ambivalence toward Elsie and also in his desire both to live comfortably in the ordinary world and to enter into transcendent regions of artistic inspiration. The latter desire pushes him toward an exploration of the mysteries that he detects in his new rooms; the new tensions in his life seem to have their true spring in this division in his character. As he follows this impulse, he cuts himself off from Elsie, from his writing, and finally from the world.

Before he discovers an active spirit in his rooms, he believes that in his own love for them, he might create such a spirit. Not until after he learns of Elsie's desire to marry him does he discover that such a spirit already occupies his home. By the time that he learns of Elsie's love, he is already under the influence of that spirit; he finds that he does not want Elsie now. For days after this discovery, he is torn between a part of himself that would welcome her love and which fears for her safety, and another part, which draws him toward the life that he feels in his rooms' hostility to Elsie. Then, one night when he finds himself as near as he has been to loving Elsie, he hears the sound of a woman brushing her hair, though no one is with him. Though he panics at first, he quickly accepts the possibility of a female spirit in his rooms, and he turns from Elsie to this beckoning fair one. At this juncture, a neighbor, a religious fanatic, accuses him of immoral activities with Elsie. Mistaken as this notion is, it proves an accurate estimate of Oleron's actual activity, which the narrator characterizes as treason against the ordinary terms and limits of human society.

Oleron begins to court the fair one, to dream of sexual union with her. Accepting her jealousy of Elsie and joining in excluding her, he concentrates on finding ways to coax the fair one into appearing. As he grows more desperate, he finally burns his manuscript, getting rid of his last connection with Elsie even as she stands outside his locked door, begging him to escape.

Eventually, he isolates himself in the womblike enclosure that his home becomes, receiving no visitors, no mail, and no food. He gives himself over to the invisible spirit. He finds the process of imagining her to be exhilarating, much as he found writing exhilarating in his younger days. This transcendent experience leads him into a slavery to the spirit which saps him; for days, he simply reclines, dreaming of the beckoner.

During this period of semiconsciousness, he seems to murder Elsie when she tries to rescue him. He has two experiences of this event. The first takes place when he is barely conscious; he then feels himself the instrument of the fair one when he strikes Elsie. In the second, he experiences a moment of apparent lucidity in which he is his old sane self. Then he seems to hear her murdered in another room. Oliver Onions never makes clear which of these is closer to the truth. Oleron quickly slips back into his insanity, in which state he is discovered by the police when they come searching for the missing Elsie.

The story ends with Oleron being carried to the hospital, accused of Elsie's murder, while his neighbors, stirred up by religious fanatics who seem to have dimly understood what he has been doing, call for his execution.

Themes and Meanings

"The Beckoning Fair One" is simultaneously the story of a man who becomes the victim of a vampiric spirit and the story of an artist who seeks to live wholly in the realm of imagination. Though there is sufficient ambiguity to lead a reader to suspect that the spirit may be merely a product of Oleron's imagination, Onions does not allow the reader to rest in such an opinion. Onions wants his ghost, ultimately, to be real. The main purpose of the ambiguity about the reality of the beckoning one is to emphasize the degree to which she is exactly the ghost most likely to entice an artist of Oleron's character. Indeed, he is the second of her known victims, an artist named Madley having previously died of starvation while living there. Because the fair one is the right ghost for an artist, the story communicates one main theme, the psychological dangers which threaten an artist who tries to conform his life to his work, to live in the ideal that he imagines.

Onions carefully details how Oleron's desire for the joy of the ideal blinds him to the absoluteness of the terror that he is pursuing: "To the man who pays heed to that voice within him which warns him that twilight and danger are settling over his soul, terror is likely to appear an absolute thing, against which his heart must be safeguarded in a twink unless there is to take place an alteration in the whole range and scale of his nature. . . . He is even content that . . . joy also, should for working purposes be placed in the category of the absolute things; and the last treason he will commit will be that breaking down of terms and limits that strikes, not at one man, but at the welfare of the souls of all." Onions represents Oleron's decline as a falling deeper into this treason until he loses his self and murders his human beloved.

Style and Technique

One of the most important features of Onion's technique is his handling of the ghost. Henry James's ghosts in *The Turn of the Screw* (1898) are seen only by the governess; that their very existence is therefore in doubt increases the psychological pressure on the reader to resolve the mystery. William Shakespeare's ghost in *Hamlet* is seen by several people, but it speaks only to Hamlet; that Hamlet doubts what the ghost tells him reveals the depths of Hamlet's character. The beckoner is more like Shakespeare's ghost than James's. Oleron's destruction reveals the fatal weaknesses of his character, but the ghost herself remains shrouded in mystery. What does she offer? Is she really an evil spirit, as Oleron finally, helplessly perceives her, or is she an absolute, amoral power, capable of raising him to transcendence had he a single will, but instead giving him the strength to destroy himself by means of the normal human contradictions of his soul? In other words, does she appear evil because she is evil or because she empowers the evil in his nature?

Though the story may seem moralistic because Onions comments directly upon Oleron's failures, it proves, nevertheless, a highly effective tale of terror, in part because of the ambiguities concerning the ghost's reality and its nature.

Terry Heller

THE BEET QUEEN

Author: Louise Erdrich (1954-   )
Type of plot: Ironic parable
Time of plot: 1932, the Depression years
Locale: Argus, North Dakota, a fictitious town on the Minnesota–North
  Dakota border, and the northern plains
First published: 1985

> *Principal characters:*
> MARY LAVELLE, the narrator
> KARL LAVELLE, her brother
> ADELAIDE and THEODOR LAVELLE, their parents
> SITA, a cousin
> FRITZIE and PETE KOZKA, their aunt and uncle
> THE GREAT OMAR, "aeronaut extraordinaire"

The Story

In the opening episode of the "The Beet Queen" (a six-paragraph prologue which displays the author's flair for the dramatic), Mary, a girl of eleven, and her fourteen-year-old brother Karl leap from a boxcar in the sugar
beet valley of fictional Argus, North Dakota, and head for the home of their
Aunt Fritzie, who, with her husband Pete, runs a reasonably successful
butcher shop. As they walk through the streets, a fierce dog frightens them.
Mary runs toward the butcher shop and Karl runs back to the boxcar in a
scene reminiscent of the flight of Mendel and Isaac from Ginzburg in Bernard Malamud's short story "Idiots First." Yet, in "The Beet Queen," it is not
Death pursuing the youngsters; it is Life. In this interplay between chance
and determination, there is the suggestion of a quest motif in the classic
mode—one which has serious and tragic consequences.

Following this prologue, recounted by a third-person narrator, the rest of
the story is told in the first-person voice of the little girl, Mary. She recounts
the events which led to this fateful train ride, as well as her experience following it, beginning her story with the grain-loading accident which killed
her father and the sad relocation of his pregnant widow and two small children to the Cities. There, they are reduced to penury and the new baby
brother is born. "We should let it die," she recalls her mother telling her, "I
won't have any milk. I'm too thin." Some weeks later, Mary recounts, with an
eviction notice in hand they stumble upon a country fair called "The Orphan's Picnic," where all three children are abandoned by their mother, who,
in a moment of weakness and excitement and carried away by her ardor, flies
into the sky with the dashing aeroacrobat "The Great Omar" and never
returns.

Mary is left holding the baby, her older brother sitting beside her "gazing into the dark sky." A "sad man" whose wife has a "new baby of her own . . . and enough milk for two" simply sits beside Mary on the sidewalk and, waiting her out, finally takes the wailing baby from her arms and disappears into the crowd. The two children walk down the empty streets to their old rooming house, and the next morning they set out for Aunt Fritzie's, clutching their mother's small "keepsake box."

During the train ride, the young female narrator sees her mother "flying close to the pulsing stars" and being thrown out of the plane by the selfish Omar when his fuel gets low. (Though readers never know whether the mother is really dead or whether, after abandoning her children, she is declared dead by the daughter, this fantasy scene contrasts with the next realistic scene of Mary walking toward the butcher shop.)

Mary is taken into the warm arms of Uncle Pete and Aunt Fritzie but is resented by her cousin Sita. She sets about making herself "essential" because she believes that she has nothing else to offer. Finally, in an effort to pay her own way, she opens the "treasure box" and is stunned to find only stickpins, buttons, and a worthless pawn ticket. Aunt Fritzie and Uncle Pete are silently sympathetic, but Sita gloats. In a conclusion worthy of all who discourse in parables, Louise Erdrich does not allow her protagonist's bad luck to overwhelm the virtues of experience and tolerance. Tenderly and unforgettably, the child narrator muses, "What is dark is light and bad news brings slow gain," acknowledging that her mother's legacy is both cruel and paltry and that the gain of which she speaks is intangible. She may be disillusioned, but she is not defeated.

Themes and Meanings

The function of a parable is to teach readers how, from the natural occurrences of life, one may discover moral and ethical attitudes essential to humankind. Louise Erdrich's work is expressive of this tradition stemming from the oral traditions of American fiction, in which the journey becomes a metaphor for life, characters are archetypal, conflicts are gradually and slowly drawn and sustained, and endings are satisfactorily resolved.

Themes which rise from the tradition of the parable are often predictable, but that does not make the story less interesting or the writer less skilled. On the contrary, these kinds of stories often loosen the spirit in ways that more complex stories do not. Erdrich is a member of the Turtle Mountain Chippewa Tribe of Indians, a cultural group whose storytelling traditions clarify the journey convention as deliberately as any other. "After that train journey I was not a child," says Mary Lavelle, her movement toward adulthood complete before she reaches her teens. "The Beet Queen" is clearly a story about a girl who has had no childhood, robbed of it by the circumstances of her grim environment.

A second theme, one of the significant recurring themes in twentieth century narrative fiction, is that of the loss of traditional values. Certainly, this
story's events and ironic tone seize upon this idea. It becomes apparent to
the careful reader, however, that in the closing lines there is a hunger
expressed by the youthful narrator for a fervent and passionate affirmation of
life in spite of its cruelty and disappointments. She reassures her listener (the
reader), "I could see a pattern to all of what happened, a pattern that suggested completion in years to come. The baby was lifted up while my mother
was dashed to earth. Karl rode west and I ran east. It is opposites that finally
meet."

Even though the first of these events is assumed to be literal and the second hallucinatory, the reader has been carefully prepared to accept the voice
of the narrator and to have confidence in her assessment of things, her oddly
compassionate response to a cruel and undeserved fate. Wise beyond her
years, Mary recognizes that life will not be easy for her, that time heals all
wounds, and that conflicting forces are often suspended and united in ways
that are not easily understood. Her attempts to fathom the mysteries of life,
though not fully articulated and clarified, result in a transcendence, an epiphany (to use James Joyce's term), and the fullness of the story is realized in
these final lines.

Style and Technique

This is one in a series of Louise Erdrich stories set in the fictitious town of
Argus, North Dakota, a place which has been compared to William Faulkner's Yoknapatawpha County. The story's protagonist, Mary Lavelle, is not
the Beet Queen of the title; indeed, the Beet Queen does not appear in this
story at all and there is only scant reference to sugar beets.

This absent persona, however, suggests a contrasting of values in the making of the character of Mary Lavelle, the daughter of failed farmers of the
beet valley, forced out by foreclosure, now orphaned, clearly an outsider,
returning to the rural region of her birth in a determined effort to find a
place for herself.

Similes much like those found in Flannery O'Connor's short stories
abound in this piece, but they are expressive of a much kinder, more compassionate outlook: "The train pulled like a string of black beads over the horizon"; "our faces stared back at us like ghosts"; "It was the baby, born heavy
as lead, dropping straight through the clouds and my mother's body"; "over
us the clouds spread into a thin sheet that covered the sky like muslin." Mary
voices these comparisons during the train ride to Argus and as the details of
life accumulate, these intricately woven similes, gentle and implicit, emphasize a transformation coming on and her metamorphosis from child to adult
is given credibility.

The subtle tone of compassionate irony, rather than broad and brittle satire, is achieved by the author's careful interplay between the literal and the abstract. "After that we moved to a rooming house in the Cities, where my mother thought that, with her figure and good looks, she would find work in a fashionable store. She didn't know when we moved that she was pregnant. In a surprisingly short time we were desperate," Mary says matter-of-factly. Of being abandoned she says, "My mind hardened, faceted and gleaming like a magic stone, and I saw my mother clearly. . . . All night she fell through the awful cold. Her coat flapped open and her pale green dress wrapped tightly around her legs. Her red hair flowed straight upward like a flame. She was a candle that gave no warmth. My heart froze. I had no love for her. That is why, by morning, I allowed her to hit the earth."

Readers of such narrative fiction, who have come to expect a kind of unreliablity of narrative voice in such writers as Flannery O'Connor, Carson McCullers, and Joyce Carol Oates, will notice a return to the traditional truthfulness of the storyteller in this Erdrich story. Indeed, the truth and purity in this narrative voice is one of the most charming devices in the story and, almost singlehandedly, it prevents the drawing of the demonic and grotesque characters so familiar in other contemporary works.

Lest one think Erdrich too kind, however, in this story which criticizes the valley folk, it is no accident that Theodor Lavelle "had smothered in oats," and that the making of orphans takes place at the church-sponsored "Orphan's Picnic" where "cowled nuns" hover and picnic goers snatch babies.

Elizabeth Cook-Lynn

BEGGAR MY NEIGHBOR

Author: Dan Jacobson (1929-   )
Type of plot: Social and political realism
Time of plot: The 1960's
Locale: A white suburb of Johannesburg, South Africa
First published: 1962

> *Principal characters:*
> MICHAEL, a white South African boy, about twelve years old
> FRANS and
> ANNIE, black South African orphans of Michael's age,
>   brother and sister
> DORA, the black cook in Michael's home

The Story

Michael, a white South African boy, is accosted by two black, raggedly dressed, almost emaciated children on his way home from school. Like so many impoverished black children, they are hungry and ask Michael for a piece of bread. At first he rejects them, but, touched by their abject posture, he offers to give them bread and jam if they follow him home.

Dora, the black cook at Michael's home, grudgingly prepares the food, and Michael, experiencing the first flush of a power he has not hitherto known, gives them the bread and patronizingly demands a thank-you from the cowed piccanins. The children begin to appear regularly, and the sense of his own generosity gradually helps to inflate Michael's ego and recently acquired power. He wishes, for example, that the children would be even more obsequious toward him. Michael, an only child, is lonely, and, compelled to rely on his own resources, he is much given to fantasizing. Michael's ambivalent feelings toward the black children—a sort of love-hate nexus—appear largely in his fantasies and the climactic dream sequence.

Yielding to a whim one day, Michael shows the children a particularly beautiful pen and pencil set, and the piccanins plead for it. Shocked by their desire for something other than food, Michael indignantly refuses and they leave, much to the delight of Dora.

Meanwhile, Michael's sense of his own importance and power increases, and his fantasies change rather noticeably: He begins to treat the children as if they were slaves, and in the real world he enacts these fantasies by deliberately keeping them waiting for bread and inflicting other acts of petty cruelty upon them. Inevitably, Michael's scorn, which has been only partially submerged, surfaces and gives way to anger, and he summarily orders them never to return. The piccanins, however, are persistent, and time and again they return to haunt Michael, as if embodying his own imperfectly understood guilt.

Shortly after dismissing them, Michael is struck down by a fever, and in his delirium he sees himself brutally attacking the boy and sexually assaulting his frail sister. The delirium deceives Michael into thinking that he is awake, the fever broken, and he is leading the abused and rejected children into his room. Here Michael yields to the impulse of love, which has also surfaced in delirium, and he kisses and caresses the piccanins. They, however, have vanished into the dark world beyond the white, comfortable suburbs, and all of Michael's efforts to find them are futile.

Themes and Meanings

Michael's final rejection of the black children is at once a symbolic and a literal act. By ordering them never to return, he is trying to reject their dreaded Africanness, which gradually becomes a persistent irritant to him. Michael, therefore, may be regarded as the embodiment of the white South African's conscious or unconscious wish to rid himself of the gnawing demands of black intransigence.

To this extent the story may be read as an allegory, but it is also a sensitive and incisive treatment of the moral ambivalences dividing an essentially decent youngster. Michael's instinctive empathy for the black children is established early in the story. The children's touching dependence on each other is particularly appealing to Michael, whose need for a sibling as well as parental affection and attention is implicit in his behavior. Even though the children are "identical in appearance to a hundred, a thousand, other piccanins," they become increasingly individualized to Michael as his contacts with them increase. The apartheid system will not permit him to relate to the children on a personal, affectionate level, but his own sensitive humanity can safely do so in dream and fantasy. Even so, Michael does make tentative attempts to reach out to the piccanins in the harsh world of reality. For example, his questions, which are ostensibly innocent and paternalistic, conceal Michael's desire to know them as persons. Therein lies the source of the tragedy. Michael's revelation—it reminds one of a Joycean epiphany—comes, significantly, in dream: His hatred of the piccanins is mutual, and it is the inevitable product of the mores of his particular society. There is more: Michael understands that the piccanins require love as much as bread. This understanding comes too late; he has lost the moment. The human urge to give love, which does not recognize racial differences in its pristine stages, has been frustrated in both black and white.

Style and Technique

This is a superbly controlled story. In a story full of political and moral resonances, the writer is undoubtedly tempted to indulge in authorial editorializing. In "Beggar My Neighbor," however, there are no authorial intrusions, and indeed the narrative voice is altogether effaced. All the moral conflicts and ambivalences in race relations are implicit in Jacobson's carefully modulated references to the white boy's perception of his own intrinsic superiority and the piccanins' instinctive obsequiousness and silence. These are deployed in strategic, and therefore effective, places in the narrative. The first time Michael gives the children bread and jam is a good example. In this scene, the white superior-black subordinate relationship is conveyed in Michael's condescending, even supercilious posture and words. The tenor of his future relationship with the children is therefore established early in the story.

Jacobson also carefully controls his use of images. Images of light, shade, and darkness are embedded in the story's idiom. Fantasy and reality, love and hate, acceptance and rejection—all these antitheses tend to coalesce, then fade and separate, at various times in the story. In the same way, various intensities of light, shadow, and darkness are called up for the reader, and they are meant to complement and enhance the tenuous link between the moral antitheses and ambivalences. The juxtaposition of these antitheses is the hub around which the story turns. On the one hand, the social and political realities of race relations in South Africa forbid intimate contact with the piccanins; in his fantasies, however, Michael can give his deeply buried desires and fears and whims their widest scope. (It is worth noting that in most of his fantasies the black children are dependent upon the white boy's courage and paternalistic assistance.)

Jacobson uses other methods to reinforce theme. Dora's hatred of the piccanins is a case in point. The author does not drive this hatred very hard; instead, he uses it rather subtly. In her role as cook in Michael's home, Dora is in a comfortable and decidedly preferred position, but her complacency and spurious security are jolted by the piccanins' inexorable persistence, which not only reminds Dora of her own dubious link with the white suburb but also, perhaps more pertinently, generates guilt feelings in her. Dora's conflicts are therefore suggested rather than stated with blunt directness.

The symbolic resonances of Michael's beautiful pen and pencil set are also worth noting. When Michael displays the set, it is a half-innocent, half-subconscious act of exhibitionism and flaunting from the middle-class white boy. When the deprived children linger over its shimmering beauty and then plead for it, however, Michael is shocked by the revelation that black children have aesthetic as well as physical needs. This undermines the assumptions about blacks which his society has nurtured in him, and so he perversely rejects them with noticeable severity. Yet this severity is counterpointed when Michael suddenly relents and offers them more bread and jam as a substitute. It is a telling moment, for it tends to crystallize all of the boy's troublesome conflicts and ambivalences.

Harold Barratt

THE BEGGARWOMAN OF LOCARNO

Author: Heinrich von Kleist (1777-1811)
Type of plot: Ghost story
Time of plot: Fifteenth or sixteenth century
Locale: A castle on the edge of the Italian Alps, near Locarno
First published: "Das Bettelweib von Locarno," 1810 (English translation, 1934)

> *Principal characters:*
> THE BEGGARWOMAN, an old sick woman
> THE MARQUIS, the lord of the castle
> THE MARQUISE, his wife
> THE NOBLEMAN, a Florentine knight

The Story

The apparent impetus for telling this strange history is the sight of a castle ruin as it might be noticed by a traveler descending into northern Italy from the St. Gotthard Pass. As if in reply to such a traveler's question of how the castle has fallen into disuse and ruin, the narrator tells the story of the beggarwoman of Locarno, in which an old woman comes begging at the castle gate, is taken in at the Marquise's orders, and is given a place to sleep for the night in one of the castle's unused rooms. When the Marquis returns from the day's hunting, however, he peevishly orders the beggarwoman from her place in one corner of the unused room to a spot behind the stove at the opposite side. In her effort to get up, her crutch slips on the polished floor, and she falls, injuring her spine. Laboriously and painfully, she finally stands and hobbles to the corner as bidden, but on reaching the spot, she collapses and dies of her injury.

The incident is evidently forgotten for some years, during which the Marquis' fortunes decline to the point that he begins to think of selling his domain, and the chance arrival of a Florentine nobleman seems to offer such an opportunity. Without further thought, the master and mistress of the house give their prospective buyer lodging in the same unused chamber for the amount of time that he may require to consider the purchase. Yet, in the middle of the night, the man comes downstairs, pale with fright, to report that his room is haunted by a spirit. He describes the ghostly presence as some invisible thing which arose from a corner of the chamber with a sound as if from a bed of straw, walked with slow, feeble steps across the room, and collapsed with moans and gasps behind the stove. The Marquis tries to reassure his guest and offers to spend the rest of the night with him in the uncanny room as proof that no harm could come to him there, but the knight declines the offer, asks to sleep until morning sitting in a chair, and with the new day continues his journey without delay.

From this time on, the rumor circulates that a ghost inhabits the castle, and several more prospective buyers are frightened off by the tale of what the first one experienced there. The Marquis therefore resolves to discredit the rumor by spending a night in the room himself. To his horror, he experiences, at the stroke of midnight, exactly what the Florentine knight had described. The following morning, he furtively tells his wife that a ghost does indeed inhabit the chamber. She is alarmed by the news but proposes that they confirm it beyond any doubt before acknowledging that the room is haunted. That same night, she, her husband, and a trusted servant all stay in the room, and all three hear the same inexplicable, ghostly sounds.

Now only their fervent wish to find an unwitting buyer and to be rid of the castle enables them to suppress their fear and insist that the uncanny events must have some harmless explanation. A third night, therefore, the husband and wife go to the room, this time with candles, sword, and pistol, and accompanied by the dog, which they decide at the last moment to keep with them. Again, at the midnight hour, the noises are heard. The sound of a crutch tapping on the floor arouses the dog, which backs, growling and barking, toward the corner, as if the animal could see what is invisible to human eyes. At this, the Marquise runs in terror from the room and orders horses hitched to leave at once for the town. Before she can pass through the gate, however, flames spring from the building. In his crazed fear, the Marquis has taken one of the candles and set fire to the place, "weary of his life." It is too late to save him from a gruesome death in the blaze, and, as the imaginary traveler is told at the conclusion, the whitened bones of the Marquis can still be seen lying in the same corner of the chamber from which he had commanded the beggarwoman of Locarno to get to her feet.

Themes and Meanings

It would be simple enough to draw from this story the lesson that a criminal act will eventually be punished, and that the punishment will fit the crime. In this case, the act amounts to murder, even if that was not the Marquis' intent, because his tormenting of the defenseless beggarwoman was gratuitous and meanspirited. Heinrich von Kleist does not prevent his reader from inferring that the Marquis' economic circumstances worsened as a consequence of his heedless brutality, but he does not imply anything more than a coincidental connection, either. The Florentine nobleman, after all, seems quite prepared to buy the property, notwithstanding the ravages of "war and bad harvests," until his own terrifying experience in the guest room changes his mind and the minds of others who might also have come to the aid of the struggling owners.

The two ideas which are much more prominent here—and more characteristic of Kleist—are guilt and the guilty one's consciousness of it. The "several years" intervening between the beggarwoman's death and the decline in the Marquis' fortunes are also years in which he forgets the unfortunate incident, or at least obliterates it from his conscious memory. At no time in the story is any word spoken or sign given by the Marquis to acknowledge what he has done, either at the time of the old woman's death or in discussions of the frightening sounds in the fateful room. Upon hearing the nobleman's report, he is thus "frightened without knowing why himself" and treats the matter with forced unconcern. On the final night, he and the Marquise take the watchdog with them "without knowing exactly why, perhaps from an instinctive desire to have the company of some third living creature." "Perhaps" is a crucial word here, as it allows the possibility of reasons for taking the dog other than simply to have its company. The deeper "instinctive desire," especially on the Marquis' part, is to confront his tormenting spirit at last in some more tangible form. Thus, when the dog sees what the humans cannot, the Marquise flees in terror; yet her husband's fear compels him to stand and complete his struggle with the ghost he has summoned to his consciousness.

What the Marquis fears most is the guilt within him, and to know one's greatest fear as he now knows his is to be driven mad. He sets the suicidal fire "maddened with terror" and "weary of his life." The novelist Thomas Mann called the first of these two phrases thoroughly Kleistian and urged readers of "The Beggarwoman of Locarno" to ponder carefully Kleist's choice of words here. As for the Marquis' weariness of his life, there is only one thing clearly known about his life to which it can refer: his responsibility for the beggarwoman's death. The life Kleist has recounted here is the exhausting, doomed struggle to deny the knowledge of guilt.

Style and Technique

Because of length, and Kleist's reputation as an early nineteenth century master of the anecdote form, one might at first think of "The Beggarwoman of Locarno" as an example of this genre. Its narrator recounts a remarkable occurrence, building to the story's critical point with the objective economy that typifies the anecdote. Yet, despite its brevity, this work is almost always named among Kleist's novellas, stories which, on average, run to more than ten times the length of this short piece. Its dramatic character is what places "The Beggarwoman of Locarno" most decisively in the category of the novella.

That the story is told with objective economy does not imply stylistic simplicity. Kleist's prose is highly individual, some would even say perversely eccentric, whether to the modern ear or to that of his own time, and his translators seem able to succeed only by simplifying his syntax and punctuation to some degree. Yet there is a strictly observed dramatic purpose in Kleist's idiosyncratic use of language. Whereas an epic narrator employs a grammatical style that is markedly sequential, emphasizing the discrete interest of the individual links of the narrative, Kleist's sentences depend heavily and crucially on interlocking grammatical subordination: hypotaxis rather than parataxis. The effect of his language in "The Beggarwoman of Locarno" is thus more nearly simultaneous than sequential; this is the essence of drama, in which the test of every element is in its purposeful relationship to the climatic moment.

"The Beggarwoman of Locarno" differs from the ghost stories of Kleist's contemporaries, such as Johann Ludwig Tieck and E. T. A. Hoffmann, in that it does not seek to generate the kind of ghostly atmosphere which is so effective in Tieck's and Hoffmann's tales of the supernatural. To do so would have risked creating moments or scenes with a substance of their own, which might divert or delay the reader's interest and thus slow the critically breathless pace of the story's events.

Michael Ritterson

BENITO CERENO

Author: Herman Melville (1819-1891)
Type of plot: Adventure
Time of plot: 1799
Locale: The harbor of St. Maria, off the southern tip of Chile
First published: 1855

> *Principal characters:*
> AMASA DELANO, a New England sea captain
> BENITO CERENO, the Spanish captain of the *San Dominick*
> BABO, the leader of the slave mutiny, apparently Cereno's
> devoted servant
> ATUFAL, Babo's lieutenant

The Story

Captain Amasa Delano anchors his ship, the *Bachelor's Delight*, in the harbor of St. Maria to take on water and food. The next day a Spanish ship, the *San Dominick*, also drifts into the harbor. Seeing the ragged state of the sails and the generally poor condition of the ship, Delano loads several baskets of fresh fish onto his whale boat to present to the other vessel.

As soon as he steps on board, he is surrounded by blacks and whites lamenting their calamitous voyage marked by plague, hunger, thirst, and contrary winds. Moved by their story, Delano sends the whaleboat back for additional supplies while he remains to visit with the ship's captain, Benito Cereno. Since Delano knows the harbor and Cereno clearly does not, the American plans to act as pilot to lead the *San Dominick* safely to shore. He also intends to refit and refurbish the Spanish merchantman so that it can sail to its destination of Lima, Peru.

Throughout the daylong visit, Delano is repeatedly appalled by Cereno's behavior. The Spaniard never expresses gratitude for offers of help. He fails to maintain discipline, allowing crew members to fight, even to stab one another. Yet he has ordered the docile Atufal to appear before him in chains every two hours until he begs forgiveness for some unnamed fault.

Delano is also troubled by Cereno's repeated private conferences with his constant black companion, Babo. The Spaniard and the black seem to be conspiring, and Delano derives no comfort from the tenor of Cereno's questions: How many men has the American on board? Is his ship well armed? Will all the men stay on board at night? Spanish sailors skulk about; a balustrade collapses, nearly plunging Delano into the ocean. Cereno's account of his voyage seems incredible—how could the *San Dominick* have taken months to travel the short distance the *Bachelor's Delight* traversed in only a few days?

Delano, however, dismisses his suspicions as unworthy, and his visit does seem likely to end uneventfully. After navigating the *San Dominick* into the harbor, he boards his whaleboat to return to his ship. At that moment, though, Cereno confirms Delano's fears. The Spaniard and his servant leap after him, followed by three Spanish sailors. Delano believes that they plan to murder him. The Americans overpower their assailants, only to discover that Cereno and the other whites have leapt into the water to escape the blacks, and that Babo has followed Cereno not to support an attack but to kill Cereno even at the cost of his own life.

At last Delano learns the true situation. On its way from Valparaiso to Callao, the *San Dominick* was seized by its cargo of slaves, who had been allowed to go about the decks unfettered. Led by Babo and Atufal, the blacks had killed all but a few Spaniards and ordered the rest to take the ship to Senegal. For their former owner, Don Alexandro Aranda, they reserved a particularly grisly fate. After murdering him, they removed all the flesh from his bones—probably by cannibalism—and substituted the skeleton for the ship's original figurehead.

Like Delano, the Spanish had come to St. Maria for water but were surprised to meet another ship. Babo then instructed Cereno as to what to say and do, threatening him with instant death if he refused. Babo intended to seize the American ship, but instead the Americans recapture the *San Dominick* and help it to reach Lima.

There, Cereno offers a full, official explanation and then retires to a monastery, a broken man. Three months later, he is dead, and he is buried in the church where the remains of Don Alexandro Aranda were deposited.

Themes and Meanings

"Benito Cereno," like so many of Melville's other works, rejects the benevolent worldview of the optimistic Transcendentalists, represented in the story by Captain Delano. Significantly, Delano comes from Massachusetts, the birthplace of Transcendentalism. Delano is charitable, well-meaning, compassionate, and trusts to the "ever-watchful Providence above." He is also a fool. Melville says as much at the beginning of the story when he describes the captain as rejecting the notion of "malign evil in man." The author then wonders whether "in view of what humanity is capable, such a trait implies . . . more than ordinary quickness and accuracy of intellectual perception."

The answer is no, as Delano repeatedly proves in the sequel. On board the *San Dominick* he sees repeated evidence that Cereno is not in control of the ship, yet he fails to draw the logical conclusion that if the Spaniard is not, the blacks must be. He notices that blacks abuse whites with impunity, that Babo uses the Spanish flag as a shaving towel, that at lunch Babo does not stand behind his supposed master but instead takes his station behind Delano, whence he can watch Cereno's every gesture. At one point a sailor tosses Delano an intricately wrought knot and urges him to "undo it, cut it, quick." Again Delano fails to understand the meaning of the scene; he does not equate the knot with the mystery aboard the ship.

Nor does Delano learn anything from his experience. Even at the end of the story, he believes that he is saved not by the actions of Cereno but by his own innocence and by Providence. He urges Cereno to forget what has passed and cannot understand why the Spaniard cannot share his happiness. "What has cast such a shadow upon you?" he asks naïvely. Cereno replies, "The negro." Though Cereno refuses to look at Babo after the rescue, he cannot ignore what Babo symbolizes. He has seen the heart of darkness that lurks in man, and that knowledge destroys him.

Style and Technique

Melville repeatedly uses irony to undercut the easy assumptions of Captain Delano. Observing Babo's constant attendance on Cereno, whom the black will not leave even for a moment, Delano comments, "Don Benito, I envy you such a friend; slave I cannot call him." Such envy is clearly out of place, but there is ironic truth in Delano's refusing to call Babo a slave, for Babo in fact is the master. Delano likens the ship to a monastery and the blacks to monks, analogies hardly appropriate to the situation. The American regards the black women as the pattern of docility, "pure tenderness and love"; later the reader learns that during the mutiny they were more vicious and bloodthirsty than the men.

Melville also employs irony to indicate that blackness is not a function of skin color. Babo demonstrates that blacks and whites are identical within when he mockingly shows the skeleton of Don Alexandro Aranda. To each of the Spaniards he puts the same question: Does not the whiteness of the bones prove that they belonged to a white man? The answer is no. Beneath the surface all men are alike, which means that all men are capable of the horrors committed aboard the *San Dominick*.

Ironic repetitions emphasize this idea. Babo's motto, "Follow your leader," is a warning to the Spaniards that if they refuse to comply with his orders they will share the fate of Don Alexandro. When the Americans recapture the *San Dominick*, the chief mate urges the sailors on with the cry, "Follow your leader!" When the blacks mutiny, they kill eighteen whites; in the recapture, "nearly a score of negroes were killed." Delano prevents Babo from stabbing the prostrate Cereno; later he stops the Spaniard Batholomew Barlo (how close that name is to Babo's) from stabbing one of the chained blacks.

Even in death, irony rules. Don Joaquin hides a jewel to present at the shrine of Our Lady of Mercy in Lima as a gift of thanks for his safe passage. The jewel goes to the church, but only after Don Joaquin dies aboard ship.

Babo warns Cereno that failure to obey will cause the captain to follow his leader, Don Alexandro, to death. When the *San Dominick* lands, Aranda's skeleton has been buried in St. Bartholomew's Church. Shortly thereafter, Cereno, too, is buried there and so does, indeed, follow his leader.

Kindness and Providence offer no protection against the blackness in man. Aranda was a kind master who allowed his slaves the freedom of the ship. His benevolence was his undoing, as it almost destroys Delano, who unwittingly guides Babo and his mutineers into a berth next to his own vulnerable ship. Though Delano emerges from his experience neither sadder nor wiser, the reader cannot be so untouched, for Melville has shown him the grimness of man's soul.

Joseph Rosenblum

THE BET

Author: Anton Chekhov (1860-1904)
Type of plot: Fable
Time of plot: November 14, 1870–November 14, 1885
Locale: An unspecified Russian city
First published: "Pari," 1888 (English translation, 1915)

Principal characters:
THE BANKER, the host at the party, an elderly man
THE YOUNG LAWYER, later the prisoner

The Story

"The Bet" is the story of a bet which stakes a banker's two million rubles against fifteen years of a young lawyer's life. As the story opens, the banker is recalling the occasion of the bet fifteen years before. Guests at a party which he was hosting that day, he remembers, fell into a discussion of capital punishment; the banker argued that capital punishment is more humane than life imprisonment, while the young lawyer disagreed, insisting that he would choose life in prison rather than death. As the argument became more heated, the banker angrily wagered two million rubles that the lawyer could not endure imprisonment, a challenge which the lawyer accepted, setting the term of his voluntary captivity at fifteen years, at the end of which he would receive the two million rubles.

The lawyer was imprisoned in the banker's garden house in complete solitude, permitted no visitors, no letters, no newspapers. He could write letters, however, and he was permitted books, music, wine, and tobacco.

The banker observed the progress of the young lawyer's adaptation to his imprisonment. During the first year, he read light books and played the piano. In the second year, he ceased being interested in music, but turned to great literature. In the fifth year, he loafed, drank wine, and played the piano. Then for four years he studied languages, history, and philosophy before moving to the New Testament and to theology. Finally, his reading became eclectic.

At the beginning of the story, the day on which the banker is recalling the events of these fifteen years, he is within a day of the final accounting, when, no longer rich but oppressed by debt, he will be ruined by paying the two million rubles. Desperate, the banker resolves to unlock the garden house door and to kill his captive, throwing the blame on the watchman. When he enters the room, he sees an emaciated man, old before his time, asleep at his table. Before him is a paper, on which he has stated that he despises everything in human life, even the books from which he has learned about it, and that, therefore, he intends to leave his room five minutes before the fifteen-year period elapses, thus forfeiting the bet.

After reading the paper, the banker despises himself. The next morning, he learns that the lawyer has indeed left the garden house. In order that no one will suspect him of a crime, the banker puts the paper in his safe.

Themes and Meanings

"The Bet" was written during a period when Chekhov was greatly influenced by Leo Tolstoy, whose simple, didactic tales were popular during the 1880's. The theme of "The Bet" is clearly the vanity of human wishes. Before his imprisonment, the young lawyer believes that life on any terms is better than death. He thinks that he can find the inner resources to live in solitude for fifteen years, and that the promise of a fortune will sustain him during the period of complete leisure in comfortable surroundings. Like the eighteenth century travelers in search of truth—Dr. Samuel Johnson's Rasselas (from *Rasselas, Prince of Abyssinia*, 1759), for example—Chekhov's captive moves from one enthusiasm to another, discarding one by one those sources of human happiness which he is permitted under the terms of his agreement.

It is interesting that the lawyer alternates between self-indulgence and disciplined study, moving from light books and music to classical literature, then back to escape through music and wine, then to intense study, first of the human world and then of the divine. At the end, Chekhov's banker observes, he has no direction, but strikes out erratically, obviously searching for something, anything, to give meaning to his life.

Unlike most truth-seekers in literature, the lawyer is deprived of human contact, love, family ties, friendship, and companionship. During the first year, Chekhov writes, the captive is lonely; evidently, solitude is less depressing during the later years. It might be said, however, that his exploration of all human possibilities is incomplete without an experience of personal relationships. Chekhov is aware of that omission and deals with it in the letter written by the lawyer at the end of his fifteen years alone. Through books, he says, he has experienced all human pleasures, from human love and the enjoyment of natural beauty to the exercise of tyrannical power, and though his emotional involvements have been vicarious, he believes that he can reject them on the basis of what he has learned.

The grounds of the lawyer's contempt for life, as expressed in the final letter, are several. First, everything is empty. Various interests last for various lengths of time, but none can justify a life. Second, all that man considers beautiful is ugly, and all that he considers true is false; in other words, man can like this world only if he sees it as it is not, and the captive has lost the capacity for illusion. Finally, nothing endures; death destroys everything and everyone. All is vanity, then, empty, illusory, and doomed.

It is significant that after he sees the shrunken, miserable captive whom he had intended to kill, after he reads the letter denouncing human existence, the banker feels contempt not for the world, but for himself. Does he feel guilt because he has destroyed a life? Does he feel shame because he was ready to commit murder rather than lose his money? Does he feel that the captive has higher ideals than he? Chekhov leaves the banker's reaction unexplained. The banker, however, is not ready to renounce life; he locks the note in his safe as insurance against any accusations which might be made.

One of the problems with this story is that the author seems uncertain as to his theme. Surely Chekhov does not agree with the captive that nothing is worthwhile, although he does realize that no enthusiasm in life seems to be permanent. The fact that Chekhov concludes "The Bet" with the banker's self-protective gesture suggests that the world is not ready to agree with the lawyer. Furthermore, the unnatural appearance of the captive leads readers to believe either that life has worn him down much faster than usual or that his life has been much harsher than the lives of most people. Is he truly wise? Or have fifteen years of solitary confinement warped his judgment? Again, Chekhov leaves the question open.

That Chekhov was uncertain about what he intended to prove in the story, other than the fact that human reactions are unpredictable, is indicated by the third section of the story, which he omitted in his collected works. In it, at a party a year after the prisoner's escape, the banker is expressing his admiration for the lawyer, the one man of principle whom he has ever encountered. Suddenly the lawyer appears, announces his love of life, declares books a poor substitute, and asks for a considerable sum of money, threatening suicide if he does not receive it. The banker agrees and then is overcome by the desire himself to renounce life, but realizing that his life is no longer happy enough to make the gesture meaningful, he rejects the impulse and declares the lawyer the winner of the bet.

Style and Technique

Because "The Bet" is cast in fable form, the characterization is not as individualized as in Chekhov's other stories, but rather, the banker and the lawyer serve as voices of two different viewpoints. Except for the letter written at the end of the fifteen-year period, Chekhov does not reveal the thoughts of the captive. On the other hand, the story begins with the banker's memories and observations, proceeds to his worries about money and his resolution to kill the prisoner rather than pay the bet, and concludes with the banker's self-contempt and with his self-protective gesture. The sequel discarded by Chekhov continues the focus on the banker's point of view. Thus it might be suggested that Chekhov is more interested in the psychological and ironic possibilities of his account than in a didactic point.

Usually Chekhov's imagery, too, reflects his psychological interest. Certainly in "The Bet" it is appropriate that the story begins on a dark rainy night and that the banker's temptaion to murder occurs on a dark, cold, rainy night, that he passes a bare bed and a cold stove on the way to the sealed room, and that the prisoner's room is dark, with a dimming candle. All these images of death are consistent with the banker's resolution, as well as with the lawyer's death-in-life. Because they are seen through the banker's eyes, however, they are particularly important as reflecting his own psychological condition, a despair which is itself a death-in-life, and which may finally be Chekhov's particular interest in "The Bet." For although Chekhov followed Tolstoy in constructing his story in the form of a fable, both the story as he finally published it and the longer, earlier version emphasize psychological realism more than certain truths about human existence.

Rosemary M. Canfield-Reisman

BEYOND THE GLASS MOUNTAIN

Author: Wallace Stegner (1909-   )
Type of plot: Psychological realism
Time of plot: A May in the late 1940's
Locale: Iowa City, Iowa
First published: 1947

> *Principal characters:*
> MARK AKER, the protagonist, a medical researcher on the
>   Yale University faculty
> MEL COTTAM, Mark's closest college friend, who runs his
>   father's former business in Iowa City
> TAMSEN COTTAM, Mel's wife and a member of the same
>   college crowd
> "CANBY," Mel and Tamsen's twelve-year-old son

The Story

Superficially, the situation in "Beyond the Glass Mountain" is an American commonplace. It concerns a very brief reunion of Mark Aker, a Yale University medical professor and researcher, with his former college friend Mel Cottam, a small businessman in Iowa City, Iowa, after a seventeen-year separation. The reunion begins for Mark with a nostalgic return to Iowa City and his recollections of the college town and the college world that gave him "the best days of his life." He returns, also, in response to what he perceives is a call for help from Mel. He hopes to repay a profound personal debt to the man who made those days possible. The reunion is cut short, however, when Mark cannot penetrate the wall that time and experience have put between them; he is unable to bring himself to pry into Mel's private world and unable to find the words that would set it all right with them again.

Mark's uneasiness about the long-delayed meeting is overcome, initially, by the power of Iowa City to trigger rich and complex memories of the good days of his youth, "the whole coltish . . . time handed back to him briefly, intact, precious." "The passionate familiarity of everything"—landmarks, names, sights, smells, and sounds—includes Mel's voice answering his phone call. Mark realizes that the poignancy of these "things" lies in the fact that they are all part of a storied past. The stories he recalls are made of modest material—sports, dating, eating, pranks—but they always involve Mel and suggest their closeness. Mark is reminded of how they had "made games of everything"; also, Mel's house had been home for both of them. The power of these memories invests Mark with the hope that the old Mel is not lost and their old relationship still lives.

Yet Mark also fears the reunion. He fears the possibility that he will find Mel drunk rather than sober, that the drinking is a sign that his friend has been deeply hurt or betrayed. His evidence for believing that Mel is an alcoholic is slim—the reader hears initially only about two drunken phone calls. When Mark calls Mel to announce his unexpected arrival in town this particular Sunday morning in May, he is relieved to hear Mel's sober voice answer, but when Mark himself falls naturally into the bantering, clownish "talk" that characterized their college days ("Hello, you poop out. . . . This is Canby"), Mel responds by falling into his old role of happy-go-lucky, jocular sot, a role he sustains, to Mark's increasing distress, beyond the "point where it should have stopped."

Mark's initial fear is reinforced when he arrives at Mel's house to find Mel and his wife, Tamsen, having Sunday-morning cocktails. The source of Mark's concern for Mel becomes even clearer in the scene that follows: Tamsen, highball in hand but also "smooth and sober and impeccable," stands in striking contrast to spraddle-legged Mel; she gives every indication that she is "in command in this familiar house." In college, Mark knew Tamsen as shrewd but dishonest ("she could lie her way out of hell"), as well as a woman of easy virtue. He has learned that Mel found out about her infidelities and considered a divorce, but that somehow the marriage was patched up.

In a brief moment the two men have together, Mark considers urging Mel to leave Tamsen, for the sake of their child as well as himself. He thinks of asking Mel to come away with him and kick his drinking habit. The plea, however, is never uttered: Despite his former closeness to Mel and his desire to be close again, Mark believes that "you simply did not say things like that. Even thinking about them made them sound self-righteous and prying." There is some invisible, transparent, but formidable barrier that separates them—a glass mountain. Even though Mel is as close as an animal seen by the hunter through the sights of his rifle, in fact Mark and Mel are as far apart as the two worlds separating the hunter from the animal he hunts—the animal seemingly indifferent to the hunter's presence.

To these unspoken reflections, Mel turns "his ear sideward like a deaf man." Mark, in turn, is shaken, refuses a second drink proposed by Tamsen, and begs the necessity of catching a 12:30 train. As the two friends part ways on the street corner, however, Mark tries once more to get his friend to "listen straight." The response is even more disturbing: He finally sees in his friend's eyes the "pained, intent, sad" expression for which he has been looking as evidence of the real Mel, but he also catches a "flicker of derision" on Mel's lips, indicating that he still does not fully understand the man behind the mask. The story ends with the reader still not sure that Mark has seen fully or judged fairly the situation or the relationship. Mel's derisive gesture marks his rejection of Mark as well as Mark's friendly overture.

Themes and Meanings

Initially the reader may see "Beyond the Glass Mountain" as Mel's story, since his "problems"—drinking and marriage—preoccupy Mark. Mel's expression of contempt for Mark at the end of the story is consistent with his stoic resolve to hold on to his marriage, however compromising, and reject advances into his private life, even from a well-intentioned "friend"; it even implies a criticism of Mark's success. They both know that Mark has "gone up and out in the world," while Mel "has been marooned behind." Mel signals his attitude toward Mark's success when he plucks at his sleeve and asks, "Where did you get that jacket?" Mark feels guilty in responding "Montreal," and shame when he finds himself justifying a trip there to attend a genetics conference.

The story is more centrally Mark's, for it presents a man of considerable worldly success facing a personal and private failure. Mark wonders how a man can act honorably when the past leaves him with debts and obligations. He fails to find an answer. Instead, he learns that his perceptions of reality are deceiving, that "friends" wear masks that hide their true feelings, and that communication between adult men is problematic.

Mark becomes angry when Mel draws attention to his worldly success: "Mel [who had everything then] had taught the whole unlicked lot of them something, how to win and how to lose, how to live with people and like them and forgive them. He had never owned a dime's worth of anything that he wasn't glad to share." Mark cannot repay his debt unless their youthful roles are reversed—with Mel the benefactor of Mark's largess. That reversal is effectively blocked by Mel's pride, the stigma of Mark's new status, and Mark's judgmental temperament.

Mark comes to the situation with strong moral biases. He can imagine pronouncing them, but he knows that it is inappropriate for a friend to voice them. His sensitivity is underlined by his unrehearsed response to the good life remembered and Mel's generous role in making it good. Faced with the present situation, however, he can only look uneasy. In his way, he is as reticent as Mel, withholding from his friend (if not the reader) his strongest sentiments about their relationship as well as his most strident judgments about Tamsen and dishonesty and bad marriages.

Both his moral probity and his success stand against him under the circumstances. While part of Mark is convinced that he and Mel remain the people they once were, that "what we were is still here, if we peel off the defenses and the gag lines," the glaze that covers Mel's eyes is all but impenetrable. When it cracks for that moment at the end of the story, it does not give Mark the reassurance that he seeks.

Style and Technique

Meaning in "Beyond the Glass Mountain" develops out of the complex relationships between the characters and between the past and the present. Mark sees his college years with Mel as a Damon and Pythias affair—the allusion to the classical legend of the loyalty of two friends appropriately underlining the idealizing tendencies of Mark's memory. As this ideal collapses under the stress of the present moment, it is the legend of the mountain man Jim Bridger hunting elk in Yellowstone that comes to Mark's mind. The connotations of the wilderness and hunting—with their hint of alienation and even violence—suggest human relationships far from the ideal in the Greek legend.

Stegner uses quite different techniques to enrich the contrast between past and present. During Mark's initial nostalgic awakening, the reader watches him literally "soak himself in the sensations he remembered," the impressionistic images flowing from a man with the heightened sensibilities of a poet rather than a biologist. Later, at the Cottam home, Mark exposes an identity in his interior monologues quite at odds with the "civil" visitor who converses wittily with both Tamsen and Mel.

Indeed, talk is a major contributor to the dramatic tension that gradually emerges between Mark and Mel. The college talk into which the two drift— the caustic, sometimes ribald name-calling—is a code language that identified a camaraderie among young college strangers but keeps middle-aged adults at bay and estranged. Mark initiates it when he introduces himself as "Canby." ("In their college crowd everybody had called everybody else Canby"). Mel responds by dropping into the "clowning voice" of his college years, a voice that feigned drunken confusion and misunderstanding at every turn. When Mark tries to straighten out the conversation—"This is Aker. Remember me?"—Mel holds to his voice: "You mean Belly Aker, the basketball player...?"

At the Cottam home, Mel's tomfoolery continues. Mark is unable to decide whether Mel has become a "drunken parody" of his former self or is using "double talk and affectionate profanity" as a defense to hide his feelings. When Mel and Tamsen's son innocently intrudes, Mel calls him "Canby" and treats him in the same roughhousing, jocular manner, suggesting that the son is being initiated into a kind of masculine, tribal discourse; as if donning the tribal mask, the son grins. Mark cannot escape the talk either, as well as the role it implies, despite his uneasiness. His farewell to Mel begins in the same spirit: "I wish you the best, you bum," he begins. When he tries to say more than this, however, he is met by Mel's pained expression and the "flicker of derision" that warns him to go no further. By invoking this series of contrasts—between ideal and real, past and present, thought and talk, the mask and the true self—Stegner reveals the difficulty of truly understanding another, of breaking through the "glass mountain."

Merrill Lewis

BEZHIN MEADOW

Author: Ivan Turgenev (1818-1883)
Type of plot: Sketch
Time of plot: Mid-nineteenth century
Locale: Province of Tula, Russia
First published: "Bezhin lug," 1852 (English translation, 1855)

>*Principal characters:*
>THE NARRATOR, a hunter
>FEDYA,
>PAVLUSHA,
>ILYUSHA,
>KOSTYA, and
>VANYA, peasant boys

The Story

As with all of Ivan Turgenev's stories in *A Sportsman's Sketches* (1852), the plot of this one is simple and straightforward. After a day of grouse-shooting, the hunter who narrates the story starts homeward but becomes lost as night approaches. Growing increasingly uneasy as he wanders beside a wood, then along the boundary of a field, around a knoll, and into a hollow, he stops short at the very edge of an abyss. At the bottom of the precipice he can barely perceive a broad river and a vast plain; he now knows where he is and descends to Bezhin Meadow, where five boys are clustered around two fires while keeping watch over a drove of grazing horses.

The narrator describes the boys, who range in age from fourteen to seven. The one who stands out from the others is twelve-year-old Pavlusha, who appears to be the leader, as the narrator, lying quietly apart from the boys, observes while listening to their conversation. They talk about goblins and water-fairies and an apparition on a drowned man's grave. Suddenly, the dogs are roused, rush off, and are immediately followed by Pavlusha, who returns shortly, saying casually that he thought a wolf might have been the source of the dogs's excitement. The conversation around the fire resumes, again concerning tales about the dead, the supernatural, wood-demons, and water-sprites. The boys share the few potatoes they have been cooking in a small pot, and Pavlusha goes off for some water. When he returns, they settle down to sleep in the deep silence that precedes dawn.

The hunter awakes just before sunrise, nods goodbye to Pavlusha, the only one of the boys who wakes up, and sets off for home as the sun rises and everything returns to life—the river, the hills, the creatures of the meadow. He hears a bell, then the drove of horses passes him, chased by the boys.

In the last paragraph, the hunter adds regretfully that Pavlusha died some months later in a fall from a horse.

Themes and Meanings

To understand the underlying ideas and significance of this sketch, one should consider the context in which this story appears. The book is a collection of landscape descriptions and character portraits based on chance encounters with peasants of all sorts and conditions. A few members of the gentry also appear occasionally, but always in relation to the peasants, as in "The Bailiff," in which the narrator recounts an unpleasant and disquieting visit with an acquaintance who embodies the worst qualities of a cruel, self-indulgent landlord. It is perhaps in that story that Turgenev's opposition to serfdom is most strongly indicated. He never expresses this opposition directly, but the theme is perfectly clear, especially if one views the sketches as parts of a whole. Taken separately, the message in each sketch is presented so subtly that it almost disappears in the wealth of detailed portraiture and description, but even in the seemingly simple and straightforward account of a night spent observing five poor, ignorant, superstitious children, the author's ideas about his subjects are strongly implied. There is, however, a universality about the hunter's experience and the boys he describes that raises the sketch far above a merely sociological discussion.

The author's love of his native land is much more explicit, as he describes the countryside, the weather, and the various settings in which the hunter finds himself, such as a cottage, an inn, an estate, a hut, or a meadow next to a river.

Both themes—an indictment of serfdom and a love of the land—are present in "Bezhin Meadow," though in this particular sketch the latter seems predominant. Yet in the tales the boys tell one another, the former is evident, too. For example, twelve-year-old Ilyusha describes the appearance of a goblin in the paper factory where he and nine other boys of his age work; quite matter-of-factly, he tells how the overseer makes the boys spend the night on the floor in the rolling-room of the factory so that they will be on hand in good time the next day for an extra amount of work. Ilyusha is more interested in his account of the goblin's appearance than he is in the working conditions of the peasant, but the reader cannot ignore the significance of Ilyusha's barely mentioned details about his life. There is no complaining, no self-pity. If the reader, along with the silent hunter, observes the boys closely, the universal qualities of boyhood become evident in all their variety, humor, courage, intelligence, gullibility, and enjoyment of life, however difficult their circumstances. Their pleasure in one another's company and in the warm, starry night, with the two feisty dogs and the horses close by, is one that any reader can share.

Style and Technique

In this sketch, Turgenev uses a combination of lyrical description (particularly in the opening paragraph, in which a day in July is related in poetic detail) and a nearly total detachment, with such minimal, brief indications of the hunter's feelings that they go almost unnoticed. In the author's treatment of the boys, there is no sentimentality, no romantic idealization. They are real boys, and their conversation is natural: direct, candid, unadorned. One can see the boys and hear them talk, just as one can feel the beauty of the night and hear its sounds—the snorting of the horses, the crackling of the fire, the eerie cry of a heron, the splash of a fish in the river. Yet one can sense, more from what Turgenev does not say than from what he does, the author's curiosity, compassion, and respect for his subjects.

The language Turgenev uses is genuine, never artificial, never overdone. The boys' stories of ghosts and goblins are given in their own words, with almost no commentary by the hunter. Their tales are mixed with references to the night and its sounds; the result is both realistic and poetic. There is a perfection in the choice of details and the dialogue that makes it possible for the reader to identify with both the hunter and the boys, and the night spent on "Bezhin Meadow" becomes a part of the reader's own memory.

Natalie Harper

BIG BLONDE

Author: Dorothy Parker (1893-1967)
Type of plot: Satiric realism
Time of plot: The 1920's, during the Prohibition era
Locale: New York City
First published: 1929

> *Principal characters:*
> MRS. (HAZEL) MORSE, the "Big Blonde," the central
>   character
> HERBIE MORSE, her first husband
> MRS. MARTIN, a friend of Mrs. Morse
> THE BOYS, the men at Jimmy's bar

The Story

In the traditional sense, the story has no plot with a tight climax and resolution. It is primarily a history, an extended portrait of "Big Blonde."

Hazel Morse, a big, fun-loving, peroxide blonde, is a caricature. Amiable, empty-headed, given to tears at the slightest provocation, she is not so much a realistic character as she is a collection of traits and attitudes which the author holds up for satiric scrutiny.

She and her first husband, Herbie, begin married life isolated from any connections, utterly content with each other. Soon, Herbie—like Hazel, a collection of mannerisms, viewed by Dorothy Parker as a specimen—wearies of Hazel's moods, her "misty melancholy." When he can take no more, he slams the door, rushes out, and gets drunk. Once tender lovers, Hazel and Herbie (their names suggest Parker's attitude toward them) become enemies. Whenever Herbie stays out late, Hazel worries; in time, however, her worry turns to anger, and she is ready for an argument when he returns. Soon, loud, violent quarrels are a regular feature of their marriage.

Hazel begins to drink, and soon all of her days run together. Sure that she is losing Herbie, she begins to frequent Jimmy's bar, the haunt of "The Boys." Mrs. Morse, as she is known at Jimmy's, makes fast friends with a forty-year-old blonde, Mrs. Martin; the two women drink together and enjoy the attentions of The Boys. One of them, Ed, from Utica and married for twenty years, plays poker with Mrs. Morse; his kisses lead the way to romance, and she becomes his "doll."

One day, Herbie packs to leave for a job in Detroit; he offers his wife, foggy with drink, the furniture and some stock. After he leaves, Mrs. Morse (so Parker refers to her for the remainder of the story) plays her favorite recording, "Ain't We Got Fun."

Ed gives her presents and suggests that she move. She agrees, because her relations with Mrs. Martin and Joe, Mrs. Martin's boyfriend, are strained. Ed gives her a flat and a black maid, Nettie. Alcohol continues to keep Mrs. Morse fat; her moods keep her gloomy and melancholy.

At Jimmy's, Mrs. Morse finds the women monotonously the same: big, heavy, ruddy, healthy. Most are married, some divorced, some have a child. Yet they are cordial and friendly. The Boys enjoy the women, above all Mrs. Morse. She needs money, so she passively responds to Ed, who continues to buy things for her. Finally, however, he is bored by her fits of gloom. He needs fun; the other women at Jimmy's are not so moody.

After three years with Mrs. Morse, Ed moves to Florida. He cries on leaving Mrs. Morse and gives her a check: she does not miss him at all, and each year when he returns to New York and rushes to see her, she remains passive.

A friend of Ed, Charley, has always liked Mrs. Morse, and now with Ed gone, he fills her life. She finds him "not so bad," but after a year, she lets Sidney, "a clever little Jew," take his place. Sidney likes her softness and size; with him, she feels lively and happy. Soon, however, he leaves her to marry a rich woman. Billy and Fred are next, but soon Mrs. Morse cannot recall how they came and went.

News comes that Herbie has a new woman, but Mrs. Morse is not moved at all. Several years have passed since she saw him; now, all the days blur together. One night, tired and blue, she sees horses stumbling and slipping, and she begins to think of death. With a drowsy cheer, she thinks "It's nice to be dead," and later she reads stories about suicides. In her drinking bouts, she has sudden intuitions of the nuisance of existing. She dreams all day of no more tight shoes, no more forced laughs, no more trying to be a "good sport." Whenever the idea of suicide becomes tangible and immediate, however, she flinches.

A new man, short and fat, comes on the scene; when he whispers "You're the best sport in the world," Mrs. Morse tries very hard to feel something. One night at Jimmy's with Art, she chats with a woman about insomnia and learns of a remedy: five grains of veronal. It can be purchased in New Jersey without a prescription. The next day, Mrs. Morse takes the train to Newark and easily buys twenty tablets of veronal. That night at home, she sends Nettie for Scotch; then, vaguely blurred, she goes to Jimmy's, where she meets Art, who has told her that he will be away for a week. Thus, the glow of the Scotch turns to gloom; this merely irritates Art, who leaves, impatient, with "Try to cheer up by Thursday when I'll be back."

She returns to her room and swallows slowly the twenty tablets of veronal. Waiting for death to come, she says, "I'm nearly dead," and chuckles at the words.

The next morning, Nettie the maid sees Mrs. Morse sprawled on the bed, making strange sounds. Nettie runs out and gets the elevator boy to run with her for a doctor. When the doctor sees the vials, he pumps out the drug, but Mrs. Morse remains unconscious for two days. When she wakes, she swears at Nettie, then apologizes. A pageant of sensations passes in her memory—Jimmy's bar, horses stumbling, men saying, "Be a good sport." Nettie gives Mrs. Morse a postcard from Art, urging her to cheer up for Thursday. Then Nettie and Mrs. Morse share a drink, with Nettie saying, "Cheer up now," and Mrs. Morse replying, "Yeah, Sure." Thus the portrait of "Big Blonde" ends.

Themes and Meanings

One of the central themes in "Big Blonde" is the futility of alcohol to fill an empty mind and heart. When Mrs. Morse cannot cope with disappointments, she has no remedy but drink, and finds that ultimately it is no panacea. She also illustrates the old cliché about "laughing on the outside." While clinging desperately to her reputation as "a good sport" and struggling to laugh the easy laugh that attracts men, Mrs. Morse succumbs often to copious crying and soon loses her appeal. Closely related to her alcoholism and her oscillations between fun and melancholy is the theme of marriage. To endure, marriage requires a modicum of love and mature understanding. Mrs. Morse lacks these assets; her marriages are superficial or short-lived. This lack of love serves to intensify the emptiness of her relations with people and her failure to find true satisfaction in life.

Style and Technique

Dorothy Parker's style is direct, lively, and fast-paced. The third-person narration holds the characters at a distance: Mrs. Morse is an admonitory example, and while readers of the story may pity her, they are not invited to identify with her.

Dialogue is natural, quick, and immediate, though used sparingly. Much of the story is given to exposition, in the historical past, again enforcing a certain detachment. Parker offers few if any close-ups of love scenes or hate scenes, or highly dramatic moments. Although the circumstances of the protagonist change, she does not undergo significant development; that is not the author's intention. Rather, Parker anatomizes a character-type.

Ann Edward

BIG TWO-HEARTED RIVER

Author: Ernest Hemingway (1899-1961)
Type of plot: Outdoor adventure
Time of plot: 1919 or 1920
Locale: The woods of Michigan's upper peninsula
First published: 1925

> *Principal character:*
> NICK ADAMS, a young American who has recently returned
> from action in World War I

The Story

"Big Two-Hearted River" is one of the best stories by one of the greatest short story writers of the twentieth century. "The story was about coming back from the war," as Ernest Hemingway later explained in *A Moveable Feast* (1964), "but there was no mention of the war in it." Unless the reader knows *In Our Time* (1924, 1925), Hemingway's first collection of short stories, "Big Two-Hearted River" will not make complete sense. The first five stories in that collection describe the young Nick Adams growing up in and around the northern Michigan woods, while the middle stories (and most of the interchapters that preface every story in the collection) concern Americans in Europe during and immediately following World War I. "Big Two-Hearted River" concludes the book and brings Nick Adams back from the wounds and trauma of war to the regenerative natural setting of woods and water, where, as a boy, he first learned about the world. "Big Two-Hearted River" is a boy's adventure of camping and fishing, but it is finally a story of a man's healing.

The story is broken into two parts (in *In Our Time* they appear as separate stories in the table of contents and are divided by a brief interchapter), but there is very little plot in either. Part 1 opens as "The train went on up the track out of sight, around one of the hills of burnt timber." This is Nick's last contact (except in his thoughts) with other humans. Nick has been dropped off in what remains of Seney, a once thriving lumber town that has been deserted and burned over and now resembles (although Nick does not say so) the war zone that he has so recently left. "Even the surface had been burned off the ground."

At a bridge across the river, Nick looks down on "the trout keeping themselves steady in the current with wavering fins." Like the trout, Nick will try to hold himself together in the next days as he recovers from the war in the restorative environment of these north woods. Nick "felt happy. He felt he had left everything behind, the need for thinking, the need to write, other needs. It was all back of him." Hiking toward the woods, Nick finds that the grasshoppers "had all turned black from living in the burned-over land"; even the insects have learned to adapt here.

Little else happens in part 1. Nick walks away from the charred land into the woods, naps, and—like Rip Van Winkle—awakens to a new adventure. He finds a good campsite by the river, pitches his tent, and crawls into it "happy."

> He had not been unhappy all day. This was different though. Now things were done. There had been this to do. Now it was done. It had been a hard trip. He was very tired. That was done. He had made his camp. He was settled. Nothing could touch him. It was a good place to camp. He was there, in the good place. He was in his home where he had made it. Now he was hungry.

Nick cooks dinner over his fire and, while he makes coffee, he thinks of Hopkins, a friend who deserted Nick and others when he became rich. "His mind was starting to work. He knew he could choke it because he was tired enough." Nick crawls into his tent and goes to sleep.

In part 2, Nick cooks and eats his breakfast, packs himself a lunch, and heads into the river. He hooks and then loses a huge trout ("He had never seen so big a trout"), but his "feeling of disappointment" slowly leaves him, and he catches two other trout. Nick sits on a log to eat his lunch and observes that the river narrows and flows into a swamp farther downstream.

> Nick did not want to go in there now. He felt a reaction against deep wading with the water deepening up under his armpits, to hook big trout in places impossible to land them. In the swamp the banks were bare, the big cedars came together overhead, the sun did not come through, except in patches; in the fast deep water, in the half light, the fishing would be tragic. In the swamp fishing was a tragic adventure. Nick did not want it. He did not want to go down the stream any further today.

Nick guts and cleans his fish and walks back to his camp. "There were plenty of days coming when he could fish the swamp," Nick thinks in the last line of the story.

Themes and Meanings

"Big Two-Hearted River" is perhaps the best example of Hemingway's theory of omission, which he discusses in *Death in the Afternoon* (1932):

> If a writer of prose knows enough about what he is writing about he may omit things that he knows and the reader, if the writer is writing truly enough, will have a feeling of those things as strongly as though the writer had stated them. The dignity of movement of an ice-berg is due to only one-eighth of it being above the water.

It is best if readers encounter "Big Two-Hearted River" first at the end of *In Our Time*, after reading the related stories of Nick Adams growing up, going to war, and being wounded. Yet even if they read the story isolated in some anthology, readers should sense from the curiously tense surface that "Big Two-Hearted River," despite its content, is no boy's adventure story.

The meaning of the story lies in Nick's ability to build a good camp and to fish well and thereby tap the restorative powers that nature holds. Just as in the fishing scenes in *The Sun Also Rises* (1926), in which Jake Barnes and his friend Bill are able to escape the meaningless whirlwind of Paris life in the pure and tranquil fishing in the mountains of Spain, so Nick in "Big Two-Hearted River" can return to his Michigan woods in order to recover from the violence and trauma of war and to gain some control over his life. Although Nick shows no scars, his psychic wounds are deep. Nick in fact resembles the trout that he guts toward the end of the story: "When he held them back up in the water they looked like live fish." Nick has been gutted by the brutality and senselessness of war, but now, like Frederic Henry in *A Farewell to Arms* (1929), he is able to escape, at least momentarily, to a sanctuary from war and the world.

Nick is restored in two ways. First, the setting itself provides some kind of natural, almost mystical, healing power. Like Henry Thoreau at Walden Pond, Nick is able in the woods to return to the elemental activities of eating, sleeping, and fishing. Fishing provides the second restoration. In Hemingway's world, fishing is one of the ritualistic activities (like boxing and bullfighting) by which man establishes and maintains his control over an arbitrarily violent world. In such activities, there is a clear set of skills (a code) and by fishing well (and not, for example, "in places impossible to land" the fish), a man can be successful and achieve his limited goals. Fishing provides one means of erecting a scaffolding of skills over the essential meaninglessness of life.

Yet the story, in its brief twenty-four hours, recounts merely the first step. As Nick says in the last line, "There were plenty of days coming when he could fish the swamp." The swamp thus represents human society, and, when Nick is whole again, he will be able to return to society for the painful task of human interaction. In the Hemingway cartography, society can be as violent and arbitrary (as "tragic") as the world of war. "Big Two-Hearted River" is about a man returning from the war, getting his psychological strength back through contact with nature and the ritual of fishing, and preparing to return to the world.

Style and Technique

"Big Two-Hearted River" is one of the most accomplished of Hemingway's early stories, ranked in the top half-dozen of this master storyteller's major achievements. The story is carried almost single-handedly through

Hemingway's style. There is only one character in "Big Two-Hearted River" and very little plot or action. Yet much occurs. Hemingway has written a story that is much like the Big Two-Hearted River itself—so spare and clean that the reader looks down into its clear water for meaning.

The power of the story comes in large part from its descriptions. There is no dialogue, and only a few times does Nick Adams allow himself to think. For most of the story, readers are observing Nick moving simply in this natural setting:

> Nick went over to the pack and found, with his fingers, a long nail in a paper sack of nails, in the bottom of the pack. He drove it into the pine tree, holding it close and hitting it gently with the flat of the ax. He hung the pack up on the nail. All his supplies were in the pack. They were off the ground and sheltered now.

Such descriptions give the action with an economy of word and picture.

This lean, economical prose actually intensifies the psychological situation of the story. The prose is dramatic and objective, but right below the surface (or, in the other seven-eighths of Hemingway's "iceberg") is a man barely under control, who must cut off his own thoughts. The tightly controlled surface of the story, in other words, reflects the struggle that is going on within Nick Adams, and this surface tension is what gives the story its actual power. The simple declarative sentences, the repetition of sentence elements, and the lack of subordination—all these add up to the story's elemental weight and force. Beneath the story's simple actions, as Hemingway knew and as he expected his readers to know, is a story of recovery from war. As the tip of the iceberg stands for what lurks just beneath the surface, so the places and things on the surface of the story (the camp, the trout, the swamp) are symbolic and stand for the things, just below the surface, that Hemingway is not telling his readers.

To read "Big Two-Hearted River" right is to glory in the physical descriptions of making the camp and fishing, and to realize what a major psychic struggle is going on just beneath the surface of Hemingway's rhythmic, almost lyrical prose.

David Peck

THE BIRTHMARK

Author: Nathaniel Hawthorne (1804-1864)
Type of plot: Allegory
Time of plot: Late eighteenth century
Locale: New England
First published: 1843

> *Principal characters:*
> AYLMER, the protagonist, a scientist
> GEORGIANA, his beautiful wife
> AMINADAB, Aylmer's beastlike lab assistant

The Story

The protagonist of this tale, Aylmer, is a scientist "proficient in every branch of natural philosophy." The plot is set in motion when he marries a beautiful young woman, Georgiana, who bears a curious birthmark on her cheek in the shape of a tiny crimson hand. Envious women sometimes say it spoils her beauty, but most men find it enchanting. Aylmer, however, becomes obsessed with the birthmark as the one flaw in an otherwise perfect beauty.

When Aylmer involuntarily shudders at the appearance of the birthmark, which waxes and wanes with the flushing or paling of the lady's cheek, Georgiana also develops a horror of her supposed blemish. Aylmer has a prophetic dream in which he seeks surgically to remove the mark, but it recedes as he probes till it clutches at her heart. In despair, Georgiana encourages Aylmer to try to remove the mark, even if it endangers her life to do so.

He secludes her in a lovely boudoir and entertains her with enchanting illusions and captivating fragrances. He and his gross, shaggy-haired assistant, Aminadab, labor mightily in Aylmer's laboratory to produce an elixer that will irradicate the imperfection of his nearly perfect bride. The laboratory's fiery furnace, its soot-blackened walls, its gaseous odors, and its test tubes and crucibles contrast grimly against the ethereal boudoir where his wife waits.

Meanwhile, Georgiana finds and reads Aylmer's journal, which records his scientific experiments. Her admiration and understanding for her husband's aspirations and intellect increase, even as she recognizes that most of his experiments are magnificent failures. Though she no longer expects to outlive the experience, she gladly and lovingly accepts the draft from her husband's hand. The birthmark does indeed fade, leaving her a vision of perfect beauty, a spirit unblemished in the flesh, but Georgiana is dead. The birthmark is mortality itself.

Themes and Meanings

Allegories seldom produce well-rounded characters, since their purpose is primarily philosophical and didactic. Aylmer is undoubtedly the Faustian man who is never satisfied with his own limitations. Ordinary nature is never good enough to fulfill his idealistic aspirations, and like both Christopher Marlowe's and Johann Wolfgang von Goethe's Faust, he is entranced with the Greek ideal of perfect beauty. In terms of visible beauty, Georgiana cannot compete with Helen of Troy, the supernatural succubus provided by Mephistopheles for Faustus. On the other hand, she can appeal to Aylmer's attraction to spiritual beauty and thus perhaps save his soul, like Gertrude, instead of assuring his damnation as the spurious Helen did for Faustus in Marlowe's version. Aylmer's ultimate fate is not resolved in the story. Presumably, he, like Ethan Brand, another of Hawthorne's protagonists, has found the one unforgivable sin in himself: intellectual pride.

Aylmer is never covetous of evil pleasures. He aspires upward, always, toward the ideal. In this sense, he is less believable as a human specimen than the Renaissance Faustus, who craved sensual experience as well as knowledge and power. Aylmer seems to have been corrupted by the idealist's tendency toward abstraction and discontent with reality. In fact, he hardly seems sufficiently empirical in orientation to make a good scientist. Yet the reader is assured that "he handled physical details as if there were nothing beyond them; yet spiritualized them all, and redeemed himself from materialism by his strong and eager aspirations towards the infinite." Science is obviously closer to alchemy and magic at this time than to modern chemistry and physics. Alchemy always had a spiritual element.

Georgiana is a one-dimensional heroine, as good as she is beautiful. In fact, the story seems to support the Platonic assumption that perfect beauty is equivalent to perfect goodness. Georgiana does gain some intellectual insight in the course of the story, loving her husband more but trusting his judgment less. She has more common sense than he, but also more selfless devotion. Modern readers may complain that the perfect goodness she attains, even before she is purified of her physical flaw, is simply the absurd exaggeration of conventional female virtue: absolute self-sacrifice and submission to the will of the beloved. Hawthorne casts all blame for the tragic outcome on the misguided husband, who is not satisfied with the ample blessings of nature.

The conflict is not really between good and evil; it lies, rather, in a fundamental incompatibility between the physical and the spiritual aspects of man. Georgiana recognizes that Aylmer's journal was "the sad confession and continual exemplification of the shortcomings of the composite man, the spirit burdened with clay, and working in matter, and of the despair that assails the higher nature at finding itself so miserably thwarted by the earthly part."

Style and Technique

Hawthorne inherited from his Puritan ancestors a brooding preoccupation with the idea of Original Sin. He created several haunting symbols to suggest that human flaw: the minister's black veil, the poisonous breath of Rappaccinni's daughter, the scarlet letter that Hester Prynne wore on her breast. The birthmark is one of these symbols. While the tiny hand is expressly associated only with the "fatal flaw" of mortality, Aylmer's peculiarly Calvinistic frame of mind expands its symbolic value to "his wife's liability to sin, sorrow, decay, and death."

Hawthorne's symbolic mode sometimes explains too much for modern tastes, yet there are ambiguities lurking even in this most allegorical of tales. The fact that Aylmer connects the physical flaw to moral sin seems to be the reason for this abhorrence of the birthmark and thus his justification for, in essence, murdering his wife. This presents a moral ambiguity akin to the situation in "Young Goodman Brown," where the author carefully suggests that Brown may indeed have met his neighbors and his wife at the Devil's sabbat, but that he may have dreamed the whole episode. If the evil vision was a dream issuing from the tortured sense of his own guilt, then Brown casts a terrible blight upon his wife and neighbors with the poisonous vapors of his Calvinistic imagination. Even more obviously does Aylmer blight his wife as though her physical imperfection were equivalent to sin.

Yet Aylmer is explicitly aligned with the spiritual, God-like side of humanity. The shadow side of man, or, more precisely, the entirely physical element that presumably serves the spirit, is represented by the grotesque Aminadab. Lest the reader miss the point, Hawthorne pushes the contrast between the servant and his master. "With his vast strength, his shaggy hair, his smoky aspect, and the indescribable earthiness that encrusted him, he seemed to represent man's physical nature, while Aylmer's slender figure, and pale, intellectual face, were no less apt a type of the spiritual element."

In spite of the didactic instruction in the symbolic significance of such figures, one must remember that the villain of the piece is not the beastly shadow figure, but the spiritual, intellectual Aylmer. This is true even though Aminadab chuckles ominously at the death of Georgiana, as though at the victory of earth over spirit. He contributes to the menacing gothic atmosphere of the alchemist's laboratory but is a relatively innocent collaborator in an intellectual crime. Who needs Mephistopheles when men can destroy in the name of perfection?

The obvious allegorical quality of "The Birthmark" makes it a less satisfactory treatment of the mad scientist theme than the more complex and polished "Rappaccinni's Daughter." They are both intermediate forms, however, between the religious allegories of the past and the science fiction of the present.

The traditional Satan or Mephistopheles has waned as literary symbol of evil, to be replaced by the machine or mutant monster which the mad scientist creates in his ambition to take over from God the control of natural forces. In "Rappaccinni's Daughter," the mutant form which in turn destroys the innocent maiden is the poisonous vegetation created by her father. In "The Birthmark," however, the scientist is described in persistently spiritual terms and creates no intermediate form, except of course the fatal potion, but brings death directly to his beloved. While the menacing Dr. Rappaccinni seems closer to the Devil in conception, Aylmer seems closer to God. Perhaps Hawthorne suffered from a dark suspicion that, after all, God must be responsible for man's imperfection and suffering. The tales of Hawthorne speak eloquently of a profoundly ambivalent mythic imagination.

Katherine Snipes

THE BISHOP

Author: Anton Chekhov (1860-1904)
Type of plot: Philosophical tale
Time of plot: The late 1890's
Locale: A nameless Russian provincial capital
First published: "Arkhierey," 1902 (English translation, 1915)

Principal characters:
BISHOP PYOTR, the suffering bishop of a diocese and the
    protagonist
MARYA TIMOFEEVNA, his mother
KATYA, his niece
FATHER SISOY, his aide

The Story

Against the solemn background of Holy Week, the most important week in the liturgical year, Anton Chekhov recounts the last days in the life of the protagonist, Bishop Pyotr, including his illness, the accompanying crisis and "awakening," and death.

Bishop Pyotr officiates at vespers as the story opens on the eve of Palm Sunday. To the bishop, who is unwell, the congregation is an indistinguishable blur with "all faces alike," "heaving like the sea." That the congregation seems shrouded in mist suggests his isolation from his flock. Even as his own mother approaches him, he is unsure of her identity. When the bishop begins to weep, and the congregation with him, his tears are no doubt brought about by these imaginings of his mother as well as of his impending death. Suddenly the weeping stops and the narrator notes, "everything was as before"—words which are echoed at the end of the story following the bishop's death. On his return to the monastery, the bishop identifies with objects in nature even if these evoke sterility and deadness. To the bishop, "everything seemed kindly, youthful, akin . . . and one longed to think that so it would be always." Despite this desire for continuity of existence, his identification with such forms of nature strengthens the motif of his estrangement from his personal identity.

Returning to the monastery, the bishop rejoices to learn that his mother was indeed in town. The news quickens memories of his "sweet precious childhood . . . which seemed brighter, fuller, and more festive than it had really been"—a childhood when "joy was quivering in the air," when he had had "naïve faith," had been called Pavlushka, and had been "infinitely happy." His pleasant reverie is rudely interrupted by the snoring of his aide, Father Sisoy, in the adjoining room—a sound which to him suggests "loneliness, forlornness, even vagrancy." Descriptions of ominous nature—the "moon peeping" into the bishop's window and a "cricket chirping"—intensify this mood; in Chekhov, such images are often associated with death.

Chapter 2, which begins on Palm Sunday, describes the everyday routine of Bishop Pyotr's office, interrupted by lunch with Marya Timofeevna, his mother, and Katya, his niece. In this setting, surprisingly, his mother treats him as a bishop rather than as her son. Surprised and disappointed by his mother's reserve, the son once again "cannot recognize her," she who was so tender and sympathetic when he was ill as a child. Cut off from warmth and simple human intercourse, the bishop feels estranged from reality and is increasingly aware of his illness. Even as he overhears the banal conversation between his mother and Father Sisoy, he recalls the course of his clerical career. The life that, eight years before, seemed to him to have "no end in sight" has now "retreated far away into the mist as though it were a dream."

Chapter 3 further details the bishop's daily routine. Illness has intensified his sensitivity toward the clergy's lack of spirituality and the ignorance, triviality, and pettiness of his suppliants. People's awe at his rank annoys him. No one speaks to him "genuinely, simply, as to a human being." Church is now the only place where he feels peace. During Tuesday's vespers, the past rises before him again, and he recalls having heard in his youth the readings about the Bridegroom who comes at night and the Heavenly Mansion. He is satisfied with his success, acknowledges having faith, and contemplates life hereafter. Yet some things remain unclear to him; he senses that something most important is still missing and that he does not want to die.

Chapter 4 opens with a lyric description of nature. Mention of "awakening trees smiling a welcome" foreshadows the bishop's "awakening" and identification with nature before dying. A visit from his eight-year-old niece, Katya, leads to genuine spontaneous communication. His mistaken impression of hearing the opening and shutting of doors, identified by Katya as the noise in his stomach, provokes his laughter and offers a moment of relief, yet it also indicates the progress of illness. His mother also visits him, observes that he is ill, and adds that, when Easter comes, he shall rest—words prophetic of his death the day before Easter. Similarly, the announcement that the horses are ready, that it is time for the Passion of the Lord, foreshadows the bishop's own approaching suffering and agony. Once again he finds relief in church, where he discovers a sense of continuity and thus a meaning to life—he sees the congregation as unchanged since the days of his childhood and senses identity in the church. At home, however, the feeling of oppression returns. He is even prepared "to give his life" merely to escape the monastery and the surrounding banality. His loneliness reaches its greatest intensity as he yearns for someone with whom he could talk openly. On the next day, Good Friday, final relief and release come in the form of a hemorrhage. He imagines himself thinner, weaker, and more insignificant than anyone and concludes "How good!" signifying his acceptance of death and the discovery of true peace. Realizing that the bishop is dying, his mother begins to comfort him and addresses him as her son, Pavlushka. Yet he no longer hears her. Rather, having identified himself with nature, he imagines that he is a simple, ordinary man, free as a bird.

Easter Sunday, the day after his death, is celebrated by everyone with no particular notice of his passing. In fact, he is "completely forgotten," and some people do not believe of his mother that her son was a bishop. Thus, the bishop's deathbed vision of being at last a free man appears to agree with a reality where no one even remembers him.

Themes and Meanings

"The Bishop," Chekhov's penultimate short story, is the tragedy of a member of the intelligentsia whose pursuit of a highly successful clerical career cuts him off from genuine human intercourse. Not until he faces death does the bishop realize that something important is missing from his life—namely, a love and respect for himself, not for his rank. His existential feeling of loneliness and isolation is evidenced by his thoughts: "If only there were one person to whom I could have talked, have opened my heart."

The bishop has two identities: a private one associated with Pavlushka, the name from his youth, and a public one associated with his present name, Bishop Pyotr. He has been unable, however, to defend this private identity against the forces of his career. His mother's nearness during the last week of his life (after a nine-year separation for which he must share the blame) has made him painfully aware of the lack of genuine love and closeness in his life. Even his mother addresses him with the formal "you" and "Your Holiness."

Now that he is dying, he wishes to return to the simple existence of his youth (clearly a Tolstoyan idea). His metamorphosis occurs both physically and spiritually. He imagines that he has become thinner, shorter, and more insignificant than anyone (the Latin root of Pavlushka means "little"). The bishop and his mother agree, whereupon his mother kisses him, calling him Pavlushka and "darling son." Then, during his final, more spiritual, thoughts, he imagines himself a simple, ordinary man, walking cheerfully through the fields under a sky bathed in sunshine, free as a bird to go anywhere he likes. His awakening before death enables him to die peacefully, thinking "How good!"

The author notes that the bishop died and was forgotten, yet this conclusion is not despairing, for the story suggests that a simple, genuine existence guided by love and respect is far more important than rank and fame. Throughout the text, an analogy is drawn between Bishop Pyotr and Christ. This likeness rightfully stops with the quiet death of the bishop. The point is, the bishop is not Christ and need not be remembered. He is only a link in a continuous chain created by Christ. Before he dies, the bishop perceives this continuity and is happy that he is part of it. His faith assures him of the Resurrection promised by the One whose own Resurrection is celebrated the day after the bishop dies. The pealing of church bells which the bishop so enjoyed on Easter morning is testimony to the perseverance of his spirit.

Style and Technique

Chekhov's impressionistic style, evident here, consists in juxtaposing complete scenes with a minimum of authorial comment. Multiple perspectives lend the story ambiguity, while a variety of rhythmic structures combined with a variety of artistic devices such as contrast, parallelism, carefully chosen metaphors and similes, dreamlike sequences, and recurring formulas make it an excellent example of the musicality of Chekhov's prose. Among the story's many symbolic elements are the ubiquitous sound of bells, the mysterious moon, the smell of pine, and the chirping cricket. The language is a masterly blending of levels of diction, including journalistic, Church Slavonic, and standard and substandard Russian (for example, the language of Father Sisoy and the mother).

Guiding the course of the story is the fatal typhoid which controls Bishop Pyotr's thoughts and actions. "The Bishop" ranks as one of Chekhov's best works portraying illness. Sharing numerous thematic and compositional features with Chekhov's mature plays, it divides into four parts: The first chapter describes the onset of the malady; chapters 2 and 3, its duration; and chapter 4, the crisis followed by death. Hints throughout suggest that the bishop will die. Besides the symptoms of his disease that are scattered here and there, each chapter contains references and allusions to death.

Leonard Polakiewicz

A BIT OF A SMASH IN MADRAS

Author: Julian Maclaren-Ross (1913-1964)
Type of plot: Social irony
Time of plot: Probably the 1940's
Locale: Madras, India
First published: 1965

> *Principal characters:*
> ADAMS, the narrator and central character, an Englishman
>   working in Madras, India
> STANTON, a friend with whom he shares quarters
> SHANKRAN, an Indian lawyer
> HOLT, the assistant commissioner
> SIR ALEC, Adams' boss
> DR. MENON, the company solicitor
> KRISHNASWAMI, witness to the accident
> TURPIN, a jockey and Krishnaswami's cohort

The Story

The flippant title of this story about an Englishman who seriously injures an Indian laborer in a drunken automobile accident is the first clue to its ironic social criticism. The very fact that the central character and narrator of the story calls such an accident merely "a bit of a smash" says more about the British arrogance and indifference to native Indians that led to the crumbling of the British Empire than do volumes of history or social commentary.

The story begins with the narrator's admission to his unidentified listener that he was so drunk when the accident occurred that he knew nothing about it until told about it by his roommate the next morning. His prejudicial attitude toward the Indians is made obvious when the police inspector arrives and the narrator identifies him as a native, but a "nice chap" anyway. Adams' white acquaintances are equally indifferent to native feelings. All are eager to "fix" things for him—his roommate, who buys off his bar bill so there will be no evidence that he was drunk; his drinking buddy, who pays for his bail; and his boss, who retains the company lawyer for him.

Native figures influenced by British rule fare no better in this story. Adams' first act is to retain an Indian lawyer whose main claim to fame is that he once defended an Englishman who crashed into a Muhammadan funeral, killing five; Adams was able to get for him a sentence of only three years. After Shankran the lawyer reassures Adams not to worry, he goes off thinking that, except for his skin, Shankran is much whiter than many Englishmen in India. The one witness to the accident, Krishnaswami, is interested only in extorting money from Adams, but he masks this by insisting that he believes the caste system should be abolished and that all men are brothers, even the poor laborer who was injured. He tries to ingratiate himself with Adams by suggesting that he should play middleman and take money from Adams to give to the laborer's family.

The British influence on Indians is further criticized by Adams' description of the company lawyer, Menon, and Krishnaswami, who negotiate a deal about the amount of the proposed payoff, both talking in Oxford English and trying to outdo each other. Shankran, who corrupts the courts and witnesses, ironically accuses Menon of corruption when the company lawyer tells him to get as much out of Adams as possible. In fact, the entire story is a complex and distasteful web of corruption, prejudice, and indifference by Englishmen and English-educated Indians alike. The only time Adams himself shows any sign of regret for his injuring the Indian laborer is when he visits him in the hospital and sees the man's family weeping and wailing around his bedside. Adams' prejudice is so deep-seated, however— so much a part of the British attitude toward the Indians—that his telling his listener that he "bloody near wept himself" rings false.

By the time the actual trial comes up, after Shankran has postponed it by fixing Adams up with a false doctor's report that he has dysentery, Shankran has frightened off Krishnaswami, has bribed another witness, and has promised to pay off the Inspector, all the while cursing his Indian countrymen as being corrupt and thinking only of money. The final judgment of the trial judge is that Adams pay 350 rupees to the injured man as compensation and two hundred rupees to the court as a fine for not stopping after the accident. He also must pay the Inspector three hundred rupees as a bribe, as well as his lawyers' fees. Instead of being chastened by his experience, Adams goes on a drinking binge for a month, is finally fired by his boss (although he is given good references), and goes back to England. His last line shows how oblivious he is of the moral weakness of his character: "Don't know of any good jobs going, do you?"

Themes and Meanings

The social criticism leveled at the British influence in India, both in terms of the white man's attitude toward the Indian and in terms of British corruption of the educated Indians, is clear in this story. The native who is seriously injured by the drunken accident and who is reported close to death remains anonymous and in the background. There is no real concern for him as a human being; rather, he is merely a nuisance, the cause of the Englishman Adams' being in trouble. The only real issue at hand seems to be who is going to get paid off to get Adams off the hook.

The story paints a thoroughly distasteful picture of prejudice and indifference so deeply seated that those guilty of it are completely unaware. It is not that the central character, Adams, is a particularly bad man, although there is little to like about him, but rather that he at no time sees his responsibility; his only concern is to get things fixed. If he is the central figure of oblivious-ness to his own prejudice and thus the central ironic voice of the story, then his Indian counterpart is the lawyer Shankran who, even as he bribes and threatens others to win his cases, accuses his countrymen of being corrupt, ironically, for accepting the very bribes that he offers. The other corrupt fig-ure who spouts talk of brotherhood and democracy, even as he tries to extort money from Adams under the guise of giving it to the injured man's family, is Krishnaswami, who carries a card identifying himself as the holder of an Ox-ford bachelor of arts. The company lawyer, Menon, also parades his Oxford degree and what Adams calls his BBC accent as a badge of superiority to his fellow countrymen.

Characteristic of the story is the word-of-mouth network among the natives (what Krishnaswami calls "systems of communications" unknown to the Europeans) that makes it seem as though everyone is watching the unfolding of a corrupt series of events without surprise but only with a sense of inevitability. Everyone is an impostor here, from Krishnaswami, who pre-tends he is the son of a trade commissioner, to Shankran, who pretends he is "straight," to Adams himself, who poses as a "good bloke" who only had a bit of a smash that has made things somewhat messy but requires simply some "fixing" to make it all right. Money is the oil to smooth over whatever problems the "bit of a smash" has caused. The reader comes away from the story with a clearer understanding of the imperialist attitude that doomed British control in India.

Style and Technique

The single most significant aspect of the style and technique of "A Bit of a Smash in Madras" is the fact that it is told solely in the first-person voice by Adams in a sort of extended dramatic monologue. Yet, even though the story is presented as if it were told to someone orally, rather than written down, the listener is never really defined or directly referred to. This technique of allowing the central figure, a character who is oblivious to his moral culpabil-ity, to tell the story, is a typical device to serve the purpose of social satire and criticism. It is obvious that the issue of slavery is all the more horrifying in Mark Twain's *The Adventures of Huckleberry Finn* (1884) because it is so easily accepted by everyone in the novel, even Huck himself. Such a tech-nique of allowing a morally oblivious character to tell his own story is often used as an effective means to allow the reader to make the moral judgment that the narrator himself cannot make.

The voice of Adams, revealing as it does his values and his attitude toward the Indians (even though he himself sees nothing extraordinary about it), is sufficient to condemn him in the eyes of the reader. His slang and idiom reveal him to be middle-class in the caste system that makes up British society, a fact he reveals further by his scorn for those Indians who have been to Oxford or who at least affect such Oxfordian airs. Adams respects only the lawyer Shankran, but only for his ability to "fix things" and get people off the hook by his political pull and bribery.

The tone of the narrator convinces the reader that corruption and prejudice are so integral to British life in India that no one in the story questions it. It simply is the way things are. At the conclusion, when Adams asks his listener if he knows of any "good jobs going," there is no reply. To the reader, who has been a close listener to the voice of prejudice, arrogance, and indifference, the very offhandedness of the question is the final repulsive indication of Adams' moral obtuseness.

Charles E. May

BITTER HONEYMOON

Author: Alberto Moravia (Alberto Pincherle, 1907-   )
Type of plot: Psychological symbolism
Time of plot: An August in the early 1950's
Locale: Anacapri, Italy
First published: "Luna di miele, sole di fiele," 1952 (English translation, 1956)

> *Principal characters:*
> GIACOMO, the bridegroom
> SIMONA, his wife, a member of the Communist Party
> LIVIO, a work associate of Simona, also a Communist

The Story

Giacomo found the first night of his honeymoon unsatisfactory. His wife had complained that she was tired and still suffering from the effects of the boat trip to Capri and had put him off. Now, on this second day of their marriage, she is as much a virgin as she was before. The thought of his failure to accomplish this prime marital responsibility preys on Giacomo's mind, as he and his wife, Simona, are walking along a path winding through a field on the heights of Anacapri. He looks around at this place that he has selected for his honeymoon with a jaundiced eye. Several months before, when he was here last, the air was clear and the fields were fresh with flowers; now the weather is sultry and oppressive, the fields have turned to dust. His wife does not like Anacapri either.

He walks several paces behind her, reflecting on their relationship, a love match "based rather on the will to love than on genuine feeling." Giacomo, however, is convinced that his wife views him with physical repulsion and that she regrets being married. He would like to take possession of her with one, single, piercing glance, a technique that has served him well with other women, but he realizes his chances are not good. He tries to figure out what he had found in her that was so physically attractive. Her legs are long and skinny, and chaste, shiny, and cold; her breasts droop and seem like extraneous and burdensome weights.

When she complains that she is being made to walk ahead, Giacomo goes on ahead, brushing her breast with his elbow as he walks past her "to test his own desire." The path winds around the summit of Monte Solaro; it goes through stretches of vineyards before descending sharply toward the sea. His wife complains, "Have we far to go? It's so hot . . . I wish we could go home." Giacomo promises that soon they will have a swim and, to pass the time, he gets her to recite some poetry. She chooses the third canto from Dante's *Inferno*. They pass a villa that once belonged to Axle Munthe, a very fashionable doctor practicing in Rome at the turn of the century. Giacomo tells his wife a story about one of Munthe's famous treatments. A woman came to him with all sorts of imaginary ailments. Munthe responded by telling her to look out the window; when her back was turned, he gave her a swift kick in the rear. Simona remarks that that is the way she should be treated because she is slightly crazy for having acted the way she did last night. She says that she was neither tired nor seasick, but simply afraid, "afraid of the whole idea." She allows that she will have to grow accustomed to the idea, and remarks, "Tonight I'll be yours."

The promise is insufficient to cure Giacomo's doubts about her and about his own virility. He decides that her aloofness has something to do with her political beliefs. She is a Communist, while he is "too much of an individualist." In fact, he has no interest in politics whatsoever, and the only thing that bothers him is "the fact that his wife did have such an interest." He taunts her by saying that if the Communists ever came to power, she would inform against him. She tells him not to worry about something that does not exist. The fact that she did not categorically deny his charge confirms Giacomo's suspicions and makes him angry. He continues to blame her for the way he feels.

They continue their walk, now going down the slope toward the water. Giacomo watches her run ahead of him and wonders what could be the importance of a political party when compared to the act of love. "And he was sure that in the moment he possessed Simona he would drive out of her every allegiance except that of love for him." Nevertheless, his jealousy of the Party continues. They reach a small inlet, but their continued togetherness is prevented by the presence of one of Simona's young Communist Party associates, Livio, to whom Giacomo takes an instant dislike. Giacomo cannot tolerate the nonchalant way Livio and his wife talk with each other. It is not so much what they say, mostly small talk about various Party workers and vacations, but the note of complicity with which it is said, the "tone of voice of two monks or two nuns meeting one another." He senses that Simona will escape him through her Party connections, but he does not want to show his annoyance and explains his scowl to her as a result of the heat.

The two honeymooners soon go off toward the shelter of some rocks to change their clothes for a swim. The sight of Simona's naked body prompts him to suggest that they make love "right here and now," but she puts him off, again promising that tonight things will be different. They put on their swimming suits and go back to the basin to take a swim. Livio is still there, now sunning himself. Livio springs into action, suggesting that Simona race him over to a distant rock. They dive into the water and swim off. Giacomo does the same, but he is no match for their athleticism; as he struggles out of the water near a rock on which they are sitting, Livio suggests that they race back. Giacomo tries to restrain his anger as he follows them.

When all three are together again, Simona serves lunch, which she shares with Livio. The conversation about Party associations continues. Although Livio's observations are commonplace, Giacomo notices that his wife seems to like them. After they have eaten, Simona decides to take a sunbath, but she refuses to allow Livio to rest his head on her lap. Now Giacomo senses that she is beginning to pay some attention to him, however, and his spirits soar. Once more he believes that there is "a possibility of love between them." At his suggestion, she accompanies him on a stroll among the rocks. They go to a more private beach to sunbathe and she allows him to rest his head on her lap. He sleeps for about an hour. When he wakes up, the sky is dark and they have to hurry back to their villa before the rain starts. Livio, in the meantime, has gone.

Before they arrive home, it starts to thunder. Simona confesses that lightning scares her to death. She runs on ahead, feeling safe only when she is inside and the door is shut. She immediately goes to the bedroom. He delays joining her, drinking a glass of white wine before he enters the bedroom. Now he goes to his wife, removes her dressing gown, and orders her into bed. He then takes off his own clothes and lies down next to her. He tries to arouse her with soft caresses, but these produce a strong desire to possess her, which he impulsively tries to do. His vigorous approach prompts a strong refusal on her part. He tries to prevail by force, but she fends him off. Finally, after a somewhat prolonged tussle, he loses his patience and gets up. He goes to the bathroom, where he purposely cuts his finger with a razor blade. Returning to the bedroom, he smears some blood from his wound on the sheets and announces to her that she is no longer a virgin. He shows her the bloodstained linen as evidence. She seems unsure, but when she sees his cut finger, she knows he is lying.

Giacomo goes into a rage. You will be a virgin forever, he shouts. He accuses her of always being hostile, of being closer to Livio than to him; he repeats that, if the Party came to power, she would inform on him. These charges reduce her to tears; she sobs that she would rather die than inform on him. Still distraught, she gets up from the bed and goes over to the window. As she looks outside, the sky is suddenly illuminated with a flash of lightning, followed by the metallic-sounding crash of the thunderbolt. Simona returns to the bed, frightened, and throws herself into her husband's arms. While she is still weeping, he has sex with her. He feels his accomplishment is somehow comparable to the power of the sun. Later, though, he decides that nothing really was settled, but he is satisfied that she had said she would kill herself for him. That will do for the time being.

Themes and Meanings

Giacomo's relationship with his wife is shaped by his sense of what is proper. He believes that love, especially marital love, is above all an act of submission which begins with his wife letting him deflower her on his wedding night. The prescribed copulation has not been accomplished, and Giacomo is extremely bitter. The feelings of his wife matter little, whether she was tired, or seasick, or anxious, or terrified. Giacomo, brooding on the consequences of his failure, fears that his whole marriage was a mistake. To get even for this insult to his masculine pride, he begins to badger his wife, accusing her of not caring about him, taking her to task for her political beliefs which he says could lead to his betrayal.

Giacomo's sexuality cannot be separated from his ingrained belief that sex is an instrument of male domination over women, a device for the achievement of total possession. A wife is there for constant reassurance that the husband is the only person who matters. Livio is therefore immediately seen as a threat. Livio is part of his wife's life to which Giacomo has not, and probably will not, be able to gain entrance. The shoptalk of Simona and Livio appears conspiratorial and sinister. Giacomo's resentment of Livio is increased because Livio is also a symbol of the very virility that Giacomo apparently lacks. Giacomo sees Livio as "a bronze statue on a stone pedestal" and observes his "trunks pulled tightly over his voluminous pubis and all the muscles of his body standing out." These thoughts continue to plague him. Livio, he decides, is "the sort of a fellow that goes in for purposeful tanning, and then wanders about showing it off, wearing skimpy tights designed to exhibit his virility as well." Livio is a worse menace because he comes from the working class, while Giacomo is bourgeois. Giacomo, preoccupied with Livio, worries that his wife will renege on her promise to give herself to him.

When the moment of truth finally comes, Giacomo's wife does refuse to go through with it. This prompts Giacomo to stain the wedding sheets with his own blood. If he cannot have the reality, he will at least have the appearance of reality. His wife refuses to cooperate in his subterfuge. Thanks to the timely intervention of the night storm, she allows herself to be "penetrated." In the aftermath of his conquest, Giacomo glories in his accomplishment, with all the self-righteousness of a wife beater—which, in a sense, he is.

Style and Technique

As in many of his other stories, Moravia is concerned here with the twisted values of the Italian bourgeoisie. Giacomo, despite his pretensions to individualism, is a prisoner of his own class and a prisoner of his conception of the lower classes, to which he feels superior. The bloody sheet incident shows his determination to convince his wife that a ritual defloration has been accomplished, but it also shows that Giacomo is little different from a primitive peasant who hangs such evidence on the balcony the next morning to show off for the villagers.

Moravia tells the story, in his lean and sparse style, from the standpoint of Giacomo. In doing so, he more effectively reveals the devastation which Giacomo visits on his wife. Through his eyes, the reader sees Simona's anxiety turn into guilt and her guilt into doubt of her own sanity and thoughts of suicide. The reader observes her attempting to escape, through petulance, by conversation with Livio, and with physical resistance. All are unsuccessful. Moravia uses Giacomo to show the vapidity of the Italian middle class, especially in its tendency to view people as property. Giacomo's alienation with his wife is presented as a kind of disease that probably will never be healed.

Part of the problem lies in man's inability to establish a proper relationship with the natural world. In "Bitter Honeymoon," this failure is symbolically rendered in Moravia's descriptions of nature, his use of climate to establish mood, his depiction of natural surroundings to reflect the characters' attitudes: "the odours of meadows and sea had given way to those of scorched stone and dried dung." The relationship of the story's characters to nature is most effectively dramatized in the account of the storm, which links fear and sexuality. The thunderstorm becomes a *deus ex machina*, but the release it produces is as transitory as the tempest itself; man is linked to nature, but forever estranged.

Wm. Laird Kleine-Ahlbrandt

BLACAMÁN THE GOOD, VENDOR OF MIRACLES

Author: Gabriel García Márquez (1928-   )
Type of plot: Picaresque fantasy
Time of plot: Mid-twentieth century
Locale: The Caribbean coast of Colombia
First published: "Blacamán el bueno vendedor de milagros," 1972 (English translation, 1984)

Principal characters:
BLACAMÁN THE BAD, a sadistic huckster
BLACAMÁN THE GOOD, the narrator and disciple of Blacamán the Bad

The Story

Blacamán the Good relates how he came to know and work for Blacamán the Bad, an itinerant confidence man who, dressed in flamboyant and preposterous garb, would sell all manner of things to the unsuspecting villagers in the north Colombian province of La Guajira. In the first scene the narrator describes in grotesque detail how Blacamán the Bad feigns a poisonous snakebite in order to sell a supposedly effective antidote. The curative illusion is so convincing that, in addition to selling out his entire stock to the naïve townspeople, Blacamán the Bad manages to deceive the admiral of the United States naval fleet, anchored offshore, into purchasing the elixir as well. Most noteworthy in this first encounter with the charlatan is his incessant, eerie laugh and his self-serving, demagogic rhetoric.

Blacamán the Bad offers to adopt Blacamán the Good as his protégé, ostensibly because of "the foolish look on my face." After a flurry of wisecracks designed to impress his new master, Blacamán the Good confesses in earnest that his desire in life is to become a fortune-teller. At first, because he is an utter failure at knowing the present, much less the future, and because the two Blacamáns must flee the navy's attempts at revenge for the credulous admiral's death, they undergo considerable hardship. Later, for his role in their travails, Blacamán the Good is subjected to various forms of mental and physical torture. When Blacamán the Bad taunts the starving victim with a dead rabbit, however, Blacamán the Good loses his temper and throws the animal against a wall. To his surprise, the cadaver regains life and walks back through the air to the budding magus.

From this point on, Blacamán the Good, a real wizard rather than the sham his master was, has nothing but good fortune. He sets out on his own and plays to overflow crowds all along the coast. He becomes a successful entrepreneur, with a chain of shops that sell curios and souvenirs designed to foster his own legend. He owns a chauffer-driven car, silk shirts, topaz teeth, and lotions imported from the Orient. At the peak of his glory he declares,

"What I am is an artist." When Blacamán the Bad finally reappears, pathetic and decrepit, Blacamán the Good refuses to employ his powers to save him from his own venomous potion. Instead, he takes revenge on his former master by burying him in his own carnival trunk and resuscitating him periodically so the old sadist can suffer for as long as the miracle worker lives: that is, forever.

Themes and Meanings

Although this fable evokes several themes of no little import, among which figure death, solitude, memory, hunger, imperialism, and revenge, none falls outside the framework or escapes the subsuming power of the motif of deception. The story ultimately is about the illusion it manifests itself to be. As a self-proclaimed artist, and in contrast to the angelically pure figure of the artist García Márquez portrayed in "La prodigiosa tarde de Baltazar" ("Baltazar's Marvellous Afternoon"), Blacamán represents the dark or demonic side of artistic creation. He is a miniature version of Melquíades, the Gypsy sage who foreordains the fate of the Buendía clan in *Cien años de soledad* (1967; *One Hundred Years of Solitude*, 1970), the masterpiece generally recognized as most responsible for García Márquez' receiving the Nobel Prize for Literature in 1982. The only thing "good" about the character so named (and naming, or rather misnaming, is an important component in elaborating a fiction)—what distinguishes him from his mentor and antagonistic namesake—is his self-revelation as a creator of simulacra. In other respects, he is every bit as rancorous, hypocritical, and sadistic as Blacamán the Bad. There is a point, in fact, where they undergo a peripeteia and reverse roles by repeating each other's gestures in only slightly altered form. Whereas the Bad laughs ceaselessly at the outset, it is the Good who enjoys the last laugh in the end. The suffering inflicted on the Good in the early going is reflected in the eternal anguish to which the Bad is ultimately condemned, and the claims of philanthropic motives amid real putrefaction of the one are emphatically reiterated in the other. "Blacamán the Good, Vendor of Miracles" is an imaginative and morbid reflection on the falsification inherent in baroque art in general and writing in particular.

The chief deception perpetrated in the story is on the reader, represented by the defunct American admiral who perishes for credulously "swallowing" the illusion whole. The reader is tempted to do the same because Blacamán, who introduces himself as "the Good" and recounts numerous hoaxes carried out by his supposedly more perverse counterpart, sets the reader up, so to speak, to be favorably disposed toward the accusing voice. Whereas Blacamán the Bad's antics are termed "incredible," Blacamán the Good claims that his tale "has nothing to do with invention." Once the reader's trust is gained, the narrator proceeds to incorporate truly unbelievable elements (he claims to remember things that happened more than a century ago as if they were last Sunday and eventually reveals himself as everlasting, for example) with cunning casualness. Once the reader realizes the essential continuity between the two Blacamáns (or that they are merely aspects of the same dissimulating entity), it becomes plain that all the preceding has the ontological status of a mirage. If the story is disingenuous, however, its telling is undeniably authentic. Therein lies the truth value of this adroit narrative sleight of hand.

The figure of Blacamán harkens back to the Spanish picaro, a young rogue who portrayed himself as living on the margins of society, avoiding conventional work, and postponing starvation by serving a series of masters. The picaresque novel, whose prototype is the anonymous autobiographical narrative *Lazarillo de Tormes* (1553), placed a concave mirror before the nether strata of a rapidly changing society in the Spanish Renaissance and Baroque periods. The results were often shocking exposés of conditions and practices, which the picaro condemned and, quite significantly, emulated. In the graphic depiction of a grotesque reality, García Márquez is remarkably faithful to the picaresque tradition, but there is more. Blacamán the Good charges the United States Navy with the wanton annihilation of natives, blacks, Chinese, and Hindus in seeking retribution for the death of their leader. Yet his parting gesture is an act of vengeance perhaps more severe in its cruelty. American military and cultural hegemony is one of the author's most ardently repeated themes—in *El otoño del patriarca* (1975; *The Autumn of the Patriarch*, 1975) the despotic leader has to sell the Caribbean Sea to the Americans in order to dissolve the nation's onerous foreign debt. In an act of admirable artistic integrity, however, García Márquez shows that no one, not even a surrogate author such as Blacamán the Good, is above reproach.

Style and Technique

As is the case with master and slave, Blacamán the Good and Blacamán the Bad are doubles. They are contrary facets, ultimately undistinguishable, of the same malicious process or phenomenon ("malicia" in Spanish means, among other things, "duplicity"): art. Their lack of a discrete personal identity is reinforced technically in the story by the use of a "floating" point of view. The voice of Blacamán the Bad is embedded in the narration of Blacamán the Good, with no quotation marks to set them apart, as in the following passage:

> From the first Sunday I saw him he reminded me of a bullring mule, . . . except that at that time he wasn't trying to sell any of that Indian mess but was asking someone to bring him a real snake so that he could demonstrate on his own flesh an antidote he had invented, *the only infallible one, ladies and gentlemen, for the bites of serpents, tarantulas, and centipedes plus all manner of poisonous mammals* [italics, to signify the voice of Blacamán the Bad, not in the original].

There is thus not one "point" from which the narration originates but a field in which it circulates. Blacamán the Bad's voice is within Blacamán the Good's, just as the opportunism and rancor of the one informs the other. In addition, the hyperbolic rhetoric of the sideshow barker, a style that runs through all of "Los funerales de la Mamá Grande" ("Big Mama's Funeral") and which Blacamán the Good adopts when he assumes the mantle of vendor of miracles, sustains the tension between appearance and reality.

The last device worth noting is the multiple use of memory. Memory, of course, is the key to all narration of events in the past. Special attention is drawn to the act of remembering in the story when the narrator claims to recall a scene from more than a century previous as clearly as if it had happened the week before. As the anecdote develops, memory becomes essential to the characters' survival, for when they are alone and starving, they use nostalgia as a means of fooling death. As a businessman, Blacamán the Good panders to the tourists' memories ("souvenirs" in French). Moreover, the desired effect of the narrator's vengeful *coup* depends on memory, for Blacamán the Bad's sentence is to live interred forever and to remember why. It is, finally, Blacamán the Good's memory of his evil double's discomfiting recollections that makes his revenge so sweet.

Jonathan Tittler

THE BLACK CAT

Author: Edgar Allan Poe (1809-1849)
Type of plot: Psychological realism
Time of plot: Mid-nineteenth century
Locale: An unnamed American city
First published: 1843

> *Principal characters:*
> THE NARRATOR, an educated man and animal lover turned
> alcoholic, ailurophobe, and murderer
> THE NARRATOR'S WIFE, sensitive and silent-suffering
> PLUTO, the husband's and wife's first pet black cat
> A SECOND BLACK CAT, one-eyed, which is adopted by the
> couple

The Story

Told in the first person by an unreliable narrator (a term designating one who either consciously or unconsciously distorts the truth), the story can be seen to be divided into two parts, each of which builds toward a climactic physical catastrophe: in the first part, the narrator's mutilation and later murder of a favorite pet, as well as a fire that destroys all he and his wife own; in the second part, the narrator's ax murder of his wife, followed by his arrest and death sentence.

Opening with both suspense and mystery in his revelation that he wants to "unburden" his soul because he will die the next day, the narrator gives details (with unwitting ironic ramifications) of his early love for animals and marriage to a woman of the same sentiments, who presents him with many pets. Among these is his favorite, a black cat, whose name, Pluto (Greek god of the underworld), foreshadows the narrator's descent into the murky regions of alcoholism, self-deception, and violence.

When he does later succumb to alcoholism, the narrator shortly thereafter begins maltreating his wife and pets, which gives a double meaning to his term for drinking, "Fiend Intemperance," referring not only to alcohol abuse but also to intemperate transgression of rational thought and behavior. Eventually the narrator maltreats "even Pluto" (which implies that the cat was valued more than his wife, whom he has maltreated earlier). One night, presumably out of frustration, he seizes the cat, which has been avoiding him. When it bites him, the narrator says he became "possessed" by a "demon" and with his pocket knife cut out one of the cat's eyes. At first grieved and then irritated by the consequences of his action, the narrator says that he was then "overthrown" by "the spirit of PERVERSENESS" (author's capitalization), Poe's definition of which anticipates by a half century psychologist Sigmund Freud's concepts of the id (unconscious desires to do all things, even wrongs, for pleasure's sake) and the death wish (the impulse within all for self-destruction). The "spirit of PERVERSENESS" causes the narrator, even while weeping, to hang Pluto in a neighboring garden. That night a fire destroys his house and all his worldly wealth, and the next day the narrator discovers on the only wall that remains standing the raised gigantic image on its surface of a hanged cat.

His alcoholism continuing, the narrator one night at a disreputable tavern discovers another black cat, which he befriends and adopts (by implication making a substitution out of guilt and remorse), as does his wife. For this double (a frequent motif in Poe's works), however, the narrator rapidly develops a loathing. First, it has only one eye, which reminds him of his crimes against Pluto. Second, it is too friendly—an ironic inversion of the common complaint that cats are too aloof, as the narrator complained about Pluto. Third, it has a white patch on its breast that to the guilty narrator's imagination looks more and more like a gallows, which points both backward to his hanging of Pluto and, unknown to him, forward to his hanging for the murder of his wife.

One day, with his wife on an errand into the cellar of their decrepit old house, the narrator, infuriated when he is almost tripped on the stairs by the cat, starts to kill it with an ax, is stopped by his wife, and then instead kills her with the ax. With insane calmness and ratiocination, the narrator concocts and implements a plan of concealing the corpse in a cellar wall. Meanwhile, the cat, which has tormented his dreams, has vanished, allowing him to sleep—despite his wife's murder. Inquiries are made about his missing wife, however, and on the fourth day after the murder the police come for a thorough search. As they are about to leave the cellar, the narrator, apparently with taunting bravado but really with unconscious guilt that seeks to delay them so he may be arrested and punished, remarks to them on the solidity of the house's walls, rapping with a cane the very spot of the concealed tomb. When a horrible scream is emitted from the wall, the police break down the bricks, discover the corpse with the black cat howling on its head, and arrest the criminal. Rationalizing to the end, the narrator blames the cat for his misdeeds and capture: "the hideous beast whose craft had seduced me into murder, and whose informing voice had consigned me to the hangman."

Themes and Meanings

The story has many themes, most of them relating to human psychology and several in the form of contraries: reason versus the irrational; human being versus animal; self-knowledge versus self-deception; sanity versus madness; love versus hate; good versus evil; the power of obsession and guilt; and the sources or motives of crime. As in many of his works, Poe is interested in the borderline between opposites and how it may be crossed.

Despite the narrator's explicit claim of sanity in the story's first paragraph, he immediately shows himself self-deceived by terming his story "a series of mere household events." Further, by the end of the first paragraph the narrator has circled to a contradictory position by expressing his hope for a calmer, more logical, and "less excitable" mind than his own to make sense of the narrative. A favorite adjective of his for pets, "sagacious," which he uses early in the story for both dogs and his cat Pluto, thus ironically indicates the wisdom he himself needs both to see life clearly and not to give in to the irrationality of drinking or violent behavior. What should distinguish man from beast—this is, the faculty of reason—the narrator too frequently abandons, a weakness expressed in the animal metaphor of his "rabid desire to say something easily" to the police searchers.

His early reference to admiring the "unselfish and self-sacrificing love" of animals reveals the narrator's blindness; ironically, his scornful words, "the paltry friendship and gossamer fidelity of mere *Man*" (author's italics), apply to himself. The narrator later reveals that his dipsomania is self-indulgent and self-loving, because he "grew . . . regardless of the feelings of others" and dimly perceived that he had lost the "humanity of feeling" (compassion) that his wife retained.

Sheer emphasis or proportion in the story—the great number of words he spends on the cats contrasted with the brevity of his remarks about the maltreatment and murder of his wife—indicates the deficiency in both the narrator's insight and his feelings. He cannot see that guilt causes him to forestall mentioning his greatest misdeed until the story's end, while his feeling for his wife was too weak to prevent his murdering her. The narrator cannot see that his killing her is not a mere deflection from his murderous purpose, but its true aim, whose motives are laid down in the sixth, sixteenth, eighteenth, and twenty-second paragraphs of the story. Mutely representing goodness, she has been a constant irritant to him, one upon whom he can vent all of his pent-up feelings in one blow.

Style and Technique

Besides the narrator's ironic self-contradiction or unwitting irony, Poe's other most pervasive technique in the story is symbolism. Symbols of perception include the narrator's particular mutilation of Pluto, for like his pet the narrator is half-blind, not only in the past, in the story he relates, but in the present, when he still cannot understand what it all means. In the past he was half-blinded by drink, and in both the past and present by guilt, rationalizing, or unwillingness to see unpleasant things. For example, though he claims to have been "half stupefied" when he first became aware of the second black cat, only a consuming if unacknowledged sense of guilt can explain his asserted failure to notice that it was one-eyed until after it was home, despite his prior continued petting of it in the tavern and detailed notice of its markings. He wanted an exact substitute, with the same injury, in order to punish himself. The words "half," "equivocal," and "blindly," which the narrator applies to himself at various times, reveal his defective vision.

Symbols of rationality and its defeat can be found in the narrator's horrible act of burying the ax in his wife's "brain"—a word which emphasizes thinking more than the word "skull" would. In this act, the narrator has in effect extinguished his own rationality, as well as its chief human representative in his sphere. Further, when the brick wall is broken down, the black cat is found perched on the corpse's head, one more indication of the narrator's guilt (recalling the site of the wound) and its cause.

Among the symbols of "humanity of feeling" is the second cat's marking. It has, in the narrator's phrasing, "a large, although indefinite splotch of white, covering nearly the whole region of the breast." Moreover, the cat has, the narrator says, a habit of "fastening its long claws in my dress" to "clamber, in this manner, to my breast." Finally, the cat will not let him sleep; he awakens with it on his chest: "its vast weight [was] . . . incumbent on my *heart!*" (Poe's italics). The repeated references to "bosom," "breast," and especially "heart" point to the narrator's fatal deficiency of love and compassion.

Finally, several strands of symbols help express the conflict between good and evil. The very scene of the crime, a cellar, recalls the suggestive name of the narrator's first black cat and represents the narrator's descent into the darkness of irrationality, the forces of the unconscious mind, and evil. Comparable imagery of spirited darkness can be found in the narrator's recollection that, prior to the murder, "the darkest and most evil thoughts" had become habitual to him; in like manner, he refers to his wife's murder as "my dark deed." The interrelation between consciousness and conscience is suggested by the narrator's keeping his wife's corpse in this dark underworld, after walling her off—analogues of psychological repression.

Finally, the cat's howl in response to the narrator's rapping of the wall is described in symbolic terms: It begins as a muffled cry, "like the sobbing of a child," but quickly swells into a "continuous scream . . . such as might have arisen only out of hell, conjointly from the throats of the damned in their agony and of the demons that exult in the damnation." In capsule form, this utterance describes the whole of the narrator's life—and death.

Norman Prinsky

THE BLACK PRINCE

Author: Shirley Ann Grau (1929-   )
Type of plot: Melodramatic romance
Time of plot: Probably the mid-twentieth century
Locale: The American South
First published: 1953

> *Principal characters:*
> STANLEY ALBERT THOMPSON, the Black Prince of the story, a
> mysterious, folklorish hero with supernatural powers
> ALBERTA LACEY, a young black girl loved by Stanley Albert
> MAGGIE MARY EVANS, a young black girl who loves Stanley
> Albert
> WILLIE, a black man who owns a bar; he loves Alberta and
> hates Stanley Albert

The Story

The emotions are so simple, primitive, and stark in this story that one realizes immediately that this tale is Shirley Ann Grau's attempt to create a legendary fantasy. The opening situates the story not only in the poorest part of the smallest and worst county in the state but also in a fairy-tale realm where the cows are wild and unmilked and the winters are short and cold. The characters, drawn simply and directly, also suggest the two-dimensional personages of a folktale romance. Alberta first appears walking down a country road proclaiming her superiority to the birds, and Stanley Albert Thompson appears out of nowhere, calling to her like some rare bird himself, claiming that he came straight out of the morning and that he saw her name in the fire.

Stanley Albert is the central figure in the story; his designation as the Black Prince, coupled with the quotation from Isaiah at the beginning of the story—"How art thou fallen from heaven, O Lucifer, son of the morning"—suggests that he is the Prince of Darkness. He is not so much an embodiment of pure evil, however, as he is the personification of the rebel, the outcast, the mysterious, powerful figure who arrives out of nowhere. As soon as he arrives in the small community (which does not even have a name on the map), he establishes his superiority by winning fights at the central gathering place, Willie's Bar. In these fights, in which razors, bottles, and knives are used, Stanley Albert gets a reputation that earns for him the fear and hatred of the men and the admiration and love of the women.

Stanley Albert's supernatural aura is established by his inexhaustible supply of silver coins—coins that he can shuffle through the air the way that other men shuffle cards and that never seem to run out, although Stanley

Albert apparently does no work to earn the money. Primarily what Stanley Albert does is stir things up. Because the men are afraid to fight him, they begin to fight one another and thus rekindle a feud that has lain dormant for several years. All this action as a result of Stanley Albert's arrival seems quite aimless, for the Black Prince has no ostensible purpose either in being in the small crossroads or in creating such turbulent activity. The only event toward which the story seems to aim is Stanley Albert's finally gaining the girl for whom he has been waiting nearly all winter—the girl he met in the beginning of the story, Alberta.

Stanley Albert's wooing of Alberta (whose similarity of name is surely not coincidental) primarily consists of singing songs to her in which he promises to give her an apron full of gold if she will only let her hair hang low. Indeed, although he does not give her gold, he manifests his supernatural power by picking off gobs of wax from the candles in his house and flipping them to Alberta, making them turn into silver coins as they flash through the air. Their courtship is marked by obsessive passion and fraught with tension as the feud rages about them and as Willie (who loves Alberta) and Maggie Mary (who loves Stanley Albert) are filled with jealousy.

The story reaches its supernaturally tinged climax when Willie uses several silver coins that he has received from Stanley Albert to make four silver bullets, with which he shoots the Black Prince. Stanley Albert and Alberta disappear, to become legendary figures who continue to haunt the area, becoming the cause of evil acts and general bad luck, such as Willie's death and weevils getting in the cotton. Children still hear the jingle of silver in Stanley Albert's pocket and the women whisper together about the legendary couple whenever there is a miscarriage or a stillbirth.

Themes and Meanings

"The Black Prince," published originally under the title "The Sound of Silver," was Shirley Ann Grau's first story to be published in a professional literary journal. When the collection of stories *The Black Prince and Other Stories* appeared in 1955, it made quite an impression on both critics and the general public, selling out its first printing in two weeks. The title story of the collection, as is typical of many of Grau's short stories, hovers uneasily between mythic legend and simplistic melodrama. Thus, it is not easy to determine whether it is a serious experiment with archetypes of universal primitive experience, or whether it is simply a commercial exploitation of stereotypes of the American black experience. The story certainly depends on enough clichés about black life to be uncomfortable reading for readers in a post–civil rights era. The black characters in the story are driven by no other emotions than sexual desire and physical violence. The men drink, cut off ears with razors, and pursue women. The women get pregnant, have abortions, and continue to pursue the men.

Stanley Albert Thompson seems to embody the classic black male wish fulfillment, at least as seen from a white point of view. Although he never works, he has enough money to buy fancy clothes, sport an expensive watch and ring, drink, and attract women. He has a mysterious sexual aura that immediately intimidates and alienates the men, even as it acts as an aphrodisiac for the women. Regardless of the title's suggestion that he is Lucifer, he is less a demoniac figure than he is the embodiment of a man who, in the vernacular, is a "real devil."

Still, although the story makes use of unpalatable stereotypes about black life and values, it seems probable that Grau intended it to be a classically simple exploration of the most primitive human emotions, a kind of legendary folktale that embodies archetypes of love and lust, hate and violence. In some respects, the story is similar to the work of such Southern women writers as Flannery O'Connor, Carson McCullers, and Eudora Welty, for it takes place less in a real world and time than in a season of dreams in which the ordinary is transformed into the mysterious and mythical. Yet this similarity is less real than apparent.

One convinced of the seriousness and value of the story might argue that its theme focuses on elemental human emotions as basic as the song "Frankie and Johnnie," but as old as the nature of story itself. For those somewhat more skeptical, the story can be seen as simply an exploitation of the clichés of black life that tells nothing valuable about either the sociology of the black experience or the psychology of love and hate.

Style and Technique

Given the folktale plot of the story, the stylized nature of its technique seems inevitable. If the events seem somewhat melodramatic and simplistic, then the language of the story is that which attempts to dignify it, for Grau tries to give the story the simple dignity of the folklore ballad or classic tale. The language is controlled and balanced; it strives to create the illusion of an oral tale even though it has the formality of a written story. In style, as well as in character and plot, the story is reminiscent of such authors as McCullers and Welty, but only as a facile imitation of writers whose stories are definitely superior in both their subtlety of theme and delicacy of tone.

Shirley Ann Grau appeared on the American literary scene in the mid-1950's amid a flurry of predictions of great things to come. Yet such a simplistic story of black life as "The Black Prince" was much more likely to be acceptable to readers in the mid-1950's than any time since; the fascination with the music of black culture was beginning to manifest itself in the birth of rock and roll music (although mostly made acceptable by being recorded by white artists) and much of American society was guilty, in that age of innocence and white conservatism, of unself-conscious racial prejudice. These factors combined to make "The Black Prince" an easily accepted confirmation of white suspicions about black life, even as it allowed white readers the mistaken sense that they understood that life.

Charles E. May

BLACK TICKETS

Author: Jayne Anne Phillips (1952-   )
Type of plot: Psychological realism
Time of plot: The 1970's
Locale: A slummy neighborhood of Philadelphia and the city jail
First published: 1979

> *Principal characters:*
> THE NARRATOR, the protagonist, a drug dealer
> JAMAICA DELILA, his girlfriend and drug partner
> RAYMOND, their other partner in the drug operation
> NEINMANN, owner of the pornography theater where they sell
>   drugs

The Story

The unnamed first-person narrator/protagonist tells this story in bits and pieces from a jail cell. The central fact of the story is his obsession with his recent girlfriend, Jamaica Delila, toward whom he has ambivalent feelings. He thinks she might have "set me up . . . to do lock-up in this cadillac of castles," and he fantasizes about beating her. Even as he imagines her falling, however, he cannot help dwelling on the way her hair spreads out and her uplifted hands glow in the light. He dwells even longer on memories of their lovemaking in the bathtub, the boy's shirts and underpants she wore, and the cartoon faces she drew on their legs with lipstick.

He also remembers her in the daytime, when, high on Benzedrine, she sold tickets at the Obelisk, a run-down pornography theater. There Jamaica entertained herself by staring at the rolls of tickets and, with an ink pen, drawing lines of tickets on her thighs. She also helped keep old Neinmann, the theater's owner, in line so that she, the narrator, and Raymond could practice their drug trade on the premises: "At first it was sideline stuff, Nembies and speed balls, a little white stuff for the joy bangers who came downtown to cop." They cut the speed with powder from the crumbling tiles of the bathroom floors and sold it to "silky Main Line debs reeling in their mommys' sports cars."

Appropriately, the three drug partners developed a close fellow-feeling for the "cinematic rodents" that overran the building. The narrator also misses "reptilian Raymond," a hunchback like Quasimodo and a self-described "nice Jewish boy, doing his bit for reverse reparations" by helping Neinmann, "that old storm trooper," save money to return to Germany. For the narrator, however, the presiding goddess of the whole operation was Jamaica: "Jamaica, you thin wonder in schoolboy clothes. I could crush them all into a burlap bag full of stones and watch them sink in a sewer named for you." The narrator's qualifications for belonging to this select group include a brief Florida jail stay for statutory rape before he came to Philadelphia.

Their Obelisk operation went smoothly for months, until Raymond decided to start selling powerful amyl nitrite, "those little extras to close down the days and promote orgasmic endings." Jamaica began using the drug herself when she and the narrator made love: As he "watched the X's come up" in her eyes, she would turn into "an electric zombie, a stiff-legged gazelle shuddering in northern catatonia." Holding his amylized lover, the narrator would have a violent urge to shake the bottled-up blackness out of her, and finally one day he succumbed. Just short of shaking her to death, however, he threw down her limp body, ran to the next room, and destroyed the supply of amyl nitrite. Raymond jumped up to pound the narrator with a nightstick, but put it away when Jamaica staggered in.

Raymond's protective gesture reveals the part he played in their three-way arrangement. The narrator was Jamaica's sexual partner, but Raymond was her big brother. Raymond slept on the living-room couch, and, whenever Jamaica had nightmares, she would get up and go sit in the room with him. He would place her legs across his lap and touch her feet to his forehead, apparently the closest they ever came to sexual contact. The trio's relationship was potentially volatile.

Jamaica seemed in particular to need a surrogate brother because her own family life was so rotten: Her mother, a West Indian, sold her and her four sisters as prostitutes when they were growing up. Little Jamaica specialized in playing a boy's role, though her mother would never let her cut off her braids. When Jamaica shears her braids over the narrator's naked body, he believes it is a message, and indeed, that day the police pick him up with sufficient evidence to send him away for years. Even worse, the police tell him that the Obelisk burned down, with Neinmann in it. The narrator suspects Jamaica of setting him up and Raymond of torching the Obelisk, though he has no proof of either. Still, waiting in jail he makes his decision: "Tomorrow I'll sing and sell you all. . . ."

Themes and Meanings

"Black Tickets" takes a look at the drug scene from inside, from the point of view of a drug dealer. Naturally, the narrator views himself and his drug partners sympathetically, even sentimentally—as human beings who have the usual emotional needs and who even form a quasi family. Naturally, too, his point of view fluctuates somewhat when he thinks his partners have stabbed him in the back. These fluctuations combine with the objective facts (insofar as the facts can be established) to set up an ironic counterpoint in the story. The counterpoint theme reveals the drug partners to be misfits in their personal relationships much as they are in society. As human beings, they are pathetic creatures, buddies of the Obelisk rats.

They are losers in society from the beginning. Raymond grew up " cracking meters" and making other "small deals," Jamaica was a child prostitute, and the narrator is coming off a bout of statutory rape. Drug dealing is merely the next step up (or down) for them. It is hard, however, to dismiss them simply as drug dealers; in one way or another, they make a play for the reader's sympathy: The narrator has the reader's ear, Jamaica has her rotten childhood, and Raymond has his hump. Except, perhaps, for the narrator, they have been dealt "black tickets" in their lives. It is also suggested that they are only part of society's general corruption: A cross section of society flocks to the Obelisk's attractions, and even "silky Main Line debs" end up "digesting the crumbling universe of Obelisk." The drug partners are as much representatives as rejects of their society.

Still, neither their personal hardships nor society's general rottenness excuses their behavior. The narrator seems as little concerned about the victims of their drugs as he is about the burnt-up Neinmann. "Black Tickets" is one of the few stories in which going to jail is a happy ending; at least there the narrator might have a chance to "learn a new career." The confused people of "Black Tickets" are not so much loving as they are addicted to one another.

Style and Technique

Surprisingly, "Black Tickets" has humor as well as pathos, the main source of humor being the first-person point of view. The narrator's style reflects his ambivalent feelings and lack of responsibility: It combines a jaunty, reminiscing tone with street talk and rich metaphors. His ability to reel off memorable phrases—probably unusual among drug dealers—suggests that he might have been a poet. Occasionally this style is overdone, however, as when the narrator describes the many varieties of blackness that flow from Jamaica or his equally numerous "sick vomits in bathrooms of restaurants, theaters, gas stations, train depots. . . ." Most "vomits" are "sick" and it seems unnecessary to specify the places, as well as a description of the "head on the bowl," the "intimate stains of countless patrons," and so forth.

Possibly these colorful details are symbolic, since the story is heavily laden with symbols that underline the sleazy lives of the characters—from the Obelisk Theater (all the world's a porno stage, so to speak) to the rats to the radiating meanings of "black tickets." By the time Jamaica's braids are mentioned, the reader might be too saturated with symbols to care. The overdone symbols, like the overdone style, show the talented young author's tendency to go to excess ("Black Tickets" is the title story of her first major collection). After reading this story, however, few people will want to rush out to buy black tickets.

Harold Branam

BLACKBERRY WINTER

Author: Robert Penn Warren (1905-   )
Type of plot: Initiation story
Time of plot: 1910
Locale: Middle Tennessee
First published: 1946

> *Principal characters:*
> SETH, a nine-year-old boy
> HIS MOTHER, a self-reliant woman
> HIS FATHER, a Southern farmer
> THE STRANGER, a sullen tramp
> DELLIE, the black family cook
> BIG JEBB, her elderly husband
> JEBB, their young son

The Story

"Blackberry Winter" describes one day in the life of a young boy on his parents' farm, but the story is told as a recollection by a grown man, thirty-five years later. Robert Penn Warren has said that the story grew out of two memories—that of being allowed to go barefoot in the summer when school is out and that of feeling betrayed when the promises of summer are forestalled by a sudden cold spell. After beginning with this nostalgic memory, Warren has said that he realized that for it to be a story something had to happen. Therefore, he introduced the mysterious stranger who seems, like the cold of "blackberry winter," to be wrong, out of place, incongruous.

Indeed, incongruity, or the child's discovery of a cold reality of which he was previously unaware, constitutes the plot line and structure of the story. It begins with the boy's astonishment that he is not allowed to go barefoot, even though it is June, because of a fierce rainstorm and the accompanying cold weather. The adult Seth examines the significance of this disruption of his expectations by relating it to the child's perception of time, which is not something that passes and has movement, but is like a climate, like something solid and permanent. The story itself is a memory in time that retains this solidity.

The stranger that appears on the farm on this particular morning is as incomprehensible to Seth as the unseasonable cold weather. First, it is strange that he should be there at all, having come out of a swamp where no one ever goes. Seth even closes his eyes, thinking that when he opens them the man will be gone, for he seems to come from nowhere and to have no reason to be there. Seth, with the self-assurance of a child, realizes, as he does about the weather, that the man does not belong, that he "ought" to be other than as he is.

The tramp is given the job of burying dead baby chicks killed by the storm, a task he performs fastidiously and with sullen resignation. The adult Seth's comment that there is nothing that looks deader than a drowned chick is the first of several images of death and incomprehensible evil that the story introduces. When Seth goes down to the creek to watch the flood with his father, he sees a dead cow come floating down the stream, bloated and looking at first like a large piece of driftwood. When the son of a poor sharecropper wonders aloud if anyone ever ate dead cow, the more immediate implications of poor crops caused by the storm are suggested, especially when an older man says that if a man lives long enough he will eat anything when the time comes.

Seth goes to the house of the family cook, Dellie, to play with her little boy, and once again is surprised by something that "ought" not to be. Dellie and her husband old Jebb have a reputation of being clean and thrifty "white folks's negroes," and Seth is surprised to see that the storm has washed trash out from under Dellie's house into the yard that she has always been proud to keep swept clean. Moreover, he cannot understand Dellie being sick and in bed, and he is shocked when she gives her son a vicious slap for making too much noise. Dellie's illness is explained to Seth by her husband as being "woman-mizry," a result of the change of life, additional realities that Seth cannot understand.

All these clashes with incongruity and the incomprehensible come to a climax when Seth returns to his house and witnesses a confrontation between his father and the tramp. After being paid a half-dollar for his half-day's work, a fair wage for 1910, the tramp utters an oath at Seth's father, who orders him off the farm. The tramp then spits at the father's feet and walks away, with Seth following him down the road. He asks the tramp where he came from and where he is going, but the only response he gets is the tramp's hurling an obscenity at him and threatening to cut his throat if he does not stop following him.

The story ends with Seth describing briefly his life since the event: the death of his father and mother, the death of Dellie, the imprisonment of little Jebb, and a meeting with old Jebb, now more than a hundred years old. The last line of the story—that he has followed the tramp all of his life—forces the reader to look back on the memory to try to determine its structure and meaning and thus understand what Seth means by this.

Themes and Meanings

"Blackberry Winter" has often been called one of the great stories in American literature. One of the reasons for its staying power is that is combines two of the most familiar themes in fiction: the rite of passage (the coming of age of a male youth) and the mysterious stranger (the encounter with inexplicable evil). The story is a classic initiation story in that it deals with the child's discovery of the possibility of disruption of his previously secure and predictable life. Blackberry winter is something Seth has never before encountered and thus seems to be a betrayal by nature itself. This atmosphere of betrayal and the irrational is the climate of time that the story reconstructs as remembered by the adult Seth. All the experiences he undergoes during this one day when he was nine are equally incongruous—the city tramp in the country, the flood during summer, the trash under Dellie's floor, her vicious slap—all are part of a mystery that old Jebb calls the "changes in life."

The central event that sticks in Seth's mind is the confrontation between the tramp and his father; the central image is the gob of spit lying between his father's boots with brass eyelits and leather thongs on one side and the sad and out-of-place broken black shoes of the tramp on the other. The boy follows the tramp all the rest of his life because he comes to an important realization—that the meaning of "a man" is not just that of his proud, gentlemanly father, but also that of the mean and bitter human being that the tramp is. It is a recognition that has been prepared for by his sympathetic identification with the poor boy, who wonders if anyone can eat drowned cow, and by his realization, in connection with Dellie's yard, that underneath the swept-clean exterior of human life lies "mizry" and the possibility of violence born out of frustration, bad luck, and the inevitable.

The proof that Seth (a persona for Robert Penn Warren) has followed the tramp all of his life is not only this story, which communicates a sympathetic understanding of human reality regardless of its frequent irrational viciousness, but perhaps all of Warren's fiction, for the artist must always follow those who, like the tramp, are victims in some way—of themselves, of society, of nature, of unreasoning reality.

Style and Technique

This is a carefully controlled story, so packed with events similar in their significance that it can truly be said to be "loaded." There is nothing superfluous to the cumulative impact of Seth's confronting incongruity and coping with how to integrate the new and mysterious into his understanding of life. Because it is told from the point of view of the adult Seth recalling a memorable day, the language of the story is that of an intelligent and thoughtful adult, one trying to understand something by means of an imaginative reconstruction; in short, it is a tale told by an artist, a miniature portrait of the artist as a young man, making a discovery about the need for sympathetic understanding of other humans that is essential for the artist.

Because the story is both a description of the boy's day and a conscious effort of the adult to understand it thirty-five years later, the reader must respond to a double perspective: the uncomprehending view of the child and the probing thoughts of the adult. Thus, although the story is told primarily as simple description and narration, it also intersperses expository philosophical passages of the man attempting to understand and explain. The very fact that the story is so firmly directed toward the classic theme and structure of the rite-of-passage initiation story and the fact that it is so loaded with obvious images of death, the unexpected, the incongruous, and the mysterious, indicate that this is an artist's story, for it is told by a writer who is well aware of the tradition of the initiation story as well as the use of conventional metaphors for death and disruption. The metaphors are handled with such naturalness and confidence, however, that they seem to exist as part of a real and tangible world, even though the reader is aware that this is a highly conventional story. Such an achievement is precisely the mark of one who has followed the tramp all of his life—that is, the true artist.

Charles E. May

THE BLANK PAGE

Author: Isak Dinesen (Baroness Karen Blixen-Finecke, 1885-1962)
Type of plot: Epiphany
Time of plot: Nineteenth century
Locale: Portugal
First published: 1957

> *Principal characters:*
> THE WRITER, who writes the story
> THE STORYTELLER, who tells the story
> THE LADY AND GENTLEMAN, who hear the story
> THE SISTERS, who keep the bridal sheets at the Convento Velho
> ROYAL PRINCESSES OF PORTUGAL, who visit the convent
> AN OLD SPINSTER, who visits the convent

The Story

There are stories and stories. Most stories are meant to entertain and up-lift the average person, who represents the vast majority of readers. "The Blank Page," however, is a unique story conferred on chosen listeners as a rare and distinct privilege. It is unique because it illustrates the loyalty of the storyteller to the true being of the story; it illustrates the storyteller's knowl-edge that when words end, silence may speak a deeper truth to one who lis-tens for it. An old storyteller, who learned the art of storytelling from her grandmother, who in turn learned it from her grandmother, tells the story to a lady and a gentleman at an ancient city gate. The writer tells the story as told by the old storyteller.

In Portugal, following an ancient tradition, whenever a princess of the royal house is married, on the morning after the wedding night the bridal sheet is displayed from a balcony by a chamberlain or a high steward, and the princess is declared to have been a virgin. The sheet is never washed or lain on again.

The sheets for the royal brides have always been provided by the Sisters of Saint Carmel at the Convento Velho. They have obtained this privilege because they grow flax and make the softest, whitest linen in the land. Their second privilege has been to have in their safekeeping the sheets from royal wedding nights. A square from the center of each sheet is cut out, framed, and decorated with a gold, coroneted plate. On it is inscribed the name of the princess whose sheet it is. The framed squares hang side by side in a row in a long gallery at the convent. In the framed canvas, people of imagination and sensibility may see signs of the zodiac, which they may use to predict the life of the married pair, or onlookers may find their own romantic ideas pictured as a rose or a sword or a heart.

Elderly princesses whose bridal sheets hang framed in the long hall come with their rich retinues on a pilgrimage to the convent. Such visits are sacred, for they are undertaken to pay homage at the altar of virginity, the acme of a virtuous life, yet they are also "secretly gay"; apparently the old princesses know some secrets that enliven their reminiscences. A very old spinster also comes. A long time ago, she had been a playmate, confidante, and maid of honor to a princess. A sister conducts her to the gallery and leaves her there by herself, respecting her wish to be alone.

The spinster is veiled in black, not unlike the storyteller herself. She nods her head, which is "skull-like," perhaps because she is very old, and she smiles and sighs in recollection as she looks at the framed sheets, remembering the omens read of her friend's life, and of the lives of other princesses, and remembering the actual events, joyful or sad, of the family and of the state, the alliances and intrigues that took place. One canvas, however, is different from all the rest, for it is blank and nameless, placed there by royal parents in full loyalty to the tradition. Such loyalty makes even the storytellers draw their veils over their faces in extreme respect.

It is in front of this spotlessly white linen more than any other that not only princesses and their old friends, but also the nuns and the mother abbess herself stand in deepest contemplation. The blank page conveys something deeper to all of them. It is not limited in meaning to a pictured page. Variously and significantly to each one who thinks upon it, the blank page becomes the revelation of a spiritual truth, an epiphany.

Themes and Meanings

A pure and ancient tradition, whenever preserved with integrity, may reveal to perceptive persons deeper truths than are ordinarily apprehended. Such a truth, a vision of truth, or an epiphany, is the revelation and the theme of "The Blank Page." Many continuing traditions intertwine and illustrate this view in this story. The tradition of storytelling itself is traced through a long lineage, back to a grandmother's grandmother and even back to the time when Scheherazade herself told a thousand and one tales. The continuing tradition and blessing of growing flax and making fine linen comes from the Holy Land, from the Jewish bride Achsah to Portugal, to the Carmelite sisters, the brides of Christ. The blessing pronounced on the Blessed Virgin, her Immaculate Conception, and the promise through Christ of spiritual salvation, continues to be a promise of spiritual salvation to the virginal sisters of the convent. The tradition of publicizing and preserving the evidence of virginity comes from olden days to within living memory, according to the storyteller.

The tradition of storytelling produces good stories. The tradition of flax growing produces good linen. The tradition of publicized morality brings about public recognition of that morality. The tradition of spiritual seeking brings about the promised salvation. By establishing the norm, traditions maintain their standards, but they also tend to stereotype and limit personal discovery.

Perceptive persons may and do see more than others beyond the preserved traditions, if they look for a special meaning for themselves: The crusader who brings back the seeds of the flax plant sees the possibility of growing flax in his homeland; the sisters' faith, stronger than the average Christian's, makes them commit themselves to the truth of their religious tradition as revealed to them. The canvases in the convent's gallery tell the standard stories of virginity and lend themselves to omen readings, which are no more than fallible predictions. Yet the blank page makes people stop before it and ponder life, true morality, or simply the truth about the unnamed princess. It may even make people look within themselves for deeper meanings.

Traditional stories with plots and character also throw some light on life and human nature. Yet the story that has no plot and no individualized characters may reveal a deeper truth. Those persons who look for a deeper meaning through their own contemplation—the lady and gentleman of the story, the old spinster who knows much about life and morality, the sisters of the convent, or the mother abbess herself—discover it in the silence beyond words. They discover it as a revealed truth, as an epiphany, upon the blank page.

Style and Technique

Isak Dinesen's primary ambition, she once said, was to invent very beautiful stories. "The Blank Page" is beautifully told, as are Dinesen's other tales, but it is different from all the others; there is no plot, and there are no individualized characters. The tone and the setting are, therefore, made the substance as well as the context within which the untold story may reveal itself upon the blank page. Both are conducive to the distinctly oral quality of Dinesen's writing.

Although there is no conventional plot, there are little stories linked into a context: the storyteller's strict training under her grandmother; the crusader bringing back the linseeds; the Blessed Virgin receiving the Annunciation; the public announcements of virginity; the pilgrimages of the old princesses; the coming of the old spinster; the framing of the blank canvas. All these are linked as hallmarks of traditions. In the beginning, the loyalty of the storyteller to the true being of the story is extolled, and, at the end, the dauntless loyalty to tradition of the parents who had their daughter's blank canvas framed is praised. These loyalties not only unify the narration but also create the context of the story.

Other associative and subtly connecting repetitions, such as the old, black-veiled storytellers and the old, black-veiled spinster, the Blessed Virgin, the virgin princesses, and the virgin sisters, enhance the rich cohesiveness and depth of the tale. The black-and-white tiles of the gallery of virtue are a symbolic and ironic motif: Ordinary events and everyday morality may be set down in black and white, in trite categories, but the deeper truth must be discovered personally on the blank page. The final unity and the ultimate epiphany occur paradoxically, through contrasts, by bringing opposites together. There cannot be a virgin mother, but to the devout, the mother of Christ is the Blessed Virgin. Silence cannot speak, but to the keen listener it is eloquent. The blank page conveys nothing, but to the contemplative it reveals a deep truth, not expounded by the writer or the storyteller but clearly indicating matters of sexual as well as spiritual significance, not only for temporal and spiritual brides, but also for all beings in relation to their spiritual destiny. In this way, Dinesen eloquently and skillfully uses words and the absence of words to tell the story of "The Blank Page."

Sita Kapadia

BLISS

Author: Katherine Mansfield (Kathleen Mansfield Beauchamp, 1888-1923)
Type of plot: Psychological impressionism
Time of plot: c. 1917
Locale: Probably London
First published: 1918

> *Principal characters:*
> BERTHA YOUNG, a thirty-year-old housewife
> HARRY YOUNG, her husband
> PEARL FULTON, a young, mysterious acquaintance
> EDDIE WARREN, a young, just-published poet
> MR. NORMAN KNIGHT, a theatrical producer
> MRS. NORMAN KNIGHT, an interior decorator

The Story

Late one afternoon, as Bertha Young turns a corner onto her street, her body and mind suddenly feel total bliss. Only the conscious constraints of "civilization" keep her from running, dancing, and laughing.

Inside her house, she tells her housekeeper to bring her a bowl of fruit so she can decorate the table where she is to give a dinner party that night. The beauty of the fruit on the table makes her laugh almost hysterically.

Bertha runs upstairs to the nursery and begs the nurse to allow her to hold her infant daughter, Little Bertha. The nurse resentfully consents. As Bertha fondles and kisses her child, bliss again overwhelms her. The nurse returns, tells her she is wanted on the telephone, and triumphantly seizes "*her* Little Bertha." On the telephone, Bertha's husband, Harry, tells her that he will be home a little late. She has an urge to tell him how she feels but represses it.

Anticipating seeing Miss Pearl Fulton, a lovely, mysterious blonde woman, a recent acquaintance, who is to attend the dinner party, Bertha feels bliss again, and goes to the drawing-room window and looks across the garden at a lovely pear tree in full, perfect bloom. To her, it is "a symbol of her own life": She is young; she and her husband are "really good pals"; she has a baby, no money worries, a house and garden, artistic friends, books, music, a wonderful dressmaker, a fine new cook; and a trip abroad is planned for the summer.

Mr. and Mrs. Norman Knight arrive for the dinner party; he is a would-be theatrical producer and she is an interior decorator. Eddie Warren, socially in demand as the author of a "little book of poems," arrives. In a characteristic explosion of energy, Bertha's husband arrives, and just behind him comes the alluring Pearl Fulton.

As the guests exchange witty remarks and gestures, Bertha, convinced her mood is shared by Pearl, watches for a "sign." When Pearl asks to see the garden, Bertha pulls the curtains and presents the pear tree, which now resembles Pearl. Bertha has a profound feeling of oneness with Pearl and wishes her husband, who behaves as if he dislikes Pearl, would share her feelings.

Suddenly, Bertha feels another powerful emotion—sexual desire for her husband, "for the first time in her life."

The guests begin to leave. As she listens to the poet express his enthusiasm for "an incredibly beautiful line" of poetry, "Why must it always be tomato soup?" Bertha looks out into the hall, where her husband appears to be arranging a romantic rendezvous with Pearl.

Bertha runs to the windows and looks out, crying "What is going to happen now?" The pear tree, however, is "as lovely as ever and as full of flower and as still."

Themes and Meanings

As an observer of human behavior, Mansfield is a psychological realist who analyzes impressionistically a single moment in her characters' lives. Bertha's moment of bliss makes her want, for a moment, to touch her husband. Later, she has a "miraculous" moment when she is certain Pearl feels what she feels. The time setting for the story is only a few hours—a moment in Bertha's life, but one prefigured in her past, and one that presages her future. Bertha's moment of bliss produces another, inseparable, key moment: her "strange . . . terrifying" realization that she desires her husband.

Complex possibilities make a single interpretation of this story indefensible. An interesting possibility is to read "Bliss" solely as an expression of Bertha's moment of bliss from start to finish; from neither Bertha, from whose point of view the reader experiences the elements of the story, nor the author does the reader receive clear, literal expressions of Bertha's having negative feelings about the scene between Harry and Pearl at the end. Mansfield's intentionally ambiguous story raises many possibilities, but no one to the exclusion of all others. Several questions arise. Why is Bertha "overcome, suddenly, by a feeling of bliss" on this particular day? Is it by cruel chance that on the same day she will, ironically, discover her husband's bliss with another woman? Would she have been able to sustain the feeling of bliss alone that night when, "for the first time," she desired him? Would the rushes of bliss cease tomorrow as suddenly as they had struck her today? Mansfield seems to insist that Bertha, and the reader, remain subject to the contingencies of each new day.

The reader follows Bertha's unconscious use of several pyschological devices: Instead of expressing her feelings, she, as is her habit, represses them; instead of acting on her feelings, she projects them onto other people, especially Pearl; instead of authenticating her own identity, she excessively identifies with Pearl, whom she imagines is her opposite. Does bliss overwhelm her on the particular day because of her subconscious anticipation of seeing and intensely identifying with Pearl, her ideal, sensual self? The only different, new element in her life on this day is Pearl. Faulty or not (considering her discovery at the end), Bertha's perception that she has guessed Pearl's mood, instantly, exactly, is a clear example of the way she projects her own mood onto another person. That projection is most powerful as she stands close to Pearl at the window admiring the pear tree. Having so perfectly identified with Pearl for a moment (as the pear tree's blossoms are perfect only for a moment), Bertha feels, for a moment, desire for her husband. Scrutiny of this psychological process raises the possibility that Bertha, frightened of her "terrible" desire for Harry, projects onto Pearl and Harry the natural consummation of her own feelings by misperceiving the significance of their gestures in the hall at the end of the story. Perhaps the distance between Bertha and Harry and Pearl contributes to the misconception. Bertha's perceptions and emotions throughout the evening would predispose her to project impulsively onto the scene what she believes, or only imagines, she sees.

Mansfield then shows the reader how—even in a moment, or a series of moments clustered in a brief time—faulty human perceptions generate rare, romantic emotions that, given the nature of their stimulus, may be doomed to shatter against reality in disillusionment. Feelings such as "absolute bliss," even when one willfully tries to sustain them, as Bertha does, are rare and fleeting, but, as Eddie the poet tells her just after her observation of the Harry-Pearl scene, mundane "tomato soup is *dreadfully* eternal." Nevertheless, such moments as Bertha's moment of bliss have their own psychological reality and intensity before external reality does its work on them, and Mansfield seems to regard those moments with awe and wonder.

Style and Technique

When a writer's meanings are intentionally ambiguous, the reader can almost always depend upon the techniques used to express those meanings to be clear. As an artist, Mansfield is an impressionist; as impressionist painters offer a single image charged with emotion, she focuses on a single image, Bertha standing with Pearl communing with the pear tree, and a single emotion, bliss. The image is sharpened, the emotion is intensified, by the controlled use of two major devices: point of view and a style that evolves most naturally out of it.

The point of view is third-person, central intelligence; that is, all elements of the story are to be taken by the reader as having been filtered through Bertha's perceptions. As Bertha responds emotionally, imaginatively, and to a lesser extent intellectually, the reader receives her psychological impressions, expressed in the third person by the author in a style carefully controlled, paragraph by paragraph, to suit Bertha, on this particular day, at each instant. The reader should anticipate that Bertha's perceptions, like those of all human beings, are likely to be in error, to be flawed, or distorted, especially considering the fact that on this day a single powerful emotion is sweeping her along through the hours: bliss.

The surprise ending is one of those literary devices most often open to abuse or misinterpretation. Commercial writers use this device to stimulate a transitory thrill. The serious writer knows that a surprise ending may generate numerous misleading, distorting ambiguities. "Bliss" is an example of an unusually ambiguous story; Mansfield chose a point of view that by its nature must rely on the technical devices of context and implication to convey its meanings. Mansfield seems to intend much of the ambiguity as a device for stimulating the reader's own imagination.

When the reader comes, with Bertha, to the surprise ending, Mansfield provides a dramatic demonstration of how Bertha's perceptions have been flawed. Having chosen the point of view most effective for her purposes, Mansfield cannot tell the reader what actually happened between Harry and Pearl; she does, however, use various devices to prepare the reader's emotions, imagination, and intellect to reevaluate, retroactively (in a second reading) all of Bertha's assumptions, preconceptions, and perceptions. For readers who believe that the Harry-Pearl scene must have had a negative effect on Bertha's bliss, the surprise ending generates ambiguities that allow for several interpretations. The reader may perceive in a rush a pattern of already implied ironies. For example, Bertha is certain that Pearl shares her blissfulness, but it is with Harry that Pearl shares bliss; when Pearl, who is like the pear tree, says, "Your lovely pear tree," at the end, the irony is that Pearl is no longer lovely in Bertha's eyes.

Given her decision to filter everything through Bertha's consciousness as a way of developing a series of misperceptions, Mansfield must employ several other devices to lead the reader toward various possible, supportable interpretations of Bertha's character. It is implied, through Bertha's actions, that she is childlike, as when she forgets her key, "as usual." The theater motif also implies Bertha's childlike quality; her guests remind her of "a play by Tchekof." Mansfield uses the device of comic contrast to stress the serious elements: Tomato soup provides comic contrast to the lovely pear tree. Some readers will see Bertha's baby "in another woman's arms" as an early parallel to her husband in another woman's arms. The pear tree is the central, symbolic image of the story, charged with implications. Images of fire contrasted with cold, of clothes, and of color enhance the central image. Appropriately, in a story focusing on bliss, Mansfield's style activates all of the reader's senses.

David Madden

THE BLIZZARD

Author: Alexander Pushkin (1799-1837)
Type of plot: Romantic anecdote
Time of plot: 1811-1816
Locale: Country estates in provincial Russia
First published: "Metel," 1831 (English translation, 1856)

>   *Principal characters:*
>   MARYA GAVRILOVNA, the heroine, a romantic young lady of
>   seventeen
>   GAVRILA GAVRILOVITCH R——, her father, a prominent
>   landowner of the estate Nenaradova near the village of
>   Zhadrino
>   PRASKOVYA PETROVNA R——, her mother
>   VLADIMIR NIKOLAYEVITCH, her secret fiancé, a poor army
>   subaltern
>   COLONEL BURMIN, a young Hussar, a war hero

The Story

Marya Gavrilovna, the seventeen-year-old daughter of a wealthy landowner in provincial Russia, has formed her ideas of romance by reading French romantic novels. She develops an infatuation for Vladimir Nikolayevitch, a poor army subaltern, who returns her love. Her parents consider him unacceptable for their daughter and forbid them to see each other. They continue, however, to meet in secret. When winter comes and their secret meetings become impossible, they agree to a secret wedding, planning to return later and throw themselves at her parents' feet, confident of receiving their forgiveness.

The night before her elopement, Marya writes letters to be delivered to her parents and a sentimental young girlfriend after the wedding. That night, her sleep is troubled by dreams foreboding her separation from Vladimir. The next day, she is restless and leaves the dinner table early to await the hour of her departure. In the meantime, a violent blizzard has arisen. At the appointed hour, she slips quietly from the house and goes to the end of the garden, where a sledge and Vladimir's coachman, Tereshka, await to take her to the little church in Zhadrino for the wedding.

During the day, Vladimir has arranged for a priest to officiate at the wedding and selected three witnesses. Two hours before the wedding, he sends his coachman to get Marya and leaves alone in his one-horse sledge for the twenty-minute ride to the church. Almost immediately, the blizzard begins. Unable to see through the raging, swirling storm, he loses all direction. Soon his sledge is off the road. Many times it turns over and has to be righted. As the hours pass, he grows desperate until he sees a small village and learns that he has overshot Zhadrino by a great distance. Hiring a guide, he retraces his steps and arrives at the village church just at dawn. The church is locked and empty. Pushkin adds, "And what news awaited him!"

The next morning, back at Marya's home, no one knows what has happened. Marya has burned the letters she wrote. Her maid, the priest, the witnesses, and Tereshka all keep a discreet silence about the events of the previous evening. That evening, however, Marya becomes quite ill. In her delirium, she talks confusedly about her love for Vladimir. Her parents, upon consultation with neighbors, relent and send him word that they now consent to the marriage. Much to their surprise, he writes back refusing their offer and stating that his only hope is death. His wish is granted when, a short time later, he is wounded in Russia's battle against Napoleon at Borodino and dies the day Napoleon enters Moscow.

A second tragedy strikes when Marya's father dies, leaving her the sole heiress of his large estate. Surrounded by too many sad memories, Marya and her mother, Praskovya Petrovna, move to an estate in another area. Many suitors seek the hand of this beautiful, wealthy heiress, but she is faithful to the memory of Vladimir.

The war against Napoleon ends victoriously and the regiments return in showers of glory. They are the pride of Russia. The appearance of any officer in a provincial town is greeted with enthusiastic applause. A charming young Hussar, Colonel Burmin, returns to his estate near Marya's home to recuperate from a battle wound. Even though it is rumored that he has formerly been a prankster, he now appears reserved. Marya is determined to break that reserve and to see him at her feet. It seems that she is succeeding, and the neighborhood expects an imminent wedding. Burmin, however, does not propose. Finally, he decides that he must give her an explanation. He begins, "I love you passionately." She expects a declaration of love like that Saint-Preux made to Julie in Jean-Jacques Rousseau's novel and is shocked when he adds that an insuperable barrier separates them: He is already married. He continues that in 1812 he was on his way to join his regiment when a terrible blizzard arose and his driver became lost in strange country. He requested the driver to stop to ask for directions at a small wooden church which was open. Several people, asking why he was so late, rushed him into the darkened church, lit by only a few candles, to the side of a bride. In a spirit of recklessness, he allowed the priest to marry them. When he turned to kiss the bride, she cried out, "No! This is not he!" and fainted. Rushing to his sledge, he hurried away. He concludes that after so many years he has no way of finding the young lady upon whom he had played such a cruel prank.

Marya seizes his hand and cries out, "So it was you? Do you not recognize me?" whereupon Burmin throws himself at her feet.

Themes and Meanings

In 1830, while Pushkin was in seclusion at Boldino, he wrote *Povesti Belkina* (1831; *The Tales of Belkin*, 1947), an experiment with a new form for him, prose narration. Actually he was breaking new ground for his nation; these five tales, of which "The Blizzard" is one, are among the first Russian short stories. Tolstoy himself credited them with having influenced his own style.

As Pushkin began writing narrative prose, he was in turn influenced by Sir Walter Scott. Like Scott, he headed his stories with suitable quotations, used fictitious narrators, and created highly romantic situations and characters. In Scott's *St. Ronan's Well*, as in "The Blizzard," the heroine does not realize that she has married the wrong man until after the ceremony. Like Scott in *The Bride of Lammermoor*, Pushkin uses the providential hand of nature (in both cases, a storm is used) to effect the action. The blizzard prevents Vladimir from arriving at his wedding on time and brings Burmin to the church where he thoughtlessly marries the unheeding Marya.

Pushkin, however, makes the outcome of the narrative depend also on the choices his characters make. Vladimir chooses to send his servant to bring Marya to the church rather than doing so himself. Burmin irresponsibly takes advantage of the wedding party's ignorance when they mistake him for the groom. Later, after being wounded in battle and falling in love with Marya, he matures and becomes a more serious person.

Marya also shows character growth. At the beginning of the story, she is almost a parody of the young, sentimental lady who sees life through romantic novels. Her reading has filled her head with romantic imagination, which feeds her nightmares and forms her concept of love between the sexes. She seals her letters with an emblem engraved with two flaming hearts, bursts into tears, faints easily. After Vladimir's death, she rejects all suitors, remaining faithful to his memory until Burmin, the charming Hussar, enters the scene. Then she becomes a coquette, determined to prompt him to a declaration of love even though she knows she cannot marry him. She reverts to her former concept of love, however, when she thinks that he is ready to propose to her.

Pushkin uses the community to respond to the events of the story. After Marya's illness, they use moral platitudes to justify her marriage to Vladimir, who is culturally beneath her. They rapturously welcome their victorious soldiers from the Napoleonic wars. They spread rumors of Burmin's rakish pranks and watch his courtship of Marya, certain that their marriage is imminent.

Style and Technique

Pushkin is more concerned with plot, point of view, and irony than he is with character development. To create suspense, he abruptly breaks the narrative at the climactic point when Vladimir arrives at the empty church. Not until the end of the story does the reader learn what he discovered there. The glorious return of the veterans from their defeat of Napoleon serves as the turning point; thereafter, the story moves toward an implied happy conclusion. There are, however, numerous coincidences and improbabilities which pave the way for that conclusion.

Seemingly because *The Tales of Belkin* was an experiment in prose fiction, Pushkin decided to publish it anonymously, attributing the authorship to a fictitious author, Ivan Petrovich Belkin, for whom he developed an elaborate biographical background. George Z. Patrick has pointed out a number of similarities between the "spiritual makeup" and biographical details of Pushkin and Belkin. Belkin's personality, however, is basically different from Pushkin's. Belkin is simple, artless, naïve; any flaws in the narrative can be attributed to him. Furthermore, Belkin indicates that he is merely recording narratives as told to him by someone else—in the case of "The Blizzard," a Miss K.I.T. The strong element of girlish sentimentality can be attributed to her influence. The point of view is further complicated when a character in the story, Burmin, tells of his experience during the blizzard and thus solves the mystery of that fatal night.

Pushkin's skill in ironic humor permeates the narrative. The snowstorm which keeps Vladimir and Marya apart ultimately produces her happiness; Marya's parents finally agree to her marriage to Vladimir only to find that he is no longer willing to marry her; Marya is determined to elicit a marriage proposal from a man who, unknown to her, is already her lawful husband. The final ironic twist brings the story to a happy conclusion. Marya and Vladimir believed that their happiness would be complete when, after their elopement (so they planned), they threw themselves at the feet of her parents, receiving their forgiveness and blessing. Instead, Marya realizes this happiness when Burmin at the end throws himself at her feet to ask her forgiveness for his heartless prank four years earlier. The reader surmises that she forgives him and that their felicity is complete.

James Smythe

BLOOD-BURNING MOON

Author: Jean Toomer (1894-1967)
Type of plot: Symbolic realism
Time of plot: The early 1920's
Locale: Rural Georgia
First published: 1923

> *Principal characters:*
> LOUISA, a black woman
> TOM BURWELL, a black man who loves her
> BOB STONE, a white man who loves her

The Story

The last of six prose pieces in the first part of the cycle of poems and stories entitled *Cane* (1923), about young black women, "Blood-Burning Moon" is the tragic story of Louisa and her two lovers, a white and a black; its action occurs in a small factory town and the surrounding sugarcane fields in rural Georgia early in the 1920's.

Louisa works in the kitchens of the Stones, a leading white family of the community, and young Bob Stone loves her; as the narrator says, "By the measure of that warm glow which came into her mind at the thought of him, he had won her." Tom Burwell, called "Big Boy" by everyone, also loves her, but since he works in the fields all day, he cannot spend as much time with Louisa as Bob Stone can. Further, even at night, when he does come to her, "Strong as he was with hands upon the ax or plow," he finds it difficult to hold her. Both men, for different reasons, have problems communicating their feelings to her. Louisa's attitude toward the pair is ambivalent; Tom's "black balanced, and pulled against, the white of Stone, when she thought of them." On the night that the action takes place, Louisa is scheduled to meet Stone in the canebrake. There is a full moon that, rising from the dusk, lights the great door of the antebellum cotton factory, an omen which the black women attempt to neutralize by means of a song:

> Red nigger moon. Sinner!
> Blood-burning moon. Sinner!
> Come out that fact'ry door.

Thus, in the first part of this story Toomer not only introduces the players and sets the stage for a confrontation and its consequences but also introduces three primary themes: the conflict between the races, the economy that historically is a source of the problem, and the black woman as sex object.

The second section opens at a clearing on the edge of the cane forest where men grind and boil the cane stalks while listening to Old David Georgia chatter about "the white folks, about moonshining and cotton picking, and about sweet nigger gals." When someone links Louisa with Bob Stone, Tom Burwell menacingly announces, "She's my gal," and threateningly brandishes a long knife, an action that foreshadows the pivotal confrontation to come. He then heads toward factory town, shuddering at the sight of the full moon and thinking about Louisa and Stone ("Better not be"). When he comes to Louisa's place, however, he is a different person: gentle and withdrawn, unable to speak. He grins and begins to move on, but she prompts him ("Youall want me, Tom? . . . You wanted to say something?"), and he bursts forth with a confession of his love and his hopes (including having his own farm, "if ole Stone'll trust me," and "silk stockings an purple dresses" for Louisa), but he also wants reassurance: "Bob Stone likes y. Course he does. But not the way folks is awhisperin. Does he, hon?" She feigns ignorance ("I dont know what you mean, Tom") but asks what he would do if the rumors were true. "Cut him," he replies, "jes like I cut a nigger . . . already cut two." Then, hand in hand, the two walk off to make love in the canebrake.

Bob Stone, meanwhile, also is thinking of Louisa; he regrets, too, the passing of the old order, when as a white master he could have gone into the house and taken Louisa ("Direct, honest, bold") without sneaking about as he now must do. He also speculates about how his mother, sister, and friends up north would react if they knew about him and Louisa, whom he considers "lovely—in her. . . Nigger way." Unable to articulate even to himself what he means by "Nigger way," he wonders if "Nigger was something . . . to be afraid of, more?" Though he rejects the idea, it leads him to think of Tom Burwell and that "Cartwell had told him that Tom went with Louisa after she reached home," but he refuses to believe this. Stone's reaction, therefore, precisely matches Burwell's, even including a threat ("No nigger had ever been with his girl. He'd like to see one try"), and when he goes off in search of her, he hears (as Burwell does) the men at the stove talking about the trio and how the affair likely will lead to violence: "Tom Burwell's been on the gang three times fo cuttin men. . . . Young Stone ain't no quitter an I ken tell y that. Blood of th old ones in his veins."

The talk has the same effect on Stone as it has on Burwell, for he must prove the truth of the overheard characterization of him. A captive of his love for Louisa and the blacks' expectations, Stone goes to the canebrake, where he normally meets her. Since this is their regular meeting time, he assumes that she is with his rival, and he tastes blood: "Tom Burwell's blood." Trying to find the pair, he trips over a dog and starts a ruckus that stirs Burwell. They confront each other and fight; when Stone starts to lose, he takes a knife from his pocket. Burwell says, "That's my game, sho," and he cuts Stone's throat.

The blacks who observe the struggle sneak into their houses and blow the lamps out; the white men, "like ants upon a forage," trap Burwell. They bind his wrists, drag him to the factory, pile rotting floorboards around a stake, pour kerosene on the boards, tie him to the stake, and fling torches onto the pile. As the ritualistic lynching reaches its climax, the triumphant yell of the mob echoes "against the skeleton stone walls and [sounds] like a hundred yells." Louisa, who has gone home and does not hear the cries of the lynching mob, apparently senses that something is wrong, for her eyes open slowly and she looks at the full moon, "an evil thing . . . an omen which she must sing to."

Themes and Meanings

"Blood-Burning Moon" brings together key thematic motifs from the earlier stories in *Cane*. Like the others, it focuses on a woman as sex object, controlled by men but at the same time exerting a powerful force over them that transcends the normal social barriers of the South at the time. The story thus addresses, too, the sexual relationship between black and white, which Toomer also examines in "Becky" (about a white woman with two black sons) and "Fern" (whose heroine, Fernie May Rosen, has a black mother and a white Jewish father). It therefore adds an extra dimension to Toomer's focus in much of the book upon what he regards as a Southern conspiracy to ignore the reality of miscegenation. In sum, the bigotry that pervades both blacks and whites in rural Georgia creates barriers to normal interpersonal relationships, exaggerates the tensions present in any evolving society, and ultimately results in sexual repression. Toomer presents the blacks, however, as having a firmer cultural basis than the whites do. Though they are not at all primitives in the conventional sense, the blacks who work in the fields are close to nature. In "Fern," the narrator says, "When one is on the soil of one's ancestors, most anything can come to one." The title "Blood-Burning Moon" and the folk song from whose refrain it comes emphasize this kinship and its spiritual and emotional significance. A third motif, which is important throughout *Cane*, is the economic situation—symbolized in large part by the cane of the title—in which the races are interdependent at the same time that they are rivals. In "Blood-Burning Moon," the cane is both reality and symbol in a more central way here than elsewhere in the book. It is a means of livelihood for both blacks and whites, for the decaying cotton factory is evidence that the old economic support is fading, and the smell of the cane pervades the town.

Style and Technique

Widely recognized as one of the foremost literary works of the Harlem Renaissance of the 1920's, *Cane* is a collection of stories, sketches, and poems that emerged from Toomer's experience as temporary head of a school for blacks in Georgia. The poems, which appear within the stories and between them, are in a variety of forms, though most are folk songs or ballads. As in "Blood-Burning Moon," they provide substantive reinforcement to the action and themes of the prose pieces, but serve primarily to enhance the pervasive wistful and mournful tone. They also heighten the impressionistic quality of the book, for though Toomer writes about real social problems and his characters are believable, he is not only a realist. The lynching of Tom Burwell, portrayed in a deliberately ritualistic manner, thus is appropriate both stylistically and symbolically.

Because of the impressionistic style and technique of *Cane* and for other reasons, the book recalls Sherwood Anderson's *Winesburg, Ohio* (1919). For example, both books have narrators who serve as mediator between author and reader, both are collections of prose cameos, and each has a group of characters that can be labeled "grotesques," in Toomer's case because of the lingering social and psychological effects of slavery.

Finally, though its subject matter may recall the naturalist movement, the style and technique of "Blood-Burning Moon" and *Cane* as a whole link it more directly to a later period, in which myth and symbol would be dominant in American fiction.

Gerald H. Strauss

BLOW-UP

Author: Julio Cortázar (1914-1984)
Type of plot: Magical realism
Time of plot: The 1950's
Locale: Paris
First published: "Las babas del diablo," 1958 (English translation, 1963)

Principal characters:
ROBERTO MICHEL, a Chilean-French translator and amateur photographer living in Paris
A TEENAGE BOY
A BLONDE WOMAN, who attempts to seduce the teenager
A MAN, sitting in a parked car

The Story

Roberto Michel opens his story not by telling what happened but by mulling over how it should be told, as well as why it must be told. Once he decides that "the best thing is to put aside all decorum and tell it, " he recounts the events of his Sunday morning stroll along the Seine. His excursion is quite uneventful until, while lighting a cigarette, his eye catches an interesting scene in which a blonde woman seems to be attempting to seduce a teenage boy.

With nothing better to do, Michel watches the scene carefully. As he notices the boy's nervous reactions to the woman's advances, Michel begins to imagine the particulars of the situation, details that he attempts to divine from his somewhat distant observations. Michel imagines in considerable detail the boy's background, his relationship with his friends, even his home life. He then begins to imagine the events of the morning that led the boy to this precarious situation. Now certain in his own mind of what is happening, Michel begins to derive a perverse pleasure from foreseeing the possible endings of the "cruel game," imagining both escape for the boy and conquest for the woman.

Michel notices a man in a parked car near the scene, but he is unable to establish his role in the seduction. Before the scene can disintegrate before his eyes, Michel readies his camera, still ruminating about the possible denouements of the story unfolding only a few feet away. When he finally snaps the photo, his action is noticed by both the woman and the boy. Irritated, the woman approaches Michel and demands the film. In the meantime, the boy seizes the opportunity to escape, "disappearing like a gossamer filament of angel-spit in the morning air." The mysterious man approaches from the parked car and joins the woman in demanding the film. Michel refuses to relinquish it and returns home.

Several days later, Michel develops the film and makes an enlargement of the photo of the woman and the boy. Fascinated by the shot, he tacks a poster-size blowup of it on the wall of his apartment. While working on a translation, he is mysteriously drawn to the photo. Examining it from several perspectives, he compares what is frozen in the picture with what happened immediately after it was taken. His contemplation of both the photo and the events surrounding it produces in him a self-satisfaction, for he feels that his intrusion allowed the boy the escape that the teenager so badly wanted. As Michel concludes, "In the last analysis, taking the photo had been a good act."

Magically, however, the figures in the photo begin to move and the scene develops beyond the point of Michel's intrusion, as if he and his camera had never been there. Michel sees that without his presence this time, "that which had not happened, but which was now going to happen, now was going to be fulfilled." He realizes that the woman had not been seducing the boy for her own pleasure but for that of the man in the parked car. As Michel points out, "The real boss was waiting there, smiling petulantly, already certain of the business; he was not the first to send a woman in the vanguard, to bring him the prisoners manacled in flowers." Michel painfully realizes that he cannot stop the order of events this time. He cannot interrupt the scene with another photograph, or even with a shout of warning to the boy. The figures are functioning in a time frame separate from his own, forcing him into the role of a powerless bystander.

Feeling helpless, Michel screams out and runs toward the photo. Surprisingly, the man, now out of the parked car, reacts to Michel's approach and turns to confront him. Once again, the boy seizes the opportunity afforded him by Michel's presence and escapes running. For the second time, Michel has helped the teenager, allowing him to get away, thus "returning him to his precarious paradise." Emotionally and physically exhausted, Michel breaks down in tears and makes his way to the window of his apartment. It is from this location that he narrates his story while watching the birds and the clouds pass by.

Themes and Meanings

A number of themes common to several of Cortázar's stories are found in "Blow-Up." One of these is the creation of a fictionalized reality that becomes accepted as truth within the story. Michel views an isolated scene about which he has little information. He nevertheless manufactures a complex reality surrounding that scene, a fictionalized reality complete with details concerning the boy writing to his aunt in Avignon, the manner in which the young man folds his pornographic magazines, the color of the comforter on the bed in the blonde's apartment, and several others. Michel establishes his own version of reality. As even he says about himself, "Michel is guilty of making literature, of indulging in fabricated unrealities."

The story also deals with Cortázar's interest in the prospect of multiple and parallel realities (either true or fictionalized). The movement of the figures in the photo contributes to the treatment of this concept in that it demonstrates a reality independent of the "main" one in which Michel and his camera are first involved. Of equal importance, however, is the duality in Michel's interpretation of the scene unfolding before him. For example, he imagines both success and failure for the seductress, thus establishing at least two separate realities, fictionalized though they both may be. By suggesting more than one possibility, more than one "truth," Cortázar, as he does in several of his works, demonstrates that "true" reality is hardly ever as simple to establish as one might logically think.

Another thematic concern of Cortázar's found in this story is the individual human being's need to tell what he knows, that to which he is privy, in an effort to cleanse himself, to rid himself of the psychological burden of his solitary knowledge. This is demonstrated in the first two pages of the story as Michel speaks of the need to tell his story, to get it out, and in doing so exorcise his soul of what he has witnessed. As he states, "Always tell it, always get rid of that tickle in the stomach that bothers you."

Style and Technique

The story is told in a somewhat complex manner. Above all, it features a self-conscious narrator who not only criticizes his own choice of words but also alternates frequently between third-person and first-person narration. The fact that Michel refers to himself in the third person is a bit disconcerting in itself. It shows, however, that he is uncomfortable associating himself with the "character" Michel who has suffered through such a psychologically painful experience. He is therefore putting distance between himself and the person who went strolling along the river with the camera. His vacillation between the two perspectives may simply demonstrate that he has not yet resigned himself fully to either position. Though certainly unorthodox, the frequent shifting from one person to the other is not a major obstacle to the reader, since it is obvious that the narrator and Michel are one and the same.

Of equal interest from a technical standpoint, and certainly more disconcerting to the reader, are the narrator's frequent references, usually within parentheses, to the birds and clouds that pass by his window as he tells his story. One reason for including these references is to show the narrator's position in the present as he tells his story. The references, which interrupt the narration, also emphasize the profound effect that the experience has had on the narrator, as he is unable to maintain a steady narrative course and alternates between what happened and what he sees outside his window. The problem for the reader here is that it is virtually impossible to understand these references at the time that they are presented, since

Michel's physical surroundings as he narrates are not revealed until the end of the story. The disquieting effect they have on the reader is quite intentional, however, as it underscores the tenuous mental state of the narrator.

Keith H. Brower

THE BLUE HOTEL

Author: Stephen Crane (1871-1900)
Type of plot: Adventure
Time of plot: The mid-1890's
Locale: Nebraska
First published: 1898

Principal characters:
PAT SCULLY, proprietor of the Blue Hotel
THE SWEDE, a visitor from New York
MR. BLANC, an Easterner
BILL, a Dakota cowboy
JOHNNIE SCULLY, the proprietor's son
THE GAMBLER, a resident of Fort Romper

The Story
   The light blue hue of the Palace Hotel, like the shade of a heron's legs, is a striking sight to railway passengers disembarking at Fort Romper, Nebraska. Its owner, Irishman Pat Scully, personally meets the morning and evening trains to "work his seductions" on potential customers. One wintry morning he collars three such "prisoners," a "shaky and quick-eyed" Swede from New York, a Dakota cowboy named Bill, and Mr. Blanc, a "little silent" Easterner. In the hotel's small front room, the guests come upon an old farmer and Scully's son Johnnie playing a card game called high-five. A conscientious host, Scully furnishes the guests with water and towels, gets Johnnie to take their baggage upstairs, and confers with his wife and daughters about the midday meal. Outside, the snow and the wind are reaching blizzard proportions.
   Almost immediately, the Swede begins behaving peculiarly. Nervous and defensive, he laughingly asserts that "some of these Western communities were very dangerous." When a quarrel terminates the card game between Johnnie and the farmer, the Swede joins the table, pairing up with Mr. Blanc against Johnnie and Bill. The latter is a "board whacker," which unhinges the Swede. Whenever the cowboy played a winning card, he "whanged" it on the table, causing Johnnie to chuckle. Suddenly, the Swede says, "I suppose there have been a good many men killed in this room." Astonished, the others take issue with him. Believing his life in danger, the Swede pleads that he does not want to fight.
   "Have you gone daffy?" Scully asks him while the Swede is packing upstairs: "We're goin' to have a line of ilictric street-cars in this town next spring. . . . Not to mintion the four churches and the smashin' big brick school-house." Refusing to accept money for the room, Scully shows him a

portrait of his deceased daughter Carrie and his elder son, who is an attorney in Lincoln. Bringing out a bottle of whiskey, he insists that the Swede take a drink.

Downstairs, the men argue about the Swede's abnormal behavior. The cowboy thinks him a phony, "some kind of a Dutchman," while Mr. Blanc figures he was frightened by Western dime-novels. Then Scully and the Swede reappear, laughing like two "roysterers from a banquet hall." When the latter is out of earshot, however, Scully confides that his strange guest thought "I was tryin' to poison 'im."

At supper the Swede behaves "like a fire-wheel," singing riotously one minute, stabbing his food menacingly the next, and all the while gazing belligerently at the others. When the meal is over, he insists upon resuming high-five. Scully has just settled down to his newspaper when he hears the Swede charge Johnnie with cheating.

Despite Scully's efforts to calm things down, both adversaries insist on going outside to fight. "I can't put up with it any longer," Scully says with resignation, adding: "I've stood this damned Swede till I'm sick."

Out in the snow, the Swede bawls out that he cannot "lick you all," but Scully assures him that it will be a fair fight. As the storm wails its "long mellow cry," the two crash together "like bullocks." The Easterner watches silently with a sense of foreboding tragedy, but the cowboy yells for Johnnie to "kill him! kill him! kill him!" Johnnie is no match for the bigger man, however, and ends up on the ground, bloody and humiliated. Afterward, Mrs. Scully is irate at her husband for having permitted their son to be so savagely beaten. "Shame be upon you, Patrick Scully," she cries.

As the Swede is leaving, the cowboy wants to fight him, but Scully again intervenes, even though the victor mimicks Bill's cry of "kill him! kill him! kill him!" Making his way to a saloon, whose entrance is made visible by "an indomitable red light," he drinks down two glasses of whiskey in large gulps and starts bragging about his conquest. After failing to persuade the bartender to have a drink, the Swede turns to four men sitting around a table. They include two merchants, the district attorney, and a gambler, who is a family man who only fleeces ignorant farmers. When they rebuff the Swede's offer of a drink, he roughly lays his hand on the gambler, calls him a "little dude," and vows, "I'll make you." He grabs the gambler's throat and starts dragging him from his chair when the gambler stabs him with a knife. His three companions flee. Wiping off the blade with a towel, the gambler tells the bartender: "I'll be home, waiting for 'em." As the bartender goes for help, the dying Swede lies with his eyes staring vacantly at a sign atop the cash-machine which reads: "This registers the amount of your purchase."

Several months later, when the cowboy and the Easterner meet, they both express sympathy for the gambler, who is serving a three-year prison sentence. The cowboy blames it all on the Swede for accusing Johnnie of cheat-

ing in a game played for fun rather than money. He *was* cheating, the Easterner replies: "I saw him. And I refused to stand up and be a man." He concludes that they were all collaborators, that the gambler was only "the apex
of a human movement." Incredulous about "this fog of mysterious theory,"
the cowboy blindly cries, "Well, I didn't do anythin', did I?"

Themes and Meanings

"The Blue Hotel" deals with man's vanities and illusions, which are absurd
but, ironically, necessary for survival. Crane's naturalistic tale presents a view
of the world as beyond comprehension and indifferent to the inconsequential
matters of mankind. According to the author, people are like lice clinging to
"a whirling, fire-smitten, ice-locked, disease-stricken, space-lost bulb."

While "The Blue Hotel" is steeped in irony, Crane explores the conun-
drum between fate and moral choice. The story is elusive on whether man
shares moral responsibility for the consequences of his actions. The Swede's
fate is tragic and of his own making, yet who is to say whether it was the
whiskey, given to him by the well-intentioned Scully, which turned him into a
reckless fool? On one thing Crane is clear: Life is fragile. Whether the Swede
is trapped by his fixed idea about the environment or whether it is the environment which traps him, his death comes as quickly and easily as the slicing
of a melon. The motto on the cash register implies that he deserves his fate,
but, ironically, the message comes too late to save him, as his eyes are
already glazed over by the shadow of death.

Perhaps literary critic J. C. Levenson best summarized the story's enigmatic quality when he wrote: "Given the facts as presented, the story constructs a universe which defies every quest for certain meaning." Yet this
much can be said: Crane's philosophy has an existential element. Had this
been merely a naturalist allegory, the author would have concluded with the
Swede's death and not included the conversation between the Easterner and
the cowboy. Despite the chaos and moral uncertainty, Crane rejects passivity.
He embraces the conceit that man has ethical obligations.

Style and Technique

Robert Louis Stevenson once wrote that in a good story, terrain and atmosphere should express and symbolize the characters and action. Crane follows Stevenson's injunction, as the images of the blizzard and the "screaming
blue" hotel foreshadow the subsequent fistfight and stabbing. In fact, just as
the blue-legged heron "declares his position" against its background, so the
Swede (called a wild loony by Johnnie) has a fixed position that is antagonistic to the environment.

The blizzard symbolizes nature's harshness, the blinding rage of a hostile
environment which can snuff out visibility, reducing the landscape to "a gray
swampish hush." Crane writes that "the conceit of man was explained by the

storm to be the very engine of life. One was a coxcomb not to die in it." The blue color of the hotel is a testimony to the owner's conceit. Scully imagines himself to be an exemplary host and entrepreneur. Rather than viewing the Blue Hotel as a tranquil haven, the Swede believes it to be a frontier outpost fraught with danger. In the end, his irrational fear becomes a self-fulfilling prophecy. Thus, man's conceit can be an agent of death as well as an engine of life.

In some ways the three travelers parody the biblical Wise Men. Scully, who "looks curiously like a priest," tells them that guests have "sacred privileges." He provides them with (baptismal) water, shows the Swede icons (pictures of his children), and offers him (sacramental) libation. Crane even describes the stove as like an altar which hums "with godlike violence." In the end, the deluded Swede runs from the safety of the temple and meets his fate in the hellish saloon.

Crane's use of vivid colors is one of his trademarks, and literary critics have debated the meaning of the hotel's heron-blue paint as well as the saloon's beckoning red light. They obviously are contrasting focal points, beacons as well as advertising gimmicks. The tranquillity and purity of the blue seem out of place; that is its charm (and Scully's conceit). The red lamp, turning the snow the color of blood, is a warning signal that the Swede ignored. The meaning of these symbols remains mysterious, in keeping with the author's philosophical skepticism.

James B. Lane

THE BOARDING HOUSE

Author: James Joyce (1882-1941)
Type of plot: Social realism
Time of plot: 1904
Locale: Dublin
First published: 1914

Principal characters:
Bob Doran, an unmarried clerk, a lodger in Mrs. Mooney's boardinghouse
Polly Mooney, an attractive single girl, the daughter of the boardinghouse proprietress
Mrs. Mooney, the owner of a shabby Dublin boardinghouse and Polly's mother
Jack Mooney, Mrs. Mooney's son, a clerk and a carouser

The Story

Mrs. Mooney, a coarse, shrewd, and determined woman, connives to marry off her daughter to one of the more responsible lodgers in her shabby, questionably respectable boardinghouse. Having given her daughter the run of the young men, Mrs. Mooney watches in silent approval as Polly seduces a meek, middle-aged clerk. As the story opens, Mrs. Mooney, having ascertained the facts of the situation from her daughter, prepares to confront the lover, Bob Doran. She is determined to make him marry the girl, under the weight of social, religious, and economic pressure. The story, told almost entirely through narrative flashbacks, recounts the collusion between mother and daughter in the entrapment of Doran. Although Doran balks inwardly against this coercion, he finds himself surrendering to the admonitions of his priest, to the middle-class conventions of Dublin life, and to his fears of scandal, of losing his job, and of reprisals by Polly's rowdy and violent brother. Despite his affection for Polly, he is repelled by her vulgarity and fears that he will be lowering himself socially by marrying her. Indeed, the narrative substantiates Doran's "notion that he was being had," while it makes clear that his capitulation is a foregone conclusion.

Since most of the story is told through exposition and flashback, very little happens in the course of the narrative, which spans only about an hour on a Sunday morning. Doran, the reluctant lover and the even more reluctant husband-to-be, is very agitated after having confessed the affair to his priest on the previous day. His anxiety increases when Polly enters, cries on his shoulder, and tells him that she has "made a clean breast of it to her mother." Feebly reassuring Polly that everything will be all right, he is summoned to an interview with Mrs. Mooney. While Mrs. Mooney has the matter out with

Doran, her daughter obediently awaits the outcome of the interview, her mind filled with pleasant reminiscences of her trysts with her lover and with still more pleasant "hopes and visions of the future." At the end of the story, Mrs. Mooney, whose name recalls "money," calls Polly downstairs to inform her of the "reparation," a promise of marriage, which she has extracted from Bob Doran.

Themes and Meanings

In discussing *Dubliners* (1914), the thematically related collection of stories in which "The Boarding House" appears, James Joyce stated, "My intention was to write a chapter of the moral history of my country and I chose Dublin for the scene because that city seemed to me the centre of paralysis. I have tried to present it to the indifferent public under four of its aspects: childhood, adolescence, maturity, and public life." Viewed in these terms, "The Boarding House" does indeed comment on the "moral history" of Ireland, as evidenced by the perversion of sexuality depicted throughout the story. On the one hand, sexuality is trivialized by the meaningless promiscuity of the transients and music hall artistes who pass through Mrs. Mooney's boardinghouse. More significantly, the marriage relationship, which should be based on love and long-term sexual commitment, is effected by entrapment of the man by the woman into a sordid monetary arrangement. Accordingly, Mrs. Mooney, one of a series of monstrous, overbearing mothers who appear throughout *Dubliners*, congratulates herself that she is not like "some mothers she knew who could not get their daughters off their hands." Clearly the story demonstrates the aptness of the nickname that the lodgers have given Mrs. Mooney: They call her "the Madam." Throughout, the narrator condemns the calculation and vulgarity of Polly's seduction of Doran and pities him for his helplessness in falling into the hands of calculating women.

Yet the story also notes that Doran, in his passivity and excessive cautiousness, is life-denying, himself a victim of the paralysis which pervades Irish life. Accordingly, Polly emerges, however crassly, as an embodiment of the life force, who, in Shavian terms, claims Doran as the father of her child and rescues him from deadness and sterility, in spite of himself. The great irony of "The Boarding House" is that, without the intervention of Polly Mooney, Doran, a self-proclaimed celibate, seems destined for the loveless, lonely existence of the mature protagonists of two other stories in the collection, Maria in "Clay" and Mr. Duffy in "A Painful Case." Fittingly, the only lively descriptions in this otherwise bare and austere story are of Polly, as Doran recalls her "wise innocence" in seducing him: "Her white instep shone in the opening of her furry slippers and the blood glowed warmly behind her perfumed skin. From her hands and wrists too as she lit and steadied her candle a faint perfume arose."

Style and Technique

In his own words, Joyce sought to describe the dilemmas of the inhabitants of "dear, dirty Dublin" in "a style of scrupulous meanness." He sought to give his countrymen "one good look at themselves" in a "nicely polished looking-glass," so as to take the first step toward their "spiritual liberation." Accordingly, the treatment is cool, detached, contemplative. The omniscient point of view often describes without comment the action of the story, as Mrs. Mooney would see it, and leaves all judgments to the reader: "she was an outraged mother. She had allowed him to live beneath her roof, assuming that he was a man of honour, and he had simply abused her hospitality." Yet, at other times, Joyce's anger and indignation show, as in his description of Polly as "a little perverse madonna" and of Mrs. Mooney: "She dealt with moral problems as a cleaver deals with meat."

The theme of paralysis is reinforced, throughout the story, by the fact that very little happens, and whatever does happen takes place offstage. Accordingly, the final scene of the story focuses on Polly daydreaming in her lover's bedroom, as her mother speaks with him downstairs, but the reader is not privy to their crucial conversation. The treatment is deliberately anticlimactic: To a character such as Bob Doran, life is what happens to him, never what he chooses or determines.

Carola M. Kaplan

BOBOK

Author: Fyodor Dostoevski (1821-1881)
Type of plot: Fantasy
Time of plot: The 1870's
Locale: St. Petersburg
First published: 1873 (English translation, 1919)

Principal characters:
IVAN IVANOVICH, the narrator and protagonist, an unsuccessful writer
PYOTR PETROVICH KLINEVICH, a baron
VASILY VASILEVICH PERVOEDOV, a fifty-seven-year-old major general
AVDOTYA IGNATYEVNA, a lady of high society
TARASEVICH, a seventy-year-old privy councillor
CATICHE BESETOVA, a young girl
PLATON NIKOLAEVICH, a philosopher, naturalist, and master of science
SEMYON EVSEICH LEBEZYATNIKOV, a court councillor
AN ENGINEER
A SHOPKEEPER
A YOUTH

The Story

The narrator, Ivan Ivanovich, is a disgruntled, unsuccessful writer who has had one novel and numerous journalistic columns rejected. He earns his living by translating from French and by writing advertisements. He is proud, resents his lack of success, and broods about his rejection. His anguished mental condition brought about by his intense feelings of inferiority leads others to regard him as insane. He himself acknowledges that something strange is happening to him. He complains of headaches and sees and hears strange visions and sounds. He is haunted by an enigmatic sound—"bobok." In order to distract himself, he attends the funeral of a distant relative, where he is treated haughtily, adding to his humiliation and resentment. After the funeral he remains in the cemetery, sits down on a tombstone, and becomes lost in reflection. He lies on a long stone shaped like a coffin and begins to hear muffled voices coming from the earth below. As he listens, he distinguishes various voices of the dead: the weighty, dignified voice of Major General Vasily Vasilevich Pervoedov; the saccharine, ingratiating voice of the court councillor Semyon Evseich Lebezyatnikov; the masculine, plebeian voice of a shopkeeper; the haughty voice of the irritable lady, Avdotya Ignatyevna; the frightened voice of a deceased youth; the lisping, peevishly imperious voice of the privy councillor, Tarasevich; the insolent, gentlemanly voice of Baron Pyotr Petrovich Klinevich; the cracked, giggling, girlish voice of the young Catiche Besetova; the bass voice of an engineer. While listening to the conversations, Ivan realizes that the life of the dead resembles the life of the living: Lebezyatnikov accuses Pervoedov of cheating in the card game they are playing; Avdotya complains of the shopkeeper's hiccuping and accuses him of shortchanging people when he was alive; the shopkeeper accuses Avdotya of not paying her debts; Lebezyatnikov suggests to Pervoedov that they tease Avdotya to relieve their boredom; Pervoedov accuses the deceased youth's doctor of overcharging his patients; Lebezyatnikov fawns and cringes before Pervoedov and Klinevich; Klinevich, a scoundrel who, while alive, passed counterfeit money and informed on his accomplice, reveals the crimes of the debauched Tarasevich, who stole money from widows and orphans; Tarasevich lusts after Catiche; everyone quarrels and engages in petty gossip. As the narrator continues to listen to the conversations of the deceased, the meaning of the enigmatic title of the story, "Bobok," is revealed. In response to Klinevich's query as to how it is possible that the dead can talk, Lebezyatnikov summarizes the theory of the philosopher Platon Nikolaevich, who maintains that after death, remnants of life become concentrated in the consciousness, which may last for two to six months until the decomposition of the body is complete. One of their number, Lebezyatnikov adds, one whose body has almost completely decomposed, nevertheless will occasionally utter a meaningless word or two, "Bobok, bobok"—a sign that even in him life "still flickers like an imperceptible spark." Klinevich suggests that before that vital spark of life disappears completely, they should arrange their lives differently, agreeing to be ashamed of nothing. All the deceased enthusiastically voice their assent as Klinevich urges them to live the last two months in shameless truth: "It's impossible to live on earth and not lie because living and lying are synonymous. But here, just for laughs, let's have no lying. Devil take it, after all, the grave does mean something!" Before the participants are able to bare their souls, Klinevich begins to tease General Pervoedov about his undue concern for rank and social standing even after death. The indignant Pervoedov defends rank and honor to the amusement and taunts of everyone. Amid the general pandemonium, the narrator, Ivan, inadvertently sneezes and everyone falls silent. Ivan leaves the cemetery disgusted by the pettiness and vulgarity of the dead in the midst of a holy and sanctified cemetery. He vows to return at a later date to learn more about the lives of the deceased. In the meantime, he will take his notes to a publisher in the hope that they will be printed.

Themes and Meanings

Dostoevski was essentially a religious writer interested in spiritual and moral questions. Throughout his career he attempted to portray moral beauty in all of its perfection. Two of his major protagonists, Prince Myshkin in *Idiot* (1868; *The Idiot*, 1887) and Alyosha in *Bratya Karamazovy* (1879-1880; *The Brothers Karamazov*, 1912), have Christlike qualities. They represent Dostoevski's attempt to portray a near-perfect, moral, compassionate human being. In contrast, the characters portrayed by Dostoevski in "Bobok" represent vice, debauchery, and pettiness. They engage in fraud, gambling, and theft. This portrait of the life of the dead reflects everything that is corrupt in an immoral, imperfect world. Dostoevski portrays moral corruption with the hope of awakening the reader's spiritual consciousness. He does this by means of a most unlikely vehicle—namely, the allegedly insane narrator, Ivan, who retains a sense of moral right and outrage. Ivan's first reaction to the graveyard and corpses is disgust at the smell of the decayed bodies. It becomes apparent, however, that the stench that overwhelms him is as much moral as physical. He is dismayed by the incongruity of true grief and feigned grief mixed with considerable ribaldry; such frivolity seems profoundly out of place in a cemetery. He is equally outraged to find one of the tombstones desecrated by a sandwich which someone has left on the tombstone. He throws it onto the ground since it is not bread (something sacred) but merely a sandwich (something profane). By the end of the story, Ivan is in complete despair over the petty conversations, debauchery, and squabbling which he has witnessed among the dead: "Debauchery in such a place, debauchery of last hopes, debauchery of flabby and rotting corpses, not even sparing the last moments of consciousness! . . . And worst of all, worst of all—in such a place! No, this I cannot tolerate."

Dostoevski uses Ivan as his vehicle for affirming the importance of spiritual consciousness. By the end of the story, Ivan has rejected the debauchery he has witnessed and has condemned the desecration of hallowed ground. He has learned the meaning of the enigmatic sound "bobok," which represents the last spark of consciousness left in human beings before the final decay of their bodies. Dostoevski valued consciousness as a source of possible spiritual regeneration and hope for humankind. By describing the bizarre afterlife of his characters, he draws attention to the threat of spiritual death, challenging readers to reevaluate their own moral standards and behavior in order to understand more clearly the importance of a spiritual existence.

Style and Technique

Dostoevski may be described as a fantastic realist. He constantly blurs the distinction between the real world and the dream world, the world of the sane and the insane. Here he achieves this effect through his use of the first-person narrator, Ivan Ivanovich, who is an alienated outsider. Dostoevski creates a feeling of emotional tension by writing in a staccato-type style, employing short syntactical units in rapid succession. When Ivan's friends suspect that he may be going insane, they recognize that a change has also occurred in Ivan's style of writing. One friend remarks: "Your style is changing... it's choppy. You chop and chop—you interpolate a clause, and then another clause within it, and then you add still something else in parenthesis, and then you start chopping and chopping again." This quotation describes accurately the style of those parts of the story in which the reader encounters Ivan's narrative voice. The reader is presented with Ivan's seemingly random thoughts in rapid succession—a device which anticipates the use of stream of consciousness in modern fiction.

By using a first-person narrator, Dostoevski draws the reader into a more personal relationship with the main protagonist and facilitates the reader's identification with the protagonist's thoughts, questions, doubts, and fantasies. It is through Ivan's reflections that Dostoevski raises the question of the standards by which society distinguishes the boundary between the normal and the abnormal. Ivan quotes a Spanish witticism directed against the first French lunatic asylum: "They've locked up all their fools in a special house to prove they are wise people themselves." He concludes that no one can prove his own sanity by stating someone else has gone mad, thereby defending himself against the charge of madness and leaving the final judgment up to the reader. The reader cannot be certain whether Ivan is sane or not, just as he cannot be sure whether Ivan is dreaming or actually hears the voices of the dead. Before Ivan hears the voices, he states simply: "At this point I sank into oblivion." He then listens to the protracted conversations of the deceased, which continue unabated until he inadvertently interrupts them by sneezing: "And here I suddenly sneezed. This was sudden and unintentional, but the effect was remarkable: All was hushed as though in a graveyard, vanished like a dream." The sneeze interrupts both the conversations of the dead and Ivan's meditations. Ivan returns to reality and vows to record and publish what he has heard. The reader is left to determine for himself the sanity of the narrator and the significance of what the narrator has learned and revealed.

Jerome J. Rinkus

BONTSHA THE SILENT

Author: Isaac Leib Peretz (1851-1915)
Type of plot: Satire
Time of plot: The late 1800's
Locale: Eastern Europe and Heaven
First published: "Bontche Shveig," 1894 (English translation, 1899)

Principal characters:
BONTSHA THE SILENT, the protagonist, a poor laborer
THE DEFENDING ANGEL, who recounts Bontsha's life
THE PROSECUTING ANGEL

The Story

In this characteristically ironic tale, Isaac Leib Peretz recounts the tragic life of one of his best-known protagonists, Bontsha the Silent. By opening with Bontsha's death, Peretz projects his narrative into the realm of the folktale, as he unveils before the readers fantastic scenes of Heaven, its host, and the proceedings of the heavenly court.

In the initial, opening phase of the story, Peretz presents a summary of Bontsha's traits and the troubled life he led. Bontsha, this insignificant man on earth, who "lived unknown, in silence, and in silence he died," is born to a poor Jewish family. He silently accepts pain from the outset when, at the age of eight days, his circumcision causes him undue bleeding and pain. Even at his Bar Mitzvah ceremony, the thirteen-year-old Bontsha remains silent, failing to deliver the traditional speech expected of young Jews entering adulthood.

Bontsha also remains silent when, as a grown-up, he uncomplainingly suffers the miseries, pain, and poverty his fate bestows upon him in a world too preoccupied with itself to notice the existence of those in need in life, illness, and death. All traces of Bontsha's shadowy existence are soon lost; the ephemeral quality of his earthly life is confirmed when the wooden marker falls off his grave, to be picked up and burned.

Surprisingly, however, Bontsha's death is known by everyone in Heaven, where his reception is excitedly anticipated. Although not noted for his holiness, fame, or righteousness, the silent Bontsha is accorded the highest honors (to the consternation of some saintly residents).

Bontsha remains, in death as in life, silent. Baffled and incredulous at the honors extended to him, he is certain that this is but a dream, soon to vanish as he again awakens to his hellish existence. Perhaps, he thinks, mistaken identity is the cause of this warm outpouring, soon to be reversed as in past experiences, when the error resulted in his becoming the brunt of embarrassed anger.

Bontsha's fear becomes magnified when, finding himself standing in the magnificently bejeweled court in Paradise, he is certain that he has been mistaken for someone else who would merit standing in so rich a palace.

Bontsha's trial begins; he, like all mortals, must pass before the heavenly tribunal to be rewarded or punished for his deeds on earth. His defending angel opens the testimony by presenting specific details to illustrate Bontsha's eternal, silent suffering at the hands of others. Beginning with Bontsha's birth, the defending angel details the sad life story of this humble man; the prosecuting angel mocks the defense's testimony, but Bontsha's advocate persists, recounting how this most silent, persevering sufferer lost his mother in his early years, only to be reared by a wicked stepmother whose stinginess with food was matched only by her generosity in meting out punishment. Bontsha was finally cast out of home (and on a cold wintry night) by his own father, a drunkard, to wander aimlessly and land in prison in the big city.

Silent even then, not questioning or protesting his imprisonment or the subsequent lowly jobs at which he works after being released, Bontsha continued to go through life. Finding a more decent job as a porter, Bontsha risked life and limb as he carried heavy loads on his back through crowded, traffic-laden streets. There too, however, he remained unchanged, often begging silently with his eyes only for the meager wages due him, accepting delays, and silently tolerating outright cheating. Bontsha never, says the defending angel, would compare his lot with that of others and would always accept his lot without a murmur against man or God.

A seemingly miraculous turn of events occurred in Bontsha's life when, having rescued a wealthy Jewish passenger from catastrophe in a runaway horse-drawn carriage, he was rewarded with a job as coachman, a marriage, and a child. Before he even had a chance to pay Bontsha, however, this philanthropist mysteriously went bankrupt. Bontsha's wife, meanwhile, ran off, leaving him with her son (who, when he grew up, threw Bontsha out of his house). Through all these troubled events, continues the defending angel, Bontsha continued to accept his fate silently and submissively, without a word of protest or complaint.

The defending angel, now speaking at length without the prosecutor's interruptions, reviews the circumstances of Bontsha's death, when he was run over by the very horse-drawn carriage of his former benefactor, who, as suddenly and mysteriously as before, recovered from bankruptcy, hired a new coachman, and continued living as before. Bontsha suffered his wounds from the accident in silence, in a hospital whose doctors and nurses ignored him and did nothing to ease his pain. Even while dying, Bontsha remained silent, never uttering a word against man or God.

Concluding his defense, the angel leaves Bontsha trembling in fear of what the prosecution will present from his murky past. Surprisingly, the prosecuting angel proclaims that "he was always silent—and now I too will be silent."

The judge, praising Bontsha's perseverance and silence in life, offers him any reward he wishes to choose in Paradise. Incredulously, Bontsha, now lifting his eyes, still needs the judge's repeated confirmation that it is indeed he who merits this highest of rewards. Bontsha's surprising request—in the light of all that is before him—is to have a roll and butter for breakfast every day.

The request lands like thunder, silencing and shaming the heavens. Only the prosecuting angel's loud laughter shatters the silence.

Themes and Meanings

In the character of Bontsha, Peretz has fashioned the supreme example of tolerance, passivity, and silent suffering. By his silence, Bontsha is as a mirror, reflecting the inhumanity of man to man in a modern world.

Like the biblical Job—who, as commentaries emphasize, did not complain when his fate turned bad, saying, "Shall we accept good from God, and not accept evil?" Bontsha is a little man in a big world, accepting his lot without a word against man or God. Unlike Job, however, Bontsha lacks the dreams, aspirations, and passion to attain a better life. Through Bontsha's story, Peretz champions those lowly and downtrodden segments of society, targets for exploitation by a ruling class preoccupied with selfish concerns.

Writing for and about the lower class of Eastern European Jewry at the turn of the twentieth century, Peretz also adopted and adapted familiar aspects of Jewish folktales (including the tales of Hasidic Jews). Thus, for example, in this and other stories, he depends on traditional tales set in Paradise; also traditional is the depiction of the heavenly court. At the same time, in presenting the latter Peretz reveals his experiences as a lawyer. By such means, the author lends his story an aura of the folktale while also keeping the ironic barbs inherent in his modern, secularized point of view.

Style and Technique

How can the lifetime of any individual be encapsulated and dramatically presented in a brief short story? In "Bontsha the Silent," Peretz has demonstrated his skills at creating tense dramatic plot by constructing events in cyclic, repeating episodes which accomplish the desired effect of deepening the character's personality while also leaving him to represent the plight of all downtrodden people.

The first cycle constitutes the story's opening, wherein the narrative recounts—briefly and with few embellishing details—the plight and travails of the protagonist in a reverse order, moving backward from his death and returning to the circumstances of the very disappearance of his grave marker.

Peretz then shifts to ironic contrast as all in Heaven are excited at the news of Bontsha's imminent arrival. Irony is indeed the most outstanding device used by the author to lend his story the dramatic force and poignancy so necessary in a satire. Also notable is the manner in which Peretz gradually silences the prosecuting angel's objections; this permits the uninterrupted flow of the defending angel's account to envelop the reader completely.

The episode of the trial provides the occasion for the second biographical cycle, wherein the defending angel shocks the reader with more explicit details of the cruelty encountered by Bontsha during his lifetime. Even more so in this instance, the author expresses his strong views concerning the injustices still going on in a world proudly calling itself modern and progressive.

Stephen Katz

THE BOTTLE IMP

Author: Robert Louis Stevenson (1850-1894)
Type of plot: Modern fairy tale
Time of plot: Late nineteenth century
Locale: Hawaii
First published: 1893

> *Principal characters:*
> KEAWE, a young Hawaiian sailor who is " poor, brave, and
> active"
> KOKUA, his wife
> LOPAKA, another Hawaiian sailor, his friend

The Story

While making a visit to San Francisco "to have a sight of the great world," Keawe, a young Hawaiian sailor, admires the opulent houses of the rich. He is particularly impressed by one house, which, while smaller than the rest, is "all finished and beautified like a toy." To his surprise, he discovers that the elderly man who lives in this beautiful house is "heavy with sorrow" and sighs constantly. The elderly man tells Keawe that his house and all his fortune came from an imp who lives in a magic bottle. The imp will grant any wish that the owner of the bottle makes, but if the owner dies before he sells the bottle, "he must burn in hell forever." The person who sells the bottle must always sell it for less than he paid for it. The elderly man tricks Keawe into buying the bottle for fifty dollars, which is all the money that Keawe has. Keawe attempts to discard the bottle or sell it for a profit, but it magically comes back to him.

When he returns to Hawaii, Keawe finds that his uncle and cousin have died, leaving him their land and a large sum of money. Resolving that he "may as well take the good along with the evil" of the bottle, Keawe has a beautiful house, called Bright House, built overlooking the ocean. His friend Lopaka persuades him to call the imp out of the bottle so that they can see what it looks like; although they are horrified at the appearance of the imp, Lopaka buys the bottle in order to enlist its power to obtain a schooner for himself.

Free of the bottle, Keawe lives in Bright House in "perpetual joy"; he could not "walk in the chambers without singing." He sees a beautiful young woman, Kokua, bathing in the sea and instantly falls in love with her. She agrees to marry him, but then Keawe discovers that he has contracted leprosy. Unwilling to marry Kokua while he has this dread disease, Keawe resolves to buy the bottle again, although "ice ran in his veins" at the thought of the evil-looking imp. He goes in search of Lopaka, and although he cannot find his friend, he succeeds in tracing the bottle, which is now in the possession of a young white man who was desperate to pay back some money that he had embezzled and paid only two cents for the bottle. It appears that anyone who buys it from him for one cent will have no opportunity to sell it for a coin of less value. Nevertheless, Keawe buys the bottle and, again resolving to "take the good along with the evil," wishes himself free of leprosy and marries Kokua.

In spite of Kokua's beauty, Keawe must "weep and groan to think upon the price that he had paid for her" because he believes that he has "no better hope but to be a cinder forever in the flames of hell." When he realizes that Kokua is blaming herself for his unhappiness, he tells her the whole story of the bottle. She tells him about a French coin, the centime, which is worth "five to the cent or thereabout," and they go to Tahiti to sell the bottle for four centimes.

When they encounter unexpected difficulty in selling the bottle, Kokua exclaims, "A love for a love, and let mine be equalled with Keawe's! A soul for a soul, and be it mine to perish!" Resolving to buy the bottle herself, she finds an old man and asks him to buy the bottle for four centimes, promising to buy it from him for three. She bravely fulfills her promise, but afterward in her imagination "all that she had heard of hell came back to her; she saw the flames blaze, and she smelled the smoke, and her flesh withered on the coals." Not realizing that his wife now owns the bottle, Keawe condemns her for not participating in his joy at being rid of it. Angry at her and feeling unacknowledged guilt over the fate of the old man who he thinks owns the bottle, he accuses Kokua of disloyalty and goes out to carouse with some friends.

One of his drinking companions is a brutal white man who has been "a boatswain of a whaler—a runaway, a digger in gold mines, a convict in prisons." The boatswain, who has a "low mind and a foul mouth," encourages Keawe to drink until he runs out of money. Returning to his house for more money, Keawe sees Kokua with the bottle and realizes her sacrifice. He slips away before Kokua sees him and resolves to become the owner of the bottle for the third time. Although his soul is "bitter with despair," he persuades the boatswain to buy the bottle for two centimes, promising to buy it from him for one. When Keawe attempts to fulfill his promise, the boatswain refuses to sell. Keawe reminds him that the owner of the bottle will go to hell, but the boatswain replies, "I reckon I'm going anyway . . . and this bottle's the best thing to go with I've struck yet." He goes away with the bottle, leaving Keawe and Kokua to the "peace of all their days in the Bright House."

Themes and Meanings

Like fairy stories and the tales from *The Arabian Nights' Entertainments* that it resembles, "The Bottle Imp" posits a clear contrast between good and evil, asserts the power of love and sacrifice in overcoming evil, and rewards its good characters with a lifetime of continuing happiness.

Keawe rather innocently entangles himself with evil because he is so deeply impressed by the opulent house in San Francisco, but once he buys the bottle—without quite realizing that he has done so—he finds it difficult to disentangle himself from its evil. The fact that his uncle and cousin die to leave him the land on which he builds his house and the coincidence that the cost of this house is exactly the sum that his uncle leaves him suggest that the evil imp in the bottle exacts a high price for his favors, but Robert Louis Stevenson does not insist on this point as the story develops.

Having relied on the imp for his house, Keawe, perhaps naturally, seeks his help in curing his leprosy, but this time an important new motive has been added: Keawe would willingly resign himself to exile in the leper colony at Molokai if it were not for his love of Kokua. The importance of love in opposition to evil is henceforth the main theme of the story.

In Tahiti, Kokua, mindful that Keawe bought the bottle the second time because of his love for her, buys the bottle herself, willing to sacrifice her own soul for Keawe. When Keawe discovers what she has done, he resolves to purchase the bottle a third time to save his wife. This time, it is important to note, he is motivated by awareness of her sacrifice rather than by delight in her beauty; his infatuation seems to have deepened into a nobler love.

Although the lovers overcome the evil of the imp, Stevenson throughout the story emphasizes the stark reality of evil. Lopaka and Keawe are figuratively "turned to stone" by the sight of the imp, and both Keawe and Kokua are cast in such despair by the prospect of an eternity in hell that they are unable to enjoy the love for which they have sacrificed themselves.

Style and Technique

As the theme of the story utilizes the clear contrast of good and evil that is characteristic of a fairy story, so are the plot devices and the style reminiscent of this genre. Keawe, motivated initially by Kokua's beauty, falls in love at first sight; after they succeed in disposing of the bottle, they live "happily ever after"—and Stevenson narrowly misses ending the story with this venerable cliché. Of the plot devices borrowed from the fairy-tale tradition, the most significant is the bottle imp himself, who can grant any wish, but who nevertheless is a sinister presence. No attempt is made to explain this bottle by any rational means or to treat it as a symbol: It is simply magic.

Stevenson's descriptions deliberately emulate the lack of specificity and the unreality of a fairy story: When Keawe builds his house, "a garden bloomed about that house with every hue of flowers," and Kokua is "so fashioned, from the hair upon her head to the nails upon her toes, that none could see her without joy." The tone of the dialogue is more conventional than real: Keawe declares that in his beautiful house his wish is "to live there without care and to make merry with my friends and relatives." Studied inversions of word order ("great was their joy that night") and occasional use of exclamations such as "behold!" give the style a deliberately archaic flavor.

Erwin Hester

A BOTTLE OF MILK FOR MOTHER

Author: Nelson Algren (1909-1981)
Type of plot: Naturalism
Time of plot: The 1930's
Locale: Chicago
First published: 1941

> *Principal characters:*
> BRUNO "LEFTY" BICEK, the protagonist, a hoodlum and boxer
> CAPTAIN KOZAK, Bruno's principal interrogator
> SERGEANT ADAMOVITCH, an older, class-conscious, Polish-
> American policeman
> A NEWSPAPER REPORTER, the witness to the interrogation

The Story

"A Bottle of Milk for Mother" is an interrogation story that pits a young Polish hoodlum against an experienced, cynical police captain. From the time that he is brought into the interrogation room until he is led to his cell, Bruno struggles to maintain his composure, to use his street knowledge of law, and to avoid implicating his friend and accomplice Benkowski. Unfortunately for Bruno, while he succeeds in shielding Benkowski, his case is "well disposed of," and he is left to tell himself, "I knew I'd never get to be twenty-one anyhow."

Rather than have his men tell their story about the robbery and shooting of the drunk, Kozak insists on Bruno telling his own story. From the start, Kozak assumes Bruno's guilt, as well as Benkowski's, and Bruno is quickly reduced from denying knowledge of the drunk to explaining how the one shot must have "bounced." Kozak dismisses out of hand the "just getting a bottle of milk for Mother" explanation, and then he attacks Bruno's ego. First, Kozak breaks Bruno's valuable spring-blade knife, a symbol of his manhood, and Bruno winces "as though he himself had received the blow." Then Kozak calls Bruno "Lefty," thereby appealing to his vanity, for he is proud of his pitching prowess, but also encouraging him to talk. Just as the appeal to motherhood fails, so do his appeals to identification ("I'm just a neighborhood kid"), to political interference (he "innocently" refers to his ties to the "alderman," Kozak's brother), to ethnicity (he claims that he spoke Polish to the drunk and tried to make him a better Polish "citizen"), and even to patriotism (his gang is not the Warriors, but the "Baldhead True American Social 'n Athletic Club").

As Bruno continues his story, Kozak abruptly intervenes with questions that assume Bruno's guilt. When Bruno talks about his pitching arm, Kozak interjects, "So you kept the rod in your left hand?" When Bruno inadvertently mentions that "we" saw the drunk, Kozak notes the reference and asks, "Who's 'we,' Left-hander?" When Bruno declares that he does not know Benkowski very well, Kozak catches him in the lie. By the time that Bruno finishes his rambling story about what "possessed" the gang to shave their heads, there is no question about his guilt; and when he refuses to implicate Benkowski, only the sentencing remains. Because he has not cooperated with Kozak, Bruno receives no mercy.

Perhaps because Benkowski has advised him, Bruno assumes that he will be able to escape relatively unscathed. He considers acting "screwy," weighs the chances of having a conviction overturned because of the newspaperman's presence, figures that the "bouncing bullet" will mean manslaughter instead of murder, and believes that because "this is a first offense 'n self-defense," he will receive only "one to fourteen" years as a sentence. Kozak asks, "Who give you *that* idea?" He appears to know that Bruno has been counseled, probably by Benkowski, and when Bruno again fails to cooperate, he explains that, in fact, he will not be able to "lam out" of the death penalty for first-degree murder.

Bruno's fate is sealed when Kozak asks, "What do you think we ought to do with a man like you, Bicek?" While Bruno notices the change from the familiar "Lefty" to the more impersonal "Bicek," he does not notice the significance of "man." Bruno has referred to himself as a "kid" to win sympathy—and to avoid the "adult" murder charge—and Kozak has called Bruno and his gang "boys." While it is true that Bruno does not want to be considered a "greenhorn sprout," he is not ready to be treated and tried as an adult.

Bruno passes from boyhood to manhood and then to a state of nonbeing. Once Kozak has "disposed" of his case, Bruno ceases to exist for the authorities. Kozak studies the charge sheet "as though Bruno Lefty Bicek were no longer in the room" and looks at Bruno with "no light of recognition." Bruno implores the policemen, "Don't look at me like I ain't nowheres," but no one listens to him. At this point, Bruno is not a person but a "case" for Kozak; for Adamovitch, the traditionalist, Bruno is a sinner who must be made to feel his guilt. When he sees Bruno go down on his knees, he is satisfied that the unrepentant sinner has turned to God. Bruno, however, is only groping for his hat. The image with which the reader is left is not one of the repentant sinner or even of a defiant young man; it is one of a man "on all fours" like an animal, certain only of his impending death.

Themes and Meanings

"A Bottle of Milk for Mother," the winner of an O. Henry Memorial Prize, is a typical Nelson Algren story in its characters, setting, and themes. In fact, the story in revised form also appears in Algren's novel *Never Come Morning* (1942), which also has Bruno "Lefty" Bicek as its protagonist. In both the short story and the novel, Bruno's world is circumscribed: the Polish ghetto of Chicago in the novel, and an interrogation room in the short story. While Bruno is ambitious and seeks to "make his fortune," he has only the illusion of freedom, and he is, in fact, a victim who cannot really "move" or escape from the fate that his environment—ethnic, economic, political— imposes on him.

In the first sentence of the story, Algren describes the murder as Bruno's "final difficulty with the Racine Street police," and the reader learns that the outcome of the story is never in doubt. Algren focuses not on what will happen, but on Bruno's growing awareness of and resignation to his fate. Though the setting remains the same, Bruno's options disappear one by one until his only "escape" is an imaginative one. Algren's theme is Bruno's entrapment, "imprisonment," so to speak, before the sentence is ever pronounced. Early in the story, Bruno feels "the semicircle about him drawing closer," even though none of the police actually moves toward him. Throughout the interrogation Bruno stands immobile. When he shuffles his feet and moves to unbutton his shirt, Adamovitch stops him; his only movements are the "scuffling" of his shoes. He does move his eyes, but only to "fix" them as a window to the outside world. In effect, the athletic Bruno is ironically rendered incapable of real action, and he "acts" only in a dramatic sense. When his act elicits only guffaws and derisive laughter from his "audience," he retreats into a fantasy world in which he "zigzags" his way to freedom; the fact that his escape is imagined in cinematic terms (he compares himself to George Raft, an actor famous for his gangster roles) implies that Bruno cannot literally see himself escaping

Style and Technique

Like many of the other stories from *The Neon Wilderness* (1946), "A Bottle of Milk for Mother" is essentially a "slice of life," a story that is short on external action, focusing instead on the protagonist's internal action, in this case the realization that he is incapable of acting. The title of the volume of Algren's short stories stresses the ironic incongruity between neon modernity and old-fashioned wilderness: There are no contemporary heroes. As in Algren's other works, irony abounds in this story, particularly in terms of the "lone wolf" motif (which is particularly appropriate to a "wilderness"). After Bruno mentions that he was acting on his own, practicing "lone-wolf stuff," that term is used, even exploited, by the newspaper reporter, who envisions using the term ironically to comment on Bruno's paralysis: "The Lone Wolf of Potomac Street waited miserably. . . ." Certainly there is irony at the end of the story when the penitent sinner turns out to be a criminal who is looking for his hat.

Algren uses a mixture of realism and impressionism to convey setting, characters, and theme. While he uses "realistic" dialogue, which effectively captures the street vernacular, with its bad grammar, slang, and colloquial expressions, Algren is hardly objective in his selection of details and his metaphors. Kozak is characterized by his "St. Bernard mouth," which renders him less human, and on another occasion his manner is compared with "the false friendliness of the insurance man urging a fleeced customer toward the door." The reporter is never identified by name; in fact, he is not a person, but a "raccoon coat" adjusting his glasses. The images of the setting that Algren presents are equally depressing. When Bruno looks out the window, he sees a January sun "glowing sullenly," almost as if it were commenting on the actions within the room. When Bruno hears "outside" sounds, the Chicago Avenue streetcar seems to screech "as though a cat were caught beneath its back wheels." There certainly are ties between the cat and Bruno, for both face death, but there are also ties between the streetcar wheels and the proverbial "wheels of justice." When the simile is followed by the shadows "within shadows" in the cell, the reader is left with images that suggest inevitable death at the hands of a mechanistic, impersonal machine.

Thomas L. Erskine

BOULE DE SUIF

Author: Guy de Maupassant (1850-1893)
Type of plot: Social realism
Time of plot: During the Franco-Prussian War, about 1870
Locale: On the road between Rouen and the port city of Havre, France
First published: 1880 (English translation, 1903)

> *Principal characters:*
> ELIZABETH ROUSSET, "Boule de Suif," a prostitute and the
>   protagonist
> MONSIEUR and MADAME LOISEAU, wholesale wine merchants
> MONSIEUR and MADAME CARRÉ-LAMADON, members of the
>   growing industrial aristocracy
> CORNUDET, a dissolute man with political ambitions
> PRUSSIAN OFFICER

The Story

A coach is making its way along the icy road to Havre. Its passengers are sitting silently, eyeing one another, trying to reach the port in spite of the war-torn countryside and the advancing Prussian troops. Self-conscious of respectability, they are uncomfortable sitting in the same coach with "a member of the courtesan class," who is nicknamed "Boule de Suif" (ball of fat) because she is so round. The journey is long and tedious, so that when Boule de Suif takes some food from her traveling basket and good-heartedly offers to share it among the others, the passengers—begrudgingly at first and then avidly—eat and drink their fill; even the two nuns indulge with comic delicacy. Before long, they are all talking amiably about patriotism and the evil Prussians.

That night, the coach stops at an inn behind the Prussian lines and the passengers are given separate rooms. During the night, officious Monsieur Loiseau keeps his eyes to the keyhole of his door, trying to observe "the mysteries of the corridor." He sees the rogue Cornudet make advances to Boule de Suif, but she rebuffs him, insisting on maintaining her dignity in the midst of the enemy. A Prussian officer, the presiding "law" in that part of the country, has set up his headquarters in the inn and is staying in a room just down the hall. Under such circumstances, she tells Cornudet, one must keep one's self-respect.

The next morning, the passengers find the coach unharnessed and themselves detained. They learn that the Prussian officer has forbidden them to leave until Boule de Suif gives herself to him. She is shocked and angry at the proposal, and, for a while, so are the other passengers. Days pass. The Prussian waits. Soon the passengers grow impatient, and the Prussian's tactic of wearing down their shallow moral indignation begins to work. They begin to hatch their own strategy for getting Boule de Suif to capitulate. The wives talk to her of romantic self-sacrifice; the nuns, too, are enlisted, preaching to her of purity of motive. The men talk of war and glorious patriotism. Throughout lunch and dinner and into the evening hours the psychological assault on Boule de Suif continues. Ironically, only Cornudet, the old rogue, refuses to have anything to do with the scheme.

Finally, exhausted, confused, and burdened with guilt over being the cause of the group's internment, Boule de Suif yields and gives herself to the Prussian. That night, the passengers celebrate victory. Loiseau "stands champagne all round." Only Cornudet is sullen. "You have done an infamous thing," he tells them.

Next morning, the passengers find the coach ready for their departure. Boule de Suif is the first to climb in, and at last they resume their journey. Now, however, the passengers snub Boule de Suif. They talk among themselves, showing her their disdain. Chatting amiably, they do not seem to care that in the dark corner of the coach Boule de Suif is silently weeping.

Themes and Meanings

"Boule de Suif" is primarily a study of character: an objective account of how people can be kind when it is easy to be so, but selfish and mean when they must endure even the most temporary of personal privations.

The coach making its way to the port is, in effect, a ship of fools and knaves. Maupassant himself tells the reader that the passengers represent "Society," a cross section of humanity, the middle class of steady virtue, smugly riding to their destination. Boule de Suif is also part of the cross section. Of strong peasant stock, she is as easy, as free with her public virtue as her fellow passengers are sternly covetous of theirs. In fact, the power of "Boule de Suif" is achieved thematically by a contrast between the public virtue practiced by the majority and the private, personal morality that only Boule de Suif truly possesses. Publicly, the characters are solid *bourgeois* playing the role society expects of them, even showing their "democratic" spirit when sharing Boule de Suif's lunch. They have already condemned her, nevertheless, because, as a prostitute, Boule de Suif has publicly played her expected role as well. In the privacy of their cabal, and in their hearts, they are as corrupt as the public image they perceive to be Boule de Suif. Their plot is demoniacally brilliant, depending as it does on the cooperation of all the members of the group—society—and appealing to the various forms of public virtue, such as patriotism and self-sacrifice. "What did you expect from that kind of woman?" is their ultimate response to the success of their scheme.

Boule de Suif ironically shows herself superior to her fellow passengers. Her initial refusal to submit to Cornudet and then to the Prussian runs contrary to her public image. Her private moral principles are inviolate; though the others talk of patriotism, they spout mere platitudes and generalities. They are thus supreme hypocrites. Only Boule de Suif is honest, and she shows true courage and patriotism in standing up for her principles. Though she ultimately submits, her surrender is not for personal gain or public approval, but motivated by guilt, by fear that she was hurting her companions. Her capitulation is thus of the same order as her sharing of her lunch with them—a generosity of spirit, a wholesomeness that her bourgeois companions would never understand. She sacrifices her body; they, their souls.

Style and Technique

Like many great literary works, "Boule de Suif" succeeds by in integration of method with subject matter. Though Maupassant is often classified as a naturalistic writer, that is, as an artist who records events with relentless objectivity, "Boule de Suif" is marked by subtle ironies of tone and detail that shrewdly comment on the action while seemingly only recording it. Though the authorial voice seems never to judge the characters or the action, narrating events swiftly and precisely, such basic narrative techniques as description of setting and the use of metaphor often amplify and deepen the meaning of the simple prose.

Maupassant takes great care in presenting the chaos of the French countryside during the Franco-Prussian War, delaying the introduction of the characters until the details of violence have established a tension which effectively prepares the reader for the real conflict between private and public virtue. The setting serves as a correlative to the battle that the coach party will wage against the principles of Boule de Suif. The season is winter, and the French are losing the war, just as the coach party coldly lays its trap, having already lost its virtue.

Even the metaphors support the idea of warfare. As the characters plot against Boule de Suif, Maupassant describes their machinations in terms of infantry besieging a "human citadel" which must "receive the enemy within its walls." Each agrees on the "plan of attack," and it is the women who begin, quoting ancient examples of self-sacrifice during wartime, from Judith and Holofernes to the Roman matrons and Hannibal. Moreover, the weather grows worse as the characters hatch their scheme. Each day of their detainment, the cold grows more intense, more painful, so that their assault on Boule de Suif takes place during a time of numbing cold, again paralleling their own heartlessness.

Finally, there is irony even in the song Cornudet sings at the close of the story. "The love of country is sacred," he sings. "Liberty, dear liberty, fight with her defenders." The true defenders of liberty are not the passengers and their bourgeois values, but the country courtesan, Boule de Suif. Thus, Maupassant reinforces a swiftly moving, simple narrative with equally simple technical devices and rhetorical descriptions to make "Boule de Suif" a masterpiece of irony.

Edward Fiorelli

THE BOWMEN OF SHU

Author: Guy Davenport (1927-   )
Type of plot: Historical reminiscence
Time of plot: 1914-1915
Locale: The World War I French-German front
First published: 1984

Principal characters:
    HENRI GAUDIER-BRZESKA, a modernist sculptor who died in
        1915
    SOPHIE, the sculptor's wife

The Story
    The title of "The Bowmen of Shu" suggests a time and place far from the World War I foxholes that readers see the story's hero, Henri Gaudier-Brzeska, inhabiting. The twenty-three-year-old French sculptor, in whose work and intelligence the poet Ezra Pound discerned the signs of a twentieth century renaissance, has left his London studio for the trenches. Readers see him sleeping on mud and ice, fighting lustily, meditating on art, war, and nature, asking London correspondents about the art culture he is cut off from, and discussing labyrinths with the scholar and fellow soldier Robert de Launay. "The Bowmen of Shu" is named for a poem of the same title by Ezra Pound which Gaudier-Brzeska quotes in letters to friends in London. The poem presents the feelings of ancient Chinese warriors fighting a lingering war with a stubborn enemy. Their fight, like that of the soldiers of World War I, is a stalemate, with many battles fought but no victory. Gaudier-Brzeska savors the closeness of the centuries-old Chinese emotions to his own. The bowman who says, "Our sorrow is bitter, but we would not return to our country," Gaudier-Brzeska echoes in a letter describing the surprising stoicism he feels about his most miserable circumstances: "Whatever the suffering may be it is soon forgotten and we want the victory."
    The story is a collection of images and anecdotes having to do with Gaudier-Brzeska's life before, as well as during, the war. Selections from his foxhole mail to friends are interspersed with scenes of his life before the war, as far back as his first day of school. As a child he loved to draw insects and flowers. He defied his parents' spankings with precociously stubborn and reasonable arguments. As an art student of seventeen he fell in love with Sophie, his senior by twenty-two years, whose biography, a testament of pure misery, is summarized in two pages of the story. As a sculptor, Gaudier-Brzeska showed a striking originality. He was part of the modernist movement which included Sir Jacob Epstein, Constantin Brancuşi, and Amedeo Modigliani, names whose fame, this story assures readers, Henri Gaudier-

Brzeska would have surpassed had he lived. His personal manifesto on sculpture was claimed by the vorticist movement in London as the clearest statement of what they were about.

The war took him. His captain praised him for the bravery and intelligence he demonstrated to others. Bullets, bombs, and gas inhibited neither his craft ("With my knife I have carved the stock of a German rifle into a woman. . . .") nor his theorizing: "Like the Africans I am constrained by the volume of my material, the figure to be found wholly within a section of trunk" ("the trunk" referring to the gun stock). Descended from the masons who built Chartres Cathedral, Gaudier-Brzeska watches as a cathedral burns to the ground, its lead roof melting onto the rubble. He savors the irony and pattern of his fate, trapped in the labyrinth of trenches which the anthropologist de Launay, who has made a career of studying mazes, now has the opportunity to study in actuality. The Germans constructed a real labyrinth during the war, a system of fortifications, tunnels, caves, and shelters out of which they would come to surprise the enemy. The primitivity of war, its brutality, Gaudier-Brzeska and de Launay both see as the expression of urges men have acted out since the days of Paleolithic hunters. They stand up to it with philosophical interest and curiosity but admit its unspeakable horror, and it claims both of them. De Launay is shot through the neck, and Gaudier-Brzeska, leading a charge, is shot through the head.

Themes and Meanings

A central thread in the story is the theme of the artist's precariousness in the world, a world which in its mysterious history turns upon itself and devours the riches of human culture that artists such as Gaudier-Brzeska create, or, in Gaudier-Brzeska's case, which destroys the maker himself. The story, however, is more than a tirade against stupid men who kill geniuses. As Gaudier-Brzeska recognized, art and contention have a mysterious linkage. Stone Age man filled caves with drawings of animals as a result of daily conflicts with real animals. Gaudier-Brzeska, known for his intense absorption while in the act of sculpting, found shooting at Germans similarly stimulating: "We shot at each other some quarter of an hour at a distance of 12 to 15 yards and the work was deadly. I brought down two great giants who stood against a burning heap of straw." The war paradoxically heightens his sense of life: "I have been fighting for two months and I can now gauge the intensity of life." That intensity took for Gaudier-Brzeska a vision of life persisting unabated by the stupendous destruction of modern war, which set out to blast every square foot of soil held by the enemy. Life ignored the bombardment. Gaudier-Brzeska explained in the manifesto he wrote in the trenches that the outline of the hills did not change as a result of the barrage of exploding shells. Life does not alter, but men alter and are altered. Gaudier-Brzeska's medium, stone, required the cutting, grinding, and biting of tools:

"You brush away, blow away the dust the fine blade has crumbled." Arguments by art critics such as T. E. Hulme required words chosen "with booming precision and attack." A model posing for one of Gaudier-Brzeska's sculptures fights her body's inclination to relax. While sculpting, Gaudier-Brzeska pauses to watch a dogfight in the street outside his studio. His nose bleeds as he works and the model ties a rag to his face to absorb the blood.

The story, then, posits the mystery of the artist's dealings with energy, the energy or passion stirred in him by what he sees, and the form of energy he establishes in a work of art. Unfortunately for Gaudier-Brzeska, the energy he was born to observe—the stance of a panther, the head of his friend Ezra Pound, the monumental curves of a woman—conflicted with another energy of which the poem's bowmen and Gaudier-Brzeska shared experience in wars. Gaudier-Brzeska's avid entry into conflict, whether with a spanking parent or a German soldier, is heroic. As a sculptor, he battled the stone to establish a form he carried in his head, a form of beauty. As a soldier, he kills and dies "pour la Patrie" (for the fatherland). To Sophie, his beloved, he was nasty because "you don't love me nearly so much as I love you," he said. The resistance of stone, the resistance of the enemy, the resistance of the beloved—"whatever the suffering may be it is soon forgotten and we want the victory."

Style and Technique

The author of this story, Guy Davenport, has his own term to describe his style. He calls it "assemblage." Blocks of narrative are arranged in a series with no chronological order. Each piece in the assemblage is titled, whether it is a two-page description of Gaudier-Brzeska's wife or a single line explaining the nickname ("La Rosalie") of the bayonet ("so called because we draw it red from the round guts of pig eyed Germans").

This "assemblage" style emphasizes the story's visual presence and structure. To heighten the visual even more, Davenport insets his drawings of Gaudier-Brzeska's statues, drawings, and photos of the sculptor. The subject of the story, Gaudier-Brzeska, presides even in the interstices. Gaudier-Brzeska contributed to the birth of a new style of sculpture, one that created emotion in the viewer through the abstract arrangement of planes. Sculpting the head of Ezra Pound, he explained that no natural resemblance would result: "It will look like your energy." Davenport's technique—the fragmenting of narrative, the uses of real historical people as characters, the quoting of real letters (and creative transpositions of real letters)—owes much to the revolution all artistic forms underwent in the early twentieth century. As a story it is a graph of the author's peculiarly bright, visualizing mind as it confronts the subject—the sculptor Henri Gaudier-Brzeska. There are sharp twists, assimilations, sudden pictures, sharp edges of single sentences which work more like a poetic line that narrative. The art of such technique lies in striking from discontinuous surfaces the desired result of irony, contrast, or restatement. French erupts to conclude the second half of a paragraph begun in English. In one fragment, Gaudier-Brzeska's captain praises him for his bravery, and in the next, the obscure mother of the dead sculptor laments his passing. The style forces the reader to pay attention to the text in a new way. It challenges the reader to interpret, to discern, without the help of transitions, introductions, and footnotes. The result, for the attentive reader, is a sense of history much brighter than history read in textbooks. In "The Bowmen of Shu," it creates a graph of an outmoded concept: the hero.

Bruce Wiebe

BOXCAR OF CHRYSANTHEMUMS

Author: Fumiko Enchi (1905-   )
Type of plot: Domestic realism
Time of plot: The 1960's
Locale: Karuizawa and vicinity
First published: "Kikuguruma," 1967 (English translation, 1982)

> *Principal characters:*
> I, the narrator, a woman writer
> ICHIGE RIE, the wife of
> ICHIGE MASUTOSHI, a mental defective who was once scion to
> a wealthy family
> KUROKAWA, a local resident whose father has told him about
> the Ichige family
> KASHIMURA, a psychiatric intern who once hoped to marry
> Rie

The Story

The narrator is a middle-aged woman, much like the author, who has left her summer home at Karuizawa to go to a nearby town to give a talk to a woman's group. She returns to Karuizawa on a train that is unexpectedly slow, not only stopping at every single station along the way but also making remarkably long stops.

At one stop the narrator finally gets off the train, partly to relieve her irritation and frustration and partly to learn the cause of the delays. She finds the station attendants loading long bundles into freight cars. At the same time, she encounters a middle-aged woman accompanied by an old man who is clearly mentally deficient. The station attendants are loading bundles of cut chrysanthemums which are being shipped on the overnight train to flower markets in Tokyo. The couple has come to the station because the old man has an obsessive concern about how his flowers are handled.

Returning to her seat on the train, the narrator learns from a local person named Kurokawa something about the odd couple she has met on the platform. He confirms that the old man is retarded and obsessed with growing chrysanthemums; he also informs the narrator that the train is going to be much slower than she had planned, but that "you might as well just get used to it and consider it an elegant way to travel." He then tells the story of the couple, Ichige Masutoshi and his wife Rie, as it was passed on to him by his father. The Ichiges had once been a wealthy family, although they have since gone bankrupt. The narrator is shocked to learn that when the family was in its heyday they arranged for Rie, one of their servants, to be a sort of human sacrifice and to marry their retarded son. Kurokawa explains that he, too, was shocked at first, but that during the war Rie had always shown up for volunteer work, had effectively managed the family garden, and, in short, had won everyone's respect by working hard and taking good care of her husband. Now that the Ichige family has lost its money, Rie has to work harder than ever to feed her husband. Indeed, Kurokawa's father saw Rie as supernaturally good, an embodiment of Kannon, the Goddess of Mercy.

Kurokawa's story reminds the narrator of yet an earlier occasion when she had heard something about the Ichige family. Many years earlier, while writing a play about a mental patient, the narrator had gotten to know some psychiatric interns from whom she learned another aspect of the Ichige family history. Because their retarded son had excessive sexual drives, the family chose to marry him to one of the maids who could look after all of his physical needs, although they had taken the precaution of having the son sterilized before he was married. At the same time, the family hired interns from the school of psychiatry to take turns standing by each night in a room next to the bedroom of the newlyweds so that they could intervene if the son turned violent. Again, censure is aimed at Rie: How could anyone agree to such a marriage, no matter how much she was being paid? Blame is also heaped upon the Ichige family for doing this. Years later, however, one of the former interns, now Dr. Kashimura, confessed to the narrator that he had fallen in love with Rie and had asked her to marry him, but she had refused, saying that she loved her husband.

At last the narrator arrives home at Karuizawa, far later than she had expected. She is still troubled about Rie and her motives for living with her retarded husband. The narrator finds Rie's devotion to be absurd; her final observation, however, is that she has reached an age when she can accept the motives and behavior of others even when their actions seem beyond comprehension.

Themes and Meanings

In this work, as in many of her stories and novels, the author explores the situation of women in the modern world. Here, she puzzles over the motives and feelings that have led Rie to devote herself to an older and mentally deficient man who has been abusive to her. In her own mind the narrator finds Rie's choice absurd, yet each time the narrator comes to this conclusion, there is a redeeming consideration. When Kurokawa tells his father's story, both the narrator and Kurokawa are appalled at Rie's fate, yet Kurokawa then goes on to depict Rie as a model wife who has won the respect of all the local people. Similarly, when the narrator recalls the experience of the psychiatric interns, she is disbelieving that anyone would put herself into such a physically and emotionally outrageous position. At precisely this point the reader learns that Dr. Kashimura asked Rie to marry him and she refused, so one knows that she was not desperately seeking some means of escape. She has chosen to live this way and makes herself an example of virtuous behavior; she truly becomes transfigured into the goddess of Mercy, as Kurokawa's father saw her. In the end, the reader is left with the narrator to ponder Rie's fate and the manner in which she has chosen to come to terms with it. Just as the narrator has to resign herself to taking a slow train and chooses to see it as a luxurious way to travel with all those fresh chrysanthemums, so too, perhaps, has Rie accepted her fate and transformed it into a life of virtue and beauty.

Style and Technique

In this complex narrative, the author presents her story as a series of stories, each laid out as a mystery which leads to a further mystery, and finally to a fuller understanding of Rie, but to no solution to the mystery. The first mystery is why the train is so slow and what the odd bundles being loaded at every station are. This leads to the encounter with the Ichiges and to Kurokawa telling the story his father had told him. This, in turn, leads deeper to the author's recollection of the mysterious duty performed nightly by the interns. Finally, the reader comes to Kashimura's confession of love; the narrator adds that he died in the war.

In terms of imagery, the reader is first presented with Ichige's favorite flower, Shiratama, which means "White Jewel." The reader does not actually see the flower at first, but is only told of its mysterious and elusive fragrance. When the author gets off the train at Karuizawa, she sees for the first time the full, white moon in the cloudless sky and associates its transcendent beauty with Rie. Finally, the story closes on a more subdued and earthly note as the narrator associates Rie's middle-aged face with the modest, white chrysanthemum, an expression of restrained beauty.

Stephen W. Kohl

THE BRIDE COMES TO YELLOW SKY

Author: Stephen Crane (1871-1900)
Type of plot: Western parody
Time of plot: c. 1900
Locale: Yellow Sky, Texas
First published: 1898

> *Principal characters:*
> JACK POTTER, the marshal in Yellow Sky
> JACK'S WIFE
> SCRATCHY WILSON, the last surviving member of a gang of
> outlaws
> A "DRUMMER" (salesman) from the East

The Story

"The Bride Comes to Yellow Sky" concerns the efforts of a town marshal bringing his new bride to the "frontier" town of Yellow Sky, Texas, at a time when the Old West is being slowly but inevitably civilized. At the climax of the story, the stereotypical and seemingly inevitable gunfight, a staple feature of Westerns, is averted, and the reader senses that all such gunplay is a thing of the past, that in fact Crane is describing the "end of an era."

Crane's four-part story concerns man's interaction with his environment. (Jack's wife is not an individualized person with a name; she is important only because she represents marriage as a civilized institution.) In part 1, Crane describes the progress of the "great Pullman" train across Texas. With its luxurious appointments ("the dazzling fittings of the coach"), the train is a foreign country to the newlyweds, whom Crane portrays as self-conscious aliens: Jack's hands "perform" in a "most conscious fashion," and his bride is "embarrassed" by her puff sleeves. The couple are so self-conscious and intimidated by their surroundings that the black porter "bullies" them, regards them with "an amused and superior grin," and generally "oppresses" them, treatment that they also receive from the black waiter, who "patronizes them." As the train nears Yellow Sky, Jack becomes "commensurately restless," primarily because he knows that he has committed an "extraordinary crime" by going "headlong over all the social hedges" and ignoring his "duty to his friends," members of an "innocent and unsuspecting community." Marshals in frontier towns apparently do not marry because they need to be free of domestic entanglements. Because Jack and his bride sense their "mutual guilt," they "slink" away from the train station and walk rapidly to his home, a "safe citadel" from which Jack can later emerge to make his peace with the community.

While Jack and his bride make their way to his house, Crane cuts to the

Weary Gentleman saloon, where six men, including the Eastern "drummer," sit drinking at the bar. While the drummer tells a story, another man appears at the door to announce that Scratchy Wilson is drunk and "has turned loose with both hands." The remainder of part 2 is exposition: The "innocent" drummer, whom Crane describes as a "foreigner," is told that there will be some shooting, that Scratchy and Jack are old adversaries, and that Scratchy is "the last one of the old gang that used to hang out along the river here."

Scratchy makes his appearance in part 3, which completes the preparation for the "show down," the anticipated gunfight of part 4. Scratchy issues unanswered challenges, shoots at a dog, and then approaches the saloon, where he demands a drink. When he is ignored, he uses the saloon door for target practice and then, remembering his traditional opponent, goes to Jack's house and howls challenges and epithets at the empty house.

In part 4, Jack and his bride encounter Scratchy near Jack's house. Scratchy gets the "drop" on Jack, accuses him of trying to sneak up on him, and warns him about trying to draw his gun. When Jack tells him that he has no gun, Scratchy is "livid" and tells him, "Don't take me for no kid." Jack answers that he is not lying, but Scratchy presses him for a reason, suggesting that perhaps he has been to "Sunday-school." Jack's response is to Scratchy almost as unlikely: "I'm married." Unable to deal with "this foreign condition," Scratchy supposes that "it's all off now" and walks away.

Themes and Meanings

Crane's frontier setting is essential to his theme, which concerns the conflict between the East and West and the passing of an era. While Yellow Sky is located in western Texas, it is accessible by train, which acts as a "vehicle" to bring Eastern civilization to the West. In fact, Yellow Sky has already been civilized, despite the anachronistic presence of Scratchy Wilson, who seems determined to preserve the "good old days." Unfortunately, Scratchy's clothes reveal the extent to which even he has been "Easternized": He wears a "maroon-coloured flannel shirt" made by "some Jewish women on the East Side of New York," and his red-topped boots have gilded imprints beloved by "little sledding boys on the hillsides of New England."

At the end of the story Crane writes of Scratchy, "In the presence of this foreign condition he was a simple child of the earlier plains," thereby indicating that Scratchy is a "holdover," a man with ties to the Old West, but also that he is a "simple child." In the story Crane depicts Scratchy not as a mature adult, but as a child-man, an adult who refuses to "grow up." His boots are related to children, and he "plays" with the town, which is described as a "toy for him." When Jack tells him that he has no gun, Scratchy is concerned that he not be taken "for no kid," and Jack himself seems to understand the importance of being treated as an adult for he assures Scratchy, "I ain't takin' you for no kid." In fact, the confrontation between Jack and Scratchy resembles the "show downs" between young boys who cannot back down, but who have to assert their own lack of fear while simultaneously not provoking their opponent. In taking a bride, Jack has broken with the traditions of the Old West and also become a civilized man, one who has truly "put away childish things."

Just as marriage is a foreign condition to Scratchy, the last vestiges of the Old West are "foreign" to the drummer, who has apparently ignored the possibility that men like Scratchy might still exist. The drummer is "innocent" of the implications of Scratchy's drinking, and his questions reveal not only his fear, but also his astonishment that someone might be killed in this "civilized" town. The townspeople strike the appropriate balance, however, for they accept Scratchy's behavior as a remnant of the past, a worn-out ritual prompted by alcohol. Jack, who "goes out and fights Scratchy when he gets on one of these tears," is a part of this *High Noon* drama. By the end of the story, however, Jack has assumed a different role in a new ritual.

Style and Technique

Although Jack believes that he is guilty of a crime and has been a traitor to the community, he takes himself, as do many Crane protagonists, much too seriously. His perceptions of himself and his situation are not shared by the other characters or by Crane's readers. The saloon conversation indicates that Jack is useful in containing Scratchy, but it does not reflect Jack's "centrality" in the community. (In fact, Jack's decision to marry must have followed his subconscious awareness that it was "safe" to marry.)

The gap between perception and reality is apparent on the train: "To the minds of the pair, their surroundings reflected the glory of their marriage." The passengers and the black porter are not impressed, however, for they see the bride's "under-class countenance," her "shy and clumsy coquetry," and the groom's self-consciousness and lack of sophistication. To Jack, his house is his "citadel" and his marriage is his new "estate." The mock-heroic style is epitomized in the bride's reaction to the meeting with Scratchy: "She was a slave to hideous rites, gazing at the apparitional snake." Crane elevates the meeting of Jack and his bride with Scratchy to myth: The "apparitional snake," the satanic force which introduces evil into the new Edenic estate, is the drunken Scratchy Wilson; Jack and his bride are the innocent Adam and Eve; the "rite" is the fall from grace. Surely, nothing could be further from reality.

In Crane's fiction, insignificant man perceives himself as the center of the universe, but the universe seems indifferent to his posturings and pretensions. Scratchy, who had thought of his "ancient antagonist" ("ancient" is also mock-heroic), goes to Jack's house. There he chants "Apache scalp-music" and howls challenges, but Crane writes that the house "regarded him as might a great stone god." Man's presumption is such that he believes he can disturb the "immobility of a house."

Part of the incongruity between man's illusions and reality is reflected in the death imagery which pervades the story. Crane describes Jack "as one announcing death" and compares his mouth to a "grave for his tongue; as Scratchy walks the streets, the stillness forms the "arch of a tomb over him." Through the use of such figurative language, Crane builds his story to its anticlimactic scene. As Scratchy walks away, dragging his feet and making "funnel-shaped tracks," the new era arrives: "Yellow Sky," "the hour of daylight," as Crane defines it, replaces the twilight of the Old West.

Thomas L. Erskine

THE BRIDGE OF DREAMS

Author: Jun'ichirō Tanizaki (1886-1965)
Type of plot: Psychological memoir
Time of plot: The 1920's
Locale: Kyoto
First published: "Yume no ukihashi," 1959 (English translation, 1963)

> *Principal characters:*
> OTOKUNI TADASU, the narrator and son of a well-to-do family
> TSUNEKO, his stepmother, who takes his mother's place and name
> HIS FATHER, a reclusive patron of the arts
> CHINU, his mother
> SAWAKO, his wife

The Story

The title of this story, "The Bridge of Dreams," is the same as that of the last chapter of the eleventh century Japanese classic, *The Tale of Genji*. The bridge is life itself, linking memories of dead loved ones with the living. In this story, a young boy becomes so confused about the identities of his real mother and his father's second wife that the two women merge into one nurturing figure.

Tadasu is a young man who loses his mother at age five. When his father remarries three years later, the boy is encouraged to rekindle his Oedipal relationship with his young new stepmother. He is both obsessed and guilt-ridden about his attraction to her, so he tries to understand his feelings in the form of a confessional memoir, which he writes years later.

Tadasu's memories of his real mother are those of a young child: her bosom and the feminine smell of hair oil. She suckles her son, as many Japanese mothers do, longer than Western mothers, and this forms a close erotic attachment. They live a quiet, secluded, and comfortable life in a traditional Japanese house called "Heron's Nest" with a large garden in the suburbs of Kyoto. (Virtually the entire story takes place in this tranquil villa.) His father seldom ventures out to his bank, enjoying the garden and its pond, concentrating his attention on his wife Chinu.

This domestic tranquillity is shattered when Chinu dies suddenly from an infected womb early in a pregnancy. The family mourns her loss for nearly a year. Then Tadasu's father brings home a young woman who plays the koto for them. She gradually becomes a presence in the household, so Tadasu is not surprised when his father announces his intention of marrying her. Only much later does he learn that his stepmother was apprenticed as a geisha at age eleven and bought by a cotton merchant at age fifteen; they divorced when she was eighteen, and two years later she married Tadasu's father. Tadasu never discovered how they met.

Tadasu suspects in his memoir that his father wanted the new wife to look and act like his lost mother, and in fact Tadasu has difficulty recalling where one left off and the other began since the two women resembled each other so much. One evening his new mother calls him into her room and cuddles him as his mother had, opening her kimono and letting him play with her breasts. He sucks her nipples, but of course there is no milk. Tadasu finds it more and more difficult to remember his real mother's face and voice, or the touch and smell of her body, as he substitutes his new mother.

Years later, when Tadasu is about nineteen, his stepmother unexpectedly becomes pregnant. His father becomes morose as he remembers his first wife's death, although the baby is born without incident. When he returns from school one day two weeks after his brother's birth, however, Tadasu is shocked to discover that he has been sent out to the countryside for adoption. Neither parent seems bereaved, and they explain that Tadasu is the only child they need. Upset, Tadasu tries to find his baby brother, but gives up and becomes resigned to the situation.

A few days later, there is an incident that haunts Tadasu for years to come. His stepmother is lactating, but with no child to suckle, she uses a milking device to relieve the swelling. Tadasu accidentally comes across her in their garden pavilion. Now nearly a man, he is embarrassed at her nakedness, but impulsively accepts her offer to taste her milk, nursing for half an hour, then running off guilt-ridden. He is disturbed by his actions and tries to understand why she put herself into such a position. He thinks his father may have encouraged it to draw the two closer together, however shameful their actions might be. Despite his guilt, he later is drawn back to her.

Tadasu soon discovers that his father is suffering from a terminal illness, tuberculosis of the kidneys. His stepmother devotes herself to his care as the disease steadily disables him. Before he dies, his father plans a marriage for Tadasu with the daughter of their gardener, a most unsuitable arrangement in the eyes of their relatives, who suspect that Tadasu and his stepmother have committed incest. They also suspect that his father wants the marriage to cover up this situation.

Soon after his father dies, Sawako, the gardener's daughter, begins paying regular visits to Tadasu and his stepmother, and a three-way relationship forms. Eventually the marriage takes place, but without enthusiasm on Tadasu's part. During and after his honeymoon, he makes sure his new wife does not become pregnant. The three seem to settle into a quiet life in the small world of the Heron's Nest, but it is shattered by the sudden and suspicious death of Tadasu's stepmother.

One evening when his new wife is massaging Tsuneko's legs, a centipede crawls on her drowsy form and bites her. She dies of shock a few hours later. Tadasu is horrified by this sudden turn of events. He harbors unexpressed feelings that his wife may have deliberately placed the poisonous insect in her mother-in-law's bed, feelings which have motivated him to write his memoir. His unconfirmed suspicions and lack of love for Sawako lead to an expensive divorce and the sale of the Heron's Nest. He seeks out his young brother, who reminds him of his dead stepmother, and there the memoir ends, the two living together in 1931.

Themes and Meanings

Tanizaki's writing has two particular traits: It focuses on the mystery of women, and it is steeped in the classical literature of Japan. Both are evident in "The Bridge of Dreams." The theme of the dimly remembered mother and the deliberate attempt of Tadasu's father to substitute Tsuneko for her suggests a search for an idealized, if erotic, relationship. Tadasu seems less an active agent than a passive observer of his life, accepting his fate without resistance. His life is determined by women; first his mother, then her substitute, Tsuneko.

There is a dark undercurrent throughout the memoir, as though it were written as a catharsis for the guilt he feels for his relationship with Tsuneko. The unnaturally late weaning at age four—although in Japan this is not as uncommon as in the West—is followed by his being drawn into a childlike role with his new mother. Yet the man-child is aware of the sexuality that has been aroused after Tsuneko bears his brother.

Readers learn that the relatives and neighbors had long suspected an incestuous affair, possibly even with his father's encouragement, but one cannot tell for sure from evidence in the story. One is left with an uneasy suspicion that perhaps all is not revealed. This suspicion is heightened by Tadasu's admission: "I do not allow myself the slightest falsehood or distortion. But there are limits even to telling the truth; there is a line one ought not to cross." Tanizaki thus leaves readers with the unstated, the possibility that there are even darker secrets at which they can only guess.

Style and Technique

Modern Japanese fiction frequently has taken the form of the "I-novel," an often intimate first-person narrative with a strong confessional tendency. Tanizaki follows this technique by utilizing a memoir which is not directed at any audience, nor is it intended to be read until after Tadasu's death. This gives the whole story an authenticity and intimacy that allows readers to see a character's innermost thoughts in an almost voyeuristic way. The use of a memoir—other Japanese authors have used long letters—creates this authenticity. One follows Tadasu's personal thoughts with almost embarrassing clarity, but at the same time one sees the other characters only through his eyes. Their motives are therefore as obscure to readers as they are to Tadasu.

The story, like all of Tanizaki's work, is heavily laden with literary and cultural references. As in Japanese poetry, he evokes the seasons with allusions to insects or the color of trees or blossoms. For example, Tadasu knows that his shocking encounter with his stepmother was in late spring, since the silk tree his grandfather had planted was in blossom. He begins massaging his stepmother when the crape myrtle is beginning to bloom and the plantain is ripening. The passing of time is marked by these familiar references from traditional Japanese literature.

Poetry, calligraphy, and other arts provide a rich background for this psychological study, giving the story a classical quality that provides a context for its eroticism. The Heron's Nest, itself a reference to *The Tale of Genji*, is a quiet eddy of Japanese culture, protected from the rapid changes of the world beyond the walls of the garden.

Richard Rice

THE BRIGADIER AND THE GOLF WIDOW

Author: John Cheever (1912-1982)
Type of plot: Social realism
Time of plot: The late 1950's
Locale: A New York City suburb
First published: 1964

> *Principal characters:*
> CHARLIE PASTERN, a businessman
> MRS. PASTERN, his wife
> MRS. FLANNAGAN, his mistress

The Story

The brigadier in John Cheever's "The Brigadier and the Golf Widow" is Charlie Pastern, who lives in a suburb of New York City and spends much of his time at the country club playing golf. He earns the nickname "brigadier" by carrying on in the locker room about America's enemies, insisting that the only way to deal with them is to drop nuclear bombs on them. Since he spends so little time at home, his wife is the "golf widow" in the title of the story. The marked difference in their personalities is initially dramatized by their attitudes toward the bomb shelter that Charlie Pastern has had constructed under their yard. Charlie is warlike and expects Armageddon, while his wife does her best to maintain appearances, decorating the ugly lump that the bomb shelter makes in the yard with a birdbath and plaster figures. She is also subtly irritable, pointing out the flaws in her neighbors' possessions to make up for the lack of fulfillment that she feels as a wife and mother—a failure that she does not consider her own fault. While her husband, Charlie, is plump and aggressive, she is gaunt and oblique.

Mrs. Pastern, like her neighbors, is active in collecting donations for medical research. Each of these suburban housewives concentrates on a given illness. Mrs. Pastern's charity is hepatitis. One autumn day, she goes around the neighborhood collecting for her charity. She covers all of her route except for two families. One of them is the Flannagan family, and while his wife is preparing dinner, Charlie Pastern, to escape the boredom of his house and the lingering boredom of his day in general, agrees to collect the remaining donations.

The fact that he does not know the Flannagans does not stop him from accepting Mrs. Flannagan's invitation for a drink in her house. Explaining that her husband has been away on business for six weeks, she proceeds to seduce Charlie, which is not difficult—he has been cheating on his wife for some time.

Charlie and Mrs. Flannagan have an affair. They meet in secret several times in New York City. Charlie succumbs to her wheedling and buys her gifts—perfume, a peignoir, a silk umbrella—which he can ill afford; because of bad investments, his finances are in disarray. After several meetings, Mrs. Flannagan stands Charlie up. When he phones her, she says that she wants to end the affair, but when he confronts her in person, she agrees to continue it if he gives her the key to his bomb shelter, which he does.

Meanwhile Mrs. Pastern is visited by her minister, Mr. Ludgate, and her bishop. What little sense of comfort she has left is all but shattered when it becomes clear that the bishop, apparently a heavy drinker, has come only to see the bomb shelter. He seems more interested in his own and his congregation's physical survival in the event of a nuclear attack than in the life after death. After the bishop leaves, the final blow to Mrs. Pastern's composure is delivered by Beatrice, the maid who comes to clean the Pastern's house twice a week. On the phone, Beatrice informs Mrs. Pastern that her husband has given Mrs. Flannagan the key to the bomb shelter.

Drunk on the remainder of the batch of Martinis that she had made for the bishop, Mrs. Pastern corners her husband when he comes home that night. Long debased by their loveless marriage and Charlie's infidelities, she tells him what she knows about the key. Charlie drives immediately to the Flannagan house, where he finds Mrs. Flannagan's newest lover hiding naked in a bathroom. Having threatened to kill her (which is in character with his melodramatic hostility against the enemies of America), Charlie goes back home, where his wife accuses him of acting the way he does because he wants the world to be destroyed along with himself. She knows that he is all but bankrupt, that he cannot pay for the bomb shelter, and that far from standing for survival, he is committed to destruction.

Though the Pasterns remain married, they lose everything. Charlie ends up in jail for failure to pay his bills, the house is sold, the children leave college, and Mrs. Pastern lives on welfare with her son in the Bronx. Mrs. Flannagan is last seen divorced and penniless, and when she makes a visit to the bomb shelter one snowy afternoon, she is turned away by the new owners of the Pastern's house.

Themes and Meanings

John Cheever's story is about social pretense and about how his middle-class characters maintain it. On the surface, Charlie Pastern, the protagonist, wants others to think of him as a strong man who is successful in life and honest about his feelings. This is why he belongs to the country club and harangues his golf cronies with his political conservatism, and why he makes no secret about his bomb shelter, which is not only an eyesore but also a blatant symbol of his patriotism and his commitment to free enterprise—as opposed, one assumes, to Communism. Yet underneath Charlie's veneer of strength and patriotic hostility lies the truth, which turns his outward demeanor into a pretense. He has, in fact, squandered everything by which spiritual and worldly success is measured in the suburban milieu that he inhabits: fidelity and money. He is habitually unfaithful to his wife—and would be, the story suggests, to Mrs. Flannagan were their affair to last long enough. He has wasted the money that his mother left him and has critically over-extended his credit. He is not, in short, a preserver of values, but a destroyer of them, victimizing in the process his wife, his children, and himself. The intelligence to which he pretends as a successful member of his suburban community is no more than stupidity. He fails to make smart investments, relies on gambling to recoup his losses, and entrusts his well-being to a woman (Mrs. Flannagan) who is too selfish to further it.

Charlie's wife is also interested in being well-thought-of by her neighbors. She tries to hide the harsh reality of the bomb shelter and of her empty life with Charlie, but she is less able than Charlie to conceal her real condition. Her wasted looks and contempt for her neighbors' tastes suggest her un-happiness. Her attempt to decorate the bomb shelter is futile; the garden ornaments that she uses for this purpose are ugly and cheap. Like Charlie's, her pretensions arise from desperation; unlike Charlie's, though, her des-peration is not self-imposed, so it is easier to sympathize with her. Indeed, she has a kind of courage that her husband lacks, for the truth about him does not drive her from their marriage, just as the truth about the bishop does not cause her to break from Christianity—or so it seems.

Mrs. Flannagan is as much a deceiver as Charlie or his wife. It becomes clear that she, like Charlie, has had many affairs, though she insists to him that he is her first extramarital lover. She seems to be naïve and childlike, but this is only a ploy that she uses to seduce men and to get them to buy gifts for her. In Charlie's case, she pretends to break up with him so she can get him to give her the key to his bomb shelter, and when he storms into her house after finding out that she has not kept her possession of the key a secret, she pretends that she is not entertaining another lover.

The story's social insight is that people who define their lives in the context of a community will go to great lengths to hide their failures, and the story's moral is that these failures—moral in nature—can be neither hidden nor made up for by pretense. Dishonesty compounds such failures, as the story demonstrates when Charlie Pastern, his wife, and Mrs. Flannagan are forced to leave the community by their own actions (Mrs. Flannagan's infidelity leads to divorce, Charlie's imprudence to bankruptcy, and Mrs. Pastern's pride to shame), thus compromising the very survival that Charlie with his bomb shelter and Mrs. Flannagan with the key to it are so anxious about.

Style and Technique

The story is told from the vantage of a narrator who owns property adjoining the Pastern's property; the narrator learns the ultimate fate of the

Pasterns and Mrs. Flannagan from a letter that his mother sends him. This narrative device suggests that the story is a form of gossip, but it also underscores the story's authority, for the narrator himself is a member of the community which the story anatomizes.

Beyond this, Cheever uses the image of the bomb shelter to focus the social meaning of the story. In itself, the shelter stands for survival selfishly conceived. For Charlie Pastern, the bishop, and Mrs. Flannagan it represents their personal survival at the expense of the survival of others and of those values that make a living community meaningful. As such, it represents failure: Charlie cannot pay for it and loses it to the new owners of his house, and Mrs. Flannagan cannot use her key to it in the end.

Mark McCloskey

THE BURROW

Author: Franz Kafka (1883-1924)
Type of plot: Interior monologue
Time of plot: Unspecified
Locale: A burrow in a forest
First published: "Der Bau," 1931 (English translation, 1946)

Principal character:
AN ANONYMOUS, BURROWING ANIMAL

The Story

"The Burrow" opens with the successful completion of the burrow and the narrator claiming that he is no longer afraid, then immediately stating his fear that someone could inadvertently discover the opening of the burrow and "destroy everything for good." Though at the zenith of his life, he cannot be tranquil, even in his burrow's strongest, innermost chamber, for some unknown, unnamed enemy may be burrowing toward him. The narrator has the advantage of knowing all the burrow's passages and each of its more than fifty rooms; he is, however, growing old. Not only do real, external enemies frighten him; so do legendary creatures of the inner earth, in whom he firmly believes. Still, the burrow is peaceful, and hunting the "small fry" that venture through it gives him a constant, if modest, food supply.

The narrator boasts particularly of his Castle Keep, the burrow's chief cell, into the construction of which he has literally poured his life's blood, pounding its walls with his forehead to harden them. In the Keep he has placed all of his food stores, the extent of which he now gloatingly contemplates. On the other hand, he sometimes fears that storing all of his food in one place may be disastrously wrong. At such times, he panics and feverishly redistributes it to several chambers, randomly. Then, reflecting on the problems with the scheme—and the cost to his conceit when he can no longer see all of his stores together—he puts them back in the Castle Keep, wishing now that he had planned and constructed several of them when he was younger. At times, the tempting smells of the stockpiled food overwhelm him: Gorging sessions ensue, followed by renewed guilt and recrimination.

Such lapses always lead to a review of the burrow's entire plan, and his gluttony necessitates his leaving the burrow to restock it. As he approaches the elaborate labyrinth just inside the entrance, he feels both pride in this theoretically brilliant tour de force and fear that it could not sustain a serious attack. In any case, it is too late now to think seriously of constructing another, absolutely impregnable labyrinth; that would take a giant's strength, of which he can only dream.

Exiting through the moss-covered trapdoor, he momentarily appreciates the freedoms of life outside: the better (if more difficult) hunting, the sense of bodily strength. Yet he can never venture too far from the burrow; indeed, the thought of its presence sustains him. Even watching the entrance for days and nights on end reaffirms his sense of its safety: He has yet to see anyone investigating the front door. Admittedly, he has had to flee at the scent of any serious enemy, so he cannot be sure of their ignorance of or attitude toward the burrow. This very reflection upon its safety inevitably leads him to consider its perils. He even briefly toys with the idea of going back to his pre-burrow existence, "one indiscriminate succession of perils," but perils whose universality kept him from focusing upon any particular one—as he now must do.

The fear of reentering the burrow also paralyzes him for days: An enemy might see him enter and, unobserved, follow him down the hole and attack. He thinks, if only he had someone, a "trusty confederate," to stand guard. Yet then the advantage of the burrow, its secrecy, would be lost, for the trustee would need to know of it, perhaps even to see inside, perhaps even to share it. Also, the narrator would be obliged to rely on the trustee, even though he could not supervise his ally. It is best after all, he concludes, not to complain that he is alone and has nobody to trust.

The narrator daydreams of a two-entrance burrow, which would allow him to watch one entrance unobserved while peeping from the other. The dream, however, shames him. Is not the burrow more than enough already, a place still and empty where he can be so at home as even to accept death calmly? Finally, worn out by the internal turmoil, he creeps exhaustedly back inside and tries to sleep.

Being back in the burrow, however, reawakens his zeal for inspecting and improving upon it, tired from his hunting, wandering, watching, and fretting though he may be. His new supply of flesh must be stored in the Castle Keep, the few small defects in the fortress repaired, and all the other rooms and passages visited and inspected. Still, the joy of being back home makes the work seem like play: He goes contentedly about it until overcome by sleep.

He wakes to an almost inaudible whistling noise. At first, he attributes it to the small fry's having burrowed a new channel somewhere, a passage which has intersected an older one and produced the bothersome sound. He sets off to find and repair the noise's source. As the search continues, however, the noise seems more pervasive, more troubling, more distinct and uniform wherever he is. Perhaps there are two noises. The whistling is audible even in the Castle Keep, where the insolent small fry apparently have penetrated, drawn by the smell of his hoard. Why has he not heard them before, though? Perhaps the intruder is a new, unknown animal—or a swarm of them. Alternating between feigned nonchalance and desperate agitation, the narrator determines to find the truth, whatever the labor and the consequence. He conceives and abandons various schemes, attempts to ignore the noise, eats and pretends it was never there, busies himself repairing the walls.

Yet as he does so the noise seems subtly louder and closer. Fearful, distracted, he wanders about the burrow, finding himself eventually at the entrance. Outside, all seems tranquil, as it used to be in the burrow, which is now "plunged into the melee of the world and all its perils." He pauses between the surface and below, his conviction growing that a single, large beast is approaching his home, burrowing at furious speed and sending reverberations great distances through the ground. The whistling must come from the beast's pointed muzzle; it works with constant freshness and vigor, never veering from its object.

Cursing himself that he has not been constantly prepared for such a foe, longing for the "petty dangers" of the past, wondering why he has not defended the burrow more elaborately against such a danger as the present one, the narrator now thinks back to an earlier, similar peril. Then, at the beginning of his work, he had heard another burrower approach, then move away. Perhaps that burrower is returning, though the narrator remains as unprepared as before. In fact, his situation is worse: He now has an elaborate burrow to defend, yet he is no longer the vigorous young apprentice who might successfully do so, but an "old architect." Even death seems preferable to this new life, filled with uncertainty and ceaseless anxiety.

At last, the narrator retreats to the Castle Keep, there to munch on the flesh of his stores and wonder about the approaching beast. Is it merely wandering, or is it digging its own burrow? Does the beast know about him? If so, how, since his own digging has been so quiet, his own movement so discreet? The narrative—apparently unfinished, the ending lost or destroyed—closes abruptly, leaving the narrator isolated, fearful, with none of his questions answered, and the noise continuing unabated.

Themes and Meanings

Because "The Burrow" is a long and finally inconclusive fragment, it is difficult to establish with certainty Kafka's thematic intent. (One version of its creation asserts that the narrator ultimately meets and defeats the unknown animal, an ending which seems at variance tonally with the rest of the story. Readers aware that this was one of Kafka's last stories tend to view the narrator as a mask for the author himself. In this view, the burrow is a metaphor for either Kafka's body—being besieged by various internal ailments as well as by Death, the unknown "outside" him—or the body of Kafka's work—the structure of puzzles he has set for readers who wish to attack the heart of Kafka's meaning, to know him.

At any rate, the story clearly deals with fear of the outside world, perhaps even paranoia, and the results of that fear. The central figure, like those in

Kafka's more finished and better-known stories "Die Verwandlung" ("Metamorphosis") and "Ein Landartzt" ("The Country Doctor") is isolated from his usual sources of security. A nightmare existence ensues, with no miraculous awakening or reversal. In the most general reading, the narrator's condition resembles that of man himself, feverishly toiling to achieve security and happiness but inevitably condemned to death. The narrator, like Albert Camus' Sisyphus, has only his work; unlike that existentialist hero, however, he cannot be imagined happy or even, within his limits, free. Instead, he is trapped in a prison of his own making, his paranoia (perhaps justified by the facts of his existence) continuing and intensifying as his end draws near.

Style and Technique

Since Kafka strictly limits the story's point of view to that of the narrator, his mode of expression becomes the most important stylistic consideration. Here Kafka, like his narrator, constructs a labyrinthine tour de force. The style might be termed "manic obsessive": Throughout the story, the narrator circles over and over the same concerns, expressing by turns his pride in his elaborate construction and his fear that it will not protect him. The ideas double back upon one another, sometimes within the same sentence, rendering concrete the narrator's mental turmoil, as do the frequent questions, unanswered and perhaps unanswerable. The style perfectly fits the narrator's psyche and situation, its shifting tone reflecting his constantly changing outlook and state of mind.

As the narrative develops, Kafka—facing his own imminent death— gradually modulates the narrator's tone. Near the story's end, he even declares, "I have reached the stage where I no longer wish to have certainty." The narrator despairs of concocting and carrying out any new defense plan or even reaching an understanding of his enemy; at the end, his only hope is that he will somehow be spared by the other beast's ignorance of him. Even as he tries to convince himself that the other beast may not have heard him, the fragment concludes, "Yet all remained unchanged," leaving him hopeless as the beast draws near.

David E. Robinson

BUT AT THE STROKE OF MIDNIGHT

Author: Sylvia Townsend Warner (1893-1978)
Type of plot: Psychological realism
Time of plot: The late 1960's
Locale: London and its environs
First published: 1971

Principal characters:

MRS. LUCY RIDPATH, a housewife, married for twenty-five
years

ASTON RIDPATH, the husband of Lucy, a "born bachelor"

VERE, Aston's sister, a "successful widow"

MRS. BARKER, the charwoman

The Story

One ordinary Saturday, Mrs. Lucy Ridpath, from all appearances a typical routine-oriented housewife, leaves her home without informing her husband or anyone where she is going. Her husband Aston feels guilty that because of an "unlucky moment of inattention," he failed to listen or attend to her, part of his practice of taking her for granted. His sister Vere advises him to call the police; otherwise, he might be suspected of murder.

Taking on the identity of Aurelia Lefanu, Lucy's cousin, whose flightiness and adventurous personality "exert a powerful intoxicating influence on her," Lucy sells her wedding ring and visits the Tate Gallery, where she meets a man working for an art publishing firm. He takes her home, marveling at her aplomb and uncalculating frankness. He plans to take her to Provence, to save her from the lunatic asylum from which he suspects she escaped, but she disappears as he is trying to secure her passport.

Lucy as Aurelia spends her time as an anonymous rider on the London buses. She sleeps in the King's Cross Station waiting room, and then finally gets Lancelot Fogg, a clergyman she meets at a funeral in Highgate Cemetery, to tell her where she can find a middle-aged hostel. The clergyman is awed at meeting a "spiritual woman" who strikes him as "exceedingly tranquil and trustful."

Lucy's stay with Miss Larke of St. Hilda's Guesthouse leads to her projecting her Lucy-self onto a tomcat, allowing her to continue as Aurelia. "Since her adoption of Lucy [the cat], she had become so unshakably Aurelia that she could contemplate being Lucy, too, so far as being Lucy would further Aurelia's designs." She then sends two letters to Aston demanding fifty pounds, one promising to return and the other promising to stay away. This equivocal or ambiguous message accurately conveys the schizoid state of Aurelia-Lucy. Aston replies with chagrin because he does not want to live with Lucy again; he prefers a "manly solitude," so he sends her four five-pound notes; Vere also replies, asking Lucy to stay away and enclosing one hundred pounds.

On a train, Lucy meets George Bastable, a builder and plumber, who rents for her a bungalow where his "young lady," now dead, once lived. Lucy spends the summer in an immunizing happiness, oblivious of past and future, living "with carefree economy" and enjoying Mr. Bastable's gifts of food. Her blackmail money spent, she begins to paint for vacationers in caravans, earning enough by the end of September to tide her over to Christmas. She busies herself gathering fuel for winter, with Lucy her cat acting as orderly timekeeper.

One foggy night, the cat comes home, dragging himself, head smashed in and jaw dangling, obviously hit by a car. His death triggers a shattering trauma and revelation: It was Aurelia's death that brought about Lucy's possession by the departed cousin. This "agony of dislocation" brings back to life Mrs. Lucy Ridpath. Amid the torrential rain, with floodwaters overwhelming the place, Lucy goes out to bury the cat, only to be swept away and killed by the roaring tumult of water.

Themes and Meanings

One of Sylvia Townsend Warner's recurring themes is the incalculable nature of human personality. Lucy Ridpath symbolizes the "nova," the aborted or inchoate possibilities in everyone. More a possessed psyche than an eccentric, Lucy stands as a pathetic but sharp indictment of the selfish insensitivity of men, a critique of hypocritical society dominated by prudence and calculating pettiness, where money dictates the terms of freedom and happiness.

When Lucy's ego is taken over by the spirit of the dead Aurelia Lefanu (the name evokes the mysterious and supernatural tales of the nineteenth century Irish writer Joseph Sheridan Le Fanu), an alternative life opens up for her. Losing her memory, she assumes a persona which functions as an empty signifier whose meaning can be filled by anyone. Thus she symbolizes spirituality to Fogg, an art object to the man she calls "Ithamore," and a surrogate sweetheart to Mr. Bastable. Oblivious of any class constraints, she delights in "a total lack of obligation" which she associates with the compline ritual.

Lucy definitively becomes Aurelia when she is able to project her old self onto the cat that she rescues, nurses, and adopts as Lucy. The theory underlying this is that identity can be fixed only with reference to another. Yet Aurelia herself is a fluid sign. The fair or carnival where Lucy finds the cat, lost and abandoned, signifies fantasy, games, free play. All of her repressed energies are released in the care and attention she gives to the cat; when he dies, she succumbs to an agonizing trauma: The beloved Aurelia, overtaken by death, restores to a particular body the social or public mask of Lucy Ridpath. Lucy is able to overcome the fixity of Aurelia's death by negating her own existence as Lucy Ridpath. What will she do with Lucy (the cat) dead? Her death in the storm indicates that she can no longer return to life in normal bourgeois society.

In retrospect, Lucy's ordinary life is precisely the death from which she has been trying to escape. She is alive only as Aurelia Lefanu.

Lucy's wanderings as Aurelia may also be interpreted as an allegory of the power of art's influence on "real" life. When Lucy disappears, Aston has to refer to William Wordsworth's Lucy to find out why. Lucy herself moves in a realm of fantasy constituted by Christopher Marlowe (the allusion to *Doctor Faustus*, 1604, suggests that her masquerade cannot escape the measure of conventional time), the picture postcard of Southern France with "a pale landscape full of cemetery trees," Claude Monet, and Giorgio Vasari's *Le vite de più eccelenti architettori, pittori, e scultori italiani* (1550; *Lives of the Most Eminent Painters, Sculptors, and Architects*, 1850-1855). Her imitation of a practical lesson from Vasari confirms the parasitism of reality on the imagination. Yet this faculty of making believe, the narrator hints, cannot long survive in a world suspicious of anything irrational or pleasurable. Lucy (as Aurelia) has to depend on the money given to her by her husband and sister-in-law, a bribe for her to maintain her disappearance. She has to submit to the demands of commissioned painting, art for sale. In effect, one can say that Lucy dies not from the violence of the flood but from the sterile, mechanical, and alienating life of middle-class society.

Style and Technique

Warner has been praised for her astringent style, for her elegance and precision in portraying eccentrics, for her ironic but "compassionate wit." This story demonstrates all these features, but it is the satire on social types such as Aston, Vere, Fogg, and Miss Larke that enables the weird behavior of Lucy to command the reader's amused and sympathetic attention.

The plot follows a chronological sequence. The initial scene depicting Lucy as the predictable housewife is followed by a quick succession of scenes showing her various possibilities: as an art object for the anonymous "Ithamore," model of piety for Fogg, harmless eccentric for Miss Larke, and memento of his vanished "nova" for Bastable. Aurelia is Lucy's "nova": the realized Other. The narrative manages to blend the fancifulness of Aurelia with the prudent tactfulness of Lucy in the plotted drifting she goes through.

The most hilarious spoof on bourgeois mores is found in Lucy's weighing of alternatives (the two letters) as she combs out the fleas in the cat "to a new rhythm of 'he loves me, he loves me not.'" The two letters condense the inescapable subordination of ethics to money and social class. The folly of the middle-class doting on the charm of the past is exposed in the exchange between the two ladies who boarded the train at Peckover Junction. Warner also ridicules the sentimental Victorian moralizing of landscapes when Lucy wonders if the tomcat's "tastes ran to the romantic, if high mountains were to him a feeling. . . ." In these moments, one feels that Lucy performs an antirealistic or countermimetic function: Like Aurelia and other artists, the authorial voice also speaks through her. Lucy's character determines the logic of the plot in its "improbable probability."

An element of semigothic melodrama intrudes when the tomcat is described in all of his gory, dying convulsions one November evening. The texture of the narrative also thickens, shifting the point of view away from Lucy's psyche to the outside, where nature accumulates its chaotic, indifferent force. The last two epithets used to fix Lucy's struggling form in the exploding landscape are "tricked and impatient," compressing the senses of fatality and of irrepressible vitality in one image. Having begun in the unperturbed kitchen of Lucy Ridpath, where bourgeois decorum concealed seething passions, the reader ends with this final scene of wild, open destructiveness that destroys public boundaries and wipes out private enclosures.

Lucy's last few months spent in happy seclusion in the remote countryside, where for the first time she is able to paint "from life," to express herself creatively and be appreciated even though for money, constitute a fable of the fulfilled life. Its disruption by the cat's unannounced departure, analogous to Lucy's own act of separating herself from her home and her past, and its mauling by a machine, qualifies that fable of solitude and suggests that community or solidarity (whose emblem is the caravan) cannot be rejected without fatal consequences. Real life and fiction interact together. To suppress either term leads to the schizoid experience of Lucy as Aurelia since each depends on the other. The companionship of Lucy the tomcat and Aurelia may be construed as the figure for the precarious interdependence of the real and the imagined, of prudence and desire: "He was happy enough out of her sight," the narrator says of the cat Lucy, "but he liked to have her within his."

E. San Juan, Jr.

THE CAMBERWELL BEAUTY

Author: V. S. Pritchett (1900-   )
Type of plot: Social satire
Time of plot: Unspecified; possibly the 1950's
Locale: London
First published: 1974

Principal characters:
>THE NARRATOR, an unnamed young man, probably in his
>twenties at the time of the story
>AUGUST, an antique dealer and petty criminal
>MRS. PRICE, August's mistress and Isabel's aunt
>PLINY, an antique dealer, tall, thin, with large ears, fiftyish
>ISABEL, fourteen years old at the beginning of the story, in her
>early twenties by its end; she marries Pliny

The Story

"The Camberwell Beauty" is told by a narrator looking back on his years in the antique trade and those years just following, when he was intimate with all the dealers in southern England. He first became involved with August, Pliny, and the other figures in this tale when he began searching for a rare piece of Staffordshire porcelain for one of his customers. In the process, he met Mrs. Price and her niece Isabel. Some time later, shortly after the death of Pliny's aged mother, he accidentally meets August, Mrs. Price, and other dealers in a Salisbury pub. They repeat the rumors that Pliny used to lock his mother in her room to prevent her giving away his merchandise and that one night a month he visits his mistress in Brixton. This precipitates an outburst by Mrs. Price against August, during which she accuses him of trying to seduce Isabel.

On a visit to Pliny's shop, the narrator again runs into August, Mrs. Price, and Isabel. He is fascinated to see the girl write her name, or rather part of it, ISAB, in the dust on an antique table. Later, he reflects that it is sad to see a young girl grow up in the eccentric world of antique dealers. During the following year, the narrator's business fails, and he is forced to quit and take a job as a real estate agent. He remains sufficiently in touch, however, to hear that August has been sentenced to two years in prison for receiving stolen goods and that Isabel has run away. Passing Pliny's shop one day, he stops for a visit but finds the store locked. Oddly, he hears what sounds like drumming and the sound of a bugle. Eventually, the rumor reaches him that Pliny has married, and when again he stops in at his shop, he is surprised to find Isabel there, although she refuses to let him come in. His curiosity now piqued, he makes several visits, eventually learning that Isabel is Pliny's wife.

Back in his own flat he realizes that, like an antique dealer with a secret passion, he now desires Isabel above all things.

Over the next several months, the narrator watches for an opportunity to visit Isabel, and when he does find a chance, he again hears the drum and bugle. Isabel reluctantly reveals that when her husband is gone she dresses in a helmet, bangs on a drum, and blows a bugle to frighten away potential thieves. Feigning interest in buying something, the narrator picks out a Dresden figurine that he knows is expensive and asks if he may buy it; Isabel, pretending to an expertise she does not have, sells it for only thirty shillings. After this, the narrator returns many times, but Isabel refuses him entry. Finally, just when the narrator thinks he is free of Isabel's spell, he sees Pliny in a pub with his former mistress and hurries to the shop to see Isabel. When he offers to return the figurine, she lets him in, and he confesses his love. She rejects him, however, saying that Pliny loves her, because unlike August, he does not come to her room, though at night he undresses her and admires her like some rare object. The narrator objects that this is not love, but Isabel remains loyal to her husband. Pliny returns unexpectedly and attacks the narrator, who easily defends himself but loses all chance to win Isabel. He leaves them and walks into the night, where people look odd under the sodium street lamps.

Themes and Meanings

"The Camberwell Beauty" is a subtle and complex study of human nature through the eccentric people of the London antique trade. They are a tragicomic group, a subculture with strange mores and dubious lusts, like August's passion for ivory figures and Pliny's for Caughley ware. This is, as the narrator says, no atmosphere in which to rear a young girl, particularly in view of the abnormal sexual neuroses that flourish among these people. August's advances on young Isabel border on the incestuous, and Pliny's relationship with his mistress and his solemn promise to his mother to give up sex are indicative of the slightly twisted mentality that reigns in the group as a whole. In comparison with the others, the narrator appears normal. At one point, he catches Isabel looking at him with unusual intensity—not because he is unusual, but precisely because he is not. What is not certain, however, is whether his love for Isabel is any less possessive than Pliny's bizarre connoisseurship, which reduces Isabel to a delicate object of art, for the narrator himself compares his obsession with her to the desire of a collector to own some rare and beautiful thing. Nevertheless, whatever the narrator's motives may be, the story takes readers beyond the strange world of antique dealing and collecting to a wider social arena, suggesting that these people and their passions are metaphors for a materialistic society in which sex is but one more commodity and people merely objects to be manipulated.

Style and Technique

V. S. Pritchett is the master of a prose style and narrative technique that are both daringly original and yet apparently traditional. All the stylistic devices and narrative techniques in this social satire have been used many times before, but Pritchett's ability to select and manipulate detail and to catch the nuances of speech and gesture lift his stories above the ordinary and invest them with a significance beyond the trivialities of their characters and events. In "The Camberwell Beauty," he paints an absolutely convincing picture of antique shops and people by weaving together bits of arcane jargon with acute descriptions of objects and people. Enveloping these unusual characters is an atmosphere of claustrophobia and suspicion worthy of a suspense thriller. Critics have frequently called his characters eccentrics, and in this instance the term is apt, but because Pritchett is so convincingly accurate in the details of their speech, habits, and mannerisms, they are never caricatures. To read a Pritchett story is to enter a fictional world in which every word, every detail, carries its full weight of meaning.

Dean Baldwin

A CANARY FOR ONE

Author: Ernest Hemingway (1899-1961)
Type of plot: Psychological realism
Time of plot: The 1920's
Locale: A train en route to Paris
First published: 1927

Principal characters:
THE WOMAN, a rich American from upstate New York
THE COUPLE, nameless Americans in their late twenties; the
husband is the narrator

The Story
Three nameless Americans—a middle-aged woman and a younger couple—travel together on an overnight train to Paris. The older woman fears
that the speed of modern transit will produce wrecks; she does most of the
talking. Although she does not mention her absent husband, who apparently
is home with their daughter, she continually asserts that only American men
make "good husbands" for American women. Her main concern is for the
marriage of her own daughter. Two years earlier, while the family was vacationing at Vevey, Switzerland, her daughter had fallen madly in love with a
Swiss gentleman of good family and prospects, and the two had wanted to
marry. The mother, however, refusing to let her daughter marry a foreigner,
had forced her family to depart for the United States. Now, she tells the
American couple, her daughter is still devastated by the affair; to cheer her
despondent daughter, the mother has purchased a caged, singing canary.
    Only the wife of the young couple participates in the conversation, giving
only vague or ambiguous responses, particularly to the question of "good"
American husbands. Only once does she extend the conversation by asking
directly if the daughter has recovered from her lost love. She also volunteers
the information that she and her husband once honeymooned one fall in
Vevey; they had lived in Paris for several years before "the Great European
War" forced them out. They are now returning to Paris for the first time
since the war.
    The young husband, who speaks aloud only once, seems satisfied to be
isolated from the women's conversation. Almost incidentally the reader
discovers that he is the first-person narrator of the story, for he steadfastly
looks out the train windows during the journey. He reports in such a flat,
unemotional tone that the reader almost forgets that he is a character in the
story until the last sentence of the story. Only as the train is pulling into Paris
does he wonder whether even trivial points of existence have remained the
same after the war. As the train enters the station, he finally reveals the truth

of his condition and the point of the story: He and his wife have returned to Paris, the city of light and love, to begin their divorce.

Themes and Meanings

As in his condemnation of the unnatural male-female relationships encouraged by the war and by postwar society in *The Sun Also Rises* (1926) and *A Farewell to Arms* (1929), Ernest Hemingway, in this very short story, questions the prevailing lack of stability and morality of that era, seeing the destruction of love and marriage as a part of the overall malaise of Western civilization. The American woman's pride, materialism, and narrow-minded prejudices against foreigners recall American greed and isolation following World War I, as do her fears, especially of speed. She wants the world to revert to the slower pace of the past. She is not only deaf but also blind to the real emotional problems in her home and in her train compartment.

The younger couple, on the other hand, have also become isolationists: They have survived the war only to become victims of emotional warfare, which has destroyed their love and marriage. Revealing their emotional state indirectly, they do not even attempt to communicate with each other. They know that the past cannot be regained, that nothing can ever be counted on for stability again for either of them, that simply being American cannot protect them in a rapidly changing world which has abandoned the old mores and verities. When marriages are wrecked, each survivor can depend only on himself.

"A Canary for One" can be grouped with other Hemingway short stories of this same period, all emphasizing the fragility of marriage in the postwar world, where values lost their meaning and the individual lost the hope of harmony. "Cat in the Rain," "Hills Like White Elephants," "Out of Season," and "Mr. and Mrs. Elliot" fall into this category.

Style and Technique

More than fifty years after their publication, Hemingway's short stories still strike the reader as highly experimental. The action and conflicts are usually internal rather than external. The traditional conclusion is abbreviated or eliminated; all authorial intrusion, by which past authors told their readers how to respond, is stripped away. Hemingway instead depends on highly stylized dialogue and carefully selected, realistic detail to produce the correct response to the story. His clean, pure line, his economy and exactness of diction, his rhythms and repetitions are here perfectly matched to the self-effacing, tightly controlled objectivity of his first-person narrator. It is only after the final sentence that the reader realizes that the story must be reassessed as an ironic tour de force. The narrator's seeming disinterest in the conversation on marriage is really a protective device to keep his emotions under control. The reader sees, however, those images on which the narrator's mind dwells. Through the train window, he notes a burning farmhouse with many spectators merely watching. He sees the fortifications around Paris, still barren from the recently ended war. He focuses on the remnants of a train wreck—splintered, sagging rail cars pulled off the main line. Each image that catches his attention is, in fact, a metaphor for the state of his marriage. Even his strange, repetitious comparisons reflect his emotional state: He is stupefied, not fully alert—unkempt and unready to face life.

Finally, Hemingway calls attention to the modernism of his story by deliberately creating ironic parallels with Henry James's famous *Daisy Miller* (1878). The references to Vevey, Switzerland, and the Trois Couronnes Hotel are unmistakable, for that is where James's story begins. The marriage tale that the American mother relates is a variation of Daisy Miller's disastrous courtship. Like Daisy, the American woman's daughter is from upstate New York. As in James's story, the father is at home, working. The daughter's courtship is a variation on the courtship of Daisy Miller. Yet the traditional values and morality that sustained the world of Henry James have disappeared in the postwar world that Hemingway has inherited. Here nothing—not marriage or train schedules—can be counted on to be the same after the war. Nor is the form of the short story the same. The authorial presence, the drawn-out plot line, and the laborious, well-mannered sentence have all disappeared. In a challenge match, Hemingway has taken on James to show that the art of fiction has been just as radically altered by the war as have the lives of his characters.

Ann E. Reynolds

A CAP FOR STEVE

Author: Morley Callaghan (1903-   )
Type of plot: Domestic realism
Time of plot: 1952
Locale: An unspecified city in North America
First published: 1952

Principal characters:
    DAVE DIAMOND, a carpenter's assistant
    ANNA, his wife
    STEVE, their twelve-year-old son
    MR. HUDSON, a lawyer
    MR. HUDSON'S SON

The Story

Twelve-year-old Steve Diamond loves baseball. Although his family is poor, he spends nearly every leisure moment playing or watching the game rather than working to supplement the family's meager income. Steve's obsession with the game is a constant source of perplexity and irritation to Dave Diamond, Steve's father, who is a carpenter's assistant. Anna Diamond, Steve's mother, does not understand her son's fascination with the sport either but is tolerant of it. When a major league team comes to town to play an exhibition game, Dave reluctantly agrees to take Steve if Steve will promise to help with some carpentry work. Steve agrees, and they go off to the stadium. Dave is unable to share his son's enthusiasm for the game and is appalled by Steve's extensive knowledge of professional teams and players. He feels that the time spent following professional baseball is time wasted. Steve feels isolated and chilled by his father's sullen disapproval.

As they are leaving the park after the game, Steve joins a throng of young autograph seekers swarming around the players, but he is too shy to get close enough to ask for a signature. Then one of the stars of the game breaks away from the crowd and strides toward the dugout. His cap falls off at Steve's feet, and Steve picks it up. He looks at the player in "an awed trance." The player, responding to the worship and appeal in Steve's eyes, tells him to keep it. Dave and Steve hurry home with the news.

In the following days, Steve is seldom without the cap on his head even though it is too big for him. Inevitably, Steve's parents tire of all the fuss that Steve and his friends make about the cap. One night, Steve is very late coming home from the park where he usually plays baseball. When he finally arrives, he desolately explains that he has been searching for the cap, which must have been stolen. Dave is furious with Steve because he does not understand how the boy could lose something that is so important to him. Steve explains that he was not careless, that he put the cap in his back pocket because it kept falling off when he ran the bases. Someone, he believes, must have taken it from there. Dave remains uncompromisingly bitter about the situation, suggesting to Steve that he lost the cap only because he did not have a right appreciation of its value. Night after night, Steve returns to the park, looking for his cap.

A few weeks later, Steve and his father are passing an ice-cream parlor when Steve spots his cap on the head of a big boy just coming out. Steve snatches it off and challenges the boy. Dave separates them and confirms the fact that it is Steve's cap. The boy coolly tells them that he bought it from another boy at the park. Moreover, his father, he warns them, is a lawyer. Dave agrees to see the boy's father in order to resolve the issue.

The boy lives in a comparatively wealthy part of the city, and when they arrive at the house, Dave is awed by it. Dave and Steve wait outside while the boy goes in to prepare his father for the meeting. The lawyer comes to the door, introduces himself as Mr. Hudson, and invites them in. Mr. Hudson is tall, well-dressed, and self-assured. He treats Dave and Steve with elaborate politeness. Dave feels shabby and confused in the man's presence but is determined to recover what belongs to his son.

Mr. Hudson asks for the details of the situation and confirms his son's story. He assures Dave, however, that legally the cap belongs to Steve; he also asserts that legally the Diamonds are required to reimburse his son for the money that he paid for it if they want it back from him. Dave contends that this is unfair but asks the amount. When he hears that it was two dollars, he is shocked and worried. Two dollars is more than he can afford, as Mr. Hudson shrewdly realizes.

Nevertheless, Dave agrees to pay, and Steve is delighted. Mr. Hudson, on the other hand, is quite surprised and disappointed. He tells Dave that his boy has grown fond of the cap and that he (Mr. Hudson) would be willing to pay five dollars to keep it. Dave nervously refuses but is not sure he is doing the right thing, since five dollars would mean so much to his family. Mr. Hudson raises the offer again, and again, finally pressing twenty dollars into Dave's hands. Twenty dollars for a cap seems impossible to refuse, but even now he turns to his son for a sign of agreement or disagreement. The boy smiles, expecting his father once again to reject the money, but Dave interprets his smile as a sign of triumph at exacting so much for so little. He accepts the money. Steve is stunned.

When they leave the Hudson's house, Steve is sullen and refuses to walk with his father. Dave tries to explain that he sold the cap because he felt sure that Steve understood and accepted the necessity. He says that Steve is being unfair, but he really means that the situation is unfair: Mr. Hudson could afford to offer far more than Dave could afford to refuse. They arrive home, and Anna Diamond tries to comfort each of them. Steve goes to bed unreconciled with his father.

Finally, Dave goes in to talk with his son. He apologizes for not understanding the importance of the cap to him, and he admits that he might have known it had he tried to share Steve's interests and aspirations. He tells his son that he is proud of him and wants to take some active part in his life. Steve responds to him with a gesture of love. He touches Dave's arm and indicates that the cap was a small price to pay for "his father's admiration and approval."

Themes and Meanings

One of the enduring themes in fiction is the importance of money and its effect on human relationships, a theme which Callaghan explores in this story. Both Mr. Hudson and Dave Diamond seek to make their sons happy; both have some claim to the cap. Yet in the world that Callaghan depicts, honest poverty is no match for money and class. It seems a foregone conclusion that Dave will relinquish the cap. He is intimidated by Mr. Hudson's dress and manner, disoriented by the lawyer's increasingly extravagant offers, and trapped by his own poverty. There is, as Callaghan makes clear, an important connection between economic and psychological independence.

If the story ended with Dave's defeat, one might describe it as a grim, naturalistic fable about the survival of the fattest. Yet it expands to embrace another, more important theme—the relationship between fathers and sons. Mr. Hudson, it is true, offers so much money for the cap that he secures it for his own son. It clearly gives him satisfaction to do this. Presumably, his son is happy to have the cap and proud of his father's display of economic power. For them the ownership of the cap remains strictly an economic issue.

Dave, however, comes to see the cap as more than simply a prize to be contested. He eventually realizes that for his own son the cap was a link to a larger, more significant world, and perhaps a pledge of future glory. Because Dave finally recognizes the importance of the cap to Steve, he begins to respond to the boy's aspirations and enthusiasms. He and his son lose possession of the cap, but it nevertheless provides them with the opportunity for an intimacy that is beyond price.

Style and Technique

The story covers a few weeks in the life of a poor family, during which a boy acquires and then loses a cap that has tremendous value to him. Only a few scenes from this period are dramatized, and they are presented in chronological order. Description is kept to essentials, while dialogue carries the story forward. The narrative voice is third person and largely objective, though occasionally revealing Dave's observations and thoughts. In general, the prose has a cinematic quality. As the story unfolds, it seems immediate, dramatic, and realistic.

In the story, the cap is not symbolic in the ordinary sense, yet some characters invest it with significance beyond its functional and market value. Hence, Callaghan is able to maintain his focus on the external world while calling attention to the existence of other, more important human realities. Also, Callaghan uses the cap as a way of structuring his story. When it is first acquired, it becomes a source of conflict between Dave and Steve; when its ownership is contested, it provides a measure of the distance and difference between the cost of something and its ultimate worth; finally, when it is relinquished, it allows the strong current of natural affection between father and son to be expressed.

Michael J. Larsen

CAREFUL

Author: Raymond Carver (1938-   )
Type of plot: Domestic realism
Time of plot: The 1970's
Locale: An unnamed city
First published: 1983

Principal characters:
    LLOYD, who is separated from his wife and trying to overcome
      a drinking problem
    INEZ, Lloyd's estranged wife
    MRS. MATTHEWS, Lloyd's landlady

The Story

In "Careful," Raymond Carver focuses on the details of a specific, small situation, giving little information about such matters as locale, the year of the action, or the occupations of the participants, except for Mrs. Matthews, who is Lloyd's landlady.

Lloyd and Inez have recently gone through what Inez calls "an assessment." The outcome of this assessment is that they decide to separate. As the story opens, Lloyd has recently moved into a two-room and bath attic apartment in Mrs. Matthews' house. The ceilings in the apartment are low and slanting, so much so that Lloyd has to stoop to look out the windows and has to be careful not to hit his head when he gets out of bed.

The reader first meets Lloyd as he enters the building in which he lives, carrying his groceries—some lunch meat and three bottles of André champagne. As he passes Mrs. Matthews' door, he looks in and sees that she is lying on the floor. He thinks that she might have collapsed, but her television set is on, and he does not venture to find out whether she is all right. She moves slightly, so he knows that she is not dead.

Lloyd's cooking facilities are minimal: A single unit contains his two-burner stove and a tiny refrigerator. Sometimes he makes himself instant coffee on the stove, but he is more likely to have a breakfast of crumb doughnuts and champagne. He switched to champagne in an attempt to wean himself away from hard liquor, but now he is drinking three or four bottles of champagne a day.

On the day of the story's action, Inez, Lloyd's estranged wife, comes unannounced to see him. Because he does not have a telephone, she has not been able to forewarn him of her visit. When she arrives at eleven o'clock in the morning, Lloyd is sitting in the apartment, not yet dressed, banging his head with his fist. His right ear passage has become blocked with wax, which he is trying to dislodge. The blockage makes all sounds seem distorted.

When Lloyd talks, he hears himself talking like someone in a barrel, and his balance is affected as well.

Inez has come to talk with him about the details of their separation, some of them having to do with money. It soon becomes evident, however, that little can be accomplished until Lloyd's ear is fixed, so Inez immediately leaps into the role of mother-nurse. Lloyd recalls that one of his schoolteachers, who was like a nurse, years ago had warned her students not to put anything smaller than their elbows in their ears, and he tells Inez of this warning. She responds, "Well, your nurse was never faced with this exact problem," and she proceeds to search for a hairpin or some other implement to stick into Lloyd's ear to dislodge the wax.

Finally, after an abortive attempt to work with a small nail file wrapped in tissue, Inez goes to ask the landlady to borrow some oil, which she heats and pours into Lloyd's ear, warning him to keep his head positioned so that the oil will not run out for at least ten minutes. While Inez is downstairs borrowing the oil, which quite significantly turns out to be baby oil, Lloyd slips into the bathroom and finishes off the bottle of champagne that he stashed there when he heard Inez arriving a few minutes earlier. Lying as he must to keep the oil in his ear, Lloyd sees everything around him from an odd perspective. All the objects in his vision seem at the far end of the room.

Finally, the oil works, and the wax is dislodged. Yet too much time has passed for Inez to talk with Lloyd about whatever it was that originally brought her to his apartment. She has other commitments to keep. Lloyd asks her where she has to go, and she replies vaguely, "I'm late for something." When she gets downstairs, Lloyd hears her talking with Mrs. Matthews, who asks her to leave her telephone number in case Lloyd should need her. Inez says that she hopes he will not, but she gives Mrs. Matthews the number. Lloyd hears her drive away in their car.

Lloyd pours some champagne into the glass in which Inez had put the baby oil. Although he has rinsed the glass out, he notices that some oil is floating on top of the champagne. He throws the champagne down the sink, gets the champagne bottle, and drinks from it.

Themes and Meanings

Carver is concerned in this story with the theme of regression to infantilism. Because the story is not set in a definite locale or in a definite time frame, the focus is on the tawdry apartment to which Lloyd has moved and on the two major characters in the story. Readers learn that the ceilings of the apartment seem to close in on Lloyd, that he does not have a telephone, that the furnished apartment has minimal housekeeping facilities, including a broken-down television, which he plays all day and all night, keeping the volume turned down. One gets the feeling that the apartment is a sort of womb into which Lloyd has retreated.

When his ear becomes clogged with wax, Lloyd has difficulty hearing, and his visit with his wife recalls the silent television images that usually inhabit the apartment with Lloyd. If Lloyd has a job, that information is not revealed. Because he is sitting home alone at eleven o'clock in the morning, one would assume that he is not employed.

Lloyd thinks back to his old teacher who warned children about putting things in their ears. The word "careful" occurs six times in the story (once as "carefully") and recalls what mothers and primary school teachers often say to children: "Be careful, dear." It is interesting that the word is used only once before Inez arrives on the scene. She immediately falls into the mothering role, and Lloyd regresses noticeably. He wants sympathy, and his blocked ear is the vehicle for his attaining it. Inez suggests that Wesson oil and Q-tips would be appropriate props for her in her mothering-nursing role. Lloyd has nothing like this in the apartment, so Inez must see whether she can borrow what she needs from the landlady.

It is significant that Inez must settle for baby oil, which she heats and, after it has cooled a little, pours into Lloyd's ear. When she leaves, and Lloyd overhears her talking with Mrs. Matthews, one is reminded of how a mother visiting school might talk in hushed tones to her child's teacher outside the classroom door.

As the story ends, Lloyd is alone in his womblike dwelling, and he is drinking his champagne from the bottle, just as a baby drinks its milk from a bottle. Inez has twice told him that she cannot linger because she is "late for something." She feels no obligation to explain anything to Lloyd, for whom she feels pity rather than love at this point; metaphorically, perhaps, her words suggest that she has, because of him, missed out on life but that something lies ahead for her despite her late start.

Style and Technique

Carver has the ability to take a commonplace event and imbue it with considerable meaning. His style is characterized by tight control and calculated understatement. He allows details to move in on the reader, who, for example, is told little about Lloyd's economic situation, but who comes immediately to understand that the man is faced with economic problems. Carver achieves this end in small, subtle ways.

First the reader is told that Lloyd is buying André champagne, which is one of the cheaper brands. Lloyd does not have a telephone. He does not have to pay for the electricity in this small, furnished apartment on the top floor, so he leaves the television on all day and all night. The implication is that if he had to pay the electric bill, he would be more conserving. Inez tells Lloyd that she has come to talk with him about necessary things including money, but she utters the word only once and apparently does not feel pressed to pursue the matter immediately.

In contrast to Lloyd's obvious poverty, Inez is carrying a new canvas hand-bag with bright flowers stitched on it, and she is dressed well. Inez is looking ahead; Lloyd is retreating from life. Carver shows that because of the separation, Lloyd does not even have a doctor to go to now. Also he has lost the car, as is evident when "he heard her start their car and drive away."

By placing the story in Lloyd's dank quarters, Carver heightens the contrast between Lloyd and Inez. Lloyd is still in his robe and is disheveled when Inez gets there. She is a well-groomed spot of brightness on an otherwise drab foreground. Lloyd is in the process of falling apart. Inez appears to be on the brink of finding a new life for herself.

R. Baird Shuman

THE CASK OF AMONTILLADO

Author: Edgar Allan Poe (1809-1849)
Type of plot: Horror
Time of plot: Unspecified
Locale: Italy
First published: 1846

Principal characters:
MONTRESOR, the narrator, an Italian nobleman
FORTUNATO, a connoisseur of wine

The Story

Told in the first person by an Italian aristocrat, "The Cask of Amontillado" engages the reader by making him or her a confidant to Montresor's macabre tale of revenge. The victim is Fortunato, who, the narrator claims, gave him a thousand injuries that he endured patiently, but when Fortunato dared insult him, he vowed revenge. It must be a perfect revenge, one in which Fortunato will know fully what is happening to him and in which Montresor will be forever undetected. To accomplish it, Montresor waits until carnival season, a time of "supreme madness," when Fortunato, already half-drunk and costumed as a jester with cap and bells, is particularly vulnerable. Montresor then informs him that he has purchased a pipe of Amontillado wine, but is not sure he has gotten the genuine article. He should, he says, have consulted Fortunato, who prides himself on being an expert on wine, adding that since Fortunato is engaged, he will go instead to Luchesi. Knowing his victim's vanity, Montresor baits him by saying that some fools argue that Luchesi's taste is as fine as Fortunato's. The latter is hooked, and Montresor conducts him to his empty palazzo and leads him down into the family catacombs, all the while plying him with drink. Through underground corridors with piles of skeletons alternating with wine casks, Montresor leads Fortunato, whose jester's bells jingle grotesquely in the funereal atmosphere. In the deepest crypt there is a small recess, and there Montresor chains Fortunato to a pair of iron staples and then begins to lay a wall of stone and mortar, with which he buries his enemy alive. While he does so, he relishes the mental torment of his victim, whom he then leaves alone in the dark, waiting in terror for his death.

Themes and Meanings

Poe himself seems to have had a morbid fear of premature burial; it is a theme he dealt with repeatedly in such stories as "The Premature Burial," "The Fall of the House of Usher," "Berenice," "Ligeia," and "Morella," all of which reverberate with a claustrophobic terror. He also turned again to walling up a victim in "The Black Cat." The fear was that the buried person would still be conscious, aware of the enveloping horror.

"The Cask of Amontillado" belongs to the Romantic movement in art; it is part of the Romantic subgenre of the Gothic, a tale of horror with the Gothic paraphernalia of dungeons, catacombs, and cadavers. At his best, though, Poe transcends the genre. As he observed, his horror was not of Germany (meaning Gothicism), but of the soul. To the extent that this is true, Poe was a pioneer in writing psychological fiction, often of extremely neurotic, if not abnormal, personalities. He also was an early advocate of art for art's sake; unlike his contemporary, Nathaniel Hawthorne, he did not write moral allegories. In "The Cask of Amontillado," the murderer gets away with his crime. Whatever meaning the tale offers lies in the portrait of Montresor, contained in his own words. D. H. Lawrence, in *Studies in Classic American Literature* (1923), says that Montresor is devoured by the lust of hate, which destroys his soul just as he destroys Fortunato. By this token, Montresor resembles Hawthorne's unpardonable sinners, who suffer from an intellectual pride and monomania that destroys their humanity. His revenge echoes (whether consciously or not) a passage from Thomas Nashe's Renaissance novel *The Unfortunate Traveller* (1594):

> Nothing so long of memorie as a dog, these Italians are old dogs, and will carrie an injurie a whole age in memorie: I have heard of a boxe on the eare that hath been revenged thirtie yeare after. The Neopolitane carrieth the bloodiest mind, and is the most secret fleering murdrer: whereupon it is growen to a common proverbe, Ile give him the Neopolitan shrug, when one intends to play the villaine, and make no boast of it.

Style and Technique

James Russell Lowell, in his satiric poem *A Fable for Critics* (1848), called Poe's work three-fifths genius and two-fifths fudge. In the genius-fudge ratio, "The Cask of Amontillado" ranks high on the genius side. A brief, concise story, it fulfills Poe's literary theory that every detail and word in a tale or poem should contribute to the intended effect. Here, there are only two characters, and though Montresor insists upon his patience in devising an appropriate and satisfying revenge, the story moves quickly and relentlessly to its climax. In contrast to the verbosity found in the works of Sir Walter Scott and James Fenimore Cooper, Poe's story, only about four pages long, has not a wasted word. Poe grips readers and plunges them right in with the opening sentence, "The thousand injuries of Fortunato I had borne as I best could, but when he ventured upon insult I vowed revenge." Readers learn almost nothing about the background of the characters; one is told nothing about their age, their families, their wives and children, if any, or their appearance. One is not even told when and where the story takes place, though the name Fortunato and references to a palazzo indicate Italy. From the last sentence, stating that Fortunato's bones have moldered in the tomb for half a century, one can deduce that they were young men at the time of the tale, which could occur no later than the end of the eighteenth century. As for character, Montresor tells readers that Fortunato was to be respected and even feared, that his only weak point was his pride in being a connoisseur of wine. This pride in such a trivial matter becomes grotesquely disproportionate and leads him into the trap.

Critics have complained that all of Poe's characters sound alike, that Poe has only one voice, but in "The Cask of Amontillado" the narrative voice— learned, passionate but cold, ironic—fits perfectly the character of the avenger. Like Shakespeare's Iago and Richard III, Montresor takes the reader into his confidence, assuming he or she will approve not only of his revenge but also of the clever and grotesque manner of it, and share his gloating satisfaction. The sensitive reader will also identify with Fortunato, however, and share his fear of the charnel-like catacombs and his horror of being walled up alive, to die slowly in the dark of starvation or suffocation among the skeletons of Montresor's ancestors.

The reader should realize, as Montresor does not, that despite his cleverness and irony, Montresor is an inhuman monster and something of a madman. Montresor's tone throughout is jocose. Repeatedly, he baits Fortunato (whose name is ironic in light of his ghastly fate) by playing upon his vanity, suggesting that Luchesi can judge the wine as well, pretending to be his concerned friend, giving his enemy chance after chance to escape. The vaults are too damp, Fortunato has a cough, his health is precious, and they should turn back. With foreknowledge, Montresor observes that Fortunato will not die of a cough and drinks to his long life. Montresor interprets his family's coat of arms—signifying, he says, that no one injures him with impunity, a warning that Fortunato has ignored. When Fortunato makes a secret gesture and asks if Montresor is a mason, the latter produces a trowel, which he will use to wall up his enemy. Thus, Montresor plays cat and mouse with his victim. After chaining his enemy, he implores him to return, then says he must render him "all the little attention in my power," and proceeds to the masonry. Clearly, he savors every moment of his murderous revenge. When Fortunato begins to scream, Montresor reveals his own madness. Unsheathing his rapier, he thrusts about with it and then responds by echoing and surpassing the cries of his victim. At the end, he returns to his jocose tone, observing that his heart grew sick on account of "the dampness of the catacombs," and concluding, fifty years later, "In pace requiescat": "May he rest in peace."

Robert E. Morsberger

THE CATBIRD SEAT

Author: James Thurber (1894-1961)
Type of plot: Comedy
Time of plot: 1942
Locale: New York City
First published: 1942

> *Principal characters:*
> ERWIN MARTIN, the department head at F & S
> ULGINE BARROWS, the new special adviser to the president
> of F & S
> MR. FITWEILER, the "F" and elderly president of F & S

The Story

"The Catbird Seat" is the story of Erwin Martin's calculated destruction of the vulgar, ruthless Ulgine Barrows, who has made life at F & S miserable since her appearance two years before the story begins. The tale might almost be called a revenge comedy, and it is even more amusing because Mr. Martin's very dullness enables him to succeed.

The story begins with an uncharacteristic action by Mr. Martin. He does not smoke; yet he is surreptitiously buying a pack of cigarettes. The purchase is part of his plan to kill Mrs. Ulgine Barrows, a plan which he has worked out during the preceding week.

Mr. Martin has no qualms about his action. Since charming the elderly Mr. Fitweiler at a party and persuading him to make her his all-powerful adviser, Mrs. Barrows has fired some employees and caused the resignations of others. As she has moved from department to department, she has changed systems and, Mr. Martin believes, is threatening the very existence of the firm, while Mr. Fitweiler, besotted, applauds. Although he is consistently annoyed by her Southern expressions, evidently picked up from a baseball announcer, such as "sitting in the catbird seat," that is, in a perfect situation, Mr. Martin has not thought that she deserved death until her appearance in the filing department, which he heads. When she suggests that his filing cabinets were not necessary, Ulgine Barrows signs her own death warrant. Mr. Martin's purchase of a brand of cigarettes which she does not smoke is only one element in a thoughtful plan.

At a time of day when the streets are relatively deserted, Mr. Martin goes to the apartment of Mrs. Barrows. She is surprised to see him, puzzled when he refuses to remove his gloves, and amused when Mr. Martin, who is known never to drink, accepts a Scotch. As he looks about for a weapon, Mr. Martin realizes that the murder he had planned is simply too difficult. Another idea comes to him, however: He can eliminate Mrs. Barrows by destroying her credibility.

When Mrs. Barrows returns with his drink, Mr. Martin smokes, drinks, announces that he takes heroin regularly, and suggests that he intends to kill Mr. Fitweiler. Commenting that he is in the "catbird seat," he leaves, goes home unseen, and goes to sleep.

At the office the next morning, Mrs. Barrows reports the incident to Mr. Fitweiler. Faced with Mr. Martin's usual propriety, Mr. Fitweiler can only assume that Mrs. Barrows has developed delusions. After consultation with his psychiatrist, Mr. Fitweiler has concluded that she must be fired. Furious, Mrs. Barrows screams at Mr. Martin, voicing her suspicions that he may have planned the whole situation. Still screaming, she is removed from the office. Accepting Mr. Fitweiler's apology, Mr. Martin permits himself a faster pace in the hall, but back in his department, he resumes his usual propriety and returns to his files.

Themes and Meanings

The familiar Thurber drawings of women in the act of seducing, menacing, attacking, or intimidating men are matched in his short stories by accounts of the ongoing war between the sexes. Armed with sex appeal, defiant illogic, physical strength, and their institution of marriage, Thurber's women seem to have the odds on their side. When a man as meek as Walter Mitty or Erwin Martin must deal with a female antagonist, only his imagination can bring him the victory.

In the battle recounted in "The Catbird Seat," each side uses characteristic weapons. Mrs. Ulgine Barrows has gained her job initially by strength and sex appeal. At a party, she rescued the elderly Mr. Fitweiler from a large drunk, and then she charmed him into offering her the job. Once committed to her, he gives her complete control; he is completely at her mercy, playing Samson to her Delilah.

Initially, Mr. Martin intended to destroy Mrs. Barrows by brute force, hoping to avoid suspicion by such detective-story devices as the use of gloves, the choice of a weapon from the victim's own apartment, and the deceptive clue of the partially smoked cigarette. He realizes, however, that violence is not his best weapon; indeed, that he cannot win in a game where the hefty Mrs. Barrows is at her best. It is his imagination, fortunately a talent that has remained hidden, which can defeat her. Therefore, like Walter Mitty, he becomes another person, but he reveals that personality only to Mrs. Barrows, who is therefore trapped into a seeming lie which can only be interpreted as madness. The silent self-control which makes Mr. Martin a good file clerk ensures his victory, for he is too disciplined ever to tell anyone what he has done, ever to reveal his secret self.

Although Thurber, like George Bernard Shaw, suggests that women are the stronger sex, it is clear that men can sometimes triumph if only they use the weapons which have always been available to the oppressed; craftiness, imagination, and the ability to keep a secret. Armed only with these, Mr. Martin has attained his victory.

Style and Technique

The comic irony which is so important an element in Thurber's stories is effected in "The Catbird Seat" by the technique of limited omniscience. From the beginning to the end of the story, Thurber reveals the thoughts only of his Mr. Martin. Yet the impression that Mr. Martin makes on others is clearly revealed through objective comments, such as the fact that the cigarette clerk did not look at him, and by comments recalled by Mr. Martin, such as those of Mr. Fitweiler and of the late Sam Schlosser. With the judgment of the outside world thus established, Thurber can produce his comic effect by letting the reader in on the secret. Only the reader shares Mr. Martin's carefully dissembled anger; only the reader follows the formulation of his plot; and only the reader anticipates and then experiences the final scene, in which no one will believe Mrs. Barrows, even though she is telling the truth.

Because the character of Mr. Martin is so important, both in the plot line and in the total comic effect, Thurber establishes his spinsterish fussiness, his bureaucratic orderliness, by the use of numerous details. He plans to eliminate Mrs. Barrows as if she were an error; he tries and convicts her in a mental courtroom, while he is drinking his milk; he shines his glasses and sharpens pencils while he waits to murder her.

The other characters are seen through Mr. Martin's eyes. Mrs. Barrows "romped . . . like a circus horse," "was constantly shouting," "demanded," "brayed," and "bawled." To the quiet Mr. Martin, her bouncy noisiness is clearly distasteful. Similarly, when Mr. Fitweiler is forced to speak to Mr. Martin about the woman's allegations, Mr. Martin notices that he is "pale and nervous," that he plays with his glasses—in other words, that his employer has less control over the situation than Martin has.

It is a final refinement of Thurber's comedy that Martin does not reveal the fact of his control. Thus, he expresses regret that his employer must fire Mrs. Barrows, and after Mr. Fitweiler's apology for the loud attacks of Mrs. Barrows, Martin agrees to forget the incident. At the end of the story, Mr. Martin is in "the catbird seat," and only the reader, who has been admitted to his thoughts as well as having watched his actions, is party to his triumph against the odds.

Rosemary M. Canfield-Reisman

THE CATCH

Author: Kenzaburō Ōe (1935-   )
Type of plot: Adventure
Time of plot: Late in World War II
Locale: A small mountain village in Japan
First published: "Shiiku," 1959 (English translation, 1959)

> *Principal characters:*
> THE YOUNG BOY, the narrator and protagonist
> THE CAPTIVE, a black American airman
> THE FATHER, an impoverished hunter
> HARELIP, the boy's playmate and the village bully
> THE CLERK, a handicapped official from the local town

The Story

It is a hot, lazy summer in an isolated mountain village in Japan. Floods have washed out the only direct link to town, a suspension bridge. The teacher refuses to travel the long, treacherous path along the ridge, so the village children find time on their hands.

The narrator of this story is searching for bone fragments in the village crematory when Harelip, the local Tom Sawyer, appears with a wild-dog puppy that he has captured. Suddenly the narrow sky of the valley is filled with the shadow and roar of an enormous airplane.

Harelip shouts that it is an enemy plane, and the dog escapes in the confusion, but a more important "catch" is at hand. The next morning, the children of the village awake to find an ominous silence and all the adults gone. They are out searching for downed American airmen. The distant war, noted only by the absence of young men from the village and an occasional death notice, does not have much meaning for the children until the adults return late in the day from the mountains. They bring with them an enormous black man. The boy is reminded of a boar hunt, the hunters silently circled around the captive, who has the chain from a boar trap around his legs.

The enemy excites both fear and curiosity among the children. He is put into the cellar of the communal storehouse and a guard is posted. The storehouse is a large building, and the boy and his younger brother live on the second floor with their father, an impoverished hunter. His gun, always at the ready on the wall, "gave a kind of focus" to their "humble home." They have no furniture, and food is hard to come by in the war years. Yet the boy is excited at the thought of sleeping in the same building as the exotic prisoner who has fallen into their midst.

At first the captive is kept under close guard and treated as a dangerous animal. His smell is overpowering, and he seems like an animal to the children. The next day the boy goes with his father to town, to sell some weasel skins and to report the capture. The boy is uncomfortable in the town, conscious of his poverty and dirtiness. The local officials will not take the prisoner off the hands of the village until they receive orders from the prefecture offices. The boy and his father return to the village at sunset with the unwelcome news.

The boy carries food down into the dark cellar, guarded by his father, who has his shotgun ready. At first the captive only stares at the food, and the boy realizes in shame that the poor dinner might be rejected. The black man, however, suddenly devours the meal. Gradually the boy loses his fear of the American as they bring him food every day, and vigilance is relaxed: "I began to feel that he was docile and quiet, like some gentle animal."

The village elders are angered when they learn from the clerk sent out from town that they will have the responsibility of guarding the prisoner until the officials decide what to do. The boy and his friends begin to have a proprietary interest in the captive. The other children are envious of the boy's privileged role, carrying food to the catch twice a day. He does share one task with Harelip, carrying out once a day the heavy wooden tub that the black man uses. They carry the evil-smelling liquid to the village manure heap.

As time passes, the adults return to their fields, and the children spend more time with the captive, hoping that orders from town will not appear. Noticing that the captive's leg is bloody from the boar trap, the boy and Harelip find a key and release him with initial trepidation, but they find him well behaved. Even the adults in the village accept the idea that the captive is actually human, as gentle as a tame animal. They let him use tools to fix the boar trap. They form an almost "human" bond, coming to trust him.

One morning, the one-legged clerk from town has a bad fall on the path to the village, damaging the metal attachment of his false leg. The children, who fear the worst, are delighted to hear that he was coming simply to tell them that there was still no word from the prefect. In good spirits, they take his leg and the village toolbox down into the cellar, where the captive quickly fixes it. He is taken outside in celebration, and the clerk gives him a cigarette.

After that, the children often invite the captive out of the cellar to walk through the village. The adults come to accept this, and he is even allowed to wander around the village alone. The women lose their fear and give him food from their own hands. The children take him to the village spring, where they all strip naked and splash in the water. The black man's wet body "shone like the body of a black horse; it was perfect and beautiful." The boy thinks that he is a splendid animal, an animal of great intelligence.

The trust and respect disappear, however, when the clerk reappears on a rainy day. As the adults assemble, the prisoner senses that he is about to be taken away, and he grabs the boy and drags him to the cellar and locks the door. The boy is shocked and hurt as he realizes his sudden danger. The airman has turned back into the dangerous beast that he was when first captured. As the grown-ups break into the cellar, the captive uses the boy as a shield. The boy's father plunges a hatchet into the boy's hand and the captive's skull.

When he recovers, the boy is in a daze with a bandaged hand. He screams until his father and the other adults leave. Gradually he learns that the villagers wanted to cremate the captive, but that the clerk brought orders calling it off. They put the body in an unused mine, but the smell penetrates the village.

The story ends in irony. Paying another visit, the clerk notices the children using the lightweight tail of the American plane as a sled on the grass. In a playful mood, he decides to give it a try, but he hurtles into a rock and is killed. He will be cremated using the wood collected to cremate the American captive.

Themes and Meanings

Kenzaburō Ōe was born in a mountain village, and perhaps this gave him insight into the poverty, insularity, and inferiority that villagers experienced in prewar Japan. "The Catch" is earthy and vivid, capturing the simplicity as well as the coarseness of farm life. It captures the unreality of war as war is brought to the village in the unexpected arrival of an American airman.

Although the story takes place in the context of the unusual hardship of the war years, its theme of coming of age is universal. The young boy finds his childhood innocence and trust betrayed by the captive, as well as by his father and the other adults who rush to rescue him in a frenzy of hatred. Like a wild exotic animal, the "catch" is dangerous when he is cornered. The boy nearly loses his life in the violence, but the loss of his childhood is more important. There are echoes of *The Adventures of Huckleberry Finn* (1884) in this story: the spirit of adventure of the young boys, their unaffected wonder and curiosity, and their rejection of adult attitudes. Yet the difference is in the bitter ending; Jim does not die in Mark Twain's story, as does the black captive in "The Catch."

The story also shows how war leads people to ignore the basic humanity of all mankind. When the airman is first captured, the villagers are on guard, but the captive's humanity eventually wins them over. As they become more familiar with their captive, they find it difficult to treat him as a dangerous animal and come to accept him as part of their community. When the outside world, the world of officials and wars, interferes in the form of the clerk, the fragile human link between the villagers and the captive is once again broken. They return in the end to hostility and fear.

Style and Technique

Ōe is one of the most original writers in Japan. He successfully uses humor and pathos, brutality and gentleness in the same work. He uses the juxtaposition to create a realistic, yet somehow absurd, view of the world. To express it another way, his writing exposes the absurdity of the world. In "The Catch," he uses the voice and innocence of a child to tell the story. The use of a young narrator allows him to introduce humorous elements of childish enthusiasm that make the final tragedy all the more appalling.

Richard Rice

THE CELEBRATED JUMPING FROG OF CALAVERAS COUNTY

Author: Mark Twain (Samuel Langhorne Clemens, 1835-1910)
Type of plot: Tall tale
Time of plot: 1850
Locale: Northern California
First published: 1865

Principal characters:
AN UNNAMED NARRATOR
SIMON WHEELER, a current resident of Angel's Camp
JIM SMILEY, a former resident of Angel's Camp

The Story

The narrator, urged by a friend from the East, decides to call on Simon Wheeler, a good-natured and garrulous old fellow who resides at Angel's Camp, a northern California mining settlement. His errand is to inquire about a certain Reverend Leonidas W. Smiley, but he, the narrator, is already half persuaded that *Leonidas W.* Smiley never existed. Asking about him will only result in releasing a torrent of Simon Wheeler's boring reminiscences about *Jim* Smiley.

Simon Wheeler, a genial man, fat and baldheaded, wears a look of perpetual simplicity and tranquillity. As the narrator suspects, Wheeler cannot place Leonidas W. Smiley, but he does recall the presence of a fellow by the name of Jim Smiley who, some years previously, had been an Angel's Camp inhabitant. Wheeler's tone never changes, his voice never wavers from a pattern of earnestness and sincerity as he launches into his tale. He declines to register anything but the utmost respect and admiration for the two heroes whose adventures he will relate.

Jim Smiley, according to Simon Wheeler, was "always betting on anything that turned up." He would lay odds on either side of a bet, and if he could not find a taker for the other side, he would simply change sides. He bet on horse races, dog fights, and chicken fights. If he had had the opportunity, he would have bet on how long a straddle bug's flight was between one destination and another—then he would have followed the bug all the way to Mexico, if he had needed to, in order to win a bet. Smiley would bet on anything.

Smiley loved to employ animals in his betting schemes. He had a mare, an old nag really, but he used to win money on her, for all that she was slow and prey to myriad diseases such as asthma, distemper, and consumption. He also had a bull-pup, named Andrew Jackson, that Smiley had taught to fight using a most peculiar strategy. Andrew Jackson always went for his opponent's hind legs, and, holding these in a viselike grip, could hold on for a year. Smiley always won money on that pup until he came up against a dog whose hind legs had been sawed off with a circular saw.

One day Smiley caught a frog and took him home, swearing that all a frog needed was a good education—he stayed home for three months educating him. Daniel Webster was the creature's name, and Jim trained him so well that all he would have to do was yell, "Flies, Dan'l, flies," and the frog would leap off counters, displaying amazing feats of skill to startled onlookers. A modest frog, too, Daniel Webster was not given to airs despite his great gift of agility. So naturally Jim Smiley began to bet on Daniel, and he would take on all comers. He was exceedingly proud of his frog, convinced that Daniel was the finest example of the species to be found.

Once a stranger saw Jim's frog and inquired as to what he was good for. Jim eagerly explained that Daniel Webster could outjump any frog in Calaveras County. "I don't see no p'ints about that frog that's any better'n any other frog," the stranger observed. Yet he sportingly declared that he would bet with Smiley, if only he, the stranger, also had a frog. Jim took that bet, and a sum of forty dollars was wagered. Then Smiley willingly went off to the swamp to look for another frog. In Smiley's absence, the stranger pried open Daniel Webster's mouth and filled him full of quail shot. When Smiley returned with the other frog, both contestants were placed on the ground, and each was given a push from behind by his respective human. The new frog hopped off immediately, but Daniel Webster remained behind, as if bolted to the ground. The stranger collected his forty dollars and readily departed.

Smiley was dumbfounded by this turn of events and picked up the frog. Feeling his radically increased weight, he turned the animal upside down and Daniel Webster belched out a double handful of shot. Smiley set out after the stranger, but he never caught him.

At this point the narrator interrupts Wheeler's tale, assuring him that further information about *Jim* Smiley would shed no light on the activities of *Leonidas W.* Smiley. Lacking the desire to hear anything further relating to Jim Smiley, he leaves.

Themes and Meanings

To load a frog with shot so that it cannot engage in a jumping match is amusing. Beyond the obvious laugh, however, the slyness with which the defeat of the champion frog is managed seems to be an indication of Mark Twain's interest in championing frontier common sense. It is not really an endorsement of cheating or deception in a malicious sense. The narrator's casual reference to an Eastern friend is followed by an indulgently superior description of Simon Wheeler. Wheeler's winning gentleness and simplicity are of primary importance to the author. This disparity establishes Twain's dislike of the affectations and hypocrisy of the East, a dislike he readily contrasts with the informality and openness of the West. If the similarities of dramatic situation at the outset of the tale seem to indicate a familiar story line—the country stooge bested by the polished urbanite—the story upsets these calculations. The narrator, as things turn out, is not as clever as he sees himself. Assuming that he is more sophisticated than the man he meets, the encounter teaches him just the reverse—it is he, not Simon Wheeler, who is simple. The innocence of Simon Wheeler's expression is a mask which he assumes to deceive the outsider by seeming to fulfill all his preconceived notions of Western simplemindedness.

Simon Wheeler's tall tale also endorses democracy by making fun of superior feelings. Gazing at Daniel Webster, the stranger is unable to see anything that makes him innately superior to any other frog in creation. The subsequent triumph of the underfrog over the highly touted excellence of Daniel Webster comically vindicates the stranger's radical democracy. The lesson here is that it does not pay to be too proud or too haughty in the egalitarian West.

Twain is not merely embellishing a well-known theme. Though not immune to the sentiments of cynicism and skepticism, Twain was imbued with the frontier spirit of openness and sincerity characteristic of the West. By poking fun at hidebound tradition, manifested through the narrator's arrogant and polite speech, he ridicules Eastern customs and manners. In creating these three "simple" characters, Simon Wheeler, Jim Smiley, and the stranger, all of whom are superior to the narrator, Mark Twain places his humorist's stamp of legitimacy on the American West.

Style and Technique

In this highly significant humorous experiment, the author incorporates the traditional form of the tall tale into a story of his own creation. He produces a sort of literary tug-of-war between town and country, provincialism and urbanity. In appropriating this apocryphal frog story for his own purposes, Twain makes numerous changes in its composition. First and foremost, he embellishes the anecdote with a frame, in which he presents the narrator, Mark Twain, who in turn explains his encounter with Simon Wheeler in the mining settlement at Angel's Camp.

The names of the bulldog, Andrew Jackson, and the frog, Daniel Webster, may suggest that Twain was merely indulging in topical political satire. In fact, however, his intention was to mock politicians and lawmakers as a species—an activity in which he gleefully engaged throughout his literary career. Simon Wheeler's tall tale does not attempt to size up recent history. Its content is purely Western in feeling and, as such, is generous in its ready acceptance of the exaggerated and the absurd. In this story, it is the vernacular, not the traditional style of polite speech, that emerges triumphant. The city slicker narrator receives, not teaches, the lesson.

This is not merely the repetition of an oft-told tall tale, redesigned and decked out in a new guise. From the beginning it is made clear that there is no Leonidas W. Smiley, especially no Reverend Leonidas W. Smiley, and that his existence is mere pretense in order to hear Simon Wheeler elucidate on the past experiences of Jim Smiley. Simon Wheeler's calculated ramblings admirably provide a platform for Twain's subtle and not-so-subtle humor. His literary greatness, in part, emanates from a perpetual malicious shrewdness which he frequently chooses to cloak under an assumed simplicity. His innocence is always pure sham, and the fact that he openly shares this secret with the reader is part of the fun.

Rhona E. Zaid

THE CELESTIAL OMNIBUS

Author: E. M. Forster (1879-1970)
Type of plot: Allegorical fantasy
Time of plot: Edwardian England
Locale: "Surbiton," a suburban town outside London
First published: 1911

> *Principal characters:*
> THE BOY, the protagonist, who is enthusiastic and instinctive
> in his pursuit of knowledge
> HIS FATHER AND MOTHER, typical middle-class parents with
> pretensions to culture
> MR. BONS, a churchwarden, a candidate for county council, a
> benefactor of the free library, the head of the literary
> society, and a pseudointellectual

The Story

E. M. Forster has filled this modern fantasy with wordplay and hidden allusions which allow it to function as an allegory on literary snobbery. The unnamed protagonist, a boy, has begun to discover the joy of literature; untutored, he plunges ahead uncritically and appreciates the popular and the classical with equal enthusiasm. He is, however, spiritually imprisoned in his parents' suburban home in "Surbiton," Agathox Lodge, appropriately a corruption of *agathos*, the Greek word for "good."

The adults who surround the boy merely stifle his curiosity. For example, when he naïvely asks the meaning of the sign which points toward a blind alley but reads "To Heaven," his flustered mother answers that it had been placed there by "naughty young men." She elaborates, though she still does not answer, by adding that one of them wrote verse and was expelled from the university, an oblique reference to Percy Bysshe Shelley. Mr. Bons ("snob" spelled backward), a family friend and frequent guest, wants the adults to know that he has caught the reference, though he does not tell the boy what he wants to know. The boy innocently admits that he has never heard of Shelley, and Mr. Bons is aghast ("...no Shelley in the house?"). There are "at least" two Shelleys in the house—not, however, collections of Shelley's poems, but rather framed prints, both of which were wedding presents. (Mr. Bons has seven Shelleys.)

Surbiton at sunset has, for the boy, the beauty of an Alpine valley. He is filled with vague stirrings "for something just a little different," and he finds it in a cryptic paper posted on the wall of "the alley to heaven." Shelley had his skylark; the boy has a celestial omnibus, which leaves for Heaven twice daily from that very alley opposite his home.

The boy's journey is a Wagnerian spectacular straight out of *Der Ring des Nibelungen* (1852). The driver (the essayist Sir Thomas Browne) heads upward through lightning and thunder, which synesthetically create a rainbow bridge to Heaven. Color and sound become one for the boy. Sir Thomas Browne and the boy pass the gulf between the real and ideal and hear the song of the Rhinemaidens. The boy does not recognize the music as being from *Das Rheingold* (1852). He knows only that it is very beautiful. His journey is an adventure into the world of literature and art, naïvely but genuinely appreciated; it is also a determined striking out against the boredom and oppression of Agathox Lodge and Surbiton. When he returns home, his father punishes the boy for the disappearance with a sound, middle-class caning and by forcing him to memorize poetry. With typical ignorance, he assigns John Keats's sonnet "To Homer" in praise of the blind poet's ability to see the enchanted world described in the *Odyssey*. Forster does not explicitly identify the poem, though he has the boy quote its first line: "Standing aloof in great ignorance." The boy's father applies the words to his son; the reader realizes that they more fittingly apply to those such as the father, who would punish joyful discovery and naïve enthusiasm.

Mr. Bons is present at the recitation and perversely curious at the boy's sudden knowledge of literary lore. He determines to "cure" the boy by accompanying him the next evening on his search for the omnibus. Indeed they find it, though the driver this time is not the freethinker Sir Thomas Browne, but someone identified explicitly only as "Dan." That the driver is Dante is clear from the emended *Inferno* quotation which is placed above the door of the coach: "Lasciate ogni baldanza voi che entrate" ("Abandon all self-importance, you who enter here"). Mr. Bons explains in a voice that "sounded as if he was in church" that "baldanza" is obviously a mistake, that it should read "speranza" ("hope"). The reader, however, knows that with Mr. Bons in the omnibus, "baldanza" is undoubtedly more appropriate.

Mr. Bons corrects the boy's literary errors during the journey. It is wrong for him to prefer Sir Thomas to Dante, Mrs. Gamp (a Charles Dickens character) to Homer, Tom Jones (the protagonist of the Henry Fielding novel) to William Shakespeare. He also lectures the boy on how to behave toward literary immortals. The boy, though he resolves to become "self-conscious, reticent, and prim," cannot resist meeting Achilles, who raises him on his shield. Mr. Bons is frightened out of his wits and wants to return; the boy would remain with Achilles forever.

Great books are the means, not the end, as Dante tells Mr. Bons, who wants to return to his vellum-bound copies of Dante's *The Divine Comedy* and his comfortable, secondhand knowledge rather than pursue this actual experience. Mr. Bons tries to escape and return to the world, but he falls through a moonlit rock, no doubt because he does not believe that it exists. The postscript "quotation" from the *Surbiton Times* reporting the discovery of Mr. Bons's mutilated body near "Bermondsey Gas-Works" provides a fittingly ironic death for a "windbag." Since Mr. Bons held both return tickets, the boy is presumably still enjoying life among the immortals.

Themes and Meanings

"The Celestial Omnibus" is one of Forster's earliest works; though fantasy, it is also one of his most personal. His Cambridge years (1897-1901), which coincided with the end of Queen Victoria's reign, were his period of intellectual awakening. The dons and fellows included Goldsworthy Lowes Dickinson, Roger Fry, G. E. Moore, Bertrand Russell, and Alfred North Whitehead. His fellow undergraduates were John Maynard Keynes, Sir Desmond MacCarthy, Lytton Strachey, and Leonard Woolf. For Dickinson and for his student Forster, Shelley became a "Daedalus," providing the most suitable literary "wings" to escape convention yet never to forget humanity. This credo would ultimately draw Forster to the Bloomsbury group.

Shelley's skylark becomes an omnibus in Forster's story, the vehicle which introduces the boy to a veritable pantheon of great authors, both classical and popular. Significantly, this pantheon is available "to everyone," though only those with an unaffected appreciation of art survive the journey to this literary Valhalla. Finally, the story's theme of self-discovery is as clear as that of Sir James Barrie's play *Peter Pan* (1904) or Lewis Carroll's Alice stories.

Style and Technique

Forster adds wordplay to symbol in "The Celestial Omnibus." Mr. Bons, for example, represents apparent good (*bon*) only; he is actually pure snob, as his name spelled backward indicates. His poetry is an ornament to be worn, something to be quoted, corrected, or criticized rather than a faith to be held or a trust to be kept. He demands that Dante return him to the world because he has "...honoured...quoted...and bound..." him, but Dante replies that he (his works) are the means, not the end. Mr. Bons's death is mere poetic justice.

Though Marxist critics have savaged this story as an escapist response to bourgeois oppression, Forster intended no political implications at the time he wrote it. The socially conscious Forster would emerge in *A Passage to India* (1924) and in the prewar political essays, but "The Celestial Omnibus" is an intelligently written fantasy, filled with the scholarly enthusiasms of a bright young man who has recently come down from Cambridge.

Robert J. Forman

A CHAIN OF LOVE

Author: Reynolds Price (1933-   )
Type of plot: Social realism
Time of plot: The 1950's or 1960's
Locale: Afton, North Carolina, a small town near the border between North Carolina and Virginia; Raleigh, North Carolina
First published: 1963

> *Principal characters:*
> ROSACOKE MUSTIAN, a teenage girl from Afton, North Carolina
> HORATIO "RATO" MUSTIAN, Rosacoke's brother
> MILO MUSTIAN, Rosacoke's brother
> SISSIE MUSTIAN, Milo's wife
> BABY SISTER, Rosacoke's six-year-old sister
> MAMA MUSTIAN, Rosacoke's mother
> PAPA, Rosacoke's grandfather, Mama's father-in-law
> WESLEY BEAVERS, Rosacoke's boyfriend
> MR. LEDWELL, a dying hospital patient

The Story

The chain of love to which the title of "A Chain of Love" refers represents the closeness of the Mustian family, three generations of whom live in Afton, North Carolina, on the Virginia–North Carolina border. Papa, a widower, has just celebrated his birthday with appropriate family festivities. The next day he falls sick, and Dr. Sledge decides that he must be hospitalized in Raleigh, an hour's drive away. As is customary among rural Southern families, all the kinfolk go to Raleigh for Papa's hospitalization.

Mama, Rosacoke's mother and the widow of Papa's son, cannot stay in Raleigh, as would be expected of her, because she is in charge of Children's Day at the Baptist Church. She must see that responsibility through. She accompanies Papa to Raleigh, bringing with her half a gallon of custard she has made to leave with him. When Papa enters the hospital, he is offered a large corner room for twelve dollars a day, but he decides there is "no use trying the good will of the Blue Cross Hospital Insurance so he took a ten-dollar room standing empty across the hall."

Mama promises to come back on Sunday, after the Children's Day festivities are over, and stay with him until he can go home. Meanwhile, she leaves her daughter Rosacoke and her son Rato to look after Papa. The two set themselves up in Papa's small room, each using a chair to sleep in through the night. They stay for several days, keeping watch over their grandfather.

Rosacoke often goes into the still vacant corner room across the hall to look out the window during her vigil with Papa. From the room she can see a statue of Jesus, head down, hands spread by his sides. The statue is bare-chested and a cloth is draped over its right shoulder. Rosacoke cannot see its face, but she remembers it as a kindly countenance from having seen it when they came into the hospital.

After two days, someone checks into the corner room, a man, later revealed to be Mr. Ledwell. He looks healthy and is able to walk in under his own power, accompanied by his wife and son. Meanwhile, Papa can find out little from the doctors about his own condition, and he tells them little except that he wants to die at home, not in a hospital.

The first day Mr. Ledwell is in his room, Rosacoke mistakes his son, who is sitting in the hall, for her boyfriend, Wesley Beavers, and embarrasses herself by saying something inane to the youth, who reacts gracefully. Before long, Rosacoke learns from Snowball, a hospital attendant from her hometown, that Mr. Ledwell is to undergo surgery for lung cancer and that one lung will have to be removed. The prognosis is bleak.

The next morning, Mr. Ledwell is operated upon and at first seems to be doing quite well, but after a few hours, his condition deteriorates and his doctor is called in the middle of the night to come in and use emergency measures to save his life. Mr. Ledwell is resuscitated, and Rosacoke decides that she should go in to visit him and his family and to offer to help them if she can.

She does not want to go in without taking anything for Mr. Ledwell, so she sends a card to her mother asking her to bring some altheas with her when she comes on Sunday to visit Papa. Rosacoke is nervous about visiting Mr. Ledwell, but feels it is her duty to do so because he has lived in Raleigh only six months, having moved there from Baltimore, and he has no friends to visit him.

On Sunday, Mama brings the altheas, not knowing what Rosacoke intends to do with them. The whole family has come to spend the day with Papa, whose room, in sharp contrast to Mr. Ledwell's, is filled with people. When things have settled down, Rosacoke puts on some makeup, wraps the altheas, ties a note to them, and knocks softly on the high oak door of Mr. Ledwell's room. There is no answer. She pushes the door gently. The room is dark except for some candles she sees burning. When her eyes adjust, Rosacoke sees that Mr. Ledwell's son is standing at the head of the bed. An old man in black, presumably a priest, is conducting some sort of rite that is foreign to Rosacoke. She suspects that she should not be there, but as she turns to leave, the son sees her and almost smiles. She watches as the dying man is anointed, not knowing the meaning of Extreme Unction but realizing what this sort of service must mean. She leaves her flowers on the chair and goes back to Papa's room to say goodbye before Milo comes by to pick her up and take her home to Afton.

Before Rosacoke goes home, Rato reveals that Mr. Ledwell has died and suggests that they leave the door open a crack so that they can see his body being removed. Rosacoke absolutely rejects this suggestion and Rato leaves the room, slamming the door behind him.

Themes and Meanings

"A Chain of Love" is a gentle story whose characters are the same people Reynolds Price wrote about in his novels *A Long and Happy Life* (1962) and *A Generous Man* (1966). Essentially, the story is about continuity from generation to generation, about family lines and family closeness. The Mustian family gathers to help Papa through an illness which could be his final one. They are with him as much of the time as they can be.

The Ledwells are quite shadowy people compared to the Mustians, as the reader sees them from Rosacoke's vantage point. She observes them from the shadows. They are unaware that she is observing them, and they never really come to know the sympathy she feels for them. From her standpoint, they are lonely and alienated because they are living as newly arrived strangers in a place where family ties are of extreme importance.

Price never reveals the Ledwells or anyone else in the story from any point of view other than Rosacoke's, and he successfully works within the limitations of this point of view. Rosacoke's innocence and naïveté color everything in the story, and soften the realities substantially. The reader is shown that not all the relatives in Papa's sickroom have Rosacoke's innocence. Milo is planning to duck out of the sick man's room to take his wife to a Chinese dinner and movie. He wears a necktie that lights up in the dark to read, "Kiss Me in the Dark!" Rosacoke, in her innocence, is learning to deal with death, which she has experienced before, but which she is now experiencing for the first time as a somewhat mature person.

Price has Rosacoke ponder questions relating to death. Mr. Ledwell was said to have been clinically dead but his doctor revived him. Rosacoke remembers the time the Phelps boy fell off the dam at Fleming's Mill and almost drowned. He, like Mr. Ledwell, was dead until they revived him. Rosacoke wonders if people who go through that experience know what lies on the other side. She suspects the Phelps boy knows, but he will not tell, saying that what he found out when he was dead for half an hour is between him and Jesus.

Style and Technique

Reynolds Price has not only managed to capture expertly the speech patterns of people from Warren County, North Carolina, but he has also managed to capture in all of its detail the rich fabric of family life in that part of the country. "A Chain of Love" exudes authenticity. If its title is a bit ironic—chains do, after all, bind—the irony is softened because the love is genuine. If the love is also a bit cloying, it seems a small price to pay for the security it offers.

The story's dialogue, both overt and internal, is rambling and discursive. It is filled with details, not all of them pertinent. Nevertheless, it is just these qualities that make the dialogue totally believable to anyone who has experienced the part of the country about which Price is writing.

Price presents his characters with considerable skill. In this story, the reader sees almost nothing of Milo's wife, Sissie, yet every word that is spent on her serves to build an unforgettable image of a woman who feels outside the family, who is frustrated at not being accepted more fully, and who is forced into doing things that she does not want to do because the family decrees it. Milo is caught in the middle and tries to humor Sissie.

Price stays in total control of his characters by remaining always within the limitations imposed by the point of view he has selected. He provides no information that is not available within his chosen viewpoint. His ability to keep his focus accurate and consistent is noteworthy.

R. Baird Shuman

CHANGE

Author: Larry Woiwode (1941-   )
Type of plot: Domestic realism
Time of plot: 1979
Locale: Chicago
First published: 1980

> *Principal characters:*
> THE HUSBAND,
> THE WIFE
> THE EIGHT-YEAR-OLD DAUGHTER
> THE INFANT SON
> THE NEIGHBORS, Bob and Betty
> "THE BOYS" of Bob and Betty

The Story

Through recall, Woiwode engages in a discursive examination of two households, particularly the home of the narrator, for a period of about six months, from April to fall.

A glowing doorknob, with its paint and grime removed in the spring, is a reminder to the narrator of the time and energy expended on it before it began to shine "like a miniature burnished sun." With the door swung against the left end of the table at which he is now sitting and "walling" him in "somewhat on one open side," the knob still shines "above the edge" of his vision in the room in a ramshackle apartment house.

It is fall now, and the narrator is at work on transcribing notes which—or so he believes at times—will be an "indisputable proof of the existence of God." These notes range over a thirteen-year period during which he has had "different opinions or interpretations of their meaning during different recastings of them." He especially desires to leave the events, not of his making, free of "subjective coloring." This new work is a "stock-taking interim."

Now "walled-in" at the table, the narrator begins to recall the effects of bolts of lightning striking twice at the apartment house. Following the first bolt, he recalls, he simply sat at the table, feeling guilty about not being able to get at the work he set for himself. Picking up a glossy magazine, he read an article on guerrilla warfare in Palestine. The account of the violence and of bystanders being injured by bombs merely sharpened the guilt he does not wish to examine.

The next bolt came within a matter of months; a week or two later, he saw a troubling cartoon in the same glossy magazine: "a pair of angels on a cloud, looking over its edge, one of them with a bunch of jagged cartoon thunderbolts under an arm, and had a caption that went something like 'Get him again!'" The bolts meant external change, at least for the "upper limbs" of the oak tree in his yard.

In the time covered by these recollections, the narrator's wife gave birth to their first son "right there in the apartment house." Soon, the baby son changes from an "indrawn center of internal listening" to a freer human being, grasping and grabbing at objects. Then, he begins to laugh, freely and heartily, especially when he plays "games" with his parents and eight-year-old sister. What is particularly thrilling is the happy occasion when the family is together in the same room and his mother lifts him up to the mirror, in which he sees the various angles from which he can view the family. When the sister gives the child a playful scare, he bursts out in such laughter that the father is amazed, unable to believe that a child of his can laugh with such "seizure of freedom."

The daughter, too, can shriek with hilarity, particularly at the father and the baby having one of "their talks," but she can change from apparent happiness to what seems to be jealousy as she silently observes in a detached manner her little brother as though each were in an "isolated room."

The work and play of most members of the household mount. The mother moves from chore to chore every hour of the day. The daughter is transformed when she pretends to be an adult, replacing her own clothes with the clothing of her mother and father. The parents know that there will be another change: Someday they will be abandoned, just as the clothes are: "seldom picked up, left lying where they have been discarded." There is yet another change that come with these foreshadowings of adolescence: At times there is a "pained evasiveness" about the daughter that causes the narrator to think of "the boys" next door.

These three boys are reminders of "the unendingness of violence." Whether they throw eggs or tomatoes at their neighbors' windows or dirt at their daughter, or set the walls of the garage on fire, or beat up one another, one of their chief characteristics is violence. The father of the boys is "a huge, unsmiling man" with a flattop; conjecturing that the man saw action in Korea, the narrator pauses in his musings to wonder how many of the men he passes on the street have been trained to kill.

The narrator's family closes itself in and keeps to itself. They study with a pastor, attend a Reformed and Presbyterian chapel, make public confession of Christ, and have their son baptized. They pray, in general, for the other family, but they also begin to ignore it.

One night, the disturbed mother of the boys phones her neighbors and urges the narrator to check on "what those kids are up to" down in his basement. The phone call is an implicit admission that the boys are out of control; it is also, more fundamentally, a cry for help, to which the narrator does not respond. The woman's husband leaves her soon after, only to return a "few nights later"—at the request of a social worker and the police—"to settle some matters." While he is there, Betty, the distressed woman, attempts to cut her wrists.

Another change comes. The mother is in a hospital under psychiatric care; the father comes back to live with the boys. The narrator tries to visit the woman, but only family can see her. He gives the boys a copy of the Gospel of John to give her, and intends to mention "the gift of Christ and the grace of God" but is unable to follow his intentions. Finally, the boys move away, and a bulldozer levels the old house next door, bringing yet another change. A parking lot begins to take shape.

It is now cool again. The thermostat needs adjusting, but the narrator desires no change in his position in order to make the adjustment. After all, he must not move until "a certain amount of work is fixed" in his files "for good."

The doorknob still glows, mirroring the narrator. He sees as he looks up at it "a meditative kingbolt," and he asks the question: "Which side do you open a door from if the door's never really closed, but more a wall that holds you inward?" The season has changed from spring to fall, and there are no fingerprints on the glowing knob.

Themes and Meanings

"Change" is a complex, penetrating vision of the complicated modern human being who hardly knows his own identity. The modern man in "Change" can participate to some extent in the joyous discoveries of his family, especially the baby boy who soon rises "from that indrawn center of internal listening" and lives and laughs without inhibitions. The narrator walls himself in and finds difficulty in knowing who he is and what he is to do.

Amid all the changes about him, he observes others busy with their own lives, apparently having found their exact niche, but he is unable to establish his place. Others work with purpose; he always intends to do something. What to do with his work, his faith, and his relation to others are problems for the narrator—this modern man.

Modern man sees the hopeful and positive; he also sees the painful and negative, but what one is to be or to do in the midst of a confused world is almost impossible to know.

Perhaps there is also an expressed concern for the artist in this short story. What must the artist do in a world in which there is violence on all levels? How can he do his work as an artist in such circumstances? Does the artist have a responsibility to fulfill to a disturbed and violent world in ways other then through his writing?

Style and Technique

Woiwode's style captures the flow of human thought as it merges past and present, and at the same time, captures the perplexity of modern man. The involuted sentences combined with the steady unraveling of the story relentlessly pull the reader into the writer's world. The musings and realities fuse in a way that disallows any neat allegorical pattern or any easily determined point. Woiwode's style, however, is never obscure; it is clear and direct. His images express his intensely personal and ambiguous response to a world that is equally ambiguous. The style makes real the intangible inner life of a sensitive human being by capturing the nuances, intricacies, and complexities of man's inner existence.

Indeed, Larry Woiwode's style demands neither more nor less than what every excellent writer deserves: complete concentration.

E. Beatrice Batson

CHARLES

Author: Shirley Jackson (1919-1965)
Type of plot: Domestic realism
Time of plot: The mid-twentieth century
Locale: Bennington, Vermont
First published: 1948

> *Principal characters:*
> LAURIE HYMAN, a kindergarten student
> THE NARRATOR, Laurie's mother
> LAURIE'S FATHER

The Story

The narrator (based on the author, whose married name was Hyman) tells the story of Laurie's first month at kindergarten. Laurie comes home each day to report on the doings of a fellow student, Charles, who behaves in an extraordinary manner. For the first two weeks, Charles is spanked or otherwise punished almost daily for being "fresh," for hitting or kicking the teachers, for injuring fellow students, and for a host of proscribed activities. Charles proves so interesting to the kindergarten class that whenever he is punished, all the students watch him; whenever he stays after school, all the students stay with him.

As a result of this behavior, Charles becomes an institution at the Hyman house. Whenever anyone does anything bad, inconsiderate, or clumsy, he or she is compared to Charles. During the third week, however, Charles undergoes a conversion. For several days, he becomes a model student, the teacher's helper. Reports of this transformation astonish the Hyman household. Then, Charles seems to return to normal, first persuading a girl to say a terrible word twice, for which her mouth is washed out with soap. The next day, Charles himself says the word several times and receives several washings.

When the day of the monthly Parent Teacher Association meeting arrives, Laurie's mother is anxious to go and to meet the mother of the remarkable Charles. At the meeting, she learns from Laurie's teacher not only that Laurie has had some difficulty adjusting to kindergarten, but also that there is no student named Charles in her class.

Themes and Meanings

After "The Lottery," "Charles" may be Shirley Jackson's best-known short story; it is often anthologized for young readers. The story's appeal seems to derive more from the irony of its surprise ending and from its humor than from any very significant thematic content. One interesting thematic aspect of the tale, however, emerges from considering the significance of Laurie's creation and characterization of Charles.

The narrator reflects, as she sends Laurie off to his first day at kindergarten, that in his change of dress from corduroy overalls with bibs to blue jeans and a belt, he has been transformed from an innocent tot into "a swaggering character who forgot to stop at the corner and wave goodbye to me." One can see Laurie as beginning the discovery of his identity. At school, he tries various modes of self-construction and self-assertion. While his stories about Charles protect him from parental wrath, they also reveal that he naturally conceives of his self as a fictional construct over which he has considerable power. The Charles he creates is also a person who can create himself, who can be extremely "bad" one day and extremely "good" the next, as he chooses.

Part of the interest of this thematic aspect of the tale is that an interest in how the self is constructed pervades Jackson's fiction, and is often near the thematic center in her horror novels and stories.

Style and Technique

"Charles" is a short sketch, originally published in *Mademoiselle* and eventually incorporated into Shirley Jackson's fictionalized memoirs of family life in Bennington, Vermont, *Life Among the Savages* (1953).

In *Shirley Jackson* (1975), Lenemaja Friedman points out that when the real Laurie Hyman went to kindergarten, there actually was a boy there who performed several of the exploits which the fictional Laurie attributes to the fictional Charles. Altering this fact enhances the dramatic and thematic effects of "Charles." The surprise discovery that Charles is Laurie's fiction produces irony, the realization that all along the story has been meaning something other than what it has been saying. What it has been meaning becomes more interesting as well, for depths of complexity become visible in the child's character. One result is a kind of wonder at the fiction-making powers which all people possess.

Terry Heller

CHEAP IN AUGUST

Author: Graham Greene (1904-   )
Type of plot: Comedy
Time of plot: The 1960's
Locale: Kingston, Jamaica
First published: 1967

> *Principal characters:*
> MARY WATSON, the protagonist, in Jamaica on an inexpensive
> month's holiday
> HENRY HICKSLAUGHTER, in his seventies, who picks up Mary
> Watson

The Story

Mary Watson, an Englishwoman married to an American university professor who is in Europe to complete a study of the eighteenth century poet James Thomson, decides to take an inexpensive month's holiday in Jamaica during the off-season. She has written her husband that an old friend from England has insisted that she accompany her on the holiday, but she has in fact gone off alone. The off-season rates explain the story's title on its simplest level.

In the first days of her holiday, yearning for a brief affair to give her life a fillip before she enters her forties, Mary is put off by the oversized St. Louis matrons who, in hair rollers and Bermuda shorts, attempt to befriend her. As she sits and dines alone on red snapper and tomatoes, she begins to review her marriage and her life as a Connecticut faculty wife. At thirty-nine she feels ready for an affair, in part as a refuge from the staleness of her marriage to a kindly although pedantic husband who is as faithful to his scholarship as he is to her, in part as a refuge from the tedium of a university community. In the off-season, however, there are few eligible men, and Mary, alone, moves into an assessment of her sexual, social, and, although she does not know this, spiritual roles.

She knows that she is by no means unhappy with either her marriage or her position—the marriage has, the reader infers, produced no children—yet she yearns for an experience that will provide her life with a restorative perspective. She hopes, too, that her husband will have such an experience, but she is fairly certain from the tenor of his daily letters to her that no such adventure is possible for him.

One morning, while sunning by the hotel pool, she observes a bald, fat man in his seventies who introduces himself to her as Henry Hickslaughter. She is amused by his "pick-up," then intrigued by his disappointed look; she glimpses a tousled child within his gross form. She is pleased when he tells her that he has been observing her for several days, and she learns that their rooms are only a few doors apart. They share a table at dinner, and Hickslaughter invites Mary to have drinks with him in his room. She begins to understand that he too is taking advantage of the off-season rates, and is further intrigued by his old-pirate demeanor.

Ostensibly looking for a maid to give her a carafe of ice water, Mary goes into Hickslaughter's room, where she has very recently seen the maid. She reads a vaguely threatening letter that Hickslaughter has written to his brother asking for money. Hickslaughter finds her in his room, asks her to have drinks with him that evening, and she agrees. She returns later to find that he has been crying. Years ago she had seen her husband cry when his volume of essays had been refused by a university press. "I'm afraid of dying, with nobody around, in the dark," Hickslaughter says to her. Moved by his fear, his loneliness, his attempt to stave off the unknown, his failure at life, Mary spends the night with the frightened old man whom she almost loves. Later, when she remembers the affair, she wonders what they had in common, except for the fact that they shared a cheap Jamaican holiday.

Themes and Meanings

Very little happens by way of action in "Cheap in August": A woman has a brief affair with a fat, old, and lonely man. Yet the texture of a human life is revealed in all of its complexities, of fear and loneliness, of courage and compassion, of truth and beauty. It is the subtext of the tale that reveals its essential truth—that connection with others is what gives life whatever meaning it possesses.

In his introduction to his *Collected Stories* (1972), Graham Greene explains that the notion for the story came to him in Kingston, Jamaica, in August of 1963. He included it in his collection entitled *May We Borrow Your Husband? and Other Comedies of the Sexual Life* (1967): "I sat over my red snapper and tomotoes watching the monstrous Bermuda shorts worn by fat parties from St. Louis, and wondered, as my character did, what possible pick-up [*sic*] were possible in this out-of-season hotel." Mary Watson's emotion of tenderness for the gross old man who picks her up fulfills her need for human connection, as she does his. Felt emotion is infinitely more conducive to meaning than action described or spoken dialogue. Perhaps the ultimate meaning of the story can be discovered in the word "cheap," which etymologically once meant "trade" or "bargain." Mary Watson and Henry Hickslaughter do strike a bargain, one that confirms their humanity as it staves off, for a brief moment, the certainty of death. The pun on the name Hickslaughter becomes equally significant.

Style and Technique

If sadness is the overarching tone of "Cheap in August," then the farcical coming together of two seemingly mismatched people undercuts the sadness to give the tale its bittersweet quality. What the story does best, by means of subtle authorial suggestions, is to reveal the reality of pain behind a comic façade. That Greene has included the story in his collection of comedies dealing with sexual experience indicates that the grotesqueness of an old man still yearning for sex and the romantic sentimentalism of a woman seeking confirmation of her attractiveness are to be seen as one more turn in the comic *ronde* that life presents to the careful onlooker. The presence of the narrator is felt strongly in the story's subtext as he directs his reader to an awareness of how simple emotion can overwhelm one and dignify life. The story achieves, as a result, a tragicomic resonance that links it to the stories and dramas of Anton Chekhov. What the reader feels as he reads through the events of the narrative is what William Wordsworth called "the still, sad music of humanity."

Mary and Hickslaughter's affair is ultimately life-enhancing as it comments on the temporality of life through the spiritual quality of a compassionate experience; it provides the reader with an insight into what it means to verify one's humanity through the sexual act.

A. A. DeVitis

THE CHEMIST'S WIFE

Author: Anton Chekhov (1860-1904)
Type of plot: Realism
Time of plot: Nineteenth century
Locale: A small town in Russia
First published: "Aptekarsha," 1886 (English translation, 1916)

> *Principal characters:*
> TCHERNOMORDIK, a chemist in the town·of B——
> MME TCHERNOMORDIK, the chemist's wife
> OBTYOSOV, a thin officer
> THE DOCTOR, another officer, "the big one"

The Story

"The Chemist's Wife" is told in the third person through the consciousness of the title character. The main action of the story occurs within the mind and the emotions of the chemist's wife, who progresses from sleeplessness and boredom to the realization that she is truly unhappy. As in so many Chekhov stories, there is very little external action; the action which is attempted is thwarted.

The story begins late at night, near dawn, in a little Russian town. The chemist is snoring contentedly, in a sleep so deep that nothing could awaken him, certainly not the restlessness of his young wife. Mme Tchernomordik cannot sleep; she does not know why. She feels close to tears; she does not know why.

Just at daybreak two officers appear, talking casually as they pass the chemist's shop. Mme Tchernomordik hears them speculating as to whether she loves her husband and imagining how she looks in bed. On impulse, Obtyosov suggests that they ring the chemist's bell and make a purchase; perhaps, he says, they will see the wife.

Now the mood of the chemist's wife changes. She puts on a dress and hurries to admit the officers, who buy some lozenges. During brief conversation, Mme Tchernomordik keeps her eyes on the slender, rosy Obtyosov. Attempting to prolong the slight adventure, the doctor orders soda, and Obtyosov thinks of seltzer-water. When the doctor asks for red wine to go into the seltzer-water, the men have an excuse to sit down at the counter, and the little flirtation progresses. Soon the chemist's wife is quite happy, and she even drinks some of the wine. At last the doctor suggests that the men return to camp. As Obtyosov pays the reckoning, he once again mentions the fact that the chemist is asleep.

When the officers leave, Mme Tchernomordik watches them walk a little distance, then stop and whisper. Obtyosov returns and rings the bell. This time, however, the chemist answers the door and sells the lozenges. Again, the chemist's wife watches; Obtyosov throws away the package of lozenges, the doctor joins him, and the two men then walk away. Angrily, Mme Tchernomordik tells her husband that she is unhappy and bursts into tears. He merely asks her to put away fourpence that he left on the counter and falls asleep again.

Themes and Meanings

Like many of Chekhov's stories, "The Chemist's Wife" deals with loneliness. Even the title is appropriate; Mme Tchernomordik has no name, either to her husband or to the officers who flirt with her. She is simply an appendage of the chemist. When Obtyosov returns to the shop, perhaps on a dare, he hopes to steal a few words, a kiss, perhaps something more, if the husband remains asleep. Yet to him it is only a casual adventure, the stuff of military boasts. Seeing the older, ugly man to whom the pretty, young woman is married, he and the doctor have sensed an opportunity. Their approach to her, however, is purely a matter of whim and chance. They happen to be passing the shop after a party; they think of her. Her husband is asleep, and she answers the door. While they are with her, the conversation rambles, leading to no certain conclusion. Only Obtyosov's repeated comment that the chemist is asleep suggests the possibility of seduction. Yet even his return is marked by irresolution; he and the doctor whisper at length before Obtyosov turns back toward the chemist's shop; on reaching the shop, the officer hesitates, passing back and forth in front of the door before finally ringing the bell. When by chance the chemist wakens and answers the summons, Obtyosov is easily defeated. When he throws away the lozenges he has been forced to purchase, he is throwing away the whim, the passing fancy for the chemist's wife. It really does not matter much to Obtyosov, nor, indeed, would have a brief relationship with her; that would have been quite as easy to discard.

To Tchernomordik, also, the young woman is unimportant. Early in the story, when she looks at him asleep, she thinks that nothing could waken him, not even an embrace. Suggestive though the officers' hints may be, the dreams of the chemist are only of business. Although Tchernomordik's dreams should not convict him of indifference toward his wife, his conduct when she announces her unhappiness and bursts into tears must do so, for he simply ignores her, worrying only about a few pennies which have been left on the counter. At the end of the story, his sleep is symbolic, for he is oblivious of the needs of his wife. When he goes to sleep, he discards her as clearly as Obtyosov did when he threw away the lozenges.

If both Obtyosov and Tchernomordik find it easy to turn away from the chemist's wife, however, she cannot discard the possibilities of a fuller life so easily. There is a depth to her emotions which neither man possesses. Her very unhappiness suggests her sensitivity, for she does not know what she lacks. Nor does she know what she wants, unlike Obtyosov, who wants a trivial adventure, and unlike Tchernomordik, who wants to make money and to sleep. While the officers stumble along unseeing in the dawn, the chemist's wife is responding to the flaming sun and to the red moon, which symbolize passion and adventure to her. Later, while the officers are flirting uncertainly, her emotions are violent. When she watches them whispering before Obtyosov returns, it is as if her fate is being decided, she thinks, again feeling intensely. At the end of the story, when nothing has happened, her tears are not casual, but well up from a real agony in her heart.

The tragedy of the chemist's wife is not only that she is viewed merely as an object of desire or of convenience, as someone to flirt with or to put money in the till, but also that the men whose attention she seeks could never give her what she deserves. Thus her own sensitivity and her capacity for a passionate response to life have doomed her to loneliness.

Style and Technique

In Chekhov's play *Tri Sestry* (1901; *The Three Sisters*, 1920), the title characters dream of going to Moscow. At the end of the play, no one has gone to Moscow, and it is clear that no one ever will. Typically, in Chekhov's works, human beings dream, but the dreams are negated by life. In depicting life as a situation in which very little happens, Chekhov considered himself a realistic writer, in contrast to the melodramatic style of much nineteenth century literature. Yet if, as in "The Chemist's Wife," very little external action occurs, in Chekhov's stories and plays there is much internal action. In revealing the emotional reactions of his characters to the slight external events, Chekhov deliberately avoided seeming to be involved, believing that his own detachment would actually produce more sympathy for characters such as the unhappy chemist's wife than would the typical nineteenth century authorial commentary.

Chekhov also differed from other realists, choosing merely to suggest setting rather than describing it in full detail. Thus, at the beginning of "The Chemist's Wife," four short sentences establish the stillness of the night, and the detail which makes it sharpest for readers is probably the brief mention of a dog's bark in the distance. The unlovely chemist is described snoring, with a flea on his nose; the officers are introduced with the sound of spurs. All the details are realistic, but they are sparse.

Finally, Chekhov typically used a small detail or a minor action at the end of a story to suggest a revelation which had come to a character or to forecast future action. At the end of "The Chemist's Wife," Mme Tchernomordik realizes not only that she is truly unhappy but also that no one is aware of the fact. As if to prove her point, the chemist asks her to see to his money and promptly falls asleep. There Chekhov stops the story. The chemist's wife has come to understand her own misery; the chemist is indifferent. It is suggested that Mme Tchernomordik's future will be no different from the moments which Chekhov has just described. Typically, she will not get to a metaphoric Moscow.

Rosemary M. Canfield-Reisman

CHICKAMAUGA

Author: Ambrose Bierce (1842-1914?)
Type of plot: Psychological realism
Time of plot: American Civil War
Locale: The Battle of Chickamauga
First published: 1891

> *Principal characters:*
> AN UNNAMED BOY, who is six years old
> CONFEDERATE SOLDIERS, who have suffered a defeat

The Story

There is actually only one character in this story—the six-year-old boy who wanders away from his home and gets lost in the forest—and even he is not individualized but rather is presented simply as "the child." When he encounters defeated soldiers in retreat from the Civil War battle of Chickamauga, his response to them is one only of childish curiosity. Although the soldiers are grotesquely wounded, maimed, and bleeding, the boy sees them as circus animals and clowns, and instead of being horrified, as the reader is, he is delighted at having someone with whom to play. He uses his toy sword to lead the men back whence he has come, leaving many of them dying in a river as he makes his way home. When he reaches his home, he discovers that it is burning and his mother is dead, her brains blown out by an artillery shell. The story ends with the boy making inarticulate cries—"a startling, soulless, unholy sound, the language of a devil." The reader's final shocking realization is that the child is a deaf-mute.

This climactic discovery "explains" the most striking aspect of the story—the disengaged and almost autistic response that the boy makes to the horrors of war. It is the gap between the boy's indifferent response and the reader's shock that gives the story the powerful impact that it has. Ambrose Bierce's most basic purpose here is to create an antiwar story; he does this by setting up a tension between an innocent, childish response to reality and an ironic adult one. The story begins with the narrator explaining that the boy is the son of a planter who had once been a soldier. As a result of the father's teaching the boy about war through books and pictures, the "warrior-fire" survives in the boy. In his play, he sees himself as the son of a heroic race, and he chases imaginary foes, putting all to death with his toy sword.

Thus, when the boy encounters the retreating soldiers, they become part of his play, creeping like babes instead of men through the forest. He has seen his father's slaves crawl on their hands and knees, playing horses with him; thus he crawls on the back of one of the dying men to ride him similarly. He laughs as he watches what to him is a merry spectacle and is as unaware as the men are of "the dramatic contrast between his laughter and their own ghastly gravity." Even when he returns to his burning home, he still reacts to the devastation as if it were merely spectacle, and he dances with glee around the fire, collecting more fuel to throw on the blaze. Only when he recognizes some of the buildings with "oddly familiar appearances, as if he had dreamed of them," does the plantation seem to swing around as if on a pivot, and he then realizes that it is his own home.

The fact that the boy is a deaf-mute emphasizes his childish fantasy world, detached from external reality, and makes more plausible the primary device of contrasting the child's view of war as a game with the adult's view of it as a horrifying actuality. It enables the author to set up a strange, dreamlike effect as the reader sees the events primarily from the boy's point of view. Even at the end of the story, the boy's inarticulate cries suggest a horrifying realization that goes beyond the ability of any language to express fully.

Themes and Meanings

The antiwar theme of Bierce's story depends on the basic tensions between the child world and the adult world and between fantasy and reality. The boy's fantasy world of playing at war is his only reality; consequently, when he encounters the genuine, external reality of war it seems curiously fantastic to him; thus he is able to integrate it effortlessly into his fantasy play world. Bierce develops the story on the ironic realization that the adult view of war often springs from childlike views in which men glorify battle in a heroic and fantasy image, only to find out too late that the reality of war is horror and death. This is a common antiwar convention, used in other Civil War stories, often in terms of the Southern gallantry of noble knights who then confront the gritty and horrifying reality of battle. It was also a common device in World War I stories, in which young American men go off to fight the honorable battle and save the Old World only to confront the horrors of the muddy trenches of Europe. The primary communicators of this fantasy image of war in Bierce's story are books and pictures that glorify war, for the boy has been taught "postures of aggression and defense" by the "engraver's art." Thus when he encounters the actuality of war, the boy responds to it as he has to the fantasy pictures that he has seen and the world of play-reality that he has known.

Style and Technique

As is typical of many Bierce stories, style and technique are practically everything in "Chickamauga." Although he wrote during a period of American literature characterized by realistic depictions of external reality, Bierce maintained his allegiance to Romanticism. Often compared with the originator of the American short story, Edgar Allan Poe, Bierce focuses not so much on external reality as he does on the strange, dreamlike world that lies somewhere between fantasy and reality. Thus, the genius of his stories lies not in their theme, which is often fairly obvious, but in the delicate and tightly controlled way that Bierce tells the story, creating a playfully nightmarish world that involves the reader emotionally.

Perhaps the most interesting aspect of "Chickamauga"—the technique which creates its unforgettable effect—is Bierce's handling of point of view and tone. On the one hand, the story depends on Bierce's developing the perspective of the child, in which the reader is made to see the maimed and bleeding soldiers as circus clowns and childlike playmates for the boy. Yet this point of view is balanced by that of an adult narrator, who counterpoints the boy's childish view, sometimes in a developed background exposition, sometimes in a flat declarative statement. For example, when the boy seems to see some strange animals that he does not recognize crawling through the forest, the narrator simply says, "They were men." When the boy sees men lying in the water as if without heads, the narrator simply says, "They were drowned."

This narrator is not named in the story but is presented as a disembodied presence who not only sees what the boy sees but also sees the boy and draws conclusions about the boy's responses. The boy's mind is as inaccessible to the narrator as it is to the reader. This technique enables the reader to respond dually, both to the boy's point of view and to the adult narrator. As the narrator says about the scene witnessed by the boy, "not all of this did the child note; it is what would have been noted by an elder observer." Indeed, it is the elder observer who establishes the ironic tone at the beginning of the story which mocks the "warrior-fire," the heroic race, and the notion of a spirit of battle in the boy which make him born to "war and dominion as a heritage."

It is indeed the subtle tension between this adult point of view and the childish perception of the boy that creates the story's impact and reflects its theme. At one point in the story, when the boy goes to sleep and (because of his deafness) sleeps through the battle that rages nearby, the adult narrator says that he was as "heedless of the grandeur of the struggle as the dead who had died to make the glory." Because of this structural counterpoint, the narrator has no need to make any more explicit comment on the action. The juxtaposition of the two perspectives creates a tragic irony of war as something more than a heroic and childish game, even as it makes the reader see how war, in order to persist, depends on precisely such a childish point of view. The boy is innocent in his playful point of view, but at the same time the playful point of view is what is responsible for the death of the men who surround the child.

Like many of Bierce's other stories, "Chickamauga" is to shock, to catch the reader up in a nightmarish reality. Also like many of his other stories, it is an artistic tour de force of romantic short fictional style. Bierce holds the reader suspended between reality and fantasy until the final grotesque realization, which retrospectively illumines the story's restrained, ironic control.

Charles E. May

THE CHILDHOOD OF LUVERS

Author: Boris Pasternak (1890-1960)
Type of plot: Poetic realism
Time of plot: Early twentieth century
Locale: Perm and Ekaterinburg (modern Sverdlovsk), Russia
First published: "Detstvo Lyuvers," 1922 (English translation, 1945)

> *Principal characters:*
> ZHENIA LUVERS, a young girl
> MR. LUVERS, her father
> MRS. LUVERS, Zhenia's mother
> LIZA DEFENDOVA, Zhenia's friend, a neighbor girl
> DIKIKH, one of Zhenia's tutors
> TSVETKOV, a friend of Dikikh
> SERËZHA, Zhenia's brother

The Story

Zhenia Luvers' first memories are of Perm, a gloomy northern city not far removed from a state of nature: Bearskin rugs are made from local animals; during the spring, weeds sprout and trees bud overnight; ice floes pass by on the river. Mr. Luvers manages a mine and spends little time with his children. Occasionally he is seen playing cards or discussing his dealings with factory owners. A series of governesses tend to Zhenia: She is educated first by an Englishwoman she scarcely remembers, and then by a French tutor who burdens her with the conjugation of difficult verbs. When Zhenia is thirteen, she feels strangely ill and inadvertently leaves bloodstains on a bearskin rug and on her clothes. She takes the maid's powder and attempts to efface the red marks, and a family confrontation takes place. Mrs. Luvers upbraids Zhenia at first, and in the end dismisses the Frenchwoman. Subsequently, and quite more insistently than for previous visits, her mother arranges for a doctor to examine Zhenia. Some time later, and quite to her surprise, Zhenia learns that the family will move southeast to a city beyond the Urals.

At first, Zhenia is enchanted with her new surroundings, which she persistently regards as "Asian." Ekaterinburg is clear, clean, and spacious. The exotic and the commonplace mingle easily. Zhenia is entranced by Tatar children from the region; she makes friends with a local girl, Liza Defendova. When she is transferred from the city's lycée and is given private lessons at home, Zhenia is more upset than her friend that they will no longer meet in school. Zhenia's lessons do not always come easily—good-naturedly, she spells some words according to her own lights, and she confuses some terms for units of weight and measure. Her tutor, who has the improbable surname Dikikh, amuses her, and she is intrigued by his friend Tsvetkov, who walks with a limp. She competes half-seriously with her brother, Serëzha, but fears the he may be steadily surpassing her in strength and endurance.

That autumn and winter are fixed in her mind more specifically and clearly than past changes of season; the days seem colder and darker than during previous years. Zhenia is aware that her mother does not leave the house, and rumors are afloat that she is pregnant. One night, as she lies in bed, Zhenia hears a scream and then another, rending, howling cries, and then she nearly runs into her father in the hallway. Hasty, disjointed questions and commands are exchanged among members of the family. Zhenia's intuition seems confirmed: Her mother has given birth again. Then she falls asleep and has some trouble convincing herself that she has not dreamed it all. The next day she is sent to stay with the Defendovs; on her way out Zhenia notices that, amid jumbled pots, pans, medical supplies, and towels, her mother lies in bed and is still moaning. While at the neighbors, Zhenia asks Liza Defendova whether she can have babies, and she is reassured when Liza tells her that all girls can.

After several weeks Zhenia returns home and resumes her lessons; she learns what has actually happened from the doctor and her tutor. One night, her mother and father were returning from the theater when their stallion inexplicably reared up and trampled a bypasser to death. The mother suffered what—in the doctor's euphemistic expression—was a "nervous upset." Zhenia infers that her little baby brother was born dead; the doctor can only confirm her worst fears. Dikikh, the tutor, finds Zhenia strangely changed; he declares that he too has lost a friend. Intuitively Zhenia associates Tsvetkov, or someone like him, with the accident outside the theater; she screams as Dikikh sets forth his recollections of that tragic evening. Later the tutor, who seemingly has accepted his friend's death, is taken aback at Zhenia's "excessive sensitivity." She seems under the power of impressions that cannot be described precisely in words. Zhenia's schoolbook must be put back on the shelf to await another day.

Themes and Meanings

The events of young Zhenia's life, both insubstantial and momentous, point to her development from a young girl to an adult woman. Largely this process takes her unawares: Continuous throbbing headaches and inexplicable effusions of blood beset her at the onset of sexual maturity. Transformation is also suggested, in quite another sense, by transportation beyond the Urals. Zhenia feels that she has reached a continental divide where much is similar, but the atmosphere seems changed somehow. The beginning of autumn seems more distinct than at other times she can recall. At one point she begins to use perfume; she becomes aware of physical differences between herself and boys her age.

Many transitions she grasps half-consciously and in passing: Her awareness of life's deeper concerns mingles with poignant everyday impressions that are still deeply felt. Her father is a remote figure and offers little in the way of guidance or understanding. Some basic issues she realizes only imperfectly and intuitively. Her mother's pregnancy, and the expectations and agonies of childbirth, are brought home to her only at a distance; only then does she understand that she, and other girls she knows, eventually will have babies of their own. During her discussions with Liza Defendova, she finds the other girl's knowledge remarkable and is shocked at the easy vulgarity with which Liza discusses procreation. The tragic end of life is revealed to Zhenia in broken, circuitous statements from the family doctor and her teacher: They cannot hold back news of the family's loss, or of the death of Dikikh's friend. Zhenia is at an awkward age: She can comprehend the beginning and end of life, but she cannot still her screams and uncontrollable outbursts of tears. She seems peculiarly sensitive to sorrow and suffering. The drama of her approaching adulthood seems darker and more profound because her character is still forming; she remains childlike in some respects even as in other ways physical and emotional maturity overtakes her.

Style and Technique

Young Zhenia's life and thoughts are presented in a rich, poetic language that, even for the most valiant and gifted translator, eludes precise rendition. The work originally was intended to be the opening portion of a novel, and it is often presented on its own as a story. The plot is uncomplicated and sometimes appears fragmented. The author tarries at some passages, whereas elsewhere time goes by unnoticed. The story is told in the third person, but draws the reader directly into the world of feeling and experience that envelops young Zhenia. There are a few interventions in the narrative on the part of the author, mostly to trace the family's movements or to supply essential facts about their work or education.

Much of the work records Zhenia's own sensations and impressions of the world around her, some of which are imprinted most vividly upon her memory. She recalls in detail lush, thick bearskin carpets of different colors. Mundane but discrete and clearly defined objects—budding trees, or ice floes on the river—are closely described, and seem set in counterpoint to the more enduring transformations engulfing her. Climatic conditions, which foreshadow stages of Zhenia's own development, are recorded with a fine sense of feeling and atmosphere. Sometimes her French lessons, the chills of early spring, and throbbing headaches are inchoately intertwined. Perceptions which often seem scattered and kaleidoscopic during the first part of the story, which presents the girl's earliest memories, become more specific and lucid as Zhenia gains in maturity. Whole, connected conversations and episodes are set down, and Zhenia's view of the world takes on a somewhat sharper, clearer focus. Dikikh, the tutor, for example, is described more specifically and at greater length than any comparable characters from the first section of the work. All the while Zhenia still seems under the spell of powerful emotional forces; she perceives people and events at times as wordless impressions, producing sudden uncontrollable impulses that accompany her own unsteady but oncoming passage into adulthoood.

J. R. Broadus

CHILDREN ON THEIR BIRTHDAYS

Author: Truman Capote (1924-1984)
Type of plot: Fantasy
Time of plot: The 1940's
Locale: Alabama
First published: 1948

Principal characters:
MISS LILY JANE BOBBIT, a precocious, ambitious, ten-year-old girl
BILLY BOB, the boy next door
PREACHER STAR, his friend
ROSALBA CAT, a black girl befriended by Miss Bobbit

The Story

Late one summer afternoon, an unusual-looking young girl, Miss Lily Jane Bobbit, arrives with her mother in a small, unidentified town in Alabama. The bus on which they arrive, the narrator of the story states in the opening lines, is the same one that will run over Miss Bobbit a year later as she prepares to move on, in pursuit of her dream of Hollywood stardom. Why she has chosen to settle briefly in this Southern town is never revealed, and very little information about her earlier experiences is given. As for her family, her father is in a penitentiary in Tennessee; her mother is a strangely silent woman. Miss Bobbit herself, from first to last, remains an enigma, a funny, delightful, not real child-woman.

The particular day of her arrival in front of the house of a boy named Billy Bob is important: Billy Bob, his friends, his mother, and his cousin, Mr. C., the narrator of the story, are celebrating Billy Bob's birthday. Offered some of the party fare, Miss Bobbit refuses it in an adult fashion. Simultaneously little girl and adult, she is obviously different from any ordinary child. In many ways her conversation and behavior seem grown-up. Her face is made-up as if she were a mature woman, although she is wearing a child's party dress. Both her dress and the occasion of Billy Bob's party symbolize Miss Bobbit's dream of what life should be: a world of beauty and happiness that is like a birthday party, particularly like children on their birthdays. Driven by her longings, she cannot take the time to be a child. She focuses all of her energy on the preparation for a dazzling existence in a place that she believes will turn her vision into reality.

During the year that she lives in a boardinghouse next door to Billy Bob and his family, Miss Bobbit becomes something of a celebrity because of her appearance, her mannerisms, and her behavior. Girls constantly walk past her house to catch glimpses of the elegant rival who keeps the boys fighting over her. Billy Bob and Preacher Star, competitors for her unavailable affection, wear themselves out trying to serve her. Rosalba Cat, the black girl whom she makes her "sister," brings further attention to her.

No matter what people think, Miss Bobbit always does as she chooses. She chooses not to go to church or school, in spite of community pressure. Neither is for her, she maintains, since her primary interest is the advancement of her career. In pursuit of her dreams of fame, she single-mindedly devotes herself to training for films. She practices her dancing, reads a dictionary, and dresses in one elegant outfit after another, made for her by her unobtrusive mother. To raise money for her travels, Miss Bobbit goes into business as an agent for magazines, putting Billy Bob and Preacher to work for her.

Miss Bobbit seems to be on her way to Hollywood, if not to the stardom that she assures her friends she will have, after she wins an amateur contest sponsored by a con man. Undaunted by the disappearance of the man who awarded her first prize—a screen test—and who also enticed a considerable number of young men to pay large sums of money in return for the promise of romantic-sounding jobs, Miss Bobbit shows her strength and ingenuity: She succeeds in tracking him down and getting the money restored. Her powers of persuasion prove to be as strong as her will when she convinces those same young men to invest their money in her future by sending her off to Hollywood.

Yet Miss Bobbitt is not destined to fulfill her heart's desire. As she rushes across the street to claim the roses that her two ardent admirers have picked for her, she is killed by the bus that delivered her to the town the summer before, when those same rose bushes were in bloom.

Themes and Meanings

Although the setting of the story is realistic, little else is. Miss Bobbit is a fantasy creature, unlike any ten-year-old girl who has ever existed. In her, Capote created a type of child who reflected much of what he believed that children longed to be: beautiful, clever, and loved. Both in statements about his own childhood and in his fiction he brooded over the sadness and disappointments that children suffer. Happiness is evanescent: Most of the children of his stories begin their years in innocence and pleasure. Then the blow falls, usually with the loss of a much-loved person. Yet his portrait of Miss Lily Jane Bobbit differs from the others in a very significant way: Like them, she lives with illusions and impossible dreams, but, unlike the others, she dies before her hopes are vanquished.

Miss Bobbit is the forerunner of the more famous Holly Golightly of Capote's *Breakfast at Tiffany's* (1958). Miss Bobbit and Holly are restless females, with longings that will never be fulfilled. Each speaks of living in the sky, a metaphor that suggests both freedom and happiness, but which also connotes separation from other people. Though the later story contains many of the same themes as the earlier one, it is ultimately more melancholy, for in it the heroine's dreams are blighted.

Capote portrayed a series of orphan characters, of whom Miss Bobbit is one, even though both of her parents are alive. She never hears from her imprisoned father, and her mother seems to play so small a role in her life that Miss Bobbit gives the impression of being completely responsible for herself. Furthermore, whatever attachments she forms are temporary, because she always plans and longs to move on. Thus, she is seen as a lone—though not lonely—and isolated figure, in spite of her popularity.

Capote often drew these "parentless" children as wanderers, seekers for a world unlike the one that they have known. Miss Bobbit has no home, no place (ironically, in a region that prides itself on place). Without roots, she imagines that she will gain both a home and glory once she crosses Hollywood's golden threshold.

Capote himself, as a boy, dreamed of becoming a famous tap dancer, a dream never realized, yet never forgotten. In this and other stories he reminds his readers, through his fantasy children, of the longings that all children have to be or do something extraordinary. The recognition that such yearnings cannot be fulfilled is a significant part of the impact of this story on readers, a reminder that all memories of childhood are a mixture of happiness and sadness. Miss Lily Jane Bobbit dies without achieving her desires, but she also dies before the disappointments and disillusionments of adulthood can touch her.

Style and Technique

Here, as in a number of other stories, Capote has blended humor and nostalgia. Much that is humorous in his fiction comes through his variation of the "tall tale," that is, the exaggeration of details in both plot and character. With only a few exceptions, the characters in the story have humorous qualities. One comic episode follows another: Miss Bobbit's quaint mixture of French and English; her platonic massage of Billy Bob; the war that she and Rosalba conduct against the dogs of the town. The behavior of the boys is equally funny as they attempt to gain the love of the wondrous Miss Lily Jane Bobbit.

The comedy, though an integral part of the story, is finally less important than the sweet-sadness, the nostalgic element in the telling of the tale. Through the use of memory, the narrator captures, as if in a bottle or a glass, the perfect moment, the brief, lost world of childhood. Yet, at the same time that the past is caught forever, there is the counterpoint of the transient images, which add both joyfulness and melancholy to the story.

Typical of Capote's imagistic style, light and color flicker everywhere. At nightfall, birds swoop, fireflies dart among the leaves, and the swift movements and brief moments of light in darkness becoming symbolic of Miss Bobbit herself. The irises bloom only briefly. The scent of roses, sweet shrub, and wisteria perfumes the air. For a time it is as though summer will never end. Furthermore, the story is a summer story; in spite of the fact that a year passes, other seasons seem unimportant.

Miss Bobbit arrives in summer and dies at the same time the following year. Winter, symbolic of time and age, never touches her. Dressed in white as she runs toward her death, she has a Communion look, an image that captures purity and innocence in endless time. A fine mist of rain is falling as she moves joyfully toward twin bouquets of yellow roses, the rain the final emblem of nostalgia and irredeemable time.

Helen S. Garson

THE CHILDREN'S CAMPAIGN

Author: Pär Lagerkvist (1891-1974)
Type of plot: Political-social satire
Time of plot: 1978
Locale: An anonymous country
First published: "Det lilla fälttåget," 1935 (English translation, 1954)

> *Principal characters:*
> THE CHILDREN, who compose an army in a militaristic nation
> THE ADULTS, who compose the army and the civilian
> population of a neighboring country

The Story

At the beginning of "The Children's Campaign," the reader is introduced to a nationalistic and militant society, in which children play an integral role in the country's defense. The children between the ages of six and fourteen constitute a highly respected and beloved children's army, which they command, train, and organize without adult intervention. The boys serve in the army corps, and the girls are allowed to volunteer as nurses.

An apparently inferior country insults, in some manner, this more powerful, unified nation, and the children's army receives permission to retaliate by launching an attack, which begins in the spring of that year.

As war is declared, the army of youths demonstrates its efficiency: Within a day, it is mobilized and ready to defend its country's honor. After a patriotic speech by the twelve-year-old commander in chief, the troops leave for the offending country, where their campaign begins victoriously.

By the summer, the children have nearly reached the enemy's capital, having won many battles and sustained comparatively few losses. Their heroism and discipline and their dedication to their mission are admired at home, where the media devotes specified times of day for reports on the progress of the popular war.

The bravery of the children is chronicled in detail: They defy death and bodily injury, and not a complaint is recorded. Moreover, the children's army is superior to the army of the enemy—a nonmilitaristic nation—in armed combat, military tactics, and troop discipline; only the physical size of the children prevents success in hand-to-hand combat and in the effective pursuit of defeated enemy forces.

As the strengths and weaknesses of the two armies are compared, it is clear that the children have important advantages: more soldiers, better organization and command, and superior skills and training. The enemy army's advantage is mainly the larger size of its soldiers, although the army's military skills do improve somewhat as the war continues.

Just before autumn, a simultaneous offensive strike results in a tragic battle in which the troops on both sides are annihilated. This battle indicates a stalemate, since after it, neither army can truthfully declare victory, although both do. Both armies are forced to regroup and continue maneuvers from trenches, while the winter rains prevent further progress.

During this time, the morale of the children's army is decidedly higher than that of the enemy. The children endure great hardships, but not a complaint is uttered. Even during Christmas, the children remain dedicated to their cause, launching several attacks.

The stalemate continues until spring, when offensives are begun in preparation for the decisive battle. At one historic point in the war, the enemy discovers a weakness in the children's formation, enabling them to force a retreat of the children's army. The children, however, are able to turn this event to full advantage by encircling the advancing enemy and pressing for victory from all sides.

As the children gain the enemy's capital, the war is declared over, the children return home to a victory parade, and the troops are dismissed. A full account of the war is entered in the nation's annals, and the date of victory is to be commemorated forever after.

Themes and Meanings

Themes of political and social nature intertwine in "The Children's Campaign" to issue a warning concerning the direction of human nature and society. Published before World War II, the story depicts a world obsessed by war, a world in which even war's tragedies are glorified.

In this setting, war is second nature, even to children. The prevailing image of childhood—innocent and free of the responsibilities of adult life— is quickly shattered as the fantasies of war games are replaced by the realities of military exercises. Indeed, these children need no adult supervision; they are proficient, exacting, and successful. Not only do they excel at military maneuvers, but also they are well adapted to the physical hardships of army life. Although forced to live in mud-filled trenches during the winter months, they nevertheless "felt at home":

> Filthy and lousy, they lived there in the darkness as though they had never done anything else. With the adaptability of children they quickly got into the way of it.... When one saw them in their small gray uniforms, which were caked thick with mud, and their small gas masks, one could easily think they had been born to this existence.

In this subtle way, the author recalls images of boys at play in mud, sleet, or snow—in short, any activity in which the dirt becomes part of their youthful attire.

The war succeeds in seizing childhood away from the army of youths;

"The war had hardened and developed them, made them men." Yet the reader is often reminded that, despite their endeavors, these are still children; there are frequent references to their small size, an account of their love of chocolate, and a reference to an unhappy soldier, homesick at Christmastime, who is eventually court-martialed and shot.

The complex role of war in society is examined as the account of the campaign unfolds. War is viewed as the natural outlet for human cruelty, in which rules and regulations provide the acceptable manner for displaying aggressive tendencies. The enemy, a nonmilitaristic nation, is often denounced for its ignorance of the proprieties of war, an ignorance which leads its civilians to resort to acts of atrocity against the children. It must be remembered that the offense committed by the enemy is never revealed; its nature is ambiguous. One is told merely that the country has "behaved in a high-handed and unseemly way toward its powerful neighbor." Clearly, this is not an act of military provocation or overt aggression, yet the offended country is quick to rally its forces and launch a full-scale war.

In its final, senseless devotion to war's uncivilized accomplishments, the society in "The Children's Campaign" proves hungry enough for the spoils of war to sacrifice its most precious commodity: its children. Ultimately, one must question the high price of nationalism and the devotion to its ideals.

Style and Technique

The sociopolitical messages of "The Children's Campaign" are expressed in a deliberately understated style. Through straight narrative that chronicles both the military and the personal aspects of the campaign, the author satirizes war.

From the opening line ("Even the children at that time received military training..."), the reader is thrust immediately and forcefully into a hostile environment. There is no gradual introduction to the times or reasons offered for its nature; rather, the lack of alternatives is as arbitrary, as inevitable, as war itself.

War is, as are many highly serious topics, a subject that lends itself effectively to humor. In fact, the more intense, the more horrific, the effects of war are, the more absurd they appear. The story's imagery lends itself to this idea. The literary implications of spring—those of renewal, rebirth, the celebration of life—are recalled in a paradoxical manner: It is spring when the children's army first sets out to wield its destructive hand and, later, when the greatest loss of life is incurred.

Another image—that of the youths' size—becomes especially striking during battle descriptions, where the children are "so small ... it was possible ... to spit several of them on the bayonet at once...." At other times, they are swarms of "little fiends," scurrying "over one and in between one's legs."

The story's most satiric description, indeed, accentuates childhood's ultimate representation: A female enemy civilian turns a child-lieutenant over
her knee and gives him a spanking, declaring that he should be at home with
his mother. The boy is consequently sent home to his family and forced to
move with them to an obscure area of the country.

While the language of "The Children's Campaign" is objective, the story
nevertheless succeeds in re-creating individual beliefs and moral convictions
concerning the polarities of human nature. The reader ends the narrative
sadly recognizing the outlines of the familiar world in the grotesque world of
this fable.

Shelly Usen

A CHILD'S DRAWINGS

Author: Varlam Shalamov (1907-1982)
Type of plot: Social realism
Time of plot: Between the mid-1930's and the mid-1950's
Locale: A forced-labor camp in the Kolyma region of northeastern Siberia
First published: "Detskie kartinki," 1978 (English translation, 1980)

> *Principal characters:*
> THE NARRATOR, a political prisoner in one of Stalin's work
> camps
> TWO OTHER POLITICAL PRISONERS, members of his brigade

The Story

The story begins as the routine day begins. The narrator, a nameless political prisoner in a nameless Kolyma labor camp, is sent out with the other prisoners for the day's work. There is no checklist for the prisoners; they are simply lined up by fives so that the guards have an easy time of counting and multiplying. Today the narrator's brigade has an easy job—sawing wood with a circular saw, a task which usually falls to a more privileged prisoner group, the common criminals. The saw, like the prisoners, moves slowly, growling in the bitter cold of the far North. The third prisoner assigned to the woodpile works separately, splitting the brittle, frozen larch logs which fall apart easily, despite the fact that he can barely wield the hatchet.

The brigade has a few minutes of free time after stacking the wood, since their guard has gone indoors to warm up, and they have to wait for the remaining brigades to finish and gather for the collective march back to camp. They take advantage of the break to comb through a nearby garbage pile, a heap of trash they have been eyeing all day long. Picking through one layer after another, they collect the scraps and cast-offs that may mean survival for another day—discarded socks, the odd crust of bread, leftover cutlets frozen hard.

The narrator keeps scratching, since he alone of the three has not yet found anything useful. He turns up something he has not seen in years—a child's drawing tablet, filled with scenes from all four of Kolyma's cold seasons. As he begins flipping the pages, he recalls his own childhood and his own drawings of fantastic folk heroes and magical animals. The recollections are vivid—his white paint box, the kerosene lamp on the kitchen table, the drawings themselves. He remembers his Ivan-Tsarevich, Prince Ivan, loping through the forest astride his trusty gray wolf, smoke rising in a curlicue, birds like check marks. The more vivid his own recollection, the more acute the realization that his own childhood is gone and that he will find no trace of it in this child's drawings.

The world in this child's tablet is one of wooden fences and wooden walls, all identical, all yellow ocher: fences, barbed wire, sentry boxes, guard towers, armed guards. The purity and brightness of the young artist's colors remind the narrator of a local legend—that God created the taiga when He was still young, before He learned to create intricate designs or a variety of birds and beasts. When He grew up and learned these things, He buried His stark taiga world in snow and left for the south.

The narrator concentrates on a winter scene, a northern hunt. Here Ivan-Tsarevich wears a military-issue fur hat with earflaps, a thick sheepskin coat and a rifle at his back. A German shepherd strains at the leash. The narrator realizes that the only world this child knows or will ever recall is one where humans hunt one another and where life is circumscribed by yellow buildings, wire fences, guards with guns, and blue sky.

Another prisoner breaks the narrator's reverie. He tests the notebook paper, then tosses it back onto the pile, remarking that newspaper works better for rolling cigarettes.

Themes and Meanings

"Nature in the north is not faceless, not indifferent—it is in league with those who sent us here." Shalamov's narrator knows from experience that the fresh air regime of the Kolyma camps is more likely to kill a prisoner than save him, especially since that prisoner is ill-clothed, ill-treated, overworked, and underfed.

Of all the "islands" in the Gulag Archipelago, the Kolyma camps were the most frightful: the final, icy grave for millions of Joseph Stalin's victims. Barely populated before the 1930's, this far corner of Siberia was "developed" for gold production in order to accommodate the vast numbers of quite innocent political prisoners arrested during the purges. If the politicals provided the state with some gold, or lead, or furs, or fish before giving in to starvation, scurvy, dystrophy, or suicide—so much the better. Technically fiction, Shalamov's *Kolymskie rasskazy* (1978; *Kolyma Tales*, 1980) are both a document and a testament.

"A Child's Drawings" bears witness to the fact that those inside the barracks and barbed wire were not the only victims of Kolyma. As the narrator leafs through the stiffened pages of the discarded notebook and remembers his own childhood, his remembrances are happy ones; although Russian folktales are far from always benign, Ivan-Tsarevich, when in trouble, can call on a host of animal allies. The natural world, in exchange for his kindness, comes to his aid—rocks, trees, rivers, winds alike. His own native goodness, cleverness, and innocence, along with the magic provided him, defeat evil sorcerers and wicked witches and, in the end, he is rewarded with prosperity and long life.

What the narrator experiences is not simply nostalgia for his own childhood, but fear at the ominous vision which has replaced his own, and perhaps everyone's. This child's vision is disturbing both in what it has and what it lacks: the bright primary colors and triangle-larches, stark and uncompromising whatever the season, man's buildings repeated in the same color, surrounded by the same barbed wire—nature and man, both hostile. Most frightening of all is Prince Ivan's transformation from the underdog hero to the pursuer and predator—this child's Ivan-Tsarevich is on a hunt not for a fierce bear or shape-changing wizard, but for men.

Nowhere in these drawings does the narrator find himself, the prisoner, for whom and by whom all these monotonous structures, these fences and towers, have been built. The hunt shows the pursuit, but not the prey. In this child's world, the prisoners are simply not there—absent from his world as they are absent from the world of their own pasts—not yet dead, but already gone.

Style and Technique

Shalamov's semiautobiographical narrator is an insider, a veteran of camp life, an observer rather than an active participant. In this story, too, his only "act" is contemplative, when he stops digging through the trash heap for anything edible or useful and looks over the notebook. It is left to a fellow prisoner to judge the paper unfit for rolling cigarettes and toss the notebook back on the heap. Though not above the scene, this narrator is removed from it by his own reticence in act and speech.

What gives this story—and the rest of the *Kolyma Tales*—their impact is the dissonance between the unbelievable, nightmare absurdity of the labor camps and the narrator's calm reportage. He avoids dramatization, embellishment, sentimentality, even sympathy. He may explain, or clarify, but he never comments. What he leaves out reveals more than any description ever could.

For example, the story begins with a brief description of camp routine. The narrator tells the reader that the prisoners are marched out in fives to make counting easier, since even the prisoner's patience wears thin if he has to wait in the cold. End of description. What the reader is left to figure out for himself is the ignorance and stupidity of those in control, and that the fear of violence—even violence by starving wrecks of men—controls the controllers.

The narrator's impartiality extends to himself as he relates how he systematically rummages through the garbage, envious of his companions' success in scavenging. His tone does not change when he describes his own reaction to the child's notebook: material boon, spiritual loss—seemingly equal value, redefined, redrawn by Kolyma.

The suggestive legend of the taiga god who discards his own crude, childish creation, covers it with snow and leaves forever, ends with a disclaimer—

"So goes the legend." Once again, the narrator makes no connections, and the reader must link the god's abandoned, snow-covered world, the narrator's lost childhood, and the Kolyma child's tablet, coated with frost as soon as it returns to the garbage heap.

Jane Ann Miller

CHRISTMAS MORNING

Author: Frank O'Connor (Michael Francis O'Donovan, 1903-1966)
Type of plot: Autobiographical narrative
Time of plot: Early twentieth century
Locale: Ireland
First published: 1946

Principal characters:
LARRY, the narrator and restless older brother, who yearns for excitement
SONNY, the smarter, younger brother
THE MOTHER, who must struggle to keep the father from drinking the household money
THE FATHER, who enjoys drinking and singing Latin hymns

The Story

The first-person narrator of this story, a young boy named Larry, learns an important lesson about growing up, about childhood beliefs, and about family relationships. Young Larry, who is not even ten years old, dislikes his younger, more studious brother, Sonny, because he believes that Sonny is mother's favorite child. Encouraged by their mother, Sonny concentrates on spelling words correctly, on displaying his learning in other subjects, and on attending school, whereas Larry, much to mother's chagrin, dislikes his studies, favors playing with his boyhood "gang," and prefers skipping school. As the story unfolds, however, Larry discovers why his mother seems to favor Sonny and simultaneously discovers an important lesson about Christmas.

Instead of studying, Larry spends his time playing with the Doherty gang and dreaming of becoming a soldier. He believes that studying is not commendable and, perhaps, is better suited to sissies.

As Christmas approaches, Larry hears, but adamantly refuses to believe, that there is no Santa Claus. The neighborhood Doherty boys, who reveal this information, are a "rough class of children you wouldn't expect Santa to come to anyway," Larry observes.

Four days before the holidays, Larry is caught skipping school. Because he has not bothered to learn his required math lessons, he and Peter Doherty have cut classes and have been spending their time in a store on the quay. When his mother reprimands him for his truancy, Larry discovers that his lies have been more offensive to her than has been his failure to attend school. Yet at this point in his life, he fails to understand why lying is such an important failing in a human being.

In contrast, Sonny behaves particularly well during the Christmas season. When the two boys retire for the night, Sonny warns Larry that Santa surely will not visit any boy who has skipped school and who has associated with the rough Doherty boys.

Larry, therefore, decides to remain awake on Christmas Eve to discuss his plight with Santa Claus—man to man. Surely Santa, because he is a man, will understand Larry's behavior. That evening, Larry rehearses several explanations of his behavior. Failing to realize that these explanations to Santa would simply be more lies, he awaits Christmas Eve and Santa's arrival.

Although the boys eagerly anticipate Christmas Eve, their mother is quite frustrated. When the father returns home after work and begrudgingly offers her only a few coins, the mother argues with him in an attempt to obtain extra housekeeping money for toys, cake, and a Christmas candle. Yet the father tosses her only two extra half-crowns, shouts at her to make the best of the situation, and storms out of the house. An embittered woman, she takes the money and realizes that the father will spend the remainder of his salary on liquor.

Returning from her shopping trip on Christmas Eve, mother carries her cake, her Christmas candle, and a few packages. When father fails to return home, the three silently eat the cake, sip tea, light the candle, and hang Christmas stockings. Around eleven o'clock, a drunken father returns home. He attempts to sing Latin hymns but does not remember the correct words.

Although he struggles against sleep, Larry finally succumbs. When he awakens early the next morning, Larry is terribly dismayed to discover that Santa has made a grievous error. In his own stocking Larry unhappily discovers a book, a pen and pencil, and a bag of sweets. In Sonny's stocking Larry discovers a bag of sweets and a popgun. Larry knows that he can use the popgun but has absolutely no use for the book and writing instruments; therefore, a clever idea pops into his head. Perhaps he could switch the presents. Sonny would never be any good in a gang, Larry reasons, and could, at least, learn many new spellings from the book. Besides, only Santa knows what gifts each boy has received. Perhaps, Larry finally reasons, Santa has indeed made a mistake. Larry carefully makes the switch and returns to bed only to be awakened later by Sonny, who has discovered the presents, and who rushes to show mother and father. Because he has nothing to fear—only Santa and himself know of the switch—Larry joins Sonny in their parents' bedroom.

When his mother asks Larry where he got the gun, Larry answers that Santa brought it to him. Instantly, and perhaps without thinking, his mother accuses Larry of stealing the gun from Sonny. The father seems to understand the boys' plight and offers them a few coins. Mother, however, does not understand Larry's lying and mentions that she does not want her child to grow up to be a liar and a thief.

The climax of the story occurs when Larry suddenly realizes that the

Dohertys were right after all: There is no Santa Claus. There are only the gifts that parents give their children. Yet perhaps the most important lesson that Larry learns is that his mother has been relying on Larry to extricate her from her miserable existence. Larry painfully understands that the fear in his mother's eyes "was the fear that, like my father, I should turn out to be mean and common and a drunkard." Thus one Christmas morning a young boy grows up to understand adult relationships and adult hardships.

Themes and Meanings

In this story, as in many of his stories, Frank O'Connor realistically treats the often harsh realities of life in rural Ireland. The story details a young boy's journey from innocence to maturity and depicts Larry's ultimate understanding of adult realities. The reader understands that Larry, the narrator and protagonist, did in fact learn important lessons on that Christmas morning, because early in the story Larry indicates that he was not very good in school until the age of nine or ten. In fact, before his epiphany on Christmas morning, Larry did not participate at all in his education: He did not understand math, he disliked reading and spelling, and he skipped school. Before the revelation that concludes the story, he is blinded by the natural selfishness of a child; because he plays with troublemakers, dreams of becoming a soldier, and is engaged in his own naïve world, he fails to see the difficulties that exist in his mother's world.

On Christmas morning, however, after he is admonished for exchanging his present for his brother's present, he suddenly realizes that his mother—a lonely, frightened woman—is at the mercy of his father, a brutal drunkard, who squanders the housekeeping money on liquor.

He also realizes that his mother's dreams of escape are focused directly on him, the older son. Although his discovery that Santa Claus is not real has been "almost more than [he] could bear," he has learned a more important lesson: The future of his family depends upon his growing up with values different from his father's.

Style and Technique

In this first-person narrative, O'Connor uses an informal, almost provincial style. Because the characters are Irish, as is O'Connor, many colloquialisms appear throughout the story to add authenticity to the realistic narration. For example, instead of skipping school, the boys "go on the lang" and engage in "mitching." Rather than say "my mother," the narrator always says "the mother." Moreover, Sonny, the "little prig," is "stuffed up" and tells the Dohertys that Larry "isn't left go out." Instead of drinking excessively, Larry's father "had a drop in." This conversational, provincial dialogue suggests a working-class Irish family.

O'Connor's deliberately repetitious use of the conjunction "and" intensifies the lesson which Larry learns at the end of the story: He sees that "Father was mean and common and a drunkard and that she [the mother] had been relying" on him. The last sentence reinforces the intensification: "And I knew... I should turn out to be mean and common and a drunkard."

Bette Adams Reagan

THE CHRYSANTHEMUMS

Author: John Steinbeck (1902-1968)
Type of plot: Domestic realism
Time of plot: 1937
Locale: The Salinas Valley in California
First published: 1938

Principal characters:
ELISA ALLEN, a woman in her thirties
HENRY ALLEN, her husband
MAN IN A WAGON, a tinker

The Story

Elisa Allen, a woman approaching middle age, is at a point in her life when she has begun to realize that her energy and creative drive far exceed the opportunities for their expression. Her marriage is reasonably happy—when she notices that her husband is proud of selling thirty head of steers he has raised, she gives him the compliment he hopes for, while he, in turn, appreciates her ability to grow flowers of exceptional quality. There is an easy banter between them, and while they have settled into a fairly familiar routine, they are still responsive to each other's moods, and eager to celebrate an achievement in each other's company with a night on the town. On the other hand, their marriage is childless, and Elisa generally wears bland, bulging clothes that tend to de-sex her. Their house is described as "hardswept" and "hard-polished"; it is the only outlet for her talents and it is an insufficient focus for her energy. She has begun to sense that an important part of her is lying dormant and that the future will be predictable and rather mundane.

Although Elisa would never consider an actual affair, when a stranger appears at their farm offering to sharpen knives and mend pots, his singularity and unconventional appearance immediately arouse her interest. In contrast to her husband, he is a kind of adventurer who lives spontaneously, a man of the road not bound by standard measures of time and place. Because he has found it useful to be able to charm his potential customers into giving him work, he is accomplished at gauging a person's emotional needs, and he has developed a facility for the kind of conversation that verges on the suggestive. He is described as big, bearded, and graying, a man who has been around, who knows something about life and people: a man with a captivating presence whose eyes are dark and "full of brooding."

Elisa is fascinated by his way of life, overlooking the harshness and uncertainty of his existence in her eagerness to romanticize his style. When she tries to get him to discuss his travels, he steers the conversation back to the possibility of employment. When it is apparent that she has no work to give him, however, he cannily praises her flowers, and when Elisa responds to his "interest," he tells her that a woman he expects to see soon on his rounds has asked him to be on the watch for good seeds. Almost desperately eager to share the one thing she is actually doing, Elisa carefully gathers some shoots, and as she instructs the stranger on the proper care of the seedlings, her passionate involvement with the process of planting becomes an expression of all the suppressed romance in her life. The stranger senses this, and to show that he shares her vision, he offers just enough encouragement to lead her into a full-scale declaration of her profound sense of what planting means to her, a declaration which is presented in powerfully sensual terms. Elisa would like this moment of intensity to continue, but the tinker reminds her that hunger overcomes inspiration, and Elisa, somewhat abashed by her own openness, finds some useless, old pots for him to mend. She believes that the man has given her something intangible but valuable and that she is obliged to give him something he needs in return. As the man leaves, Elisa looks away after him, whispering to herself, "There's a bright direction. There's a glowing there."

The consequence of their conversation is very dramatic. Elisa feels energized and appreciated, delighted by her opportunity to share her special skill and excited by the chance to share, at least in her imagination, a totally different kind of life. As she prepares for the evening, the power she usually puts into scrubbing the house is redirected into her preparation to make herself as attractive as she now feels. Her husband is both surprised and pleased by her appearance, and their conversation is mixed with a pleasant uncertainty and a kind of unexpected delight as they both enjoy the animating effect of Elisa's encounter. Their mood remains distinctly elevated as they head for town, but then, Elisa sees a small speck on the road in the distance. Instantly, she realizes that this is the treasure she so avidly prepared. The tinker has discarded the flowers on the road to save the pot that contained them, the only object of value to him.

Elisa is shattered by the callous manner in which he has drawn something from her secret self and then completely betrayed her "gift" by not even taking the trouble to hide the flowers. She attempts to override her disappointment by maintaining a mood of gaiety, suggesting that they have wine at dinner, a bold gesture in the context of their lives. This, however, is not sufficient to help her restore her feelings of confidence and expectation, so she asks her husband if they might go to a prizefight, a request so completely out of character that her husband is totally baffled. She presses further, searching for that "special" feeling she held briefly, and asks if men "hurt each other very much." This is part of an effort to focus her own violent and angry feelings, but it is completely futile as an attempt to sustain and resurrect her sense of self-control and command. In a few moments, she completely gives up the pose, her whole body collapsing into the seat in an exhibition of defeat. As the story concludes, Elisa is struggling to hide her real feeling of pain from her husband. She is anticipating a dreadful future in which she pictures herself "crying weakly—like an old woman."

Themes and Meanings

John Steinbeck published "The Chrysanthemums" in a collection of stories called *The Long Valley* (1938). They are set in the Salinas Valley in California where he was born, the fertile farmland that the "Okies" settled after their flight from the Dust Bowl. Freed from the crushing burden of absolute poverty and social disintegration, Steinbeck's characters, like Henry Allen, are quite pleased to be able to make a decent living, but equally important, like Elisa Allen, they are beginning to sense that not everybody can be satisfied by bread alone.

In a subtle prefiguration of feminist philosophy, Steinbeck challenges the tradition of woman's "place"; while Henry Allen is well-meaning and basically decent, his concentration on his own role as provider, organizer, and decision-maker has blinded him to the fact that Elisa needs something more in her life than a neat house and a good garden. He is ready to offer what he can (a share in the work; brighter lights and bigger cities for occasional recreation), but Elisa's urgent need for someone to talk to who can understand the essential nature of her yearning for a poetic vision of the cosmos is, unfortunately, beyond Henry's range and insight. The question Steinbeck poses is whether one should settle for security and a lack of pain, or risk one's dreams in an attempt to live more completely and intensely. The retreat from action at the conclusion suggests that the risks are high, but there is a possibility that Elisa might not be permanently crushed by her pain.

The situation recalls D. H. Lawrence's story "The Shades of Spring," in which a woman reconciles herself to a steady man when the sparkling boy of her youth goes off to seek his fortune. Yet she knows what she misses, and tells him on his return, "The stars are different with you." Elisa Allen is not ungrateful for her husband's kindness and for his provision of security, but the dark stranger brings thoughts of a life she has only sensed she was missing, and her response to his vague romantic encouragement startles her in its suddenness and its force. The paradox here is that the stranger has actually lost his spontaneity and manipulates her emotions not to satisfy his own romantic longings, but to earn the money he needs for survival: money she no longer has to be concerned with.

Style and Technique

It is clear from Steinbeck's epic novel of American experience, *The Grapes of Wrath* (1939), that he is particularly sensitive to the effect of landscape on a person's life. Because Elisa Allen's sense of her own self-worth is so closely tied to the land, Steinbeck has chosen to connect her psychic state to the season, the climate, and the terrain she inhabits. The mood of the story is set by his description of a fogbound valley in winter, a description which is also applicable to Elisa's mood. She is entering middle age, and when the valley is likened to a "closed pot" with "no sunshine ... in December," there is a close parallel to the condition of her life at that point, a sealed vessel with little light available. Steinbeck calls it "a time of quiet and waiting," and the land, Elisa's only field of action, is dormant, with "little work to be done."

Elisa is earthbound, rooted securely in her garden but also held down by her connection to it. It is significant that her excitement in talking to the stranger is expressed by a vision of the stars and by her exclamation that "you rise up and up!" The stranger is not bound to a particular place, and while his freedom to roam is only a step removed from endless exile and rootlessness (as exemplified by Elisa's uprooting her plants, only to have them thrown away and left to die on the road), it is appealing in contrast to her chainlike connections to the earth.

Elisa is also seen alternately as a part of a larger landscape and as a small figure in an enclosed area. The story unfolds from an inventive cinematic perspective, as Steinbeck first describes the entire valley in a panoramic view, then moves closer to focus on the ranch in the valley, and then moves in for a close-up of Elisa working in her garden. Throughout the story, the perspective shifts from Elisa's narrow and cramped domain, walled or fenced in, to the entire ranch, and to the world beyond. Then, in a final shift, Elisa's shock is reflected by an image of multiple confinement, as she is enclosed by a wagon, surrounded by her seat and hidden within a coat that covers her face. It is not an image designed to create confidence in Elisa's prospects.

Leon Lewis

CINNAMON SHOPS

Author: Bruno Schulz (1892-1942)
Type of plot: Fantasy
Time of plot: Early twentieth century
Locale: A small city in Poland
First published: "Sklepy cynamanowe," 1934 (English translation, 1963)

> *Principal characters:*
> THE NARRATOR, a boy of high school age
> THE NARRATOR'S FATHER
> THE NARRATOR'S MOTHER
> PROFESSOR ARENDT, the narrator's drawing teacher
> AN OLD CAB HORSE

The Story

On winter days, the narrator's father communes with an invisible world that he shares with the family cat. To distract him, his mother arranges to have the family attend the theater. Before the curtain rises, however, the father notices that he has left at home his "wallet containing money and certain most important documents." The boy is sent home to fetch it.

He steps into a clear winter night and soon finds his imagination creating "illusory maps of the apparently familiar districts." Soon the town dissolves into "the tissue of dreams." He looks for his beloved cinnamon shops, replete with curiosities from and books about exotic places. He turns into a street he knows, but it presents him with an unknown vista of orchards, parks, and ornate villas—which metamorphose into the back of the high school building. He recalls the late-evening drawing classes taught there by Professor Arendt, an enthusiastic and inspiring teacher.

Seeking out the professor's classroom, the narrator instead finds himself in an unfamiliar wing of the school building, which houses the headmaster's magnificently luxurious apartment. Embarrassed to be caught prying into private quarters, he runs into the street and hails a horse-drawn cab, which circles the city. The cabdriver catches sight of a crowd of fellow cabbies gathered in front of an inn and jumps off the carriage to join them, abandoning his vehicle to the narrator and his old horse, which " inspired confidence—it seemed smarter than its driver." The narrator yields himself to the horse's will.

The cab leaves the city and enters a hilly landscape, while the boy enjoys the unforgettable sight of a starry sky and the haunting scent of the violet-perfumed night air. He is happy. At last the horse stops, panting. The narrator remarks tears in its eyes, a wound on its belly. He asks the horse why it did not reveal its injury sooner. The horse replies, " 'My dearest, I did it for you' . . . and became very small, like a wooden toy."

The narrator leaves the horse, still feeling "light and happy," and runs most of the distance back to the city. He keeps admiring the changing shapes of the sky's many configurations. In the city's central square he meets people whose faces, like his, are uplifted with delight as they gaze at the sky's silvery magic and he "completely stop[s] worrying about Father's wallet," assuming that his father had most likely forgotten about it by now. Meeting with school friends who have been awakened by the brightly illuminated sky, the boy accompanies them, "uncertain whether it was the magic of the night which lay like silver on the snow or whether it was the light of dawn. . . ."

Themes and Meanings

A thin, reclusive, shy, and sickly man, Bruno Schulz earned his living as a high school drawing instructor in his native southeastern Poland and wrote stories in his spare time but was too timid to submit them to publishers until friends arranged an introduction to Zofia Nalkowska, a highly regarded Warsaw novelist. She arranged for the publication of a slender volume of his short stories in 1934. Titled *Sklepy cynamanowe*, it was translated into English by Celina Wieniewska and published in 1963, in Britain under the title of *Cinnamon Shops* and in the United States as *The Street of Crocodiles*. Schulz was subsequently to produce one more collection of stories, a novella, and the manuscript of a novel before his death at the hands of the Nazis in 1942.

In Schulz's fiction, the narrator typically related phantasmagoric incidents wherein everyday reality is transfigured into a dream by the protagonist's surrealistic imagination. In an interview, Schulz termed the collection *Cinnamon Shops* "a biographical novel" whose spiritual genealogy vanishes into "mythological hallucination." This is evident in the title story, which lyrically celebrates a teenage boy's separation and individuation from his parents and commitment to a fictive family of animistic creatures and phenomena.

Central to most of the tales in *Cinnamon Shops* is the father, causing critics to compare Schulz to another Slavic-Jewish writer, Franz Kafka (1883-1924). Yet whereas Kafka magnifies the progenitor to a potent, punitive, stern patriarch of God-like authority, Schulz reduces him to an eccentric but frail, antic and confused occultist dominated by his wife and maid. In "Cinnamon Shops," the father is a foolish fumbler, on speaking terms with an unseen world of imps and demons, escaping the demands of everyday routine and the needs of his family by engaging in interior monologues inaccessible to the outer world. The mother receives short, undefined shrift in this story; in other texts she is portrayed as energetic, practical, but unloving. Schulz's art can be more illuminatingly related to that of Isaac Bashevis Singer (born 1904), another Polish Jew, with whom he shares an engrossment in folk motifs and supernatural powers. While both Kafka and Singer are rooted in the tradition of Jewish religiosity, however, Schulz is a secularist whose mythological world is individualized, formless, fragmented, contingent, and isolated.

It is a world of animism in which reality is frequently irrational and fluid. Schulz is Platonic in rejecting the objective evidence of the senses. Matter and creatures can change shapes and faculties, can distort space or time. The father is more intimate with his cat than he is with his family; the boy's imagination accords credibility to fantasized streets, doorless houses, classic gods, mirrors exchanging glances, friezes panicking, and a horse addressing him intelligibly. The boy is the story's mythmaker: He is an artist of the fantastic, reminiscent of Marc Chagall (1887-1985), another Slavic Jew, in his glowing, occult visions that celebrate the ethereal manifestations of a magic universe in the landscape of the night sky.

Style and Technique

Schulz makes his hero's mythological hallucinations plausible by enveloping them in bold similes and metaphors brimming with intensely pictorial effects. Thus, mid-winter is "edged on both sides with the furry dusk of mornings and evenings"; a park's bushes are "full of confusion, secret gestures, conniving looks"; cabs loom in the street "like crippled, dozing crabs or cockroaches"; the air "shimmered like silver gauze"; hills "rose like sighs of bliss"; the narrator is "touched by the divine finger of poetry." The imagery is sharp, immediate, and unforgettably lyrical.

Animism and anthropomorphism charge the story's texture. Gardens becomes parks which become forests. The night's stillness is interrupted by the "sighs and whispers of the crumbling gods" depicted in the statuary collected by the art professor. Mounted weasels and martens leave their school cabinets to mate nocturnally in park thickets. Schulz's language teems with a pan-masquerade of changed dimensions and roles, an intense hymn that expresses the narrator's delight with a universe alive with amazement and mystery. While limited in scope and range, his talent is one of the most richly imaginative among European prose writers who matured between World Wars I and II.

Gerhard Brand

THE CIRCULAR RUINS

Author: Jorge Luis Borges (1899-1986)
Type of plot: Fantasy
Time of plot: Unspecified
Locale: An unnamed jungle
First published: "Las ruinas circulares," 1940 (English translation, 1962)

> *Principal characters:*
> THE DREAMER, a worshiper of the fire god
> HIS "SON"

The Story

In "The Circular Ruins," from a nameless home in a time not marked on calendars, a figure known only as "the taciturn man" or "the gray man" beaches a bamboo canoe on the bank of a jungle river. When he lands, he kisses the mud and heads inland to the circular ruins: the ruins of an abandoned temple to a god no longer worshiped. He sleeps there in the ruins, and when he awakes, he will begin a task of creation.

He awakes in the morning and sees tracks around him, which inform him that natives of the area have observed him during the night. Those visitors suit his purpose: He has come to this region, as Borges says, "to dream a man." He wants to dream this creation in every detail—every hair, every pore—and through the intensity and thoroughness of his dreaming, make it real. He has come to the ruins seeking their aid in the accomplishment of his task, seeking their loneliness and their barrenness. There will be less to distract him from his work. The natives of the place will not intrude on him during the day but, filled with superstition, will supply his bodily needs with their offerings each night.

He begins by dreaming of an enormous lecture hall filled with students, candidates for the honor of being dreamed into reality. He considers all of them until he selects one, the likeliest, on whom to concentrate. After a few private lessons in his dreams, however, what he calls a catastrophe takes place. The dreamer is unable to sleep. After the dreamer begins to appreciate the difficulty of his task, he gives up conscious intention and no longer tries to direct his dreams. He abandons premeditation and lets the dreams come when they will.

On the night of the full moon, he falls asleep "with his heart throbbing"; it is of a heart that he dreams, a beating heart within a body whose form he cannot yet see. For two weeks he concentrates on that heart in his dreams, merely observing, not interfering. There is a hint that the dreamer is a magician: He lectures on magic to the imaginary students; he calls on the names of gods and planets. He works this sort of spell before dreaming of the next organ of his creation. When that one is finished, he goes on to another. A year passes before he comes to the skeleton. The "innumerable hair" is the hardest of all, but eventually he dreams an entire sleeping young man.

When the dreamer finally awakens his creation, it is crude and clumsy, like Frankenstein's monster, and the dreamer almost despairs. In his exhaustion, he throws himself before the strangely shaped statue of the god of the ruins and pleads with it to help him. Then, the fire god appears before the dreamer in his sleep and agrees to bring his creation to life in a special way: To all but the fire god and the dreamer, the creation will seem to be a normal man. Yet there is a price for this gift. The dreamer must educate his creation in the ritual of the fire god, and when this child of his mind has learned the mysteries of that worship, he must be sent downstream to the next ruined temple to reestablish the worship of the fire god.

The dreamer agrees and, in the months that follow, instructs the created being whom he is now beginning to think of as his son. He cuts his waking hours down to an irreducible minimum, looking forward to sleep and the company of his creation.

He starts to introduce his son to "reality." For example, as always in a dream, he instructs the young man to place a flag on a mountaintop. When the dreamer awakes, he finds the flag where it was planted, flying in place in the waking world. After other such trials, he believes that his son is ready to be "born," to enter the waking world of the dreamer. In his dream that night, he kisses his son and sends him to the temple ruins downstream to take up his duties. He gives the youth one last gift, however: So that his creation will not think himself different from any other man, the dreamer erases from his mind the memory of his years of instruction.

Having achieved his greatest desire, the dreamer's life begins to interest him less and less. One night he is awakened by two natives who tell him of a man of strange powers in a nearby temple, a man who is able to walk on fire without being burned. He at once realizes that this man is his son, and he worries that his son's peculiar power might cause him to doubt his own reality. He imagines how humiliating it would be for one to realize that one is merely the creation of another's mind.

Eventually, these doubts of the dreamer pass. A night comes, however, on which the circular ruins, ages ago destroyed by fire, catch fire again. As the flames rise around him, the dreamer is not alarmed; his life's work has been done and he is ready to die. Rather than try to escape, he walks toward the flames. When he enters them, however, they do not burn him. In a flash he realizes that this immunity to fire is the same as his son's, and he understands that he too is an illusion, the dream-child of another.

Themes and Meanings

Borges was a great admirer of Lewis Carroll's comic fantasies, as seen in

Borges' neatly summarizing the theme of "The Circular Ruins" with a quotation that stands at the head of the story: "And if he left off dreaming about you . . ." from Lewis Carroll's *Through the Looking-Glass and What Alice Found There* (1871). The reference is from a chapter of Carroll's book in which Tweedledee shows Alice the sleeping Red King, tells her that the king is dreaming about her, and asks, "And if he left off dreaming about you, where do you suppose you'd be?" Alice says she would be where she is now, but Tweedledee disagrees "contemptuously." He says, "You'd be nowhere. Why, you're only a sort of thing in his dream!"

Borges puts this notion, used for comedy in Carroll's book, to chilling effect in "The Circular Ruins" as the realization of the dreamer at the end of the story comes with enormous impact. Critics have called the story one of the most horrifying of Borges' works, yet it is simply the logical extension of a philosophical notion that informs the majority of Borges' fiction.

This notion, usually called "idealism" with various adjectives prefixed to it, can be traced to a number of philosophers whom Borges himself cites in various works. For example, the eighteenth century English philosopher George Berkeley developed a philosophy called "pluralistic idealism," which holds that the so-called real world perceived as around one exists only in one's consciousness. His German contemporary Immanuel Kant took this idea even further. Kant's "critical idealism" holds that matter does not exist if it is not sensed by the individual. The often-quoted question, "If a tree falls in the forest and no one hears it, does it make a sound?" is a question to which the idealist answers "No."

Style and Technique

The word "circular" in the title accurately describes the form that Borges' story takes. At the end of the story the pieces fall neatly into place: Remembering that the dreamer erased all memories of his beginning from his son's mind, the reader recalls with new understanding the mysterious origin of the dreamer himself. The reader is never told where the dreamer comes from, except that it is upstream. His history is scanted, and the reader is never told how it is that he knows about the ritual of the fire god, or how he has acquired his magical powers. When the dreamer realizes that he is merely one revolution in a cycle, the reader realizes that the dreamer's memory has been wiped clean by his "father," just as the dreamer has done for his "son."

Borges' reliance on philosophical idealism in his fiction should not be taken as evidence that he seriously believed that human perception creates the universe. Rather, the philosophy is one that he could put to work in art; in "The Circular Ruins," it allows an ending of great power and surprise. Borges had a thorough familiarity with English and American literature, even with what is sometimes called "popular" literature—the detective story, for example. He often expressed an admiration for the classic detective story, especially for its ending, in which all the pieces of the mystery must fall into place in a revelation which is both surprising and satisfying to the reader. Just such a story, transposed into fantasy, is "The Circular Ruins."

Walter E. Meyers

CLAY

Author: James Joyce (1882-1941)
Type of plot: Symbolic realism
Time of plot: c. 1900
Locale: Dublin, Ireland
First published: 1914

Principal characters:
> MARIA, the protagonist, a middle-aged spinster, a kitchen
> helper in a Dublin laundry
> JOE DONNELLY, her former nursling

The Story

Halloween (October 31) is the Celtic New Year's Eve and Feast of the Dead, Christianized as the Feasts of the Blessed Virgin and All Saints (November 1) and All Souls (November 2). In Irish folk custom, it is a night of remembrance of dead ancestors and anticipation of the future through various fortune-telling games. This Halloween story, "Clay," is about Maria, a middle-aged spinster, who works in the kitchen of a laundry established for the reform of prostitutes. Readers follow Maria from the routine of her job there, as she makes her way across the city of Dublin to the seasonal festivities at the home of her former nursling, Joe Donnelly. In these few scenes, Joyce draws a complex character portrait which, by means of its symbolic devices, conveys much of Maria's past, present, and future.

The story unfolds by means of the contrasts between the narrator's view of Maria and her own emotionally limited self-awareness. The story develops in three scenes: at the laundry, on the journey across the city, and at the Halloween party. In the first, readers observe Maria's prim, fussy personality as she prepares the women's tea while privately anticipating her reunion with Joe and Mrs. Donnelly and their family. She suffers many slights in this institution, set apart by temperament and experience from the inmates, and by her Catholic piety from its Protestant management. On this particular occasion, the search for the wedding band hidden in the traditional Halloween cake causes some pointed disquiet for Maria. Indeed, her private chagrin at her single state is a recurring embarrassment throughout the evening.

As she travels northward across Dublin, stopping off at the city center to purchase her gifts, she is again reminded of her isolation: first by the irritation of the girl in the cakeshop, and again by the polite attentions of the gentleman in the tram. She is so flustered at this that she evidently leaves the rather expensive cake behind her.

At the Donnelly household she is greeted dutifully, and with mixed emotions. She irritates the children by interrupting their party, and by suggesting that they stole the lost cake intended for their parents. Joe and Mrs. Donnelly make her welcome, though, and she is soon relaxed enough to raise a question about Alphy, Joe's estranged brother. This again disrupts the festive atmosphere, only restored by the traditional fortune-telling games. When the children's fortunes are told (the prayer book, signifying the religious life; the water, emigration; and the ring, marriage, respectively), Maria—oddly enough, as an adult—is invited to play. When her lot turns out to be clay (signifying the fortune of death), however, the rules are changed and she gets the consolation of religion. The evening concludes with Maria's song, "I Dreamt I Dwelt" (from Michael William Balfe's opera *The Bohemian Girl*, 1843), but she sings the first verse twice, forgetting or censoring the references to lovers and knights of the second verse. When she is finished, the story focuses on Joe's response: His eyes fill with tears motivated by a mixture of drunken nostalgia and guilt.

Themes and Meanings

This story can be viewed as an astute study of a psychologically repressed personality. The setting implies frames of reference encompassing the social, religious, cultural, and political circumstances of that repression.

First, Maria's character is marked by persistent self-deception: To herself, she is tidy, pious, proper, and nice; to others, she is well-meaning, dull, sometimes vindictive, and pitiable. She is dutiful, generous, and punctilious, yet her officiousness and tactlessness cause offense and resentment in others. It is clear, too, that she feels that life has betrayed her, that she has never found a husband and probably never will. She consoles herself with attention to the duties of her job and religion while retaining some small connection with the Donnellys, whose Halloween party is the nearest to family life she will know. Yet even there, her resentments break out, and the pathos of that revelation is barely restrained.

These conflicts in Maria's character are developed by means of several sets of contrasts in the story, the most notable of which is that between images of the Blessed Virgin Mary and a witch, or Celtic *cailleach* (old hag). These images (for example, Maria as a quasi-virgin and mother, versus the recurring representation of her profile) correspond to the positive image Maria has of herself, and the less flattering one suggested by the concealed narrator. These correspondences reflect, in turn, the historical Christianization of what was originally the Celtic Feast of the Dead, as conveyed in the contrast between the religious and fortune-telling rituals in the story. Thus, while Maria consciously regards herself in the light of the Christian promise, her story takes place among shadows cast by a darker past.

In these contexts, then, Maria can be considered as a type of her race, or as an allegorical representation of Mother Ireland. She is a typical Dubliner, in Joyce's view, in that she is paralyzed by circumstances beyond her control or awareness (her appearance, her apparent ejection from the Donnelly household, for example), while not examining too critically what lies behind the flattery and patronization of her employers, fellow workers, and personal friends. As a victim of division of the household, feeling herself a stranger in her own home, observing outsiders in control, and appealing, in vain, for a liberating hero, she is a version of the ancient symbolic representation of Mother Ireland dominated by imperial England.

Style and Technique

"Clay" is told in language very close to Maria's own: The sentences are simple, the vocabulary limited and repetitive, and the tone naïve, even prissy. Note the repeated use of the words "nice" and "right," for example. This tone is finely managed. At first reading, it seems naïve and objective. Closer observation, however, shows it to be a complex interweaving of controlled irony, sentiment, and cool understatement. The narrator describes the various sides of Maria's character by means of subtle innuendo, suggestive images and symbols, delicate restraint or even silence. Consider here the repeated description of Maria's profile, the references to witchcraft sprinkled throughout the narrative, and the pointed suppression of the title in the body of the story. The story is very expressive on theses terms, but gains in power if attention is paid to its historical, cultural, and religious allusions.

Joyce's personal background and education made him deeply aware of the tragic history of Ireland, including the destruction of its ancient Celtic civilization. He was alert to elements from this national past surviving into the modern age in the language, songs, and folklore of the ordinary people. He was also thoroughly conversant with the teachings, history, and rituals of the Catholic Church. A reader sensitive to these various influences will derive a more complex pleasure from "Clay," because it is situated at precisely that time in the Celtic calendar when the normal laws of nature are suspended, when past and future are indistinguishable, and when the dead pay a visit on their living relatives. The Christianization of these traditions, Ireland's subsequent conquest by the English, and the inertia that Joyce observed in the Dublin of his time are all recurring themes in Joyce's fiction. In this particular case, he is able to exploit the rich fictional possibilities afforded a Halloween story about a poor, pious, disappointed spinster whose profile is like Ireland's battered western coastline. "Clay" is scrupulously accurate in respect to all "objective" details while at the same time resonating with echoes from ancient and popular culture. Joyce's integration of these realistic, psychological, and symbolic themes is masterful.

Cóilín Owens

A CLEAN, WELL-LIGHTED PLACE

Author: Ernest Hemingway (1899-1961)
Type of plot: Naturalism
Time of plot: The 1930's
Locale: Spain
First published: 1933

> *Principal characters:*
> AN OLDER WAITER and
> A YOUNGER WAITER, workers in a Spanish café
> AN OLD MAN, their customer

The Story

Two waiters in a Spanish café are waiting late one night for their last customer, an old man, to leave. As they wait, they talk about the old man's recent suicide attempt. The younger waiter is impatient to leave and tells the deaf old man he wishes the suicide attempt had been successful. The young waiter has a wife waiting in bed for him and is unsympathetic when the older waiter says that the old man once also had a wife. The old man finally leaves when the younger waiter refuses to serve him further.

The older waiter argues that they should have allowed their customer to stay, that being in the café is not the same as drinking at home. He explains that he is also one of those "who like to stay late at the café. . . . With all those who do not want to go to bed. With all those who need a light for the night." He is reluctant to close, since there may be someone who needs the café. When the young waiter says there are bodegas open all night, the other points out that the bright atmosphere of the café makes it different.

After the younger waiter goes home, the older one asks himself why he needs a clean, pleasant, quiet, well-lighted place. The answer is that he requires some such semblance of order because of "a nothing that he knew too well." He begins a mocking prayer: "Our nada who art in nada, nada be thy name thy kingdom nada thy will be nada in nada as it is in nada." He then finds himself at a bodega which is a poor substitute for a clean, well-lighted café. He goes home to lie awake until daylight may finally bring him some sleep: "After all, he said to himself, it is probably only insomnia. Many must have it."

Themes and Meanings

One of Hemingway's shortest stories, "A Clean, Well-Lighted Place" has been the subject of considerable critical analysis, much of it focusing on the significance of *nada*, or nothingness. This concept of *nada* is clearly central to Hemingway's worldview; characters obsessed by death, by the apparent meaninglessness of life, appear throughout his fiction. In a century in which religion, politics, and various philosophical stances have failed for so many, modern life has devolved into spiritual emptiness and moral anarchy. *Nada* in "A Clean, Well-Lighted Place" becomes a metaphor for this modern chaos; the older waiter's nothing represents an absence of light—including that word's associations with reason and belief—of order, of meaning.

What is important for a Hemingway character, however, is how to respond to this seemingly meaningless universe. Hemingway dramatizes this dilemma through contrasting the two waiters; as the older one explains, "We are of two different kinds." The young waiter is selfish and cynical, lacking in empathy, inexperienced at life without realizing it. "I have confidence. I am all confidence," he tells the older waiter. He is like many young people who think that they and their world are as they should be and will always be the same. The older waiter responds ironically, "You have youth, confidence, and a job. . . . You have everything." This "everything" will last only until experience, as it must, teaches the young waiter about life's disappointments, about the chaos that youthful confidence now allows him to ignore.

The older waiter is one of the initiated, one who understands the true nature of the world, who clearly sees the distinction between cafés and bodegas, between day and night, between values as they should be and harsh reality. He represents the so-called Hemingway code, which can be seen as a humanistic, as opposed to theological, effort to create a dimension of meaning. The Hemingway code character recognizes the seeming futility of man's headlong rush toward death and, instead of despairing, attempts to create what meanings or values he can, as with the hero's "separate peace" in *A Farewell to Arms* (1929). Thus, the older waiter wants to keep the café open, since someone like the old man, like the waiter himself—someone bruised by the dark, disordered world—may need it.

The café, rather than *nada*, becomes the most important symbol in the story since it represents a kind of hope, pathetic though it may be. The old man's despair at home leads him to try to hang himself; in the café he can drink his brandy with dignity. The older waiter recognizes this dignity: "This old man is clean. He drinks without spilling. Even now, drunk." (The young waiter spills the brandy he pours for the old man.) The café is a place where those without the innocence of youth, the illusions of belief, can pass the time with dignity. It is a refuge from meaninglessness but only a refuge, not an escape. The café must eventually close; all must go home. The older waiter finds the bodega to which he wanders "very bright and pleasant," but the bar is unpolished. It is a temporary substitute for the café just as the café is a temporary respite from the chaos of the dark world outside.

"A Clean, Well-Lighted Place" dramatizes modern man's quest for dignity amid the destruction of the old values. The individual needs to escape his responsibilities while realizing that this escape is but momentary. The individual's responsibility to himself is to find a clean, well-lighted place or create one of his own. The ironic paradox of the story is that meaning can be created only through an awareness of its absence.

Style and Technique

"A Clean, Well-Lighted Place" is one of the best examples of Hemingway's distinctive style: objective point of view; short, active declarative sentences; frequent repetition of key words; heavy reliance on dialogue in which the characters speak in short, clipped sentences or fragments, an impressionistic representation of everyday speech: "This is a clean and pleasant café. It is well lighted. The light is very good and also, now, there are shadows of the leaves."

In *A Moveable Feast* (1964), Hemingway identifies one of the key elements of his technique as recognizing that what is left out of a story is just as important as what is included, as when Nick Adams' recent return from the chaos of war is not directly mentioned in "Big Two-Hearted River" (1925). This approach can be seen in "A Clean, Well-Lighted Place" in which there is no overt reference to the disappointments the young waiter will certainly experience, the nights he will not be so eager to run home to his loving wife, there is no explanation of why the old man attempts suicide, no evidence of what has specifically taught the older waiter about *nada*. Considerable dramatic tension, as well as universality, is created by revealing so little about the characters and the time and place.

A corollary to this technique is that everything in the story must be there for a reason. A brief reference early in the story to a soldier and girl, apparently a prostitute, passing by the café is significant to illustrate the younger waiter's concern only with the practical, the immediate: "He had better get off the street now. The guard will get him." The older waiter's view is more worldly: "What does it matter if he gets what he's after?" As the couple pass, "The street light shone on the brass number on his collar." By ignoring the rules, the soldier has captured a moment in the light. Ironically, he is similar to the young waiter so restless to join his wife in bed. Such economic, perfectly controlled storytelling is the epitome of Hemingway's style at its best.

Michael Adams

CLOUD, CASTLE, LAKE

Author: Vladimir Nabokov (1899-1977)
Type of plot: Fable
Time of plot: 1936 or 1937
Locale: Berlin and surrounding countryside
First published: "Oblako, ozero, bashnya," 1937 (English translation, 1941)

Principal characters:
VASILI IVANOVICH, Russian émigré, the narrator's
    "representative"
THE NARRATOR, who wrote the story
GERMAN MEMBERS OF A TOUR GROUP
THE TOUR LEADER
SCHRAMM, a "stimulator" from the Bureau of Pleasantrips

The Story

Vasili Ivanovich, a mild-mannered Russian émigré living in Berlin, wins a pleasure trip at a charity ball. Although Vasili is reluctant to travel anywhere, he finally decides to go when he discovers that getting out of the trip would involve cutting through all sorts of red tape in the bureaucracy. The tour group gathered at the railway station consists of four women and four men, each a kind of double of the other. The group leader is assisted by a sinister man called Schramm, from the Bureau of Pleasantrips. After their train departs, it soon becomes obvious that Vasili Ivanovich is the odd man out. When he attempts to read Russian lyrical poetry or observe the beauties of nature, his German companions interrupt him and force him to join them in singing uplifting songs or playing games. At first their teasing is good-natured; later, as nightfall approaches, it turns malevolent.

The group disembarks from the train and begins hiking through the countryside, eventually arriving at a blue lake with an old black castle on its far side and a beautiful cloud hanging over it. The insensitive Germans ignore the view, but Vasili is enthralled by its beauty. He sneaks away from the group, follows the shore, and comes to an inn. After the innkeeper shows him a room for rent, with a view of the cloud, castle, and lake, Vasili decides to take the room for the rest of his life. He runs joyfully down to the meadow to inform his companions. The collective of pleasure trippers, however, refuses to accept what they see as a betrayal of their common venture. Infuriated, they seize Vasili and drag him, "as in a hideous fairy tale," down a forest road to the train. On the return journey they torture him, using a corkscrew and a homemade knout. Upon his arrival back in Berlin, Vasili goes to see the narrator, his employer. He tells the story of what happened and begs to be released from his position and from humanity: "He had not the strength to belong to mankind any longer." The narrator graciously lets him go.

Themes and Meanings

As in two of Nabokov's novels, *Invitation to a Beheading* (1938) and *Bend Sinister* (1947), the main theme here is collectivist tyranny. The story illustrates how an imaginative, sensitive individual is forced to conform to the vulgar Philistinism of the unimaginative collective. Although the word "Nazi" is never mentioned, the story is obviously a condemnation of the Nazi regime under which Nabokov himself lived for a time in Berlin. It also is an implicit condemnation of collectivist oppression in the Soviet Union and of a widespread human inclination to embrace stagnant conformity and attempt to stifle creative eccentricity.

"Cloud, Castle, Lake" may also be an allegory of life, which is a sometimes unpleasant "pleasure trip" through time toward inevitable death. Before his departure, Vasili has a dim vision of some perfect, timeless world full of happiness. That world seems attainable when he comes upon "the lake with its cloud and its castle, in a motionless and perfect correlation of happiness." Here, so he senses, he can stop time, abandon the "pleasure trip" of life, and enter into the realm of motionless serenity. As he is soon horrified to discover, however, one is not allowed to abandon the journey. Furthermore, nothing really is motionless; even beautiful nature is constantly changing. The ideal of static serenity, for which Vasili yearns, does not exist on earth.

A strange twist in the final paragraph illustrates why Nabokov's works cannot be read as realistic fiction. The disillusioned Vasili visits his maker, the writer, and asks to resign from mankind. Although he has just learned that life does not accept such resignations, the writer grants him that release without demur. Note that in the first line of the story the narrator terms Vasili "one of my representatives." Throughout the world of his fiction, Nabokov uses the words "representative" and "agent" to refer to imaginary personages or alter egos that he creates to perform any number of functions in his works. In addition to serving as the protagonist of this story, Vasili Ivanovich appears to work for his creator as a collector of fine detail from nature, to be used by the writer in his fiction. See, for example, the passage in which "his precious, experienced eyes noted what was necessary," followed by a lovely description of a dry needle hanging in a fir grove. Furthermore, in many of his works Nabokov, or the narrator who writes in his name, plays the role of benevolent god of the fiction, mercifully releasing tormented characters. Each of the two novels that have the closest affinities with "Cloud, Castle, Lake" (*Invitation to a Beheading* and *Bend Sinister*) ends with a similar sort of release. It is as if the writer were saying, "Yes, in real life there is no escape from time and human cruelty, but since I am inventing all of this, I

can let poor Vasili go." What happens, however, to a fictional character after
he is released from his role as a human being? The disintegration of his personality amounts to an escape resembling death. Is the writer who "releases"
Vasili really so benevolent after all? Complex philosophical questions are
raised when Nabokov openly treats his characters as fictive rather than
pretending, as do most writers, that they are real human beings.

Style and Technique

The story's most obvious message, a condemnation of collectivist tyranny,
is subtly convincing because the author distances himself from the brutality
rather than blatantly condemning it. He describes it in matter-of-fact tones
and even tempers it with humor. One cannot help laughing when Vasili loses
the nonsensical game on the train and is forced to eat a cigarette butt as punishment. The genuine horror of his situation is epitomized by the black humor in the description of how he is beaten: "The post-office clerk, who had
been to Russia, fashioned a knout out of a stick and a belt, and began to use
it with devilish dexterity. Atta boy! . . . All had a wonderful time." Here the
irony is obvious. When used in descriptions of brutal events, humor intensifies the shock effect on the reader and makes the horror even more palpable.

Descriptions of nature also play an important stylistic role throughout the
story, contrasting the beauty of mans' surroundings with the beastliness of his
life. In this tale about human inhumanity, it is significant that only the beautiful nature Vasili loves seems to have any sympathy for him in his plight. As
the Germans are dragging him back through the forest to the train, "the dark
firs fretted but could not interfere."

The overriding theme of most of Nabokov's works is the artistic process
itself, and "Cloud, Castle, Lake" is no exception. The narrator of the story is
a central character, and the most interesting stylistic features involve the way
he insinuates himself into the action as he tells it. The reader is shocked (or
should be) from the story's beginning, when he learns that the narrator is not
even sure of his character's name: "I cannot remember his name at the moment. I think it was Vasili Ivanovich." Later, the narrator blends with his
character ("We both, Vasili Ivanovich and I, have always been impressed by
the anonymity of all parts of a landscape"), and thenceforth descriptions of
nature suggest the enthusiasms of the writer as well as those of the character.
Three times, exuberant lyrical passages end with the words "my love," obviously the narrator's words, not Vasili's. To whom do they refer? Probably to
the muse of the writer, the great love of his life, his art. The most exalted of
these invocations of the muse ("my love! My obedient one!") comes amid the
description of the harmonious beauty of the cloud, castle, and lake.

These subtleties of style suggest that the story may involve the narrator's
search for ideal beauty and serenity as much as Vasili's. Unlike his character,
however, the writer is attempting to transcend mundane vulgarity by creating

a lyrical world in beautiful words. He yearns to merge with his muse: "if one could stop the train and go thither, forever, to you, my love." When he describes the castle as "arising from dactyl to dactyl," the meter of the passage is dactylic, as is the meter of the original Russian title: "Oblako, ozero, bashnja." This use of metrical terminology and meter implies that the story is a castle built of poetry, epitomizing the joy that a writer takes in creating a work of art.

In the end, the narrator may think that his art has transformed a "hideous fairy tale" into a thing of beauty, but does the fanciful edifice he has built in his mind really provide the transcendence of vicious reality that Vasili sought at the inn on the lake? Is the joy that the artist takes in his creation even somehow reprehensible in the light of the tale's context of horrible human suffering? In a word, is the ideal of art simply another illusion, a sophistry? These are the questions that Nabokov raises in nearly all of his works. They are not easily answered.

Robert L. Bowie

THE COLLECTOR OF TREASURES

Author: Bessie Head (1937-   )
Type of plot: Social realism
Time of plot: 1966-1975
Locale: The villages of Puleng and Gaborone, in Botswana
First published: 1977

> *Principal characters:*
> DIKELEDI MOKOPI, the protagonist, who murders her husband
> GARESEGO, her husband, the antagonist, an administrative
>   clerk
> BANABOTHE, their eldest son
> PAUL THEBOLO, the principal of the Puleng primary school
> KENALEPE, the wife of Paul Thebolo and Dikeledi's first
>   genuine friend

The Story

Bessie Head's vignette of a village woman abandoned and abused by her husband begins *in medias res*. In the first of the story's four sections, Dikeledi is on her way to prison in Gaborone, the country's new capital city, from her village, Puleng. She gazes indifferently at the passing landscape of the bush as she rides in the police truck. As a result of the long day's lonely journey and her emotional turmoil, she finally collapses, "oblivious to everything but her pain." Upon her arrival at the prison that night, she is stirred to consciousness by the police, who dutifully record her crime, "man-slaughter," and her life sentence. As Dikeledi is led to her barren cell, the wardress remarks sarcastically that she will be the fifth woman currently in the prison to have been sentenced for the same offense, murdering her husband, and notes that the crime is "becoming the fashion these days." Having been locked up, Dikeledi is left to her own silence in the dark cell.

Upon rising early the next morning, the other four women—Kebonye, Otsetswe, Galeboe, and Monwana—introduce themselves. Kebonye asks Dikeledi why her parents have named her *tears*, and she replies that it was after her mother, who died when Dikeledi was six years old, her father having died in the year of her birth. In the ensuing conversation, Dikeledi expresses little sorrow for her crime, which was murder by castration. As the women begin their work in the prison, they observe that Dikeledi's "hands of strange power" are especially skillful with sewing, knitting, and weaving. She has, in fact, reared her three children largely through her own efforts, because her husband abandoned her after four years of marriage. After the day passes in intimate disclosure among the five women, the third-person, omniscient narrator describes Dikeledi's newfound friendships as "gold amidst the ash, deep loves that had joined her heart to the hearts of others." In this "phase three of a life that had been ashen in its loneliness and unhappiness," Dikeledi accepts the tender compassion possible in friendship: "She was the collector of such treasures."

Having established the protagonist's complexity of character, yet with-holding the comprehension of it from the reader, the narrator begins the second section with a digression on the "two kinds of men in the society." With cultural background analyzing the evolution of the type of man who bears no responsibility for his family or for his community, Garesego is introduced as the model of the man who is "a broken wreck with no inner resources at all." For Garesego, national independence has brought a two-hundred-percent increase in salary that permits him to engage "in a dizzy kind of death dance of wild destruction and dissipation." He leaves his wife and three sons in favor of drinking and prostitutes. Ironically, he does so in the same year, 1966, of Botswana's independence. Against Garesego, the narrator sets the second type of man, modeled by Paul Thebolo. He devotes himself entirely to his family's stability and to the community's well-being. Not only is he principal of the primary school, but also he is the epitome of the caring neighbor. Further, he is an example of leadership, moderating discussions of politics and assisting the villagers whenever they require his skills in literacy. His inner resources give him "the power to create himself anew."

Dikeledi meets Paul when he arrives in Puleng to build his house. She, re-nowned for her ability to thatch a roof, offers to assist in setting up the household. Not long after, his wife, Kenalepe Thebolo, arrives; the two women develop an intimate, enduring friendship. Because of the Thebolos' reputation, Dikeledi's dressmaking business begins to boom. Throughout the next eight years, the friendship deepens. By virtue of her craft skills, Dikeledi becomes nearly self-sufficient. Kenalepe even offers to "loan" her husband to Dikeledi in order to share the joy of sexuality, which she has renounced, never having experienced sexual pleasure with Garesego. Dikeledi refuses Kenalepe's offer, but when Kenalepe is hospitalized after a miscarriage, Dikeledi cares for her children and household. As she cleans the kitchen hut one night while Paul is visiting his wife, he returns to find her hard at work, and they share a moment of intimacy, one that does not rest on a sexual perception of each other: "it was too beautiful to be love." Such an affirmation that a man can possess goodness yields one more "nugget of gold" for Dikeledi. This second phase of her life has led to a sense of hope and joy in her independence and friendship.

During the developing intimacy with Kenalepe and Paul, Dikeledi con-fides much of her past. In reply to Kenalepe's question of why she married Garesego in the first place, Dikeledi explains that, having been orphaned at six, she was reared by an uncle, who regarded her as a servant; even her cousins thought of her as their servant. Consequently, she was forced to leave school early, and she was never included or loved as a member of the family.

When Garesego proposed through her uncle, Dikeledi married him to escape the bondage of her uncle's family. While this first phase of Dikeledi's life continued, she tolerated Garesego's irresponsibility, drunkenness, and unfaithfulness, nurturing a fragile pride based on his claim to prefer her for her traditional values and an uncertain hope for love within a family of her own. Garesego, however, regarded traditional women as primarily servants; thus, he abandoned her and the children altogether as soon as his postindependence promotion made it financially feasible.

Dikeledi's crisis comes when she learns that her eldest son, Banabothe, has been accepted for secondary school. Remembering the disruption in her own education and having witnessed Banabothe's dedication to his studies, she is distraught to learn that she has not saved enough money to pay all of Banabothe's fees and still pay the primary school fees for her two younger sons. Out of a desperate refusal to interrupt the education of one son, Dikeledi decides to seek Garesego's help to pay the fees for all of them; they are his sons, too. When she approaches him as he leaves his office, she is shocked not so much at his hesitation as at his accusation that she is the mistress of Paul, who, Garesego argues, should bear the cost of the fees. Paul, later hearing of the slander against himself, confronts Garesego; after an exchange of insults, Paul punches Garesego, giving him cause for further slander. He tells the villagers that his "wife's lover" did it. They in turn spread the gossip about the man who many consider "too good to be true," but they also criticize Garesego for failing in his duty to Banabothe.

To save face with the village and to provoke Dikeledi, Garesego sends a note to her, announcing that he will return home and requesting that she prepare a meal and a bath for him. Despite his stated intention for a reconciliation, Dikeledi knows that he is coming home to demand sex in exchange for even considering the partial payment of the fees; she agrees to the visit, and she begins her extensive preparations—including the sharpening of "a large kitchen knife used to cut meat." When Garesego arrives that evening, he responds to her with callous indifference and ignores his children, further convincing Dikeledi of the righteousness of her plan.

After drinking beer and feasting, Garesego believes that he has won his claim to his wife over Paul, because he does not see him next door. He dismisses Dikeledi's request about the fees without a firm commitment. While she bathes him, he drifts naked into a smug, self-satisfied sleep. Dikeledi leaves him, kisses her children goodnight, and, in a detached trance, unconsciously attempts to wake him with the noise of her clean-up. When he sleeps on, "lost to the world," she kneels by the bed, removes the knife from where she had hidden it, and castrates him in a single stroke. Garesego's bellowing as he bleeds to death brings Banabothe, who is sent to summon the police, and Kenalepe, who flees in terror. Paul, too, arrives and, after staring dumbfoundedly at Dikeledi, promises to rear and to educate her sons.

Themes and Meanings

Bessie Head's brutal, despairing tragedy of contemporary village life in postindependent Africa grounds itself clearly in the historical and cultural background of the story. Aware of a non-African audience, she offers at once a scathing condemnation of masculine dominance and an affirming challenge to local leadership. The three phases of Dikeledi's life parallel Head's analysis of the evolution of Bamangwato society. In tracing the three periods of moral decay, she notes that while traditional laws may have provided discipline for society as a whole, they failed to acknowledge the individual's needs; further, traditional society doubly compounded the error for women, regarding them as inferior to the male. In the second period, colonialism, migratory labor patterns to South African mines further eroded traditional family life. Men were forced to be absent from their families for long periods of time in order to earn enough to pay the British poll tax. With men demeaned by their racially inferior status under colonialism, the third period, independence, presented the challenge for a new order of family life, but both men and women, suffering from legacies of simplistic traditional custom and of colonial degradation, had little more than their own inner stamina to draw upon in shaping that necessarily new order.

In *Serowe: Village of the Rain-Wind* (1981), Head describes two additional factors in the story's central theme: "the complete breakdown of family life." Head claims that "of every one hundred children born in Serowe, three on the average are legitimate." This widespread anonymity and, subsequently, irresponsibility of fathers results from erosion in traditional customs of polygamy and *bogadi*, "the bride price or the offering of a gift of cattle by a man to his wife's family at the time of marriage." Without polygamy, women are no longer assured a husband (provider); without *bogadi*, there is no guarantee of legitimacy for her children. Head, however, does not advocate a return to these practices, charging that polygamy promoted "jealousy and strife" while *bogadi* had "undertones of a sale-bargain" in which "women were merely a marketable commodity." Rather, she argues through her fiction, the inner resources necessary to reverse the family's collapse are the treasures of compassion.

"The Collector of Treasures," then, provides a study in the origins of postindependent family misery and contrasts two divergent responses to the family's collapse. The Mokopi marriage models the plunge into an ever-increasing despair, while the Thebolo marriage provides the creative challenge. Garesego's moral decay, not exclusively of his own making, is obvious; Paul's ability to act out of integrity and dignity in order to shape self-respect in the village family is equally obvious. The story is, in fact, a polemical challenge to the new African male: He must act with traditional respect for the community but do so in the modern context of individuality which confronts him.

Style and Technique

Blending polemic, history, and anthropology without compromising aesthetic merit tests the skill of any writer. Bessie Head's achievement is that she can address African readers while informing her audience abroad. Although origins of eroding family life in this story are specific to Botswana, the threat of materialistic moral decay to modern families is universal. By beginning her story with Dikeledi's affirmation of love and intimacy, she involves her readers in a complex character, yet the detached narrative voice withholds judgment of the character for her crime. As one questions Dikeledi's motives, the narrative flashback unfolds not only her background but also the complexity of Kenalepe, Garesego, and Paul, who all sustain the developing characterization and provide parallels and contrasts.

Simple, direct imagery plays an important part in the story, from the title motif of fellow feeling as a kind of "treasure" to the animal images used to describe Garesego. While Head employs dialogue sparingly, she does so effectively. Her characters speak openly and directly to one another, embodying the intimacy achieved first among the prisoners and later in the friendship between Dikeledi and Kenalepe; the authenticity of human compassion and its power to create new stability in the family and community are thus affirmed. Ironically, Dikeledi creates a new order of stability that excludes the very society which sentenced her; symbolically, she finds her deepest freedom in prison.

Michael Loudon

COLOR OF DARKNESS

Author: James Purdy (1923-   )
Type of plot: Psychological realism
Time of plot: 1956
Locale: United States
First published: 1957

> *Principal characters:*
> THE FATHER, twenty-eight years old, a success
> BAXTER, his young son
> MRS. ZILKE, a housekeeper, past middle age

The Story

The father in "Color of Darkness" is disconcerted because he cannot remember the color of his wife's eyes. She left him and their son, Baxter, some years back, and her features have almost entirely slipped from his memory. Eager for his father's attention, the child stays as close to him as possible and attempts to draw him into conversation. The father's work requires that he be absent most of the time; even when at home, however, he seems to be psychologically absent. The housekeeper, Mrs. Zilke, is not an adequate replacement for Baxter's mother; indeed, she is more a mother figure for the father than for his son. To the father, Mrs. Zilke appears as a repository of wisdom, as someone secure in her relationship to the world about her, as someone for whom the world was "round, firm, and perfectly illuminated," as it was not for him. His world is as amorphous, unstable, and hazy as the pipe smoke that swirls around his head. His inability to remember the color of his wife's eyes reflects not only his lack of connection with her, but also his inability to achieve any vital emotional connection with anybody. He soon realizes that he cannot remember the color of Baxter's eyes, either.

When Mrs. Zilke tells the father that Baxter is lonely, he confides to Mrs. Zilke that he does not know children, that he does not know what they know, so he does not know how to talk to them. She reassures him that since he is a success at work, it is not necessary that he worry about anything else. In effect, Mrs. Zilke mouths the platitudes of society which endorse the public life at the expense of the private or personal life. As a token of his appreciation of her support, he invites her to join him in a glass of brandy. This symbol of communal understanding fails, however, as she does not drink. When he closes his eyes, he realizes that he does not remember the color of her eyes, either.

One night, the father becomes uncomfortable when he discovers that Baxter sometimes sleeps with a stuffed crocodile; consequently, he readily agrees when Mrs. Zilke suggests that Baxter needs a dog. Baxter does not take to the puppy; he especially does not want to sleep with it, for he needs a father, not a dog. Baxter has become to the father like "a gift someone has awarded him," rather than as someone intimately connected with his own being. In addition, "as the gift increased in value and liability, his own relation to it was more and more ambiguous and obscure."

Baxter tries to find a connection between himself and his father by asking him whether he had a dog when he was young, but the father's responses are, as usual, vacuous. In response to his father's absentmindedness, the boy begins to retreat into himself, declaring that he does not want anything. Noticing that Baxter has something in his mouth, Mrs. Zilke and the father demand to know what it is. For the first time Baxter allows himself to feel resentment toward them, and defiantly lies about the object and refuses to spit it out. When the father touches Baxter in his attempt to remove the object, Baxter declares that he hates him and swears at him. The object the father forces from his son's mouth turns out to be the wedding ring the father took off his finger the previous night for the first time since his marriage. As they stare at the ring, Baxter sharply kicks his father in the groin, and runs upstairs, calling him an obscenity connected to his conception. The story ends with the father refusing Mrs. Zilke's offer of help as he writhes on the floor in pain.

Themes and Meanings

The primary theme of "Color of Darkness" is the central theme of Purdy's work: the pain that comes to human beings through their failure to bridge the gaps between individuals, a failure deriving from man's tendency to transform his existential experience into abstractions. The information that Baxter is lonely leads to the father's generalization that commitment to work precludes any commitment to people. All the generalizing discussion between the father and Mrs. Zilke results in this abstracting of experience. The father's concern about what Baxter knows becomes the abstraction that children know everything. Mrs. Zilke's comment about the bouquet of the brandy leads to his assertion that she knows everything. This tendency to generalize creates a barrier between the self and the immediate. Baxter complains that his father is always thinking about something other than the immediate or looking as if he "didn't know anything." The inability to remember the color of people's eyes reveals his inability to know the particular or the specific.

This failure to know specifics translates into failure to commit himself to people or to empathize with anyone, even his son. He knows intellectually that Baxter is lonely, he even feels guilty about not fulfilling Baxter's need for a closer emotional relationship with a father, but all he is able to do in response is to buy him a dog.

Baxter reacts to the pain that comes from his father's abstractedness in two ways: He inflicts pain on his father by kicking him and he retreats into abstraction himself. The kick is Baxter's last attempt to make his presence real to his father. Baxter has learned that to be aware is to be aware of pain; the father, writhing in pain on the floor, is at last sharing Baxter's world. In refusing the puppy, Baxter generalizes that he does not want anything. His father's use of the word "son" makes Baxter feel nauseous; the obscenity he calls his father reduces the father to an abstraction, just as the father's use of "son" has made Baxter feel that he is merely an abstraction.

Style and Technique

Purdy achieves much of the intensity of his story through the contrast between the inertness of the generalizations spoken by the characters and the vitality of his symbols. The abstract assertions of both Mrs. Zilke and the father are the deadest of social clichés, meaningless abstractions: "You know everything," "As long as a parent is living, any parent, a child has something." Every conversation degenerates into such meaningless, trite, vague nonstatements with the repetition of highly abstract nouns such as "something," "everything," "thing," or equally vaporous verbs such as "know" or "seems." Such generalizing vitiates all of their perceptions.

The images, on the other hand, accrue meaning or significance as Purdy either directly associates them with characteristics of his characters or takes images with strong traditional meanings and gives them deliberate twists. The pipe smoke of the father and the cigarette smoke of Mrs. Zilke, which are examples of the first use of symbols, represent the amorphous deadness of their thoughts and feelings expressed in the equally dead words that issue from their mouths. As the smoke obscures their faces, so their words obscure reality by acting as a screen between themselves and their feelings as well as the world about them. The image of the title is symbolic in the same way. The color of darkness is a noncolor or the most abstract of colors. It represents the opposite of the particular blue of Baxter's eyes, which stand for phenomenological specifics. The color of darkness, then, is the color of abstraction.

As the phrase "color of darkness" contains within itself its own negation, so many of Purdy's major images have their traditional meanings reversed by the context of the story. The symbolic significance of the brandy, which traditionally would serve to suggest sharing, is reversed. The adults discuss the look, the smell, and the taste of it, sharing their experience of it, but as usual, the discussion becomes generalized in the extreme. Finally, Mrs. Zilke does not drink it. There is no real bond among these people; the bond of abstraction can be no more real than the color of darkness. The dog bought to replace the crocodile wets on the floor, bites Baxter, and leads to Baxter's attack on his father. In like manner, the wedding ring, a traditional symbol of the communion between people, becomes a symbol of the absence of any communion. These images of the denial of communion culminate in that of the father crying in pain after refusing Mrs. Zilke's offer of help: an image that expresses the theme of the story in uniting the specific with the abstract. Baxter's kick has penetrated the father's shell of abstraction, making him feel the pain of being alive.

William J. McDonald

COMING, APHRODITE

Author: Willa Cather (1873-1947)
Type of plot: Psychological realism
Time of plot: Early twentieth century
Locale: New York City
First published: 1920

> *Principal characters:*
> DON HEDGER, a young artist
> CAESAR III, Hedger's dog
> EDEN BOWER, an aspiring singer

The Story

Don Hedger, a talented young painter who lives in a dingy top-floor apartment in Washington Square, leads a solitary life of dedication to his art. His only close companion is his dog, Caesar, a fierce English bulldog whose character mirrors that of his owner in many ways, and who also is the self-appointed protector of Hedger's privacy. Although he is far from rich, Hedger is successful by his own standards; indeed, when, as has happened on several occasions previously, he is on the verge of commercial success, he deliberately refuses to pursue this success.

Into this ascetic way of life comes Eden Bower, who moves into the apartment next to Hedger's. Eden, a beautiful and ambitious young girl from the West, plans to study singing in Paris. Hedger hears her singing but soon forgets about her, as he forgets everything when absorbed in his painting. When they do meet, however, he is overwhelmed by her beauty. Some time later, as Hedger is rummaging through his closet, he discovers a knothole in the wall which allows him to see into Eden's apartment. In the middle of a sun-drenched room, Eden stands naked, engaged in a series of gymnastic exercises. Hedger watches, enthralled. The richly suggestive imagery evokes a sense of Eden's beauty and energy, and appears to confer upon her the status of a divine being. Hedger views her with the eyes of an artist, but as he continues to gaze raptly at the shower of golden sun pouring in through the windows after Eden has finished her exercises, the echoes of the story of Zeus impregnating Danae in a shower of gold not only add to the mythological overtones but also give a strong sexual suggestiveness to the entire scene.

Hedger becomes obsessed by Eden and is no longer able to paint. The two become friends, and one day she agrees to accompany him on an expedition to Coney Island, where they observe a friend of Don executing the daring feat of ascending in a balloon. Eden is so enthralled by this sight that, unknown to Don, she arranges to go up in the balloon herself. Furious at Eden for taking such a foolish risk, Don is moved against his will by the beautiful sight as she descends from the sky like a "slowly falling silver star."

Eden's daring has charged the air with sexual excitement for both of them, and over dinner that evening Hedger tells her an ancient Aztec story called "The Forty Lovers of the Queen." This queen has been dedicated to the gods from early childhood, and taught the mysteries of rainmaking. Her chief qualities are her voracious sexuality and her miraculous ability to bring fertility to the land. This power endures until she tries to save the life of one of her lovers, thus violating the unspoken law that such lovers must die after having sexual relations with her. She is put to death and a drought follows. This extraordinary and powerful myth has clear symbolic connections with the story of Eden and Don. The woman, like Eden, is seen as having divine powers; her sexuality has a primeval quality which transcends the personal. That night, Eden and Don become lovers. As they embrace for the first time, they are "two figures, one white and one dark, and nothing whatever distinguishable about them but that they were male and female."

Inevitably, the relationship breaks down when Eden tries to help Don get ahead. She enlists the assistance of Burton Ives, a successful artist whose department-store conception of art Hedger loathes. Desperately hurt by the revelation that Eden has no understanding of his idea of art, Hedger takes a train to Long Beach and stays away for several days. He returns, however, because Eden "was older than art," but she has left for Paris with the Chicago millionaire who is financing her studies. Thus, Hedger is left, saddened and lonely, in the knowledge that the rest of his life will be spent in solitary dedication to his painting.

Twenty years pass, and Eden returns from Paris, where she has become a famous opera singer. "Coming, Aphrodite," the legend which announces her name in lights at the opera house, refers both to the opera in which she will perform and, once again, to her association with the goddess of love. Curious to know what has become of Don Hedger, she asks an art dealer of her acquaintance about him. She learns that he enjoys a considerable reputation but has never become commercially successful. The story concludes with an image of her face, hard and settled in the glow of an ugly orange light. The contrast with Hedger is clear. Eden has succeeded in getting everything she wants, and has led a very exciting life in conventional terms. Moreover, when she sings, she has the capacity to become the divine Aphrodite, in the eyes of her audience at least. Yet, as Cather has commented earlier, Hedger "has had more tempestuous adventures sitting in his dark studio than she would have in all the capitals of Europe." Eden's art as well as her life are empty by comparison with Hedger's.

Themes and Meanings

Through the two central characters of this story, Cather asks the question of what it means to be an artist, and she examines the dangers which lie in wait for those who have chosen to follow this path. Both Don Hedger and

Eden Bower are artist figures, but whereas Hedger understands the real nature of art and remains true to his ideals, Eden, although gifted, chooses commercial success and does not understand that there can be a difference between being a good artist and achieving material success. The title of the collection in which the story first appeared, *Youth and the Bright Medusa* (1920), indicates Cather's continuing obsession with this theme. Although the indifference of society can harm the artist, the bright Medusa of success can also lure him to his downfall. Hedger realizes that in order to achieve success by his own definition, he must remain always open to new ideas and always ready to discard what is old or outworn, even though it may be what the public wants.

Cather also explores the artist's encounter with elemental beauty and sexuality in the form of a woman. The mythological resonance of the story of the Aztec queen, with its emphasis on a primitive sexuality stripped of all the superficialities of civilization, lends power and dignity to the love affair between the young couple. Yet solitude must be the way for Hedger in the end: The true artist must place his art above everything else. Although it is Eden who literally leaves Hedger behind, in her zeal to get ahead, the implication is that the permanency of human relationships is not permitted to the artist. Unlike the Aztec queen who tries to save her lover and dies, bringing about drought, Hedger remains alone but also remains an artist.

Style and Technique

There are a number of recurrent image patterns in the story which underline its themes and meanings. Romantic images of light and beauty are associated with Eden. The sun, the moon, and the stars are all connected with her, and her apartment is airy and full of light. Hedger, by contrast, is seen in terms of images of darkness. His apartment is dark and dingy and his desperate attempts to clean it up after he has met Eden are to no avail. He is also seen as living in a kind of fish tank, suggestive of the artist's necessary isolation from the more active pursuits of life. Animal images add to this idea of isolation: Hedger is compared to a wolf, and also to his dog Caesar.

The mythic dimension of the story is another significant aspect of Cather's technique. As a kind of modern-day Venus, Eden Bower takes on an allegorical dimension, yet there are many ambiguities in this view of her. On one level, she transcends the triviality of her own individual nature and is certainly viewed with sympathy and even admiration by Cather. Similarly, Cather can mock Hedger because of his lack of interest in worldly things. Yet Hedger remains the type of the true artist, while Eden, possessing both artistic talent and a powerful, almost superhuman, beauty which connects her to the world of myth, is perhaps not really an artist at all by Cather's definition.

Anne Thompson Lee

CONSOLATION

Author: Giovanni Verga (1840-1922)
Type of plot: Social realism (*verismo*)
Time of plot: c. 1880
Locale: Milan, Italy
First published: "Conforti," 1883 (English translation, 1958)

> *Principal characters:*
> ARLÌA, the protagonist, a hairdresser
> MANICA, her husband, a barber
> FATHER CALOGERO, her uncle, a parish rector
> FORTUNATA, the daughter of Arlìa and Manica
> ANGIOLINO, Fortunata's brother
> SILVIO LIOTTI, Fortunata's lover and, later, her husband
> A FORTUNETELLER

The Story

A healthy young couple, a barber named Manica and a hairdresser named Arlìa, marry, in spite of the misgivings of Arlìa's uncle, Father Calogero, who knows that tuberculosis runs in their family. He had become a parish priest, thereby keeping moderately healthy and avoiding many of the troubles that beset the urban poor.

Each year, Arlìa becomes pregnant, affecting adversely her work; Manica, too, is unsuccessful financially as a barber. Child after child dies of tuberculosis; the costs of medicine, special broths and food, and burial expenses offset any economic gains of the working couple.

One of the boys is named Angiolino; he is bitter at having been born, when facing death. Arlìa seeks help for the child from the Church, through prayer and a mass, though Manica is cynical. Finally Arlìa has recourse to a woman who tells fortunes from the whites of eggs. She has been told that a countess who had wanted to have her hair cut because of unhappiness in love had found consolation from the fortuneteller. The fortuneteller tells Arlìa that she will be happy, but that she will have troubles first. Her uncle believes that the prophecy is a Satanic fraud, but Arlìa's despair is overcome temporarily by the hope that Angiolino will recover. The child grows worse, however, and Father Calogero offers to pay for his funeral. Still, Arlìa persists in her faith in the prophecy and pities Manica for his lack of belief. Her hope is finally dashed by the death of the boy. Filled with despair, she wonders what the fortuneteller's promise could have meant.

The suffering causes Manica to turn to drink; Arlìa persists in her trust in the prophecy. A daughter, Fortunata, is the only child who survives. The family's economic situation becomes worse, debts pile up, and customers desert Arlìa and Manica. Arlìa seeks reassurance from her daughter that the prophecy of the fortuneteller will come true, but Fortunata is interested in a young man, a clerk named Silvio Liotti.

When questioned by her mother, Fortunata says that she does not want to die like her brothers; the neighbors and the girl's father warn the mother to be careful about her daughter's relationship with Silvio. Finally, Fortunata confesses to her mother that she has been seduced by Silvio.

Through an intermediary to Father Calogero, Silvio learns that Manica cannot afford a dowry for his daughter; thus, any marriage seems impossible. Fortunata begins to show signs of developing tuberculosis, as well as a tendency toward suicide, so that Arlìa fears that she will lose her daughter also and that Manica will learn about Fortunata's affair. Arlìa finds solace in the prophecy and turns to gambling, buying lottery tickets each week, as a key to financial success, and to her daughter's health and happiness. One day, Manica, looking for money with which to pay for liquor at the tavern, finds some of the lottery tickets and becomes angry. Arlìa explains that they must allow good luck to come to them. He demands money from her and later returns drunk from the tavern.

Fortunata, however, finds no consolation. Arlìa continues to be certain of their future happiness; they invite Father Calogero to a fine meal at their home on Christmas Day. He becomes touched by their problems and arranges for a dowry for Fortunata, making possible her marriage to Silvio.

The marriage does not work out well; Silvio spends the dowry and beats Fortunata. Each year, as her mother had before her, she gives birth to a child. Her children are healthy and have huge appetites, putting a strain on family finances. Arlìa is forced to continue to work in her old age, running errands for shopkeepers. Manica, too, continues to work each Saturday at his trade, spending the remainder of the week at home or in the tavern. Arlìa now spends the lottery-ticket money for brandy, deriving a measure of consolation from her secret drinking.

Themes and Meanings

"Consolation" is the English translation of the Italian title, which literally means "comforts." A key to the meaning of the story is immediately provided in the opening words, which announce the prophecy of the fortuneteller that Arlìa will be happy after passing through hardships and troubles. The theme of the story is how this illusory hope permits a poor woman, representative of Milan's urban poor, to survive and to find partial, temporary consolation amid the suffering.

Father Calogero expresses well the situation facing Arlìa and her family and, by extension, all the urban poor: "The world is full of troubles. It's best to keep away from it." This formula for surviving in a hostile world seems to work well for Calogero, who has "purposely become a priest so that he wouldn't have to listen to the troubles of the world." He has managed "to put a little fat on himself," as well as having the money to pay for little Angiolino's funeral and Fortunata's dowry.

The other characters seem, to be facing a life that seems to contain nothing more than hunger, fatigue, illness, and early death. Whatever progress is made is eaten up by the ills of life. The children, before dying, "gobbled up the small profit of the year," the son-in-law Silvio "ate up his wife's dowry." Even Fortunata's healthy babies eat "like horses," bringing more trouble to their overworked grandparents.

The answering refrain to Calogero's formula for survival comes from the fortuneteller: "You will be happy, but first you'll have troubles," or, as Arlìa interprets it, "We have to leave the door open to luck." Arlìa, until the end, believes and hopes for the best. Her heart, which was "black with bitterness," becomes "like a burning lamp," filled with hope. When hope fails, each character finds his own form of consolation: Fortunata (her name, ironically, means "happy") chooses love; Manica uses drink; Arlìa, because she holds more tenaciously to her hopes, tries magic, the Church, gambling, and, finally, drink.

Ultimately, however, there is only death, evoked by the window from which Fortunata thinks of jumping: "See that window, Mamma? . . . See how high it is?" The "terror of that window," and thus of death, drives the characters to work, to scheme, to hope, but in the end they all must face it: Manica's nose is "pressed against the clouded window" of his shop; Fortunata confesses to her dishonor "in front of the open window"; and at the end, with only the consolation of brandy, Arlìa sits "before the window thinking of nothing, looking out at the wet, dripping roofs." Her heart, once lit by hope, is warmed only by drink.

Style and Technique

Giovanni Verga's name is associated with *verismo*, or Verism, in which the prime purpose of the writer is to present the truth, without avoidance of unpleasant or depressing aspects of life, and at the same time with no attempt at moralizing or other subjective interference. In "Consolation," Verga paints a bleak picture of the lives of the poor.

One device which helps him do this is "free indirect discourse," wherein a character's attitude, thoughts, or words are expressed indirectly, as if part of the author's commentary. For example, when the lottery ticket is first bought, Arlìa's motivation is suggested by the following statement: "The blessed souls of her children would take care of it from above." Again, when Arlìa's husband takes to drinking, "she" (actually the narrator) thinks: "Now that all the troubles had fallen on her shoulders, happiness would come. That's the way it often is with the poor!" Although it is the narrator's voice here, referring to Arlìa in the third person, it is only Arlìa's perceptions—her deluded hopes—that the narrator relates. The ironic contrast between Arlìa's view and Verga's probable skepticism (happiness never comes to the poor in this story) thereby emphasizes the theme: the futility of hope in a hopeless world.

In addition to free indirect discourse, Verga makes prodigious use of eye and sight imagery to point up the contrast between the characters' perception of their situation and the dark reality: The reader is constantly presented with images of the characters' eyes—consumptive "mother-of-pearl eyes," "eyes circled black," eyes fixed on other characters or "fixed on a point that only she could see." Similarly, the big barbershop that Arlìa's husband envisions owning at the story's beginning, "with perfumes in the window," stands in contrast to the poor, empty facility where he "waited for customers all day long, his nose against the clouded window."

Perhaps the most telling device used in this story, however, is the contrast established between the fortuneteller and Father Calogero, the priest: Each is representative of a force which influences or controls the human condition—chance and God—yet neither can offer a solution to the poverty and disease the characters suffer. The fortuneteller offers hope without truth—mere self-delusion; the priest rightly denounces the deception but can offer nothing but the cold fact of death in its place. In such a world of false hope versus unmitigated suffering, the characters end by choosing the meager *conforti* of the title.

Edgar C. Knowlton, Jr.

THE CONVERSION OF THE JEWS

Author: Philip Roth (1933-   )
Type of plot: Anecdote
Time of plot: The 1950's
Locale: An American city
First published: 1958

Principal characters:
OSCAR (OZZIE) FREEDMAN, a thirteen-year-old Jewish
    student
MRS. FREEDMAN, his widowed mother
ITZIE LIEBERMAN, his friend and classmate
RABBI MARVIN BINDER, a thirty-year-old Hebrew teacher
YAKOV BLOTNIK, a seventy-one-year-old synagogue custodian

The Story

Ozzie Freedman has been attending a synagogue Hebrew school in preparation for his Bar Mitzvah confirmation. He is a bright student, but entirely too inquisitive for the comfort of his teacher, Rabbi Marvin Binder. Binder is irritated by Ozzie's inability to accept traditional doctrinal answers to fundamental religious questions, and he has summoned Mrs. Freedman three times to discuss her son's disruptive influence on his class.

During the Wednesday afternoon class prior to their third scheduled meeting, tensions between Ozzie and Binder precipitate a crisis. Earlier, Ozzie resisted Binder's facile dismissal of Christian claims for the divinity of Jesus. He was also dissatisfied with Binder's explanation for an airplane crash and for why Jews were particularly grieved over the number of Jews on board. Now they clash over the issue of God's omnipotence.

During the free discussion period, none of the boys volunteers any comments or questions. Binder, however, sensing that Ozzie has something on his mind, goads him into speaking. Ozzie wants to know why, if God can do absolutely anything, it was not possible for Him to have arranged a virgin birth for Jesus. His insistence that Binder does not know what he is talking about provokes an uproar in the class and an angry reaction from the rabbi.

When Binder slaps him, Ozzie runs up onto the roof of the synagogue. The fire department is summoned, and Ozzie soon finds himself looking down at a growing crowd of spectators. Binder first demands and then pleads that Ozzie come down from the roof, but Ozzie's fellow students cheer his stand against the rabbi and urge him to jump. Ozzie's mother, arriving for her appointment with Binder, becomes part of his audience.

Stimulated by this unexpected turn of events, Ozzie exerts his power over the assembled crowd. He declares that he will jump off the building unless everyone—Binder, his mother, the students, the firefighters, even pious old Yakov Blotnik the synagogue's custodian—kneels before him on the ground. Then he demands that Binder and all the others acknowledge vocally that they believe "God can make a child without intercourse." Finally, after exacting a promise that no one will ever be punished because of God, Ozzie descends—by jumping into the yellow net held up by the kneeling firefighters below.

Themes and Meanings

"The Conversion of the Jews" is the story of the coming-of-age of a boy on the brink of manhood as defined by the Jewish ritual of Bar Mitzvah. Set in a modern American city where Jews are a tolerated minority, it raises questions about the continuing vitality of Jewish culture and about the coherence of a Jewish community within a pluralistic society. In Ozzie's refusal to accept traditional dogma, it also takes a critical look at strategies to justify the ways of God to young men.

As befits his last name, Freedman, Ozzie is not tied to historical explanations for fundamental questions that he is confronting for the first time. Alone of all his classmates, Ozzie dares to challenge the authority of the rabbi, whose name, Binder, suggests his own fealty to tradition. Binder, a tall, handsome, and imposing man, is a sort of surrogate father to Ozzie, whose deceased father is commemorated by the ceremonial sabbath candles his mother lights each Friday at sunset. Ozzie is intoxicated by the sense of power he feels his defiant, independent stance can exert over the others. He sees himself as a lone champion of truth battling the obscurantist forces of tribal superstition. He is also asserting his own personal dignity against a condescending elder who is merely patronizing toward the young man's quest for explanations.

When he climbs up onto the roof alone, Ozzie realizes that he has passed a turning point in his life and that there is no possibility of reversal. His mother begs him to come back, not to become a martyr. Though they do not understand the term, his classmates invert the request, urging him indeed to be a "Martin." Caught in this dramatic situation, Ozzie feels too committed to retreat from the principles that suddenly seem more important to him than life. His dedication to the ideals of free thought provides him with the moral force to perform, symbolically, a task that is proverbially impossible: convert the Jews. When he finally jumps off the roof, into the safety net provided by the community, it is as if Ozzie the child has died and Ozzie the man is born.

The transformation of this bold adolescent is explicitly related to a sexual theme: the possibility that Mary conceived Jesus without having had intercourse. The very euphemism "to have intercourse" is somewhat shocking and titillating to the boys when they hear it employed by their rabbi. Binder would just as soon not discuss the subject at all, but, when Ozzie refuses to accept Binder's dismissal of Jesus as merely historical, the teacher is forced to deal directly with that feature of the Christian story that most troubles the boys: Mary's sexuality. The thirteen-year-old's curiosity over the mysteries of religion also suggests a burgeoning interest in sex.

The Gentile firefighters are bemused by and impatient with the entire confrontation. They do not understand Jewish separatism any more than the Jewish boy on the roof does. Ozzie can find no reason why his mother is most distressed about eight of the fifty-eight casualties in a plane crash, simply because they were Jews. For him, Jewish tradition is represented by grotesque, incoherent old Blotnik and the tyranny of a Hebrew school that attempts to inculcate by rote ideas that do not accord with reason. Written in the 1950's, when American Jewish literature was emerging as a major and respected force, "The Conversion of the Jews" helped establish Philip Roth as a peer of Saul Bellow and Bernard Malamud, yet it also marked his alienation from an ethnic tradition that he was often to satirize as having grown complacent and obtuse. His assimilated Jews cling to meaningless vestiges of ancient allegiances and values.

Style and Technique

A brief conversation between Ozzie and his friend Itzie, who has missed a previous class, helps to establish the background of Ozzie's conflict with Binder. Then, five short paragraphs describing the Freedman household on a Friday evening provide useful information on Ozzie's family background. The remainder of the story concentrates on the crucial Wednesday afternoon on which Ozzie challenges the rabbi. With considerable narrative economy, Roth depicts a compelling battle of wills.

Much of "The Conversion of the Jews" is presented as the dialogue of the principal characters. Most of the rest conveys important information through detached, third-person assertions. Simply by stating, for example, that class discussion time is often devoted to Hank Greenberg, a baseball star who was Jewish, Roth makes a telling point about the tenuousness of Jewish identity in a secular, tolerant society. Rarely does the author intrude with his own commentary. The effect of organizing the material so that it shows rather than tells is to provide a paradigm of the resistance to authority that Ozzie represents; readers cannot rely on a privileged voice for perspective but must arrive at their own conclusions.

As Ozzie is the focus of the reader's perceptions, one tends to be sympathetic to his aspirations and frustrations. The motivations of Binder are not nearly as well developed as are those of his defiant student. Because of the detached mode of narration, Ozzie's fundamental theological questions are made to seem highly pertinent, impossible to dismiss from the perspective of an impatient adult. Yet, posed in the vernacular of a self-righteous thirteen-year-old, they are also simplisitc and naïve. Roth maintains an ambivalent at-

432 Masterplots II

titude toward the conflicts between faith and reason and between tradition and the individual talent he depicts. He relates, without commentary, how the young man in effect accomplishes what he sets out to do. Yet the story's final sentence recounts Ozzie's return to earth, albeit with an aura, only partially ironic, of the sacred—"into the center of the yellow net that glowed in the evening's edge like an overgrown halo."

Steven G. Kellman

COUNTERPARTS

Author: James Joyce (1882-1941)
Type of plot: Symbolic realism
Time of plot: c. 1900
Locale: Dublin
First published: 1914

> *Principal characters:*
> FARRINGTON, a middle-aged scrivener
> MR. ALLEYNE, a lawyer, Farrington's boss

The Story

The action of "Counterparts," one of Joyce's *Dubliners* stories, occurs during a February afternoon and evening in the life of a lawyer's scrivener in Dublin. Farrington, the heavyset protagonist, is frustrated by his demeaning, monotonous job of copying legal documents. Mr. Alleyne, his boss, chastises him for taking an extended lunch hour, and rather than complete the work in hand, Farrington slips away from his desk to a nearby pub for a quick mid-afternoon drink.

Unable to finish the task before closing time, he turns it in two documents short while attempting to conceal his negligence. This time he is reprimanded by Mr. Alleyne for the compounded dereliction before his fellow clerks and an attractive, wealthy client. Faced with this public humiliation, and affected by the combination of alcohol and suppressed rage, he blunders into an impertinent and accidentally witty answer, which sinks him in deeper trouble: He may now lose his job.

To drown these accumulated anxieties, when his workday is over he pawns his watch and spends the proceeds boozing with his pals. His embellished retelling of the confrontation with Mr. Alleyne earns for him their temporary admiration. As the evening progresses, however, and as they move from bar to bar, he pays for almost all the alcohol consumed in his honor, feels snubbed by a passing actress, and is defeated in Indian wrestling by an English vaudeville acrobat. He feels abused, cheated, and betrayed. When he finally arrives late that night at his cold, dark home to find his wife away at church, he turns in violent exasperation on his own son as the most convenient victim of his accumulated anger.

Themes and Meanings

Farrington is James Joyce's most brutal creation. Evidently devoid of redeeming social or personal qualities, he does not appear to be respected by anyone. His relationships at work and home are marked by threats, evasion, and fear. His leads a life of desperate routine, never realizing an ennobling or liberating moment. Instead, he escapes into the temporary and insincere refuge of his drinking friends. The mood of the story suggests that their fates are very much like his: Their evening together does not lead to enlightenment or solidarity; rather, it is the occasion of mutual exploitation. Thus, when Farrington at the end of the story realizes his abandonment, his sadistic response amounts to an implicit admission of self-hatred. The design of the story, however, suggests that Farrington is not really a free agent and is not fully responsible for his actions.

"Counterparts" is Joyce's portrait of alienated labor. Farrington has little or no control over his own life, and his work is utterly mechanical and repetitious. His employers clearly belong to a higher social class—as various details, such as the hats and the accents, attest—and they deal imperiously with their employees, as shown by the two dramatic encounters in the first part of the story. Farrington's work, moreover, is the mind-numbing transcription of legal documents which mean nothing to him. He is kept to this treadmill by sheer intimidation, but the reader sees his mind and feelings constantly wandering to more pleasurable arenas and fixing on thoughts of vengeance. Whatever human feelings he posseses are perverted by the endless round of repression, repetition, and recrimination.

"Counterparts" traces the chain reaction of violence as it spreads, partially fulfilled, frustrated, reversed, and finally displaced, to an innocent and defenseless victim. The story illustrates how relationships based on power and control perpetuate and reproduce themselves, as brutality and bitterness pass from one level of authority to the next and from generation to generation. Farrington responds to his employer's abuse by repeating his offense, provoking even heavier censure. His several attempted escapes from humiliation in the office are encouraged by the appearance of success: in the bravado of the smart answer to Mr. Alleyne, its subsequent improvements, the extra shilling yielded on the watch at Terry Kelly's, and even the chastisement of his child at home. Yet Farrington must also face the reality of accumulating defeats: the apology to Mr. Alleyne, the "hornet's nest" his office will henceforth be, the defeat in Indian wrestling, the extra shilling now owed to the pawnbroker, and the browbeating that awaits him when his wife gets home.

As each victory has a corresponding defeat forward or backward in time, so has each character and relationship in the story its own counterpart, horizontal or vertical in the power structure. From this study of a very plain citizen, the reader is invited to infer something of the quality of the network of relationships in the larger society. It can be observed, for example, that, saving his infamous retort, Farrington's self-expression derives its substance and style from his boss: He copies Mr. Alleyne's documents, mimics his accent, bullies his underlings, and unconsciously imitates his rhetoric. Further, the mechanical imagery ("ring," "shoot," "vibrate," "manikin"), the click of Miss

Parker's machine, and the silent supervision of the clock all conspire to chill the atmosphere and formalize the relationships at Crosbie & Alleyne's.

Style and Technique

The various dictionary meanings of the word "counterpart" hold the key to the symbolic technique of this story, which proceeds by means of a complex set of corresponding, reduplicative, and complementary elements. Each character in the social scale has his or her counterpart: from Crosbie and Alleyne to Charlie and Tom ("twin" in Aramaic). Ultimately, in one sense or another, all are counterparts of Farrington: his fellow office-workers, his drinking cronies, and his wife (horizontally); Alleyne, Weathers, and Tom (vertically). In addition, each of these latter counterparts is associated with a woman, a different shade of red, and a distinguishing accent. Thus, they are all counterparts of one another. This pattern of correspondences and repetitions embraces the "rounds system" of buying drinks, Farrington's imitation of Weathers' taste for Appollinaris (a relatively expensive English mineral water), Farrington's and Higgins' retelling of the retort, and O'Halloran's corresponding experiences at Callan's of Fownes Street. This structural and symbolic pattern enlarges Farrington's very ordinary experiences and suggests, among other things, that they are self-perpetuating: The paralysis is contagious. Farrington is scarcely aware of the design of the events that determine his life. This perspective is cleverly suggested, for example, in that every character has a double letter in his or her name, and that Farrington has only a fleeting awareness of the repeated b's in one of the documents he is required to copy.

Farrington's employment as a legal scrivener suggests another structural pattern: The story makes use of some forty legal terms ("counterpart," "consignor," "trial," "fair," and so on) and is designed according to the consecutive, formal stages in a legal action. The import of this symbolic structure is to cast Farrington as the victim of an unfair trial, and the function of this theme is best understood in conjunction with Farrington's allegorical representation of Irish manhood.

The reader may observe that he is almost exclusively referred to as "the man" in the first and third scenes, while, in the bar scenes, he is called almost exclusively by his surname. This contrast of alienation and acceptance is clearly thematic. Yet if one considers that Joyce's naming of Farrington owes something to the Irish word for "man" (*fear*, pronounced as the English "far"), that he is called upon "to uphold the national honour" against the Englishman Weathers, and that in the course of the story he is seen as failing every test of manhood (as servant, sexual object, athlete, father), a larger conclusion presents itself: that the story has a theme related to political justice. And indeed it does.

Farrington is a figure of brutalized Irish manhood, the victim of the colonial legal establishment, abetted by a succession of publicans and pawn-brokers. These figures form a collective symbol of British-capitalist interests preying on the energies of native Ireland while at the same time criminalizing their victims. Here in "Counterparts," as in all the *Dubliners* stories, Joyce interweaves a scrupulous attention to realistic detail and multiple symbolic patterns. The result is a complex theme which, like Farrington's chance witticism, gives the dull human drama of his characters an unexpected moment.

Cóilín Owens

A COUNTRY DOCTOR

Author: Franz Kafka (1883-1924)
Type of plot: Modern fable
Time of plot: The late nineteenth or early twentieth century
Locale: Possibly rural Bohemia
First published: "Ein Landarzt," 1919 (English translation, 1940)

> *Principal characters:*
> A COUNTRY DOCTOR, the narrator and protagonist
> A YOUNG BOY, his patient
> ROSA, his maid

The Story

On a snowy night, a country doctor desperately seeks a way to reach a very sick patient in a village some fifty miles away. His own horse died from overexertion the night before, and Rosa, his servant girl, has found no other horse in the village for his carriage. While absentmindedly searching his barnyard, he accidentally knocks open the door to an unused pigsty, only to find there two powerfully built horses and a groom. He instructs Rosa to help the groom hitch the horses to his carriage, but the groom attacks her as soon as she gets near him. The doctor climbs into the carriage, but is reluctant to leave when the groom says that he plans to stay behind with Rosa, which causes her to run screaming into the house. The doctor protests in vain, as the horses whisk him away and arrive seemingly instantaneously at the patient's door.

The parents and sister of the patient rush out to greet the doctor and practically carry him into the poorly ventilated room of the sick boy. The boy, thin but without a fever, whispers to the doctor that he wants to die. At a loss as to what to do, the doctor aimlessly takes out his instruments and curses the miraculous assistance that has been provided him. He suddenly remembers Rosa, toward whom he has never paid much attention but whose fate now troubles him.

The horses manage to open a window in order to observe the sick boy. One neighs loudly when the doctor approaches the bed. As an underpaid employee of the district in which he works, the doctor believes that he is taken advantage of by his impoverished clientele. He convinces himself that the boy is not sick after all and prepares to leave, but is interrupted by the disappointed parents. Their intervention brings him to admit that the boy might be sick after all, and when he approaches the bed a second time, both horses neigh loudly in approval.

The doctor discovers that the boy is indeed very sick. There is a hand-sized wound on his right hip, pink ("rosa," in German), with many shadings and containing worms the size of his fingers. While the family is overjoyed to see the doctor's activity, he thinks to himself that there is no possible way to save the boy. These people always "demand the impossible from the doctor," he thinks; "they've lost their old faith; the minister sits at home and pulls apart his vestments, one after another; and the doctor is supposed to do everything with his delicate surgical hand."

As a school choir sings, "If you undress him, he will heal," the family and the recently arrived village elders undress the doctor, place him in the bed next to the boy's wound, and then leave the room. When the boy tells the doctor that he has very little confidence in him, the doctor tries to excuse his shortcomings and tells the boy that his wound is not so uncommon—many people, he claims, sacrifice their sides to two strokes of a mattock in the forest. Although sensing that the doctor is deceiving him, the boy does not question him further.

The horses have faithfully remained at the window. The doctor gathers up his clothes and instruments. Thinking that the return trip will be as swift as the arrival, the doctor hastily hitches the horses to his wagon and commands them to take him home, but slowly, "like old men," they plod through the snowy wasteland. Behind him the doctor hears another song of the schoolchildren: "Rejoice, you patients, the doctor has been laid in bed for you."

Never will he arrive home, the doctor complains to himself; he has lost his practice, a successor is robbing him, the groom rages in his house, and Rosa has been sacrificed. "Naked, exposed to the frost of the most unhappy of times, I, an old man, drive around with an earthly wagon and unearthly horses. . . . Deceived! Deceived! There can be no making amends for having once followed the false ringing of my night bell."

Themes and Meanings

One of the richest and most suggestive of Franz Kafka's texts, "A Country Doctor" depicts the tragic self-deception of an individual faced with his own loss of faith in his profession. The doctor readily blames other factors—the conditions of his employment, his patients, the decline of religious belief—for his failure to carry out his responsibilities, principally, to heal those in need. Once he fails to perform his duties as a healer, his life loses all sense of purpose and meaning.

The doctor's existential crisis is partly of his own making and partly the result of his extreme social isolation. He has neglected Rosa for years, says that it is very difficult to reach a mutual understanding with his patients, and feels tormented by the allegedly false ringing of his night bell. Although there does seem to be a breakdown in a viable social community—the doctor is an official of a political district and thus part of a bureaucratic system at some remove from the people (illustrated in the text by the distance that he must travel this particular night)—the strong subjective bias of his report of his relationships to other people puts into question his whole understanding of who he is and what he does. The reader needs to approach the doctor's own assessment of his situation with skepticism and ask what is the reality behind his self-pitying failure to heal, or even begin to treat, the boy's horrible wound.

Style and Technique

Despite his failure to heal, the doctor tells his story in a remarkably poetic and convincing way. So convincing is it, in fact, that the reader is likely at first to be fully taken in by the doctor's account. The doctor begins innocently enough by saying, "I was in a dilemma," namely, that he lacked a horse to take him to the distant patient. A change in the doctor's story first becomes noticeable when he breaks into the present tense at the point when he tells of the groom's attack on Rosa. He continues to use the historical present until he says that the patient accepted his story about the origin of the wound and fell silent. This change in tense sets off the story's long middle section, in which the doctor's self-pitying complaints, hesitations, and doubts about his profession predominate.

The reader must keep in mind that the doctor relates the details of his final sickbed visit in a state of utter despair, as he is driven in a seemingly endless winter night by a pair of horses over which he has absolutely no control. The desperateness of his situation, however, does not become clear until the last paragraph of his story. At first the doctor's detached narration draws the reader's sympathies and blocks any skeptical response to what is being told. As the account unfolds, there are more and more indications that the doctor's consciousness is clouded by his own fears and anxieties—his sudden concern for Rosa, his paranoia about the miraculous assistance of the horses, who seem at the disposal of higher forces, his need to justify to himself his failure to act. Thus, the most fantastic elements of the story—the horses' speed during the initial journey, the terrible beauty of the boy's wound, and the undressing of the doctor—reflect the unreality of the doctor's distorted consciousness rather than a fantastic reality that might have confronted him. The artistic skill with which the doctor turns his failure to cope with the realities of his work into a brilliantly seductive narrative suggests that his real calling is as a storyteller and not as a healer.

Peter West Nutting

THE COUNTRY HUSBAND

Author: John Cheever (1912-1982)
Type of plot: Domestic realism
Time of plot: The early 1950's
Locale: Shady Hill, a fictional suburb of New York City
First published: 1954

> *Principal characters:*
> FRANCIS WEED, a businessman and father of four
> JULIA, his wife
> ANNE MURCHISON, their teenage baby-sitter
> CLAYTON THOMAS, Anne's fiancé

The Story

"The Country Husband" recounts Francis Weed's brief rebellion against the mundane norms of his prosperous, dull community. Francis and Julia Weed have long been at the center of social life in Shady Hill, experiencing the conventional joys of suburban marriage and child rearing. Events conspire to jog Francis out of complacency and make him question his satisfaction with life.

The first of these events is a plane crash. Returning from a trip to Minneapolis, Francis and his fellow travelers experience an emergency landing in a field outside Philadelphia. They are shepherded to a nearby barn, and Francis takes a train to New York which arrives in time for him to catch his normal commuter train to Shady Hill. Naturally shaken by this occurrence, Francis is dismayed to discover that no one at home seems able to understand his brush with death. He arrived home on time, he looked fine—all his family went on with their normal routine. In fact, his children are more quarrelsome than usual, and Francis irritably compares his home to a battlefield, sending his wife upstairs in tears.

The next day, Francis is again disconcerted when he recognizes the new French maid at a neighbor's dinner party. After some pondering, he realizes where he has seen her before: At the end of World War II, he had witnessed her public humiliation by the people of her town in Normandy. She had been accused of living with a German officer during the occupation of France. As punishment, her head had been shaved and she had been made to stand naked before the townspeople. This memory overwhelms Francis, all the more because he does not feel able to share it with anyone, not even his wife. This experience, combined with the trauma of the plane crash, has made Francis suddenly aware of mortality, of danger, of passion, and his senses are heightened. Something is bound to happen.

That something comes, rather anticlimactically, in the form of Anne Murchison, the baby-sitter who is waiting for Francis to drive her home when the Weeds return from the neighbors' party. Anne strikes Francis as impossibly beautiful—"he experienced in his consciousness that moment when music breaks glass, and felt a pang of recognition as strange, deep, and wonderful as anything in his life." For the next several days, lustful fantasies about Anne fill his waking thoughts and his dreams. He buys a bracelet for her and carries it in his pocket, awaiting the right moment to give it to her and take her in his arms. Although terms such as "statutory rape" enter his thoughts, he nevertheless imagines sneaking off with her to a lovers' lane.

Francis' obsession with Anne has two immediate consequences. On the one hand, it heightens his enjoyment of physical reality. He is thrilled when he sights the first frost of autumn; the view of an express train hurtling down the platform excites him with "the miraculous physicalness of everything." On the other hand, Francis' passion makes him dangerously cavalier about the social proprieties on which a town such as Shady Hill depends. Accosted on the train platform by a boring chatterbox, Francis explicitly insults her. Later his wife reminds him that this woman is the town's social arbiter and might prevent their daughter's invitation to the important dances. This reminder precipitates a dreary, tearful fight in which Julia accuses Francis of leaving his dirty clothes on the floor to torment her.

The next morning, Francis again escapes this domestic banality by imagining that he sees Anne on the morning train. He chases after her only to discover that he has been mistaken—the woman he has followed is much older than Anne. Later that day, however, he realizes the folly of his obsession. He receives a call asking him to recommend for a job a college boy, Clayton Thomas, who visited the Weeds the night before. During the visit, Clayton— a rather earnest and immature young man—announced his engagement to Anne Murchison. To his own horror, Francis finds himself telling his caller that he cannot recommend Clayton Thomas, that in fact the boy is a thief. Recoiling at what he has done, Francis telephones a psychiatrist.

The story ends with a view of Francis building a coffee table in the cellar of his house: The psychiatrist has recommended woodworking as therapy. He is absorbed in "the holy smell of new wood"; for the moment, at least, his crisis seems to have been resolved in a straightforward way. Life is back to normal.

Themes and Meanings

It would be possible to read "The Country Husband" as an ironic commentary on what has come to be known as a "mid-life crisis," in which a man approaching middle age suddenly becomes infatuated with a much younger woman. While Cheever gently satirizes the particular form that Francis Weed's crisis takes, however, he treats more seriously Francis' realization that he and his friends have stopped paying attention to the meaning of life. This realization is most explicit in the moments following his recognition of the French maid: "The people in the Farquarsons' living room seemed united in their tacit claim that there had been no past, no war—that there was no danger or trouble in the world."

One theme of the story, then, is suggested by the question: How can life be meaningful in the absence of the sharp awareness brought on by crises such as death and war? Cheever suggests several answers. First, a consciousness of the past—of possible "danger or trouble"—is important to maintain. Francis has never had a good memory; as Cheever says: "It was not his limitation at all to be unable to escape the past; it was perhaps his limitation that he had escaped it so successfully." The thoughtful person, Cheever suggests, maintains a balance between the ordinary surface of daily life and an awareness that the extraordinary has happened in the past, and will happen again, for better or worse.

Second, the story suggests that in the absence of the extraordinary, individuals can heighten their perception of life by concentrating on the small pleasures of physical life (as Francis is encouraged to do first by his love for Anne and later by his psychiatrist). The beauty of architectural detail, the smell of ink rising from the morning paper, a random glimpse of a beautiful woman on a train—all these common moments can seem like revelations to the heightened awareness. What is more, occasional flights of fancy may be good for the soul. One of the last images in the story shows Francis' youngest son, Toby, struggling out of his cowboy outfit and putting on his "space suit" with a "magic cape." As he "flies the short distance to the floor," Toby proves that people have the resources within them to escape the ordinary, if only for a moment at a time.

Style and Technique

Consistent with the story's theme that even the mundane world contains much that is worthy of notice, Cheever's writing is rich in detail; for example, in his careful description of the Weeds' preparation for their yearly Christmas photograph. Moreover, the pattern of classical allusions which recur in the story emphasizes the reality of history, and in fact the lingering presence of the past in the modern world.

The classical allusions are diverse. The Weeds' living room is said to be "divided like Gaul into three parts." A neighbor says of his wife, "She makes me feel like Hannibal crossing the Alps." Francis notes on Fifth Avenue the statue of Atlas bearing the globe on his shoulders, and his love for Anne, it is suggested, may result from some "capriciousness of Venus and Eros." The beautiful woman glimpsed on the train becomes "Venus combing and combing her hair." The classical allusions are capped by fact that the neighbors' retriever—"black as coal, with a long, alert, intelligent, rakehell face"—is called Jupiter. Although these allusions are used with an ironic tone, their cumulative pattern is enough to suggest that the distant classical world can still provide an enriching presence in the modern world. To see one's neighbors, their living rooms and their pets, as analogues to the heroes and gods of classical antiquity endows them all with a certain dignity, even if tempered by gentle irony. At the end of the story, as Francis works happily in the basement, Jupiter comes prancing through the garden, and the evening suddenly seems "a night where kings in golden suits ride elephants over the mountains." Romance and beauty can be found in the modern world, even in Shady Hill.

Diane M. Ross

A COUNTRY LOVE STORY

Author: Jean Stafford (1915-1979)
Type of plot: Domestic and psychological realism
Time of plot: c. 1950
Locale: Rural New England
First published: 1950

> *Principal characters:*
> MAY, a housewife, nearly thirty years old
> DANIEL, her husband, a college professor, nearly fifty years
>   old
> DR. TELLENBACH, Daniel's Swiss physician

The Story

"A Country Love Story" focuses on a couple, May and her much older husband, Daniel—a college professor recuperating from an illness (presumably tuberculosis)—and their relationship set against the rural isolation of an old house in the country, to which they have just moved to aid in Daniel's convalescence.

Though the story begins with emphasis on May's and Daniel's failure to follow through on their plan to remove an antique sleigh that stands in the yard (a symbol of both erosion and hope that resurfaces throughout the story), upon their increasing silence as winter comes on, and upon May's original lack of enthusiasm for the seeming exile from Boston, these negatives are balanced by the couple's love for the country house, their regained intimacy ("it was like a second honeymoon"), and their mutual pleasure in reading, gardening, and repairing the new home. The crucial change occurs with the arrival of autumn, when Daniel withdraws to his historical research and May finds that she has nothing to fill her days; her complaints elicit from Daniel a heretofore unrecognized tendency toward passive-aggressive behavior. He puts May on the defensive and keeps her there by means of his self-pity, his preoccupation with blame, his condescending to her as childish, and his ambiguous accusation, "I almost believe there's something you haven't told me."

May does not seem to understand the sources or implications of his changes: His year in the sanitarium Dr. Tellenbach describes as "like living with an exacting mistress," an image that hints at Daniel's suspicion that May had an affair during their separation. It also does not occur to her that the year's illness has made mortality very clear and personal to her husband and that he now resents her for her youthfulness and health. All this is disguised as repeated attacks on her mental state: "You know, you may really have a slight disorder of the mind . . . you could go to a sanitarium." May does seem to understand subconsciously, however, for she creates a lover where none existed before and through the winter concentrates on bringing him more and more to life, until finally he sits in the sleigh, a pale young man from an earlier era, a kind of romantic and antique image of Daniel himself.

In the final scene, Daniel unwittingly but appropriately superimposes himself upon the image of the lover in May's dream, bringing May back to the unpleasant reality and the shock of admitting that he is "old" and "ill" and now very much dependent upon her, that the imaginary lover is gone forever, and that she is "like an orphan in solitary confinement." There is not the smallest spark to brighten or warm the cold and damp of this last morning.

Themes and Meanings

The double irony of Jean Stafford's title—May's love for Daniel ends, and her imagined adulterous love also disappears—hints at the deceptive nature of her story. The surface of May and Daniel's domestic life in their country home shows only a steady decline into mutual distrust and almost total silence; though there are brief quarrels, there are no truly dramatic events. Stafford creates here a kind of gothic configuration: The female protagonist is trapped in the dark house with an enemy, while her rescuer-lover appears just outside. That the ogre is May's once-adored husband and that the lover is only an imaginary expression of her desire for revenge and her wish to escape make for further irony, as does the presence of the derelict sleigh as a romantic symbol, but all of it is entirely without humor.

Stafford's title suggests that some of the story's meanings cohere around notions of the pastoral, specifically as a place of simplicity and calm which will somehow engender the same qualities in those who venture there. Early in the story, Dr. Tellenbach makes clear his belief that life in Boston will, with its "strain," "pandemonium," "excitements," and "intrigues," hinder Daniel's recovery, and that the purity and solitude of country life will further it. Behind his belief lies the assumption that self-absorption and "little talk" are beneficial, and that complexity of any sort is to be avoided. The narrative demonstrates the fallacies of these positions, hinting that the condition of married love is a social one and needs the stimulation of a society outside.

On the other hand, the presence of individuals outside but very close to a marriage creates the threat of triangles, and there are several in this story. The most destructive third person is Dr. Tellenbach: He speaks to May in a "courtly" way but is "authoritative" and treats her like a child; his mention of Daniel's mistress-disease furthers the triangle theme. May herself is bothered by what she perceives to be a greater intimacy between the doctor and her husband than she enjoys herself. Daniel, for his part, creates but does not name the imaginary-lover motif, and by rejecting May verbally and presumably sexually as well he sets in motion a strange sort of gestation in her: she "felt a certain stirring of life in her solitude," and "nursed" her injury, "hugged it," and feared that others sensed the "incubus of her sins." The result, her lover-in-the-sleigh, completes the series of triangles, and though the implied betrayal does not destroy the marriage, this lover's presence signifies that the marriage has already failed, just as his disappearance signals that May has no alternatives to comfort her.

Another, related theme is May's initiation into an awareness of her sensuous needs and her ability to desire revenge. At the beginning of the story, her eagerness to please the men and to stifle her objections makes her essentially passive. Daniel's abuse gradually forces her rebellion, and her breaking out takes the form of a rejection of the retentive influence of the Swiss doctor in Boston. Not coincidentally, she discovers on Christmas Day both her "weighty but unviolent dislike" for Daniel and her connecting the sleigh with her attraction to the "passionate, sweating, running life" of the animals which once pulled it. This transformation changes the significance of the sleigh: It becomes the setting for her desire. Thus, her decision not to go to the scent-filled barn for firewood at the story's end hints that she understands desire now, and knows that a life with Daniel cannot accommodate it.

Style and Technique

Typical of Stafford's work, this story does not call attention to its stylistic features; nevertheless, it shows meticulous care in its strategies. The story's purpose, to reveal May's growing consciousness of despair, is well served by the unobtrusive voice and the restriction of the third-person narrative to May's own consciousness. There is much that May does not recognize in the early part of the story, but by refusing to reserve the highest consciousness for her narrator, Stafford avoids condescending to May, allows her to retain full stature, and emphasizes her gradually maturing vision. The persona who tells the story implies a sympathy exclusively for May, but does so only in arranging events: Daniel speaks his intolerance and retreats to his study. The narrative voice itself is unfailingly objective, following realism's assumption that the events, told completely, will interpret themselves.

The arrangement of events and placement of images shows Stafford at her masterful best. For example, descriptions of the earlier years of the marriage emphasize their intellectual sharing. Daniel's refusal to converse with May about his research or his year in the sanitarium reveals his inability to speak of what actually preoccupies him: jealousy and suspicion. The story's imagery, however, implies in other ways that May has never wished to be unfaithful: May's dream of canoeing with her lover in a meadow of water lilies parallels exactly an earlier scene wherein she rowed with Daniel and first noticed changes in him; the lover himself, as mentioned above, is physically like Daniel, only younger. Similarly, Stafford handles the adultery theme with reference not to human beings but to animals: During Daniel's exile, May takes refuge from her guilty sexual longings by "imitating the cats," sleeping. This initiates the series of images connecting the barn and its passionate animals with the sleigh and May's desires, all of which culminates in the cold final scene's "lion foot" unlit stove and the blacksmith's cat which climbs into the sleigh. These elements allow Stafford to develop themes never explicitly named by the characters, and to show the developing of May's psyche as she responds to Daniel's accusations though never consciously understanding them. The technique allows May to retain essential innocence, but also a truly human complexity.

Finally, there is in both the setting (the claustrophobia of the old house, the ghostly horses and lover, the lone woman) and the action (especially Daniel's mysterious and vaguely threatening behavior) more than a small hint of the gothic horror story. By means of a quiet irony, Stafford manages to create a rescue scene in Daniel's kisses and brusque supplication ("You must," he says, "forgive the hallucinations of a sick man") and at the same time to leave her protagonist more trapped than ever. By technique, she reveals that initiation is not always hopeful.

Kerry Ahearn

THE COUNT'S WIFE

Author: Dino Buzzati (1906-1972)
Type of plot: Fantasy
Time of plot: The 1970's
Locale: The home and estate of the protagonist
First published: "La moglie con le ali," 1971 (English translation, 1983)

> *Principal characters:*
> COUNT GIORGIO VENANZI, the protagonist, a wealthy farm
> owner
> LUCINA, his wife
> GIORGIO VENANZI'S MOTHER
> DON FRANCESCO, the family chaplain
> MASSIMO LAURETTA, the best friend of the Count and Lucina

The Story

Giorgio Venanzi, a thirty-eight-year-old count and squire of a province, is caressing the back of his wife, Lucina, when he feels a small protuberance on her left shoulder blade. Alarmed, Giorgio inspects the lump carefully with two magnifying glasses, which reveal only that the lump is covered with a fine down.

The next morning, Giorgio examines his wife's back again and finds another lump matching the first, at the apex of her right shoulder blade. The lumps are significantly wider now and contain minuscule soft, white feathers. His wife seems to be growing wings. Giorgio's anxiety has turned to depression; the monstrous growths suggest to him witchcraft rather than miracle.

Giorgio's depression cannot be attributed to concern for his wife, but rather to a fearful reaction to the unknown. University-educated in agriculture, vigorous, and apparently active, he is nevertheless conventional to a fault, unimaginative, poorly cultured, and painfully jealous. His wife, eighteen years old, delicately small and beautiful, married him not out of love, but to please her parents, who wanted her to marry someone of their own noble class. Lucina lives a fairly restricted life, mainly because of her husband's jealousy, but she does not complain, having grown accustomed to Giorgio, who is, after all, greatly enamored of her.

Giorgio questions Lucina about her recent activities, suspecting the work of Gypsies, then insists that Lucina see no doctors. He leaves the house, mainly not to be looking at her back the whole day. He is still obsessed, however, with his wife's monstrosity. For his beautiful wife to sprout wings and become a spectacle is horrible enough, but the threat of scandal, the threat that his dignified family may be subject to ridicule, troubles him even more.

When Giorgio returns home, his worst fears are materialized: The two protuberances have taken the unmistakable form of wings, similar to those on angels in churches. Lucina, to Giorgio's irritation, is undisturbed and apparently enjoying herself, even laughing through these changes in her.

Giorgio consults his mother, who is equally horrified—reminding Giorgio that she never liked the marriage—and she recommends their talking with Don Francesco, the family chaplain. At first incredulous, the good-humored old priest views the wings of Lucina, who reveals them by unzipping the two vertical zippers she has put on the back of a cotton dress she has made. Don Francesco decides that the wings are either the work of the Devil, in which case they are merely illusory, or a gift of God, in which case they are genuine, and functional, wings. To determine which is the case, Lucina must soon attempt flying. Against his wishes, Giorgio agrees to a test flight.

Accordingly, one night Giorgio, Lucina, Giorgio's mother, and Don Francesco drive out to a clearing in a remote forest of Giorgio's holdings, and Lucina attempts a flight. It is not long before the wings, which are now more than three meters across when fully spread, lift the light, frail body of Lucina, who is immediately intoxicated with exhilaration, feeling more happy and beautiful than ever before. Don Francesco, moved by the flight as well as by Lucina's beauty, declares that the wings are a divine investiture. Lucina is an angel. Though Don Francesco argues that Lucina must not be locked up in secrecy, believing she has some divine mission, perhaps as "a sort of new messiah, of the female sex," Giorgio insists on keeping her change a secret. He curses the possibilities of "gross headlines . . . interviews . . . every kind of annoyance."

Giorgio is convinced that his wife will accept her imprisonment at home, but she grows increasingly restless, unable to accept this fate: "less than twenty years old . . . chained in her house without being able to . . . look out the window." She takes advantage of the dense October fog by taking clandestine flights from her garden, which bring her "a blissful delirium."

One afternoon, Lucina's confidence betrays her, and she is seen flying by Massimo Lauretta, a brilliant young man who is best friend to her and her husband. She must speak to him while still in flight so that he will not mistake her for a bird and shoot her. At sight of Lucina alighting before him, Massimo kneels and begins praying the "Hail Mary." Both of them nervous and excited—Massimo by Lucina's angelic beauty and Lucina by the delirium of flight and, perhaps, the wonderful freedom to be with someone—they have a brief, tender exchange. Massimo offers to take her into a cabin, out of the cold, and Lucina declines, fearful of being seen by the gamekeeper within. Then:

> They stood a little while watching one another puzzled. Then Lucina said:
> "I'm cold, I told you. At least hold me."
> Although the young man was still trembling, he didn't need to be told twice.

In the next scene of the story, Giorgio is returning home to find his wife, wingless, calmly sewing in the parlor. Giorgio is confused, shocked, and relieved. Some months later, Giorgio explains to Lucina, "God really loves you. . . . You were able to meet the Devil at the right moment." He has overcome his jealousy and possessiveness for the relief of having his wife normal again, safely returned to a conventional existence with him.

Themes and Meanings

"The Count's Wife" dramatizes one of Buzzati's characteristic interests, man's preoccupation with fear, particularly of the unknown or anything that transcends his understanding. In this story, it is the protagonist who is preoccupied, and his fear is of the monstrous, inexplicable deformity of his wife. Buzzati has created here a man without imagination, who is easily challenged by anything outside the conventions of his household and village. His own life is routine and unimaginative. He has married a beautiful young woman of nobility, apparently because of his great attraction to her ("he regarded her as the most fascinating woman in the town"), and he keeps her fairly isolated from the rest of the world while he occupies himself with tending his farms and pursuing the peasant girls. He is, in other words, in control of his world. He thus becomes an ideal target for fear and ironic reversal. His wife's wings threaten to wrest him from his privileged position of control, by exposing his family to unwanted attention and subjecting his name to scandal. It is one of the protagonist's weaknesses that he can imagine no result of his wife's being appointed by God other than the ruin of his own quiet, conventionally respectable life. He and his wife are both victimized by this weakness. If Buzzati enjoyed depicting man as mainly fearful in face of things unexplainable, he has here made his point especially clear by portraying a man whose small-mindedness is easily transcended.

Style and Technique

Many qualities of this tale are reminiscent of fables. It is simply and directly told in the third person, lacking in ornament and almost devoid of explanation. It is almost purely narrative, moving action quickly and keeping dialogue spare. The opening lines, "One night Count Giorgio Venanzi, a thirty-eight-year-old landowner and squire of his province . . ." echo many qualities of fables: the nonspecific time reference "One night" (echoic of "Once upon a time"), the title of the protagonist, and the medieval sounding "squire of his province." It is a story in which one might be prepared to find winged angels and possible allegorical suggestions. The angelically pure wife falling, as a result of the influence of her husband's spiritual blindness, does invite an allegorical reading (purity loses to the evil of ignorance or self-centeredness).

Irony is the dominating literary device of the story. The plot leads step by step to the bitterly humorous, final irony: The formerly jealous, possessive husband is relieved to know that his wife has been adulterous, for by meeting the Devil she returned their life to normal. This irony is made more striking by Buzzati's careful preparation for it. The husband's jealousy is depicted more and more intensely as his protectiveness becomes a mania. At the same time, his horror at the possibility of his wife's bringing shame to his name and personal ruin to him also crescendos so that at the end these two emotions are nearly indistinguishable. The concluding irony is the focal point, or target, of the story, resolving these two tensions simultaneously.

Dennis C. Chowenhill

CRAZY SUNDAY

Author: F. Scott Fitzgerald (1896-1940)
Type of plot: Social realism
Time of plot: 1931
Locale: Hollywood
First published: 1932

> *Principal characters:*
> JOEL COLES, a motion-picture scriptwriter new to Hollywood, the son of a once-successful actress
> MILES CALMAN, a famed motion-picture director for whom Joel has written
> STELLA CALMAN, the motion-picture star Stella Walker and wife to Miles Calman

The Story

Joel Coles, a twenty-eight-year-old screenwriter, son of a once-successful stage actress, has spent his childhood between New York and London, trying to separate the real from the unreal. For six months he has been in Hollywood writing scenes and sequences for films as a continuity writer. He is invited to a Sunday cocktail party at the home of the Miles Calmans, a mansion in Beverly Hills "built for great emotional moments." Miles Calman is the most significant director at the studio; his wife is the star Stella Walker, whom Miles has created ("brought that little gamin alive and made her a sort of masterpiece"). Joel sees the invitation as evidence that he is getting somewhere in his career, as well as an opportunity to mix with the important people of the industry.

Though he resolves not to drink at the party—Miles Calman is "audibly tired of rummies"—Joel breaks his vow. As a result, he performs for the crowd a tasteless impersonation of a crass independent producer, Dave Silverstein, burlesquing the man's cultural limitations. Tempted to show off for the attentive Stella Calman, Joel seizes upon this routine, which has been well received at other parties. The result is disastrous: The feeling of the audience is expressed by the booing from an actor, the Great Lover of filmdom. "It was the resentment of the professional toward the amateur, of the community toward the stranger, the thumbs-down of the clan."

The next day, back at the studio lot, abashed and alarmed, Joel writes an apology to Miles but receives the following day a letter of praise from Stella and an invitation to her sister's Sunday buffet supper.

At the buffet, Joel learns of the Calmans' troubles—Miles's affair with actress Eva Goebel, his jealousy of Stella, his trials with his psychoanalyst, his mother fixation and its linking of sex with dependency. Joel is informed of this by the Calmans themselves, mostly Stella, back at the Calmans' house. It is obvious by now that Joel is falling in love with Stella and that Stella is using Joel to spur Miles's jealousy so that his attraction to Eva will be neutralized. The Pygmalion story of Miles and Stella—the creation which he brought to life with the marriage—is in peril, both Miles and Stella feeling they might lose the dream: he as artist/fairy godmother, she as Pygmalion/Cinderella. Eva is Stella's best friend; Joel is considered by Miles a friend and confidant.

Monday, at the studio, Joel is invited by Stella to escort her to the Perry's Saturday dinner and theater party, for Miles is flying to the football game at South Bend.

On Wednesday Joel asks Miles about the flight to the football game and about the party, finding that Miles is indecisive because of his jealousy and guilt: He might stay, he thinks, and escort Stella safely to the party. Reassured when Joel says that he is not even planning to go to the party, Miles asks him to go, for he likes Joel. The problem, says Miles, is that he has trained Stella to like the men he likes.

Miles flies east to attend the game and sends Stella telegrams from there, yet she insists that he could have had the telegrams sent falsely and could be observing what she does. What she has done is to take Joel into her house and seduce him, or anyway, to invite his seduction of her. This occurs just before midnight, but the result is that Joel becomes aware that she still loves Miles, a fact she admits. Just past midnight, on the third Sunday of the story, a phone call informs Stella of Miles's death in an airplane crash.

With the news of Miles's death, which Stella refuses to accept, Stella's attitude toward Joel changes, from the distancing which accompanied and followed their lovemaking to begging him to stay the night with her and to make love to her. Joel realizes that Stella is trying to keep Miles alive by sustaining a situation and a problem in which he played an important part; she will play the role of the unfaithful wife that Miles's jealousy created, for she has found her existence in the roles Miles molded for her, and, in fact, has believed her very being to be a creation of his genius.

Joel will not give in to her, this time, under the circumstances. He takes charge, insists on and calls a doctor, and requests her friends to come to Stella's side. Is this an act showing that Joel has taken control of his life, or is it a tribute to the memory of Miles Calman and his creative genius? Joel will not stay with Stella, but he will be back if she needs him.

Themes and Meanings

"Crazy Sunday" is a story about the interrelationship of illusions and reality (or make-believe and actuality), of the difficulty people have separating them, and of the confusion of identity that results. Since the story's characters work in a profession which creates and markets illusions, the problem of personal identity is heightened and the thin line between acting and being is blurred. On Sundays, when they are not making films, they are thrown into the challenge of coping with the world of actuality. Since it is psychologically frustrating for them to contend with real problems of fidelity, jealousy, illness, and death, they tend to extend their work week and to find faith in the profession itself, to live in the office of creation. Their weekend lives are staged at parties in theaterlike mansions. Yet they are vulnerable: Miles is marked for death, Joel has a problem with alcohol, and Stella verges on hysteria with her insecurity.

Miles tries to turn his artistic creation, Stella Walker, into his real-life wife, but he cannot cope with that step in her transformation. Stella, with Miles's death and the loss of her creator-director, believes she cannot manage and pleads for Joel's support. Joel does not accept the real plea for help from Stella, for he still sees her as the little gamin whom Miles turned into a star.

Another theme in "Crazy Sunday" is the coexistence of the characters' glamour and emotional instability—Miles's psychological confusion and weariness of mind and body, Stella's insecurity amounting to complete dependence, Joel's drinking and naïveté. This dark side is also evidenced in the coarse makeup of the film extras and the rummies who write the film scripts. The fact is that these are necessary accompaniments to the dream world they produce for the public and in which they themselves are caught.

Style and Technique

The point of view of "Crazy Sunday" is that of a limited omniscient, or selected omniscient, narrator. Everything is seen as Joel sees it or could see it; thus, dramatic irony is provided by the contrast between Joel's perception of events and the deeper understanding afforded to the reader. When Joel makes a fool of himself at the Calman's party, he is conscious of his error, but when, at the end of the story, he makes a much more serious mistake, abandoning Stella, only the reader grasps the significance of Joel's action. Joel himself has lost the ability to distinguish between reality and fantasy, and thus he fails to see the reality of Stella's suffering.

This is a dramatic story with cinematic effects. There is a five-part structure, with three strong Sunday scenes separated by interims at the studio. The interims set up the logical business of the Sunday scenes. Each Sunday shows the humiliation of a different main character, first of Joel at the Calman's party, then of Miles being attacked for his adultery, and finally of Stella's collapse with grief at the news of Miles's death. In each scene, Joel's love for Stella progresses a step further, a commitment from which he later retreats.

The fully dramatized Sunday scenes (which include the Saturday of the Perrys' party, extending to the tragic early hours of Sunday) are visually oriented. Readers are constantly being directed to appearances, shapes, colors, positions. Moreover, the characters are always *looking, seeing, noticing*. In the world of "Crazy Sunday," only appearances count.

As usual with good Fitzgerald stories, there is crisp, concise observation: "an Italian-colored sweater," "a dress like ice-water, made in a thousand pale-blue pieces, with icicles trickling at the throat," "under the pure grain of light hair." The descriptive language works well with the theme of glamorous make-believe threatened by reality.

William E. Morris

A CRITICAL INTRODUCTION TO *THE BEST OF S. J. PERELMAN* BY SIDNEY NAMLEREP

Author: S. J. Perelman (1904-1979)
Type of plot: Parody
Time of plot: 1944
Locale: New York
First published: 1947

> *Principal characters:*
> SIDNEY NAMLEREP, a literary critic
> S. J. PERELMAN, a prominent American humorist

The Story

S. J. Perelman uses Sidney Namlerep to comment on his style and subjects and to make fun of himself and any possible detractors in this "Critical Introduction" to *The Best of S. J. Perelman* (1947), a collection of forty-nine stories from four previous volumes. Namlerep (Perelman spelled backward) writes from 1626 Broadway (Perelman's office address) this "consideration" of a humorist who "certainly deserves the same consideration one accords old ladies on streetcars, babies traveling unescorted on planes, and the feebleminded generally."

Many of Perelman's stories begin as essays only to develop elaborate plots, but in "A Critical Introduction to *The Best of S. J. Perelman* by Sidney Namlerep," his narrator is concerned solely with attacking, while ostensibly explaining, the writer's supposed talent, his physique, and his sanity. All three defects are conjoined by the critic's claim that Perelman's "entire output over the past two decades has been achieved without benefit of brain."

Namlerep questions the writer's morality and his insistence upon using arcane language. The two complaints merge when Namlerep analyzes a lengthy passage from a story entitled "Scenario," which ridicules the clichés of melodrama: "It is all very well to condone Perelman on the ground that he wrote the foregoing after extended servitude in Hollywood, but what if such passages were to fall into the hands of children? Particularly children who did not know the meaning of words like 'patchouli'?"

Namlerep also accuses his subject of being a phony. References to a Tattersall vest and the Cesarewitch Sweepstakes in "Kitchen Bouquet" imply that the writer is "an habitué of the tracks." Yet the ever-diligent critic uncovers the truth. Twenty-four years previously Perelman borrowed a Tattersall vest to wear to a tea dance at his university, and ten years later he overheard two elderly jockeys discussing the Cesarewitch. "It was therefore inevitable," Namlerep concludes, "that, since Perelman suffers from what psychologists euphemistically term total recall, he should have dredged up these references when the opportunity arose."

The critic predicts a "disastrous future" for his subject since "the two most dominant themes" in his work are those involving women and money: "Obvious infantilism of this sort can be forgiven a gifted writer; in one so patently devoid of talent as Perelman, his continual absorption with the flesh-pots indicates the need for speedy therapy." Namlerep suggests he "betake himself to that good five-cent psychiatrist he is forever prating about."

Themes and Meanings

In "A Critical Introduction to *The Best of S. J. Perelman* by Sidney Namlerep," Perelman lampoons both introductions to books and literary criticism. He ridicules the pomposity of Namlerep by having him accuse Perelman himself of that and similar literary sins. Namlerep's ego, humorlessness, literal-mindedness, and vindictiveness represent both the narrowness and the excesses of literary criticism at its worst. Perelman's tongue-in-cheek presentation of Namlerep's inability to separate the man from the writer, his obsession with puerile psychological insights, and his almost religious fervor for the omnipotence of modern psychiatry show that such critics are not to be taken seriously.

Namlerep indicates both the triviality and the pedantry of his method when he supports his money-and-women theory by counting "thirty-seven direct allusions to the former and twenty-four to the latter." Most enjoyable of all is how blissfully unaware Namlerep is that he evinces all of Perelman's supposed weaknesses and superfluities in his own writing. Such an approach by Perelman is particularly appropriate since he is a practitioner of what his friend and colleague Robert Benchley called the "dementia praecox" school of humor.

In passing, Perelman comments on some of his usual subjects involving what passes for normality in twentieth century America. For example, Namlerep wonders how his subject "contrives to fulfil the ordinary obligations of everyday life—to get to his office, philander with his secretary, bedevil his wife, and terrorize his children."

Style and Technique

All the elements which have made Perelman not only one of the best American humorists but also one of the most distinctive literary stylists are on display here. He has the largest working vocabulary of any American writer, rivaled only by Vladimir Nabokov, and, with boyish glee, he works the most uncommon words into his narrative: "bayaderes," "equinoctial," "lubricity," "midden," "palliate," "yokefellow," "zeugma." He also employs more familiar words in unusual senses: "blinked" to mean ignored.

Perelman's main subject is language, and he finds as much pleasure in the vernacular as in the esoteric. He glories in such clichés as "cheek by jowl" and "grain of sense." Even the occasional slang term such as "moola" slips in. The slang, clichés, and elevated language are not that amusing in themselves but rather in the masterful way that Perelman juxtaposes them. He is a literary vaudevillian, constantly juggling the sophisticated and the sophomoric.

Non sequiturs and plain silliness abound in "A Critical Introduction to *The Best of S. J. Perelman* by Sidney Namlerep." Mysteries of science include not only the common cold but also mixed bathing, and Namlerep describes the anger of the aroused author: "At the least suspicion of an affront, Perelman, who has the pride of a Spanish grandee, has been known to whip out his sword-cane and hide in the nearest closet."

Central to Perelman's style is hyperbole: "With fiendish nonchalance and a complete lack of reverence for good form, he plucks words out of context, ravishes them, and makes off whistling as his victims sob brokenly into the bolster." Namlerep charges that "what Flaubert did to the French bourgeois in *Bouvard and Pecuchet*, what Pizarro did to the Incas, what Jack Dempsey did to Paolino Uzcudun, S. J. Perelman has done to American belles-lettres." The latter example also illustrates the humorist's penchant for allusions, for the incongruous grouping of the famous and infamous, for the bizarre name.

"A Critical Introduction to *The Best of S. J. Perelman* by Sidney Namlerep" is a virtual catalog of this slapstick linguist's stylistic devices. It ends appropriately with the last of a long series of puns: "A plague on all his grouses!" Perelman epitomizes the joy of lexicology.

Michael Adams

CRITIQUE DE LA VIE QUOTIDIENNE

Author: Donald Barthelme (1931-   )
Type of plot: Domestic realism and satire
Time of plot: Probably the 1970's
Locale: Probably New York City
First published: 1972

> *Principal characters:*
> THE NARRATOR, who is separated from his wife
> WANDA, his wife
> THE CHILD, their son

The Story

"Critique de la Vie Quotidienne" (critique of daily life) records the disintegration of the marriage of a young urban couple. The narrator, given to excessive drinking, retrospectively sketches a series of domestic clashes that highlight the nature of the conflicts between him and his wife, Wanda, and their child.

The narrator and his wife quarrel, sometimes violently and finally almost lethally, about various domestic matters, among them the child's behavior, a game of chess, the narrator's stinginess, and his abandonment of her. The father's relationship with the child is marked by his irritation with the child's requests, by his exasperation with the child's behavior, and by his fury at the child's inferences about his character.

In the final section, a separation has taken place, and the wife is visiting the narrator's bachelor quarters. A round of friendly toasts to each other quickly degenerates into mutual recriminations, and Wanda pulls a large pistol from her bosom and fires at her husband. She misses and instead shatters the bottle of liquor on the mantel. The concluding scene shows the wife in Nanterre, France, studying Marxist sociology while the husband is at home, content with his favorite brand of scotch: "And I, I have my J&B. The J&B company keeps manufacturing it, case after case, year in and year out, and there is, I am told, no immediate danger of a dearth."

Themes and Meanings

Like many other stories by Donald Barthelme, "Critique de la Vie Quotidienne" is about failed relationships. The narrator, probably in his thirties, is thoroughly disenchanted with domestic life. He attributes his drinking to his boring evenings at home: "Our evenings lacked promise. The world in the evening seems fraught with the absence of promise, if you are a married man. There is nothing to do but go home and drink your nine drinks and forget about it."

The narrator scorns Wanda's attachment to *Elle*, the French magazine for women, to which she turns for trendy advice on food, fashions, interior decorating, and entertainment. Wanda herself is discontented. A French major in college, she now has little to do except "take care of a child and look out of the window." Sex is also a problem; Wanda withholds her sexual favors if the narrator does not behave properly, and he is inclined to visit a prostitute after fights with his wife. After the separation, Wanda charges the narrator with other failings, including stinginess when he hid the charge card or refused to pay to have her overbite corrected. Once he also forced Wanda to don a chauffeur's cap, drive him to the Argentine embassy, and wait outside with other chauffeurs while he chatted with the ambassador.

The narrator's relationship with the child is marked by deep hostility. The child, who significantly is never called by his first name, angers his father by asking for a horse. Also, the father remembers an unpleasant incident when the child, sleeping with them in a narrow hotel bed, urinated on the sheets. The father is aggravated, as well, by the child's constant, pervasive, and unpleasant singing, augmented by the television set and the transistor radio. The narrator does record one moment of a happy father-son relationship when he fixed the seat on the child's bicycle (after his wife had berated him for buying a cheap bicycle in the first place), but this is one of only two transitory interludes in a generally unhappy relationship.

Part of the hostility between them is rooted in the child's discerning understanding of his father's failing and fears. A discussion with his father about the life masks for a school project exposes the father's dread of death and his regret of the course that his life has taken. The discussion ends in a "certain amount of physical abuse" of the child by the father. The father's anxiety about getting old, which the son uncovers, is revealed as well in the final confrontation with the wife, when her attempt at murder is directly precipitated by his untactful remarks about signs of aging in her face.

"Critique de la Vie Quotidienne," then, as the title suggests, is an analysis of daily life. The narrator, bored with his domesticity, in conflict with his wife and child, and bedeviled by his own mortality, seeks relief in alcohol, which in turn exacerbates his relationships with his family and leads to eventual alienation and an attempt on his life. In a larger context, Barthelme is examining the prevalence of failed relationships in modern American society. At one point the narrator tells Wanda, "There has been a sixty percent increase in single-person households in the last ten years, according to the Bureau of the Census." She, however, fails to be consoled by his subsequent statement that they are part of a trend.

Barthelme's fiction in general shows a remarkable awareness of the surfaces of contemporary American life. He has a keen satiric eye for faddish brand names and trends and an accurate parodist's ear for clichés and fashionable phrases. "Critique de la Vie Quotidienne" reflects the ambience of a postbaccalaureate crowd of an urban center on the East Coast, probably New York City (the mention of a brownstone apartment and the *Times* is evidence for this), which is the location for some of his stories, many of which appeared, appropriately enough, in *The New Yorker* magazine. The narrator reads the *Journal of Sensory Deprivation*, a publication, probably fictional, whose subject matter was in style at the time of the story. Yet it is Wanda who is most afflicted by the desire to be *au courant*. On the advice of *Elle*, she cultivates "the schoolgirl look." She dotes on pictures of restored mills in Brittany, and she comes to resemble, says the narrator, Anna Karina, an actress about whom the magazine has run innumerable pieces. Her choice of wines, sauces, and flatware all reflect a sharp concern with products and brands favored by a chic group. Her trip to France to study Marxist sociology with Henri Lefevre, the author of a book also entitled *Critique de la Vie Quotidienne*, indicates her fashionably leftist tendencies. In France, Wanda also makes sure that her son does not suffer from a conventional education. She enrolls him in an experimental school conducted "in accord with the best Piagetian principles," an appropriate continuation of the child's progressive school in the United States.

Style and Technique

Unlike many stories by Barthelme in which he ignores or distorts traditional techniques of fiction, "Critique de la Vie Quotidienne" is a readable and conventionally coherent story with clear plot and characterization. The self-revelation of the first-person narrator-protagonist is of particular interest. Although he is telling an essentially sad tale of domestic abuse, neglect, alcoholism, and separation, his manner of telling his story—detached, wry, and self-excusing—enhances the reader's perception of the irony. Although the narrator reveals his own flaws, he fails to criticize himself or to feel guilty for his role in the dissolution of his family.

Another distinctive aspect of the narration is the humor. The narrator tells his story by employing devices that Barthelme's narrators have used in many other stories, such as repetition. On learning about the child's making of life masks as a school project, the narrator says: "I cursed the school then, in my mind. It was not the first time I had cursed the school, in my mind." The story also displays the odd turns of phrase and unexpected juxtapositions which are part of Barthelme's distinctive style.

The most enjoyable aspect of the narration, however, is the narrator's antic and whimsical recording of events. Beneath the surface of the serious conversation between father and son about life masks lies a vein of intensely comic repartee. After a fight with his wife, the narrator decides to visit a prostitute but cannot because he has only three dollars, and the bordello will not accept his MasterCharge credit card. When the narrator forces Wanda to act like a chauffeur on his visit to the Argentine ambassador's residence (an improbable social call in the context of the story), he explains to his wife, who wants to be included, "You know no Spanish." When Wanda attempts to murder her husband, she "withdrew from her bosom an extremely large horse pistol," a ludicrous action considering the disparity between the size of the weapon and its place of concealment.

The pistol also emerges as a key symbol. When Wanda's aim wavers, and she hits a bottle of J&B scotch instead, it is clear that Wanda, herself a little drunk, has inadvertently taken action against her principal enemy—alcohol. Their marriage is beset by many problems—the child and their mutual discontent with each other and with the patterns of their daily life—and it could be argued that the narrator's alcoholism is a symptom as well as a cause of their difficulties, but it is, in the story, the most prominent, tangible, and immediate source of the failure of the relationship.

Walter Herrscher